War in the Modern World

WAR

IN THE MODERN WORLD

THEODORE ROPP

NEW, REVISED EDITION

With a New Introduction by Alex Roland

The Johns Hopkins University Press
Baltimore and London

Originally published by Duke University Press, 1959
New, revised edition published by Macmillan Publishing Company, 1962
Johns Hopkins Paperbacks edition, 2000
2 4 6 8 9 7 5 3 1

The Johns Hopkins University Press
2715 North Charles Street
Baltimore, Maryland 21218-4363
www.press.jhu.edu

Library of Congress Cataloging-in-Publication Data

Ropp, Theodore, 1911–
War in the modern world / Theodore Ropp.—New rev. ed.
p. cm.
Includes bibliographical references and index.
ISBN 0-8018-6445-3 (alk. paper)
1. Military art and science—History. 2. Military history, Modern. I. Title.
U39 .R6 2000
355′.009′03—dc21
99-087565

A catalog record for this book is available from the British Library.

Contents

Preface   ix
Introduction to the Johns Hopkins Edition,
  by Alex Roland   3
Introduction to the Original Edition   11

THE AGE OF THE GREAT CAPTAINS

1. Land Warfare from the Renaissance to the
   Neoclassical Age (1415–1789)   19
      New Techniques and Types of Military
        Organization   19
      The Wars for Italy and the
        Rise of Spain (1494–1559)   25
      The Army of the Spanish Hapsburgs   29
      Spain's Decline (1559–1659)   37
      The Age of Louis XIV (1643–1715)   40
      The Age of Frederick the Great:
        Neoclassical Warfare   44
      The Common Soldier in the Neoclassical Age   53

2. Naval Warfare from the Renaissance to the
   Neoclassical Age (1417–1789)   60
      The Command of the Sea   60
      Portuguese and Spanish Sea Power   62
      The Rise of English Sea Power   66
      Navies in the Neoclassical Age   70

3. The Anglo-American Military Tradition   76
      The Weakness of the Standing Army   76
      Problems of Imperial Defense   80
      The Break with Britain   86
      The Continental Army and Navy   88
      The British in the American Revolution   93

4. The French Revolution and Napoleon   98
      French Military Reformers   98
      The Revolution   102
      The Organizer of Victory   107
      The Napoleonic Empire   117

The Opposition to Napoleon: The Peninsula   124
The Opposition to Napoleon in Eastern Europe   132

THE INDUSTRIAL REVOLUTION AND WAR

5. The First Half of the Nineteenth
    Century (1815–1853)   143
      Britain and the Long Peace   143
      Austria, Russia, and France   147
      Prussia   152

6. The Wars of the Mid-Nineteenth
    Century (1854–1871)   161
      The New Weapons of the Industrial Revolution   161
      The Crimean and Italian Wars   164
      The Rise of Germany   169
      The American Civil War: Men and Tactics   175
      The American Civil War: Strategy   184

7. The Years of Uneasy Peace (1871–1914)   195
      Military Organization: The Spread of
        Prussian Doctrine   195
      Mobilization and Intellectual Preparation
        of the Mass Army   200
      The Race for Colonies and Sea Power   206
      Land Tactics with the New Fire Weapons   215
      The War Plans of the Continental Powers   222
      British Participation in a Continental War   230

THE AGE OF VIOLENCE

8. The First World War   239
      The Opening Battles (1914)   239
      Deadlock in the West (1915–1916)   245
      German Victory in the East (1915–1916)   251
      The United States and the War (1917)   257
      Years of Decision (1917–1918)   261

9. The Long Armistice (1919–1939)   275
      The Peace Settlements   275
      The Totalitarian State: Bolshevik Russia   285
      Italian Fascism and the Theories of
        Giulio Douhet   290
      The Military Recovery of Germany   294
      The Three Democracies   303

10. The Second World War   314
    The Opening Battles   314
    Britain, the Mediterranean, and the Atlantic   321
    The Russo-German War   333
    Allied Deployment:
        Decision in Western Europe   345
    The East Asian and Pacific Wars:
        The Japanese Raid   359
    The Allied Counterattack in the Pacific   371
    The War for East Asia   382

    Epilogue   393

    Index   405

Preface

THIS BOOK is the result of nearly twenty years of teaching naval and military history. It is written for civilians with some knowledge of history and for military men interested in the ways in which their profession has been changed by political, social, and economic developments. The works of the great military writers are quoted in some detail; this book is in some ways an introduction to the major military classics. It stresses the wars of the twentieth century and Anglo-American concepts of sea, land, and air war, because both civilian and military readers may be particularly interested in their own age and their own countries' military traditions. Campaigns and battles are used only to illustrate more general trends. Such studies must be very detailed to be meaningful and cannot be incorporated easily in a general history. I have indicated the most important and readable of such studies in the hope that readers will be led farther into the fascinating and crucial subject of military history. The long footnotes are largely bibliographical. Though these bibliographies cannot be exhaustive, it is hoped that they contain all of the classics and those works which the author and his students have found interesting. The mountains of military literature have not recently been surveyed. The author hopes that his short bibliographical introductions to the many subjects which relate to the vast subject of modern warfare are an original contribution to scholarship. The bibliographies of personal accounts and war novels are matters of individual preference. The author can only hope that selections from his own favorites will lead readers to further exploration.

Geography is the bones of strategy; the terrain and lines of communication have governed the course of many campaigns and battles. Pictures and diagrams of weapons tell more than many paragraphs, but only detailed maps and pictures are really meaningful. Since adequate illustrations and maps would be prohibitively expensive, the author must assume that the reader will have access to standard maps and that he will depend on the maps which must accompany any scholarly study of campaigns or battles.

Any general introduction to so vast a subject is built on the work of many other scholars. Richard A. Preston of the Royal

Military College of Canada and Jay Luvaas of Allegheny College read the entire work. The latter corrected proof while the author was traveling on another research project. Harry Stevens of Ohio University and Harold T. Parker of Duke read most of the manuscript and offered many suggestions. Earlier versions and the earlier chapters were read by Alan K. Manchester, Wesley Williams, and Frederick and Mary Bernheim of Duke, Alexander De Conde of the University of Michigan, William T. Jones of Pomona College, by Vice Admiral Ralph Earle, Jr., and Captain Clyde J. Van Arsdall, United States Navy, and by Richard M. Leighton and George F. Howe of the Office of the Chief of Military History, Department of the Army. Many other suggestions were made by John R. Alden, John S. Curtiss, Arthur B. Ferguson, Irving B. Holley, Frederic B. M. Hollyday, and Richard L. Watson, Jr., of the Duke University Department of History. The Duke University Research Council provided clerical help and subsidized publication. My wife typed much of the manuscript and displayed an admirable degree of patience throughout the whole long process. Most of Captain Liddell Hart's comments arrived after the book was in press. The second printing incorporated many of his suggestions and some additional bibliography. I am deeply grateful for the interest and advice of one of the world's greatest military critics and historians and for the suggestions of the students on whom this work has been tried. None of these persons is in any way responsible for the errors of commission and omission which surely remain in a work of this nature.

Numerous new titles, a personal list for serious-minded beginners in this field, and a personal list of novels of the First World War have been added to this edition. But some important works have surely been left out, and I am eager for additional comments from readers. For such comments I am most grateful to G. A. Hayes-McCoy of University College, Galway, Robin D. S. Higham of the University of North Carolina, Arthur Marder of the University of Hawaii, Walter Millis of the Center for the Study of Democratic Institutions, Charles P. Stacey of the University of Toronto, and Ian Wards of the New Zealand War History Branch.

War in the Modern World

Introduction to the Johns Hopkins Edition

THE return to print of *War in the Modern World* affords me the opportunity to offer a personal appreciation of both the book and its author. Ted Ropp was my graduate mentor in the early 1970s. In 1981, I returned to Duke to succeed him when he retired. Succeeding your mentor can be a wonderful experience or a nightmare; mine was a wonderful experience. Ted and I even taught a course together during my first semester (his last) on the Duke faculty. He was as kind and solicitous in that setting as I had remembered him being when he was my teacher.

War in the Modern World has been in print for most of the last forty years, a testament to the soundness of the original book, unrevised since 1962. But even good books age, and few command attention after four decades. *War in the Modern World* clearly speaks to us from an earlier generation of scholarship, but it also retains timeless qualities that more than justify its reissue. Three of those qualities are particularly noteworthy.

First, the book draws on twenty years of experience teaching military history. In the late 1950s, Theodore Ropp was a tenured associate professor of history at Duke University, where he had been teaching since 1938, a year after having taken his doctorate in European History with William Langer at Harvard University. He had not yet published a book. His colleagues suggested that promotion to full professor would depend on that accomplishment. Always more interested in reading than writing, Ted turned to the only book-length corpus of material at his disposal: his class notes. Since World War II he had taught a legendary undergraduate course in Western military history. The notes for that course became *War in the Modern World*.

The origins of this book bring to mind John Keegan's *The Face of Battle*. Keegan had been teaching for fourteen years at Sandhurst, the British military academy, when he wrote his first book, *The Face of Battle*, also based on his teaching experience.[1] Like Keegan's now-classic study, *War in the Modern World* rings with the detail, anecdotes, humor, and insight that come from trying to engage the interest and capture the imagination of undergraduates. Both books mask greater purposes and high ambition. Keegan sought to

[1] John Keegan, *The Face of Battle* (New York: Viking, 1976).

understand war from the bottom up, from the vantage point of soldiers on the ground. Ropp sought to understand war from the perspective of politics, economics, and society. Both were innovative approaches to military history in their time. Both became part of much larger movements that redirected the historiography of war.

Unlike Keegan, Ropp never wrote another book. *War in the Modern World* won him the promotion to full professor with which he always seemed content. His passion was to understand, not to persuade. He read voraciously and wrote extensively, but displayed little interest in publication or scholarly reputation of the traditional sort. In 1984, Clark Reynolds, a former student, published one of Ted's recent, extended essays, "Continuity and Change in Military and Revolutionary History," in a slim book entitled *History and War*.[2] Reynolds added a long, personal reminiscence of his experience as Ted's student, colleague, and friend, but he attributed authorship of the book entirely to Ted. At a testimonial marking his mentor's retirement, Clark presented the volume with the observation that Ted now had two books to his credit. In 1987, Ropp's Harvard dissertation was published by the United States Naval Institute Press, having been edited with his approval by Stephen S. Roberts.[3] Still, *War in the Modern World* is the book that made his reputation.

To say that Ted Ropp published little is not to say that he wrote little. I still have a file drawer filled with the unpublished papers that he produced, reproduced, and circulated among his students and colleagues. They read like trail markers along the routes of his intellectual journey. They bear titles such as "Continuity and Change" (1968), "Political and Other Considerations in the Infliction of Mass Casualties" (1965), "Military Genius" (1965), and "Main Current of Modern Strategy" (1968). Some were prepared specifically for classes he taught at Duke, some for lectures he gave elsewhere—he preferred to speak from, but not read, a prepared text—and some for the Historical Evaluation and Research Organization (HERO), a military history consulting group with which he was associated. Many of these papers deserved publication, but Ted had little patience with the demands of that practice. He wrestled with the ideas, established sufficient intellectual control to write for his

[2] Theodore Ropp, *History and War* (Augusta, Ga.: Hamburg Press, 1984).
[3] Theodore Ropp, *The Development of a Modern Navy: French Naval Policy, 1871–1904* (Annapolis, Md.: Naval Institute Press, 1987).

colleagues, and then moved on. For better or for worse, he cared little about sharing his insights with the larger world or with testing his ideas against the critiques of editors and referees.

As with the footnotes in *War in the Modern World*, Ted's unpublished papers attest to the catholicity of his reading and to his prodigious memory. In the graduate seminars I took with him in the early 1970s, the students attempted to catch him out, to find a book even remotely connected with military history that he did not know. Two years' assault on fortress Ropp proved unavailing. I suspected we had him once, but he managed the encounter so smoothly that I could never be sure. Ted usually came to campus twice a week, on Tuesdays and Thursdays. In the morning, he taught his undergraduate military history course and then moved across the hall to meet his graduate colloquium. He stayed on campus for lunch, often with his students, and met individually after that with those who sought him out. Then he was gone. He eschewed university politics (though he served for many years as a regional representative of the American Association of University Professors) and he seldom found himself called to committee service. He told me once that if I performed badly enough on these committees I would not be invited again.

Ted spent his time reading at home. The inner sanctum of his intellectual life was an attic reached by a pull-down ladder. Up there, amidst the thousands of books that made up his personal library, Ted bent his large frame to keep from hitting the rafters and settled into the modest table and chair that was his workplace. His office at Duke was where he hung his hat; this attic library was where his heart lay. It was here, preparing his undergraduate lectures, that he amassed the wealth of information shared in *War in the Modern World*.

The second great reason for continuing to read *War in the Modern World* is the complicated, penetrating mind that lay behind it. The legend of Ted Ropp, both on the Duke campus and in the military history community, stemmed from a unique combination of erudition and eccentricity. No one doubted the depth of his knowledge or the sheer intellectual power with which he manipulated it. But neither could anyone be quite sure, on any given occasion, if he was being entirely serious. Colleagues in the Duke history department still ask me if I understood Ted. They mean the question in two ways. First, could I follow the curious streams of consciousness that often passed for conversation with Ted? Second, did I know what made him tick? Ted lives in blissful retirement just a couple blocks from me as I write this; one imagines that I might simply go over and put those questions to him. But those who know Ted would understand why I don't. This is not the kind of question Ted Ropp would answer directly. A response, if it came at all, would take the form of riddles and impenetrable allusions. "We all know what grandmother thought about that," he would intone in the middle of a conversation. While the listener tried to imagine who "grandmother" was (Queen Victoria), Ted would seize the conversation and lead it in a direction more to his liking. His conversations always made sense, but it often took days of reflection to figure out where you had been. I have come to believe that these rhetorical ploys alternated between pedagogic devices to keep his students on their toes and defensive tactics to mask Ted's fundamental shyness. Whatever they were, all his colleagues and associates came to expect them and perhaps to write them off to professorial eccentricity.

If Ted is or was an eccentric, it was by design. When I returned to Duke in 1981, he offered only two pieces of advice. First, he said, I should write my class notes on high-quality paper, so that they would not yellow with the years. This counsel dripped of irony, coming from a man who never gave the same lecture twice in his forty-three years at Duke. Second, he said, I should "cultivate an eccentricity." It would, he assured me, amuse the students and confound my colleagues. Ted achieved both in his career, no doubt by design.

His students, of course, needed more from him than amusement. The undergraduates needed grades. The graduate students needed mentoring and recommendations. Most of us felt some obligation to figure him out, to learn the code. One contemporary of mine later reported that a review of his notes from Ted's undergraduate course in military history proved to be absolutely impenetrable. They made no sense at all. But I always believed that they did make sense. Ted conducted an ongoing internal dialogue with himself. When it came time for class, he just drew the students into the conversation. Often the lectures in his undergraduate military history course began with an article in that morning's local newspaper. One suspected at first that he had not prepared for class, that he was killing time. But always it came around to the material at hand. Always there emerged another example of history, no matter how remote or how esoteric, being as current and as relevant as today's headline. One imagines that he saw the connection each morning at breakfast, comparing the newspaper with the topic of that day's lesson. And he could always extemporize a narrative thread connecting one to the other.

For this reason, in part, his undergraduate course was legendary. Alumni still ask me about "Professor Ropp" and share with me their fond memories of his morning class. It did not hurt that he cared as little for grades as he did for committees. But the appeal of his course was not just an easy grade; it was Ropp himself, the consummate performer who entertained and instructed with equal facility. *War in the Modern World* is filled with the same asides and nuggets that salted his lectures. It reports the etymology of everyday terms whose original meanings convey new understanding and insight. It traces the origins of modern military practice in ancient tradition. It offers strong, blunt opinions on the wide range of literature that Ted internalized and relished. It reports what Ted found interesting in his vast reading. Not surprisingly, his taste for the interesting was as eccentric, original, and fascinating as he himself.

The third and most important reason to read *War in the Modern World* is that it marked a turning point in the historiography of war. Just as Keegan's *The Face of Battle* marked the transition to the social history of the military, so Ropp's classic coincided with the first full flowering of what would later be called the "new military history." In 1959, when this book first appeared, military history was still dominated by operational history, the study of wars, campaigns, and battles, told from the perspective of the great captains. It was designed to convey lessons that military practitioners might apply in their own careers. Since the days of Sun Tzu and Thucydides military history had served this instrumental function, which gained impetus through the example of the Prussian military reformers of the nineteenth century. Gerhard von Scharnhorst, Karl von Clausewitz, and their colleagues studied military history to educate themselves in the art of war.[4] The success of the Prussian system in the wars of German unification, 1864–71, convinced most of the developed world to follow their example. Military academies,

---

[4] Charles E. White, *The Enlightened Soldier: Scharnhorst and the Militärische Gesellschaft in Berlin, 1801–1805* (New York: Preager, 1988).

such as our own West Point, already existed on the model developed in France during the wars of the French Revolution and Napoleon. But the emphasis on history was a peculiarly Prussian contribution.

When Ted Ropp took up military history in the 1930s, the leading scholars in the English-speaking world were Charles Oman, Spenser Wilkinson, and Cyril Falls, all at one time Chichele Professors of History at Oxford.[5] The most influential public historians, along with Wilkinson, were J. F. C. Fuller and Basil Liddell Hart, both former British Army officers. Fuller and Liddell Hart had American counterparts in Theodore Dodge, Oliver Spaulding, Hoffman Nickerson, and John Wright. But there were no academic students of war to compare with Oman, Wilkinson, and Falls. All of these writers focused on the battlefield. Like John Keegan, they studied warfare, not war. In their history, war existed independent of society. It responded to its own imperative. It was best viewed from horseback, at the elbow of the great captains. Even Spenser Wilkinson's institutional history, *The Brain of an Army* (1890), betrayed a fascination with the commander's view of war, leavened perhaps by the insights of practitioners such as Scharnhorst and Clausewitz.[6]

Ropp had more in common with Oman, Wilkinson, and Falls than with Fuller, Liddell Hart, and their American counterparts, though he respected all of them. He wanted to understand war not as an operational exercise but as a historical phenomenon. He wanted to place war in its historical context. Specifically, he sought to understand the social, economic, and political dimensions of war. These threads run throughout *War in the Modern World*. While not slighting the operational art, Ropp focuses on the political causes of war, its economic drives and constraints, the social composition of armies and navies, and the technological capabilities that shaped the tools of war. In his own way he pursued what military historian Hans Delbrück, and his mentor Leopold von Ranke, called "universal history."[7]

---

[5] Oman held the Chichele chair in modern history, Wilkinson and Falls the Chichele chair in the history of war.
[6] Spenser Wilkinson, *The Brain of an Army: A Popular Account of the German General Staff* (London: Macmillan, 1890).
[7] Delbrück in turn had the term from the great nineteenth-century German historian, Leopold von Ranke. See Hans Delbrück, *History of the Art of War within the Framework of Political History*, trans. Walter J. Renfroe, Jr., 4 vols. (Westport, Conn.: Greenwood Press, [1920], 1975–1985).

Ropp was among the first to take this step. *War in the Modern World* bears comparison with a near-contemporary history, Richard A. Preston, Sydney F. Wise, and Herman O. Werner, *Men in Arms: A History of Warfare and Its Interrelationships with Western Society*.[8] In Ropp's pages and theirs, armies and navies are social institutions. Wars are continuations of politics. Campaigns are exercises in logistics and management as much as strategy. And battles are contingent events where chance, training, technology, morale, and tactics collide to produce results that range from the banal to the momentous. The actual clash of arms receives slight attention in these books. This was the new military history, appearing in its nascent form.

War in the Modern World made an enormous splash. Liddell Hart hailed it as "a brilliant survey of the history of warfare . . . the best yet produced anywhere." Collier Books acquired the rights from Duke University Press and published a revised edition in 1962. Military academies and war colleges around the world adopted it, and Ted became a much-sought-after speaker, commentator, and reviewer. Duke became a mecca for students like myself who wanted to study with the master. And Ted became for a while the dean of military historians in the English-speaking world. He wrested that unofficial title from the likes of Falls and Liddell Hart, although in time it returned to England to rest with Michael Howard and John Keegan. Two British ex-patriots, Paul Kennedy and Geoffrey Parker, are also contenders within the generation after Ropp's. All of these, save Keegan, profess to be European historians, though most of their scholarship has been in military history. The same is true of Richard Preston and Sydney Wise. Perhaps this training and inclination allowed them to see military history from a different perspective, to see it as part of a larger historical context. None of them denied its significance, but neither did any of them (with the possible exception of Liddell Hart) believe that it could be understood independently of Ranke's universal history. When I showed Ted a draft of this introduction, his only suggestion was that I mention Frederick B. Artz, his beloved mentor at Oberlin College, who instilled in him an abiding interest in European history conceived on the broadest possible scale. Ted once told me that no one trained in military history had ever amounted to much, one of his calculated barbs designed, I think, to warn me of the

[8] New York: Preager, 1956.

parochialism that tainted so much of the field. It is ironic that one of the great teachers of military history, whose only book flowed from his lecture notes, should warn his own student to eschew the narrowness and circumscription that constrain so much of the literature on war.

War in the Modern World has none of that. Instead, one finds insights and curiosities at every turn. Here the etymology of the "forlorns." There the chatty footnote reporting that Saint Simon, one of the founders of modern socialism, served with the French Fleet of Admiral DeGrasse, which led away the British and left Cornwallis trapped at Yorktown. In place of theories and paradigms, one finds common sense and straightforward explanation. Soldiers and officers learned to fight by fighting, asserts Ropp, a truth so obvious that one seldom finds it in other histories. Ted claims that he never created a school of historical theory or a consistent style among his students because he was never sure himself exactly what he thought about war. He simply applied great erudition, exhaustive reading, and common sense to explain what we know. He himself possessed what he always recommended to his students: a firm grasp of the obvious.

Of course any book that is forty years old has some weaknesses. The bibliography amassed in the footnotes is increasingly dated. Ropp quotes overmuch perhaps, a reflection of his note-taking style in the age before ubiquitous computers and photocopying machines. The book concentrates on Anglo-American military experience to the neglect of other histories. It displays Ropp's reluctance to move from insight to generalization. And it necessarily relied on a secondary literature that has been largely superseded.

The marvel is that the text holds up as well as it does. Theodore Ropp found truth in facts. Always suspicious of theory, he collected and manipulated facts to tell his story. Theories and interpretations may have changed in the last forty years, but the facts have not. This is still good, reliable history, told with clarity, wit, insight, and understanding. It rewards reading just as much as when the new military history was new.

Alex Roland
Chair, Department of History
Duke University

Introduction to the Original Edition

IN 1933 the great British military critic, B. H. Liddell Hart, ended the Lees Knowles Lectures at Trinity College, Cambridge, with a call for the wider study of war as a social phenomenon.

We live in a time when 'war' is on everyone's lips; when everything contemporary is dated in relation to the last war; when those, who dislike the subject most, talk about it most—if their talk be only about the prevention of war.

That volume of talk is proof of their subconscious realization of the part that war has played in . . . their lives, and the life of modern Europe. Subconscious, because they give astoundingly little recognition, in a practical sense, to the importance of the subject. They talk much *about* war, but rarely do they talk *of* it—as a subject so serious as to be worth the serious study of every thinking man and woman. They appear to regard it as a disturbance of Nature similar to an earthquake, . . . rather than as a disease that might be prevented, . . . and the danger of which might at least be curtailed by scientific treatment. . . .

For the failure to treat it as a branch of scientific knowledge, responsibility lies as much on men of learning as on men of war. By the nature of their profession, soldiers are practitioners, not detached researchers. . . . They are general practitioners, so occupied in administering immediate remedies and compounding drugs, that they have not the freedom for research, if peradventure they have the bent for it. Even a Staff College training is more akin to walking the wards than to work in a laboratory.

The study of war as a branch of knowledge, requires the method of work that prevails in a University as well as the attitude of mind which is inculcated there. But it is not likely that these needs will be fulfilled until men of learning change their attitude of mind towards war, and learn to regard it as a branch of knowledge worthy of exploration.[1]

1 *The Ghost of Napoleon* (London, 1933), 145-147. The classic work is Hans Delbrück, *Geschichte des Kriegskunst im Rahmen der politischen Geschichte* (7 vols., Berlin, 1900-1936). For campaigns and battles, General J. F. C. Fuller's brilliant and prejudiced *A Military History of the Western World* (3 vols., New York, 1954-1956) and Lynn Montross, *War Through the Ages* (3d ed., New York, 1960) are good. So are Henri Bernard, *La Guerre et son évolution à travers les siècles* (2 vols., Brussels, 1955-1957), Richard A. Preston, Sydney F. Wise, and Herman O. Werner, *Men in Arms: A History of Warfare and Its Interrelationships with Western Society* (New York, 1956); Theodore A. Dodge, *Great Captains* (Boston, 1895), and Oliver L. Spaulding, Hoffman Nickerson, and John W. Wright, *Warfare* (Washington, 1937). Gordon B.

When soldiers speak of the "principles of war," they are referring to those principles of action which can be illustrated by the military events of any historical period, the maxims of the soldier's trade. The United States Army lists nine of them: the Objective, the Offensive, Mass, Maneuver, Surprise, Security, Economy of Force, Unity of Command, and Simplicity. Most of them were boiled down in Nathan Bedford Forrest's famous phrase, "fustest with the mostest." They lie in the background of military history as the principles of politics lie in the background of political history. Though he must be familiar with them, the historian does well to focus, however, on the process of change. In the case of this outline, we are particularly interested in those changes which have occurred in modern times, roughly defined as the last five centuries. The factors producing these changes can be roughly classified as (1) political, (2) technological, and (3) organizational, institutional, or administrative.[2]

Since a war by definition—to distinguish it from other kinds of social violence—is a violent conflict between states, many problems can be approached first from the political angle. The political factors include those matters which were once grouped under the broad heading of "political economy": the aims of the opposing states and the resources—social, economic, and diplomatic—which each has at its disposal. These were the factors stressed by the nineteenth-century Prussian military philosopher Karl von Clausewitz in his famous definitions of the nature of war, its means, its object, and the gradations between limited and total warfare.

We shall not begin here with a clumsy, pedantic definition of war, but confine ourselves to its essence, the duel. . . . Each tries by

Turner, ed., *A History of Military Affairs in Western Society* (New York, 1953) is a good source book. On military thought use Edward Meade Earle, ed., *Makers of Modern Strategy* (Princeton, 1943). The fine *West Point Atlas of American Wars*, ed. Vincent J. Esposito (2 vols., New York, 1959) covers that field only. The most detailed encyclopedia is *Handbuch der neuzeitlichen Wehrwissenschaften* (4 vols., Berlin, 1937).

2 The Italian strategist Giulio Douhet defined the principles of war as "the rules of the game." They "remained unchanged, because the players were always alike and the game always the same, even though the forms of the pawns changed. But even if the main principles did not change, their application in specific cases depended on the player." *The Command of the Air*, trans. Dino Ferrari (London, 1943), 122. The best recent short summaries of these principles and some of the problems presented by them are D. K. Palit, *The Essentials of Military Knowledge* (Aldershot, 1950) and Edgar J. Kingston-McCloughry, *The Direction of War* (London, 1955).

physical force to compel the other to do his will; his immediate
object is to overthrow his adversary and thereby make him incapable
of any further resistance.

*War is thus an act of force to compel our adversary to do our
will. . . .*

Force, that is to say physical force (for no moral force exists
apart from the conception of a state and law), is thus the *means:*
to impose our will upon the enemy is the *object.* To achieve this
object with certainty we must disarm the enemy, and thus disarming
is by definition the proper aim of military action.

If we want to overthrow our opponent, we must proportion our
effort to his powers of resistance . . . expressed as a product of two
inseparable factors: *the extent of the means at his disposal and the
strength of his will.* The extent of the means at his disposal would
be capable of estimation, as it rests (though not entirely) on figures,
but the strength of the will is much less so and only approximately
to be measured by the strength of the motive behind it. . . .

To avoid underestimating the value of these various shorter ways
to our aim . . . we have only to bear in mind the diversity of political
objects which may cause a war, or . . . the distance which separates
a death struggle for political existence from a war which a forced
or tottering alliance makes a . . . disagreeable duty. . . . If we reject
one of these gradations, we might with equal right reject them all,
that is to say, lose sight of the real world entirely.[3]

The second set of factors is technological—"Force armed
with the inventions of art and science." The increasing importance of technology is a major feature of modern warfare,
as it is of modern life. Competition in weapons is older than
recorded history, but only in modern times has technological
innovation been so rapid, so conscious, and so continuous that
scientists have become as important in warfare as politicians
or soldiers. One of the changes which marked the beginning
of the modern period was the increasing utilization of gunpowder. The reinforcement of the national state by the nineteenth-century Industrial Revolution and twentieth-century
applied science—in Alexander Herzen's phrase, "Ghenghiz
Khan with the telegraph"—now threatens to obliterate Western
civilization. Destruction, in the words of General H. H. Arnold,

---

[3] *On War*, trans. O. J. Matthjis Jollis (New York, 1943), 3-6, 24. A fine condensation is *The Living Thoughts of Clausewitz*, ed. A. O. Mendel (New York,
1943). For the relations between international law and military history, see
Quincy Wright, *A Study of War* (2 vols., Chicago, 1942) and Lothar Kotzsh,
The Concept of War in Contemporary History and International Law (Geneva, 1956). A recent sociological treatment of war is Gaston Bouthoul, *Les
Guerres, éléments de polémologie* (Paris, 1951). *La Guerre* (Paris, 1953) is
a condensation of the larger work.

the head of the United States Army Air Forces during the Second World War, has become "too cheap and easy."[4]

The institutional, administrative, and organizational factors in military history are related to both politics and technology. They are the particular concern of the professional soldier, a specialist who, in Clausewitz' view, "is levied, clothed, armed, trained, sleeps, eats, drinks, and marches *merely to fight at the right place and the right time."* Getting the soldier to do this has required an increasingly complex social organization. The organizational factors cover a host of specialties—strategy, tactics, logistics, communications, and training. Strategy may be defined roughly as the art of bringing an enemy to battle. Tactics is the means of defeating him in battle. All tactical systems, it has often been noted, ultimately rest on the dominant weapon in use. Troops are, or should be, trained to exploit their dominant weapon's strong points and to minimize its weak ones. War is a chess game in which both the values of the pieces and the nature of their possible moves vary both with the training of the pieces and the skill of the individual player. Logistics, a term which came into common use only in this century, has to deal with movement and supply. An army is composed of organisms with stomachs. One of the most important of military gifts, in the words of Lord Wavell,

is what the French call *le sens du practicable*, . . . a really sound knowledge of the 'mechanisms of war,' *i.e.* topography, movement, and supply. It is the lack of this knowledge . . . which puts what we call amateur strategists wrong, not the principles of strategy themselves, which can be apprehended in a very short time by any reasonable intelligence. . . . A homely analogy can be made from contract bridge. The calling is strategy, the play of the hand tactics. . . . Calling is to a certain degree mechanical and subject to conventions; so is strategy. . . . There is, of course, wide scope in both for judgment, boldness, and originality. . . . But in the end it is the result of the manner in which the cards are played . . . that is

4 "Air Force in the Atomic Age" (*One World or None*, ed. Dexter Masters and Katharine Way, New York, 1946), 26. On the *Tools of War*, see James R. Newman's work of that title (Garden City, 1942). Another sound summary is Stanton H. Coblentz, *From Arrow to Atom Bomb* (New York, 1953). Tom Wintringham, *Weapons and Tactics* (London, 1942) and J. F. C. Fuller, *Armament and History* (New York, 1945) are written from opposite ends of the political spectrum. Fuller is heavily indebted to Lewis Mumford, *Technics and Civilization* (New York, 1934) and to Werner Sombart's famous *Krieg und Kapitalismus* (3 vols., Munich, 1913). Unfortunately, John U. Nef, *War and Human Progress* (Cambridge, 1950), has demolished Sombart. See also Nef's brilliant paper on military history, "La Guerre" (*IXᵉ Congrès International des Sciences Historiques*, I, *Rapports*, Paris, 1950, 595-606).

put down on the score sheets. . . . Therefore I rate the skilful tactician above the skilful strategist, especially him who plays the bad cards well.[5]

Military histories have been written to stress the importance of one or the other of these groups of factors—political, technological, or organizational. Military history has been told as a tale of great states, key inventions, or great captains. But such partial views of a complex social phenomenon are usually false. War, as Clausewitz put it, "is a veritable chameleon, because in each concrete case it changes somewhat its character . . . composed of the original violence of its essence, . . . of the play of probabilities and chance, . . . and of the subordinate character of a political tool, through which it belongs to the province of pure intelligence." For this reason, "the work of war, plain and simple though it appears, can never be conducted with distinguished success by people without distinguished intellectual powers." But intelligence alone is not enough. In war, as in other aspects of politics, "there is always a great difference . . . between knowing what to do and being able to do it. Man always gets his strongest impulses to action . . . from those amalgamations of temperament and character which we have learned to recognize as resolution, firmness, staunchness and strength of character."[6]

[5] *The Good Soldier* (London, 1948), 10, 32.
[6] *On War*, 18, 44, 46.

THE AGE OF THE
GREAT CAPTAINS

Chapter 1

Land Warfare from the Renaissance to the Neoclassical Age (1415-1789)

LAND warfare during the first three and one half centuries of the modern period can be studied best in the armies of the Spanish Hapsburgs and Prussia, each of which had at one time the best army in Continental Europe. The army of the sixteenth-century Hapsburgs was typical of the years of transition from medieval to modern times, while the eighteenth-century Prussian army represented the highest development of what can be called the neoclassical age of modern warfare. Though an exact definition of "modern" is impossible, both of these armies had the same distinguishing characteristics. (1) They were the *political* instruments of dynastic monarchies and not of feudal barons, private mercenary captains, or city states. (2) They were *armed*, at least partially, with gunpowder weapons. (3) They were *organized* around a permanent (or "standing") body of professional infantry.[1]

New Techniques and Types of Military Organization

The medieval feudal array—of men serving for a limited time in return for land tenure—had been built around the heavily armored lancer. The dismounted men carried pikes, short swords, and shields like those of the Romans, but their duties toward the mounted men had made it impossible for them to fight as organized infantry. As in modern armored battles, the fate of the knights had usually decided the fate of their "soft" auxiliaries. During the centuries since the break-

[1] Antiquity's heavy infantry reached its peak when the flexible Roman sword lines replaced the spear squares of the Greek phalanx. Armored cavalry was the late Roman answer to the Asian plainsman's high saddle, stirrups, and iron horseshoes. Key works are J. F. C. Fuller, *The Generalship of Alexander the Great* (London, 1958), F. E. Adcock, *The Roman Art of War under the Republic* (Cambridge, Mass., 1940) and *The Greek and Macedonian Art of War* (Berkeley, 1957), and Oliver L. Spaulding, *Pen and Sword in Greece and Rome* (Princeton, 1937). On military technology before 1900 use Charles J. Singer, *et al., A History of Technology* (5 vols., Oxford, 1954-1958), or the condensation of this great work by T. K. Derry and Trevor I. Williams, *A Short History of Technology* (Oxford, 1960), or for earlier eras, R. Ewart Oakeshott, *The Archaeology of Weapons* (New York, 1960). The definition of a professional is as difficult in war as in athletics. The medieval soldier was, perhaps, a semi-professional. See J. F. Verbruggen, *Die Krijgskunst in West-Europa in de Middeleeuwen* (Brussels, 1954).

19

down of Rome, the landowners had also erected great fortifications of stone, an immense tax on the resources of Europe's localized economy. Since field armies could feed themselves for only a few weeks during the summer, an inferior medieval force had only to retire behind its ramparts to be almost impregnable. On hilltops, in marshes, or at the nodal points of transportation, these man-made obstacles compounded the difficulty of movement on the decayed Roman roads and waterways. In terms of the categories used in this outline, the characteristic features of the medieval system of warfare were: (1) an extreme localization of military power following from and contributing to the extreme localization of economic and political life, (2) the technological superiority of the defensive over the offensive, and (3) a military organization centered around the heavily armed and armored horsemen, who could move faster and hit harder within this localized framework than any force of footsoldiers.[2]

The first missile weapon which decisively affected medieval warfare was the primitive longbow, taken over by the English from the savage Welsh and Scots. Though not as powerful as the crossbow—a one-man version of the Roman ballista—the longbow outranged it and had four or five times as great a rate of fire. It was especially effective whenever the moving mass of horses could be halted and piled up by a ditch or some other obstacle. The combination used by the English kings for over a century was a mass of dismounted men-at-arms behind temporary field fortifications with sleeves of bowmen who shot the opposition to pieces from the flanks while it was "fixed" by the dismounted knights in the center.

2 When these local jealousies were submerged by the extra-political force of religious fanaticism and water transportation was available, medieval armies accomplished great things: in the Third and Fourth Crusades and the conquest and settlement of Iceland, the Azores, and the Canaries. Little has been done on medieval river and barge traffic, or on such military transport in the early modern era. On land frontiers chains of castles (with surprisingly small garrisons of military monks or other professionals) had replaced the continuous Roman screening walls. These castles sheltered the settlers and their stock and provided bases for "punitive expeditions" or new conquests. Key works are Steven Runciman, *A History of the Crusades* (3 vols., Cambridge, 1951-1954), Roger R. Sellman, *Medieval English Warfare* (London, 1960), Robin Fedden and John Thomson, *Crusader Castles* (London, 1957), Ferdinand Lot's superb *L'Art militaire et les armées au moyen age* (2 vols., Paris, 1946) and a new edition of Charles W. C. Oman, *The Art of War in the Middle Ages, 375-1515*, rev. and ed. John H. Beeler (Ithaca, 1953). Other fine works are Frederick G. Heymann, *John Ziska and the Hussite Revolution* (Princeton, 1955), Sidney Toy, *A History of Fortification from 3000 B.C. to 1700* (New York, 1955), and R. C. Smail, *Crusading Warfare (1097-1193)* (London, 1956).

The French answer to such tactics, especially during the first half (1339-1380) of the Hundred Years' War had been logical, but essentially regressive. The French had dismounted their own knights, who advanced on foot against the numerically weaker English center. But fighting on foot in full armor was a tactical blind alley, since heavy cavalry depend on the shock effect of both men and horses.[3]

Some of the bands of the Hundred Years' War were raised by individuals with royal commissions; others—the "Free Companies"—were military societies like the trading guilds. They were supported by cash levy-money, regular sums for each man enrolled, and by promises and hopes of lands, titles, and plunder. When these sources dried up, these professional soldiers turned to banditry or took service with the great nobility. Under the medieval system of finance, the king could not pay soldiers for not fighting, and he could not defeat them with his own forces. Long practice had made the bands' discipline so effective that no feudal levy could stand up to them. One way to get rid of them was to lure them out of the country. As a result, many of the German and English bands who were devastating France were pushed or pulled over the Alps and Pyrenees into Italy and Spain. The Italian adventurers who imitated them were known as *condottieri*. The larger Italian cities were able and eager to hire heavy cavalry. Their local militia were useless for offensive purposes against their rivals. The *condottieri* companies often drew recruits from specific local territories and were commanded by a permanent captain, who signed a long-term contract—the *condotta*—with the state or city which employed him. The citizens could go about their business relatively unmolested, since the captains did not wish to imperil their steady incomes by allowing their men to plunder their employers. Occasionally, as in other professional sports, the captains of both sides were

---

[3] The French decision to fight on foot was a matter of tactical doctrine and fear of arming the peasantry with the longbow. In spite of the plate needed to keep out arrows, a knight could still lift himself onto his horse. See Claud Blair, *European Armour circa 1066 to circa 1700* (New York, 1959), and Eduard Wagner, ed., *Medieval Costume, Armour and Weapons* (London, 1959). The French fell back to the final defenses of any medieval state, their fixed fortifications. See Edouard Perroy, *The Hundred Years' War* (New York, 1951), Alfred H. Burne, *The Crecy War* (New York, 1955) and *The Agincourt War* (New York, 1956), P. E. Russell, *The English Intervention in Spain and Portugal in the Time of Edward III and Richard II* (Oxford, 1956), and H. J. Hewitt, *The Black Prince's Expedition of 1355-1357* (Manchester, 1958). This last is particularly good on recruiting, as is, for an earlier period, I. J. Sanders, *Feudal Military Service in England* (Oxford, 1956).

accused of arranging the show beforehand. Battles used up the captains' capital, and everyone preferred live prisoners who could be ransomed to dead men whose relatives or friends might take revenge. Readers should not take Machiavelli's contemptuous account of the *condottieri* too seriously. Some of their battles were very bloody, and reprisals for unsportsmanlike conduct often knew no bounds. Paolo Vitelli, whose treachery so impressed Machiavelli, plucked out the eyes and cut off the hands of captured gunners after seeing his friends killed by the new weapons.

Meanwhile the Swiss cantons had developed a heavy infantry which could stand in the open and, eventually, maneuver in the field instead of waiting behind ditches, stake barricades, and other field fortifications. Its principal arm—and the arm of the town militia everywhere—was the pike, a long spear which had been revived in the late Roman Empire to enable legionnaires to cope with cavalry. The pike was held at shoulder height with the point slightly downward when advancing against dismounted knights or bowmen, or with the shaft sunk in the ground to form a hedgehog against cavalry. The points of the first four ranks reached to the front of the square. The other men carried their pikes upright until they stepped in to take the places of the fallen. The ordinary Swiss peasant or townsman could not afford much armor, but the steel cap and breast plate of ancient times provided sufficient protection against arrows.

The Swiss pikemen were disciplined citizens. Elsewhere the citizens were not disciplined, or the disciplined were not citizens. Elsewhere military service had become the monopoly of a single class. The ordinary peasant did not fight at all, or was called out only for labor service or to repel full-scale invasion. The new national monarchs gave the townsmen the choice of serving or taxation. The townsman would rather pay than serve; the king preferred money anyway, because it enabled him to hire far more useful professionals. As a result, the Swiss defeated the armies raised by potentially far more powerful political units. At the same time, however, the Swiss Confederation—like the other leagues of city states which had won local victories in Germany, Italy, and the Netherlands—could not take the offensive as successfully as the new dynastic monarchies. The Confederation finally became (like Nepal in more recent times) a recruiting ground for other states with more centralized governments and greater political ambitions. These mercenaries seem to have been recruited voluntarily at first, but after soldiers became a major Swiss article of commerce the magistrates acted as middlemen, taking some of the profits and compelling the men to fulfil the obligations they had contracted for them.[4]

Employed in other armies, the Swiss did much to introduce common tactical ideas and standards. Their pikemen remained the backbone of most European armies throughout the wars for Italy. They were combined with swordsmen and bowmen until, about the beginning of the sixteenth century, the handgun gave footsoldiers a missile weapon superior to either type of bow. Pike and "shot" were to become the standard for all infantry during the next two hundred years in a Europe increasingly dominated by the armies of the dynastic monarchs. The most powerful of these monarchs was the king of France. During the last phases of the Hundred Years' War he had gradually created the best army in Europe. This long war had greatly weakened the French Estates' resistance to royal taxation. The kings had gradually succeeded in getting the Estates to grant them the permanent revenues necessary for the support of a standing ("standing" in the sense of "standing committee") military force. In 1445 the French king had hired twenty companies on a yearly rather than on a monthly basis. The favored companies ("of ordnance"—of a standard size or strength) were those already commanded by good officers. A guarantee of permanent employment bound them more tightly to the king and made it possible for him to demand more from them. Each company consisted of a hundred "lances" and four officers. A "lance" included the man-at-arms, his squire ("coutillier"—the modern French term for can opener—to collect upset knights and hold them for ransom), two archers, a valet, and a page. All six of them had horses, though they usually fought on foot. This mobile force was just what was needed for defeating the inferior English forces in the field. The English fortresses were then battered into submission by the French siege train in which the exact proportion of guns to other siege weapons

---

[4] The number of these mercenaries is hard to determine. They mustered armies of 25,000 men in their wars with the Burgundians. There were usually about 10,000 Swiss in the Italian campaigns, though perhaps 20,000 took part in the campaign against Milan in 1495. The population of the cantons was then about a million; the proportion of men under arms was as high as in France at any time before the Revolution. W. Bickel, *Bevölkerungsgeschichte und Bevölkerungspolitik der Schweiz seit dem Ausgang des Mittelalters* (Zurich, 1947), 293-294.

is still unknown. After the English had been driven from all their holdings but Calais, the French king quartered the royal companies in strategic points throughout France, where they were equally efficient at suppressing the old soldiers who had turned to banditry and the small private armies of the king's own relatives and vassals.

The French *"Compagnies d'Ordonnance"* are usually considered to be the direct ancestors of most modern European armies, though they were a force of mounted rather than regular infantry and the way in which they were recruited perhaps even widened the old feudal gap between the military specialist and the rest of society. Even within the nobility a gulf began to open between the ordinary landlords and those who had turned to full-time professional service. The former did less and less real military service, though they kept their immunity from taxation, as the feudal "ban" was used less and less frequently. The *"arrière ban"* which called out the peasant militia also fell into disuse. It was easier and perhaps safer to hire Swiss and German infantry than to train French peasants for this purpose. When regular French infantry regiments were organized by Swiss instructors, they were not taken from the ordinary peasantry, but from its dregs, *"enfants perdus"* who were faithful hired hands of what might be called the royal revolution. This pattern of recruiting both officers and men from limited groups in the population was to last almost everywhere until the French Revolution.

The French standing army of the latter part of the fifteenth century was, however, an army which was modern in a good many of its essential features. It was the *political* instrument of a dynastic monarchy. It was *armed* with a mixture of gunpowder and other weapons. And its companies—with their permanent organization and special loyalties—were much more tightly *organized* than the feudal array. When the unification of France had been substantially completed by the extinction of the House of Burgundy, Charles VIII (1483-1498) was free to turn his attention to Italian politics. Whatever the numbers of Charles's first expedition to Italy (1494), his forces were much stronger than anything which the Italian states or any rival outside dynasty could bring against them. And since the French expedition was observed by some of the best minds of a very great age of intellectual inquiry, the French army of 1494 is perhaps the first modern army of which there is a really accurate description. One of the best is that of the Florentine historian, diplomat, administrator, and soldier Francesco Guicciardini (1482-1540), who credited Charles with 200 gentlemen of the royal guard, 1,600 men-at-arms ("with two archers, according to the French custom, for each, so that every lance included six horses"), 6,000 Swiss and 6,000 French infantry, and "a great quantity of siege and field artillery, the like of which Italy had never seen."[5]

"This plague," Guicciardini continued, had been brought into Italy by the Venetians from Germany about 1380. But the old iron or brass "bombards" had been so hard to transport and so slow in firing that the defenders could repair their works between shots. Charles's

cannon, using iron balls instead of stone, were drawn on wheels, not by oxen . . . but by horses, . . . with such speed that they almost kept up with the army. . . . They were planted with such speed and left such short intervals between shots, . . . that the work of days was accomplished in a few hours. [Charles's army was also] feared, not for the number but for the valor of the soldiers. . . . Almost all the men-at-arms were his subjects, not commoners but gentlemen, . . . paid and disciplined not only by their captains but also by royal officers. Their companies were up to strength and were composed of picked men with good horses and sound armor. . . . The captains had no reason, either of ambition or greed, to change their employers or to compete with each other for better contracts. . . . There was no less difference between the Italian infantry and those of Charles. The Italians did not fight with firm and ordered ranks, but . . . dispersed . . . often retiring to take advantage of hills or ditches. The Swiss, a most war-like nation, . . . stood against their enemies like a wall, firm and almost invincible.[6]

The Wars for Italy and the Rise of Spain (1494-1559)

The great military historian Charles Oman described the military history of the fifteenth century as "shut up in many water-tight compartments. . . . These can all be treated as separate stories, having few and infrequent cross-relations

[5] Charles may have had as many as 65,000 men, though Nef, *War and Human Progress*, 91-92, notes that 30,000 men was a big army 140 years later. A minute description of the Burgundian army has been given by Charles Brusten, *L'Armée bourguignonne de 1465 à 1468* (Brussels, 1954).

[6] *Storia d'Italia*, ed. Costantino Panigada (5 vols., Bari, 1929), I, 71-74. Gunpowder affected siegecraft first. See B. H. St. J. O'Neil, *Castles and Cannon: A Study of Early Artillery Fortifications in England* (New York, 1960).

with each other." But in the sixteenth century, after the opening of the wars for Italy, "all the old local groups of war gradually grow into one single complex, in which Spain, Italy, France, Germany, the Netherlands, Hungary, and the Ottoman Empire are all involved together." In 1494 the five Italian "great powers" controlled somewhat more of that peninsula's total area than the six European great powers controlled in their peninsula in 1914. But the individual weakness of the Italian states is apparent in the estimates of their populations—one of the best rough guides to military potential in an agrarian society. Naples, with two and a half millions at the very most, had fewer people than England and Wales or the Netherlands. Milan, the States of the Church, and Venice may have had a million people each, and Florence only half a million. France had about fifteen million people, and Spain about six. The ruin of the Italian states was to require only four years more (1494-1529) than the thirty-one years (1914-1945) which were to ruin the great powers of Western and Central Europe just four centuries later.

The Italian wars began with Charles VIII's revival of an old claim to the throne of Naples, from which, by controlling communications the length of the peninsula, he might be able to dominate the whole area. But instead of forming a common front, the Milanese allowed the French to cross the Alps and to recruit mercenaries in their territories, the Florentines overthrew the Medicis and re-established a republic favorable to France, and the Pope made no resistance whatever. As a result, the French occupied the whole kingdom of Naples, while the French siege train battered down the old-fashioned fortifications to which the Neapolitan king had retired—in the best medieval manner—while waiting for the other powers to come to his assistance. This happened in 1495. Spain, the Holy Roman Emperor, the Pope, Milan, and Venice united; and the French were expelled, but two other "barbarian" rulers (Ferdinand of Aragon and the Holy Roman Emperor) had been called in and one of the most famous of the *condottieri* generals had been badly beaten by the retreating French in a pitched battle at Fornovo.

Though the French had been driven out, both the military and political lessons had been very clear to intelligent Italians. These observers, who can be said to have founded modern military and political theory, saw that Italian armies had to be ready for serious fighting and not just for tournaments and that if the Italian states failed to unite under a single dynasty, all of them would be conquered individually by the "barbarians." These were the solutions proposed in many works, of which the greatest were those of the Florentine diplomat Niccolò Machiavelli (1469-1527), whose *The Prince* (1513, but not published until 1532) and *Art of War* (1521) summarize the changes in the arts of politics and war during the early sixteenth century. These changes were most apparent on the political level. *The Prince* was a classic study of the mechanics and morals of state building and a plea for unity under a strong sovereign. Machiavelli's military experiences had strongly impressed him with the military ineptitude and political unreliability of the *condottieri*. The Roman historian Livy provided him with many arguments for a citizen army. Machiavelli's own hero, Cesare Borgia, had successfully substituted his own subjects for alien troops, and Machiavelli was placed in charge of a new ministry for raising a citizen militia in the country districts around Florence. Though this militia was not effective against the Medici party, one of the central ideas of the *Art of War* is the superiority of native over foreign armies. In this connection native is a better word than national—a sovereign should depend on troops raised from his own subjects.

Machiavelli was the weakest on the details of techniques and tactics. He was not a professional soldier, but even professionals could hardly have been expected to pick the weapons of the future from the many then competing for attention. Partly because of their similarity to the legionnaires, Machiavelli was greatly impressed by the Spanish swordsmen. They were stationed inside or behind the pikes and went into action when the original spear walls had become entangled. In this situation the pikemen (following the experiences of the Greek phalanx against the legion) had to drop their heavy spears and try to fence with skilled swordsmen with more armor and shields. Machiavelli has been charged, incorrectly, with paying too little attention to gunpowder. He was greatly interested in gunpowder weapons, but was naturally unable to predict which ones would be the weapons of the future. Missile weapons did not really dominate the battlefield until the middle of the nineteenth century. Leonardo da Vinci was already designing breech-loading guns, submarines, and flying machines, but none of his many inventions had much practical significance. Except in the fields of fortification and surgery, the demands of war did not stimulate Renaissance science as much as has been sometimes believed.[7]

These theoretical writings, like the brilliant political works of the Greek fourth century B.C. or the equally cogent arguments for European unity in the twentieth century, did not unify Italy. The people who learned the most from the early Italian wars were the foreign "barbarians." Of these foreign monarchs, Ferdinand of Aragon (1479-1516) and his wife, Isabella of Castile (1474-1504), were perhaps the most able and enterprising. Like the other royal armies, the Spanish had begun as a royal bodyguard of about a thousand men, augmented by forces raised by the towns, the church, and the loyal nobility for the suppression of banditry. These forces, for local operations in states just emerging from dynastic crises, had been largely composed of cavalry. The sovereigns had also attempted to give their army a permanent financial foundation by forced loans levied on the clergy and to raise the standards of the town militia, or, failing that, to collect taxes from the towns to pay their own forces. Once their internal enemies had been brought under control, Ferdinand and Isabella had then taken up the most popular cause in Spain, the conquest of the mountainous Moorish state of Granada. This had involved numerous siege operations, which had increased the need for long-service professional soldiers and for heavy artillery imported from foreign countries. After their initial defeats in Italy, the Spanish captains improved on the Swiss model to create the best heavy infantry in Europe, while diplomacy united Spain, the Netherlands, and the Hapsburg lands in the person of the Emperor Charles V (1516-1555). The most noteworthy pitched battle of the Italian wars was at Pavia (1525), in which the Spanish infantry decisively defeated the Swiss. Four years later in the Treaty of

[7] Nef, *War and Human Progress*, 64. On the great surgeon Paré, see Francis R. Packard, *Life and Times of Ambroise Paré* (New York, 1926). On Machiavelli, see Felix Gilbert's essay in Earle, *Modern Strategy, The Prince and Discourses*, Introduction Max Lerner (New York, 1940), and the edition and translation of these works and the *Art of War* by Allan H. Gilbert, *Machiavelli: The Chief Works* (3 vols., Duke Press, 1962). C. C. Bayley, *War and Society in Renaissance Florence: The De Militia of Leonardo Bruni* (Toronto, 1961) is equally important. Two brilliant surveys are F. L. Taylor, *The Art of War in Italy, 1484-1529* (Cambridge, England, 1921) and Piero Pieri, *Il Rinascimento e la crisi militare italiana* (Turin, 1952). See also Allan H. Gilbert, "Machiavelli on Fire Weapons" (*Italica*, XXIII, 1946, 275-286), David Ayalon's remarkable *Gunpowder and Firearms in the Mamluk Kingdom* (London, 1956), and J. R. Hale's fine chapter in *The New Cambridge Modern History* (I, ed. G. R. Potter, Cambridge, 1957), 259-291, and his *Machiavelli and Renaissance Italy* (London, 1961).

Cambrai the French king gave up his claims to Milan and the Hapsburgs became the leading power in Italy.[8]

The Army of the Spanish Hapsburgs

The conquest of Granada in 1492 had left only two states in addition to Spain in the Iberian peninsula: Portugal, with about a fifth of the land area, already committed to vast colonial enterprises, and the tiny kingdom of Navarre astride the passes at the Atlantic end of the Pyrenees. Charles VIII of France, settling with his neighbors before invading Italy, had ceded the counties which controlled the more important passes at the other end of the Pyrenees into Catalonia. Strategically Spain was "almost an island" (the literal meaning of peninsula), a situation which was to affect the Spanish Hapsburgs' armies in many ways—in weapons as well as in military organization. The Spaniards, generally speaking, were the first soldiers to use guns in large numbers in the infantry. During the early Italian wars about half of the Spanish infantry were pikemen. A third were armed with short swords and javelins. A sixth carried guns, which then consisted of two general types: the ten-pound four-foot arquebus and the fifteen-pound six-foot musket. The two-man musket, which was fired from a forked muzzle rest (possibly a Spanish invention), was the Spanish infantry's basic missile weapon by the second quarter of the sixteenth century. Its two-ounce ball could smash any existing armor at close range and might disable a horse at three hundred yards. Each of the three arms had serious logistical problems, but the infantry met these problems more efficiently than either the cavalry or the artillery until the middle of the nineteenth century. If the gun is considered as an internal combustion engine, mechanization can be said to have been used tactically for killing men and battering down fortifications for centuries before it was applied to moving men, guns, and supplies into position. The muscles of men and horses were an army's only prime movers at the fighting front as late as the First World War.[9]

8 The ablest Spanish commander of the Italian wars was the "Great Captain" Gonzalo de Cordoba. See Gerald de Gaury's new biography, *The Grand Captain, Gonzalo de Cordoba* (London, 1955).
9 In that war the British army shipped more oats and hay (nearly 5,500,000 tons) to the Western Front than ammunition. Oil and motor stores accounted for only 750,000 tons; tanks and tank stores were less than a tenth of that figure. J. F. C. Fuller, preface to G. C. Shaw, *Supply in Modern War* (London, 1938), 12-13. On the importance of logistics, see the remarks of Richard Glover, "War and Civilian Historians" (*Journal of the History of Ideas*, XVIII, Jan., 1957, 84-100).

Though individual athletes may approximate Superman, the carrying power of the ordinary man is a reasonably fixed quantity. He cannot march more than a dozen to eighteen miles a day nor carry more than eighty pounds along with him. Modern medical men think that his most efficient load is about a third of his body weight, or about fifty pounds for the average American soldier. Within these limits the infantryman's range and carrying power are directly related; the most rigorous physical conditioning cannot raise them. The horse's hauling capacity had been revolutionized by the medieval invention of the horse collar, but horses are neither as tough nor as omnivorous as men and demand fuel in bales instead of capsules. Horse mobility, except on the grassy plains of Asia and North America, has often, therefore, been something of a delusion. The horse's concentrated muscle power has been more useful tactically than strategically. Horse-powered wagons are also "soft" transport. They add nothing to the army's fighting power, and must be serviced and defended. For this reason modern generals (except Cromwell, Napoleon, and Stonewall Jackson) have consistently tended to overload their men, until the common soldier has been little more than a pack animal, who had to be rested before he could fight and could not pursue an enemy far under any circumstances. The Roman legionary—a specially picked man on good roads—carried about eighty pounds; the redcoats carried as much into battle at Bunker Hill. The average commander learned that overloaded mules or horses would die. The average infantryman consistently tried to discard part of his impedimenta, no matter how stern the rules against such conduct.[10]

The Roman infantryman had carried a short sword and a javelin and a defensive shield, helmet, and breastplate. With these, he might also pack as much as two weeks' short rations and a rampart stake and spade for field fortification. The Spaniard's musket, sword, rest, ramrod, and ammunition were much heavier than the legionnaire's offensive equipment,

[10] The great work on the horse is Lefebvre des Noëttes, *L'Attelage, le cheval de selle à travers les ages* (2 vols., Paris, 1931). Equally important is S. L. A. Marshall, *The Soldier's Load and the Mobility of a Nation* (Washington, 1950). Vehicles to relieve the soldier of his duties as packer to the front, and air transport, which made him less road-bound, appeared almost simultaneously. The new inventions were not adopted at once, however, and Americans landed on Omaha Beach during the Second World War as overloaded as the British at Bunker Hill.

while his defensive armor (no shield, but a helmet, breast, and backplates to turn more powerful missiles) was about as heavy. This meant that he could carry almost no food, which tied him to his wagons or pack trains and greatly restricted his mobility. The great marches of the Roman legions had been made possible by centuries of political achievement—the building of roads, lines of fortifications to hold off barbarians, and the certainty of securing supplies in a friendly country. Since that time roads had deteriorated and sixteenth-century Western Europe still bristled with obstacles to movement, for the castles which the kings had battered down were soon improved, for the royal service, by some of the very same inquiring minds which had been working to exploit their weaknesses. Since sixteenth-century agriculture was perhaps not yet as productive as that of the third century, supplies were still very scarce and likely to be well defended. Because of the cavalry, almost never present in the west in Roman times, infantrymen were safe only in large bodies. It was neither wise militarily nor prudent politically, considering the unreliable character of the troops and their commanders, to allow the men to forage for themselves. Spoiled food and bad water killed men more effectively than gunpowder, though gunshot wounds, for which the only treatment was cauterization in boiling oil or amputation, were much harder to treat than those made by "clean" personal contact weapons.

Another major difference, if not the chief one, lay in the fact that the Roman soldier did not use up his equipment in battle. Javelins or arrows could be manufactured or repaired on the spot by the blacksmiths and soldiers. Shot and powder, on the other hand, were both expendable and irreplaceable. What was lost or shot away had to be provided by some central authority. Then too, an ancient battle was a hand-to-hand affair which could not be broken off and usually ended in the massacre of the defeated. A sixteenth-century army could often withdraw to fight another day. The victorious commander often had to worry about "the battle after the morrow," the political loyalty of his own forces, and the safety of his artillery train, magazines, and food convoys. For all of these problems the most popular Roman textbook on the art of war—Vegetius' late fourth century *De re militari*—provided no answers. But it was these difficulties of supply and transportation which first set sixteenth century soldiers thinking about strategy—"grand" as distinct from "petty"—tactics.[11]

The "shot" were usually drawn up eight ranks deep, with the front rank passing to the rear to reload or holding fast while the other ranks advanced. The men were thus in constant motion within the formation. In addition to their muskets and rests, the musketeers carried leather bags of bullets, separate containers for the fine priming and coarse main charges, swords, ramrods, and nine foot pieces of lighted wick or match. Their matches were always going out in rain, wind, or fog. Their glow gave away the troops' positions in night operations. Loading and firing demanded nearly a hundred separate motions, all of which had to be carried out in the tightly confined space between the pikemen and the other gunners. Since a single man on foot in the open was at the mercy of a horseman until the middle of the nineteenth century, the secret of infantry fighting for the Spanish, as for their Swiss predecessors and their Prussian successors, lay in absolutely automatic physical discipline.[12]

Field artillery consisted of various little guns which could be manhandled and that part of the siege train which happened to be present on the field of battle. When the French invaded Italy they used wheeled guns up to nine feet long firing balls as big as oranges, but even these guns had been more useful against fixed defenses than in field operations. The gunners were still hired specialists. They did not furnish their own transportation, but hired it locally—one more source of graft, inefficiency, and tactical confusion. Though these guns were sometimes very effective against the heavy pike squares, they were usually used only for an opening bombardment. The pikemen could avoid their fire by lying down. After the close-quarters bulldozing had begun, they

11 Though widely read, Vegetius' work was largely of antiquarian interest. Significantly enough, Machiavelli, like Montesquieu later, depended chiefly on the Roman historians. See *The Military Institutions of the Romans,* trans. John Clark and ed. T. R. Phillips (Harrisburg, 1944).
12 Owing to the usual factors of conservatism and expanse, there was much overlap in the various methods of ignition—the matchlock, wheel lock, and flintlock. The Spanish were apparently the first to use matchlocks in large numbers, but it is impossible to make comparisons in this period. Gunmaking required the services of a number of crafts—blacksmiths, locksmiths, joiners, and others—and guns were assembled from parts supplied by various makers. Spanish barrels, for example, were regarded as the best in Europe. The standard history of infantry is still E. M. Lloyd, *A Review of the History of Infantry* (London, 1908). For the French army of this period see G. Dickinson's introduction to *Fourquevaux's Instructions sur le Faict de la Guerre* (London, 1954).

were often masked by their own infantry or cavalry. The Spanish musket was actually a very effective light artillery, and the pike and musket became the basic Spanish weapons precisely because they were so portable.[13]

The cavalry had saved itself by discarding most of its armor, getting back on its horses, and supplementing its lances and sabers with pistols. But horsemen never again made up more than a third of a normal field army. Though the Spanish armies of the Moorish wars had been made up largely of light cavalry, the difficulties of transporting horses by sea often made the Spanish forces weaker than their rivals in this arm.[14]

The building blocks of the new army were still the companies of about 250 men. This number was often reduced by disease and payroll padding. The captain recruited his men, collected their pay and distributed it, and chose his assistant (ensign) in the same way that a naval captain appointed the rest of the ship's officers. The sergeant—whose status was almost that of a commissioned officer—was sometimes elected by the men from among the old soldiers. The first permanently constituted units larger than the company were known as *tercios;* a ten- or twelve-company tercio was about the size of a modern regiment, though the latter's organization is dif-

[13] Rough roads sometimes shook the gunpowder down into its component elements of charcoal, saltpeter, and sulphur. The careful gunner often mixed his own on the spot. On weapons see the popular summaries by Edmund Burke, *A History of Archery* (New York, 1957), Robert Held, *The Age of Firearms* (New York, 1957), and W. Y. Carman, *A History of Firearms, from Earliest Times to 1914* (London, 1955). Howard L. Blackmore, *British Military Firearms, 1650-1850* (London, 1961) and Harold L. Peterson, *Arms and Armor in Colonial America, 1526-1783* (Harrisburg, 1956) are excellent. On artillery see Henry W. Hime's scarce *The Origin of Artillery* (London, 1915), Charles Ffoulkes, *Arms and Armament, an historical survey of the weapons of the British Army* (London, 1945), the magnificent work of Giovanni Canestrini, *Arte militare meccanica medievale* (Milan, 1946), and the first volume of Jorge Vigon, *Historia de la Artillería Española* (3 vols., Madrid, 1947).

[14] The transportation of horses to the New World was immensely difficult. Cortez' sixteen horses cost as much as five hundred pesos ($6000) each. It is no wonder that Bernal Diaz' information about them was "minute enough for . . . a sporting calendar." Cortez had 110 sailors, 553 soldiers, and 200 Caribs. There were 32 crossbowmen and 13 arquebusiers. He had 4 little falconets and 10 larger guns. The classics are still William H. Prescott, *History of the Conquest of Mexico* (New York, 1940) and Bernal Díaz del Castillo, *The Bernal Díaz Chronicles; The True Story of the Conquest of Mexico,* trans. and ed. Albert Idele (Garden City, 1956). George Millar's fictional *A Crossbowman's Story of the First Exploration of the Amazon* (New York, 1955) is excellent. The best book on cavalry is George T. Denison, *A History of Cavalry* (2d ed., London, 1913), but there is fascinating source material in H. C. B. Rogers, *The Mounted Troops of the British Army, 1066-1945* (London, 1959).

ferent because of the necessity of supporting the rifle companies with heavier weapons and the greater complexities of
communication and administration. The basic tactical, as distinct from recruiting and training, unit was the battalion—a
square or rectangle formed by the pikes of several companies,
with the companies of shot disposed inside or outside of
them. The anomalous position of the battalion officers was
the source of some confusion, but this organization reflected
the social realities of an age in which each captain was the
proprietor of the company which he had raised and trained
and each colonel was the proprietor of the regiment which
he had been commissioned to raise for the king. This situation
persisted throughout the *ancien régime* in spite of increasing
royal centralization and standardization. The captain remained the lord of his company. A colonelcy was a place of
honor and profit in armies which consisted of collections of
regiments. The British generals of the Napoleonic period, for
example, received no pay for their ranks as such, though
they did receive extra pay and allowances while on active
duty as generals. But a man might be a lieutenant-general and
draw the pay of the lieutenant-colonel of his regiment. If his
regiment was disbanded—which often happened to new regiments raised during hostilities—he would then revert to the
half-pay of a lieutenant-colonel. He would still retain the resounding rank and title of lieutenant-general.[15]

These old regiments were the core of the Spanish army.
Almost continuous service abroad contributed to their professional pride, which was drummed into the recruits by the
old soldiers. Each unit also formed a semireligious brother-
hood, and the heavy leavening of chaplains, as in Cromwell's
later New Model, suggests that they performed some of the
duties of the modern political officer. The impoverished
Spanish nobility were now eager to serve in the infantry, and

15 Each company of 250 men had 2 commissioned officers. An infantry rifle
company in World War II consisted of about 200 men and 6 officers. Only 6
of the 19 persons on the *tercio's* staff were combat officers. The regiment carried 3 medical men, 13 chaplains, and 35 musicians. The drum major was
expected to be familiar with the music of all other armies, including the
Turkish, so that he could interpret the din for the colonel. Each *tercio* had
attached to it a squadron of 300 heavy and 300 light cavalry. Charles W.
Oman, *Art of War in the Sixteenth Century* (New York, 1937), 59-61.
Roger B. Merriman, *The Rise of the Spanish Empire in the Old World and
the New* (4 vols., New York, 1918-1934), II, 158-160, gives quite a different
set of figures. On military rank see the brilliant article by T. H. McGuffie,
"Bibliographical Aids to Research. XIV.—The Significance of military rank
in the British Army between 1790 and 1820" (*Bulletin of the Institute of
Historical Research*, XXX, No. 82, Nov., 1957, 207-224).

the infantryman, no matter what his social origins, began to consider himself a gentleman just because he had served in the infantry. "Love of plunder and of glory drew adventurers and furnished a host of volunteers whom the kings gladly enrolled to get rid of them. . . . The cities of Spain passed off to Italy and America the very best and their very worst, their most degraded and their most idealistic, their most generous and their most grasping, in a word, the rubbish and the honor of their population."[16]

Since most nobles were expected, though not required, to serve in the army and recruiting required the permission of those who were normally in contact with the peasantry, a sixteenth-century army carried two sets of officers. The sergeants, sergeant majors, and sergeant major general trained and moved the troops. These old soldiers took care of the complicated preliminary deployment of the army into "battles," "wings," and "forlorns" (it is easy to guess what a "forlorn" was, the word came from the German *verloren*). The noble colonels and generals, who could not, in view of their local interests, be expected to do military housekeeping, then led the army and, as was appropriate to their station, collected most of the glory. Higher units and commands were a matter of administrative convenience. They provided a means of moving men and guns to the spot, after which the battalions and regiments were formed up in accordance with the situation in which the field commander found himself. This—the job of the sergeant majors or the sergeant major general— always took much time—and might cost the army the day, if it was caught before its battle formation was ready. But all of this grew out of the vast uncertainties of supply, communications, and the uncertain loyalties, fighting abilities, and numbers of even supposedly comparable units. There is, then, no such thing as a typical sixteenth-century battle formation. Each battle was a separate tactical problem. It was a game in which not only the numbers but the value of the pieces varied with each situation. Some combination of guns, pikes, artillery, and horse would be used throughout the sixteenth and seventeenth centuries, though the proportion of shot to pikes gradually increased and the bowmen and swordsmen vanished.

Since Spain was a strategic island, only a small portion of the Spanish army was regularly stationed there, and the mili-

16 J. H. Mariejol, *L'Espagne sous Ferdinand et Isabelle* (Paris, 1892), 202.

tia lost all of their importance after the conquest of Granada. When it took two weeks for news to travel from Spain to Flanders and a whole season for men to march from Milan to the Netherlands, the *tercios* were only the core of forces recruited, for the most part, in those areas which the Hapsburgs' enemies were immediately threatening. At St. Quentin in 1557—the biggest battle of that century—Philip II had only 9000 Spaniards in an army which may have numbered 53,000 men. The problems of high command were also particularly difficult for the Hapsburgs. Since the Hapsburg "Empire" was really a coalition, the Hapsburg commanders had constantly to take both military and political decisions with little guidance from a central authority. The ideal solution to the problems of high command during this period was a monarch who was both politician and soldier. A king who was only a soldier might see his state disintegrate behind his back. A military incompetent might, like Francis I of France at Pavia, commit fatal tactical blunders. When the king was not present in person the command devolved upon the constable, marshal, or captain general, a man always related to the royal family or of the very highest nobility. Under the feudal system these offices, like places in the line of battle, had been hereditary, a source of great danger to the dynasty if the holder should himself aspire to the kingship. The outright desertion of important military and political leaders was still not too uncommon, as was the case when the French Constable Charles of Bourbon joined the Emperor in 1512. These problems plagued all of the new dynastic monarchies, but they were especially acute for the Hapsburgs, whose territories were scattered over such great distances.[17]

Charles V wore himself out wandering around Europe. His Spanish successor, Philip II, wisely or not, tried to direct things from the center, only to find that his orders often

17 The high commander of the Allied fleet at Lepanto was Don Juan, the twenty-three-year-old half-brother of Philip II, who was both Captain General of the League and High Admiral of Spain. The Turkish commander was an able politician, who had risen from the job of muezzin in a mosque, where his voice, so it was said, had attracted the attention of a wife of the Sultan. The allied commanders, in turn, depended upon the technical advice of professional soldiers and sailors, given in councils of war which might be trying to interpret royal orders weeks or months old. The treaty of alliance set out, first, the men, ships, and supplies to be furnished by each party. Each year in March or April, the objective for the season would be chosen. If nothing was agreed on, each contingent of the allied navy could act independently. The three generals were to manage the campaign, and the commander was their chief executive. William L. Rodgers, *Naval Warfare under Oars, 4th to 16th Centuries* (Annapolis, 1939), 168.

could not be carried out, owing to local conditions of which he had been ignorant when writing his orders. Perhaps the Hapsburgs' diplomatic problems were insoluble. The coalition arranged by Charles's grandfather was held together primarily by fear—of the Turks in the western Mediterranean and the Danube, of the French in Italy and the lands which had belonged to Burgundy. When one element of this coalition, the Spanish, became so strong that it seemed to be more dangerous to the traditional liberties of some of its parts than the French, its break-up was more or less inevitable. There was no way in which the Hapsburgs could unite both interests and liberties by deliberately helping to create a Hapsburg nationalism, the real cement of modern states after dynastic loyalties began to be outmoded.

Spain's Decline (1559-1659)

When Charles V abdicated in 1555 his lands were divided into two parts, the younger or Austrian branch of the Hapsburgs getting the German possessions, Austria, Bohemia, and the western fringe of Hungary. This saddled them with the problems of German unification and the defense of Central Europe against the Turks. Philip II could concentrate on the Netherlands, Spain, the New World, and the naval defense of Italy and the western Mediterranean. By this time the Hapsburgs were supreme in Italy and in the Counter-Reformation church. They could count on religious supporters in every country in Northern Europe. The income from the Indies (a fifth of all the bullion that was produced theoretically belonged to the crown) provided the surplus with which Philip II conducted his foreign policy and recruited troops, though many German mercenaries were now replaced by men from Flanders and North Italy. The winter before Philip sent his Armada against England, to take one example, the Americas yielded twice as much bullion as the English queen's income for an entire year, almost enough to pay for outfitting the whole Armada. Though the mercantilist theory of warfare—that a state's power was directly related to its supply of bullion—was no invention of the Spanish, their example powerfully supported its conclusions. And the decline in Spanish political power has even been correlated with the Spanish bankruptcies of 1557, 1575, 1596, 1607, 1627, and 1647.

Things went very well for Philip during the first twenty-five years of his reign (1556-1598). The Catholic Mary had succeeded to the English throne in 1553 and had married Philip a year later. In 1559 France made peace with Spain, just before the death of the French king and the outbreak of a generation of religious and dynastic war in that country. The Turks were defeated in the naval battle of Lepanto in 1571. In 1578 the king of Portugal was killed by the Moors at the battle of Alcazar, and Philip made good his claim to the Portuguese throne two years later. This union of the Iberian peninsula and of two great maritime empires brought Spain closer to the domination of Western Europe than ever before. But

the rest of Europe . . . was appalled at the incredible rapidity of Spain's rise, in little more than a century, from a position of comparative insignificance to the leadership of the most extensive empire the world has ever seen. And not only did the suddenness of the transformation put the rest of Europe up in arms . . . , it was also fatal to Spain's hope of a successful defense. Such widely scattered . . . territories could not possibly be welded together, under an efficient imperial organization, in such a comparatively short space of time.[18]

The center of the resistance to Philip lay in the Netherlands, parts of which had been in revolt since 1568. The rebels' strongholds were the two isolated Dutch provinces of Holland and Zeeland, covered by the mouths of the Meuse, Scheldt, and Rhine rivers. The revolt was dependent upon a mixture of national and Protestant sentiment, the fortified towns which studded this water-logged area, and on the help which could be brought in by sea from other Protestant countries. As is often the case with revolutionary armies, the rebels' first attempts to stand up to the Spanish veterans with local militia ended disastrously. Their leader, William the Silent, gradually formed the usual mercenary army of Germans, Scots, English, French, and native volunteers. The crisis came after 1580, when Spain fell heir to Portugal and the able Duke of Parma began a methodical reconquest of the north from Luxembourg and the Catholic southern Netherlands. William the Silent was assassinated in 1584; the next year the Spanish recaptured Antwerp. But these events forced Elizabeth of England (who had succeeded Mary in

[18] Merriman, *Rise of the Spanish Empire*, IV, 674-675. E. W. Bovill, *The Battle of Alcazar* (London, 1952) is good. This is the battle which ended Portugal's pretensions as a military power.

1558) to intervene openly on the side of the Dutch and Philip had to turn his major attention to England.

In the north Spain fought at a geographical disadvantage. A French offensive at any point from Milan to Flanders could imperil the long land route from northern Italy to the Netherlands. The sea route depended on the friendship of either France or England. In 1588 the Spanish Armada failed in its attempt to invade England and dethrone Elizabeth. Soon afterward Philip's enemy Henry IV made good his claim to the throne of France and expelled the Spanish troops who were aiding his rivals. These events had also given the Dutch a breathing spell. William the Silent's son, the great soldier Maurice of Nassau, finally recovered all the territory behind the river line and established a number of bridgeheads south of it. The Dutch revolt played the same role in the decline of Spain that the Spanish revolt was to play in the fall of Napoleon. It was the "running sore" which drained off Spanish soldiers, Spanish morale, and Spanish money.[19]

The Thirty Years' War (1618-1648) marked the end of a century which had seen "more organized fighting, more devastation, and more misery bred of both, than at any earlier age since the Western Europeans had begun to advance economically in the eleventh century." Germany, Bohemia, Austria, the Spanish Netherlands, and parts of Italy, Spain, and France had been hard hit, though the Dutch fortifications had kept the worst of the fighting away from the United Provinces. These wars were a nearly unmitigated social calamity, though they finally resulted in a measure of religious toleration and in the mutual observance of some international rules of warfare. The military genius of the Thirty Years' War was Gustavus Adolphus II, King of Sweden (1611-1632), though Albrecht von Wallenstein (1583-1634) almost carved out a German principality for himself with the professional army which the Emperor had commissioned him to raise. The

[19] "In Flanders the Spaniards found no romantic interest whatever. They could never keep warm; and the unpleasant tasks which they carried out so thoroughly . . . were a duty best done and forgotten. The Spanish proverbial phrase, 'trailing a pike in Flanders' brings with it the hopelessness and despair of defending a lost cause in a flat, water-logged country—a cause which was never really theirs, but only their king's." J. B. Trend, *The Civilization of Spain* (New York, 1944), 111. For a discussion of the importance of geography and the "river line," see Pieter Geyl, *The Revolt of the Netherlands* (2d ed., New York, 1958), and *The Netherlands Divided* (London, 1936). There is no good study of Maurice in English. The standard work is Jan Willem Wijn, *Het krijgswezen in den tijd van prins Maurits* (Utrecht, 1934).

French did not make peace with the Spanish Hapsburgs until 1659, eleven years after the general Peace of Westphalia. The Spanish fleet had come north for the last time in 1639, and had been destroyed by the Dutch in English territorial waters. The decisive test between the Spanish and the French infantry had taken place in 1643 at Rocroi, a little town near the modern French-Belgian border a few miles from the scene of the two battles of Sedan (1870, 1940). Half of the Spanish field army in the Netherlands had been killed and most of the rest captured. Seventy years later the Spanish Empire was to be partitioned in the Treaty of Utrecht. A few years previous the Turks had been driven out of Hungary. Both the Spanish and the Ottoman Empires had become international problems.[20]

The Age of Louis XIV (1643-1715)

During the reign of Louis XIV (1643-1715) France was again the strongest military power in Europe, a state with roughly three times as many subjects as Great Britain, the Austrian Hapsburgs, or Spain, and more than six times as many as the Dutch Republic. Louis XIV's wars (1667-1668, 1672-1678, 1688-1697, and 1701-1713) left his monarchy bankrupt. The other major wars of these years involved the Austrian Hapsburgs and the Turks (1663-1664 and 1682-1699), while Russia, Poland, Saxony, Denmark, Prussia, and Hanover began the partition of the Swedish Empire in the

[20] Nef, *War and Human Progress*, 20-21, challenges the idea that war aided the development of the middle class advanced in Richard Ehrenberg, *Capital and Finance in the Age of the Renaissance* (London, 1928). The literature of the Thirty Years' War is enormous. A recent critique of German work on that war is Robert Ergang, *The Myth of the All-Destructive Fury of the Thirty Years War* (Pocono Pines, Pa., 1956). The best single volume is C. V. Wedgwood, *The Thirty Years War* (London, 1938). Nils Ahnlund, *Gustav Adolf the Great*, trans. Michael Roberts (Princeton, 1940) is not very satisfactory on military matters. The standard work by Michael Roberts, *Gustavus Adolphus: A History of Sweden, 1611-1632* (2 vols., New York, 1953-1958) should be supplemented by the same author's *The Military Revolution, 1560-1660* (Belfast, 1956). A fine short summary of the Swedish contribution to military thought is Olof Ribbing, "Characteristiques de l'art nordique de la guerre" (*Révue internationale d'histoire militaire*, No. 15, 1955, 223-249). On the development of international law, the best short history is Arthur Nussbaum, *A Concise History of the Law of Nations* (New York, 1953).

Each generation of historians produces its own explanation for the decline of Spain and the Ottoman Empire—religious intolerance, pride, the decline of intellectual life, or economic maladministration. Three outstanding works on Spain are Bohdan Chudoba, *Spain and the Empire, 1519-1643* (Chicago, 1952), Richard Konetsky, *Das Spanische Weltreich* (Munich, 1943), and Fernand Braudel, *La Meditérranée et le monde méditerranéen à l'époque de Philippe II* (Paris, 1949).

Great Northern War of 1700-1721. The most famous commanders of the age were the French generals Condé and Turenne, the English Duke of Marlborough, the Hapsburg commander Eugene of Savoy, and Charles XII of Sweden. Louis XIV's finance minister, Colbert, tried to cut down waste, to increase revenues by increasing the country's prosperity, and to pay off old debts or convert them at lower rates of interest. The war minister, Louvois, saw that the army's units were kept at full strength, and that they were equipped and inspected efficiently. The name of Inspector General Martinet has even passed into the English language. (In French it is the word for the cat-o'-nine-tails.) Colbert was the son of a merchant. Turenne and Louis' great fortifications expert, Vauban, came from the lesser nobility.[21]

To these able administrators, military efficiency came from standardization and centralization rather than from tactical innovation. Part of the apparent increase in the size of armies during the age of Louis XIV was due to the steady absorption of the auxiliary services into the royal establishment. When Louis XIV attacked the Spanish Netherlands in 1667, his army numbered some 73,000 men. At the end of his second war in 1678, he had 279,000 men in the army. It was not to fall below 200,000 during the rest of his reign. During the latter part of the eighteenth century the various European states kept at least half a million soldiers in peacetime, nearly as many in proportion to their total population as they were to keep at the end of the nineteenth century. The difference between the two centuries did not lie in the development of larger peacetime armies, but in the nineteenth century's practice of creating enormous reserves by training nearly every eligible citizen for a short time.

[21] John B. Wolf, *The Emergence of the Great Powers, 1685-1715* (New York, 1951) and Frank Taylor, *The Wars of Marlborough* (2 vols., Oxford, 1921) are brilliant works. For individual generals see Maxime Weygand, *Turenne, Marshal of France,* trans. George B. Ives (Boston, 1930), Henri Malo, *Le Grand Condé* (Paris, 1937), O. Redlich, *Prinz Eugen* (Vienna, 1922), Winston Churchill, *Marlborough, His Life and Times* (4 vols., London, 1933-1938), Louis André, *Michel le Tellier et l'organisation de l'armée monarchique* (Paris, 1906), is very important. The standard works on Charles XII are Otto Haintz, *König Karl XII von Schweden* (3 vols., Berlin, 1958), and Frans G. Bengtsson, *The Life of Charles XII,* tr. Naomi Walford (London, 1960). There is an excellent survey of Polish military institutions in *Révue internationale d'histoire militaire,* No. 12 (1952). Number 10 (1951) of this same periodical contains a brilliant essay by Piero Pieri on the persistence of classical military ideas in this period: "La formazione dottrinale di Raimondo Montecuccoli," 92-115. There is nothing very new in Sir George Clark, *War and Society in the Seventeenth Century* (Cambridge, 1958).

The militarization of transport and supply owed much to Gustavus Adolphus, who had fought some of the first winter campaigns in modern history. By the end of the seventeenth century governments were supplying rations, tents, and field bakeries, though the soldiers were still given money to secure their own food in winter and were billeted on civilians during that season. Supply trains (with six days' bread and nine days' flour rations) and the larger siege guns required to deal with stronger fortifications demanded more horses—twenty of them for each three-ton siege gun and twenty-four more for its six ammunition wagons. Military accountants supervised payments and requisitions. Better roads and wagons encouraged other impedimenta. Officers took their current mistresses, and the great eighteenth-century general Maurice de Saxe was accompanied by his private troupe of actors. In practice, of course, an army's increased requirements were not always met. Many states were still "incapable of providing the substance—the fuel, the metal, the gunpowder, the cheap quick transport of munitions, the swift-moving attack—which would have been required to kill enough men to produce decisive results."[22]

The campaigns of the early eighteenth century were still long-drawn-out, but they may have done less damage to the civilian population than those of the previous century. Some of the worst atrocities of the religious wars had been as much due to hunger as to religious fanaticism. Noncombatants in the sixteenth century armies—the usual reckoning had been a woman and a boy for every man—had been more numerous than the soldiers; when these hordes were not paid and fed with some regularity, they had become as dangerous to their commanders as to the civilian population. A great Spanish victory at Mookerheide in 1574, for example, had been neutralized by a mutiny of the Spanish troops who won it. The

[22] Nef, *War and Human Progress,* 213. A British officer summed up the whole process as follows: "1. Plunder pure and simple. 2. Plunder systematized into the creation (more or less) of magazines. 3. . . . The soldier . . . mulct of pay for subsistence . . . from magazines furnished by plunder. 4. Organized plunder, or the creation of magazines by requisition. 5. . . . A population will fill magazines more readily if paid, and the organization of this system under the Treasury. 6. . . . Requisition . . . supplemented by supplies brought from a distance. A commissary . . . to manage this . . . . Transport . . . to extend the areas fed by the magazines . . . . Transport and Supply thereupon become . . . semi-military and then . . . completely military." John W. Fortescue, *The British Army, 1783-1802* (London, 1905), 134. See also Fritz Redlich, *De Praeda Militari: Looting and Booty, 1500-1815* (Weisbaden, 1956).

mutineers had demanded their pay, chosen a general of their own, and held the loyal city of Amsterdam for ransom. Two years later the Spanish garrison in the Antwerp citadel had again mutinied, sent for aid from other mutinous garrisons, defeated the militia which had been gathered to watch them, killed seven thousand people, plundered the city, and burned a third of it. Such atrocities as these had almost lost the Catholic southern Netherlands for Spain. The standardizing and centralizing tendencies of the later seventeenth centuries were as much in the cause of political and military efficiency as in that of humanity.

During the Italian wars the attack and defense of entire cities had become much more important than the reduction of isolated castles. The great Italian military engineers had also begun to think of active defense, or siting artillery to reply to the guns of the attackers. Their most brilliant successor, the mathematician Simon Stevin (1548-1620), designed—or rather rebuilt—the fortifications which held the river line for Maurice of Nassau. Vauban (1633-1707) developed a new system of attacking fixed defenses by digging parallels to approach the walls and a chain of fortified sites to protect the whole French kingdom. His triple ring of fortified places in French Flanders and the Austrian and Dutch fortifications opposite them were to be the scene of many a tedious campaign. Though individual works could always be taken, Vauban's fortresses probably saved Paris during both the wars of the Spanish Succession and the French Revolution. In these fortresses armies collected vast stores of provisions and equipment. No country could then produce enough weapons from current production, and there was then no danger that these accumulated stocks would suddenly be rendered obsolete by technological progress. These fortresses also reinforced the trend toward limited warfare. Sieges became as highly formalized as *condottieri* battles or medieval tournaments. Louis XIV ruled that a commander might surrender honorably after a small breach had been made in the citadel and the repulse of one assault. The previous rule had required a large breach and several assaults. The new rule held until the French revolutionaries executed both a commander and his wife for such a *pro forma* resistance. As the revolutionary leader and engineer Lazare Carnot remarked, "What was taught in the military schools was not the art of defending strong places, but that of surrendering them honorably after certain conventional formalities."[23]

The Age of Frederick the Great: Neoclassical Warfare

Russia had become recognized as a great power during the reign of Peter the Great (1689-1726), the real victor of the Great Northern War. By the middle of the eighteenth century Russia's population was second only to that of France, and the Russian army was about as large as that of Austria. But then, as later, the military importance of Russian manpower was somewhat lessened by "inability to utilize it, by lack of organization and modern training, equipment and communications, by very grave social and economic disharmonies." The same was also true of Austria. The Hapsburgs were "unable to tap, let alone organize or develop the vast financial and military resources of the Hapsburg dominions." This backwardness of the Austrian political administration explains in part the sensational victories of Brandenburg-Prussia, a state in the middle of the seventeenth century of only 600,000 inhabitants. This was just about the number of inhabitants in Machiavelli's Florentine Republic, which had been the weakest of the great powers of Renaissance Italy.[24]

The rise of Prussia was so dramatic that it gave birth to a number of historical legends—that Prussia was created by its landed aristocracy, the *Junkers,* or that it was primarily the work of the Prussian army. Modern Prussia was really the creation of a very able ruling family, who worked with the

[23] *De la défense des places fortes* (3d ed., Paris, 1812), xiii. See Gaston Zeller, *L'Organisation défensive des frontières du nord et de l'est au XVIIIe siècle* (Paris, 1928). P. E. Lazard, *Vauban, 1633-1703* (Paris, 1934) is the best biography. Reginald Blomfield, *Sebastien le Prestre de Vauban* (London, 1938) is a good book which depends heavily on Lazard.

Stockpiling kept the arsenals and other armament industries busy. During this period—in which campaigning was limited to a few areas—warfare did furnish an important stimulus to business development. At this time, as in the 1950's, "Preparations for war, without the damage done by heavy wars, can be represented as contributing to progress in the direction of industrial civilization." Nef, *War and Human Progress,* 219. Nef's figures on the casualties of armies during this period of limited war must be treated with great reserve. He seems to be much too anxious to make a good case for limited warfare. Battle casualties—which he quotes—were comparatively low. But casualties from disease were very high. There are no really reliable figures for losses of life during the War of the Spanish Succession. See Gaston Bodart, *Losses of Life in Modern Wars: Austria-Hungary; France,* and Vernon Lyman Kellogg, *Military Selection and Race Deterioration* (Oxford, 1916), 89-97.

[24] B. H. Sumner, *A Short History of Russia* (New York, 1943), 380-381. Walter Dorn, *Competition for Empire, 1740-1763* (New York, 1940), 43.

materials they had at hand to create both a state and an army. Still another feature of the Prussian story is the wealth of its historical documentation. While the unification of France or England—and, incidentally, the history of almost all of the great technological innovations of the anarchic years around 1450—must be pieced together from very incomplete records, Prussia's rise, greatness, and decline took place in the full light of modern history. The Prussian records form a pattern as important for modern politicians and military men as the Roman historical records were for Montesquieu or Machiavelli. The growth of modern historical science in Prussia, one can believe, was not accidental, nor was the Prussian army's pre-eminence in military philosophy.

The foundations of the later Prussian state were laid by Frederick William, the Great Elector of Brandenburg (1640-1688). At his death Brandenburg was the most powerful of the middle-sized German states, with a population of about a million and a half and an army of about 18,000. These were a little larger than the corresponding figures for the Elector of Bavaria, a prince whose ambitions ended unhappily when he rushed to the aid of the loser in the War of the Spanish Succession. But Prussia (which had become a kingdom in 1701) was made into a great power by two eighteenth-century rulers—Frederick William I (1713-1740) and his son Frederick II (1740-1786). When Frederick William I came to the throne, there had been "little to distinguish Prussia from other fair-sized German states with rulers imitating Louis XIV—court etiquette, architecture, extravagance, impending bankruptcy." As Frederick II said, Berlin had been trying to become a northern Athens. Frederick William I made his state into a Sparta. He ran the whole country along strictly business-like lines and invested the proceeds in his war chest and a superbly trained standing army. By 1740 the Prussian army of 80,000 men was the fourth in Europe, just behind the armies of France, Russia, and Austria. Though Austria had many times Prussia's population, she had less than 100,-000 professional soldiers. Where France kept one soldier for every 150 inhabitants, Prussia supported one for every 25. The new ruthlessness which Frederick William I brought into preparation for war—the relentless punishments and almost daily floggings—has been seen as the first ominous sign of the breakdown of the system of limited warfare characteristic of the age of Louis XIV.[25]

Frederick William I "built up the capital, human as well as material, which his son invested so riskily and so successfully in national greatness." Frederick II was one of the greatest soldiers in history, a man who, as a foreign officer had noted of Gustavus Adolphus, "was not content to be commander-in-chief, he must needs be captain, subaltern, engineer, gunner, and private—in short, everything." Frederick's attack on Austria (the War of the Austrian Succession, 1740-1748), the skill with which he held his gains against overwhelming odds during the Seven Years' War (1756-1763), and his gains from the partition of Poland made Prussia into a real great power with about 6,000,000 people. This figure was still only a quarter of that of Austria, but it was far larger than that for any of the other German states. From it Prussia now supported a standing army of 162,000 men, only 11,000 less than that of France. Massive British financial aid and Frederick's careful management had left Prussia without a substantial public debt, while France was again bankrupt. Prussia, in short, had made a business of war and that business had paid off, though there was to be some irony in Napoleon's later suggestion that he ought to "do Europe the service of abolishing the system of enormous standing armies begun by Prussia."[26]

The political background of eighteenth-century warfare was not new. The so-called Benevolent Despots (of whom Frederick II was one) continued to work within the established

[25] Penfield Roberts, *The Quest for Security, 1715-1840* (New York, 1947), 62-65. The standard English biography of the Great Elector is Ferdinand Schevill, *The Great Elector* (Chicago, 1947). Like many fanatics Frederick William I was a most unlovable character and the butt of much contemporary gossip. Robert Ergang, *The Potsdam Führer* (New York, 1941).

During the War of the Spanish Succession the Bavarian army of 17,000 men, contingents of which had fought as far away as Belgrade, was completely destroyed by Marlborough in the first stages of the Blenheim campaign (1704).

[26] Roberts, *Quest for Security*, 65. The best short biography in English is Pierre Gaxotte, *Frederick the Great* (New Haven, 1942). There are very illuminating comments in G. P. Gooch, *Frederick the Great, the Ruler, the Writer, the Man* (New York, 1947), and Gerhard Ritter, *Friedrich der Grosse: eine historisches Profil* (rev. ed., Heidelberg, 1954). The classic multi-volume study of the Seven Years' War is Richard Waddington, *La Guerre de Sept Ans* (5 vols., Paris, 1899-1914).

Prussia can be considered an eighteenth-century Sweden, a state which had raised itself far above its normal rank by excellent military leadership. The Swedish empire lasted ninety-two years—from the Truce of Altmark (1629) to the end of the Great Northern War (1721). Just ninety-three years after the accession of Frederick William I, Napoleon destroyed both the old Prussian state and the old Prussian army.

traditions of dynastic statecraft. The art of politics lay in the skilful use of the old rules rather than in the invention of new ones. The same thing was true in military technology after the invention of the bayonet and the substitution of the flintlock for the matchlock toward the end of the seventeenth century. The introduction of the bayonet reduced the infantry from two kinds to one—a major step in standardization and simplification. The infantry was now armed with a single muscle-mechanical weapon which could be produced by the artisans of every great power in Europe. During the eighteenth century technological, like political, progress, lay chiefly in refining existing weapons. In 1718 the Prussians introduced a double-ended iron ramrod and a funnel-shaped touch-hole. Both of these innovations increased the musket's rate of fire without changing its basic characteristics. The eleven-pound, six-foot (with bayonet) muzzle-loading flint-lock musket of 1840 was to be almost identical with the weapon used a century and a half earlier, a short-range gun-pike combination. Battles were still to be decided by the push of pike—now a bayonet charge—at the decisive moment. At Borodino (1812—one of the bloodiest battles of the Napoleonic period) the average French infantryman used only ten rounds of ammunition. Conservative officers—who had reluctantly given up the pike—were to think of the muscle-powered bayonet as the ultimate weapon until the early twentieth century. As the French military historian Jean Colin was to remark, "More than a thousand years were needed before the invention of gunpowder really transformed war." [27]

The same standardization had also taken place in the artillery. Order had been brought out of the chaos of calibers (a seventeenth-century English list gives fourteen different guns

[27] *Les Transformations de la guerre* (Paris, 1912), 14. There is a scarce English translation of this work published in London in 1912. The plug bayonet—a dagger stuck into the end of the gun barrel—was introduced between 1660 and 1690. Socket bayonets—which permitted the soldier to fire with a fixed bayonet—were first used by the armies of Charles XII. Marshal Maurice de Saxe, whose *Reveries on the Art of War* (trans. and ed. Thomas R. Phillips, Harrisburg, 1944) was a curious mixture of conservative and progressive ideas, was reluctant to abandon the pike. He proposed two ranks of men with muskets and two with half-pikes and muskets slung over their shoulders. He also thought plug bayonets better than the socket type "because they enable the commander to reserve his fire."
, Professor Nef believes that Western European soldiers were hesitant to use the bayonet because it was so frightful. It was more widely used during the French Revolution because the soldiers were more fanatic. *War and Human Progress*, 251. His evidence on these points seems inconclusive.

under eight and a half inches), and carriages, wheels, and axles were now built to standard patterns. The two and three pounders, which had been used so effectively by the Swedes, were manhandled by the gunners themselves for direct infantry fire support. The larger five and six pounders, with a range of about half a mile, sometimes did great damage with their ricocheting iron balls during a cross fire. Powder and ball were too expensive for practice firing. Artillery, like infantry, drill consisted of dry runs, limbering, and unlimbering. The Prussian infantry's losses during the Seven Years' War compelled Frederick to develop his horse artillery, but Napoleon was the first commander to have enough field guns to use them in masses. Each improvement in firearms made the cavalry's job more difficult. Surprise became more difficult as forests were cut down and the medieval open fields cut up by hedges, ditches, and other obstacles. The eighteenth century saw various experiments with mounted infantry—or dragoons—but the cavalry continued its slow decline as the other horsed arm—the artillery—slowly increased in importance. Cavalry was most successful as an assault arm when it could achieve surprise or strike the enemy's flank and rear. It was not used for large-scale reconnaissance. Napoleon, like a number of other great generals, used his cavalry to screen his own movements and depended largely on information from spies and agents. Information gathered by the cavalry might arrive too late to be useful and the cavalry which had obtained it would not be available for battle. At Eylau, Dresden, and Leipzig Napoleon's cavalry successfully charged unshaken infantry, but was to fail badly at Waterloo.[28]

The Queen of Battles was still the infantry. Its power could be increased by greater numbers, improved training, or improved weapons. The French revolutionists were to use the first method; the Prussians the second. In spite of many improvements in ballistics, neither greatly improved the musket. Gun barrels had been grooved or rifled during the Renaissance. But a rifle was much more expensive than a smoothbore, and it was hard to get the ball down the grooved barrel. Since a hunter, unlike an infantryman, could take time to hammer the ball home with a mallet, the early rifles were used chiefly for hunting big game in the forests of Eastern Europe. Early

[28] The best book on eighteenth century cavalry is the first volume of a French General Staff study, Edouard Desbrière and Maurice Soutai, *La Cavalerie de 1740 à 1789* (Paris, 1906).

breech-loaders had to be taken apart after each shot; later models were too expensive for infantry use.[29]

So the infantryman still carried a simple iron tube and discharged it after a complicated series of physical contortions. Constant drilling led to perfection. The infantryman had now discarded his armor and had stuck his dagger on the end of his gun. But he still had to deal with the gun, its cartridges (measured charges wrapped with a ball in a piece of paper), the priming powder, and the ramrod. To make sure that the flash reached the main charge and was not "a flash in the pan" the cartridge was bitten open, the powder and ball poured in and the paper rammed on top of them for wadding. The soldier then replaced the ramrod, opened the pan, poured in the priming powder, closed the pan (with the flintlock, the pan opened automatically at the moment of firing), aimed, and fired. Though the original 98 motions of loading (requiring 6 to 8 times as long as firing), had been reduced to under 30 (twice the time of firing), they were still very complicated. In spite of the endless drill, they must often have been performed badly in battle. They still had to be carried out in close formation for defense against cavalry, who might sneak to within a hundred yards before being observed in the quite literal "fog" of battle. And the powder might still be too damp or the flint, good for anywhere from 10 to 70 rounds, might still have to be unscrewed and a new one inserted. With a somewhat simpler and faster musket, moreover, soldiers had discovered the tremendous effects of volley firing, which still further increased the need for physical discipline. The old six- or eight-rank squares (which had roughly corresponded to the comparative times of loading and firing) now gave way to three-rank lines which could fire either

---

[29] The German hunting rifle was the direct ancestor of the famous Pennsylvania or Kentucky rifle. The American frontiersman wrapped the ball in a greased linen patch, which made loading much easier and also served as a temporary obturator (to prevent the escape of gas around the ball). The resulting higher pressures made it possible to decrease the size of the ball, a major improvement in Frontiersman's logistics. The rifle, incidentally, did not play a major part in the American Revolution, in spite of the legend of the fabulous shooting of a few American riflemen. Most American troops used French muskets or American copies. These muskets, with barrels which were not always very straight and as much as .05″ windage between the ball and the barrel, were hardly triumphs of gunsmithery. But they were cheap, quick-loading, and deadly at close quarters. The best book for the reader who does not want to be a gun collector is Joseph W. Shields, Jr., *From Flintlock to M 1* (New York, 1954). On the science of ballistics see A. R. Hall's excellent, *Ballistics in the Seventeenth Century: A Study in the Relations of Science and War with reference particularly to England* (New York, 1952).

separately or simultaneously, a clear example of the influence of technics on tactics.

Into these lines the "linear" tacticians of the eighteenth century tried to crowd all the muskets (and thus as much fire-power) possible. Their weak points were on the flanks (protected by cavalry), or at the joints between the various units, and in the difficulties of changing front or maneuvering side-wise, at night, or in broken country. Frederick's famous "oblique" order consisted in sudden sidewise maneuvers (impossible for all but superbly trained troops) to overpower a less agile enemy on one flank, while the rest of his forces fixed the remainder. In firing, a man only a few inches out of line would have his eardrums blown in by the muskets of the men behind him; a mistake or halt by one unit would open up a fatal gap in the whole order of battle. Under these conditions the famous "goose" or parade step of the Prussian army was of real military value. The tight knee, the exact tempo and step enabled the whole line to advance without halting to dress the line.

With guns which pitched curves on a field covered with smoke, there was no reason for giving the ordinary infantry-man special training in marksmanship. He was lucky to have fired five rounds before he went into battle. The soldier's training consisted of endless dry runs and physical hardening. His job was to go through the complex motions of loading as quickly as possible, level his weapon at the opposing line, and let them have it. What they received was a literal hail of lead—of ounce balls three quarters of an inch in diameter, larger and heavier than the biggest glass marbles. What was wanted was speed and volume—now obtained automatically with the machine gun or the automatic rifle. Normal musket range was about the forty yards of Bunker Hill. The usual rule was not to fire until you could see the whites of their eyes. Since this distance could be covered by the other side in about half a minute or the time taken to reload, each side tried to wait until the last minute before firing the first volley.[30]

The deployment of troops from marching order remained slow and difficult. At Blenheim (1704) with the English ad-

---

[30] The legend of Fontenoy—"Gentlemen of the French Guard, fire first! No, gentlemen, we never fire first!"—makes sense in this connection. The British army's "Brown Bess" could hit a foot square target every time at 40 yards. At 100 yards, however, a skilled marksman got only 24 hits in 42 shots at a four-foot square. A longbowman hit this target 31 times.

vancing only a mile toward the French camp, this process took from seven in the morning to nearly one in the afternoon. During this period each commander could see the whole field and identify the enemy units by their distinctive uniforms and flags. The French held their fire until the English were only thirty yards away; the English fired in the faces of the French when the leading brigadier struck the French barricades with his sword. The fighting which followed lasted for over three hours, a period which would be close to the moral and physical limits of the men. Exhaustion and the dreadful casualties suffered by the most closely engaged units made the pursuit of a beaten enemy very difficult, if not impossible. Eighteenth-century warfare, like that of antiquity, was thus dominated by the physical skills which could be gained on the parade ground. In the words of Marshal de Saxe, "All the mystery of maneuvers and combats is in the legs." Trained arms and legs could do everything—move, fire, and fight with the bayonet—just a bit better. As the Prussian king put it, "The discipline of these troops, now evolved into habit, has such effect that in the greatest disorder of an action and the most evident perils their disorder still is more orderly than the good order of their enemies."[81]

Political and technological standardization were thus accompanied by a similar standardization of military concepts and institutions. As the Chevalier Folard put it, "War is a trade for the ignorant and a science for the expert." It had again become an "art"—in the eighteenth-century sense—governed by rules nearly as rigid as those prescribed by Vegetius. The eighteenth century can properly be called the neoclassical age of modern warfare because success in battle depended upon the sophisticated use of tools and rules known to everyone. The extensive military literature of this age is closer to Vegetius than to Machiavelli. The writings of its Great Captains—Marshal de Saxe, Frederick the Great, and even Napoleon—are largely collections of tactical and training maxims, which assume that the reader is familiar with the underlying political and technological framework. Their

[81] The officers, whose positions seem to be so terribly exposed, were in no greater danger than anyone else, unless the enemy adopted the unusual and unsporting practice of aiming at individuals. Frederick the Great, *Instructions for his Generals*, trans. Thomas R. Phillips (Harrisburg, 1944), 12. This work, and those of Sun Tzu, Vegetius, Maurice de Saxe, and Napoleon are also available as a single volume, Thomas R. Phillips, ed., *Roots of Strategy* (Harrisburg, 1940).

writings remind one of works on chess or contract bridge and
are just about as interesting to the layman. Lesser minds saw
the "secret" in the drill sergeant's pacing stick and pendulum.
The great practitioners spoke of the *coup d'oeil* or sense (as
we speak of baseball or football "sense") that combined intuition and experience. As Frederick expressed it,

> The *coup d'oeil* of a general is the talent which great men have
> of conceiving in a moment all the advantages of the terrain and
> the use they can make of it with their army. . . . Within a single
> square mile a hundred different orders of battle can be formed.
> The clever general . . . gains advantage from the slightest hillock,
> from a tiny marsh; he advances or withdraws a wing, . . .
> strengthens either his right or his left, . . . [and] perceive[s] at first
> glance the weak spot of the enemy. . . . This is the result of
> experience.[32]

All that Frederick's definition reveals is the difficulty of
putting the "secret" of craftsmanship on paper. The best that
could be done with most officers was to make them good tacticians. There were many, like Frederick's famous mule, who
had been through twenty campaigns and knew no more about
generalship than they had at the beginning. Like many other
great generals Frederick was a gambler. He was not afraid
to fight battles; he was, in fact, as eager to destroy the enemy
in battle as Napoleon. But Frederick's military capital was
very slender. He could never have boasted, as Napoleon was
to do, of his unlimited military resources. Like all successful
gamblers, Frederick was lucky. His kingdom was probably
saved from partition by the death of the Empress Elizabeth
of Russia in 1762. In any case Frederick retired with his
winnings, while Napoleon was to lose everything. At one
point Frederick himself claimed that

> Extravagant projects of campaigns are worthless. . . . In pushing
> too far into the enemy's country you weaken yourself, . . . and in
> order to make assured conquests it is necessary always to proceed

---

[32] Frederick, *Instructions*, 41-42. Napoleon defined it as "a faculty to be able
. . . to grasp instantaneously the relation of the ground with the general nature
of the country, . . . a gift . . . which great generals have received from nature."
(Conrad H. Lanza, ed., *Napoleon and Modern War: His Military Maxims Revised and Annotated*, Harrisburg, 1943, 147-148.) There is no modern edition
of the Chevalier Jean Charles Folard's *Histoire de Polybe* (6 vols., Paris, 1727-
1730). This literature is summarized in Max Jähns, *Geschichte der Kriegswis-
senschaften* (3 vols., Berlin, 1889-1891).

within the rules: to advance, to establish yourself solidly, to advance again . . . always within reach of . . . your resources.[32]

The Common Soldier in the Neoclassical Age

The eighteenth century, it has already been suggested, was the great age of the standing army. The royal troops—only six regiments at the accession of Louis XIV—by the time of his death had swallowed up most of the foreign mercenary units and the militia. Some soldiers—like the Hessians who served with the British army during the American Revolution—were still rented out by Swift's "beggarly princes not able to make war by themselves," but most foreign soldiers now came in as individuals. This helped to curb payroll padding and did away with the great differences in training between units of the same army. Mutiny and the desertion of whole units was much less common. When men ran away—as they continued to do in large numbers—they did it as individuals. The number of foreigners—Germans, Belgians, Swedes, Poles, Danes, Italians, Irish, Scots, and Hungarians—varied with the needs and resources of each of the great powers. Each tried to get as many of them as possible because of the chronic shortages of skilled labor. A French minister even claimed that each foreigner was worth three men: one more for the French, one less for the enemy, and a Frenchman left to pay taxes. The proportion of foreigners in the British army was generally very high because Britain was now the wealthiest power in Europe.[34]

In the words of Marshal de Saxe, "Troops are raised by enlistment with a fixed term, without a fixed term, by compulsion sometimes, and most frequently by tricky devices."[35]

[33] Frederick, *Instructions*, 12-13. Frederick's position with regard to a strategy of attrition or one of destruction was much disputed after Hans Delbrück expressed the former view in his famous *Die Strategie des Perikles erläutert durch die Strategie Friedrichs des Grossen* (Berlin, 1890). Delbrück's summary of the literature is in *Geschichte der Kriegskunst*, IV, 426-444. The subject came up again after Hitler's invasion of Russia. See especially Gert Buchheit, *Vernichtungs- oder Ermattungsstrategie?* (Berlin, 1942).

A good account of the eighteenth-century Great Captains is Elbridge Colby, *Masters of Mobile Warfare* (Princeton, 1943). Nothing new is said in *The New Cambridge Modern History* (VII, ed. J. O. Lindsay, Cambridge, 1957). The best short description of eighteenth-century armies is still Spenser Wilkinson, *The Defence of Piedmont, 1742-1748* (Oxford, 1927), 67-73.

[34] During the American Revolution the six contracting Hessian states furnished 30,000 men, a larger force than the whole Continental army. Each prince got seventy-five cents a head and an annual subsidy—about $300,000 for the Landgrave of Hesse. The men got British army pay, seven cents a day for a private. More than a third of this was deducted for their rations: two and a half pounds of beef and a pound and a half of flour a day.

[35] *Reveries on the Art of War*, 21.

The Prussians ran a military slave trade, and even sent armed crimping gangs into surrounding principalities. Though enlistments in the Prussian army were for life, the turnover was high. Old age, disease, and desertion made it necessary to replace about a fifth of the army every year. As many as a thousand recruiters (one for every eighty men) were stationed in foreign countries. Frederick's father gave them special prizes for bagging even one recruit for his only hobby, the Potsdam Giants. Every man of the regiment was at least six feet and the tallest were nearly eight. A six-foot recruit for this collection of "walking colossi" was worth from seven hundred to a thousand thalers and real giants were even more expensive at a time when a common soldier drew two and a half thalers a month and a lieutenant only twelve. The practical Frederick disbanded his father's giants, but did not abandon crimping. Voltaire's classic description of eighteenth-century recruiting refers to his former patron's army:

He halted sadly at the door of an inn. Two men dressed in blue noticed him. . . . They went up to Candide and very civilly invited him to dinner. "Gentlemen," said Candide with charming modesty, "you do me a great honour, but I have no money to pay my share." "Ah, sir," said one of the men in blue, "persons of your figure and merit never pay anything; are you not five feet tall?" "Yes, gentlemen," said he, bowing, "that is my height." "Ah, sir, come to table; we will not only pay your expenses, we will never allow a man like you to be short of money; men are only made to help each other." . . .
"We were asking you if you do not tenderly love the King of the Bulgarians." "Not a bit," said he, "for I have never seen him." "What! He is the most charming of kings, and you must drink to his health." "Oh, gladly, gentlemen." And he drank. "That is sufficient," he was told, "You are now the support, the aid, the defender, the hero of the Bulgarians; your fortune is made and your glory assured."
They immediately put irons on his legs and took him to a regiment. He was made to turn to the right and left, to raise the ramrod and return the ramrod, to take aim, to fire, to double up, and he was given thirty strokes with a stick; the next day he drilled not quite so badly, and received only twenty strokes; the day after, he had only ten and was looked on as a prodigy by his comrades.[36]

Though Marshal de Saxe thought that some form of uni-

[36] *Candide*, chap. ii. If Frederick William could not kidnap a man, he would try to obtain him by barter. One man cost him a skilled bassoon player, and a Spanish stallion was traded for thirty tall recruits. A giant Irishman cost 8,862 thalers, nearly twice the annual pay of a Prussian general. Ergang, *Potsdam Führer*, chap. vi.

versal service would be preferable to this combination of force and fraud, his arguments ran into two major obstacles. The first came from the class distinctions of a society in which, in the words of General Charles de Gaulle, "a host of privileges, contracts and traditions limited, complicated and modified the rights of each social group: class, province, township, statutory body or corporation. On whatever category of citizens compulsory service had been imposed, the whole fabric of society would have been rent from top to bottom." The other objection—which has reappeared in the age of mechanized war—was that the five years suggested by Marshal de Saxe was much too short a time to make real soldiers. Universal conscription was to prove practicable only when the term of peacetime service could be cut to three years or under. Various forms of compulsion were in use almost everywhere in the eighteenth century. They differed from modern conscription in their extreme severity, their less systematic application, and the existence of more numerous causes for exemption. Russian landed proprietors were required to furnish men according to the number of serfs on their lands, and the Prussian regiments, except the Guards, recruited their quotas of Prussian subjects from certain assigned districts. Convicts and the unemployed were pressed into service everywhere, for the colonies as well as for the armed services. Eighteenth-century service was, in short, really selective. "Recruits were provided . . . by those isolated individuals whose absence would inconvenience nobody: young men with a distaste for a humdrum existence . . . and a taste for adventure; . . . down-and-outs, ready to exchange their liberty for food and clothing; bad characters with little choice in life except that between military service or the gallows."[87]

[87] Charles de Gaulle, *France and Her Army* (London, 1941), 23. G. A. M. Girard, *Le Service militaire en France à la fin du règne de Louis XIV, Racolage et milice, 1701-1715* (Paris, 1922). Frederick boasted that he could carry on war without disturbing Prussian merchants and manufacturers. See Edmond Silberner, *La Guerre dans la pensée économique du xvie au xviiie siècles* (Paris, 1939). About a tenth of Frederick's army escaped each year, in spite of the rules given his generals in the *Instructions*, 11-13.

Marshal de Saxe's arguments for universal conscription have remained unchanged for two centuries. "It is natural and just that all citizens should participate in the defense of the nation. No hardship could result if they were chosen between the ages of twenty and thirty years . . . when youth . . . is of little comfort to parents. This . . . would provide an inexhaustible reservoir of fine recruits who would not be so much inclined to desert. . . . It would be regarded as an honor to have completed one military service. But to produce this result it is essential to make no distinctions, . . . and to enforce the law particularly on the nobles and the rich." *Reveries*, 21-22.

The men were kept in line by the nearly universal application of corporal punishment. Many officers felt that it was essential to discipline; every army contained many hardened criminals. Punishments in the French and Austrian armies seem to have been less severe than in the Prussian, but those armies were also less effective in battle. East European peasants were still accustomed to being beaten by their masters, but some observers claimed that the British army's discipline was more brutal than either the Prussian or the Russian. Perhaps Prussian brutality was simply more systematic. Voltaire wrote that the philosopher king Frederick would stand at his window talking about ethics while he watched condemned soldiers run the gauntlet, ride the wooden horse with a couple of muskets on each foot, or drag a cannon ball strapped to an ankle. Since the days when Charles V lifted his hat to the gallows as the first servant of his state, beating had been part of the routine of the professional army. Tolstoy's description of the training of the Russian soldier in the nineteenth century could have been applied to most European armies a century earlier.

We spent the night at the house of a ninety-five-year-old soldier. He had served under Alexander I and Nicholas I. . . .
"The soldiers spoke well of Alexander. He was kind, people said."
I thought back to the last days of Alexander when, out of a hundred men, twenty were flogged to death. Nicholas must have been kind indeed if Alexander was called kind by comparison with him.
"How was it in those days? In those days it was not worth while for them to take down their breeches for fifty lashes. A hundred and fifty, two hundred, three hundred—they flogged people to death!"
He said it without horror and aversion, and not without pride in the achievements of the past. "And when they used the stick—not a week went by without their beating one or two men of the regiment to death. Today nobody really knows what a stick is. In those days the word was always and always in the men's mouths. 'The stick! The stick!'
"Our soldiers gave Nicholas the patronymic of Bigstick. Nicholas Pavlovitch—but the men always said Nicholas Bigstick. That was his second name. . . .
"The subalterns beat the young soldiers to death. With a gunstock or with his fist he hammers the particular spot, in the chest or on the head, and the man dies. And nobody enquires. The man

dies of the blows, and the superior writes, 'Died by act of God,' and an end of it. . . ."

I thought of the dreadful things besides the clubbings which he had had to take part in—how he had had to hound people to death by flogging through the line, by shooting, by murder and sacking of cities in war. . . . I asked him about flogging through the line.

He told at length about this fearful practice. How the man, who is tied to the guns, is led through between the soldiers, who are arranged in a line with the switches in their hands, and how they all hit out; and the officers walk behind the soldiers, yelling, "Hit harder! Hit harder!"

The old man yelled this in a tone of command, and one could tell that the memory of this tone . . . gave him a certain satisfaction.

He told all the details without a trace of remorse, as if he were explaining how oxen are butchered and their meat dressed.[38]

The middle classes, most craftsmen, and free farmers remained outside the military system. They were properly regarded as the support of the state's finances, too valuable to be wasted on muscle work in the army. The public's attitude toward the common soldier mingled fear and contempt, reflecting both his social origins and his degraded existence. This attitude was to survive far longer in Britain and America, with their old-fashioned volunteer armies, than in France, which adopted universal conscription much earlier. Under these conditions the hatred of the free farmer or artisan for military service is quite understandable; with the equally well-founded fear of military despotism, it was to form the hard core of nineteenth century Anglo-American pacifism.

In the officer corps the key changes had also begun much earlier—when the great nobles had been deprived of their hereditary rights to certain high offices—but here again the seventeenth and eighteenth centuries saw a process of centralization and standardization. Illiterate old soldiers from the ranks found it more difficult to obtain commissions. The sons of the great families had to go through some type of professional training. Louvois had drawn up a roster of commissioned officers for the whole French army and had compelled them to stay with their troops from the formal opening of the year's campaigns until the men went into winter quarters.

[38] *The Living Thoughts of Tolstoy* (New York, 1939), 93-95. Scott Claver, *Under the Lash, A History of Corporal Punishment in the British Armed Services* (London, 1954).

Officers could leave the service only by formal resignation. There was no more nonsense about not taking orders from their social inferiors. As the nobility's economic position became more precarious, the once dubious honor of serving the state for pay became a privilege. Soldiering became the standard trade of the lower nobility, one of the few compatible with a code of honor which was in some ways the antithesis of the anarchic code of medieval chivalry. The French nobles' success in squeezing the middle class out of many army appointments was to do much to alienate the latter from the bankrupt, fumbling monarchy.[39]

The Prussian army was officered by the Junker aristocracy, a class more tightly integrated than any nobility in the west by family ties and common economic interests. Their cadet school training was reinforced by service in an army which was always on a war footing. A Prussian officer's career was spent in a great military prison, one far more confining than the "wooden world" of the British naval officer. The pressure to conform was irresistible; both the king and his officers freely exercised their right to blackball nonconformists. As a result of these factors the Prussian army represented the eighteenth century's highest development of what Alfred Vagts has called the "military way"—"a primary concentration of men and materials on winning specific objectives of power with the utmost efficiency, that is, with the least expenditure of blood and treasure." The example of the neoclassical age has led to the hope that similar rules and limits can somehow be applied to warfare in the age of nuclear weapons. But the rules of eighteenth century warfare were enforced by other factors than those of morals, chivalry, and fear of reprisal. The rules held because of a static military technology and because the monarchs could not reorganize their potential military resources without social revolutions

[39] Louis XIV and Louis XV dissipated new sources of income almost as quickly as they were uncovered. Both military and civilian offices were sold; since there were so many more officers than commands, the latter went to persons with court influence. By the end of the Seven Years' War some regiments had several colonels, who took command in rotation. The government even resold the right to supply the troops; a third of the French army deserted on the field at Rossbach because of poor food. See Franklin L. Ford, *Robe and Sword: The Regrouping of the French Aristocracy after Louis XIV* (Cambridge, Mass., 1953). The best short description of the French army at this time is Frédéric Reboul, *L'Armée* (Paris, 1931). On the British see E. S. Turner, *Gallant Gentleman: A Portrait of the British Officer, 1600-1956* (London, 1956).

which would be more dangerous to themselves than to their enemies.[40]

[40] *A History of Militarism* (rev. ed., New York, 1959), 11. Militarism is an "array of customs, interest, prestige, actions and thought associated with armies and wars and yet transcending true military purpose. Indeed . . . it may hamper and defeat the purposes of the military way. . . . Rejecting the scientific character of the military way, militarism displays the qualities of caste and cult, authority and belief."

Fuller, *Armament and History*, B. H. Liddell Hart, *The Revolution in Warfare* (New Haven, 1947), Hoffman Nickerson, *The Armed Horde* (2d ed., New York, 1942), and Henry A. Kissinger, *Nuclear Weapons and Foreign Policy* (New York, 1957) are excellent examples of the now common hope for new limits of warfare.

Chapter 2

Naval Warfare from the Renaissance to the Neoclassical Age (1417-1789)

The Command of the Sea

NAVAL, as distinct from military, history is connected with a special type of transportation and thus presents some problems of its own. Though both ancient and early modern states understood the general principles of sea power, these were first worked into a consistent theory by an American naval officer, Alfred Thayer Mahan. The core of his most famous book, *The Influence of Sea Power upon History, 1660-1783*, published in Boston in 1890, is his emphasis on the ocean as a highway leading to almost all the coasts of the world.

The first and most obvious light in which the sea presents itself from the political and social point of view is that of a great highway; or better, perhaps, of a wide common, over which men may pass in all directions, but on which some well worn paths show that controlling reasons have led them to choose certain lines of travel rather than others. These lines of travel are called trade routes; and the reasons which have determined them are to be sought in the history of the world.

Notwithstanding all the familiar and unfamiliar dangers of the sea, both travel and traffic by water have always been easier and cheaper than by land; [an] advantage [which] . . . was yet more marked in the period when roads were few and very bad, wars frequent and society unsettled, as was the case two hundred years ago.[1]

Since sea power deals with transportation—in the early modern period water transportation was not only the cheapest and fastest, but also the only means of moving heavy commodities—the primary objective of a navy is to get the general right to move men and supplies by sea and to deny this right to the enemy. Mahan called this control of the ocean highway "the command of the sea." Giulio Douhet's concep-

[1] Page 25. There are full bibliographies in William E. Livezey, *Mahan on Sea Power* (Norman, Okla., 1947). The standard life of Mahan is W. D. Puleston, *The Life and Work of Captain Alfred Thayer Mahan* (New York, 1940).

tion of the "command of the air" was to be exactly comparable: "the ability to fly against an enemy so as to injure him, while he has been deprived of the power to do likewise." The backbone of a country's sea power is its battle fleet, whose first function is to win the command of the sea by destroying the enemy's battle forces. The second function of a navy is to exploit that command, to use its control of water transportation to bring pressure on "the military power, the territory, and the will of the enemy." This may involve amphibious operations and the transportation of land forces overseas, defense against enemy landings, the protection of merchant shipping, and the blockade of enemy seaports.[2]

Since a ship is a machine, the technological aspects of naval history have always been very important. Ships have also been handled by professional seamen, a closely knit guild whose lives have necessarily been lived apart from those of the majority of people. For this and other reasons naval warfare has often presented difficult administrative and organizational problems. Quarrels between generals and admirals over defense policy, coast defense, and the conduct of landing operations have a long history. The nature of his work, however, has placed the sailor in a less favorable political position than the soldier. Navies, it has been argued with a good deal of truth, are far less dangerous to free institutions than standing armies. Because of their greater dependence on technology, navies have also been comparatively expensive—the estimate for the sailing period was that a man on ship cost twice as much as one on shore—requiring more developed political structures behind them.[3]

The navy's role in a given war varies with the importance of water transportation. During the Second World War, for example, the economic structures of both Britain and Japan were completely dependent on sea power. The United States' economy did not depend on the uninterrupted command of the sea, but the United States could not undertake either land or air offensives until these forces were deployed overseas.

[2] This paragraph is highly oversimplified. Only occasionally is the command of the sea so complete that it can be "exploited" immediately. Often one or even both opponents must try to accomplish some of these other missions before the command of the sea has been decided. Mahan knew this, but he was anxious to stress the priority of the command of the sea and of the battle forces which win it. Bernard Brodie, *A Guide to Naval Strategy* (4th ed., Princeton, 1958), is excellent. He compares a navy consisting only of battle forces to a railway with nothing but locomotives.

[3] One of the best books on the command of amphibious operations is John Creswell, *Generals and Admirals* (London, 1952).

The oceans were barriers—or watery deserts—rather than highways throughout most of recorded history. Even after the great discoveries of the Renaissance many coasts remained inaccessible because of unfavorable winds and currents. So naval history is a study in comparatives. In each specific case it is necessary to assess the importance of this form of transportation to a given government and society, and to compare the hitting, carrying, and staying powers of the navy's weapons with the comparable powers of the other arms of national defense.[4]

Portuguese and Spanish Sea Power

The early modern history of sea power can be divided into about the same chronological periods as the history of land warfare. The Renaissance saw a series of developments in ships, weapons, and navigational methods which paralleled the introduction of gunpowder and the revival of the infantry. The opening of the oceans was as important an event as the invention of printing. It, too, gave men mobility at a time when Western European society was still characterized by formidable immobilities. Within a generation of Vasco da Gama's first voyage to India, both the Portuguese and the Spanish had strikingly demonstrated the military, economic, and political profits of superior "mobility and miscibility." In both empires, to use the words of the Brazilian historian Gilberto Freyre,

Individuals . . . were shifted about by the colonial administration . . . from Asia to America and from there to Africa, dependent upon the exigencies of the moment or of the region. From Madeira technicians in the manufacture of sugar are sent to the plantations of northern Brazil. . . . From Africa whole nations, almost, of Negroes are transported for agricultural labor in Brazil. An astounding mobility. An imperial domain achieved by an all but ridiculous number of Europeans running from one end to the other of the known world as in a formidable game of puss-in-the-corner.[5]

[4] E. B. Potter, ed., Fleet Admiral Chester W. Nimitz, associate ed., *Sea Power: A Naval History* (Englewood Cliffs, 1960) is the most usable text, though it overstresses recent and American naval history. Michael Lewis' excellent *History of the British Navy* (Harmondsworth, 1957) is too short.
[5] *The Masters and the Slaves: A Study in the Development of Brazilian Civilization* (New York, 1946), 10-11. On the Portuguese see Gilbert Renault, *The Caravels of Christ* (New York, 1959), Bailey W. Diffie, *Prelude to Empire: Portugal Overseas before Henry the Navigator* (Lincoln, 1960), Frédéric Mauro, *Le Portugal et l'Atlantique au XVIIe siècle* (Paris, 1960), and C. R. Boxer, *Fidalgos in the Far East* (The Hague, 1948), *The Dutch in Brazil,*

Since ancient times sailing ships had been used to carry cargo for long distances. The galley, with auxiliary sail power, had usually dominated naval warfare, particularly in the Mediterranean. For centuries, however, the galley had been up against its technological ceiling; the ordinary two-hundred-ton war galley of the Renaissance was little different from the galleys of the Greeks. Faster and more maneuverable than any sailing ship, the galley held her own as long as naval battles were personal-contact encounters between sea-going infantry. She was doomed by the big gun. She could not mount guns in ports on her sides, which were taken up by the oars. And muscles could not move a big ship efficiently.[6]

The revolution in sailing ships took place during the first half of the fifteenth century. In 1400 an ordinary sailing vessel had one big mast and one large sail. In 1450 she would be much bigger, with three masts and five or six sails. She was now as truly a prototype of the eighteenth-century sailing

1624-1654 (Oxford, 1957), and, as ed., *The Tragic History of the Sea, 1589-1622* (Cambridge, 1959). On the discoveries see Boies Penrose, *Travel and Discovery in the Renaissance, 1420-1620* (Cambridge, Mass., 1952), J. H. Parry, *Europe and a Wider World, 1415-1715* (London, 1949), and Samuel Eliot Morison's *Admiral of the Ocean Sea* (2 vols., Boston, 1946). On navigation use: J. B. Hewson, *A History of the Practice of Navigation* (Glasgow, 1951), Per Collinder, *History of Marine Navigation* (London, 1954), E. G. R. Taylor, *The Haven-Finding Art* (New York, 1957), and David W. Waters, *The Art of Navigation in England in Elizabethan and Early Stuart Times* (London, 1958).

6 The Greeks had hit on all the methods for crowding power into each foot of side. In Columbus's day 3 men worked each 36 foot, 125 pound oar, which was balanced by lead weights on the handle. A fourth man might be used on each oar, but 150 men (for the 25 oars on each side) normally rowed the ship, and 75 fought her. Most rowers were slaves or convicts. Each man rose from his seat with his unchained foot braced on the bench ahead of him, pushed the oar forward, and fell back with all his weight. The men could take the racing stroke of twenty-six times a minute for twenty minutes. The ship could make some six knots and might do four knots for two hours with a slower stroke. She carried rations for forty days, but water for only twenty. Really long open sea voyages were impossible, even with auxiliary sail power.

See Lionel Casson, *The Ancient Mariners* (New York, 1959), and Archibald R. Lewis, *Naval Power and Trade in the Mediterranean A.D. 500-1000* (Princeton, 1951) and *The Northern Seas: Shipping and Commerce in Northern Europe A.D. 300-1100* (Princeton, 1958). The basic work on ancient ships, Paul Serre, *Marines de guerre de l'antiquité et du moyen âge* (2 pts., Paris, 1885-1891), was brought up to date by William L. Rodgers, *Greek and Roman Naval Warfare* (Annapolis, 1937) and *Naval Warfare under Oars, 4th to 16th Centuries* (Annapolis, 1939). Rodgers did not use Lefebvre des Noëttes' pioneer, *De la marine antique à la marine moderne: la révolution du gouvernail* (Paris, 1935). Frederick C. Lane, *Venetian Ships and Shipbuilders of the Renaissance* (Baltimore, 1934) is very fine. So is A. W. Brogger and Haakon Shetelig, *The Viking Ships: Their Ancestry and Evolution* (Los Angeles, 1953). For life on the French galleys see Michel Bourdet-Pléville, *Justice in Chains,* tr. Anthony Rippon (London, 1960).

ship as the bombard and arquebus were the prototypes of the eighteenth century's field guns and muskets. The new sail plan —which increased the number of sails, while decreasing their size for easier handling—made it possible to develop the art of sailing close to the wind, an art which had never been necessary and was never discovered in the monsoon seas of Asia. Both galleys and sailing ships were used for war for more than a century and numerous hybrids were developed, but the sailing ship was definitely superior in firepower, range, and protection. Lepanto was the last major sea battle in which galleys played the major role. By the time of the Spanish Armada both sides regarded the sailing ship as the backbone of the fleet.[7]

The Hapsburg navy, like their armies, drew on the resources of several maritime states. Aragon had been a major Mediterranean trading power, and the Hapsburgs hired many Italian ships and seamen. Other ships were furnished by their territories in the Netherlands and by Portugal, after Philip II's annexation of Portugal in 1580. These maritime resources proved to be sufficient to check the Turks in the western Mediterranean and to control the sea routes to the Indies, but not to smother the Dutch revolt. Spain was nearly a thousand miles closer to the West Indies than any of her northern rivals. From the first, because of the lack of trained pilots, merchantmen had sailed in convoy. The bulk of Europe's overseas trade was still very small in proportion to its value. Only one fleet a year was sent from Spain to the Americas. After French Huguenot and Barbary pirates became troublesome, this fleet left under heavy escort in the late spring for the Canaries. There it left part of its escort behind and crossed to the Lesser Antilles, where it was split into two fleets—one for Mexico and one for South America. The two rejoined at Havana before the opening of the hurricane season the next year. The most dangerous part of the return voyage was the passage through the Straits of Florida and along the Carolinas, where both unofficial and official marauders had their best chance of picking up stragglers. At the Azores the convoy's escort was again strengthened by ships sent out from Spain. Since the times of arrival and departure, the exact route, and even the methods of navigation

[7] The best books are Romola and R. C. Anderson, *The Sailing Ship: Six Thousand Years of History* (New York, 1947), and Jean de la Varende, *Cherish the Sea: A History of Sail,* trans. Mervyn Savill (New York, 1956).

were state secrets, the initiative always lay with the convoy.[8]

The marauders' hardest task was to find the convoy. Since communications between ships at sea were limited to flag signals, it was nearly impossible to come up with a fleet or a convoy in the open sea. Attacks on the ports of arrival and departure were more frequent than they were successful. The treasure might not have arrived in port, or the convoy might have left, or the gold might have been taken into the jungle and buried. Its sources were high inside Spanish America, defended by difficult terrain and the formidable Spanish army. For these reasons Elizabeth's victory over the Armada was never successfully exploited; expeditions against Lisbon, Porto Bello, Cadiz, and the Azores were comparative failures. At the end of her reign the English queen had again reverted to cruiser warfare and to supporting Philip II's other continental enemies. The weak spot in the Spanish system—in spite of the lure of Spanish treasure—was in northern Europe.

In the Armada campaign both the English and the Spanish depended on their big guns, though the English ships were rather lower and faster. The big Spanish ships convoyed their transport up the Channel in a half-moon formation. The English fought in groups of half a dozen ships. These hung on the flanks and rear of the Spanish mass like wolves on the edges of a buffalo herd, but they never pressed home against the formidable Spanish soldiers. In the ten days' fighting in the Channel about 7 per cent of the Spaniards were killed or wounded, and both sides used enormous quantities of ammunition (over 100,000 rounds for the Armada) in a futile long-range cannonade. The Armada reached Calais with fairly small losses, but found neither troops nor provisions. The Catholic uprising in England had failed. After they had been driven from Calais Roads by English fireships, the Spanish commanders made the fatal decision to return to Spain by way of Scotland instead of facing the reprovisioned English in the Channel. The English shepherded them north and then

---

[8] An office at Seville collated hydrographic information. Pilots were often blamed for matters outside of their control, but many of them surely pretended to more knowledge than they possessed. See Huguette and Pierre Chaunu, *Séville et l'Atlantique, 1504-1650* (5 vols., Paris, 1955-1957), Rayner Unwin, *The Defeat of John Hawkins* (New York, 1960), P. K. Kemp and Christopher Lloyd, *Brethren of the Coast: Buccaneers of the South Seas* (New York, 1961), and Godfrey Fisher, *Barbary Legend: War, Trade and Piracy in North Africa, 1415-1830* (Oxford, 1957). On Mexico see C. Harvey Gardiner, *Naval Power in the Conquest of Mexico* (Austin, 1956).

returned to port with many of their men sick of fever. Both fleets were composed of hired merchantment with small nuclei —only 16 per cent in the English fleet—of royal warships. Both were commanded by members of the great nobility, with the professional seamen in subordinate positions. Neither had been equal to the demands of a long campaign.[9]

The Rise of English Sea Power

By the early seventeenth century the Dutch, English, and French had broken the Spanish and Portuguese monopoly of extra-European trade and colonization and were breaking into the trade of the eastern Mediterranean. The United Netherlands was the greatest maritime power in Europe, with as many ships in the general carrying trade as all the other seafaring nations together. The Netherlands then furnished the best example of the ways in which, according to the English economist William Petty, "a small country, and few People, may by their Situation, Trade, and Policy, be equivalent in Wealth and Strength, to a far greater People and Territory. And particularly, How conveniences for Shipping, and Water Carriage, do most Eminently, and Fundamentally, conduce thereunto." But Dutch prosperity only set the stage for new conflicts as soon as England and France turned their attention to overseas commerce. Since the total amount of trade was then assumed to be a fixed quantity, England and France could only increase their commerce, according to Colbert, "by making inroads on the Dutch." The aim of the complex of trading, colonial, and industrial regulations known as mercantilism was not only to secure an excess of exports over imports and a favorable flow of bullion into the country, but also to cut into Dutch trade and shipping wherever possible.

[9] See Garrett Mattingly's superb *The Armada* (New York, 1959) or Michael Lewis, *The Spanish Armada* (New York, 1960). Spain's strategic position in the north was like Britain's later position in the Mediterranean. The Hapsburgs supported Scotland, Irish and Breton separatism, and friendly candidates for the English and French thrones. Britain supported Portugal, Catalan and Sicilian separatism, and the Austrian candidate for the Spanish throne. W. F. Monk, *Britain in the Western Mediterranean* (New York, 1953).

On British sea power in general see Thomas Woodroofe's popular *Vantage at Sea* (London, 1959), Michael Lewis, *The Navy of Britain* (London, 1948), Admiral Herbert Richmond's classics, *Statesmen and Sea Power* (Oxford, 1946) and *The Navy as an Instrument of Policy, 1558-1727* (Cambridge, 1953), and Julian S. Corbett, *Drake and the Tudor Navy* (2 vols., London, 1898). James A. Williamson, *The Age of Drake* (New York, 1938), *The Ocean in English History* (Oxford, 1941), and *The English Channel* (London, 1959) are very fine. For the difficulties of organizing amphibious operations, see C. G. Cruickshank, *Elizabeth's Army* (London, 1947) and Cyril Falls, *Elizabeth's Irish Wars* (London, 1950).

The merchant and fishing fleets were particular objects of governmental concern. Though they no longer supplied navies with major warships, they furnished them with auxiliary and transport craft and served as "nurseries" of seamen. When all manpower was trained on the job, the long voyage and fishing trades gave employment and training to large numbers of sailors.[10]

These commercial rivalries were one factor in the long series of wars between England, France, and the Netherlands which marked the second half of the seventeenth century. In the First Anglo-Dutch War (1652-1654) both navies still centered their efforts on the attack and defense of convoys; during the Second (1665-1667) they began to realize that the issue depended on their battle forces. France and England both attacked the Dutch in 1672 (though the English withdrew in 1674 from a war which lasted until 1678) and the Netherlands were nearly conquered by the French army. From this time on the Netherlands were forced to spend so much on mercenary troops and fortifications that their navy fell below that of England. The Dutch were also handicapped by geography. England and France flanked their routes to the open ocean. Their harbors were so shallow that their warships were smaller and somewhat lighter than their French or English counterparts. France's population was eight and England's three times that of the Netherlands. The wonder is that the great Dutch admirals Tromp and de Ruyter—in Mahan's opinion the ablest sea fighters of the age—"played the bad cards so well."[11]

[10] Petty's title sums up the objectives of mercantilist policy. *Political Arithmetick, or a Discourse Concerning, the Extent and Value of Lands, People, Buildings; Husbandry, Manufacture, Commerce, Fishery, Artizans, Seamen, Soldiers; Publick Revenues, Interest, Taxes, Superlucration, Registries, Banks; Valuation of Men, Increasing of Seamen, of Militia's, Harbours, Situation, Shipping, Power at Sea, etc. As the same related to every Country in general, but more particularly to the Territories of his Majesty of Great Britain, and his Neighbours of Holland, Zeeland, and France* (London, 1690), reprinted in *The Economic Writings of Sir William Petty* (ed. Charles Henry Hull, 2 vols., Cambridge, 1899), I, 249.

Volume II of Eli F. Heckscher's classic *Mercantilism* (rev. E. F. Söderlund, 2 vols., London, 1956) retreats somewhat from the positions taken in "Mercantilism as a System of Power." Charles Wilson, *Profit and Power: A Study of England and the Dutch Wars* (London, 1957) is excellent. On the Navigation Acts and the colonies see Bernhard Kollenberg, *Origin of the American Revolution* (New York, 1960), Carl Ubbelohde, *The Vice-Admiralty Courts and the American Revolution* (Chapel Hill, 1960), E. Arnot Robertson, *The Spanish Town Papers* (London, 1959), Lawrence A. Harper, *The English Navigation Laws* (New York, 1939), and O. M. Dickerson, *The Navigation Acts and the American Revolution* (Philadelphia, 1951).

[11] There is not much in English on the Dutch. A satisfactory general survey is Francis Vere, *Salt in Their Blood* (London, 1956).

At the beginning of the War of the League of Augsburg (1689-1697) the French navy was larger than the combined navies of England and the Netherlands. The Dutch were exhausted from the previous war and the English were engaged in new internal quarrels. But much of the French fleet was stationed in the Mediterranean and could not be brought around to the Channel in time to play a part in the events which, in 1688-1689, placed Louis XIV's great enemy, William of Orange, the Stadtholder of Holland, on the throne of England. William's army of some 15,000 men—the largest professional army that ever landed in England—got over without a naval battle. The same "Protestant wind" which blew the Dutch down the English Channel prevented the English fleet from getting out of its anchorages near London to challenge them. Later in the year, however, the French fleet convoyed the ousted English King, James II, and a small French force to Ireland, while the English fleet convoyed an English army to the same destination. In the spring of 1690 the combined French Mediterranean and Atlantic fleets defeated the English and Dutch at Beachy Head (the English letting the Dutch do most of the fighting) and drove them back into the Thames. But the French could not use their temporary command of the Channel. They had no army ready to invade England, and the next day James II was badly defeated in Ireland. Louis XIV gathered an army to invade England in 1692, but his Mediterranean fleet was delayed in joining the Atlantic squadron. The French admiral commanding the latter force decided to attack anyway, hoping for political defections from the combined English and Dutch forces. Fighting with greatly inferior forces too near Cape La Hogue, the French fleet was caught in a shifting tide after an indecisive battle. Fifteen ships were either burned by their crews or destroyed by the allies.[12]

The French navy never recovered from the defeat off Cape La Hogue. Louis XIV now concentrated on continental objectives. Many of his remaining warships were chartered out to private capitalists for commerce raiding. The naval campaigns in the War of the Spanish Succession were overshadowed by the more dramatic land operations, but there were

[12] E. P. Powley, *The English Navy in the Revolution of 1688* (Cambridge, 1928) and John Ehrman, *The Navy in the War of William III, 1689-1697* (Cambridge, 1953). On the Stuarts see the important works by C. D. Penn, *The Navy under the Early Stuarts* (London, 1920), and Arthur W. Tedder, *The Navy of the Restoration from the Death of Cromwell to the Treaty of Breda: Its Work, Growth, and Influence* (Cambridge, 1916).

continuous British convoy operations and a number of amphibious expeditions. As far as the command of the sea was concerned, the later wars of the mid-eighteenth century were anti-climactic. The British fleet was usually about twice as large as that of France; without naval support, the French traders in Canada and India were doomed. The Treaty of Utrecht—which confirmed Britain's acquisition of Newfoundland, Nova Scotia, Hudson's Bay, Gibraltar, Minorca, and certain trading rights in Spain's American colonies—marked the real beginning of British maritime supremacy.

Before the war [Mahan wrote], "England was one of the sea powers; after it she was *the* sea power, without any second. . . . She alone was rich, and in her control of the sea and her extensive shipping had the sources of wealth so much in her hands that there was no present danger of a rival on the ocean. . . . Is it meant, it may be asked, to attribute to sea power alone the greatness or wealth of any State? Certainly not. The due use and control of the sea is but one link in the chain of exchange by which wealth accumulates; but it is the central link, which, . . . history seems to assert, most surely of all gathers itself riches.[18]

Britain extended like a great breakwater between Northern Europe and the Atlantic, in the center of the half circle from Brest to Bergen. Gibraltar, Minorca, and the alliance with Portugal extended that barrier for another thousand miles, without correspondingly weakening British security. For this reason Geographical Position was to be the first in Mahan's list of the elements necessary for sea power, a list reflecting the main factors in Britain's victory in the three-cornered struggle of the late seventeenth century. The other factors were Physical Conformation, Extent of Territory, Number of Population ("not only the grand total, but the number following the sea, or at least readily available for employment on ship-board and for the creation of naval material"), National Character (especially "the capacity for planting healthy colonies"), and Character of the Government. "The various traits of a country and its people constitute the natural characteristics with which a nation, like a man, begins its career:

18 *Influence of Sea Power,* 225-226. Note the mercantilistic trend of Mahan's thought. See also Elizabeth Boody Schumpeter, *English Overseas Trade Statistics, 1697-1808* (Oxford, 1961), J. H. Owen, *War at Sea under Queen Anne* (Cambridge, 1938), Julian S. Corbett, *England in the Mediterranean* (2 vols., London, 1904), Charles de La Roncière, *Histoire de la marine française* (6 vols., Paris, 1899-1934), René Mémain, *La Marine de guerre sous Louis XIV* (Paris, 1937), and especially Raoul Castex, *Les Idées militaires de la marine au XVIIIe siècle* (Paris, 1911).

the conduct of government in turn corresponds to the exercise of intelligent willpower, which . . . causes success or failure in a man's life or a nation's history."[14]

Navies in the Neoclassical Age

The decisive battles for the command of the sea took place during the latter half of the seventeenth century. By the eighteenth century the sailing ship-of-the-line and the big naval gun were both close to their technological ceilings. Naval tactics were as stereotyped as those of eighteenth-century armies. It had long been realized that the single "line ahead" was for sailing ships the most effective formation for delivering broadsides—the galley had been weakest at the sides and strongest at the ends—but a tight line required fine seamanship and a much better system of order transmission than the "line abreast" of the galleys. Keeping station with the clumsy sailing ships was more difficult than with the galleys, so the new tactics had stressed the importance of keeping in line and following the orders of the admirals. Though the writers of the sailing period seem never to have doubted that there was such a thing as naval strategy, those of the eighteenth century were preoccupied with minute tactical considerations.[15]

The Dutch wars had forced the converted merchantmen out of the battle line entirely. By the eighteenth century warships were divided into two general categories—ships "of the line" and those "below" it. The big ships could handle anything afloat; two smaller ships could not normally fight a big

[14] *Influence of Sea Power,* 29-74. Though Gibraltar's guns could not prevent passage of fleets through the Straits, the British could be certain of discovering any movement of forces out of or into the Mediterranean.
[15] This may have been due, in part, to the lack of those fixed points, like roads and fortifications, which first turned military writers to grand strategy. "It was not possible for the admiral to convert his distances into days, as the general did into so many marches." Even tactical combinations were uncertain enough; winds and currents might upset the best tactical science. Alfred Thayer Mahan, *Naval Strategy* (Boston, 1911), 114.
    British fleets usually preferred the windward, which enabled them to attack or break off at will, though high winds or seas might keep them from using their lowest gunports. The French usually chose the leeward. They might be hampered by smoke but their guns would be elevated for maximum range to damage the enemy's rigging while he was bearing down and thus prevent him from closing. The classic on the English Fighting Instructions and their later over-formalization of fleet tactics is Julian S. Corbett, ed., *Fighting Instructions, 1530-1816* (London, 1905). A delightfully scurrilous description of many of the "tarpaulin," officers who had come in from the merchant marine, is Ned Ward's *The Wooden World Dissected* (1706: London, 1929). This pamphlet and Ward's *Mars Stript of His Armour* (1708) were the prototypes of Smollett's *Roderick Random* (1748), and Defoe's *Memoirs of a Cavalier* (1720).

one because of their clumsiness and the small training arcs of their guns. The two-foot oak sides of the big ships were almost impervious even to heavy shot, hits below the water-line were very rare, and shot holes in a wooden ship were partially self-sealing. As a result most fleet battles were decided by sheer butchery. Both sides slugged it out "yard-arm to yard-arm" until one was so helpless that her clumsy opponent could "rake" her weak ends or take her by boarding. Ships "below the line" were used for cruiser duties. The majority of British ships of the line at the end of the eighteenth century were 74's. Below them were 36- or 38-gun frigates.[16]

A sailing ship of the line was the largest and most complicated machine produced by eighteenth-century European craftsmanship, a machine built chiefly of organic materials and worked by wind and muscle. Two thousand oak trees went into each 74—perhaps half of them from the dwindling Western European forests, the rest from America or the Baltic. The oak was cured for at least a year before the framing members were bent after boiling or pickling. Then the frame was set up in the open for an additional year's seasoning. The planks were held by long wooden pins or "treenails." If the treenails were driven too tightly, they would swell and split the planks. When they worked loose, the ship became a timber basket held together by the pressure of the water. A wooden ship, like a wooden house, required constant repair and renovation. She might fall apart in three years or a hundred. After 1758 many ships were covered with thin sheet copper. The copper discouraged teredo worms and barnacles but corroded all the iron with which it came in contact. Each vessel had her own personality. The art of getting the most from her and the wind and weather could be learned only by experience.[17]

16 The 64-gun battleship was too light and those over 80 guns were too heavy. Very heavy frigates were too costly for cruiser and too light for battleship work. The very heavy American frigates of the 1790's could run from most existing British battleships and overpower most existing cruisers.

At the Nile (1798) nearly half the French and 12 per cent of the British were casualties in a single evening's fight, as great a slaughter as at Borodino. Forty-eight ships-of-the-line were captured by the British in the major battles of the French Revolutionary period. Only two were sunk, though some of the prizes were surrendered in a sinking condition.

17 The best books on shipbuilding are Westcott Abell, *The Shipwright's Trade* (Cambridge, 1948), and C. N. Longridge, *The Anatomy of Nelson's Ships* (London, 1953). On the timber problem there are Robert G. Albion, *Forests and Sea Power: The Timber Problem of the Royal Navy, 1652-1862* (Cambridge, Mass., 1926), and Paul W. Bamford, *Forests and French Sea Power, 1660-1789* (Toronto, 1956).

Each of the warship's component parts—pumps, sails, anchors, or guns—was limited by the powers of human muscle. The three-ton 32-pounder naval gun was the biggest that could be handled on shipboard. It required a fourteen- to sixteen-man crew; more men would simply be in each others' way. The guns did not recoil inboard until about the time of the Dutch wars. It was not until then that all the ships in a line could deliver a continuous fire, like that developed by the infantry during the same period. Naval, like land, guns were still inaccurate. Their effective range of less than three hundred yards was only a tenth of their extreme carry. Good gunnery was a matter of speed and volume. At sea as on land, there was little qualitative competition. There were no secret weapons; there was no problem of obsolescence. One Spanish battleship at Trafalgar was as old as Farragut's flagship would be today, and Nelson's *Victory* would have been built during the presidency of Theodore Roosevelt. Since it was comparatively easy to lay ships up "in ordinary" during peacetime, it was much more difficult to upset the status quo than it has been since the Industrial Revolution. The nation which possessed the largest number of these long-lived and virtually unsinkable battle-wagons was almost unassailable.[18]

The same men both worked and fought the ship. Everything depended on her crew's strength and experience. Since even the wealthiest states kept only small fleets in peacetime, the conscription of merchant sailors was a universal practice. Their distinctive walk and habits almost always betrayed them to the press, and many of their countrymen were eager to turn them in for a share in the bounty. Crude muscle power was provided by the jails or flushed from the dives which the press gangs worked for real sailors. The British sailor's pay remained the same from the time of Cromwell to 1797, though prices had risen considerably. An able seaman got

---

18 They were just that. Broad and heavy to carry the enormous weight of their guns without breaking their backs, their usual ratio of length to beam was only 2½ to 1. The *Missouri* is finer than even the finest clipper, over eight times as long as she is broad.

About the time of the American Revolution the British Navy began to use a sawed-off version of the standard long gun, known as a carronade or smasher. At close ranges the standard shot at a lower velocity produced a hail of splinters which was as deadly as the hail of lead from the quick-firing Prussian infantry. But this concentration on short-range volume fire left a gap for American marksmanship with the older long guns, like the one left open on land for the aimed fire of the American rifle. Frederick Leslie Robertson, *The Evolution of Naval Armament* (New York, 1921).

twenty-two shillings and six pence a month until the mutinies of the Channel fleet in that year forced a raise to the shilling a day of the common soldier. A merchant seaman was a skilled laborer whose wages rose on the outbreak of war when both the navy and shipowners wanted his services. The mingling of these skilled workers with real grievances and common criminals was largely responsible for the mutinies. The French government was supposed to pay its naval conscripts small pensions, but was often unable to meet its commitments. Some old British seamen were provided for in charitable institutions.[19]

Perhaps the worst victualing problem during the sailing period was the lack of good drinking water. Though most of the water drunk by the soldier must have been polluted, all of that drunk on shipboard was abominable. At best it was not quite as bad as the beer (a gallon per man per day), which was the normal drink of northern seamen during the Middle Ages. The brandy or rum which was later issued in place of beer was drunk neat until the mid-eighteenth century, when Admiral Vernon is supposed to have invented grog by diluting it with three parts of water. Since the water was powerful enough to spoil the whole concoction in a few days, this was an additional way of ensuring its immediate consumption. The noon issue was a half pint of rum with three half pints of water and a little lemon juice and sugar; the supper allowance omitted the last two ingredients. A good portion of the crew was generally befuddled during the night watches, one cause of the accidents which killed far more men than did battles. Though almost all sailors ended up as confirmed alcoholics, grog was a real support for men who were doing heavy and dangerous work in the open in cold climates, with little warm food and no waterproof clothing. The dietary staples were still the ship's biscuit, salt meat, and

19 J. R. Hutchinson, *The Press Gang, Afloat and Ashore* (London, 1913); C. N. Robinson, *The British Tar in Fact and Fiction* (London, 1909). The men were paid in "tickets" on the Pay Office in London. The sailors sold these at heavy discounts to various land sharks. The average sailor ran through three or four years' wages in short order and was then ready to be sold to the press gang for the bounty. Lewis, *Navy of Britain*, 298-318, believes that no more than 15 per cent of the men entered voluntarily during the Napoleonic period. Abandoned children accounted for 10 per cent, 10 per cent were foreigners, and 15 per cent direct from the jails. On the French *inscription maritime* see Eugene L. Asher, *The Resistance of the Maritime Classes: The Survival of Feudalism in the France of Colbert* (Berkeley, 1960). Many men felt that flogging was necessary to keep order, but the mutineers wanted to end illegal flogging without a court martial. John G. Bullocke, *Sailors' Rebellion* (London, 1938) is the latest work.

fish of Columbus' day. Each man was supposed to get a pound and a half of biscuit and two pounds of meat (or a pound and a half of fish) per day, but six men often ate four men's rations and were granted an allowance from the purser for the saving. The biscuits were baked of mixed wheat and pea flour with such additional bone dust as the dockyard bakers could get away with. The pea flour separated into yellow lumps which were wholly inedible, until the whole biscuit was sufficiently sour, maggoty, and musty to fall into that category. Old stores of salt beef and pork were issued first, the meat was dragged after the ship in a net to wash out the worst of the salt before it was eaten. There were also raisins, plums, prunes, and heavily salted butter and cheese, which bred a specially voracious species of long red maggots. Some fresh fruits and vegetables might be served, but northern Europeans were used to a very heavy bread and meat diet, and fruits and vegetables in the tropics are notoriously tricky. To vary the monotony and get the salt out of their mouths, the sailors would eat, drink, or chew almost anything—mixed vitriol and cider, oakum, or the melted salt fat with which the topmen greased the rigging.[20]

Besides the pay and provisions, the Channel mutineers listed the lack of leave and the treatment of the sick as major grievances. They complained especially of the embezzlement of medical supplies and the discharge without pay or pensions of men who were not fully recovered from wounds or sickness. Naval medicine had made a good deal of progress in stamping out scurvy and the epidemics of typhus which had often immobilized fleets in the sixteenth century. This was often an important strategic factor. Where the French and Spanish, for example, landed twelve hundred sick after their voyage to the West Indies in 1805, their British pursuers had lost only a few dozen. Constant scrubbing kept wooden ships very damp, while work in wet clothing brought on rheumatism, arthritis, and many respiratory infections. Disease and desertion still caused much greater wastage than battle. Ships

[20] See John Masefield's classic account, *Sea Life in Nelson's Time* (2d ed., London, 1920) and three splendid histories of nautical medicine: Richard S. Allison, *Sea Diseases* (London, 1943); L. H. Roddis, *James Lind: Founder of Nautical Medicine* (New York, 1951); and the late J. J. Keevil's unfinished *Medicine and the Navy, 1200-1900* (Vols. I–III, London, 1957-1961). Dr. Keevil suggests that older men and those impressed from the cities had more resistance than young countrymen, and gives numerous fascinating details from the records. Many men preferred salt water or urine to the beer, which as late as 1789 was reported to include " 'great heapes of stuff not unlike to men's guts, which has alarmed the seamen to a strange degree.' "

were deliberately overcrowded when they were first commissioned, and this overcrowding helped, in turn, to spread disease. In the eighteenth century ambulatory cases were allowed to loaf in the galley, the only warm, dry place in the ship. Other sick men lay in their hammocks, next to the healthy. Falls were common and often fatal, since compound fractures, like gunshot wounds, usually became infected and there were few ways of rescuing men overboard.[21]

The British and French navies were officered by younger sons of the gentry and the middle classes. Any thirteen- or fourteen-year-old who could persuade a captain to take him could become a midshipman in the British navy. The schoolmaster or the officers then taught him enough navigation and seamanship to pass the perfunctory examination for lieutenant. Promotion to the rank of captain was by selection, from that point by seniority. An officer had to reach captain's rank in his early twenties—usually through family or other influence—to become a rear admiral at fifty. Nelson was a captain before he became of age; the reverse of the medal was a glut of middle-aged officers in the lower ranks without hope of promotion. Half-pay, at first given only to a few pensioners, was little more than a retaining fee. Officers of good family were not expected to live on it; others found employment in the merchant marine. But this system was probably better than the French army's practice of multiplying officers' jobs, while promotion by strict seniority in the upper ranks created so many admirals that good men were usually available for major commands.[22]

21 In the four years 1776-1779, 1243 British sailors were killed, 18,541 died of disease, and 42,069 deserted. William L. Clowes, ed., *The Royal Navy* (7 vols., London, 1897-1903), III, 339. Five hundred of the 1872 seamen and marines on George Anson's voyage around the world (1740-1744) were impressed pensioners. Every one of them died during the voyage. Boyle Somerville, *Commodore Anson's Voyage into the South Seas and around the World* (London, 1934), J. C. Beaglehole, *The Exploration of the Pacific* (2d ed., London, 1947), Bern Anderson, *Surveyor of the Sea: The Life and Voyages of Captain George Vancouver* (Seattle, 1959), and Ernest S. Dodge, *Northwest by Sea* (New York, 1961) deal with the later explorers.

22 An obvious incompetent might become a "Yellow" admiral (the reference was to Admirals of the Red, the White, and the Blue) without ever being given a command. The senior British Vice-Admiral in 1857 was eighty-nine years old, had been on half-pay since 1812, and had never hoisted his flag. On naval education see Michael Lewis, *England's Sea Officers: The Story of the Naval Profession* (London, 1939) and E. C. Millington, *Seamen in the Making, a Short History of Nautical Training* (London, 1935). The schoolmasters, like the chaplains and surgeons, were usually quite incompetent. See especially James Anthony Gardner's recollections, *Above and under Hatches* (New York, 1955).

Chapter 3

The Anglo-American Military Tradition

The Weakness of the Standing Army

THE AMERICAN military system is of course English in origin. Its distinguishing features at the time of the first English settlements in North America were the absence of a standing army and a series of bitter constitutional conflicts over military matters. Only a few of these conflicts involved the navy. Though there were quarrels over naval finance and Parliament occasionally tried to influence naval strategy by direct legislation, the navy was always regarded as essential to national safety and no great danger to liberty. All fit men from sixteen to sixty were eligible for the militia, who could not be called outside their counties except in case of invasion, but only a few "trained bands" were drilled in peacetime. The Tudors still raised and disbanded foreign-service troops for each expedition. Each shire had a quota of volunteers, and local officials had the power to press undesirables, if real volunteers were lacking.[1]

The Stuarts' political, financial, and military difficulties were closely related. Parliament opposed a standing army, the permanent system of taxes necessary to support one, and the Stuarts' political aims simultaneously. When Parliament refused to vote enough money for Charles I's wars with Spain and France in 1625 and 1626, the king resorted to forced loans. The returning soldiers were billeted on the citizens in-

[1] Henry VIII's navy had been financed by the plunder of the monasteries. Charles I tried to finance his fleet with ship-money, a tax originally paid by the coastal towns, but eventually extended by Charles to the rest of the kingdom. The opposition claimed that this was a new tax which could be granted only by Parliament. It feared that the king would not spend the money on ships, but would use it to make himself independent of Parliament. Most of the ship money was spent on ships, but the sailors were so poorly paid that Charles's whole fleet went over to Parliament in the crisis. In the eighteenth century Parliament tried to specify the number of ships to be used in commerce protection in the "convoys and cruisers" bills. Ruth Bourne, *Queen Anne's Navy in the West Indies* (New Haven, 1939); Richard Pares, *War and Trade in the West Indies, 1739-1763* (Oxford, 1936).

A rich landowner supplied and equipped a horseman and a middle farmer a footsoldier for the militia. A group of small proprietors sent one man to the muster. The Lord Lieutenant in each county appointed the officers and helped the militia commissioners determine the quotas.

stead of being paid off. It was suspected that most of the soldiers were billeted on those who had resisted the loan. Two years later Parliament forced Charles to sign the Petition of Right, which dealt specifically with forced loans, martial law, illegal taxes, billeting, and arbitrary arrest and imprisonment. Charles then ruled without Parliament until the Scotch revolt of 1639-1640. He tried to raise an army by calling on the feudal contingents. When this force was defeated, he was forced to call Parliament. Parliament appointed its own officers for the militia, a direct challenge to his authority, and sent him the ultimatum known as the "Nineteen Propositions." Three of these dealt with the militia, forts, and castles. One asked the discharge of "the extraordinary guards and military forces now attending your Majesty."

In the civil war which followed both sides began from scratch. The military potential of the country consisted of officers and soldiers who had once served abroad, the trained bands, and the equipment supplied by the Board of Ordnance to the county magazines and the fleet. King and Parliament each summoned the militia, tried to secure the magazines, and appealed for volunteers. Parliament controlled both the financial machinery and the Board of Ordnance and was not wholly dependent upon the volunteer efforts of its supporters. Its control of the fleet prevented the King from getting supplies and men from his foreign supporters. Both sides had to resort to conscription after enthusiasm died down, but the Parliamentary armies were better paid and often had better equipment. The King got most of the better generals, and the early Parliamentary advantages were frittered away until Fairfax and Skippon succeeded in forming a "New Model" army from the forces of the Eastern Association and two other Parliamentary armies.

When the King had been defeated, Parliament tried to disband the army without compensation. This forced most of the officers and men to stick together and led in part to the army's direct intervention in Parliamentary politics. The result was a second short civil war against the royalists, the Scotch, and part of the old Parliamentary forces. This time part of the navy went with the King. After his defeat and execution, it continued the war from the western islands and bases in Holland. The victorious army leaders purged Parliament of all but their own supporters, abolished the House of Lords, executed Charles, and finally defeated both the Scotch and the

Irish. For a decade England was controlled by Cromwell and his army, about 70,000 men in 1652, but reduced to 42,000 at his death in 1658. This army was a true standing army, well paid and well disciplined, and the English got a real taste of military dictatorship. The continued existence of a refugee royalist navy and wars with the Netherlands and Spain also forced Cromwell to increase the navy. The sale of royalist estates paid the bills until 1654; then the bankrupt Protector borrowed from everyone in England who could be forced to lend him money.[2]

At the end of the period of political confusion which followed Cromwell's death, the commander-in-chief in Scotland, General Monk, called a new Parliament, which restored Charles II (1660-1685). All of the army, except for a few units, was paid off, but Charles was allowed to maintain in England a small number of regiments—with a total of about three thousand men at first—to guard his person and to garrison the fortresses. Monk's own regiment became the Coldstream Guards; the later Grenadier Guards were trusted Royalists. The King managed to increase these forces a bit during his reign, partly by means of the funds which he was secretly getting from Louis XIV. The quarrel between King and Parliament again came to a head when Charles was succeeded by his brother, James II (1685-1688). Among other things, James was charged with not disbanding regiments which had been raised to suppress Monmouth's rebellion and with recruiting Irishmen and Catholics. When the test came in 1688 the army's commander-in-chief, the later Duke of Marlborough, deserted to William of Orange. James fled to France and most of his army was paid off.

2 The navy's wage debt alone was £371,000. In 1657 the navy cost £809,000 and the army £1,100,000, at a time when the total public income was about £1,050,000. W. A. Shaw, "The Commonwealth and the Protectorate" (*The Cambridge Modern History*, IV, New York, 1934), 454-458; M. Oppenheim, *History of the Administration of the Royal Navy, 1509-1660* (London, 1896), 219, 368; Stephen B. Baxter, *The Development of the Treasury, 1660-1702* (London, 1957).

The best book on the Civil War is now C. V. Wedgwood, *The Great Rebellion* (2 vols. to date, London, 1955-1958), but Sir Charles Firth's classics, *Cromwell's Army* (London, 1902), *Oliver Cromwell and the Rule of the Puritans in England* (1900, Oxford, 1955), and, with Godfrey Davies, *The Regimental History of Cromwell's Army* (2 vols., Oxford, 1940) are still worth reading. Other interesting books are Alfred H. Burne and Peter Young, *The Great Civil War* (London, 1959), Leo F. Solt, *Saints in Arms: Puritanism and Democracy in Cromwell's Army* (Stanford, 1959), Bernard Fergusson, *Rupert of the Rhine* (London, 1952), and Maurice P. Ashley, *Cromwell's Generals* (London, 1954) and *The Greatness of Oliver Cromwell* (London, 1957).

The revolution of 1688 put Parliament in the saddle, but involved Britain in war with Louis XIV, who was certain to help James II regain the throne. William needed more troops than those he had brought with him, so Parliament allowed him to raise an army—subject to the safeguards which it wrote into the Bill of Rights and other acts of this period. The Bill of Rights stated, "That the raising or keeping of a standing army within the kingdom in time of peace, unless it be with the consent of parliament, is against law" and "That the subjects which are Protestants may have arms for their defence suitable to their conditions, and as allowed by law." When one regiment mutinied and declared for James, William found that he had no legal power to punish them. The result was the passage of the Mutiny Act which, after carefully repeating the provisions of the Bill of Rights about the illegality of martial law, gave the Crown power to set up courts-martial to deal with mutiny and desertion. The Mutiny Act was for one year. If it lapsed, the army would be automatically disbanded. It was also made illegal for soldiers to appear at election places, except to vote, or in the House of Commons, unless they were members or witnesses called before the House. Soldiers were to be confined to their barracks during the sittings of the Assize Courts, lest they try to influence the proceedings. These measures, and the reaffirmation of Parliament's control over finance, were the heart of the English answer to the problem of creating a standing army which could not be used to coerce Parliament. They also provided the precedents for the military clauses of the Constitution of the United States. Two of the ten amendments which were necessary to get the Constitution ratified also dealt with military matters—the old problems of the militia and billeting.[3]

3 The Mutiny Act was for many years the only Act forcing annual sessions of Parliament. For Britain see C. M. Clode, *The Military Forces of the Crown: their Administration and Government* (2 vols., London, 1867), C. E. Walton, *History of the British Standing Army: A.D. 1600 to 1700* (London, 1894), and J. S. Omond, *Parliament and the Army, 1642-1904* (Cambridge, 1933). For the United States use Elias Huzar, *The Purse and the Sword: Control of the Army by Congress through Military Appropriations* (Ithaca, 1950); Arthur A. Ekirch, *The Civilian and the Military* (New York, 1956); Louis Smith, *American Democracy and Military Power* (Chicago, 1951); Walter Millis, *Arms and Men: A Study in American Military History* (New York, 1956); and Walter Millis, with Harvey C. Mansfield and Harold Stein, *Arms and the State* (New York, 1958) on the period since the thirties.

These Congressional controls are defined in Article I, Section 8 of the Constitution. "The Congress shall have power . . . 11. To declare war, grant letters of marque and reprisal, and make rules concerning captures on land and

As might have been expected under these conditions of conflict between king and Parliament, eighteenth-century British army administration was unbelievably complicated. The feudal Commander-in-Chief, appointed by the King, was still the supreme field commander, but since the army was traditionally disbanded at the end of every war, there was usually no Commander-in-Chief in peacetime. The job was handled between wars by the Secretary at War, originally the Commander-in-Chief's civilian secretary. He represented the army in Parliament but did not sit in the cabinet. He was theoretically responsible to the Secretary of State who handled home matters. The Master-General of the Ordnance issued guns to both the army and the navy and controlled the artillery and the engineers. The Home Office controlled the militia and the volunteers, the Treasury managed supplies and transportation, and the Paymaster of the Forces, a very lucrative post, doled out the money. Colonial affairs, with their special military problems, were managed by still another Secretary of State. A Board of Control supervised the military and political affairs of the East India Company, and there were separate financial administrations for the Irish and Scottish forces.[4]

Problems of Imperial Defense

The seventeenth-century British monarchy gave little thought and less money to the problems of imperial defense.

water. 12. To raise and support armies, but no appropriation of money to that use shall be for a longer term than two years. 13. To provide and maintain a navy. 14. To make rules for the government and regulation of the land and naval forces. 15. To provide for calling forth the militia to execute the laws of the Union, suppress insurrections and repel invasions. 16. To provide for organizing, arming, and disciplining the militia, and for governing such part of them as may be employed in the service of the United States, reserving to the States respectively the appointment of the officers, and the authority of training the militia according to the discipline prescribed by Congress. 17. To exercise . . . authority over all places purchased by the consent of the Legislature of the State in which the same shall be, for the erection of forts, magazines, arsenals, dock-yards, and other needful buildings." The Second Amendment reads: "A well regulated militia, being necessary to the security of a free State, the right of the people to keep and bear arms, shall not be infringed." The Third is: "No soldier shall, in time of peace be quartered in any house, without the consent of the owner, nor in time of war, but in a manner to be prescribed by law."

4 The navy, being less of a threat to civil liberties, had a somewhat less complicated administration. The present Board of Admiralty is legally a commission for administering the powers of another feudal functionary, the Lord High Admiral. The First Lord is a kind of naval prime minister responsible to Parliament. The other Lords, some naval officers and some civilians, might be called the First Lord's cabinet. All of the British armed services are now administered by similar boards.

Troops were sent to Jamaica and Tangier, but the problem of overseas naval stations was not a major one before the capture of Gibraltar. The hard-pressed Stuarts had greater worries than those subjects whom profit, adventure, religion, and politics had drawn to their overseas domains. These subjects were expected to defend themselves, at least against those savages who lived on the lands the Crown was granting away. The home government gave the settlers—especially those in the valuable and vulnerable West Indian plantations —occasional grants of munitions and some protection for their shipping. A colony might also be loaned some soldiers— like those who helped to put down Bacon's Rebellion in Virginia—but in such case they were fed and paid by the colony. The settlers usually included a number of old soldiers, like Captains John Smith and John Underhill, who helped in the organization of the militia. Militia service was compulsory, but the periods of service were very short and there were many exemptions. Most of the settlers were accustomed to the use of weapons and little time was spent in formal training. The Indians of the North American forests belonged to many different tribes with varying levels of military proficiency; even the semi-agricultural Iroquois society could not supply many warriors for a long campaign. The simplest wood blockhouse could usually outlast its attackers. So the system of conquest and settlement developed in centuries of frontier warfare in Europe—blockhouses, militia, and punitive expeditions into the native country—was to prove quite adequate. The horse Indians of the Great Plains never reached the levels of military organization reached by the plainsmen of Asia and Africa and proved to be a much less formidable barrier to settlement than the Eastern forest tribes. Romantic as they are, the American Indian wars are not important militarily.[5]

[5] The best works are Henry Holbert Turney-High, *Primitive War, Its Practice and Concepts* (Columbia, S. C., 1949), John Tebbel and Keith Jennison, *The American Indian Wars* (New York, 1960), and Louis Morton, "The Origins of American Military Policy" (*Military Affairs*, XXII, Summer, 1958, 75-82). Other major works are Carl P. Russell, *Guns on the Early Frontiers: A History of Firearms from Colonial Times through the Years of the Western Fur Trade* (Berkeley, 1957); Robert L. D. Davidson, *War Comes to Quaker Pennsylvania, 1682-1756* (New York, 1957); George T. Hunt, *The Wars of the Iroquois* (Madison, 1940); John Richard Alden, *John Stuart and the Southern Colonial Frontier* (Ann Arbor, 1944); and Douglas Edward Leach, *Flintlock and Tomahawk: New England in King Philip's War* (New York, 1958). Much can be learned from E. A. Ritter's fine *Shaka Zulu: The Rise of the Zulu Empire* (New York, 1957).

The Indians of the forests were about at the military level of the New Zea-

There was little fighting on the North American mainland during the early stages of the wars between the English, French, and Dutch. Only New York, of the thirteen colonies, had British troops stationed within its borders for the entire period of British rule. For most of that time the New York garrison consisted of four independent infantry companies, not attached to any regiment. Their history "presents such a series of horrors, miseries, frauds, stupidities and sheer neglects as is rare in either colonial or military annals." Part of the trouble lay in the fact that such overseas troops were always recruited for service in a specific fortress or colony, allowing few chances of promotion for their officers and no way of rotating the men. Their ranks were filled with deserters and criminals. One of their officers had the reputation of being "for twenty years the worst captain in the worst company in the British army." Such troops gave colonists the worst possible opinion of life in the regular army. The soldiers, in return, found army life in the colonies even worse than life at home. The troops were usually too few to raise serious constitutional issues, though the New York companies were used by Governor Edmund Andros in his attempt to abolish the New England colonial assemblies in 1686. The colonial assemblies welcomed British protection as long as it did not cost them much. New York lived up to the letter of its contract by regularly voting money for quarters, forts, firewood, and candles. When attacked or threatened, the colonial legislators loudly called on their neighbors and the British government for help. The other legislatures' contributions were usually in exact proportion to the danger to each colony, a formula which was to hold good in the later British Commonwealth.[6]

land Maori. They were defeated before their tactics—which seem rather more sensible to modern soldiers than to those of the eighteenth century—could be studied in detail. As a result, perhaps, the plains Indians have been greatly overrated in American legend.

6 The misery of these companies was due to two things: policy and bureaucratic routine. The ministers were more concerned about the sugar islands, and believed that New York was amply protected by its own inhabitants and its Indian allies. Their failure to withdraw the companies was due to the pressure of routine. "The fact that in this comparatively small sphere England failed to devise any method of meeting the conditions of the New World, or of adapting the appropriate departments of government for the service of troops at a distance, is a damaging commentary upon the temper and competence of English officialdom." Stanley M. Pargellis, "The Four Independent Companies of New York" (*Essays in Colonial History Presented to Charles McLean Andrews by His Students*, New Haven, 1931), 122, 97. See the same author's *Lord Loudoun in North America* (New Haven, 1933); John W. Fortescue, *History of the British Army* (13 vols. in 20, London, 1899-1930), C. P.

Since 1689, Mahan believed, England had begun to concentrate on colonial and maritime objectives, while leaving the Dutch to carry the weight of the war on land. (The proportion of the English to the Dutch fleets was about five to three, but the Dutch had to furnish 102,000 soldiers to England's 40,000.) In spite of Marlborough's great victories, the War of the Spanish Succession seemed to prove that the small English army could accomplish little on the European continent, while the Treaty of Utrecht greatly strengthened the British position in North America. During the War of the Austrian Succession (King George's War, 1742-1748) a New England force and the navy captured the French fortress of Louisburg. Though it was returned to France by the peace treaty, the British began the new fortress of Halifax in the same area. The British colonists, so long protected by the wilderness from the French and Spanish, were now actively competing with the French in the Ohio country and with the Spaniards on the frontiers of the semimilitary colony which General James Oglethorpe had planted in Georgia in 1733. At the beginning of the Seven Years' (French and Indian) War, which broke out in the colonies in 1755, the British colonies were discussing common defense schemes, though they had rejected the plan proposed by the Albany Convention the year before.

The French settlements on the North American continent were fur trading posts linked by the waterways of the St. Lawrence, Great Lakes, and Mississippi. A few regular soldiers—five thousand men in 1757—were supported by ten to twenty thousand militia, almost the whole male population. Quebec, Montreal, and Louisburg were fortified on the European pattern. The other French posts were wood blockhouses. The colony was not economically self-sufficient. This limited the reinforcements which could be sent from France and even the concentration of the militia. Even France's Indian allies were a severe drain on the colony's resources. Montcalm, the French commander, wished to stand on the defensive. The native-born governor wished to follow up the ambush of General Braddock by allowing the Indians to raid the English frontier settlements. This united the English colonists behind William Pitt's ambitious scheme for eliminating Canada once and for all. Canada's weakest point was its

Stacey, *Canada and the British Army, 1846-1871: A Study in the Practice of Responsible Government* (London, 1936), and Rex Whitworth, *Field Marshal Lord Ligonier* (Oxford, 1958).

single line of communications by the St. Lawrence; the capture of Quebec would isolate all the posts in the interior. The best the outnumbered French could hope for was to hold out. At least parts of Canada might still be under the French flag when the powers sat down to trade the Continental pawns taken by the French army for the colonial pawns seized by the British navy.[7]

The Pitt-Newcastle ministry took office in the summer of 1757, after the series of British defeats which began with Braddock and culminated in the French capture of Minorca. Disgust with these defeats gave Pitt almost dictatorial powers. Though his ally Frederick the Great did not care for Pitt's policy of concentrating on colonial objectives—except for landings to tie down parts of the French army—Frederick was in no position to bargain. Britain's command of the sea left her free to determine when and where to throw her land forces into the balance. The French could sneak reinforcements into their colonies, but the British threw larger ones into theirs. And French plans for the invasion of England and Scotland were wrecked by the old difficulty of uniting the Mediterranean and Atlantic fleets. The Toulon fleet was defeated off the coast of Portugal (Lagos) in August, 1759, and the Brest fleet was destroyed at Quiberon Bay a few months later.

The total British forces sent to North America seem small enough—perhaps 20,000 regulars to add to the same number of colonials—but they were very large by the standards of previous wars in this area. Well-placed land guns were perhaps three times as effective—according to the eighteenth century rule of thumb—as those on shipboard, but an eighteenth century fleet carried big guns in overwhelming numbers. By the end of 1758 the British had captured Ft. Duquesne and Louisburg. In 1759 they took Niagara, Ticonderoga, Crown Point, and Quebec; in 1760 the rest of French Canada surrendered. The next year Pitt planned to capture the remaining French posts in the East and West Indies, while Spain considered joining France. Pitt proposed to take the initiative and intercept the Spanish treasure, but this was too drastic for George III and part of the ministry, and Pitt was

7 Lawrence H. Gipson, *Zones of International Friction: The Great Lakes Frontier, Canada, the West Indies, India* (Vol. V in *The British Empire before the American Revolution*, New York, 1942), 350. Working from the great wealth of colonial records, Gipson may have exaggerated the defenseless condition of the English colonies and the favorable factors in the French military situation. For a different view see Dorn, *Competition for Empire*, 357-362.

forced from office. Spain declared war after the treasure arrived, and Pitt's successors picked up additional French and Spanish posts. They retained Canada and Bengal, one of the keys to India.[8]

The North American colonists had been as determined as Pitt to eliminate France from North America. They supplied five times as many men as they had furnished in any previous war, and almost as many as were to serve at any one time during the American Revolution. Pitt had met one of their previous grievances (a sore point in the Spanish colonies too) by giving some important commands to colonial officers. The colonial troops could shoot and take cover expertly, but their sickness rate had been comparatively high when the army stayed too long in one place. The regulars had taken charge of siege operations. If the British army could get at the French posts, it could usually take them. Special companies of Rangers had taught the regulars the tricks of frontier warfare. The militia had furnished the muscle power to build roads and boats and to drag them over the portages. Eight hundred boats had been required to carry Amherst's army on Lake George, and fleets of gun vessels or row galleys had won the command of the interior waterways from similar miniscule French navies.[9]

[8] Illness had reduced the British before the battle at Quebec. Wolfe had 4000 regulars to 4500 French, only 3000 of them regulars, many of them from Canada. The French fired three volleys, beginning at 130 yards. The British held their fire; then two volleys and a bayonet charge decided the issue. The British almost lost Quebec during the winter, but the French could not move from Montreal against them because of a similar lack of provisions. The French won a pitched battle in April, but could not capture Quebec before the arrival of British reinforcements. The Indians and the French militia then went home, and the 2400 French regulars surrendered Montreal to a British army of over 10,000, which had come by way of the Mohawk valley. See Charles P. Stacey, *Quebec, 1759: The Siege and the Battle* (New York, 1959); Christopher Lloyd, *The Capture of Quebec* (London, 1959); and John R. Cuneo, *Robert Rogers of the Rangers* (New York, 1959).

Volumes VI-VIII of Gipson's *British Empire before the American Revolution* and Julian Corbett, *England in the Seven Years War* (2 vols., London, 1907) are the standard accounts. Volume II of O. A. Sherrard, *Lord Chatham* (London, 1955) deals with the war and Geoffrey Marcus with *Quiberon Bay* (London, 1960). The best survey is Gerald S. Graham, *Empire of the North Atlantic: The Maritime Struggle for North America* (Toronto, 1950).

[9] "Canada was fortified with vast outworks of . . . savage forests, marshes, and mountains. . . . The thoroughfares were streams choked with fallen trees and obstructed by cataracts. Never was the problem of moving troops encumbered by artillery and baggage a more difficult one. The question was less how to fight an enemy than how to get at him." Francis Parkman, *Montcalm and Wolfe* (2 vols., Boston, 1911-1912), II, 380. A good condensation of Parkman's classic is *The Battle for North America*, ed. John Tebbel (Garden City, 1948). On tactics see J. F. C. Fuller, *British Light Infantry in the Eighteenth*

The Break with Britain

As soon as the French danger had been removed, the British North American colonists began to quarrel with Parliament. Numerous suggestions for financing imperial defense were considered, and none was found satisfactory to all parties. The colonists could not be expected to pay the whole cost of garrisoning the newly conquered French and Spanish territories and the forts in the Indian country. There were serious objections to a colonial union for defense purposes, to colonial units in British pay, or to British army units paid for by the colonies. Ten thousand men (out of a total of about 45,000) were finally stationed in North America and the West Indies. The government hoped to get the colonists to pay about a third of their annual cost of £300,000. The French posts in the Great Lakes region had been occupied by one regiment and a few Rangers. All but three of them fell to the Indians in Pontiac's uprising of 1763. Militarily, this flare-up was not a very large affair, but it again demonstrated the colonial legislatures' reluctance to vote money for even the most necessary peacetime defenses and caused the British army to abandon many of the smaller posts. This threw the responsibility for frontier defense back to the colonial legislatures and, incidentally, left the Ohio country open to rebel conquest during the coming American Revolution.[10]

The British government first tried to collect the already existing customs duties in the colonies, which were then bringing in only £2000 a year. They accompanied this action by a new tax on foreign sugar, a Stamp Act, and a Quartering Act. The colonial authorities, like the local authorities in Britain, were to see that the troops were furnished with the billets, candles, and ale specified in the army regulations. The Stamp Act was soon nullified. A Stamp Act Congress declared

---

Century (London, 1925), and Lee McCardell, *Ill-Starred General: Braddock of the Coldstream Guards* (Pittsburgh, 1958).

[10] There were 120 men at Detroit and 250 at Ft. Pitt, but the 10 posts captured or abandoned were held by tiny forces. Michilimackinac had 35 men, but there were only 15 men or less at Sandusky, Miamis, and Venango. Reinforcements reached Detroit by water after two months. Ft. Pitt was rescued by 460 men, including two famous Scotch regiments with 214 and 133 men fit for duty. The Virginia legislature refused to pay the volunteers who had accompanied the forces sent into Ohio. They were finally paid by Pennsylvania, after armed frontiersmen had marched into Philadelphia and threatened the lawmakers. Howard H. Peckham, *Pontiac and the Indian Uprising* (Princeton, 1947). This war was "the most formidable Indian resistance that the English speaking peoples ever faced" in North America.

that no taxes could be levied without the consent of the colonial legislatures and threatened a boycott of British goods. This threat was one factor in Parliament's repeal of the Stamp Act and seemed to demonstrate the power of a commercial boycott. At the same time, however, Parliament (in the Declaratory Act) had asserted that the Stamp Act had been constitutional, and reopened the controversy the next year by levying new duties and by sending over royal customs commissioners. The Boston merchants took the lead in resisting these acts; the commander-in-chief in North America, General Thomas Gage, sent troops to Boston to protect the unpopular officials. In 1770 Parliament repealed most of the new duties, but kept the tax on tea. There were a number of clashes between the Bostonians and the soldiers. Four years later, as a result of the Boston Tea Party, Parliament passed a new series of measures directed chiefly against Massachusetts. Gage, who had been on leave, was sent back as commander-in-chief and governor of Massachusetts, thus linking the army and civilian authority. The result of these measures was the meeting of the first Continental Congress, another boycott, and preparation for active military resistance. A competent officer, Gage believed that a show of force—by as many as 20,000 men—would put down open resistance. But the government gave him only 3500, and rejected his alternative proposal to withdraw the army and establish a naval blockade.[11]

By the summer of 1774 Gage was expecting real trouble. He fortified Boston on the land side. The Massachusetts Assembly reorganized itself as a provincial Congress. The Congress began to replace the Tory militia officers and to enlist companies of "minute men" for immediate service. Gage was particularly worried by the storing of military supplies immediately outside Boston; a move to seize these supplies

[11] See especially John R. Alden, *General Gage in America* (Baton Rouge, 1949). As usual, the regiments in North America were much under strength, the total of all ranks usually being under 500. In 1767 there were 15 infantry regiments in North America: 4 in Quebec, 2 in the west, 2 in Nova Scotia, 3 in the Floridas, Georgia, and South Carolina, and 4 for the other colonies. In 1775 there were 18 infantry regiments, with a paper total of 8580 officers and men, scattered over an enormous area. F. E. Whitton, *The American War of Independence* (New York, 1931), 30. Edward E. Curtis, *The Organization of the British Army in the American Revolution* (New Haven, 1926), 2-3. On the patriots see Allen French, *The First Year of the American Revolution* (Boston, 1934) and Arthur Bernon Tourtellot, *William Diamond's Drum: The Beginning of the War of the American Revolution* (Garden City, 1959).

brought on the battle of Lexington and Concord. Within a few days perhaps 16,000 militia and minute men had gathered around Boston. Since none of these men was liable for a whole summer's service, the Massachusetts Congress tried to enlist them in an eight months' army and called for similar action by the legislatures of the three other New England colonies. Gage withdrew his men from positions outside the town and ordered the troops in New York to join him. Late in May a convoy arrived from Britain, bringing his forces up to about 6000, still too few to occupy all of Massachusetts. Gage decided to reoccupy the heights which he had recently abandoned, but found that the rebels had already begun to fortify Breed's Hill. The British captured the hill, but their losses of 1,054 killed and wounded out of 2500 men were a tribute to the effectiveness of the militia in positions where they were not required to maneuver.[12]

The Continental Army and Navy

After the fighting began, the Continental Congress in Philadelphia took charge of the four New England armies, called for men from the other colonies, and issued $2,000,000 in bills of credit to buy supplies. Washington was appointed commander-in-chief to commit Virginia and the other Southern colonies to the cause. Then 42, Washington was a year younger than Cromwell had been when he had taken command of his first cavalry company. The major generals were Artemas Ward, a 48-year-old Massachusetts farmer who had been a lieutenant colonel in the French and Indian War, Charles Lee, a 44-year-old half-pay British lieutenant colonel,

12 The best survey of the work now being done on the Revolution is John R. Alden, "The Military Side of the Revolution" (*Manuscripts*, IX, Winter, 1957, 38-42). See the same author's *The American Revolution, 1775-1783* (New York, 1954), *General Charles Lee, Traitor or Patriot?* (Baton Rouge, 1951), and, as ed., Christopher Ward, *The War of the Revolution* (2 vols., New York, 1952); Willard M. Wallace, *Appeal to Arms* (New York, 1951); Charles R. Ritcheson, *British Politics and the American Revolution* (Norman, 1954); Howard H. Peckham, *The War for Independence: A Military History* (Chicago, 1958); William A. Wallace, *Traitorous Hero: The Life and Fortunes of Benedict Arnold* (New York, 1954); and Fairfax Downey, *Sound of the Guns: The Story of American Artillery* (New York, 1956). Carl L. Baurmeister, *Revolution in America*, trans. Bernard A. Uhlendorf (New Brunswick, N. J.; 1957), is a Hessian source. The best anthologies are Richard M. Dorson, ed., *Narratives of the Patriots* (New York, 1953), George F. Scheer and Hugh F. Rankin, *Rebels and Redcoats* (New York, 1957), and Henry Steele Commager and Richard B. Morris, eds., *The Spirit of Seventy-Six: The Story of the American Revolution as Told by Participants* (2 vols., New York, 1958).

41-year-old Philip Schuyler of New York, and Israel Putnam, a 57-year-old Connecticut farmer who had also fought in the French and Indian war. The 47-year-old Adjutant General was a half-pay British major, Horatio Gates. Possibly the ablest of the former British officers was Brigadier General Richard Montgomery, an Irishman who was to be killed in the attack on Quebec during the coming winter. The other brigadiers were all from New England. Four were veterans, three of them over 60 and the fourth 50. The three brigadiers who were under 40 had had no military experience. The youngest, 33-year-old Nathanael Greene of Rhode Island, was the son of a wealthy Quaker. Henry Knox, Washington's future chief of artillery and Secretary of War from 1785 to 1794, was a 25-year-old Boston bookseller. Another able young man, 34-year-old Benedict Arnold, came up with the idea of capturing the stores in the almost deserted British forts along the Lake Champlain corridor to Canada. With Ethan Allen of Vermont, Arnold took over 300 guns at Ticonderoga and Crown Point. While Knox was dragging the cannon to Washington's army, Arnold helped to organize an expedition through the Maine woods against Canada, then held by only 800 British regulars. These officers, as in most revolutions, were a mixed lot—solid citizens, young enthusiasts, adventurers on the make, and foreign soldiers of fortune.

Washington's worst problem was holding his army together. He did his best to get additional militia, but many men refused to come and others came for incredibly short periods, often less than a month. But by spring Washington had a few regulars, the cannon from Ticonderoga, and powder from captured British supply ships. The British were forced out of Boston in the first success for the new Continental Army. This army—later enlisted for three years or the duration—was the nucleus. Not too much is known about these men—whose numbers seem to have varied from 6,000 to 10,000—how many of them were foreigners and how many came from each colony. The total number of men under arms at any one time—Continentals, state troops, and militia—seems never to have been greater than 35,000 out of nearly 400,000 separate enlistments. Perhaps the worst crisis occurred after the loss of New York in 1776. When Washington struck at the British detachments in New Jersey, half of his 6,000 men were militia. The enlistments of half of the remaining men were to run out in six days.[13]

As in most revolutions, supply partly depended on the credit of the rebels, on paper money which would be worthless if they failed and was almost worthless when they succeeded. In 1776 a quarter of the army had no guns. Local committees were set up to disarm suspected Tories, to purchase guns from men too old to serve, and to set up gun shops and powder manufacturing. In the retreat from New York large quantities of stores were destroyed by the colonials or captured by the British. Poor transportation caused other shortages and the provisions which could be obtained locally varied with the prospects of the rebel government. Some supplies were captured from British store ships. Other supplies were smuggled in by private arms traders secretly supported by the French government. Nine-tenths of all the gunpowder used during the war was imported. French financial aid was far more important than their direct (though not their indirect) military assistance. Considering the length of the war and the lack of supplies and money, Washington was fortunate in having to face only one major mutiny, one plot to replace him as commander, and one threatened officers' coup.[14]

Terrible as the winters were, Washington used them for training, as Frederick had drilled his new recruits after his opponents had been forced into winter quarters. The French Minister of War sent Washington Inspector General "von" Steuben, an unemployed drillmaster who had served with the Prussians and Russians. American agents also hired a number of French military engineers. Their chief, Louis Duportail,

13 These guesses are from Francis Vinton Greene's old The Revolutionary War and the Military Policy of the United States (New York, 1911), 291. Alfred Hoyt Bill, The Campaign of Princeton, 1776-1777 (Princeton, 1948), and Bruce Bliven, Battle for Manhattan (New York, 1956) are excellent. So are William Bell Clark, George Washington's Navy (Baton Rouge, 1960) and George Athan Billias, General John Glover and His Marblehead Mariners (New York, 1960).

14 A few days before Lexington, there were 21,549 guns available in Massachusetts, but only 17,144 pounds of powder and 22,191 of ball. Charles K. Bolton, The Private Soldier under Washington (New York, 1902), 105.

On New Year's Day 1781 about half of the Pennsylvania Line mutinied and marched on Philadelphia. Their grievances were familiar enough: no pay for over a year, not enough food and clothing, and the expiration of their original enlistments. The mutineers were discharged and then allowed to re-enlist for the bounties given to new recruits. Carl Van Doren, Mutiny in January (New York, 1943). On these plots see John Bakeless, Turncoats, Traitors and Heroes (Philadelphia, [1959]).

was to become French Minister of War for a brief period in the early days of the French Revolution. Thaddeus Kosciuszko, who was to lead the Polish national resistance of 1794, was also a fortifications expert. It is very difficult to evaluate the work of these foreign soldiers. The field works which pushed the British out of Boston were planned by Colonel Richard Gridley, a sixty-four-year-old veteran of the colonials' capture of Louisburg thirty years before. Historians of the Revolutionary War have not always realized that there was no secret key to the arts of war and fortification in the neoclassical age. There were many available books and manuals of fortification. The real problem was to get men and keep them long enough for them to learn the fundamentals.[15]

Though the Continentals won no pitched battles in the open, they were sometimes able to escape from positions which would have been fatal for militia. Cornwallis drove them from the field at Guilford Court House but lost more than a quarter of his army. This battle, however, was exceptional. The British regulars usually outnumbered the Continentals. The British command of the sea enabled them to move faster and hit harder. Most British attacks on major seaports were successful; the Continental forces committed to such points were usually badly beaten. The rebel army was almost captured in New York in 1776 and was nearly wiped out again in front of Philadelphia in 1777. Three years later the same thing happened at Charleston. Five thousand rebel regulars and militia were overwhelmed by fourteen thousand British. Most of the rebels' successes were won in the back country. As long as they could keep an army in the field they could claim foreign and domestic support for their government.[16]

[15] See especially John M. Palmer, *General von Steuben* (New Haven, 1937), and Elizabeth S. Kite, *Brigadier-General Louis Lebègue Duportail* (Baltimore, 1933). The latter, an expert in a service usually supplied by the British, planned the defenses of Valley Forge and those which secured the passage across the Hudson at West Point.

[16] At Guilford Court House some 1700 American regulars and 2600 militia faced 1900 British regulars with a few loyalists. All the militia but 200 Virginians fled during the first half hour. Cornwallis is supposed to have lost 525 men and Greene 250. The North Carolina militia who ran away were sentenced to a year in the regulars. The key works on the militia are John M. Palmer, *America in Arms* (Washington, 1943) and John K. Mahon, *The American Militia: Decade of Decision, 1789-1800* (Gainesville, 1960). More than half of the 527,654 men who served in the War of 1812 put in less than three months. Many regulars believed the militia worthless, but New Orleans confirmed the faith of militia partisans.

The militia had performed real services during the war. They were the only force that the colonies had possessed at the beginning of the war and were to be the only army that the bankrupt Confederation could afford once it was over. They had been most effective on the defensive, where their lack of formal training was more than counterbalanced by their skill with firearms. After the war Washington proposed that they be further improved by more regular training and by providing them with a corps of professional officers. In a number of campaigns the militia had decisively supplemented the regulars. Men who could not serve for a long campaign would come out to defend their own homes and corncribs. After the war, however, public opinion, in line with English tradition, exaggerated the merits of the militia and forgot their shortcomings. It forgot that the militia could not stand in the open against the bayonet, a decisive factor in many cases because of the time lag between volleys, and that the Americans had been weak in engineers, cavalry, artillery, and the other services traditionally provided by the British.[17]

Since new states without financial resources find it more difficult to improvise navies than armies, the greatest weakness of the revolutionists was at sea. In spite of the colonies' large seafaring population, the Continental and state navies, at their largest in 1776, consisted of 27 ships of about 20 guns each—against 71 British ships with an average of 28 guns each in American waters. Only one of the three ships-of-the-line voted by Congress was ever completed, and she was then turned over to France. Twelve of the eighteen frigates were either never completed or were lost when the British captured the major seaports. Four of the remainder were captured at sea and a fifth blew up in action. Only one American-built frigate—John Paul Jones' *Alliance*—and the French built *Deane* were still in service in 1783. Privateers, both state and continental, outnumbered the regular navies by at least ten to one. In 1781 there were about 450 priva-

[17] James R. Jacobs, *The Beginnings of the United States Army, 1783-1812* (Princeton, 1947) is excellent. For the War of 1812 see Charles R. Brooks, *The Siege of New Orleans* (Seattle, 1961), Jane Lucas de Grummond, *The Baratarians and the Battle of New Orleans* (Baton Rouge, 1961), and popular surveys by Francis F. Beirne, *The War of 1812* (New York, 1949) and Glenn Tucker, *Poltroons and Patriots: A Popular Account of the War of 1812* (2 vols., Indianapolis, 1954). More general surveys are C. Joseph Bernardo and Eugene H. Bacon, *American Military Policy: Its Development since 1775* (Harrisburg, 1955), R. Ernest and Trevor N. Dupuy, *The Military Heritage of America* (New York, 1956), and T. Harry Williams, *Americans at War: The Development of the American Military System* (Baton Rouge, 1960).

teers with a maximum of 20,000 men, a force larger than the Continental army. The average privateer, like the average merchantman, was quite small, mounting 10 guns or less and carrying a crew of 35 or 40. And the damage privateering did to British trade—without bases near the focal zones of British shipping—was considerably exaggerated by the generation which had fought the Revolution. The most important single service of the rebel naval forces was on Lake Champlain—where Benedict Arnold's little flotilla delayed the British and helped to set the stage for Burgoyne's disaster.[18]

The British in the American Revolution

As in the case of most revolutions, the strategy of the American Revolution was shaped by events, initially by the armed clash in the colony of Massachusetts. Boston was not the strategic center of the colonies or a major British naval base. The government had sent its troops there because the Boston merchants had challenged its authority. Though the rebels had two assets which revolutionaries do not always have—elected assemblies with the confidence of part of the population and a partly trained militia—they won in the end, Washington believed, because of the difficulties and mistakes of the British government. The greatest difficulty was that of distance. The uncertain communications which had been partly responsible for the outbreak of the revolt enormously increased the task of suppressing it. George III's ministers needed peace. Their first concern after 1763 had been to raise money and to reduce British armaments. These concerns had been partly responsible for their underestimation of colonial resistance. But after Gage had been pinned down in Boston and replaced by General William Howe, the British government reacted very vigorously. They raised the British army establishment by 20,000 men and hired an equal number of

[18] On sea as on land the War of 1812 repeated some of the experiences of the Revolution. The big American frigates won some victories, but were captured or blockaded by the end of the war. Privateers outnumbered the regular navy and destroyed a small portion of the British merchant fleet, but American trade was ruined. The most important actions again took place on the lakes. C. S. Forester, *The Naval War of 1812* (London, 1957) is old-fashioned. Use A. T. Mahan's *Sea Power in Its Relation to the War of 1812* (2 vols., Boston, 1905) and *Major Operations of the Navies in the War of American Independence* (Boston, 1913); Howard I. Chapelle, *The History of the American Sailing Navy* (New York, 1949); Harold and Margaret Sprout, *The Rise of American Naval Power 1776-1918* (Princeton, 1939); Gardner Weld Allen, *A Naval History of the American Revolution* (2 vols., Boston, 1913); Charles O. Paullin, *The Navy of the American Revolution* (Cleveland, 1906); Samuel Eliot Morison's definitive *John Paul Jones: A Sailor's Biography* (Boston, 1959); and Marshall Smelser, *The Congress Founds the Navy, 1787-1798* (Notre Dame, 1959).

German mercenaries. By the summer of 1776 there were 16,000 British troops in Canada and nearly 25,000 more off New York, which both Howe and Washington knew was the strategic center of the colonies.

New York was almost surrounded by deep water. Withdrawal from this dangerous position without a fight would have seriously damaged the rebels' morale and their hopes of foreign recognition. Washington's escape from this trap was due to a combination of energy and good luck, to Howe's healthy respect for American field fortifications, and to the fact that the British were already thinking of winter. Many Whig officers, including the commander-in-chief, Lord Amherst, had refused to take the field against the colonists. Perhaps Howe was not anxious to win, but "in every case where it can be maintained that he had the enemy in his grasp, it is apparent that the action that he took was supported by reasons well founded in the military ideas of his day." Howe's critics have also underestimated the physical difficulties of campaigning in North America. On the scene, Howe found that loyalist sentiment had been overestimated at home; his discouragement was another reason for caution. Cornwallis, Howe's subordinate, pushed after Washington as fast as he could, but finally gave up and put his men into winter quarters. Nobody can now say that he would have caught Washington's forces or that he could have withdrawn to New York without raising the rebels' morale as much as it was raised by Washington's successful attacks on the British forces at Trenton and Princeton. The problems of partisan warfare are among the most difficult of all military problems. Cornwallis was not to be the only general who has failed to solve them.[19]

During the summer of 1777 Burgoyne was to advance to Albany from Canada. Howe hoped to take the rebel capital of Philadelphia. Burgoyne was to be defeated by the factors

[19] Troyer S. Anderson, *The Command of the Howe Brothers during the American Revolution* (New York, 1936), 198. Eric Robson, *The American Revolution* (London, 1955), believed that the British had little chance of suppressing the revolt. Many critics also think that a single commander should have been appointed for the campaign of 1777, but his control would have been very nominal because of communications difficulties. The British had not used this system in the conquest of Canada. In 1777 both Howe and Burgoyne were weak in transport, cavalry, and artillery. Howe's lack of cavalry was to be partly responsible for his failure to follow up his victory at Brandywine. Howe could not start his campaign until the grass was high enough for his horses. The voyage from New York to Philadelphia took twice as long as expected and many horses had to be thrown overboard. A key point in Howe's defense is that the Allies displayed no greater energy in their early campaigns against the French revolutionaries.

that later defeated Cornwallis in the South—the unexpected resistance of the Americans and the difficulties of supply in a hostile frontier country. Howe and Burgoyne were to keep each other informed, but were to act independently. As he advanced through the wilderness Burgoyne reported that all was going well. His troubles began when he struck overland from the headwaters of Lake Champlain to the Hudson. Early in August he decided to mount his cavalry by capturing the horses and stores which were being gathered at Bennington, Vermont. The raiders and a rescue party ran into a large force of American militia and lost 500 men and four guns. This defeat brought out more American militia. Burgoyne spent another month getting supplies from Canada to last him for thirty days and building boats to transport them down the Hudson. His 6,000 men had to break through 9,000 to 12,000 Americans entrenched on a plateau above the river. On September 19, at the first battle of Bemis Heights, Burgoyne failed to reach the main American positions. A second attempt three weeks later led to the surrender of his entire army on October 17.[20]

France signed treaties of commerce and alliance with the United States in February, 1778. Spain entered the war in June, 1779, and Holland entered in 1780. The strategy of the contestants in the colonies largely depended on the movements of the British and French fleets. In the spring of 1778 the French Mediterranean fleet left for North America. General Henry Clinton, who had replaced Howe in Philadelphia, loaded his stores, some uncertain German troops, and most of the loyalists on his transports, and marched the rest of the army across New Jersey. Washington was unable to stop or capture him. The British were gone when the French arrived off Philadelphia. When the French reached Sandy Hook, Clinton's army was safe in New York and the British fleet barred the way into the harbor. The heavier French ships could enter only on a northeast wind and a high tide. They had one chance to cross the bar but, after getting under way, Admiral D'Estaing decided not to try it.[21]

---

20 For similar difficulties of supply in India see H. A. Young's fascinating *The East India Company's Arsenals and Manufactories* (Oxford, 1937).
21 The colonists had furnished eighteen thousand men to the British navy during the Seven Years' War, as many as the total in that navy in 1775. With so many people opposed to the war and so little chance of prize money recruiting was very slow. The Lord Mayor of London even arrested naval officers who were pressing men within his jurisdiction. George O. Trevelyan, *The American Revolution* (rev. ed., 4 vols., New York, 1905-1912), III, 190 ff.

D'Estaing then sailed to help the Continental and New England militia capture Newport. The British fleet arrived just as he was landing his troops, and D'Estaing recalled his men. The two fleets sparred until a gale scattered them both. The British went to New York for repairs; D'Estaing went to Boston. The New England militia went home. After D'Estaing had also gone home, the British captured Savannah. Washington's army, which sat outside New York for three years, was powerless to stop them or to recapture New York. The next summer (1779) D'Estaing reappeared and became involved in an unsuccessful siege of Savannah, while the French and Spanish home fleets botched an invasion of England. That winter the British evacuated Newport, but captured Charleston. These details show how important sea power was to the little fortified towns strung along the American coast, the ineffectiveness of naval action when neither side has more than local command of the sea, and the fact that some French naval commanders were as inept as some British generals. The first French troops had been landed in the colonies in 1780. Finally Washington made a personal appeal for some real help from the French navy.

Next to a loan of money, a constant naval superiority on these coasts is the object most interesting. . . . Indeed, it is not to be conceived how they would subsist a large force in this country if we had the command of the seas. . . . This superiority, with an aid in money, would enable us to convert the war into a vigorous offensive.[22]

The new French commander, the able Admiral de Grasse, sailed for the West Indies at the end of March, 1781, broke up the British blockade of Martinique, and captured Tobago. At San Domingo he found Washington's appeal for help against New York or against Cornwallis' army in the Chesa-

22 Allen, *Naval History,* II, 547. Washington used the *Alliance,* one of the few remaining ships in the navy, to carry his letter. Even getting her to sea was difficult enough. The Boston merchants would not allow pressing. Six men were recruited from the Continental army and twenty from the Massachusetts guard at Castle Island after they had been given a bounty of £100 silver. Most of the able seamen were British prisoners, who plotted a mutiny under the leadership of one of the quartermasters. On the way back with 2,500,000 francs on board, the captain uncovered the plot and flogged the ringleaders until they revealed their accomplices. Three men were sentenced to hang, but their sentences were commuted to service for the rest of the war in the Continental army. Dudley W. Knox, *The Naval Genius of George Washington* (Boston, 1932), W. M. James, *The British Navy in Adversity* (London, 1936). Alexander Laurence has written a model study of the siege of Savannah, *Storm over Savannah* (Athens, Ga., 1951).

peake. De Grasse chose the latter objective because he thought that his heavy ships would be more useful there. The British West Indian fleet started north five days after De Grasse and passed him on the way. Finding Cornwallis safe, the British admiral had gone to New York before returning to Yorktown to intercept a small French squadron which had left Newport. The French came out and the two fleets exchanged fire for three hours before nightfall. During the next three days they maneuvered for position. De Grasse could not catch the British. When the wind shifted he hurried back to block the entrance to Chesapeake Bay. The British, badly hit aloft, returned to New York. Meanwhile the French Newport squadron with Rochambeau's siege train had slipped into the Bay. Washington and Rochambeau marched overland from New York and Newport to the head of the Bay and then took boats to Yorktown. The siege lasted three weeks. Outnumbered two to one, Cornwallis surrendered 7,157 soldiers and 840 sailors. Two thousand of these men had been in hospital. He lost 156 men killed and 326 wounded, 4 frigates, 30 transports, and 15 galleys. Counting sailors serving on shore, the French forces outnumbered the Americans. The next year De Grasse was defeated and taken prisoner in the West Indies, but both sides were now war weary. Peace was concluded in Paris on November 3, 1783. The British saved Gibraltar, but gave up most of their American colonies, East Florida, Minorca, Tobago, and some minor posts in India and Africa.[23]

[23] See Stephen Bonsal's delightful *When the French Were Here* (Garden City, 1945) and C. L. Lewis, *Admiral De Grasse and American Independence* (Annapolis, 1945). Twenty-five hundred of the captives were German, though Gneisenau, one of the Prussian reformers of the Napoleonic era, arrived too late to see action. Napoleon's chief of staff, Berthier, may have been with the French. Saint Simon, one of the founders of modern socialism, was serving with the French fleet. One of Rochambeau's aides-de-camp kept a detailed account of the movement of his forces from Brest to Rhode Island and Yorktown in *The Revolutionary Journal of Baron Ludwig von Closen, 1780-1783*, trans., ed., intro., Evelyn M. Acomb (Chapel Hill, 1958). On the Franco-Spanish attempt to invade England in 1779 see A. Temple Patterson, *The Other Armada* (Manchester, 1961).

Chapter 4

The French Revolution and Napoleon

French Military Reformers

DURING the American Revolution both sides had been forced to violate many of the rules of eighteenth-century warfare in order to be able to move and fight in this thinly settled area. Long before this, however, self-criticism had been growing in the French army as a result of the series of defeats which had culminated in the Seven Years' War. At the close of that war, the French secretary of state for war, the Duc de Choiseul (1719-1785), began the general army reorganization which was to end in the victories of the wars of the French Revolution and Napoleon. The reformers' writings reflected both the intellectual ferment of the age and its antithetical tendencies to doctrinaire statement and scientific experiment. Its mathematical bias was clearly apparent in many formal tactical systems which failed to meet the tests of the drill ground. Marshal de Saxe (1696-1750), the only Great Captain among the reformers, "dreamed" of changing everything from artillery to victualing. Other critics, like Choiseul's protégé, the Comte de Saint Germain (1707-1778), were old soldiers who hoped to make the French army as efficient as that of Prussia. Still others hoped to make the army over in accordance with the new ideals of liberty, equality, and a "natural" society. The greatest of these theoretical writers was the Comte Jacques de Guibert (1743-1790). His *Essai général de tactique* (Liége, 1775) covered both tactics and strategy. The purchase of commissions was gradually abolished, and some of the money previously spent on purely decorative court units was used to establish schools—the boys were still too young to speak of higher military education—for future officers. Some of these men were to develope the reformers' ideas into what can be called—after the greatest of these younger officers—the Napoleonic system of warfare.[1]

[1] There is no modern edition of the *Essai*. See Robert S. Quimby's excellent *The Background of Napoleonic Warfare* (New York, 1957). Emile G. Léonard, *L'armée et ses problèmes au XVIIIe siècle* (Paris, 1958), and Louis H. Bacquet, *L'infanterie au XVIIIe siècle: L'organisation* (Paris, 1907) supplement Quimby on the social status of the officer. There were twelve military schools run by religious orders. Napoleon went to Brienne at nine, after proving that his family were poor and had been noble for four generations. Some boys were sent to Paris for an additional year at fifteen or sixteen.

The primary infantry tactical unit was still the battalion, standardized by Choiseul at 584 officers and men, 8 companies of musketeers and a company of grenadiers. Most regiments now consisted of two battalions. The key tactical problem had been posed by the invention of the bayonet, which had finally given the infantryman a single shock and fire weapon. The partisans of bayonet shock action called for a deep column formation or *ordre profond*. The partisans of fire held that the line or *ordre mince* must be the basic formation. The problem was further complicated by the development of light infantry trained to fight in open or skirmishing order. This order had been used since the introduction of firearms, but chiefly by poorly trained or otherwise undependable auxiliaries. Frederick had been reluctant to use good troops as skirmishers. With training in musketry marksmanship both difficult and costly, the Prussians depended on the unaimed volume fire learned by dry runs on the parade ground. But the tight line was also a fine target. Austrian irregulars and American riflemen somewhat later had occasionally caused heavy casualties, particularly among the officers. The French drill book of 1764 recommended that the two wing half-sections of an infantry battalion deploy in front as skirmishers and rejoin the battalion just before contact with the enemy. Five light regiments were also provided for, a mixture of infantry and dragoons, essentially mounted infantry equipped with muskets, bayonets, long straight swords, and entrenching tools. The Americans who had fought so well in open order had done so, however, because they had had something to fight for. The partisans of open order argued that such troops must be recruited from all classes of the population, that promotion should depend on merit, and that the soldier must be inspired to fight for his country. Since people generally see the brighter side of their own opinions, most of these noble reformers seem never to have thought that an army of citizens might endanger the old social order, or that the new national army might become the instrument of a new national tyranny.[2]

Skirmishers might weaken an enemy line, but they could not break it. Frederick had been able to overpower his opponents' lines because his troops could fire faster; his oblique

---

[2] See Orville T. Murphy, "The American Revolutionary Army and the Concept of *Levée en Masse*" (*Military Affairs*, XXIII, Spring, 1959, 13-20). Gunther Erich Rothenberg's fine *The Austrian Military Border in Croatia, 1522-1747* (Urbana, 1960) does not deal with the Austrian irregulars' tactics.

order had enabled him to throw line after line at the decisive point. But when other troops learned to fire as rapidly and to maneuver sidewise as well as the Prussians the result was often a stalemate. The French reformers knew that a line can deliver more fire than a column, but they also knew that a column could break a line if it advanced quickly enough to cover the distance at which the smoothbore musket was dangerous. They suggested that less attention be given to parade ground perfection and more to quick changes from line into column. Guibert advocated an *ordre mixte,* or columns intercalated with lines. His compromise formula—reflected in the drill manuals issued to the newly formed National Guard and the regular infantry in 1791—was "Column for maneuver and approach; the line for fighting." This was where matters stood at the beginning of the Revolutionary wars, but many of the officers of the early Revolutionary period soon found that the three rank firing line did not work with unskilled troops. As Marshal Gouvion St. Cyr put it, "Our third rank places *hors de combat* a quarter of our men who are wounded. . . . They all fire together as soon as the balls of the enemy whistle in their ears, and this even without the command of their chief, if he delays giving it." Though Napoleon possibly preferred the line, some of his generals apparently preferred to try to smash through in heavy columns. In any case, the *ordre mixte* was the first ingredient in the Napoleonic formula.

These tactical discussions did not reflect further changes in the musket, and cavalry weapons remained equally stable. But the last half of the eighteenth century had seen important changes in the artillery. Though many of Saint Germain's ideas were too Prussian to suit the French court, his dismissal after two years as war minister (1775-1777) did not affect the able artillery inspector Jean de Gribeauval (1715-1789) who remained at his post until his death. Gribeauval's aims were standardization and mobility. Interchangeable parts were used in the guns, carriages, and ammunition wagons. The ball and charge were packaged into cartridges. Gunsights, elevating screws, and constant drill made for much greater speed and accuracy in firing. Though none of these changes was really revolutionary, the perfecting of the details of the smoothbore field gun was to be as important for Napoleon as the perfecting of musketry fire had been for Frederick.

The use of unprecedented masses of mobile artillery was another of the major ingredients in the Napoleonic system.[3]

The column—as Guibert's formula recognized—is inherently a marching and maneuvering formation. Men in column can always move ahead faster than a line can fall back to reform. If columns could take the losses necessary to break all three of the lines of battle of armies using the Prussian system, they could rapidly exploit the gaps. So another part of the new French tactical formula was an insistence on all-out pursuit to decisive victory. This was related to the reformers' search for greater strategical mobility, a search related, in turn, to the great improvement of Western European roads and bridges during the late eighteenth century. The first result of these improved means of transportation had been a tendency for armies to carry more baggage, a trend which, by the end of the eighteenth century, had certainly gone too far. A Prussian infantry regiment of 2200 men was now accompanied by 2400 noncombatants and 1200 draft horses. Certainly such an army violated Napoleon's maxim that "An army can march anywhere and at any time of the year, where even two men can place their feet."

Many soldiers, like the Marshal de Saxe or Pierre de Bourcet (1700-1780), an expert in mountain warfare, had also become convinced that armies should be broken into smaller, more manageable units or divisions. The French Revolutionary division or army corps (neither unit was then standardized) which had gradually been evolved from these proposals was essentially a miniature army with its own infantry, cavalry, and artillery. Instead of using a single road, the army might use several parallel roads, as long as the marching columns did not become too widely separated. Bourcet suggested that this formation would also achieve strategic surprise. The army's units would advance like a screen of blockers and concentrate against one of the defenders before his teammates could shift to his rescue. The small size of his army and his distrust of his subordinates had forced Frederick to keep his army concentrated. Decentralization required some relaxation of this system of personal supervision.

[3] See the splendid work of the Finnish artillerist Matti Lauerma, *L'Artillerie de campagne française pendant les guerres de la Révolution: Evolution de l'organisation et de la tactique* (Helsinki, 1956). Guibert had emphasized precision and mobility. Napoleon came close to taking the then extreme position that "artillery is the soul of armies." He was, of course, trained as an artilleryman.

Napoleon expected his divisional commanders to put up a stout defense if they happened to run into superior forces and to march "to the sound of the guns" if an adjoining division ran into trouble. The divisional commanders were to keep in touch with each other, but were not to "waste time waiting for orders. . . . They should move toward a fixed point at which they are to unite . . . without hesitation and without new orders."

During the eighteenth century Western Europe's military potential had greatly increased. There were more men, more food, more metals, and better transportation. In spite of the weakness of the French monarchy, France was still the greatest power in Europe. Her population equaled the combined population of England, Austria, and Prussia. The people on her frontiers—Belgians, Swiss, Piedmontese, West Germans, and to a certain extent the Spanish—had long been affected by her cultural and political ideas. A revolution in France was bound to bring on a general upheaval. The most brilliant of the French military reformers, Guibert, was the prophet both of a new kind of national army and of the new doctrine of strategic mobility. The two things, he believed, were closely related.

When an army knows how to maneuver and wants to fight, there are few positions which it cannot attack from the rear or cause to be abandoned by the enemy. . . . A general who, in this respect, shakes off established prejudices will throw his enemy into consternation, stun him, give him no chance to breathe, and either force him to fight or to retreat continuously. But such a general will need an army differently constituted from our armies today, an army which, formed and trained by himself, was prepared for the new kind of operations which he would require it to execute.

Insofar as such matters can be proved, Napoleon was the pupil of Guibert.[4]

The Revolution

The French army of 1789, like most institutions in most times and places, contained officers and men who were actually or potentially discontented, but their discontents did not cause the revolution or cause the army to take an active part on one side or the other. The army, like Louis XVI,

---

[4] *Essai général de tactique* (2d ed., 2 vols., Paris, [1785]), II, 102, 104. Guibert, in turn, stressed his debt to Montesquieu. See Robert R. Palmer's brilliant chapter in Earle, *Modern Strategy*, 49-76.

simply drifted. Though its character was gradually changed by the pressure of events, it was neither dissolved nor forced to take a stand one way or the other. It was not until the king was finally dethroned and the revolution had become recognizable as such that it was possible to appreciate the unreliability of the royal army as a political instrument. In the words of the great French historian H. A. Taine,

In the hundred and fifty thousand men who maintain order, dispositions are the same as in the twenty-six millions of men who are subject to it, while abuses, disaffection, and all the causes that dissolve the nation, dissolve the army. . . . Strange recruits these, for the protection of society, all selected from the attacking class, . . . disheartened, excited, and easily tempted, . . . at one time, rioters and, at another, soldiers. . . . In this state of things the soldier ought not to meditate on his lot, and yet this is just what his officers incite him to do. They also have become politicians and fault-finders.[5]

Violence broke out in July, the month after the formation of the National Assembly. Several foreign regiments had been ordered into positions around Paris. The French Guards, who policed Paris, were discontented with the Prussian discipline imposed by their colonel and some of their officers had been hit by decrees reserving high rank to the nobility. On July 8 the Assembly demanded the removal of the foreign regiments. Louis XVI secretly dismissed Necker, the popular finance minister. Finally the Royal German regiment fired on a crowd, the tocsin was sounded, and people gathered at the churches to volunteer for a citizens' militia. Arms were taken from the gun shops in the working class sections. On July 13 a crowd broke into the Invalides, a military hospital and storage depot, and took away twenty-eight thousand muskets and some cannon. The next day the new city government asked the governor of the Bastille, a prison and storage depot, to surrender his military stores. By mistake, some of his men fired on the city authorities who were coming in under a flag of truce. The mob, aided by some of the French Guards who

[5] *The Ancient Regime,* trans. John Durand (new ed., New York, 1891), 390-393. A decree of 1781 required all future officers to have sixteen noble ancestors. Non-nobles could still be taken as sublieutenants, but could never be promoted to captain. This antagonized both the middle class officers who had bought commissions and the few who had come up from the ranks. The poorer nobles had the usual complaints about those of the court. It would have been almost as difficult for Napoleon to rise to really high rank as a non-noble. About two-thirds of the officers were nobles in 1789 and half of the members of the Nobles' Estate were army officers.

brought up cannon, broke into the Bastille and lynched the governor. This was the classic victory of the "people," a mob of armed civilians. The old monarchy—with its rudimentary police services and an army trained in formal tactics—was helpless. The king gave up without a fight. Other towns organized militias (now known as the National Guard) and chose new municipal authorities. The king was forbidden to use regulars to maintain order; only the municipal authorities could call out the Guard. Since the citizens who officered the National Guard, which was commanded by Lafayette, also controlled the new municipal governments, these regulations consolidated the position of the middle class.[6]

The army was required to take a new oath stressing allegiance to the "Nation." Officers had to swear an additional oath—in the presence of their men and the municipal authorities—never to employ their men against the citizens except at the express request of the civil authority. The officers' corps was thrown open to everyone; the king's powers of promotion were curtailed by a complicated combination of seniority with selection. The king was to vacate his office if he retracted his oath to the nation, the law, and the constitution, or if he led a military force against the nation, failed to condemn such an undertaking begun by others in his name, or left the country and did not return within a time limit fixed by the Assembly. These last provisions proved to be very important. The counterrevolutionists could not openly rally around the king, but had to conspire in secret in France or emigrate and be officially condemned by their sovereign. Finally, the king's personal guard could be no larger than twelve hundred foot and six hundred horse. They were to be paid from the Civil List and could not be promoted to posts in other units. Thus the king could not pack the army with officers who had first served in elite court units. These significant details reflect much of the history of standing armies and dynastic monarchies.

Meanwhile political clubs had been organized in many army units. When juries of privates and noncommissioned officers were introduced into the military courts the commanders had difficulty in enforcing even rudimentary discipline. Some of the political clubs tried to get control of regimental funds and to oust unpopular officers. The Na-

[6] See especially Katharine Chorley, *Armies and the Art of Revolution* (London, 1943).

tional Assembly did little to support the officers; usually the offending regiments were simply disbanded. Since nobody brought back deserters and there were few new recruits, the remaining regiments were far under strength. In June, 1791, while the finishing touches were being put on the new constitution, Louis XVI attempted to flee the country. After he had been brought back the National Assembly ordered the army to take a new oath which omitted all mention of the king's person. The officers who took this new oath were bound to the Revolution. More than half of the total officers' corps, however, either accepted pensions equal to a quarter of their pay or fled the country. The road to promotion was now wide open for the others.

Though Louis XVI accepted the new constitution, his flight had made war almost inevitable. France declared war on Austria (and by implication on Austria's ally Prussia) on April 20, 1792. Since the new constitution had specifically renounced "war with a view to making conquests," Europe was assured that the constitutional monarchy was taking up arms "only for the maintenance of its liberty and independence; that the war which it is obliged to undertake is not a war of nation against nation, but the just defense of a free people against the unjust aggression of a king." It was to be waged only against those parts of the enemy population which had been "enslaved" in the professional armies of the dynastic monarchs and their adherents. The Legislative Assembly (1791-1792) called for one-campaign volunteers from the National Guard to reinforce the regulars, as Lafayette had seen the American militia reinforce the Continentals. The French made their traditional opening move into the Austrian Netherlands, whose French-speaking inhabitants were supposedly ready to revolt at the first opportunity. Instead the French broke at their first encounter with the enemy. One divisional commander was murdered by his men and another barely escaped.

The Revolution was saved by what was left of the old army and by Austrian and Prussian inactivity. The allies had been engaged in the Second Partition of Poland and were not ready to move into France before the end of July. For thirty years there had been little fighting in Western Europe; the allied armies were parade-ground armies which had seen little active service. The emigrés had also persuaded the Austrian and Prussian monarchs that a show of force would be all that would be necessary. The Prussian commander, the Duke of Brunswick, was ordered to try political warfare before crossing the Rhine on July 30. He proclaimed that all who resisted him would be punished as rebels. If Paris harmed Louis XVI the city would be destroyed. This declaration proved to be a boomerang. The Paris mob invaded the palace and massacred the Swiss Guards, the king was suspended, and many suspected royalists were thrown into prison. At this news Lafayette tried to get his men to turn back to rescue the king and save the constitution. When they refused, he went over to the Austrians; a short time later the allies broke through the frontier fortresses at Longwy and Verdun. This news helped to bring on the September Massacres. The royalist suspects were murdered, France was declared a republic, and a new Convention (1792-1795) was elected to draw up a republican constitution.

A bewildering series of shuffles left Generals Dumouriez and Kellerman commanding the two armies on the northeast frontier. The energetic and optimistic Dumouriez, a soldier of fortune who had served in several European armies, let the Prussians get between him and Paris. But Brunswick decided to follow the rules and attack the French army before advancing farther. On the foggy morning of September 20, 1792, just fifteen years after the first battle at Saratoga, the Prussians came up with Kellerman's regulars on a hill near the village of Valmy. Dumouriez' army, which came up in support, was about two-thirds volunteer. The French began a violent cannonade. About one o'clock the Prussians advanced through the mud and then halted while the artillery battle continued. Some of the French fled when a chance shot exploded some ammunition wagons, but the main body stood firm. Brunswick again followed the rules. He would not try a frontal attack against superior forces, even though many of the French were untried. Late in the afternoon it began to rain again and the artillery duel ceased. Ten days later Brunswick withdrew. His tents were useless in the constant rain. His army was only half its original strength and he had lost an even larger proportion of his horses. In November Dumouriez occupied most of the Austrian Netherlands after a pitched battle at Jemappes. Clausewitz later wrote that this campaign had sounded the death knell of the old "restricted, shriveled-up form of war."

If the generals of the Revolution did not . . . immediately lay in ruins the monarchies of Europe . . . the cause really lay in that technical imperfection with which the French had to contend, . . . first among the common soldiers, then in the generals, lastly, at the time of the Directory, in the government itself.[7]

The Organizer of Victory

During the winter of 1792-1793 the volunteer system broke down completely. After the execution of Louis XVI the Convention declared war on Holland, Spain, and England (in addition to Austria, Prussia, and Sardinia). As Dumouriez pushed into Holland, the Convention voted the conscription of three hundred thousand men, roughly doubling the army. Except for the obligation to take bachelors from twenty to twenty-five, the departmental authorities could choose their own methods to fill their quotas. The usual procedure was to draw lots, but some departments rounded up the usual vagabonds and criminals. Conscription was partly responsible for an armed rebellion of the peasantry in the marshy Vendée near the Loire River. Royalists from other parts of France, émigrés, and foreign agents came to the aid of the rebels. Dumouriez' army was defeated and most of the Netherlands was lost. Dumouriez attempted to organize a march on Paris and then went over to the enemy. That summer many of the major provincial cities rose against the Convention. The Republic was at the mercy of the First Coalition.

As it turned out, the allies again managed to waste most of the summer, while the Convention set to work to put down internal opposition and strengthen its armies. In April the Convention had set up a twelve-man executive known as the Committee of Public Safety, a revolutionary police under a Committee of General Security, and a Revolutionary Tribunal. The local authorities were empowered to set up similar tribunals and committees, while two members of the Convention were sent to each department to speed the raising of the new armies. Three of these "deputies on mission," one of whom was to be replaced each month, were also sent to each army. They were to "exercise the most active kind of supervision over the operation of the agents of the executive council, over the generals, officers, and soldiers . . . and to

---

[7] *On War*, 580-583. The French had fired over 20,000 rounds at Valmy in the greatest artillery battle yet seen in Europe. The Prussians lost 180 men and the French about 300.

investigate most severely . . . all the supplies and contractors." The Convention thus re-established many of the principles of royal centralization. The Convention had planned to organize the new troops into separate units, but most military men had seen enough of the volunteers and their elected officers. So the differences in pay and organization between the new units and the old were abolished. France had the first "national" army in modern European history.[8]

Dumouriez had deserted on April 5. Four days later the allies invaded France. Only a small, badly demoralized force stood between them and Paris, but they laid siege to Condé and Valenciennes. These places held out for over three months, until July 10 and July 26. Then the allies maneuvered the French field forces out of another entrenched camp, the third of the campaign. The French built another camp farther west, but this new camp did not cover the road to Paris. For the second consecutive summer the allies were between the French capital and the French army. But instead of advancing on Paris—a ten days' march for infantry and four for cavalry—the allies were more interested in pawns for the coming peace conference. The English marched toward Dunkirk and the Austrians went in the opposite direction toward Maubeuge. The Convention was left free to complete the military reorganization which had been touched off by the news of the fall of Valenciennes. On August 9 the fourth commander of the army since Dumouriez was replaced. The next day all of the remaining officers of noble birth were cashiered (though the decree was not strictly enforced). On August 14 two engineer captains, Lazare Carnot and Prieur of the Côte d'Or, were elected to the Committee of Public Safety. Prieur, at thirty, was the youngest member of the Committee. Carnot, who was placed in charge of military affairs, was ten years older. Like most middle-class officers, Carnot thoroughly believed in the idea of a national army and of careers open to talent. A first-rate executive, Carnot surrounded himself with some of the ablest partisans of the new system of war. While some 400,000 allied soldiers were still spread out along the frontiers, the French began to mass their troops at a few decisive points, instead of attempting to

[8] On the Vendée, see Gérard Walter, *La Guerre de Vendée* (Paris, 1953).

attack or defend every fortified town, river crossing, and road junction.[9]

By September the total French force in the north had been brought up to 100,000, of whom 42,000 had been told off to rescue Dunkirk. Houchard, their commander, was a fifty-five-year-old Lorrainer of German descent. A captain before the Revolution, Houchard had never commanded more than a company until that spring, when he had been advanced to colonel and then to brigadier-general. "His face was hideous with the scars of three sabre cuts and a bullet wound, with a mouth twisted toward the left ear, an upper lip split in two, and a right cheek carved by long parallel gashes." A typical old soldier who knew nothing of theory, Houchard went along with the plan of his war council to try to encircle the English and drive them into the sea. But at the last minute the plan seemed to be too risky. Houchard relieved Dunkirk in the good old way, but the English army escaped. When the deputies on mission returned to Paris they reported that the original plan would have been successful. To placate the Convention, the Committee of Public Safety "discovered" that Houchard had been in treasonable correspondence with the enemy. He was relieved, imprisoned with twenty-four other generals, and guillotined, as Napoleon put it, "to encourage the others." Republican generals were not only expected to win; they had to win decisively. The next February Carnot instructed his generals "to act offensively and in masses. Use the bayonet at every opportunity. Fight great battles and pursue the enemy until he is utterly destroyed." Commanders who could do this were rapidly brought to the front; before the spring of 1794 Bonaparte and eight of his eighteen future marshals had been made generals, at an average age of thirty-three. Almost all of the new men had been connected with the old army. Though many of them had held

[9] Before the Revolution Carnot, as a military engineer, does not seem to have been a partisan of the new theories. He had gone about as far as a non-noble usually went in the old army. "His private world was a mathematical one, in which he was just short of being a genius. . . . In normal times he might have left his name simply as a scholar, as his two sons did when the hurricane was over." Robert R. Palmer, *Twelve Who Ruled: The Committee of Public Safety during the Terror* (Princeton, 1941), 7.

The standard biography is now Marcel Reinhard, *Le Grand Carnot* (2 vols., Paris, 1950). In English there are Huntley Dupre, *Lazare Carnot, Republican Patriot* (Oxford, Ohio, 1940) and S. J. Watson, *Carnot* (London, 1954). See also Georges Bouchard, *Prieur de la Côte d'Or* (Paris, 1946).

commissions, few would have advanced beyond the rank of captain.[10]

How much the successful commanders had learned from the earlier reformers is hard to say. The great Swiss military critic Antoine Henri Jomini thought that events had been more important than theory.

War was commenced in 1792 as it had been in 1762: the French encamped near their strong places, the allies besieged them. Not until 1793 . . . was this system changed. Thoroughly aroused, [France] threw upon her enemies a million men in fourteen armies. These armies had neither tents, provisions, nor money. On their marches they bivouacked or were quartered in towns; their mobility was increased also. The troops were put in columns, which were much more easily handled than deployed lines, and on account of the broken character of the country of Flanders and the Vosges they threw out . . . skirmishers to protect and cover the columns. . . . [This] disconcerted the methodical Austrian and Prussian troops as well as their generals. . . . It . . . never occurred to [them] . . . that while the skirmishers made the noise the columns carried the positions.

Practice soon made the French expert foragers, especially in the rich lands on the French frontiers where many of the early battles were fought. An army had to move to eat; but, if it could keep moving, a large army could feed itself almost as well as a small one tethered to its bakeries. Sometimes the French went without, but they had also gone without when their commissary had broken down. By 1794 the new French army was beginning to enjoy the advantages of both mass and mobility. Its strategy, tactics, and organization were beginning to meet the requirements of the army reformers.[11]

[10] Palmer, *Twelve Who Ruled*, 85. The three most important of these generals, who were placed in command of the three major field armies in the single month between September 24 and October 22, had never even gone to the military schools, but had all been noncommissioned officers or sublieutenants in the old army. Jourdan was the 31-year-old son of a surgeon. He had run away to join the army at 16 and served six years in the ranks. After five campaigns during the American Revolution, he had opened a dry goods shop, and in 1790 had been elected a lieutenant in the National Guard. Pichegru was a year older, and had begun as a noncommisisoned officer. Hoche was only 25, the son of an old soldier. He had been a groom in the royal stables and a sublieutenant in the French Guards at the time of the storming of the Bastille. He was a captain during the retreat from Belgium during the spring; six months later he was in command of an army. The classic work in English is Ramsay W. Phipps, *The Armies of the First French Republic* (5 vols., London, 1926-1939).

[11] *Jomini and His Summary of the Art of War*, cond. and ed. J. D. Hittle (Harrisburg, 1947), 85-86. The French soldiers built rude lean-tos or slept in their overcoats. In 1806 the Prussians spent the cold October night before Jena

At the same time the Committee of Public Safety had also been directing a remarkable program of economic mobilization. Many of the elements of this program had been tried before. What was new was their combination, their extension to the entire nation, and the deliberate mobilization of scientific talent. A typical member of one of these special arms committees was Gaspard Monge, forty-seven years old in 1793, the founder of descriptive geometry. Great publicly owned musket shops were set up in the Paris parks and gardens, and thousands of Paris workers were drafted to work in them. By 1794 Paris was the largest small arms center in the world, producing something like 750 muskets a day, where all Europe had previously never produced more than a thousand. On the voyage to Egypt with Bonaparte in 1798, Monge told Savary, another famous French scientist, how they had done it.

To get men, we called out everyone who, no matter what his trade, knew how to work iron, and we gave them models of the Charleville musket to work with. There were no pattern makers, so we drafted sculptors and cabinet makers. . . . After a few defective trial pieces, they succeeded. Nobody knew how to make gunlocks, since the average metal worker was simply not used to working with steel. . . . So we finally had to collect the old gunlocks stored in the arsenals, bring them in at great expense, rework them, and fit them into new muskets. But we needed guns, and we got them, finally, almost 750 a day.[12]

Though quality was sometimes sacrificed, the authorities did succeed in working the existing foundries to capacity and in furnishing them with manpower and materials in a time

in the open. Forbidden to build shelters or light fires, the men dropped in the ranks from cold and hunger. A French peasant was familiar with early rising and long hours of work in fields several miles from his village. The French usually began the day's march at four and could make sixteen to twenty miles a day and remain fairly fit for fighting. Their march seemed disorderly to armies which tried to keep their files on the march, but the French had enough men to trade stragglers for speed.

12 Palmer, *Twelve Who Ruled*, 237-238. Louis de Launay, *Monge, fondateur de l'Ecole Polytechnique* (Paris, 1933), 109-110. See also Paul-V. Aubry, *Monge, le savant ami de Napoléon Bonaparte, 1748-1818* (Paris, 1954). Monge may have been denied admission to the army engineers' school because he was not well enough born for the bourgeoisie, who tended to monopolize that branch. But colleges hire teachers who could never make the right fraternities. Monge became the teacher of Carnot and Prieur and a member of the Academy of Sciences, a kind of scientific clearing house where mathematicans, physicists, and chemists worked on both theoretical and practical projects. In 1787, for example, Monge and a colleague had reported on the new English process of melting iron with coke instead of charcoal. Six years later three of this same committee were members of the Convention's arms committee.

of great economic disorder. Propaganda did its part too. The law of September 1, 1793, exhorted citizens, "in the name of patriotism" to comb cellars, barns, and abandoned buildings for the saltpeter normally imported from the Ottoman Empire. Very simple directions were printed and sent out through the provinces, so that anyone could recognize saltpeter when he found it, as today's old sourdoughs are sent out with Geiger counters. The saltpeter, charcoal, and sulphur were then ground up in requisitioned flour mills. When the committee had determined the exact number of turns required for perfect grinding, they sent out six thousand primitive automatic computators, with bells which were rung when the required number of turns had been completed. There were also the familiar labor troubles. The gun shops were a natural haven for draft dodgers, and the conscripted workers took off for every possible political meeting or holiday. A tough foreman might be denounced to the local Jacobin club as a monarchist. The most turbulent workers were sometimes counterattacked as saboteurs in the pay of the Austrians and English. There was even forced draft technical education. In February, 1794, the Convention directed each district to send two citizens to Paris for a month's course on the casting of bronze and iron cannon, the extraction of saltpeter, and Berthollet's new method of powder manufacture.

The battles of the fall of 1793 were fought with the stockpiles—730,000 muskets and more than 2000 field guns—left by the old monarchy, but the armies of 1794 and 1795 benefited from the new weapons. When the Convention adjourned at the end of October, 1795, Belgium and Holland had been overrun, Prussia had withdrawn from the war in a secret treaty which gave France the left bank of the Rhine, and Spain had also abandoned the coalition. Carnot, the "Organizer of Victory," became the only member of the new Directory (1795-1799) who had also served on the Committee of Public Safety. He was in charge of the military operations which culminated in Bonaparte's sensational victories over Sardinia in 1796 and a preliminary peace with Austria in the spring of 1797. Even England, the last member of the First Coalition, now seemed ready to participate in a general settlement.[18]

18 Of the many studies of Bonaparte's first Italian campaign, one of the most readable is W. G. F. Jackson, *Attack in the West; Napoleon's First Campaign Re-read Today* (London, 1953). Another fine book is R. A. Hall's little-known *Studies in Napoleonic Strategy* (London, 1918).

The more moderate members of the Directory, now led by Carnot, faced some of the same problems that had faced the English just 150 years before. The French New Model of over a quarter of a million men was supporting both itself and the home government through the plunder of Italy. Even if the men could be demobilized, the officers had to be taken care of. The generals, as Bonaparte remarked, had not been "winning fame for the lawyers. Let them try to remove me from my command and they will soon see what will happen." France was tired of war. In the elections of 1797 the moderates won control of both houses of the legislature. When the three radical Directors found themselves faced with a hostile legislature, they began to plot with the generals. They turned first to Hoche and then to Bonaparte, who cautiously sent one of his generals, Augereau, to arrange a coup d'état. Carnot managed to escape to Switzerland, but many of his supporters were either executed or banished to Guiana. The war with Britain went on. In 1798, under cover of an invasion threat to England, Bonaparte persuaded the Directors to strike at India by way of Egypt.

Bonaparte's Egyptian expedition was to be a strategic failure. At sea the Committee of Public Safety's revolutionary methods had not brought victory. In the American war British sea power had been checked by a coalition of the French, Spanish, and Dutch navies, but the French naval revival of that war proved to be only temporary. In 1793 the Spanish and Dutch navies were on the British side, and the French navy had been badly demoralized by the Revolution. Many of the French ships were in no condition to put to sea, two-thirds of the officers had resigned, and many of the sailors were mutinous. In August 1793 royalist mutineers handed Toulon over to the British, and the Atlantic fleet, which had put to sea to intercept a possible British landing in the Vendée, had been forced to return to Brest by another mutiny. Two members of the Committee of Public Safety had to be sent to Brest to keep that arsenal too from being handed over. Jeanbon Saint-André, who took over the Brest arsenal, was as able and energetic as Carnot and might have made as great a reputation if he had had as much to work with. He reorganized the work of the arsenal and impressed everyone he could lay hands on. Like Carnot he protected the officers who had remained loyal and filled the gaps with merchant captains, who knew the handling of ships if not the details of naval tactics and discipline. He finally succeeded in getting the fleet to sea to cover a food convoy from America during one of the most critical stages of the Revolution. In the battle of the First of June, 1794, the French fleet saved the convoy. But it lost seven of its twenty-six ships-of-the-line and 5000 men killed and wounded to 1100 for the British.[14]

The French fleet never again came out with such confidence and enthusiasm. Enthusiasm, in any case, was only part of the Revolutionary military formula. The other ingredient was mass, which largely made up for the conscripts' deficiencies in training. Here the French navy was at a hopeless disadvantage. France was as far behind Britain in maritime resources as Britain was behind France in total population. It took six months to make a passable soldier, but at least four years to train a man to work in a ship's tops without falling. The French navy could never take advantage of the army's victories, the renewal of the French alliances with Spain and Holland, the unrest in Ireland, or the mutinies which nearly immobilized the British during the early months of 1797. Later that year the Spanish and Dutch fleets were badly beaten at Cape St. Vincent and Camperdown. In 1798 Bonaparte's Egyptian expedition, after miraculously escaping destruction en route, was isolated by the annihilation of its supporting fleet at the Battle of the Nile. The victor, Horatio Nelson, had broken with eighteenth-century naval routine as decisively as the French generals had broken with routine on land. Nelson concentrated on part of the enemy line by breaking it in the center or by putting two ships on one where the enemy had no room to maneuver. Most of Nelson's captains at the Nile were his own age, forty. They had been promoted to captain's rank at the close of the American war.[15]

14 See L. Lévy-Schneider's fine *Le Conventionnel Jeanbon Saint-André* (2 vols., Paris, 1901). Neither Brest nor Toulon was a commercial port. There were few of the middle class merchants, lawyers, and intellectuals who elsewhere provided the backbone of the Revolution. The Committee of Public Safety had to deal with the suspected and disgruntled officers and the illiterate mass of sailors and arsenal workers. The story in Brest was very much like that in Toulon—a combination of real or imaginary royalist plots with mob violence as the workers struck for higher pay, the abolition of piecework, and free bread and wine from the naval stores. The British command of the Channel deprived Brest of Baltic timber. Rigging, spars, and cordage had to be carried overland in wagons.
15 Michael Lewis's fascinating *Social History of the Navy, 1793-1815* (London, 1960), 348, 442, estimates that Britain lost only ten ships of 28 guns or upwards from enemy action in this twenty-year war. Their less well-trained enemies lost 377 such ships and suffered six to ten times as many battle casu-

Bonaparte was lucky as well as able. The English fleet had just missed him on two separate occasions on the voyage to Egypt. After his army was imprisoned there, he was able to return to France to save the revolutionary politicians from their own blunders. With the Corsican supposedly out of the way, England, Austria, and Russia had formed a Second Coalition. By the fall of 1799 they had driven the French out of Italy and were preparing to invade France once more. The elections of 1798 had again gone against the Directors; they had again annulled the results. When they again lost ground in the elections of 1799, one faction plotted to change the constitution. At this point Bonaparte escaped from Egypt and landed in France. Within a month the plotters had replaced the Directory with a Consulate with Bonaparte as the First Consul. During that month the Russians had withdrawn from the coalition. In 1800 Bonaparte again drove the Austrians from Italy. In 1802 England signed the Peace of Amiens, a few months before Bonaparte extended his term as First Consul from ten years to life, with the right to appoint his own successor. He was to make himself Emperor of the French in 1804, after what had now become the customary stacked plebiscite.

One of the Directory's final legacies had been the Conscription Act of 1798, an act which, in its essentials, remained the basis of the French army's recruiting until the disasters of 1870. Its chief feature was its combination of volunteering with conscription, now simply an efficient form of crimping.

---

alties. He places British battle deaths at 6,540, while 97,120 men died from disease or accidents. The British lost 101 ships in accidents, their enemies only 24.

The literature on Nelson, the greatest of naval tacticians and—to use one of St. Vincent's milder phrases—a complete "booby" ashore, is almost as extensive as that on Napoleon. The best short book is Russell Grenfell, *Nelson, the Sailor* (London, 1949), but A. T. Mahan, *The Life of Nelson: the Embodiment of the Sea Power of Great Britain* (2 vols., Boston, 1897) is still worth reading. Carola Oman, *Nelson* (Garden City, 1946) is now the standard work. See also W. M. James, *The Durable Monument, Nelson* (London, 1948), Ludovic Kennedy, *Nelson's Band of Brothers* (London, 1951), and Oliver Warner, *Victory: The Life of Lord Nelson* (Boston, 1958).

Wellington met Nelson only once. As Wellington later told it to his friend J. W. Croker, their conversation at first, "If I can call it conversation, for it was almost all on his side and all about himself, . . . [was] so vain and so silly as to surprise and almost disgust me." When Nelson found out that Wellington was "somebody, . . . he was altogether a different man, both in manner and matter. . . . He talked of the state of this country, and . . . of affairs on the Continent with a good sense, and a knowledge of subjects at home and abroad that surprised me; . . . in fact he talked like an officer and a statesman." *The Correspondence and Diaries of . . . J. W. Croker*, ed. Louis J. Jennings (3 vols., London, 1884), II, 233.

"Every Frenchman is a soldier and owes himself to the defense of the Fatherland," the law began. It then added that no *true* patriot would hire a substitute. Though the Directors fixed a quota of 200,000 unmarried men between twenty and twenty-one, they never succeeded in procuring more than 37,000. They were afraid to apply the law in the *Vendée;* desertions, false marriages, and self-mutilation continued in spite of threats and punishments. Though Napoleon was to boast that he could afford to lose 30,000 men a month, he never seems to have procured more than 100,000 men annually within the boundaries of the old French monarchy.[16]

As always the burden fell most heavily on the peasants, who had to learn to fight by fighting, in an army which at least now offered them a chance for advancement. In spite of the tricks which his memory played him, the reminiscences of the seventy-two-year-old Jean-Roch Coignet give a vivid picture of the life of one French conscript.

One day I was summoned to the *mairie*. There they asked me my name, . . . profession and age. . . . "What in the devil do they want with me? I have done nothing." . . . My master and mistress . . . replied, "They wish to enroll you for conscription." . . .

Two gendarmes came and left with me a way-bill and an order to start for Fontainebleu, . . . where some very unenthusiastic officers received us and put us in barracks which were in wretched condition. Our fine battalion was formed, . . . and half of them left and went home. . . . Each man was allowed fifteen days to rejoin his battalion, or . . . be regarded as a deserter. . . . The stragglers were brought by the gendarmes, and we were in order again.

Sunday was the *décadi*. . . . We had to sing *"La Victoire,"* and the officers flourished their sabres. . . . Every evening, around the liberty-pole in the principal street, we had to sing, "Les aristocrates à la lanterne." . . .

This sort of life had lasted nearly two months, when a report was circulated that General Bonaparte had landed, and was on his way to Paris. . . . Our officers went crazy about it, because the chief of our battalion knew him, and the whole battalion was delighted to hear it. . . .

[Coignet was present at Bonaparte's coup.] The grenadiers . . . were in line in the front court; a half-brigade of infantry were sta-

16 Even during the crises of 1812 and 1813 more than half the eligible men escaped service. The price of substitutes rose as Napoleon's fortunes fell. It rose from 1500 francs in 1805 to 15,000 in 1812. Georges Lefebvre, *Napoléon* (3d ed., Paris, 1947), 190-192. See also the careful study of Robert Legrand, *Le Recrutement des armées et les désertions (1791-1815): Aspects de la Révolution en Picardie* (Abbéville, 1957).

tioned near the great gate, and four companies of infantry behind
the guard of the Directory.

Cries of *"Vive Bonaparte"* were heard on all sides, and he appeared. . . . He passed in front of the . . . grenadiers, saluted
every one, ordered us into line of battle, and spoke to the officers.
. . . He went up the steps alone. Suddenly we heard cries, and
Bonaparte came out, drew his sword, and went up again with a
platoon of grenadiers of the guard. Then the noise increased. We
saw stout gentlemen jumping out of the windows; cloaks, fine hats,
and plumes were thrown on the ground, and the grenadiers pulled
the lace off the elegant cloaks. [The self-perpetuating "representatives of the French nation" wore elegant parliamentary uniforms.][17]

The Napoleonic Empire

The Peace of Amiens lasted a bit more than a year. When
England and France again went to war in May, 1803, Bonaparte gathered his Grand Army on the Channel coast. His
schemes for invading England all called for avoiding a naval
battle. The French would row across the Channel in small
boats while the British fleet was becalmed, or the French and
Spanish fleets would suddenly concentrate at the entrance to
the Channel while the British fleet was diverted to other
waters. For two years French and Spanish naval forces feinted
from the Mediterranean to the West Indies. The British were
not diverted. The French and Spanish failed to push into the
Channel after a brush with the British off Cape Finisterre. At
the Battle of Trafalgar on October 21, 1805, Nelson captured
or destroyed twenty-two of the allies' thirty-three ships-of-
the-line as they headed out of Cadiz for the Mediterranean.
This was Napoleon's last real invasion threat. Some historians
think that he had never intended to invade England. Others
feel that he had already sent his Grand Army against Austria
and Russia (who had formed a Third Coalition with England
and Sweden) in the summer of 1805 "to regain the prestige
he had lost in the recent fiasco." The great victories of the
Grand Army, in any case, confirmed "the expansive tendencies of France upon the Continent." Napoleon entered "the
vicious circle which eventually led to his ruin."

17 *The Narrative of Captain Coignet*, ed. Lordan Larchey, trans. M. Carey
(New York, 1890), 49-54. See also Jacques Godechot's fine *La Grande nation: l'expansion révolutionnaire de la France dans le monde, 1789-1799* (2
vols., Paris, 1956), G. Ferrero's imaginative *The Gamble: Bonaparte in Italy,
1796-1797*, tr. Bertha C. Pritchard and Lily C. Freeman (London, 1961), and
John Eldred Howard, ed. and tr., *Letters and Documents of Napoleon* (I,
London, 1961).

In order to equalize the inevitable advantage of his enemy on the seas and in the colonies, he was forced to keep on the offensive upon the Continent; but as the tentacles of his power spread over Europe, they provided the bases for further coalitions until the magnificent edifice he had built up collapsed of its own weight.[18]

Napoleon's Grand Army of 1805 was undoubtedly his best. About half of the men were veterans, a quarter went back to the desperate early years of the Revolution. Four years of peace and intensive training had made them as skilled in the new tactics as the Prussians had been in the old. Many inefficient officers had been pensioned off. The average age of the generals was about forty. Six of the nine marshals had been general officers since 1793. Masséna, the oldest of them, was fifty. Marmont, the youngest, was thirty-two. All of them had seen a soldier seat himself on the throne of Europe's greatest power. That soldier was to make two of them kings. All of the others were to become dukes—Castiglione, Auerstadt, Ragusa, Elchingen, Montebello, Rivoli, Dalmatia—a whole new Central European nobility. The Emperor himself directed the concentration of his divisions. His favorite maneuver, if he had any favorite, was to unite them across the enemy's line of retreat, forcing his opponent to turn about and give battle under conditions where a defeat became a disaster. Jomini, who had seen him at work, wrote that Napoleon

was his own chief staff officer. Provided with a pair of dividers opened to . . . the scale of from seventeen to twenty miles in a straight line, . . . bending over and sometimes stretched at full length upon his map where the positions of the enemy were marked, . . . he decided in a moment the number of marches necessary for each of his columns to arrive at the desired point by a certain day. Then, . . . he dictated those instructions which are alone enough to make any man famous.[19]

18 Harold C. Deutsch, "Napoleonic Policy and the Project of a Descent upon England" (*Journal of Modern History*, II, Dec., 1930, 541-568). See the same author's *The Genesis of Napoleonic Imperialism* (Cambridge, Mass., 1938); A. T. Mahan, *The Influence of Sea Power upon the French Revolution and Empire* (2 vols., Boston, 1892); Julian Corbett, *The Campaign of Trafalgar* (London, 1910); E. Desbrière, *The Naval Campaign of 1805*, trans. and ed. Constance Eastwick (2 vols., Oxford, 1933); A. A. Thomazi, *Napoleon et ses marins* (Paris, 1950); René Maine, *Trafalgar* (London, 1957); Piers Mackesy, *The War in the Mediterranean, 1803-1810* (Cambridge, Mass., 1957); Oliver Warner, *The Battle of the Nile* (London, 1960); and Dudley Pope, *Decision at Trafalgar* (London, 1960).
19 *Art of War*, 139-140. For his army see Jean Morvan, *Le Soldat impérial* (2 vols., Paris, 1904). The classic strategical studies are Yorck von Warten-

Though the Allies' land forces were again slightly more numerous than those of the French, they were smashed in three masterly campaigns. Napoleon marched across the communications of the Austrians in south Germany and forced their surrender. The main Austrian army in Italy tried to rescue Vienna by marching around through Hungary and was completely out of the picture when Napoleon defeated the Austrian and Russian emperors at Austerlitz (December 2, 1805). After Austria withdrew from the coalition, Prussia decided to join. The Prussian army was somewhat larger than Napoleon's forces in south Germany, but was handicapped by its old-fashioned supply system, tactics, and commanders. Brunswick, the Prussian commander, was seventy-one, not quite double Napoleon's age. Mollendorf was eighty-two. Blücher, one of the few Prussian generals to do well, was only sixty-four. Napoleon surprised the Prussians by striking them on the east, forcing them to hurry back to protect Berlin. At Jena (October 14, 1806) Napoleon defeated part of the Prussian army, while Davout defeated a force twice as large as his own at Auerstadt. The old Prussian army simply dissolved; many fortified towns gave up without a fight. Napoleon pushed on into East Prussia and fought the Russians at Eylau in February, 1807. In this case the vast distances of Russia worked against the Russian army. East Prussia is as close to France as to Moscow. Bad as the east German roads then were, they were not as bad as the roads in Russia. Reinforcements joined the French more quickly than they came up for the Russians. At Friedland (June 14, 1806) the outnumbered Russians were defeated. These campaigns show the

burg, *Napoleon as a General* (2 vols., London, 1897), and Hubert Camon, *Quand et comment Napoléon a conçu son système de manoeuvre* (Paris, 1931). A fine source medley is Jean Savant, *Napoleon in His Time*, trans. Katherine John (New York, 1958). For his chief staff officer see S. J. Watson, *By Command of the Emperor: A Life of Marshal Berthier* (London, 1957).

There is a Napoleon, like a Lincoln, for every taste. The best older books are Theodore A. Dodge, *Napoleon* (4 vols., Boston, 1904), H. A. L. Fisher, *Bonaparte* (New York, 1913), Spenser Wilkinson, *The French Army before Napoleon* (Oxford, 1915), and J. Colin, *L'Education militaire de Napoléon* (Paris, 1900). The standard glorifications are Louis Madelin, *Napoléon* (Paris, 1935), and Jacques Bainville, *Napoléon* (Paris, 1931). The standard multivolume life is F. M. Kircheisen, *Napoleon* (2 vol. abridgement, New York, 1932). Geoffrey Bruun, *Europe and the French Imperium, 1799-1814* (New York, 1938) surveys the entire period. Eugene Tarlé, *Bonaparte*, trans. John Cournos (New York, 1937) is a fine work by a Soviet Russian historian. Harold T. Parker, *Three Napoleonic Battles* (Durham, N. C., 1944), studies the decline of the Great Captain. The outstanding works of the last decade are P. Geyl, *Napoleon, For and Against* (New Haven, 1949), and J. M. Thompson, *Napoleon Bonaparte: His Rise and His Fall* (Oxford, 1951).

French system at its best. (1) Their forces were usually superior in numbers at the decisive point. (2) Their tactics at Auerstadt enabled them to defeat superior numbers. (3) They were able to live off the country hundreds of miles from France.

The English and Swedes had done nothing. The Russian Emperor Alexander I was tired of his allies and was afraid to retreat into Russia because of the possibility of revolt among the peasantry. (The great Pugachev rebellion had been suppressed only thirty-two years before.) Both Alexander and Napoleon were ready to bargain. At Tilsit Alexander agreed to the partition of Prussia and the establishment of the new Grand Duchy of Warsaw. He also declared war on England and excluded British ships and goods from Russia. In return Napoleon agreed to let Russia have certain Turkish territories and to take Finland from Sweden. Denmark was also forced to exclude British goods, and even the Swedes eventually joined Napoleon's boycott of British goods and chose Napoleon's Marshal Bernadotte as Crown Prince. The son of a lawyer, Bernadotte had run away to join the army at seventeen. As Minister of War under the Directory, Bernadotte had pursued a "correct" policy. He had refused to join the plot to make Napoleon First Consul, but had also refused to use the army against the plotters. Never a great tactician, Bernadotte was a careful military administrator. He was to be the only one of the revolutionary adventurers to found a dynasty.

The only great power with which the Grand Army had not been able to come to grips was Britain. As usual, the most spectacular use of British sea power had been to protect Britain against invasion. As usual, too, the British army had been too weak to do France much damage in Europe. The capture of the remaining Dutch and French colonies had tightened the British monopoly of colonial trade and had cut down losses from French privateers without affecting the war in Europe. Some French forces had always been tied down by the threat of British landings, but British amphibious operations in northern Europe had been uniformly unsuccessful. In 1793 the British had failed to support the Vendean uprising; their army had marched away to Dunkirk when the allies might possibly have taken Paris. During the Second Coalition an Anglo-Russian force had landed at the extreme northwestern tip of Holland, but had been checked before it had advanced more than a few miles inland. During the final phases of the war of the Third Coalition, the British had prepared an Anglo-Swedish force to threaten Napoleon's exposed communications in north Germany. This force did not leave Britain until June. It landed on one of the Baltic islands after Russia had made peace at Tilsit. Since the British *had* managed to send troops to Egypt, South America, Guiana, Turkey, Tobago, and the Cape of Good Hope, it is no wonder that Alexander felt that he had been left in the lurch while the British were pursuing their colonial enterprises. Two years later, when Austria was to rise against the conqueror, the British were to give them a subsidy but no help for the national uprising in northern Germany. Instead, they were to try to take Antwerp. Forty thousand soldiers and nearly forty ships-of-the-line—the largest force to leave Britain during sailing days—got started after the Austrians had been beaten. The expedition got stuck on Walcheren Island near Antwerp and withdrew after losing 106 men in action and over 4000 from disease. The Revolutionary armies were so much larger than those of the eighteenth century that an amphibious force of the old type could accomplish little. And better land communications now made it possible to move much more quickly to any threatened point.[20]

French cruisers and privateers did less damage to British trade than other French measures against their enemy's commerce. The economic warfare between Britain and France was still essentially mercantilistic in its outlook. Both opponents were still largely self-sufficient. Napoleon hoped to bring down the British government by a financial crisis caused by the exclusion of British goods from European markets.

[20] Some of the earlier British expeditions are described in Alfred H. Burne, *The Noble Duke of York* (London, 1949). The greatest British military thinker of the nineteenth century pointed out that Napoleon's winter campaign in East Prussia had been very risky. Even a small British force might have made "the campaign of Eylau . . . as disastrous to Napoleon as that of Leipzig. The presence of 20,000 men at the great battle [where the French were fought to a standstill by the Russians] would surely have turned the scale in favor of the Allies. Yet, although the men were available, . . . His Majesty's ministers, forgetful of Marlborough's glories, were so imbued with the idea that the British army was too insignificant to take part in a Continental war, that the opportunity was let slip. . . . Their idea of a diversion was a series of isolated efforts, made at far distant points." One of the reasons for Clausewitz' failure to recognize the importance of the British contribution to the winning of the war was certainly that the British government itself failed to grasp "the principles which should have controlled its [the British army's] use when the command of the sea had been obtained." G. F. R. Henderson, *The Science of War*, ed. Neill Malcolm (6th imp., London, 1913), 30-32.

Napoleon's Continental System was not a blockade, but a boycott. Such boycotts had been attempted before, but never on so large a scale. The French could not touch the sources of the British re-export trade, but if British colonial goods and manufactures could not be sold, that government's income—then derived from customs duties and land taxes—would drop disastrously. The carrying charges on the huge British debt might then force Britain into one of those bankruptcies which had played such important roles in eighteenth-century politics. The Continental System was not militarily self-defeating. It was primarily concerned with luxuries or semiluxuries of little military value—sugar, tea, coffee, tobacco, textiles, and certain types of hardware. It was also warmly supported by French manufacturers. The conquered peoples came to feel that the chief economic difference between the British and the French was that the British had given them better goods at lower prices. Neutral American traders were caught between the French regulations and the British retaliatory Orders-in-Council. A ship might be caught by British patrols if she tried to make a French port without first touching Britain. Her cargo might be confiscated by the French port authorities if they found British goods on board or evidence that she had paid British duties or port charges.

The Continental System was perhaps the closest to success after Napoleon's victory over Austria in 1809. Austria agreed to break all connections with Britain about the time that Holland and the German North Sea coast were annexed to France. The British continued to smuggle some goods in from their remaining bases—Malta, Minorca, Sicily, and Heligoland—around the French perimeter. Many people were willing to do almost anything to get such exotic and habit-forming necessities as tobacco and coffee, and centuries of mercantilist regulations had taught many ways of evading them. Napoleon's seizure of Spain in 1808 had opened Latin-America to British merchants, but the American Embargo and Non-Intercourse Acts (1807 and 1809) had seriously cut British trade with the United States. There were several bad harvests and some historians think that Napoleon could have starved Britain if he had cut off French wheat exports at this time. He preferred instead to sell French wheat for British gold, a typically mercantilist measure. There was widespread discontent among the British workers—many of the hardships later charged to the early Industrial Revolution were surely due to the war—but it is hard to say whether this discontent, among a wholly unrepresented class, could have brought down the British government. In any case Napoleon believed that the weak point was British credit, and the Continental System should be judged in those terms rather than by present ideas of economic warfare. The flexibility of British sea power also stands out quite clearly. During the whole exhausting struggle it gave the British economy alternative sources of supply and alternative overseas markets.[21]

Most important of all, the British economy was not disrupted by invasion and plundering. Though Britain's population was still little more than half that of France, she made greater industrial progress during the French Revolutionary period than at any previous period in her history. In 1790 British iron production was still somewhat smaller than that of France. By 1801 it had trebled, giving Britain a commanding lead during the final phases of the war. The British government held to its course. In spite of a debt that has been estimated at three times the national income, the government managed to borrow £22 million in 1809, £21 million in 1810, £41 million in 1811, and £45 million in 1812. During the three latter years there were nearly 150,000 seamen and marines in the British navy, compared to 100,000 the year of Trafalgar. Following the rule that a man on shipboard was worth two on shore and doubling the figure again because of Britain's smaller population, this was equivalent to a French army of 600,000. In addition, Britain also maintained an army of 250,000 men (equivalent to 500,000 for France) and paid large subsidies to her allies. This army did intervene effectively in Spain, beat back an American invasion of Canada, and captured the new American capital city. British subsidies were to save all three of the impoverished Eastern European powers during the final campaigns in Germany, while British arms equipped their new armies. British

21 François Crouzet, *L'économie britannique et le blocus continental, 1806-1813* (2 vols., Paris, 1958), Eli F. Heckscher, *The Continental System: An Economic Interpretation* (Oxford, 1922), W. F. Galpin, *The Grain Supply of England during the Napoleonic Period* (Philadelphia, 1925), C. N. Parkinson, ed., *The Trade Winds: A Study of British Overseas Trade during the French Wars, 1793-1815* (London, 1948). Since her armies lived on conquest, France came out in a better financial position than Britain. But peace saw commercial crises everywhere—a crisis of overproduction in Britain, a crisis of being thrown back on the home market in France, and a crisis of British competition in other Continental countries.

sea power, arms, and money tipped the balance in what might otherwise have been a stalemate.[22]

The Opposition to Napoleon: The Peninsula

What, then, were the weaknesses in Napoleon's system? Again there are almost as many explanations as there are historians. Many French historians—who have, perhaps, paid too much attention to France—believe that Napoleon overstrained French resources, while other writers hold just the opposite view. The latter believe that, because Napoleon had to be popular in France, he failed to organize French manpower efficiently. In addition, Napoleon could not organize his conquests except in the interests of the French merchants and manufacturers. Those people, in Italy and Germany especially, who had originally welcomed French Liberty, Equality, and Fraternity, gradually learned that "some were more equal than others." The nationalism which had once aided the Revolution turned, in time, against it. Tactically, the French armies were not unbeatable. The column could still be beaten by a line of steady professionals under certain conditions. Logistically, the new French system of living off the country worked in rich territories against an enemy who could be overpowered in a single tremendous campaign. In poorer areas against more stubborn opposition, there was much to be said for the old eighteenth-century system of careful logistical planning.

Napoleon himself—in spite of his boast that "I am not like other men, the laws of convention and morality do not apply to me"—was not immune to the weaknesses of despots. Middle age and overwork slowed him down. He was unwilling to delegate power to his subordinates and failed to develop a proper staff system. Perhaps he had no material with which to create one. He gradually broke with such independent characters as Bernadotte and Jomini. He failed to use the

[22] The United States' debt in 1945 has been estimated at one and one half times the national income. No eighteenth-century government had the taxing power of a modern state and interest rates were much higher. In 1815 the carrying charges on the old debt took half the British government's income. Carnot believed that the British ranked highest of all in national patriotism. This is not surprising. If modern nationalism is somehow related to the growth of the middle class, Britain should have been capable of a greater national effort than any other country of the late eighteenth century.

During the early phases of the War of 1812, which British statesmen had finally made every effort to avoid, the British had 35 to 40 battalions of regulars—perhaps 20,000 men—to defend a position extending from Detroit to Bermuda. A third of these men had been recruited locally. They were reinforced, on occasion, by militia and, in 1814, by 16,000 Peninsular veterans.

talents of men like Carnot. Most of his subordinates were military adventurers utterly lacking in civic courage or character, stout tacticians without a spark of statesmanship or military genius. Most of these men had risen from the lower middle class and the lower nobility. Their love for glory was matched by their love for gold. A "niggling avarice" was their most common characteristic. In short, Napoleon's great military machine gradually became militaristic. It seemed to exist only to serve the dictator, his grasping quarrelsome relatives, and the rough "battlefield nobility" around him. "Still undismayed, and still resolved to tempt Providence once more, he suddenly found himself without soldiers or weapons, and saw, towering above him and ready to break, the swollen wave of ill will, of cowardice and treachery which was to engulf his genius."[23]

These weaknesses first became apparent in Spain, where the Peninsula War developed out of Napoleon's economic policy. After the collapse of the Third Coalition and the extension of the Continental System to the Baltic, the chief remaining leak was through Portugal, a British ally since 1703 (though the alliance had been theoretically renounced in 1801 after a Spanish invasion of Portugal). To get at Portugal, the French armies would have to pass through Spain, a French ally since 1796 (and throughout most of the eighteenth century). One event of this alliance between Spain and the revolutionaries had been the return of Louisiana to France in 1800, with a guarantee that France would not transfer it to a third power. Napoleon had honored this promise by selling the territory to the United States two weeks before the renewal of the war with England in 1803. Soon after Tilsit the French and Spanish invaded Portugal and captured Lisbon. On paper, the whole coastline of Europe was now closed to British goods. More French troops entered Spain the next winter on the pretext of guarding their communications with Portugal. In the spring of 1808 Napoleon lured the Spanish king and his son to Bayonne and forced them to renounce their throne, which Napoleon then gave to his

---

[23] De Gaulle, *France and Her Army*, 60. "To carry with him a generation whose minds had been saturated with the epic deeds and fiery passions of the Revolution, he turned to the spirit of emulation, of honour, to the desire for personal glory. He placed the stamp of his own greatness on everything. . . . It was as if the army were for ever engaged in a competition organized and judged by the Emperor, with glory as the prize." *Ibid.*, 47-48. A damning study of Napoleon's paladins is Georges Six, *Les Généraux de la Révolution et de l'Empire* (Paris, 1947), 295-305.

brother Joseph. These events touched off a national revolt in Spain. A whole French army corps was captured by the rebels and units of the Spanish regular army. Though the troops who had been captured were recent conscripts under a general who had never before held an independent command, the Spanish had beaten "the victors of Jena and Austerlitz." About the same time a British army landed in Portugal, defeated the French in a pitched battle, and compelled them to give up the whole country.

The legend of French invulnerability had been badly shaken. National unrest stirred in Germany, and the Austrian government began to arm for a general uprising. Napoleon hastily called Alexander I to a conference at Erfurt and tried to get his ally to hold Austria back. But his plans were betrayed by the French foreign minister, Talleyrand, who told Alexander that Napoleon was beginning to overreach himself and that many Frenchmen would welcome his overthrow. After the conference Napoleon left for Spain. Two hundred thousand French veterans soon recaptured most of the Spanish cities, but a British army under Sir John Moore escaped by sea while the rebels melted into the hills and then reassembled. Without consulting his brother Napoleon added to his troubles by hastily reorganizing the Spanish administration, confiscating certain Church lands, and abolishing the Inquisition. Though Napoleon defeated Austria in 1809, his generals in Spain were unable to drive the British out of Portugal or to put down stubborn Spanish guerrilla resistance. Those who like their history in neat packets find the Spanish resistance to Napoleon almost as hard to understand as did Napoleon himself. It was national, but not liberal, a super Vendée, peasant, Catholic, and royalist. Here the new mass army which fed itself on conquest met its first mass resistance, a combination of modern national fanaticism with the fanaticism of the Wars of Religion. At the same time, however, the patriots found it difficult to keep up a regular army to support the guerrillas, since the peasants were as hostile to conscription as they were to the other French innovations. There were also French guerrilla bands—the *Afrancescados* —and the line between banditry and patriotism was a very fine one. This was the war of Goya's famous *The Disasters of War*. Probably more people lost their lives in it than in any other war of the Napoleonic era. As many French officers were killed there as in Russia or Germany.[24]

The British supplied many regular troops and that command of the sea which, Jomini estimated, quintupled the Spanish power of resistance,

not only on account of the facility of feeding the insurrection and of alarming the enemy on all the points he may occupy but still more by the difficulties . . . thrown in the way of his procuring supplies by sea. [In a country like Spain] the invader has only an army, whereas his adversaries have both an army and a people in arms. . . . These obstacles become almost insurmountable when the country is difficult. Each armed inhabitant knows the smallest paths and their connections; he finds everywhere a relative or friend who aids him, . . . and, learning immediately the slightest movement on the part of the invader, can adopt the best measures to defeat his projects. The enemy, without information . . . and certain of safety only in the concentration of his columns, is like a blind man. . . . When, after the most carefully concerted movements and the most rapid and fatiguing marches he thinks he is about to . . . deal a terrible blow, he finds no signs of the enemy but his campfires. . . . No army, however disciplined, can contend successfully against such national resistance unless it be strong enough to hold all the essential points, . . . cover its communications, and . . . furnish an active force sufficient to beat the enemy wherever he may present himself. If this enemy has a regular army . . . around which to rally the people, what force will be sufficient to be superior everywhere and to assure the safety of the long lines of communications?[25]

During the last phases of the Napoleonic era the British recruiting system did not greatly differ from that of the French. Both rested on a combination of compulsion and volunteering. The British army was composed of two forces: the traditional volunteer army and a conscript full-time home service militia, a quite different force from that which is

24 The Spanish guerrillas, "like avenging vultures, followed the French columns at a distance, to murder such of the soldiers as, fatigued or wounded, remained behind. . . . The women . . . threw themselves with horrible shrieks upon the wounded, and disputed who should kill them by the most cruel tortures; they stabbed their eyes with knives and scissors, and seemed to exult . . . at the sight of their blood." M. de Rocca, *Mémoires sur la guerre des Français en Espagne* (Paris, 1814), 145, 191. Two of C. S. Forester's best novels deal with the Peninsula, *Rifleman Dodd* and *The Gun* (published in one volume, London, 1942). There are few French works on the Spanish war. H. Lucas-Dubreton, *Napoléon devant l'Espagne* (Paris, 1946) is good.
25 *Art of War*, 50-51. Jomini had served in Spain, Clausewitz did not.

usually associated with that name. They were volunteers too young for the regulars or men chosen by ballot, or lot, to fill district quotas. Those with the bad numbers could buy substitutes. Most of them, after a year's militia service, then volunteered for the higher pay and bounty offered by the regulars. The remainder faced an indefinite term of service at lower pay with no chance of adventure. The ordinary militia was now a third-line force; all remaining men between eighteen and thirty were required to do some training. The regulars maintained four field armies abroad—in India, the West Indies, the Mediterranean (mostly in Sicily), and the Peninsula—in addition to supplying garrisons for posts stretching from Gibraltar and Malta to West Africa and New South Wales. The men who were siphoned from the militia into the regulars were undoubtedly as good as the conscripts who reinforced Napoleon's veterans. They were surely as nationalistic as the average man in the ranks in France. Men under thirty could hardly remember when Britain had not been at war with France. Certainly many of them thoroughly believed that Britain was fighting for her life against the Corsican.[26]

The first British forces to arrive in Portugal had been diverted from expeditions to other destinations, a good example of the mobility conferred on the British army by the British navy's command of the sea. Lieutenant General Sir Arthur Wellesley, their first and—after a winter's interlude—final commander, was just the age of Napoleon. The fourth son of an Anglo-Irish peer who had been most famous as a musician, Wellesley (he became Viscount Wellington in 1809 and Duke in 1814) had been educated at Eton, in Brussels, and at a French military college. He had been commissioned at eighteen and had taken part in the campaign in Flanders in 1794. After his brilliant elder brother became Governor-General of India, he had held important commands there be-

[26] For the militia in this era see John W. Fortescue, *The County Lieutenancies and the Army, 1803-1814* (London, 1909). The classic is still W. F. P. Napier, *History of the War in the Peninsula* . . . (1828-1840, 6 vols., London, 1900). C. W. C. Oman, *Wellington's Army* (London, 1912), based on his *History of the Peninsular War* (7 vols., Oxford, 1902-1930), is his best work. D. J. Goodspeed, *The British Campaigns in the Peninsula, 1808-1814* (Ottawa, 1958), Carola Oman, *Sir John Moore* (London, 1953), Douglas H. Bell, *Wellington's Officers* (London, 1938), and Godfrey Davies, *Wellington and His Army* (San Marino, Cal., 1954), are very good. There are many accounts by participants. *The Recollections of Rifleman Harris*, ed. Henry Curling (London, 1929) and *The Letters of Private Wheeler*, ed. B. H. Liddell Hart (Boston, 1951) are very interesting. Sir George Bell's *Rough Notes of an Old Soldier* has been edited by Brian Stuart as *Soldier's Glory* (London, 1955).

fore returning to England in 1805. By training and experience this "Sepoy general," as Napoleon is supposed to have called him, was an infantryman. As usual for a British expeditionary force in the eighteenth century, his army was weak in cavalry and artillery. It had been sent to Portugal without a siege train or engineers. This was not Wellington's own fault. He was always very careful about logistic and other details. Before he set sail a friend of his had recorded his thoughts on the French.

I have not seen them since the campaign in Flanders, when they were capital soldiers, and a dozen years of victory under Buona-parte must have made them better still. They have . . . a new system of strategy, which has out-manoeuvred and overwhelmed all the armies of Europe. . . . They may overwhelm me, but I don't think they will out-manoeuvre me. First, because I am not afraid of them, as everybody else seems to be; and secondly, be-cause if what I hear of their system of manoeuvres be true, I think it a false one against steady troops. I suspect that all the continental armies were more than half beaten before the battle was begun.[27]

Like many other infantry officers, Wellington knew that the third rank in the firing line was more or less useless. Instead of adopting the French *ordre mixte* the British abolished the third rank and gave their men rigorous musketry training. In the earlier wars French columns had pushed through lines which had already been weakened by the fire of skirmishers and artillery. In the Peninsula the order was often reversed. Napoleon's overconfident generals pushed columns into the fire of light infantry covering intact firing lines of well-trained regulars. One of the ablest of French nineteenth-century soldiers, the later Marshal Bugeaud, described Wellington's tactics as follows:

The English generally held good defensive positions . . . usually on rising ground, behind the crest of which they found cover for

[27] Jennings, *Correspondence and Diaries of . . . J. W. Croker*, I, 13. "In a series of memoranda of extraordinary detail [about a proposed South Ameri-can expedition, Wellington] . . . not only specified the number of troops to be employed, the places where they should be landed, the character of the popu-lation, . . . and the forms of government to be set up, . . . but he drew up *in his own handwriting* long lists of ordnance and stores, . . . even to the number of flints for Brown Bess, carbine, and pistol." Herbert Maxwell, *The Life of Wellington: The Restoration of the Martial Power of Great Britain* (2 vols., London, 1899), I, 91. For a careful account of Wellington's meticulous staff work see S. P. G. Ward, *Wellington's Headquarters: A Study of the Ad-ministrative Problems in the Peninsula, 1809-1814* (Oxford, 1957).

a good part of their men. The usual obligatory cannonade would commence the operation, then, in haste, . . . without ascertaining whether the ground afforded any facilities for lateral or turning movements, we marched straight forward, "taking the bull by the horns." . . . About a thousand yards from the English line the men would begin to grow restless. . . . The quick-step became a run; the ranks began to be mixed up; . . . many soldiers began to fire as they ran. . . . The red English line . . . seemed to take no notice of the storm which was about to beat upon it. . . . At this moment of painful expectation the English line would make a quarter turn—the muskets were going up to the "ready." An indefinable sensation nailed to the spot many of our men, who halted and opened a wavering fire. The enemy's return—a volley of simultaneous precision and deadly effect crashed in upon us. . . . We reeled together . . . trying to recover. . . . But to our great surprise, they did not pursue . . . for more than a hundred yards, and went back to their former lines, to await another attack. We rarely failed to deliver it . . . with the same want of success.[28]

The French failed to achieve decisive numerical superiority over Wellington in the Peninsula because of poor communications, the guerrillas, and the organization of Portuguese regulars under British officers. By 1810 Napoleon had moved 370,000 men into Spain. Masséna, the oldest and one of the ablest of the French marshals, was given 130,000 of them to conquer Portugal, which was defended by about 50,000 regulars, half British and half Portuguese. As the French advanced the Portuguese peasants destroyed their crops and retired inside the triple line of fortifications which Wellington had constructed across the peninsula on which Lisbon stands. Guerrillas struck at Masséna's communications so successfully that he had detached over half his forces when he came up with Wellington on a steep range of hills near Busaco. Know-

---

[28] Quoted in Oman, *Wellington's Army*, 90-91. Quimby's sound criticism of Oman's conclusions, *Background of Napoleonic Warfare*, 326-343, is due to the fact that Oman's ideas were drawn almost solely from the Peninsular War. On the other hand many British generals—basing their ideas on the same limited experience—felt that the French depended too heavily on their columns. After Waterloo, Wellington summed up the battle in a letter to his old friend Lord Beresford, the organizer of the Portuguese army. "Napoleon did not manoeuvre at all. He just moved forward in the old style, in columns, and was driven off in the old style. The only difference was, that he mixed cavalry with his infantry, and supported both with an enormous quantity of artillery." *The Dispatches . . . of Wellington . . . from 1799 to 1815,* compiled by Lieut. Colonel Gurwood (12 vols. and Index, London, 1837-1839), XII, 529. This was Wellington's one experience with Napoleon, many of whose infantry were little better trained than in 1793. Lloyd, *History of Infantry*, 188-229, is excellent.

ing that half of Wellington's men were Portuguese, the French tried to take the position by storm. They lost five generals and four times as many men as Wellington in an hour's battle. Masséna then outflanked the position, but Wellington was now inside his fortifications, which Masséna had not even suspected until he came up to them. The French were too weak to force the lines of Torres Vedras. The British and Portuguese were fed by sea. The besiegers, attempting to live from the wasted Portuguese countryside, lost a third of their men and most of their horses. On November 10, 1810, the French began to retire up the Tagus River. Wellington did not attack them. He thought, "the sure game, and that in which I am likely to lose fewest men, the most consistent with my instructions." Reinforcements would "only add to their distress, and increase the difficulties of their retreat. . . . If I should make any attack, the advantage must be very obvious before I adopt a measure which must be attended . . . by . . . losing my men by sickness."[29]

On March 11, 1811, Masséna began his final retreat from Portugal. His defeat had been due to the same factors which were to cause Napoleon's own defeat in Russia the next year: stout military resistance, guerrilla warfare, hunger, disease, and overstrained communications. In his memorandum on the Russian war, Wellington, who hated everything the Revolution stood for, saw the whole French system as one of plunder,

to render war a resource . . . and to throw the burthen upon the country which unfortunately became the seat of its operations. . . . Terror and the misery of the people in France; and the conscription, the execution of which was facilitated by the first; placed at the disposal of the government . . . the whole of the serviceable male population. . . . All that the government had to do . . . was to organize them into military bodies, arm them and have them taught the first movements of their arms and of their military exercises. They were then poured into some foreign country to live upon its resources. Their numbers stifled or overcame all local opposition. . . . Napoleon was educated in this system. . . . His object was to surprise his enemy by the rapidity of his marches, to fight a great battle, levy contributions, make peace, and return to Paris. But these objects were always attained at the expense of the utmost privations to his troops. These privations . . . relieved by plunder and its consequences, occasioned all these evils, till

[29] *Dispatches,* VI, 528, 583.

the army, however well composed originally . . . became at last a horde of banditti . . . destroying itself by its irregularities.[30]

The Opposition to Napoleon in Eastern Europe

Wellington was only one of a number of soldiers who believed that the French were not unbeatable. In Germany too, military reform had been in the air before the outbreak of the Revolution. One Austrian military reformer was the Emperor's brother, the Archduke Charles (1771-1847), who had advocated the divisional system, careers open to talents, and conscription in the 1790's. Under his leadership in 1809 the Austrian army had given a better account of itself than in any previous war of this period, but had again been defeated. The leader of the Prussian reformers was a former Hanoverian officer, Gerhard Johann Scharnhorst (1755-1813), the son of a farmer who had been a sergeant-major in the Hanoverian artillery. Scharnhorst had gone to the famous military school of Count Wilhelm of Schaumburg-Lippe, one of the first champions of the idea of a national army. Scharnhorst was the best known military writer in Germany in 1801 when he had asked the Prussians for a commission, a promotion, a patent of nobility, and a free hand in suggesting reforms for the Prussian army. He had been placed in charge of a section of the Quartermaster-General's Staff and had been allowed to form a military discussion society. This society had attracted some of the best officers in the Prussian army, men like Karl von Clausewitz and Hans von Yorck (later Count Yorck von Wartenburg, 1742-1819), who had served with the Dutch army in Africa and Java. Massenbach, another of the section chiefs of the Quartermaster-General's Staff, had proposed a special group of officers to study war plans. Its members were to be rotated to command posts at regular intervals to keep them from getting too involved in theory. None of these proposals came to much before the Prussian army was overwhelmed in 1806. Scharnhorst, who had fallen in with Blücher during the Prussian retreat, did well, and was placed in charge of a military reform commission.

The Treaty of Tilsit cut Prussia in half, forced it to support 150,000 French troops until the payment of a large indem-

<hr/>

[30] Quoted in Richard Aldington, *The Duke* (New York, 1943), 382-383. This work, Philip Guedalla, *Wellington* (London, 1931), and Sir Charles Petrie, *Wellington: A Reassessment* (London, 1956) are the most readable biographies. There is new material in the Seventh Duke's edition of *The Conversations of the First Duke of Wellington with William Chad* (London, 1956) and Antony Brett-James's reader, *Wellington at War, 1794-1815* (London, 1961).

nity, and limited the Prussian army to 42,000 men, only half its size at the accession of Frederick II. It also touched off a conservative social revolution which resulted in the end of serfdom and many other economic and social restrictions. Army careers were opened to all seventeen-year-olds by competitive examination. All but two of the cadet schools were replaced by military colleges. A new higher military school (the later *Kriegsakademie* or War College) gave selected officers a three-year course in strategy and other advanced military subjects. The treaty did not allow the Prussian army to raise a special militia, but the reformers talked about the principle of universal service and the formation of a national militia or *Landwehr*. Though they managed to build up a small illegal reserve (the total of this reserve and the army was only 65,000 men by 1812), Napoleon soon forced the Prussian king to dismiss Scharnhorst and to assign most of his collaborators to other military duties. When Napoleon invaded Russia in 1812, he took half of the Prussian army and about a fifth of the Austrian army (which had also been limited by treaty to 180,000 men) with him.[31]

Though the Russians had adopted certain elements of the French system after their defeat in 1807, the reformers' influence was comparatively weak in the Russian army. Many of the Prussian reformers fled to Russia after Napoleon forced the king of Prussia to dismiss them, but the Russians seem not to have been greatly influenced by their ideas. The Russians had fought Frederick the Great to a standstill during the Seven Years' War. Their greatest general, Alexander Suvorov (1739-1801), a veteran of that war, the Pugachev rebellion, and wars with the Turks and Poles, had done well against the French during the Second Coalition. And the Russians had been defeated, but not disgraced, during the Third Coalition. The Russian army, like the British, was a tough eighteenth-century professional force, well adapted to the rugged conditions of Eastern Europe. All foreign observers were impressed by the Cossack cavalry. The British painter, Robert Ker Porter, described them as "robust and fit for service: their horses, . . . mean in shape, and slouching in motion, . . . will travel incalculable journeys, and remain ex-

---

[31] A study of army reform in Austria and the other German states is badly needed. Material on the Prussians is very voluminous. William O. Shanahan, *Prussian Military Reforms, 1786-1813* (New York, 1945) is excellent, as is Rudolf Stadelmann, *Scharnhorst: Schicksal und Geistige Welt* (Wiesbaden, 1952).

posed to the heat or cold, day and night, without manifesting any sense of inconvenience." Their uniform, devoid of "expensive and needless ornaments is . . . the most soldierlike and serviceable dress I have met with in any country."[32]

Napoleon had first hoped to lure the Russian army into Poland. Then he had planned to destroy it in western Russia. These hopes had been frustrated by a combination of Russian indecision and their numerical inferiority (only 180,000-200,000 to more than twice that many in the Grand Army). By August 1, 1812—some five weeks after the French invasion had begun—the Russians were around Smolensk and Napoleon had given up trying to trap them. He had already lost nearly 100,000 men. The weather had been wet. The nights had been cold, the days as hot as in Spain or Egypt. Without mills to grind the little grain that had been found in Lithuania and White Russia—among the poorest agricultural regions in Europe—the men lived on boiled rye porridge. Plunderers destroy or spoil twice as much food as they eat. The Russians and the French advance guard had left little for the rear echelons. Napoleon's horses (there must have been well over 200,000 of them) had fared even worse than his men because of his violation of the old rule against campaigning before the grain had ripened. Five hundred ammunition wagons and a hundred guns had already been left behind. Part of the cavalry was dismounted. Such losses were not unusual. The French system of living off the country had always been hard on the men; in 1805 many men had begun their long march with only one pair of shoes. But Russia was poorer than Germany in both food and communications, while the French army was larger than that of 1805. When Napoleon was forced to concentrate "his army in great masses upon one single road in a manner never heard of before, and thus caused privations equally unparalleled" he was also fol-

[32] *Travelling Sketches in Russia and Sweden, 1805, 1806, 1807, 1808* (London, 1809), 162, 172. The most convenient edition of British travel accounts in Russia, with many extracts from Robert T. Wilson's famous *Narrative of Events during the Invasion of Russia and r.v.te ...ury of Travels . . .* (both London, 1860), is Peter Putnam, ed., *Seven Britons in Imperial Russia, 1698-1812* (Princeton, 1952).

Peter the Great had forced Russian nobles to serve the state for life; each estate had been required to furnish a quota of recruits for the army. Peter had been at war continuously for twenty-eight years. Russia had been as much of a "barracks state" as contemporary Prussia. During the eighteenth century the nobility had gradually been emancipated from their obligations to the state, but the peasants had not been emancipated from their obligations to the nobility. On Suvorov see W. Lyon Blease, *Suvorov* (London, 1920), and K. Osipov, *Alexander Suvorov*, trans. Edith Bone (London, 1944).

lowing the rule that "It is impossible to be too strong at the decisive point." If he had split his forces, his difficulties might have been even greater.[33]

Some critics, but not Clausewitz, have held that Napoleon should have prepared winter quarters during the middle of August, at the very onset of the usual campaigning season. After his experiences in East Prussia in 1806 the idea of wintering in Lithuania could not have been attractive. So conspicuous a failure would have disastrously shaken his prestige in Europe. Napoleon could not now revert to the old rules. He had to push on or perish. The Grand Army, now only slightly superior in numbers, brought the Russians to bay at Borodino. At the critical moment Napoleon refused to risk the Guard and failed to annihilate the Russians. Napoleon occupied Moscow, but Alexander made no move to surrender. More and more mystical, the Tsar had come to believe that God had chosen him to destroy the Anti-Christ. After more than a month of indecision, Napoleon withdrew. Prevented by the Russians from taking a new, but rather longer, route, Napoleon lost the rest of the Grand Army. Perhaps 100,000 men were taken prisoner; 400,000 died in battle or from exposure.

If . . . Alexander had agreed to a peace [Clausewitz wrote later], . . . the campaign would have ranked with those of Austerlitz, Friedland, and Wagram. But these campaigns also, if they had not led to peace, would in all probability have ended in similar catastrophes. . . . Instead of burdening himself with an interminable costly defensive war in the East, such as he had on his hand in the West, Bonaparte tried one bold stroke. . . . The destruction of his army was the stake in the game. . . . If this destruction . . . was more complete than it need have been, this fault was not in his having penetrated too far, . . . but in the late period at which the campaign opened, the sacrifice of life occasioned by his tactics, the lack of due care for . . . supply . . . and for his line of retreat, and, lastly, in his somewhat delayed march from Moscow.[34]

---

[33] Clausewitz, *On War*, 153.

[34] *Ibid.*, 620-621, 104-105. If they judge only by results, why bother with historians? Tolstoy used this campaign to illustrate man's fate in the "swarm, in which a man must inevitably follow the laws laid down for him." See the brilliant analysis of his view of history in Isaiah Berlin, *The Hedgehog and the Fox* (New York, 1953).

Perhaps 580,000 men, including reserves, crossed into Russia. No more than 30,000 were under Murat after the retreat across the Berezina. See M. G. Fry and J. P. Fox, "The Grand Army and the Invasion of Russia" (*History Today*, X, April 1960, 255, 265), and the best recent work, Eugene Tarlé, *Na-*

The remnants of the Grand Army reached the Grand Duchy of Warsaw about the middle of December. By the next spring Napoleon had gathered a quarter of a million men in eastern Germany and new levies were hurrying in from France. The Russians, as in 1807, could not bring men up from the Russian interior as rapidly as Napoleon could move men from France. They were outnumbered about two to one. The Austrians, who had struck too soon in 1809, preferred to wait. The first action had come from Yorck—an opponent of the reformers in military matters—then commanding the Prussian contingent in Courland. On December 30, 1812, he had signed a convention with the Russians, taking his troops out of the war and permitting the Russians to occupy much of East Prussia. Frederick William III repudiated Yorck, but the Russians commissioned the political leader of the reformers, Baron vom Stein, to organize the military resources of East and West Prussia. The provincial Estates then ratified Clausewitz' suggested proposals for raising a *Landwehr*. The other reformers had now rejoined the army. Scharnhorst had become a *de facto* Chief of Staff under the pretext of raising Prussian forces to assist Napoleon. The East Prussian revolt had been something like the local revolts in Spain. French exactions had made Napoleon more unpopular with the nobles and peasants than all of the German nationalist propagandists.

The French garrison commander, fearful of a general Prussian uprising, had evacuated Berlin, isolating the French in Poland and assisting the concentration of other Prussian forces before Frederick William declared war on France on March 16, 1813. The next day he appealed for a war of national liberation and announced a national *Landwehr*, with the quotas to be filled first by volunteers and then by lot from men seventeen to forty. These men were without training or equipment, but the Prussian regulars—though only a third as numerous as in 1806—might tip the balance in favor of the Russians. Political considerations forced Napoleon to try to recover eastern Germany; the princes of his Confederation

poleon's Invasion of Russia, 1812, trans. G. M. (London, 1942), 40. The classics are Clausewitz, *The Campaign of 1812 in Russia* (London, 1843), Count Phillipe-Paul de Ségur, *Napoleon's Russian Campaign,* trans. J. David Townsend, intro. William L. Langer (Boston, 1958), and Armand de Caulaincourt, *With Napoleon in Russia,* ed. Jean Hanoteau, abr. ed. with intro. George Libaire (New York, 1935). Logistics is discussed by Intendant-General Mazars, "L'Administration impériale: la campagne de Russie" (*Révue historique de l'Armée,* Oct.-Dec., 1947, 32-52).

of the Rhine were wavering. He won two battles, but his numerically superior but inexperienced forces could not win another Jena. He then signed an armistice, an action which Jomini felt and Napoleon himself later concluded was one of his worst blunders. His enemies were then worse off than the French. During the next two months the British sent large subsidies to Prussia and Russia, and Sweden joined the coalition. After news of the defeat of the French army in Spain, Austria offered to mediate on terms which would have meant the end of the Confederation of the Rhine and the Continental System. Napoleon refused these terms and Austria joined the allies. Meanwhile British supplies had equipped the Prussian conscripts. When the armistice expired the Prussian field army was twice as large as it had been in the spring, the Austrians and Russians had been concentrated and reinforced, and the French were slightly outnumbered. Partly to encourage his wavering German allies, Napoleon made his stand in Saxony, east of the line reached by the American First Army in the Second World War. Here he threatened each of the three allied armies, but he was far from France and close to the Prussian, Russian, and Austrian bases. He had the advantage of interior lines, but his position became a trap when he failed to annihilate the enemy. He was finally defeated in the three-day battle of Leipzig, just seven years after Jena. Perhaps seventy thousand men returned to France; for the second summer in succession Napoleon had lost an entire army.[35]

The allies made mistakes, but not the supreme mistake of giving Napoleon a winter to recuperate. Half a million men invaded France. Napoleon called up conscripts by the hundreds of thousands, but his administrators could deliver no more than 125,000. He did not have time to train the ones who had been caught, even by the low standards of Napoleonic warfare. His reserve weapons were locked up in fortresses on the Elbe or the Vistula. The new conscripts got muskets with barrels that burst, with touch-holes that were poorly bored, or triggers that failed to work. There were still many able-bodied men in France, but the French people watched the Corsican's veterans go down as apathetically as the Prussians had watched the rout of their army after Jena.

[35] Napoleon had won a major battle at Dresden, only to have it canceled by disasters to isolated columns. Each of three allied armies (defending Bohemia, Silesia, and Berlin) had been directed to avoid battle with Napoleon himself, but to act vigorously against his subordinates.

When the allies entered Paris at the end of March, 1814, they could not find out whether the people were monarchist or republican. Historians of this last campaign in France have pointed out that none of the allied generals was a match for Napoleon. But they were not afraid of him and they knew most of his tricks. This time the allies had not made the mistake of surrounding France with "a girdle of armies, while fifty different small objects are aimed at, not one of which has the power to overcome inertia, friction, and extraneous influences, which everywhere, but more especially in allied armies, are generated and forever born anew." Napoleon was exiled to Elba in April, 1814. His return to the throne and defeat at Waterloo the next year were anticlimactic. There remained only the ideals of the Revolution that the revolutionaries had betrayed and striking examples of the adventurer's military genius. What Liddell Hart has so well termed "The Ghost of Napoleon" was to prove more real than his ephemeral Empire.[36]

The German War of Liberation gave rise to many legends, among them the Liberal one that the entire victory had been due to the *Landwehr*. It was supported by such tales as that of an incident at Leipzig where a *Landwehr* battalion under a Prussian civil servant had carried a position which the regulars had refused to assault. As always, many conscripts had come unwillingly. Some had run at the first encounter. The rest had learned to march by marching and to fight by fighting. The Prussian corps which had taken the field in the Leipzig campaign had been one-third regular, one-third reservist, and one-third *Landwehr*. As Prussian Minister of War, Boyen, one of the reformers, had drafted the conscription law which remained the basis of Prussian recruiting for the rest of the century. This law was in some ways more democratic than the French recruiting law of 1818. "Monarchial Prussia, with its feudal landowners and its social hierarchy, emerged with a method of recruitment more in accord with the spirit of the new century than that of Revolutionary France. This was a decisive factor in the history of the nineteenth century."

[36] Clausewitz, *On War*, 631. Recent fine works on Waterloo are John Naylor, *Waterloo* (New York, 1960) and Henry Lachouque, *Le Secrete de Waterloo* (Paris, 1952). See also the latter's *The Anatomy of Glory: Napoleon and his Guard*, adapted Anne S. K. Brown, (Providence, 1961), and biographies of Wellington's cavalry leaders, Antony Brett-James, *General Graham: Lord Lynedoch* (New York, 1959) and The Marquess of Anglesey, *One-Leg: The Life and Letters of Henry Wililam Paget, 1st Marquess of Anglesey, 1768-1854* (London, 1961).

Estimates of the casualties of this Great War still vary widely. Military dead have been put at two million. Estimates of civilian casualties from disease and guerrilla warfare range from two to eight million. It is thus impossible to evaluate the claim that the new system of an all-out offensive for a quick victory was somewhat less expensive than the more careful methods of the neoclassical age. But if what happened is no more important than what people thought had happened, there is no denying that many Europeans were now convinced that the ideas of the revolutionaries had led only to untold bloodshed and suffering.[37]

[37] Godefroy de Cavaignac, *La Formation de la Prusse contemporaine* (2 vols., Paris, 1891-1898), II, 402. See also Walter M. Simon, *The Failure of the Prussian Reform Movement, 1807-1819* (Ithaca, 1955).

There are wide differences in the casualty estimates, particularly for those who died of their wounds or disease. With a few notable exceptions, Napoleon's medical personnel were very poor. Hospitals and ambulances, like everything else under the new system, were improvised. Napoleon did not wish to endanger civilian morale by allowing the wounded to return to France. Jean Lagorgette, *Le Rôle de la guerre: étude de sociologie générale* (Paris, 1906), 571-572; A. Meynier, *Une Erreur historique: Les morts de la Grand Armée et des armées ennemies* (Paris, 1934).

"The whole post-Napoleonic generation lay under the shadow of a great disillusionment." Frederick B. Artz, *Reaction and Revolution, 1814-1832* (New York, 1934), 49. For the conservative philosopher Joseph de Maistre's views on war see L. Lederer, ed., *Joseph de Maistre* (Paris, 1949).

THE INDUSTRIAL REVOLUTION AND WAR

Chapter 5

The First Half of the Nineteenth Century (1815-1853)

Britain and the Long Peace

THE CENTURY after the fall of Napoleon now looks like the golden century of Western European civilization, the most peaceful since the emergence of the modern state. This comparative peace was at least partly due to the treaties of 1815, which restored the balance of power and seemed to settle the main diplomatic problems of the eighteenth century. Many people were dissatisfied with the peace treaties, but these dissatisfied elements were not in places of power. The ruling classes were rightly obsessed with the problems of maintaining domestic order. Any sovereign who might wish to upset things could usually be brought to reason by reminding him of the horrors of war and the connection between war and revolution. The great powers now held fairly regular international conferences, the "Concert of Europe" which lasted in some respects until 1914. These conferences could not prevent a great power from defying the others in areas where the others could not intervene effectively, but there was no major war for forty years, a longer period of peace than neoclassical statesmanship had ever managed to secure. Because each state tended to tailor its army to its domestic situation and to its particular problem of internal security, it is difficult to follow common threads of military policy in this period. Additional complications were introduced by the uneven spread of the Industrial Revolution and differing interpretations of the possible effects of the new weapons of the Industrial Revolution on warfare. Still others were presented by varying interpretations of the lessons of the Napoleonic wars and varying answers to the host of political and military problems presented by conscription.[1]

[1] Each post-war generation examines Metternich's system. See Henry A. Kissinger, *A World Restored: Metternich, Castlereagh and the Problems of Peace, 1812-22* (Boston, 1957). Though Dr. Kissinger has dealt with current military problems, he pays little attention to military problems in this work and none to those of the army and internal security. Next to nothing has been done on this aspect of a neglected period in military history. The only synthesis is Alessio Chapperon, *L'Organica militare fra le due guerre mondiale, 1814-1914* (Rome, 1921).

The British army hardly faced these problems at all for many years, though British statesmen were vitally concerned with the Low Countries, a future passage to India through the Mediterranean, and a balance of power stable enough to allow everyone to demobilize and to lift the crushing burden of taxation. The navy remained the first line of British defense. The Netherlands and Spain were no longer naval powers, and the French navy did not recover from its defeats for a generation. The Russian fleet was now third, but the danger of a Franco-Russian alliance against Britain remained remote during most of this period. Britain grew rapidly in wealth and population during this phase of the Industrial Revolution. Her population increased from nineteen to twenty-eight millions in the quarter century from 1815 to 1840. The United States had the world's second largest merchant marine, but no battle fleet. There were only 7600 men in the United States navy in 1861 to 77,000 for the British. During the change from sail to steam the French navy threatened to catch up with the British, but that threat vanished with the French defeat in the Franco-Prussian War of 1870-1871. Until the middle eighties the British navy was usually as large as all the other navies of the world together.[2]

From the days of Castlereagh to those of Disraeli British naval supremacy was thus a reasonably constant factor in international relations. The technological changes in naval warfare will be discussed later. For the moment it is only necessary to note: (1) that the Industrial Revolution affected navies before it affected armies, (2) that the rise of private warship building yards gave the doctrine of British naval supremacy additional support in both Parliament and public opinion, and (3) that the navy was more closely connected with the middle classes than the army and thus with what were to become the main currents of nineteenth-century British life. Britain's chief territorial gains during the French Revolutionary wars had been naval bases—Malta, Ceylon,

---

[2] One puzzling problem is that of the so-called *Pax Britannica*. To what extent was the peaceful character of the nineteenth century due to British policy? One distinguished historian has commented privately, "I think that the *Pax Britannica* is a myth foisted on us by naval historians. Peace was kept until 1854 by a consensus of the Powers, which led them to show restraint and to observe treaties." Albert H. Imlah, *Economic Elements in the Pax Britannica: Studies in British Foreign Trade in the Nineteenth Century* (Cambridge, Mass., 1958) approaches the problem. Christopher Lloyd, *Short History of the Royal Navy, 1805 to 1918* (3d ed., London, 1946) is very short. There is much material in John Henry Briggs, *Naval Administrations, 1827 to 1892* (London, 1897).

and the Cape of Good Hope were the most important. As her commercial and colonial interests extended she took over other bases and trading stations—such as Aden, the Falkland Islands, and Hong Kong—and took the lead in the international effort to stamp out the slave trade and piracy. Nobody would claim that British policy was wholly altruistic, but Britain's overwhelming sea power was used to promote rather than to hinder the development of international trade. And, as Adam Smith had predicted, international trade did benefit all parties.[3]

The British army increased from 120,000 men in the 1820's to 140,000 before the Crimean War. This was a bit more than double the army of the late eighteenth century, but still small by Continental standards. It "grew" to about 200,000 with the acquisition of various East India Company units after the Mutiny, and remained around that figure until 1939. The regular army did not keep pace with the growth in Britain's population. Britain had acquired numerous new non-European colonies and, still more important, Continental armies had grown more rapidly than their total populations. Most garrisons were withdrawn from the older self-governing British colonies during the Cardwell reforms of the 1870's. This change and better transportation enabled Cardwell to introduce a "short" six-year term of enlistment and a "linked-battalion" system which provided regular reliefs for troops on foreign service. As a result of these trends the British home army became a recruiting and training force for the units abroad. As Wellington had noted in his last speech in the House of Lords, the home army was barely large enough "to relieve the sentries on duty in different parts of the world." Parliament continued to look on standing armies as necessary evils and the middle classes showed little interest in military life. This left the army to the country gentry and the farm laborers at the very time when these two classes were becoming less important in British national life. Until the Cardwell

[3] There is little on the process by which the Liberals encouraged the growth of private arms manufacturing. The Admiralty dockyards were hard hit by the Industrial Revolution, which had made both their equipment and their methods obsolete. There are few studies of the influence of the arms trade on Parliament during this period. Most later studies rehash Richard Cobden's famous *Three Panics* (London, 1862). Christopher Lloyd, *The Nation and the Navy* (London, 1954) is a fine study of the place of the navy in the national life. On the slave trade see the same author's *The Navy and the Slave Trade* (London, 1949). Few other reforms affected as many people or cost the British as many lives and as much money, or brought the British as little thanks and profit.

reforms officers still purchased their commissions, and usually spent about two-thirds of their army careers abroad. They looked after their men and took pride in spit-and-polish, but they had little time or inclination for serious military study. Their sturdy political conservatism was matched by an equally sturdy hostility to military innovations. Instead of being among the first, the British army was among the last to adopt some of the new techniques of industrialized war.[4]

Men enlisted for the uniform and bounty. At fifteen shillings a head, recruiters were interested only in getting the men past the physical examination. Most of the recruits were countrymen. They were whipped into shape in the good old way, fed boiled beef and salt pork, and shipped to the colonies. Each man now had a bed to himself instead of sleeping four in a crib, but British army sanitation was not much better than it had been during the eighteenth century. The disease rate in the London garrison was higher than that in the London tenements. The later Victorians liked to read about their army's imperial exploits, but showed little interest in increasing its numbers. Its greatest weakness was the lack of a large trained reserve. Increasing numbers of Continental reservists were conscripted and trained with the regulars. The British militia and volunteers were volunteer week-end and summer soldiers. The British public was still confident that troops could be improvised after war had broken out. The public got what it wanted: naval supremacy and a good colonial army at relatively low cost. That army pacified India and carried on "small wars" to protect the advance of white settlement. By the 1870's Britain had neglected her land power until she had little to offer but good advice on major Continental issues. This reinforced the doctrine of "splendid isolation" and a "Blue Water" view of British strategy. The

---

[4] See Raymond Aron, *War and Industrial Society*, trans. Mary Bottomore (London, 1958). The regiment was still "a little close society—a kind of military congregation." Purchase was "illogical, iniquitous, and indefensible," but it saved the nation the cost of a real pension system and the officers accepted it. Fortescue, *British Army*, XIII, 576. See Arvel B. Ericĸson, "Abolition of Purchase in the British Army," (*Military Affairs*, XXIII, Summer, 1959, 65-76). The Minié rifle, based on two British inventions, was perfected in France. Wellington (then over eighty) remarked that he did not wᵢsh to call it a rifle because the whole infantry might wish to wear green. Lord Wolseley was one of the most influential British soldiers of the late Victorian era. See his *Story of a Soldier's Life* (2 vols., London, 1903) and Sir Frederick Maurice and Sir George Arthur, *The Life of Lord Wolseley* (London, 1924).

Blue Water school's idea that large British armies ought never be sent to the Continent again made a virtue of necessity.[5]

Austria, Russia and France

Metternich's Austria—with thirty million people to twelve million for Prussia—was the bulwark of the Conservative system in Central Europe. The principle of universal liability to service had been established in Austria, but the Hapsburg army remained very conservative. Everything was complicated by the problem of nationalism, and Austrian units were normally stationed far from their home provinces, Czechs in Hungary, Poles in Italy, etc. This policy proved its worth in 1848, when the army saved the Empire, but made the Austrian mobilization system—with reservists traveling across the Empire to join their units — correspondingly cumbersome. Marshal Joseph Radetsky, the hero of the Italian campaign of 1849, did not retire from the high command until he was ninety-one. Ludwig von Benedek, who was to face the Prussians in 1866, was an able officer of the old school, who emphasized physical training and bayonet tactics rather than fire power, and had little faith in the "complicated combinations" of modern staff work.[6]

Russia, with forty million people, was potentially a greater military power than Austria, but her position was weakened by her economic backwardness and the perennial Polish prob-

[5] Russell Grenfell, *Sea Power* (Garden City, 1941) is a modern Blue Water work. The British escaped the "blood tax" of conscription and may have spent less of their national income on armaments than the Continental powers. See the optimistic estimates by Michael Mulhall, *Industries and Wealth of Nations* (London, 1896), 105. The great possibilities for a re-examination of Indian military history can be seen in such diverse works as Philip Woodruff, *The Men Who Ruled India* (2 vols., London, 1954-1955), the novelist John Masters' memoirs of this century, *Bugles and a Tiger* (London, 1956) and *The Road Past Mandalay* (London, 1961), M. Malgonkar's novel of the new army, *Distant Drum* (London, 1961), and, for colonial warfare in general, H. Moyse-Bartlett, *The King's African Rifles* (Aldershot, 1956). On the Mutiny see General Richard Hilton, *The Indian Mutiny: A Centenary History* (London, 1957) and the fascinating official study by Surendra Nath Sen, *Eighteen Fifty-Seven* (Delhi, 1957).

[6] There is almost nothing in English on the Austrian army, the Italian campaign of 1849, and the bloody war in Hungary. John Presland [Gladys Skelton], *Vae Victis: The Life of Ludwig von Benedek* (New York, 1934), is good. W. E. Mosse, *The European Powers and the German Question, 1848-71* (Cambridge, 1958) fails to deal with the Prussian military revolution. All studies of the Austrian army must start with Nikolaus von Preradovich, *Die Führungsschichten in Österreich und Preussen (1804-1918), mit einem Ausblick bis zum Jahre 1945* (Wiesbaden, 1955), and Oskar Regele, *Feldmarschall Radetsky: Leben, Leistung, Erbe* (Vienna, 1957).

lem. Though Alexander I became increasingly conservative in military matters, a few officers, who had been in contact with Western armies, continued to work to improve the lot of the Russian common soldier. Some of them organized societies to discuss the new ideas; the Society of Salvation, for example, met under the colonel of one of the regiments of the guard. After these societies had been dissolved because of their suspected Liberalism, a few of their more radical members tried to continue their work underground. When Alexander I died in 1825, one of these underground groups touched off the Decembrist revolt. Its failure marked the end of the Russian military reform movement. Alexander's successor, Nicholas I, was both politically and militarily conservative.[7]

France, with thirty million people, was still the strongest single power in Europe, though she was hemmed in by buffer states on the north and east and the Quadruple Alliance against her remained nominally in force for twenty years. Conscription had been one of the most unpopular of the Revolutionary reforms. The constitution of 1814 specifically abolished it. Conservatives talked of returning to a volunteer army with officers chosen from the nobility. But conscription was too useful. In 1818 the Napoleonic system was restored under another name. Men twenty years old drew lots and those with the "bad numbers" filled the quotas which had not been filled by volunteers. Both volunteers and conscripts served from six to eight years in the army (the terms of service were changed in 1824 and 1832) and the same period in the reserves. The army of Napoleon III's Second Empire was very much like that of Napoleon I. It was a long service pro-

[7] One of Alexander's military experiments was the establishment of military colonies in frontier areas. The idea of settling soldiers on the land was a common one. It would save money and improve morale, since the men would have their families with them. Even the children in these villages wore uniforms. Some recent historians have suggested that Alexander was deliberately trying to divorce the army from the nobility. In any case, these colonies, like the somewhat similar French military colonies in Algeria, were a failure.

"Military service in those times was terrible. A man was required to serve twenty-five years, . . . and the life of a soldier was hard in the extreme. . . . A gloomy terror used to spread through our house when . . . one of the servants was to be sent to the recruiting boards. The man was chained and placed under guard in the office, to prevent suicide. . . . His mother and his other female relatives began to sing out their lamentations . . . exactly in the same way in which they sang their lamentations at burial, and with the same words." Peter Kropotkin, *Memoirs of a Revolutionist* (Boston, 1899), 54-55. A fine short survey is John Shelton Curtiss, "The Army of Nicholas I: Its Role and Character" (*The American Historical Review,* LXIII, July, 1958, 880-889).

fessional army (an *armée de métier*) using conscription to fill the gaps left by volunteering. The landlords and middle classes who controlled parliament were either exempt or could purchase substitutes. Napoleon III regularized the collection of "blood money" by setting a fixed charge for commutations and using the proceeds to offer bounties for reenlistment. Since many city workers were medically unfit, the burden of service still fell largely on the peasants.[8]

Napoleon and his marshals had all been "practical" soldiers, trained in the same hard school of revolution and war. The marshals—Soult, Marmont, St. Cyr, Gérard, Mortier—dominated the French army, as Wellington dominated the British, after Napoleon's fall and, with Bonapartist propagandists, passed on the Napoleonic legend. Under these conditions there was little informed criticism of Napoleon I and very little interest in military theory. The campaigns in the new French colonial empire and their victories over Russia and Austria in the 1850's confirmed the French generals in their complacency, their distrust of military theory, and their faith in the *armée de métier*. Marshal MacMahon supposedly said that he would not promote any officer who had written a book, and Colonel Ardant du Picq was not anxious to publish his *Studies on Combat* during his lifetime.[9]

A French officer, or an officer in any army but the Prussian, who took up the study of military theory during the first

[8] There had been fewer difficulties with demobilization in France than in Spain and Italy, where disgruntled former officers had played a major part in the revolutionary movements of 1820 and 1830. The Spanish army now had one officer for every half-dozen men. See the suggestions in Gerald Brenan, *The Spanish Labyrinth* (New York, 1943), and A. Ramos Oliviera, *Politics, Economics, and Men of Modern Spain, 1808-1946* (London, 1946).

On the French army see Alfred Vigny's famous *The Military Necessity* (New York, 1953), P. Chalmin, *L'Officier français de 1815 à 1870* (Paris, 1956), Jean Vidalenc, *Les Demi-soldes: Étude d'une catégorie sociale* (Paris, 1955), and Brison D. Gooch, *The New Bonapartist Generals in the Crimean War* (The Hague, 1960).

[9] [Auguste] Marmont's *On Modern Armies*, trans. Captain Lendy (London, 1865) was much used at the time. See L. Nachin, ed., *Marmont* (Paris, 1938). [Thomas Robert] Bugeaud—who seems to have been a very able military thinker—was chiefly concerned with colonial warfare. The best collection from his writings is *Par l'épée et par la charrue*, ed. Paul Azan (Paris, 1938). See the fascinating article by Georges Bourgin, "Bugeaud social en Afrique" (*Révue historique de l'Armée*, April-June, 1948, 38-50).

The French had first tried to fight the Arabs with Napoleonic heavy columns and artillery. Finally, they imitated the Arabs with special light units of Zouaves and Spahis. These units reintroduced an Arab motif into western military dress. A number of units set out for the American Civil War in Turkish pants and turbans. Both sides used a French uniform, even to the characteristic flat hat or kepi. A witty book on military costume is James Laver, *British Military Uniforms* (Harmondsworth, 1943).

half of the nineteenth century, usually began with Jomini (1779-1869) whose life nearly spanned the century from Bonaparte's birth to the crash of his nephew's Second Empire. A year older than Clausewitz, Jomini had been working in a Paris bank when Bonaparte first burst on the world. Jomini read the bulletins of Bonaparte's victories and then turned to military theory himself in the hope of discovering "the fundamental principles, . . . independent of the kind of weapons, of historical time, and of place" on which these victories rested. He volunteered for the French army, served as an aid to the puppet Swiss minister of war, and went back to accounting in 1801 while he completed the manuscript which, he hoped, would show that Bonaparte's and Frederick's victories had been based on

one great principle, . . . embraced in the following maxims: 1. To throw . . . the mass of an army, successively, upon the decisive points of a theatre of war, and also upon the communications of the enemy as much as possible without compromising one's own. 2. To manoeuvre to engage fractions of the hostile army with the bulk of one's forces. 3. On the battlefield, to throw the mass of the forces upon the decisive point. . . . 4. . . . at the proper times and with ample energy. . . . It may be laid down as a general principle that the decisive points . . . are on that flank of the enemy . . . upon which . . . he can . . . more easily [be] . . . cut off from his bases. . . . If the enemy's forces are . . . too much extended the decisive point is his center, for by piercing that his forces will be more divided, their weakness increased, and the fractions crushed separately.[10]

Jomini finally took his manuscript to Ney, who allowed him to draft his daily orders of march. Jomini took Ney's report on the 1805 campaign to Napoleon's headquarters and included a copy of his own work. Napoleon found time to read it and appointed Jomini to his own staff. Friction with Napoleon's chief staff officer, Berthier, who had little use for this amateur, finally led Jomini to join the Russians during the armistice of 1813. He was a Russian general for the next fifty-six years, though he spent much of his time in the Paris suburb of Passy, where he held a kind of military salon and turned out quantities of military literature. It is easy to see how Jomini, rather than Clausewitz, became the first high

10 Art of War, 39-41, 67-73. This work was Traité des grands operations militaires (8 vols., Paris, 1804-1816). The best biography is Xavier de Courville, Jomini, ou le devin de Napoléon (Paris, 1935).

priest of the Napoleonic legend. He had known the last of the Great Captains. He was a clear and prolific writer, whose maxims and geometrical illustrations appealed to soldiers who were familiar with similar works by other military writers. And he lived nearly forty years longer than Clausewitz. Jomini's definitions and much of his terminology are still used by military theorists. His emphasis on mobility and concentration had seized the secret of Napoleonic strategy. It was not Jomini's fault that his doctrines were oversystematized by some of his followers.

Jomini's analysis of the Russian campaign is actually quite similar to the summaries of Wellington and Clausewitz. The differences are in style and outlook. Wellington, with an eye to the care of horses and men, is the old campaigner. The philosopher Clausewitz stresses the intangibles of leadership and politics. Jomini's account displays the successful teacher's tendency to oversimplification.

Although so ruinous to Napoleon, . . . he had neglected no humanly possible precaution in order to base himself safely. . . . If Napoleon erred in this contest, it was in neglecting diplomatic precautions; in not uniting . . . the different bodies of troops on the Dwina and Dnieper; in remaining ten days too long at Wilna; in giving the command of his right to his brother, who was unequal to it; and in confiding to Prince Schwarzenberg a duty which that general could not perform with the devotedness of a Frenchman. I do not speak now of his error in remaining in Moscow after the conflagration since there was no remedy for the misfortune, although it would not have been so great if the retreat had taken place immediately. . . . It is doubtless true that Napoleon neglected too much the resentment of Austria, Prussia, and Sweden and counted too surely upon a *dénouement* between Wilna and the Dwina. Although he fully appreciated the bravery of the Russian armies, he did not realize the spirit and energy of the people. . . . The only maxim to be given is "never to attempt [such enterprises] without having secured the hearty and constant alliance of a respectable power near enough . . . to afford a proper base. . . ." The safety of deep lines of operations and the establishment of eventual bases give all the military means of lessening the danger.[11]

11 *The Art of War*, 96-97. Col. Eugène Carrias believes that it "is wholly erroneous to consider him [Jomini] as the theorist of the Napoleonic method. He confined himself to defining it and personally preferred the Frederician doctrine." *La Pensée militaire allemande* (Paris, 1948), 222. Jomini had remarked that he preferred "the good old times when the French and English Guards courteously invited each other to fire first . . . to the frightful epoch when priests, women, and children throughout Spain plotted the murder of

After Prussia's victory over Austria in 1866, Napoleon III tried to increase and rejuvenate the French army, but he was years too late. His critics held that if the French army was as good as it had always claimed that it was, there was no cause for alarm. The French generals did not want a short service army of the Prussian type. They wanted a still longer term of service for the *armée de métier*, nine years in place of seven. The middle classes did not wish to give up their right to purchase substitutes. The republicans saw no reason to vote more arms for a declining dictatorship. They were also the victims of their legend of the wars of the First Republic. They believed that the *levée en masse* would repel any invasion. Napoleon III had just "liberalized" his government. He could not defy the parliament he had established without touching off a revolution. Finally the term of service in the French army was reduced to five years (instead of the Prussian three), and a National Guard was to be formed of those who had drawn the good numbers. But this National Guard was never allowed to train. The government feared that such a measure might increase popular discontent and give arms to the republicans. So the French army entered the war with Prussia with practically no trained reserve. Once the *armée de métier* had been defeated and captured, there remained only the untrained masses.[12]

Prussia

Prussia was still the weakest of the great powers. Her need for Austrian support against France on the Rhine tied her, in Clausewitz' opinion, tightly into Metternich's diplomatic system. The reformers who had planned Prussia's military recovery after Jena were not all squeezed out of the army by

isolated soldiers." *Art of War,* 52. The standard full-scale history is Rudolf von Caemmerer, *The Development of Strategical Science during the Nineteenth Century,* trans. Karl von Donat (London, 1905). See also René Pichené, *Histoire de la tactique et de la stratégie jusqu'à la guerre mondiale* (Paris, 1957).

12 Most of the great French historians of this era—Mignet, Thiers, Tocqueville, Taine, and Michelet—concentrated on the Revolution. It was not until 1867 that Lanfrey began to dissect the Napoleonic legend. The French army was little affected by the Prussian intellectual revolution. See the criticisms of General Louis J. Trochu, *L'armée française en 1867* (Paris, 1867); Dallas D. Irvine, "The Origin of Capital Staffs" (*Journal of Modern History,* X, June, 1938, 161-179); Gordon Wright, "Public Opinion and Conscription in France, 1866-1870" (*Journal of Modern History,* XIV, March, 1942, 26-45); and Lynn M. Case, *French Opinion on War and Diplomacy during the Second Empire* (Philadelphia, 1954). Napoleon III was well informed about the Prussian army. See the famous reports of Baron Stoffel, his military attaché in Berlin, *Rapports militaires écrits de Berlin, 1866-1870* (Paris, 1871).

the "practical" soldiers after 1815. Though few of them attained high positions during the conservative reaction, most of the distinguishing features of the Prussian army of the 1860's—"short service" conscription, the General Staff, and a comparatively wide interest in military education and military theory—were legacies of Scharnhorst and the other reformers of the late Napoleonic period. Boyen's law had set the term of regular army service at three years (two years after 1834), plus two years in the army reserve, and additional service in the militia or *Landwehr*. The *Landwehr* officers were selected from "one year volunteers." These were members of the bourgeoisie or Junker classes with certain educational qualifications. They served only one year in the regular army, but paid for their own arms and equipment. The *Landwehr* was thus a separate force with a separate organization. But, unlike Napoleon III's abortive National Guard and the Anglo-American militia, service in the *Landwehr* was compulsory and all of its members had passed through the regular army.

Landwehr units were to be brigaded in wartime—as in the French army of 1792 or the Prussian army of 1813—with regulars. In this way, Boyen believed, the regulars' efficiency might be combined with the national spirit of a militia.

The old school places all its trust in the standing army, though on occasion it has to be complemented by a *levée en masse*. . . . The modern school believes, on the contrary, that the country cannot be defended by a standing army alone, if only because of the expense which its upkeep imposes on the country. Because of this it is necessary to have a numerous reserve, which ought to be given serious training and not be regarded as entirely subsidiary to the regulars. . . . The old school believes that arbitrary authority and discipline alone make soldiers, the new school that it is necessary for the army to follow changing civilian custom. . . . The old school wishes to consider military questions without the participation of the public; the new school holds that the defense of the state is impossible without the material and moral cooperation of the entire nation.[13]

This organization met its first real test during the revolution of 1848. Some *Landwehr* units sided with the Liberals; many of them failed to mobilize rapidly enough during the war scares of 1850 and 1859. The result was another army reform movement led by the Prince Regent (later King) Wil-

13 Quoted in Carrias, *Pensée militaire allemande*, 169-170.

liam. This reorganization—from 1857 to the middle 1860's—
(1) doubled the Prussian field army, (2) decapitated the
Landwehr, and (3) after the reorganized army's victories in
1864, 1866, and 1870-1871 overcame the increasingly routine parliamentary opposition to these changes. William first
tried to increase the annual number of conscripts, which had
remained the same since 1816 though the number of eligible
young men had nearly doubled. The legal obligation to serve
was still universal but, as in France, the men with the bad
numbers—40,000 out of 150,000 eligible by the 1850's—
bore the whole burden. William wished to increase the annual
number of conscripts to 63,000 and to make them liable to
three years of active and four years of army reserve (instead
of two and two) duty. The *Landwehr*, shorn of its youngest
men (its first three classes) would no longer take the field
with the regulars, but would be used for second-line duties.
These proposals satisfied neither the extreme Conservatives
nor the Liberals. Three-year service was still too short for the
partisans of an *armée de métier*. And half the field army
would still consist of reservists, though these were now incorporated in regular units instead of being brigaded with them.
The Liberals objected to the relegation of the *Landwehr* to
the second line, to the purge of Liberal *Landwehr* officers,
and to the methods by which the reforms were eventually
carried out without giving Parliament a greater rôle in the
government.[14]

One major military objection to the Prussian system—in
both its old and new versions—was the difficulty of mobilization. An *armée de métier* was supposedly ready to move at
any time; its relatively few reservists joined their units either
en route or at the front. But half the Prussian field army were

[14] Even with the quota set at 63,000, more than half of each year's class still
escaped conscription. Like the French system of 1793, this was not universal
military service, but it was a longer step toward such a system than had been
taken by any other great power at that time. The constitutional conflict turned
on the King's power to raise money to train this larger number of conscripts.
The King held that his constitutional control over the army included the right
to raise money to support an army equivalent to the increase in Prussia's population since 1814. Parliament hoped to force the King to grant responsible
government by withholding funds from the army. William eventually accepted
Bismarck's argument that, in the case of a deadlock between King and Parliament, he could spend the money anyway. Eugene N. Anderson, *The Social
and Political Conflict in Prussia, 1856-1864* (Lincoln, 1954), is about the only
work in English. Gerhard Ritter's superb *Staatskunst und Kriegshandwerk:
Das Problem des "Militarismus" in Deutschland* (2 vols., Munich, 1954-1960)
now covers the period 1740-1914. See also Reinhard Höhn, *Verfassungskampf
und Heereseid: Der Kampf des Bürgertums um das Heer (1815-1850)* (Leipzig, 1938).

civilians; it could not begin to move until they had come in. With territories stretching from Russia to the Rhine, the Prussian army had to be prepared to face any one of three great powers. In peacetime it was not stationed on the frontiers but spread throughout the country. All units were raised and mobilized on a territorial basis, drawing their recruits and reserves from the districts in which they were usually stationed. In theory the new Prussian army sacrificed mobility for mass, the exact opposite of the old army of Frederick the Great. In practice, however, the Prussian General Staff overcame these handicaps so well that Prussia had the advantages of both mass and mobility.

Since the time of Gustavus Adolphus staff officers had been primarily administrative assistants to the commander-in-chief. Graduates of the French staff officers school of 1818, for example, remained in administrative posts for the rest of their army careers. The significant features of the Prussian staff system—all of which went back to the days of Scharnhorst—were (1) the General Staff's quasi-autonomy within the much larger War Ministry, (2) its particular attention to military theory, doctrine, and what can be called postgraduate education for older officers, and (3) the rotation of General Staff officers between the Great General Staff (*Grosser Generalstab*) and positions with the field forces (*Truppengeneralstab*). Entrance to the War College was by competitive examination. Its graduates (at the end of the nineteenth century around a third of the 150 who had been admitted) were then assigned to the Great General Staff for two years further experience in topographical work, map exercises, and war games. After they had participated in the annual staff ride under the personal supervision of the Chief of the General Staff, three or four candidates were made permanent members of the General Staff. (Even when serving in command positions, they were allowed to wear the red trouser stripes of the General Staff.) The others broadcast the General Staff's doctrines, since officers who had completed the War College and General Staff training were usually given better assignments and more rapid promotion. By 1870 most of the higher Prussian officers had been trained in this fashion.[15]

15 The General Staff and the Military Cabinet, which handled personnel matters, became administratively independent of the War Ministry in 1883. There was no Imperial War Minister after 1871, only a Prussian War Minister. In 1821 there were fifty-six officers in the Great General Staff and its attached bureaus, forty-seven officers were with the field forces, and six were attachés

The staff officers of other armies can be compared to skilled carpenters, working for builders who were still guided by the traditional rules of thumb. The Chief of the Prussian General Staff can be compared to an architect, divorced from the day-to-day problems of plumbing and carpentry, though he was supposed to be thoroughly familiar with them. The Prussian King (the client) gave the contractor (the War Minister) freedom to carry out the architect's plans and held him responsible for their execution. But the architect stood ready to help the builder if the latter had trouble with the blueprints. A staff officer serving with the troops can be compared with the architect's young assistant, or even to a French Revolutionary deputy on mission. He was supposed to be familiar with the Great General Staff's ideas and plans and was to make them clear to the field commander. The field commander, who had usually been trained in the War College, could generally see what his chief of staff was talking about. When the field commander issued an order, his chief of staff worked out the details so that they fitted into the general plan.

There have been two major criticisms of this system. One is the tendency of the General Staff to form an elite—a caste within a caste—a tendency which Scharnhorst had hoped to check by his insistence on rotating staff officers to other duties. The other was the potential division between planning and execution. The 1883 system of a separate War Ministry and General Staff, it must be remembered, was the work of staunch monarchists. A Hohenzollern monarch, by tradition, had to be a Supreme Warlord. The system, perhaps accidentally, was evolved to serve the three unmilitary kings (1786-1861) who happened to follow Frederick William I and Frederick II (1713-1786). Suitable variants have proved just as useful to representative governments in which the heads of the armed services are traditionally civilians. The Prussian system worked well at this time because of the personalities of the King, his War Minister, and the Chief of the General Staff. Sixty-one when he became Prince Regent, William I had spent most of his life in the army. William knew enough about military matters to make intelligent decisions. He was willing, as Napoleon and Frederick II had not been,

---

abroad. Walter Görlitz, *History of the German General Staff, 1657-1945*, trans. Brian Battershaw (New York, 1953).

There was no similar system of higher military education in the French army. The students at the French staff school entered it immediately after their graduation from the military academy (St. Cyr) or the *Ecole Polytechnique*.

to take advice from and delegate real responsibility to his subordinates. Though he was one of the last hereditary monarchs to play an important military role, historians have paid little attention to William the Great. The Chief of the Prussian General Staff, Helmuth von Moltke, three years younger than William, had transferred from the Danish to the Prussian army at the age of twenty-two. Moltke had been made provisional Chief of the General Staff in 1857, but seems to have become a close personal friend of William only after the Danish War of 1864. The War Minister, Albrecht von Roon, had naturally played a larger part in the conflict with the Liberals in parliament.

The disadvantages of a general staff are overbalanced by two facts. (1) This seems to be the only way by which large modern armies can be handled in the field, even with methods of communication which were not available in the mid-nineteenth century. Even the greatest of the Great Captains proved unable to handle everything himself. (2) It seems to be the only system by which an army can formulate, and be educated in, a "doctrine of war." This phrase still has a forbidding Prussian sound. It is primarily a set of patterns, of methods for handling the intricate business of modern war, which have proved to be as important to success in war as the genius of a Great Captain was in the neoclassical age. A modern general staff is both *collective* and *decentralized*. It draws up plans which are far too complex to be improvised by individuals. It then sees that the various parts of the machine function in accordance with these plans. Great Captains are rare. But generals can be trained in the same ways that both governments and large corporations now train junior executives. In its particular historical environment, the Prussian General Staff's autonomy undoubtedly contributed to the development of a doctrine of war. If they had not belonged to a separate planning and educational branch (as separate as the artillery or the engineers), the Prussian army's theorists would have been isolated from each other, swamped by the demands of military routine, and defeated by the hostility and inertia of the "practical" soldiers. A young British or French officer could only win distinction and promotion by "practical" service. Moltke rose to a high position in the Prussian peacetime army through intellectual achievement. During the half-century from the defeat of Napoleon to the Danish War, the Prussians, to borrow the title of one of the first English works on this subject, had developed *The Brain of an Army*.[16]

Clausewitz' contribution to early nineteenth-century Prussian military doctrine was probably less important than the development of the General Staff and of higher military education. As a protégé of Scharnhorst, Clausewitz was always suspected of radicalism. He was made director of the War College in 1818, but was not allowed to lecture there. This post was administrative; like Mahan, Clausewitz was not a very good administrator. Moltke, who was there at the time, came under his influence only after Clausewitz' death. Disappointment may have been partly responsible for Clausewitz' decision to set down the ideas which he had not been allowed to teach, as exile had been partly responsible for Machiavelli's decision to write *The Prince*. In 1831 Gneisenau, for many years without a command, was given an army to prevent revolution in Prussian Poland. Gneisenau made Clausewitz, then fifty-one, his chief of staff. Both men died in the cholera epidemic of that year. Clausewitz' unfinished masterpiece is not as difficult going as is often supposed, if the reader skips many passages and understands the author's general philosophical method. Many passages are comparable to the classical illustrations in *The Prince* or the *Discourses on the First Ten Books of Titus Livius*. They are the rules about river crossings, night marches, etc., the subjects of the eighteenth-century handbooks. Other sections contain Clausewitz' criticism of other military theories, many of them the result of the eighteenth century's search for mathematical rules and universal principles.

Jomini's greatest weakness was his tendency to formulate such rules and to illustrate his ideas by lines and diagrams. Clausewitz' stress on personality, will, and the other intangibles of war represented the Romantic—or an historically-minded participant's—reaction against these efforts to represent complex social phenomena by charts and formulas. Clausewitz' comment on Jomini was that

Even the two fundamental principles of the theory of war . . . developed only in our own time, the *breadth of the base* by Bülow, and the *position on interior lines* by Jomini, if applied to

16 By Spenser Wilkinson (London, 1891). The French army's colonial campaigns had not, as has often been asserted, unfitted it for war in Europe. But, in a modern army, "the lack of a doctrine of war can never be corrected." J. Regnault, "Les Campagnes d'Algérie et leur influence de 1830 à 1870" (*Révue historique de l'Armée*, Dec., 1953, 23-38). There is a fine explanation of modern staff work in Dwight D. Eisenhower, *Crusade in Europe* (Garden City, 1948), 74-76.

the defense of a theatre of war have actually in no instance shown themselves absolute and effective.

Jomini, who was acutely conscious of his European reputation, charged Clausewitz with being hostile to all military theory.

One cannot deny to General Clausewitz great learning and a facile pen. But this pen . . . is above all too pretentious for a didactic discussion, in which simplicity and clearness ought to come first. . . . The author shows himself far too sceptical in point of military science; his first volume is but a declamation of all science of war, whilst the two succeeding volumes, full of theoretic maxims, prove that the author believes in the efficacy of his own doctrines, if he does not believe in those of others.[17]

Clausewitz' method was to attempt to define the real nature of war and then to compare it with warfare as soldiers practiced it. The absolute—or abstract—concept of war is a concept of absolute violence. Bonaparte, Clausewitz felt, had approached this absolute concept.

We might doubt whether our notion of its absolute nature had any reality, if we had not seen real warfare make its appearance in this absolute completeness right in our own time. After a short introduction performed by the French Revolution, the ruthless Bonaparte quickly brought it to this point. Under him war was carried on without slackening for a moment until the enemy was laid low, and the counterstrokes [of 1813 and 1814] followed almost with as little remission.

Or, as the British naval reformer Admiral Sir John Fisher put it in 1905: "The essence of war is Violence. Moderation in war is Imbecility. Hit first! Hit hard! and hit *anywhere!*"[18]

Yet warfare in practice has often been quite remote from this abstract concept. It has often been described as long stretches of boredom punctuated by moments of acute danger. Quite correctly Clausewitz pointed out that,

We must decide upon this point, for we can say nothing intelligent on the plan of [any particular] war until we have made up our minds whether war is to be only of this kind, or whether it may be of yet another kind. If we give an affirmative answer to the first question [as many of Clausewitz' interpreters have done], then our theory

17 *On War*, 499. *The Art of War*, 42.
18 *On War*, 570. Arthur J. Marder, ed., *Fear God and Dread Nought: The Correspondence of Admiral of the Fleet Lord Fisher of Kilverstone* (3 vols., London, 1953-1959), II, 52.

will, in all respects come nearer to logical necessity; it will be . . .
clearer and . . . more settled.

It might, indeed, satisfy the systematizers. But what of practice? Must we reject almost all of the wars which have been
fought

from Alexander and certain campaigns of the Romans down to
Bonaparte? . . . We must say to ourselves that in the next ten
years there may perhaps be a war of that same [limited] kind
again, in spite of our theory, and that this theory, in spite of its
rigorous logic, is still quite powerless against the force of circumstances. We must, therefore, be prepared to construe war as it is
to be, not from pure conception, but by allowing room for everything of a foreign nature which is involved in it and attaches itself to it—all the natural inertia and friction of its parts, the
whole of the inconsistency, the vagueness and timidity of the
human mind.

As both Liddell Hart and Jomini have complained, Clausewitz was too subtle. Some of his followers improved his ideas
by refining the contradictions—and the life—out of them.
The gist of Clausewitz is that soldiers should always remember that war is an act of violence and that battle is the cul-
minating point toward which all military preparations should
be directed. Whether future wars would be, in fact, more
violent was a question which Clausewitz was too sensible to
try to answer. He did believe, however, that, once aroused,
national passions would not easily be curbed.

Since the time of Bonaparte, war . . . had approached more nearly
to its real nature, to its absolute perfection. . . . The cause was the
participation of the people in this great affair of state, and this
participation arose partly from the effects of the French Revolution on the internal affairs of countries, partly from the threatening attitude of the French toward all nations. Now, whether this
will always be the case, . . . would be a difficult point to settle.
. . . But everyone will agree . . . that bounds, when once thrown
down, are not easily built up again; and that, at least, whenever
great interests are in question, mutual hostility will discharge itself . . . as it has done in our time.[19]

19 *Ibid.,* 583-584. This frightening analysis of the combined effects of democ-
racy and nationalism on war is a thoroughly Romantic passage. The best short
English account of Clausewitz is Hans Rothfel's chapter in Earle, *Modern
Strategy.* Rothfels wrote the best biography, *Carl von Clausewitz, Politik und
Krieg* (Berlin, 1920). See also Walther M. Schering, *Die Kriegsphilosophie
von Clausewitz* (Berlin, 1940), Ernst Hagemann, *Von Berenhorst zu Clause-
witz* (Berlin, 1940), and Franz Mielke, *Clausewitz: sein Leben und Werk*
(Berlin, 1957).

Chapter 6

The Wars of the Mid-Nineteenth Century (1854-1871)

The New Weapons of the Industrial Revolution

THE THIRD quarter of the nineteenth century saw two of the greatest territorial revolutions in modern European history, the unifications of Germany and of Italy, and the end of France's long military preponderance. Though there was no general war, every great power in Europe was involved in war and every one but Britain went through a political reorganization. These wars were the first to be fought with the new weapons and techniques of the Industrial Revolution. In every one but the Franco-Prussian War, a "modern" industrial state defeated a "backward" agrarian one. Strategically, the most important of the new inventions were the railway and the telegraph, which made it possible to solve the practical problems of mobilizing, supplying, and commanding mass armies. The railway boom of the generation between 1840 and 1870 revolutionized strategic geography. It ended the long wastage of marches to the scene of action, marches which had drained an army's numbers, courage, and supplies before it even reached the frontier. For the first time, a whole army could put its whole strength into the enemy's country. It was the railway, in short, which made mass armies practical.

The decisive factor in 1866 and 1870 was not the mere existence of railways, but the uses to which the Prussian General Staff put them. The French railways were as good as the German in 1870, but the French had no detailed plans for moving troops by rail, while the timetable of mobilization, concentration, and the first moves of an offensive was the center of Prussian staff planning. In the American Civil War neither side had an army or trained reserves to mobilize, but the enormous size of the Confederacy made railway and steamship transportation absolutely essential. After General Rosecrans' disaster at Chickamauga the Union army moved 23,000 reinforcements nearly 1200 miles in a week—twice the distance from Paris to Berlin or exactly the distance from Berlin to Moscow. Though military thinkers had at first believed that the railway would strengthen the defense, the wars of 1859, 1866, and 1870 turned out to be the shortest major wars in modern history. Prussia's victories, in particular, were a striking example of mass multiplied by impulsion.[1]

The rifle became an effective infantry weapon after the development of the modern bullet, a conical projectile with a hollow or brass base which expands to take the grooves in the barrel. The percussion cap was an improvement over the flintlock. Breech loading increased the rate of fire and made it possible to load from a prone or running position. The muzzle loader hung on for a time because it was easier to manufacture and existing stocks of muskets could be converted into rifles, but all of these inventions eventually enabled the infantry to deliver more fire at longer ranges. This outmoded Napoleonic artillery tactics, which had smashed at the enemy's tight formations with case shot (which had the same effect as the later shrapnel) from outside musket range. The rifle forced the artillery back to ranges at which it had to use solid shot, which do little damage to infantry. Attacking infantry had thus to take both the infantry and the artillery fire of the defenders. Breech-loading rifled artillery came in slowly because it was very expensive, but it also strengthened the defensive. A unit could now hold a much wider front, which made flank movements more difficult. The skirmishing formation was now the normal tactical order. Command problems were more complicated because armies were much larger and because each rifleman could hold more territory. Field fortifications became much more extensive. In the American Civil War a superiority of at least three to one was required to carry them.

The chief tactical trend of these wars, as we can see them now, was the power which these new weapons gave the tactical defensive. But this trend was not at all clear at the time. It was obscured by the glaring strategical errors of the French and Austrian high commands and by the striking success of the Prussian General Staff's strategic offensives. In addition, no single weapon was the decisive factor in any single war. On both land and sea the new weapons were not to become reasonably stabilized until after the invention of smokeless powder in the 1880's. In 1866 the Prussian breech-loading rifle (the "needle gun") was superior to the Austrian muzzle

[1] On railways see E. A. Pratt, *The Rise of Rail-Power in War and Conquest, 1833-1914* (London, 1915).

loader, but the Prussian artillery was inferior. In 1870 the situation was reversed. The Prussian rifle was inferior to the new French *chassepot*, but the new Krupp steel breech-loading cannon was much superior to the French artillery. It is still difficult to estimate the effectiveness of the French *mitrailleuse*, a one-ton, twenty-five barreled machine gun which fired seventy-five shots a minute by rotating the barrels like the chambers of a Colt revolver. It had been guarded so carefully that few officers knew how to use their new secret weapon. It was as big as a field gun and was towed by four horses. Even the name "grape shot gun" indicated that it was regarded as part of the artillery. As a result it was usually placed with the artillery, where it was quite ineffective.[2]

Nineteenth-century soldiers were a conservative lot, by training, social origin, experience, and political conviction. Perhaps the members of hierarchic institutions are always conservatives. The same charge of innate conservatism has often been leveled at priests, lawyers, and university administrators. Since the bayonet was an infantry weapon and the infantry was still clearly the Queen of Battles, it was easy for conservative tacticians to place undue stress on bayonet drill and close order marching. It was easy to lay the bayonet's failure in the American Civil War to the poor training of the American soldier. But many thoughtful soldiers could see that lance and saber cavalry tactics were outmoded. Horsemen were still useful for raiding and scouting, but there was strong sentiment for arming them with rifles or carbines. The old superiority of a lancer on a horse to a single man on foot with a blunderbuss had at last disappeared. With it disappeared still another reason for keeping the infantry in close formation. The difficulty of analyzing the changes brought by new invention were even more apparent in naval than in land warfare. Mechanization was devastatingly rapid in naval warfare. "Mechanics" began to demand to be treated as of-

---

[2] Weapons analysis in the Civil War was even more difficult. Repeating rifles had been used, but they were so far from being foolproof that the army adopted a more reliable single-shot breechloader after the war.

The fragile paper musket cartridge was a weak point for a long time. The needle gun was a bolt-action breechloader, with the main charge behind the primer. In the *chassepot* the primer was placed in its proper position at the base of the cartridge. Development of a satisfactory metal cartridge case took a long time. The case has to be very tough at the base (to stand the shocks of firing and extraction) and very thin at the edges (to prevent gas leakage and to take the rifling). A fascinating contemporary account of the technical and other difficulties facing artillerymen is J. Emerson Tennent, *The Story of the Guns* (London, 1864).

ficers and gentlemen. The nineteenth century was also the great age of the private inventor. The line between the crank and the genius—as in the case of Charles Goodyear—was a very thin one. Newspaper reporters had discovered that science fiction sells papers and that Colonel Blimp is a fine popular target. Armies and navies were deluged with military gadgets. The inventor and his backers—some of whom might be members of parliament—were always after some of the taxpayers' money. Without scientific training themselves and without the buffers now provided by committees of government scientists, the military authorities usually rejected the inventions. They were certain to look foolish when any particular gadget turned out to have practical value.[3]

The Crimean and Italian Wars

The wars of this period can be divided into three groups: the Crimean and Italian Wars, Prussia's victories over Austria and France, and the Civil War in America. The Crimean War (1854-1856) was the longest European war of this period and the greatest amphibious war of this century. Turkey declared war on Russia (who had occupied the Danubian Provinces, later part of Rumania) in October, 1853. England and France declared war in March and sent an army to the Provinces in June, 1854. But the Russians had withdrawn and Austria had occupied the disputed area. The British and French stayed there all summer—losing a quarter of their men to cholera—before deciding to teach Russia a lesson by taking the Black Sea base at Sebastopol. Of a sea famous for its fall storms—in the words of Edward Hamley, an artilleryman who became one of the two greatest British military critics of this century—they knew "as little . . . as knight errants, heroes of the romances of Don Quixote, knew of the dim, enchanted region where, amid vague perils, and trusting

---

[3] The most famous case of successful high-pressure tactics by the inventor resulted in the British Admiralty's forced acceptance of Captain Cowper Coles's turret battleship *Captain*. She turned turtle with all hands, the inventor included, on her first commission.

There are three excellent studies of mechanization in naval warfare: Bernard Brodie, *Sea Power in the Machine Age* (Princeton, 1941); James P. Baxter, *The Introduction of the Ironclad Warship* (Cambridge, Mass., 1933); and William Hovgaard's scarce *Modern History of Warships* (New York, 1920). There are also two fine studies of the difficulty of amalgamating the naval engineer into the officers' corps: Edgar C. Smith, *A Short History of Naval and Marine Engineering* (Cambridge, 1937), and Geoffrey Penn, *Up Funnel, Down Screw: The Story of the Naval Engineer* (London, 1955). On the problem of invention during the American Civil War see R. V. Bruce, *Lincoln and the Tools of War* (Indianapolis, 1956).

so much to happy chance, they were to seek some predatory giant."[4]

The Anglo-French landing was unopposed, on a beach about thirty miles north of Sebastopol without a harbor to support an extended operation. The sixty-six-year-old British commander had lost an arm at Waterloo. His sole experience since that time had been as Military Secretary at the Horse Guards. "But he was a courteous, dignified, and amiable man, and his qualities and rank were such as might well be of advantage in preserving relations with our Allies." The able engineer who became his chief adviser—the seventy-two-year-old son of Burgoyne of Saratoga—had last seen action at New Orleans. Saint Arnaud, the fifty-three-year-old commander of the much larger French contingent, had seen much service in Africa and had helped to organize Napoleon III's coup. Hamley thought him "vainglorious to a notable degree —and much too anxious to represent himself as taking the chief part." Too ill to talk during the voyage, he died ten days after the landing. In any case—in the words of G. F. R. Henderson, the greatest British military critic of the next generation—"Generals and staff officers relied simply on their experience and common sense; all were on the same footing, and there was seldom reason to fear that the enemy would display a superior science or a higher capacity for devising irresistible maneuvers."[5]

The French and British infantry carried muzzle-loading rifles. Most of the Russian infantry still carried muskets and depended heavily on the bayonet. Five days after the landing the allies marched south and defeated an inferior Russian force on a height about halfway to the town. The allies, who had lost about 3,300 men, camped on the field for two days and did not pursue the Russians. By the end of a week the allies were in sight of the fortress; the main Russian army had withdrawn into the interior around the allied flank. Many of the allied soldiers were too weak to make more than five or six miles a day, though they had left some of their equipment and had taken only one blanket per man. During this week

[4] *The War in the Crimea* (London, 1890), 36. Hamley's major work was *The Operations of War explained and illustrated* (1866, ed. Sir George Aston, Edinburgh, 1923). Meanwhile the most powerful steam fleet yet assembled had appeared before Cronstadt and had taken and abandoned Bomarsund in the Baltic. The Russians had to watch five fronts—Danube, Baltic, Caucasus, Crimea, and the Austrians. Though the Russian sailing fleet had not yet been brought to action, the allied steam fleet in the Black Sea was superior.
[5] *Ibid.*, 32, 35. Henderson, *Science of War*, 401.

the Russians had sunk some of their sailing ships at the entrance to the harbor and had mounted their guns on land.

Sebastopol was defended by about twenty thousand sailors and marines, under the supervision of an able thirty-six-year-old chief engineer, Lieutenant Colonel Todleben. The sailors, trained to handle big naval guns, were more valuable during the coming siege than ordinary infantry. Since the allied fleet could not get close enough to support an attack on the northern side of the town, the allies marched around to the southern side, which had been practically undefended. This also enabled them to establish bases in two small harbors. When they got to the southern side, they found that Todleben's men had constructed new fortifications. Instead of trying to storm these works, the allies decided to wait for their siege train from Rumania. A month after the original landing the fleet assaulted the granite forts on the sea side while the siege guns battered the earthworks. Eleven hundred naval guns fired forty thousand rounds and barely nicked the forts, while several heavy warships were badly damaged. A week later the reinforced Russian army reappeared and twice tried to drive the allies into the sea. Both attacks were poorly prepared and failed to carry the allied positions. Todleben, in the meantime, had

developed a new feature in trench warfare, which the range and accuracy of the rifle had rendered possible, . . . rows of pits, each fitted to hold a man, and having in front a few sandbags . . . to protect his head. . . . To direct guns on objects so small as these pits . . . seemed but a doubtful policy, and they were therefore opposed by men, similarly covered by sandbags, from the parapets. After a time, . . . the rows of rifle pits were connected, by trenches, in parts of which shelter was given to continuous ranks of riflemen.[6]

After two months one of the Black Sea storms finally broke, wrecking forty-eight transports and damaging the warships far more severely than they had been damaged in their brush with the forts. The tents were blown away; the seven miles from the harbors to the front became impassable. The allies had not wanted to spare men to build roads which they would not need when they had taken Sebastopol. The Turks who had been hired as road builders could scarcely bury their own dead. Supplies had been hauled over the open plain dur-

6 Hamley, *War in the Crimea*, 197.

ing the long Indian summer. The few horses which had been brought along or captured—these were not many since the Russian army controlled the interior—starved, though boats could hardly row through the floating bales of hay in the harbor. The men who replaced the horses could barely carry up their own rations. "The sick, the wounded, and the weary lay down in mud. The trenches were often deep in water, and when night put an end to the rifle fire on both sides, the soldiers sat there, cramped, with their backs against the cold, wet earth." They suffered from frostbite and trench foot. "Coming from the trenches the men had to go far afield to seek for roots . . . to cook their food; it is hardly surprising that many . . . ate their salt pork uncooked; and as, under such diet and exposure, the numbers of the sick increased, so was more work thrown on those who remained."[7]

The French made up their losses. By the end of January, 1855, their force was up to 78,000 men, while the British were down to 11,000. The British cabinet had fallen under the impact of newspaper accounts of conditions in the expeditionary force. Nicholas I was dead, perhaps of disappointment at the showing of his army. The mobility of sea power was making itself felt. By spring the allied force numbered 150,000, though it was dependent on sea transportation even for firewood. Late in May, 1855, allied steamers captured positions leading into the Sea of Azov and stopped practically

[7] "At the end of November we had nearly 8000 men in hospital. . . . Lifted from the mud of the hospital tent, and wrapt in their wet blankets, the sick were placed on horses. . . . Bound for the great hospital of Scutari, the ghostly train would toil on, wading and slipping past the dying horses, the half-buried bullocks, the skeletons, . . . the waggon-load of dead Turks going to that yawning pit beside the road, . . . the artillery waggons, returning at dusk with the forage they had set out at daybreak to fetch—and on, always through deep mire, to the place of embarkation.

"New miseries lay in that last word. Lying amid crowds of other sick and wounded, on the bare planks, . . . without proper food, medicine, or attendance, they were launched on the wintry sea. Their covering was scanty, the roll and plunge of the ship were agony to the fevered and the maimed. . . . Not infrequently the machinery of the overladen ship broke down, and they lay tossing for days, a hell upon the waters.

"Scutari, the longed-for haven, was for weeks the very climax . . . of suffering, . . . misery, . . . [and] despair." *Ibid.,* 167-173.

Tolstoi's account is in *Sevastopol and Other Military Tales,* trans. Louise and Aylmer Maude (Oxford, 1935). See the classic by Alexander W. Kinglake, *The Invasion of the Crimea* (8 vols., Edinburgh, 1863-1887) and more recent works by C. E. Vulliamy, *Crimea* (London, 1939), C. B. F. Woodham-Smith, *The Reason Why* (London, 1953) and *Florence Nightingale* (New York, 1951), Rupert Furneaux, *William Howard Russell of the Times* (London, 1944), Maurice Garcot, *Sébastopol* (Paris, 1955), and for war correspondents generally, Joseph J. Mathews, *Reporting the Wars* (Minneapolis, 1957).

all Russian shipping. Sebastopol was finally taken on September 8, after a battle in which 19 generals and 23,000 men were killed or wounded. The war-weary French had lost 93,000 dead. A new Austrian ultimatum brought Russia— soon to be shaken by a series of internal crises—to a peace conference at Paris. The Concert of Europe had been shattered. The split between Russia and Austria was the prelude to the unification of both Germany and Italy, and the hunt for new weapons—such as the ironclad steamship and the mines which the Russians had used in the defense of Cronstadt—was accelerated.

The War of Italian Unification, the first in which all the infantry of both sides carried rifles, lasted only four months. Both sides had limited political objectives, the French and Piedmontese hoped to drive the Austrians from Lombardy and Venetia as a prelude to Italian confederation. The Austrians did not use their railway across the Alps to defeat Piedmont before the French came up, but waited on the frontier until the opposing forces were about equal. The battles of Magenta and Solferino took place in June, 1859. The latter was perhaps decided by bayonet charges against the Austrian center. Piedmont had lost a quarter of her army. Worried about Prussia and discontent at home, Napoleon III was afraid to test the Austrian fortifications in Venetia. Austria kept that province and gave up Lombardy. Napoleon III could not check the movement toward a strong national Italian state instead of a confederation. Revolutions swept through central Italy, and Garibaldi won the Two Sicilies. Venetia was taken in 1866, as Italy's price for joining Prussia against Austria, though the new Italian army and navy were beaten at Custozza and Lissa. Rome was occupied when the Franco-Prussian War caused the withdrawal of the French garrison protecting the Pope. Italy was now a great power, with more people than Austria-Hungary, huge debts, and the highest taxes in Europe to support armed forces and other great power symbols of poor quality.[8]

8 The 1861-1865 campaigns against southern "brigands" cost more lives than "all the other wars of the *risorgimento* put together." Fifty years later, a fifth of the conscripts in some areas still took to the hills. The unrest which followed the Italian defeat by the Ethiopians at Adowa in 1896 was climaxed by riots which took nearly a hundred lives in Milan alone in 1898. Dennis Mack Smith, *Italy: A Modern History* (Ann Arbor, 1959), 75, 79, 192. This superb work has many suggestions for students of other nationalistic movements. In Germany, where national unification was accompanied by immediate economic progress, the old particularisms tended to give way to a flamboyant nationalism. For many ordinary Italians, however, national

The Rise of Germany

Though the American Civil War was to be fought before the Prussian army saw action against Denmark, Austria, and France, the latter wars will be considered first because they affected European military thought more directly. In 1866 Italy tied down about a quarter of the Austrian army, but the combined armies of Austria and the smaller German states were still larger than that of Prussia. The Prussians detailed 50,000 men to occupy Hannover and the other North German states between Brandenburg and the Rhine provinces, and largely ignored the South Germans, who were hoping that their big rivals would fight each other to a standstill. This left 250,000 Prussians to face a slightly larger number of Austrians and Saxons. The Austrians had had more combat experience, and their artillery and cavalry were better than those of the Prussians, but the Hapsburgs were so short of money that many of their infantry had had insufficient training. The Prussians wished to win a quick victory to keep Napoleon III from intervening in the war. To do this Moltke's armies had to advance through the mountains into Bohemia by three widely separated passes. Benedek, the Austrian commander, did not move fast enough to defeat the Prussian armies in detail. Within a week the Prussians had pushed through the mountains and roughly handled three Austrian army corps. Benedek had telegraphed Vienna that he would probably be defeated in a major battle. Even without many later examples, it is easy to see how later strategists convinced themselves that the strategic offensive was the Prussian secret for victory.

The decisive battle of Königgratz or Sadowa was won by good luck and hard fighting as much as by superior strategy. Neither command knew much about the other, since both were holding their cavalry in reserve for shock action. Benedek was in a good tactical position, but with his back to the Elbe River. The Prussians, thinking that Benedek was across the river—a better textbook position—began to move around

unity had meant a change for the worse, a change which was harder to bear because so many nationalists had assumed that all of Italy's problems would be solved by getting rid of the Austrians. In this connection see also Bolton King and Thomas Okey, *Italy Today* (London, 1901), and Cecil J. S. Sprigge, *The Development of Modern Italy* (New Haven, 1944). The new Italian army deliberately "nationalized" its conscripts by mixing them in units which were cross-sections of the whole population. What this did to the Italian mobilization system is another matter. Charles Martel [Charles à Court Repington], *Military Italy* (London, 1884).

the Austrians' flank to cut them off from Vienna. The commander of one Prussian army blundered into Benedek and a major battle. He was saved by the arrival of other Prussian units, whose commanders attacked without waiting for orders. A quarter of the Prussians never reached the field; the rest inflicted roughly three times as many casualties as they suffered. The Austrians lost somewhat less than a fifth of their army, but got the rest across the river. The Prussians were too tired and hungry for pursuit. Superior artillery and cavalry probably saved the Austrians from annihilation. As always, luck seemed to be with the side which was willing to take chances. A bold Prussian move through a heavy fog was the tactical turning point of the battle. The fighting had lasted only two weeks. Peace was made within seven weeks after the declaration of war.[9]

Napoleon III had obtained nothing at all from a belated attempt to mediate in 1866. But his attempt to get some Rhenish territory as compensation for Prussia's formation of the new North German Confederation enabled that Confederation to pose as the protector of the now isolated states of South Germany. In the crisis of 1870 German nationalism, Bismarck's diplomacy, and French folly rallied all of these South German states to North Germany. Austria-Hungary and Russia remained neutral and English opinion was outraged by this new manifestation, as they thought it to be, of Napoleonic aggressiveness. The combined German field armies in 1870 were almost double those of the French, though the two countries were approximately equal in population and industrial production. Since 1866 the Prussians had cut their mobilization time almost in half—from five weeks to eighteen days. Moltke was confident that the French could not move fast enough to interfere with a Prussian concentration west of the Rhine at the mouth of the Lorraine gateway. This was the only path open to either army without

[9] F. E. Whitton, *Moltke* (London, 1921) is the only English biography. The best books are Eberhard Kessel, *Moltke* (Stuttgart, 1959), Rudolf Stadelmann, *Moltke und der Staat* (Crefeld, 1950), and the classics by Generals von Schlichting, *Moltke und Benedek* (Berlin, 1900) and H. Bonnal, *Sadowa: A Study* (London, 1907).

The French attaché, Baron Stoffel, stressed the superiority of the Prussian officer down to the company level. The Prussian infantryman knew that he could load and fire the needle gun from a prone position, but he did not fight that way. His fire power standing up and advancing was so great that the Austrians were beaten anyway. The Austrians placed their superior artillery too far back; the inferior Prussian guns, more boldly handled, found fine targets in the bunched Austrian reserves. This is a good example of the way in which technological superiority can be nullified by mistaken tactics.

going through Belgium, since the narrow Belfort gap (south of Alsace to the Swiss border) was closed, as in 1914 and 1940, by French fortifications. From the Rhine the Germans could strike at the flank of a French drive through Belgium or come down on the opposite flank of a French invasion from the Belfort region. Moltke's mobilization plan was detailed, but his battle plans were flexible. The whole German army would concentrate and then move forward to attack the outnumbered French wherever they could be found. Geography and diplomacy had forced Moltke to gamble in 1866, but he was not a gambler by nature.

Napoleon III's war plans were mostly concerned with grand strategy. Like all other armies except the Prussian, the French army did not yet see that a modern plan involves minute details as well as broad objectives. The peacetime Prussian army was organized in divisions, corps, and field armies. In France, as in the eighteenth century, the highest peacetime formation was the regiment. Larger units were formed only after war was declared, which made it easy for Napoleon III to move pins and draw lines on maps with every change in the political situation. His most detailed war plan had been a strictly defensive one, with armies forming at Paris, Lyons, and Toulouse, a scheme which would have left many of his troops out of action. Napoleon had abandoned this plan after consulting the Archduke Albert of Austria, but he forgot to tell the War Minister of the change until eight days before the declaration of war. With the Paris crowds demanding a march on Berlin, Napoleon then decided to strike across southern Germany while his vastly superior fleet landed men on the lower Elbe or in the Baltic. His only hope lay in speed, and most of the French *armée de métier* was normally stationed in northeastern France. The French railways did well enough, but the French high command lost time sorting its regiments into armies, corps, and divisions, and many of the supplies supposed to be stored on the spot were found to be nonexistent.[10]

Fourteen days after war was declared Napoleon III ad-

10 Some of the troops in Metz had to be fed from the reserves stored for siege operations. At Chalons the army wagons had been impounded behind strong walls with only one gate. The Prussian reservists joined their units before the unit moved to its appointed place. A French reservist—of course a much smaller proportion of the field army was composed of reserves—was expected to go to his regimental depot and then catch up to his unit. Reservists crowded the railway stations all over France. One man reported in Strasbourg, was sent to Marseilles and then to Africa for his equipment, and finally joined his unit in Strasbourg, where he had started.

vanced two or three miles into the Saar to pacify French public opinion. Eight Germans were killed, though the French newspapers reported that whole companies had been mowed down by the *mitrailleuse*. The Germans began their advance the next day. Their main force pushed into the Lorraine gap, while a second force moved into Alsace to protect its flank and to prevent a junction of the French forces in Alsace with the main army. Outnumbered more than two to one at Wörth, the French forces in Alsace were nearly surrounded before they escaped west over the mountains. The main French army was pushed back at Spicheren because troops within supporting distance did not join in the battle. In both battles the Germans had lost more killed and wounded than the French, but they had finished the legend of French superiority. The Germans had taken their losses and kept on attacking. They then united all their forces for a wide sweep after the French, whom they thought must be retreating. Napoleon III had ordered his armies to retire toward Paris, the textbook solution which the Germans expected. The Empress feared that retreat would cause a revolution and the main army was ordered to stay at Metz under Marshal Bazaine, while MacMahon gathered the reserve and the remnants of the Alsatian army at Chalons. Bazaine then decided that he could not hold Metz and began to retreat westward, but was so slow that the German right wing—sweeping on Chalons—suddenly found itself in the midst of Bazaine's forces. The German corps commander attacked anyway at Mars La Tour, losing a quarter of his men before he was rescued. This French "victory" caused Bazaine to decide that Metz might be held and to turn back eastward. The Germans were now between Bazaine and MacMahon and Paris. At Gravelotte, as at Valmy, both armies faced the wrong way. The Germans—in a series of badly co-ordinated frontal attacks—lost more men than the French, but Bazaine went back into Metz. The Germans had cut the French army in two and had surrounded its larger portion. MacMahon wanted to fall back on Paris, but this was countermanded by the War Minister. Napoleon III wished to go to Paris in person, but the Empress told him to stay with MacMahon's army.

Finally MacMahon was ordered to relieve Metz by advancing northeastward. His army and his ailing Emperor were surrounded at Sedan in the angle of the Meuse River, a few miles from the Belgian border. The Germans captured 104,-

000 men—the largest field force yet to be captured in modern times—and caused 17,000 other casualties, mostly from artillery fire. The details of these "elementary" French strategic blunders (like those of both sides in the Crimea and Italy or Benedek's mistakes in 1866) are very important, if we are to see how profoundly war was to be changed by the Prussian example. It is easy to emphasize railways, steamships, and rifles, but much more difficult to see the nature of the Prussian educational revolution. As G. F. R. Henderson was to note,

Nothing is more noticeable in the history of warfare prior to the victories of Moltke than the common level of ability of the body of officers. In many campaigns, . . . the commanders on both sides were men of such mediocre abilities that the issue seems to have been the sport of fortune. In others, a great mind ruled supreme, or was limited only by dearth of material resources; but in all, the subordinate leaders . . . were cast in the same mould. . . . If they had experience of war so much the better; if they were without it they were probably no worse off than their prospective adversaries. But with the advent of Moltke, . . . this comfortable system came to an abrupt end. . . . The generals and staff officers of Austria and France, though they had far more warlike experience, were inferior in every respect, save physical courage. . . . In small enterprises as in great, . . . the lore of camp and barrack [proved] utterly incapable of dealing with the judgment and science of the Kriegsakademie.[11]

The news of Sedan caused a revolution in Paris and the proclamation of the Third Republic. Its President was General Trochu, a bombastic critic of the old army, who had recently sworn to die defending the dynasty. The key figure was the thirty-two-year-old Minister of the Interior, Léon Gambetta, who proclaimed a national war, with Paris as the symbol of national and republican resistance. The Germans held a nar-

11 *Science of War*, 401-402. Henderson's possible exaggeration of Moltke's role is further evidence of the impact of these events on military thought. One consequence of any revolution is the realization that it has taken place. The dates are also important. In warfare, too, the mid-nineteenth century saw the end of many of the old rules of thumb and the beginning of systematic application of general principles. This does not mean, of course, that war or any other branch of politics became an exact "science" in the sense that many people would use that term.

At Sedan the wounded MacMahon had turned the command over to Ducrot. Ducrot was about to try to break out of the trap when he was relieved by Wimpffen, who arrived from Paris with new orders from the War Minister. Wimpffen did not appreciate the situation until too late. Napoleon III then took the responsibility for surrender.

row corridor leading to Paris. Napoleon III had mobilized only a part of France's resources. The French command of the sea enabled them to procure supplies from Britain, Belgium, and the United States. What the Third Republic needed most was time, the gift of the old monarchies to the First Republic in 1792 and 1793. Paris was strongly fortified. The fleet had been recalled from a futile blockade of the German coast. With the sailors and marines who manned the big guns of the fortifications there were 72,000 trained men inside the lines. The Paris National Guard and other forces brought the total up to 300,000. A Carnot might have forged an effective army, but Trochu had little faith in improvised soldiers. And the National Guard had just as little faith in Napoleon III's officers. The regulars were used to man the forts and to spearhead the counter-offensives, while the Guard trained under their elected officers. The Germans surrounded Paris on September 19. With 147,000 men for fifty miles of siege lines, they had to depend on starvation. The rest of the German armies were besieging Metz and other French fortresses, guarding communications, and watching the armies forming outside of Paris. But this also meant that the improvised French forces in the provinces faced the most difficult of all military tasks for unseasoned troops, attacking the enemy in his field fortifications.[12]

Because of the nature of the country from the Loire—where most of the new forces were gathered—to Paris, these amateur armies were thrown into battle in open terrain, in desperate attempts to win before Metz surrendered. The republican leaders were the victims of the legend of 1793; they felt that they could keep up morale only by a show of revolutionary activity. They might have done better with a little more time, but Bazaine surrendered the last of October. The republicans fought on through the winter, keeping their untrained men in the open because they were afraid that their armies might break up if they took cover in the towns and villages. One bold plan after another was tried. These were the battles in which the French suffered their greatest casualties—40,000 to 20,000 for the armies of the Loire, 12,000 to 5000 in the north, and so on. Many more men were lost to cold, typhus, and smallpox before Paris surrendered on Jan-

12 Trochu's most important book was *L'Armée française en 1867*. See Jean Brunet-Moret, *Le Général Trochu (1815-1896)* (Paris, 1955).

uary 28. The Revolutionary *levée en masse* had been defeated by an organized nation in arms.[13]

The American Civil War: Men and Tactics

The United States entered the Civil War with the military system which had come down from the first settlers, slightly modified by the experiences of two wars with Britain and one with Mexico. The United States Army numbered 16,357 officers and men. Of its 198 companies or company-sized units, 183 were scattered among 79 posts on the Indian frontier and the Pacific coast. The other 15 companies "guarded" the Atlantic coast, the Canadian border, and the 23 arsenals. About a sixth of the entire regular army was lost when Brevet Major General David E. Twiggs surrendered the Department of Texas. The only other military force was the militia, then numbering 3,163,711 officers and men. This figure represents the total for all states reporting to the Adjutant General. No record existed for Iowa and Oregon; Delaware had last reported in 1827; and Pennsylvania had sent in a round figure of 350,000 officers and men in 1858. Some militia units, like the trained bands of Stuart times, had some training and glorious uniforms. The militia of the "militant" South were a bit better organized than those of the mercantile North. In the former case, "There is every reason to doubt the efficacy of the [quarterly and annual] muster and review as an instrument of military training and organization, . . . [but] little reason to doubt . . . its effectiveness in suffusing a kind of martial spirit, however ill-defined and misdirected, in the

[13] Jacques Desmaret, *La Défense nationale, 1870-1871* (Paris, 1949) and Melvin Kranzberg, *The Siege of Paris, 1870-1871: A Political and Social History* (Ithaca, 1950). On March 1, 1871, the Third Republic still had 1,137,000 men under arms, out of a mobilized total of 1,980,000. Of the 1,450,000 mobilized Germans, 1,113,000 had crossed the frontier. Of these men, 720,000 were in France on March 1. Perhaps 280,000 French and 140,000 German were killed, wounded, or dead of disease. Perhaps the French could have struck more effectively at German communications. Both French guerrilla activity and German reprisals were greatly exaggerated at the time. There was nothing like the systematic massacres which followed the French Commune.

The crushing of the Commune shattered another legend, that of the armed uprising of the proletariat. Here again the Industrial Revolution has profoundly affected strategy. Modern armies now have weapons which revolutionaries cannot match, but are more sensitive to sabotage. Revolutions, in short, must be planned by professionals who study their art as general staffs study war. There are several recent works on the Commune. Michael Howard's excellent *The Franco-Prussian War* (London, 1961) is a long-awaited reinterpretation of a subject which had been exhaustively treated by the vast general staff publications of both sides.

people who attended." The United States Army, as an army, hardly influenced the war. There were never more than 26,000 regulars at any one time. Its trained officers and men were kept busy by the Indians instead of being used to stiffen the volunteers. Both governments turned most of the problems of recruiting over to the states. Both armies were composed of volunteers, either raised in new units or enlisted from the most active militia as the Minute Men had been recruited in New England. President Jefferson Davis, a West Pointer who had been Secretary of War, supervised the raising of the Confederate armies. The inexperienced Abraham Lincoln depended on the aged and infirm, but not senile, Winfield Scott, a veteran of the War of 1812 and hero of the Mexican War. Scott tried to see that the volunteers were enlisted for long enough terms to make real soldiers. Both governments were eventually forced to adopt conscription. The hard-pressed Confederacy adopted conscription before the United States and enforced it more effectively. Together they mobilized upwards of two and a quarter million men.[14]

14 See Marvin A. Kreidberg and Merton G. Henry, *History of Military Mobilization in the United States Army* (Washington, 1955), 83-140; John Hope Franklin, *The Militant South, 1800-1861* (Cambridge, Mass., 1956), 181. The latter author edited *The Diary of James T. Ayers: Civil War Recruiter* (Springfield, Ill., 1947). Ayers recruited Negroes. See also Dudley Taylor Cornish, *The Sable Arm: Negro Troops in the Union Army, 1861-1865* (New York, 1956), and Otis A. Singletary, *Negro Militia and Reconstruction* (Austin, 1957).

Thomas L. Livermore, *Numbers and Losses in the Civil War in America, 1861-65* (reprinted with an intro. by Edward E. Barthell, Bloomington, 1957), gave 1,556,778 Union and 1,082,119 Confederate enlistments. The latter is too high, the 600,000 of some southern writers low. E. Merton Coulter, *The Confederate States of America, 1861-1865* (Baton Rouge, 1951) settles for 750,000. The Union forces reached a peak of about 750,000 in 1865, the Confederates a peak of 300,000 in 1863. Battle deaths have been placed at 110.000 and 94,000, total deaths at 360,000 to 258.000. Perhaps 170,000 Union soldiers were "furnished" by the draft, about 120,000 of them were substitutes who probably would have enlisted anyway. The conscripts gave less trouble than the professional bounty jumpers and the state governors on both sides. See Fred A. Shannon, *The Organization and Administration of the Union Army, 1861-1865* (2 vols., Cleveland, 1928); William B. Hesseltine, *Lincoln and the War Governors* (New York, 1948); Albert B. Moore, *Conscription and Conflict in the Confederacy* (New York, 1924); and Ella Lonn, *Desertion during the Civil War* (New York, 1928), *Foreigners in the Confederacy* (Chapel Hill, 1940), and *Foreigners in the Union Army and Navy* (Baton Rouge, 1951). On the New York draft riots see Irving Werstein, *July, 1863* (New York, 1957); on medicine, H. H. Cunningham, *Doctors in Gray: The Confederate Army Medical Service* (Baton Rouge, 1958), and George Worthington Adams, *Doctors in Blue: The Medical History of the Union Army in the Civil War* (New York, 1952); on supply, Russell F. Weigley, *Quartermaster General of the Union Army: A Biography of M. C. Meigs* (New York, 1959).

During the Mexican War Congress had tried to double the 8000 man regular army and had enlisted 50,000 one-year volunteers. Halfway to Mexico City, Scott had to replace a third of his 10,000 men, a process which took from May

A larger proportion of the Confederate soldiers were farm boys, but Northern farmers at this time were equally familiar with small arms and hunting. There were more recent immigrants in the Northern armies and some fresh arrivals were crimped by unscrupulous bounty agents, but most of the men on both sides were from rural America. The average volunteer could shoot, but was not used to military discipline or to taking even elementary sanitary precautions. Some city men, even in the South, made better soldiers than the men from very poor country districts. A man's general educational level played a surprising part in his fitness for battle. The Northern states commissioned volunteer officers from major generals on down, but Davis and his adjutant general, Samuel Cooper, who had held the same position in the United States Army, appointed all the Southern generals. The Southern planter, as such, seems to have displayed no greater aptitude for command than the businessman or lawyer. The Confederate army was better led because the Confederate government used its professional officers more wisely. Most generals on both sides learned to fight by fighting; most of them would surely have welcomed more professional assistance. General John M. Palmer once worked with "one of these so-called 'politican generals,'" his grandfather John M. Palmer, later Governor of Illinois, United States Senator, and Gold Democratic candidate for President.

He felt his lack of experience keenly and [hoped for] . . . a trained officer . . . [as] brigade commander. But the War Department . . . could not spare any officers to serve as brigadier generals of volunteers because they were needed as lieutenants and captains and majors in the new regular regiments. . . . Without the immediate leadership of a trained senior and without the assistance of trained subordinates, . . . he entered the Battle of Stone Mountain, and . . . won his second star as a major general. . . . [Then] the War Department loosened up and began to send more of its trained officers to the volunteers. . . . Many of the regulars

---

to August. The best books are Justin H. Smith, *The War with Mexico* (2 vols., New York, 1919), Robert S. Henry, *The Story of the Mexican War* (Indianapolis, 1959), and Otis A. Singletary, *The Mexican War* (Chicago, 1960). On the peacetime army see William H. Goetzmann, *Army Exploration in the American West, 1803-1863* (New Haven, 1959), Francis P. Prucha, *Broadax and Bayonet: The Role of the United States Army in the Development of the Northwest* (Madison, 1953), and *Army Life on the Western Frontier* (Norman, 1958); Averam B. Bender, *The March of Empire: Frontier Defense in the Southwest, 1848-1860* (Lawrence, 1952); Robert G. Athearn, *William Tecumseh Sherman and the Settlement of the West* (Norman, 1956); and Forest G. Hill, *Roads, Rails, and Waterways: The Army Engineers and Early Transportation* (Norman, 1957).

decried the citizen army leaders as mere politicians and many of the latter had good reason to believe that the professionals were intriguing to replace them.[15]

When the war began no West Pointer had yet reached the permanent rank of general, but West Pointers were to dominate the high commands of both armies. At West Point these men had received a military education patterned on that given by the technical and engineering schools set up in France after the Revolution. A General Staff was not even thought of, though American strategic planning was certainly no worse than that of the armies in the Crimea. The Confederacy happened to get all three of the officers best fitted to command a field army at the start of the war, Lee and the two Johnstons. At Bull Run the Confederates had better men in the brigade commands—Early, Jackson, Longstreet, and Stuart among them—and they won the battle. McClellan, who was given command of the defeated Union forces six days after Bull Run, was a brilliant officer of thirty-five. He seemed to be a good choice at the time and his plan for taking Richmond from the sea side was a sound one. In 1862, as Grant remarked later, none of the other generals could have done much better. This was certainly true of Grant himself. His victory at Shiloh—with his men surprised as they were camping in the woods—was due to good luck and hard fighting rather than to good generalship. The same thing was true of the Confederates defending Richmond. Johnston's plan for driving McClellan back was neither written out nor carefully explained to his subordinates.[16]

15 *America in Arms*, 95-96. On the common soldier see Bell I. Wiley, *The Life of Johnny Reb* (Indianapolis, 1946), and *The Life of Billy Yank* (Indianapolis, 1952); Bruce Catton's trilogy, *Mr. Lincoln's Army, Glory Road, A Stillness at Appomattox* (New York, 1951-1953); and John F. Pullen, *The Twentieth Maine: A Volunteer Regiment in the Civil War* (Philadelphia, 1957).

16 At West Point mathematics and engineering took the place of Latin and Greek as fundamental disciplines, a stiff enough exchange for boys from the South and West with sketchy grammar school training. Some 300 of the 800 West Pointers who fought in the war went South. State military academies may have furnished 700 more Confederate officers, a small proportion of the 25,000 infantry officers. Robert R. Ellis, "The Confederate Infantry Officer" (*The Infantry Journal*, Nov., 1949); Frank E. Vandiver, *Rebel Brass: The Confederate Command System* (Baton Rouge, 1956). Many West Pointers had been out of the army and in much closer contact with civilians than many European officers. For Jomini's influence see David H. Donald's "Refighting the Civil War" in his *Lincoln Reconsidered: Essays on the Civil War Era* (New York, 1956).

The best short accounts are Robert S. Henry, *The Story of the Confederacy* (rev. ed., Indianapolis, 1956) and David L. Donald, ed., *Why the North Won the Civil War* (Baton Rouge, 1960). The most recent multi-volume study is Allan Nevins, *The War for the Union* (2 vols. to date, New York, 1959-   ).

The victorious Northern general, Grant, had been a comparative failure in the past and was to be a worse failure in the future, but he was a great soldier. His "Find out where your enemy is. Get at him as soon as you can. Strike at him as hard as you can and as often as you can, and keep moving on" is as able a summary of the art of war as Forrest's "fustest with the mostest." In Henderson's words Grant employed the Army of the Potomac "as if it was a battering ram, without consciousness and without feeling. It was a machine, perhaps unskillfully used, but challenging admiration by the manner in which it answered every touch of the manipulater. . . . The truth was at last recognized that even indifferent tactics have a better chance of success, where those who carry them out are in accord." Against a commander as great as Lee, only numbers could annihilate. Lee had to be badgered and harrassed and hemmed in by armies whose commanders were sound, if not brilliant, soldiers. There was good reason for Sherman's belief that Grant would become "the typical hero of the great Civil War in America." In a different theater against a different, though almost equally able commander, Sherman himself was to become one of the war's greatest masters of strategic maneuver. By combining offensive strategy with defensive tactics, he was able to capture Atlanta and to destroy much of the opposing army along with it. Neither Grant nor Sherman had ever read Clausewitz, but they kept the main ends of war in view: "the *military forces,* the *country,* and the *will of the enemy.*"[17]

Everyone should begin with Henderson, *Science of War,* and dip into Douglas Southall Freeman, *R. E. Lee: A Biography* (4 vols., New York, 1935) and *Lee's Lieutenants: A Study in Command* (3 vols., New York, 1945), and Kenneth P. Williams, *Lincoln Finds a General* (5 vols., New York, 1949-1959). Outstanding biographies are Lloyd Lewis, *Sherman, Fighting Prophet* (New York, 1932) and *Captain Sam Grant* (2 vols., II by Bruce Catton, Boston, 1950-1960), Frank E. Vandiver, *Mighty Stonewall* (New York, 1957), and G. F. R. Henderson, *Stonewall Jackson and the American Civil War* (2 vols., New York, 1898). Henderson's shorter Civil War works are in Jay Luvaas, ed., *The Civil War: A Soldier's View* (Chicago, 1958). On various commanders see T. Harry Williams, *Lincoln and his Generals* (New York, 1952) and *P. G. T. Beauregard: Napoleon in Gray* (Baton Rouge, 1955), Warren H. Hassler, Jr., *General George B. McClellan: Shield of the Union* (Baton Rouge, 1957), Freeman Cleaves, *Rock of Chickamauga: The Life of General George H. Thomas* (Norman, 1948), Earl Schenck Miers, *The Web of Victory: Grant at Vicksburg* (New York, 1955), Alfred H. Burne, *Lee, Grant, and Sherman* (New York, 1939), and J. F. C. Fuller, *Grant and Lee: A Study in Personality and Generalship* (2d ed., Bloomington, 1957).

17 Henderson, *Science of War,* 213-214. To Lord Wolseley's belief that Lee "towered above all men on either side," Sherman replied that Lee had never risen "to the grand problem which involved a continent. . . . His Virginia was to him the world. . . . He stood at the front porch battling with the flames

The tactics of both sides were worked out by the men themselves; both armies used the skirmish line rather than the Napoleonic heavy column. The average Northern soldier was a realist. In the words of one private,

We heard all through the war, that the army was eager to be led against the enemy. It must have been so, for truthful correspondents said so, and editors confirmed it: but when you came to hunt for this particular itch it was always the next regiment that had it. The truth is, when bullets are whacking against tree trunks and solid shot are cracking skulls like egg shells, the consuming passion in the heart of the average man is to get out of the way.

The Confederate soldier, according to D. H. Hill, fought the same way.

Self-reliant always, obedient when he chose to be, impatient of drill and discipline, he was unsurpassed as a scout or on the skirmish line. Of the shoulder-to-shoulder courage, bred of drill and discipline, he knew nothing and cared less. Hence, on the battlefield, he was more of a free lance than a machine. Who ever saw a Confederate line advancing that was not crooked as a ram's horn? Each ragged rebel yelling on his hook and aligning on himself.[18]

The men opened out of their own accord. Most infantry

---

whilst the kitchen and the house were burning, sure in the end to consume the whole." Lewis, *Sherman*, 644.

Liddell Hart notes Sherman's use of indirect approach in *Sherman: Soldier, Realist, American* (reissue, New York, 1958). Schofield, one of his corps commanders, thought that Sherman's skill was partly due to the practical nature of the American soldier. "Intelligent soldiers . . . they felt very strongly against attacking entrenchments . . . felt no necessity of fighting on unequal terms . . . veterans, they were very loath to attack unless they saw a chance for success . . . they fought much like they worked farms or sawmills, demanding a fair prospect that it would pay. Commanding such an army, the general must maneuver to fight the enemy on fairly even terms." Lewis, *Sherman*, 359.

18 *Battles and Leaders of the Civil War* (4 vols., New York, 1884-1888, reissued, intro. Roy F. Nichols, 1956), II, 662. See also the accounts in Francis Trevelyan Miller, ed., *The Photographic History of the Civil War* (10 vols., New York, 1911, reissued in 5 vols., 1958), and in David H. Donald, ed., *Divided We Fought: A Pictorial History of the Civil War, 1861-1865* (New York, 1952).

The Civil War was the first great war in which really large numbers of literate men fought as common soldiers. Many of their accounts have been reprinted. Outstanding among the reprints are W. W. Blackford, *War Years with Jeb Stuart* (New York, 1945), John W. De Forest, *A Volunteer's Adventures* (New Haven, 1946), and George A. Townsend, *Rustics in Rebellion* (Chapel Hill, 1950). The best source collection is Henry S. Commager, *The Blue and the Gray: The Story of the Civil War as Told by Participants* (2 vols., Indianapolis, 1951). There is much information in Francis A. Lord, *They Fought for the Union* (Harrisburg, 1960).

battles were fire fights pure and simple. They advanced in successive rushes, taking advantage of cover whenever possible—trees, roads, and quickly built log barricades, as notable a part of the Civil War as the log huts, the corduroy roads, or the wooden railway bridges. By 1862 both armies threw up these barricades as a normal procedure. Since the Confederates were usually on the defensive, their fortifications were often more finished, but both kinds could stop most infantry charges. Skirmishers dug rifle pits wherever they could dig them. Sherman's men threw away their bayonets and kept their spades, as they had thrown away their knapsacks and carried their gear in far more comfortable and less soldierly looking blanket rolls. When the supporting forces came up, they linked these rifle pits into combined barricades and trenches. Dirt was thrown over the logs from both outside and inside, more logs were piled on top to provide loopholes and head protection, and additional trees were felled with their tops pointed toward the enemy. These fortifications performed the jobs of the barbed wire and trenches of the First World War. They covered the defenders and formed physical obstacles to massed enemy attackers. These fortifications were nearly impervious to artillery fire, since the gunners could be picked off at ranges close enough for them to hit the entrenchments.

In 1862 and 1863 the commanders on both sides often tried Napoleonic frontal attacks, throwing wave after wave at critical tactical objectives as Lee did at Gettysburg. Almost all of these frontal attacks were failures. Though most of these failures have been charged to poor staff work, the staffs were not entirely to blame, though their work was usually as bad as the critics have claimed that it was. The real trouble lay in the ability of a few entrenched men to hold up a whole army and in poor battlefield communications behind the much broader fronts held by such armies. Both sides had excellent secret service systems and strategic intelligence, one mark, incidentally, of a true "civil war." The telegraph had benefited strategy, but not tactics. In battle messages still had to be carried by staff officers on horseback or sent by flag signals, which were always open to interception. When one line of earthworks was carried, as was the case with the Bloody Angle at Spotsylvania, it could often be retaken by a counterattack, or there would be a second line of entrenchments behind it. But most frontal attacks never carried even the first obstacle. The few men who reached the breastworks usually failed to take them. Field entrenchments were used constantly in the West, where the two armies were always moving and digging, and on a very large scale during the later phases of the war in Virginia. In the Wilderness the soldiers of both sides threw up barricades without orders and then sent out infantry patrols to get information. In these woods and swamps the only way of locating the enemy was to flush him. Most foreign observers noted the tremendous waste of ammunition. American soldiers preferred to save lives by spraying bullets at every suspicious object, no matter what the cost to the taxpayer.[19]

Except for siege operations, observers were surprised at the comparative ineffectiveness of the excellent Northern artillery, though commanders were careful to keep their men out of sight and range as long as possible. Sometimes the artillery was used to make the defenders keep their heads down while the attacking infantry was advancing. At other times infantry attacks were used to pin the defenders under artillery fire, for the defending infantry could not take better cover if other infantry was attacking. In the woods and swamps of rural America, there was little chance for cavalry shock action. As Sherman remarked, "the infantryman steps into the bushes and is safe, or can block a road in five minutes and laugh at the man on horseback." Cavalry was effectively used for long-range raids against communications and supplies and the nerves of the opposing commanders. Because of its inferiority at shock action, the Northern cavalry often fought on foot. When armed with Spencer repeating carbines, it was a very formidable mounted infantry. Strategically this mounted infantry was used like modern paratroopers or tank units to seize road junctions and hold them until the reinforcing infantry arrived. Lee's use of dismounted cavalry to take

[19] Since the armies themselves were not very large—those at Gettysburg being less than half the size of those at Leipzig or Sadowa—the trouble lay in the extension of their fronts. There is little evidence that Pickett's charge would have been successful if it had been lau ched earlier in the day at Gettysburg, or that Longstreet was sulki ıg. His ow ı idea of working around Meaʲe's flank to get between the Union army anꓸ Washington was somewhat like Moꞏtke's maneuver at Sadowa, though it wou d have been more risky, since the two American armies were already in co ıtact with each other. Would Meade have attacked during this operation or have been forced into action by a corps commander? Perhaps Lee and Meaʲe relied too much on their corps commanders, but this was also true of Moltke. See Dona d Bridgman Sanger and Thomas Robson Hay, *James Longstreet* (Baton Rouge, 1952) and for the Wilderness, Edward Steere's excellent *The Wilderness Campaign* (Harrisburg, 1960).

the road junction at Spotsylvania in 1864 was one of his most brilliant strokes. But the Civil War was primarily an infantry war. Only the ubiquitous footsoldier could move and dig and fight in the forests and mountains and swamps defending the Confederacy. Some of Sherman's men marched twenty-five hundred miles in a year and a half, as far as from France to Moscow and back. An observer who saw them in 1865 described them as "nothing but bone and muscle." [20]

Long lines of blue or gray or butternut troops charging across open fields were only the highlights of the war. Especially during the last two years, set piece battles gave way to that constant contact with the enemy which was to be one of the most striking features of early twentieth-century warfare. An Ohio soldier later described his battle this way:

The details were moving out through the timber towards the Johnnies. They had only proceeded a few rods, and the regiment had barely stepped back from their stacked guns, when the rebels started forward with one of their unearthly yells. . . . The rebel advance took us a good deal by surprise, but soon . . . the boys commenced pumping lead at the Johnnies. . . . They came to a standstill, . . . and with a yell that would have put a Comanche Indian to shame, our men sprang forward. . . .

There was so much timber . . . that our alignment had entirely collapsed. Each man, or squad of men, were helping to keep the rebs a moving towards the point from which they started . . . to the edge of the woods. . . . When I arrived at the rail fence running along the edge of the woods, . . . the majority of the rebel force had skedadled across the opening to the timber beyond. To

[20] Except where water transportation was available, the old problem of logistics licked the artillery. McClellan proposed a standard of three guns per thousand men, but this was not always reached in inland operations. Lee had 3.4 guns per thousand men in the Gettysburg campaign and Meade 4 per thousand. This can be compared to 3.5 for the Prussians in 1870 and 5 for the French army in 1813. Sherman had 254 guns and 100,000 men at the beginning of the Atlanta campaign. At Raleigh he had only 91 guns for 81,000 men. During his winter march through the Carolinas, "The soil melted away under rain. Even where the surface looked firm and solid, wagon wheels . . . would sink to the hubs. . . . Instead of . . . streams with well-defined, solid banks, we came across tangled swamps. . . . The regular crossing was by roads, at long intervals, . . . on raised causeways . . . defended by batteries. . . . Sometimes a place above or below could be found where the streams were fordable, and the troops waded through and then bridged the streams." John G. Barrett, *Sherman's March through the Carolinas* (Chapel Hill, 1956) is excellent. There are no recent studies of infantry, cavalry, engineering, or fortification. Fairfax Downey, *The Guns at Gettysburg* (New York, 1958), the reprint of Jennings Cropper Wise, *The Long Arm of Lee: The History of the Artillery of the Army of Northern Virginia* (New York, 1959), and L. Van Loan Naisawald, *Grape and Canister: The Story of the Field Artillery of the Army of the Potomac, 1861-1865* (New York, 1960) are excellent on artillery.

the left, . . . however, were quite a lively squad of rebels still hanging to their side of the fence with determined looks, as much as to say, we would rather die right here than to run, and sure enough nearly the whole lot were killed and wounded, as when one attempted to retreat across the open field, our fellows in the edge of the woods had a cinch on them. . . . I found that sixty rounds of ammunition out of eighty . . . had been fired. . . . I stepped behind . . . a tree . . . while I should transfer my cartridges.

At the south end of this clear land . . . was a lane . . . fenced on both sides with . . . worm rail fence. . . . At the west end of this lane . . . stood a log house, . . . a fine fortification for the rebs. . . . They had a clear sweep of the open field between their line and ours. We had to charge across this opening. . . . I moved diagonally across the open field to the left, striking the lane some twenty rods from the log house. . . .

At the word of command from someone, I know not whether he was an officer or a private, . . . every one who had come to do or die, made a rush for the Johnnies' stronghold. . . . Well this relieved us from this hot point, but the cross fire from the rebel line over to the left . . . was dropping some of our men. . . . I was squatting down on my feet with my left elbow resting on one knee and my hand supporting my gun. . . . A number of . . . the 24th Kentucky Infantry . . . were firing rapidly, whooping and cussing the Rebs. Several of them had been hit by this cross fire, the bullets passing between the rails . . . from one to two feet from the ground.[21]

The American Civil War: Strategy

The industrialized North's defeat of the agricultural South is a familiar theme. But this war can also be thought of as the last of the great wars for North America, one in which the power which commanded the sea defeated a people who were too dependent on water transportation. The South ex-

[21] Private H. P. Chapman, *Personal Reminiscences and Experiences: By Members of the One Hundred and Third Ohio Volunteer Infantry* (Oberlin, 1903), 164-169. Private Chapman was hit in the thigh a few moments later. This action was part of the siege of Knoxville, Nov. 25, 1863. "The surgeon was from a Michigan regiment. He looked at my wound, run his finger along the passage of the bullet, but he could not find it. Then he inserted a crooked probe . . . in search of that ball until the hair on my head stood up stiff enough to be cut into wire nails. But it was no use. It . . . still refuses to come to light after thirty-five years."

This was the sort of fighting that was to produce one of the great war novels of modern times, written by a youth of twenty-one who was born six years after the war started. His synthesis of other men's experiences was one of the first attempts to deal with the problem of individual courage in war, as it was one of the first great achievements of American realism—Stephen Crane, *The Red Badge of Courage* (which was published serially in a Philadelphia newspaper in 1894).

ported agricultural commodities and imported manufactures and even food by water. Its cities were still located on the water, though the Confederacy held only 10 of the 102 American cities of more than 10,000 people. The Confederate seaports, protected by long sandbars, were hard to blockade; all were close to neutral Bermuda or the West Indies. But, as Mahan put it, "The streams that had carried the wealth . . . of the seceding States turned against them, and admitted their enemies to their hearts." To replace these water routes the Southern rebels, like the rebels of 1776, had little land transportation. The North had three east-west railway systems, plus railways leading south to Washington and fanning out from Kentucky into Tennessee, Mississippi, and Georgia. In the Confederacy one line ran from Richmond to Wilmington, North Carolina, and another linked Richmond with the east-west line running from Charleston to Memphis. These lines joined at Chattanooga, a Unionist area open to Northern attack up the valleys of the Tennessee and Cumberland rivers. During the war the Confederates finished a second east-west line from Vicksburg to Charleston. But this road also was to be cut at Atlanta, 125 miles from Chattanooga. There were a few short lines across the Mississippi, but none into Texas or Florida.[22]

In white manpower the Confederates were outnumbered four to one, in total manpower two and a half to one. In industry the North's superiority was overwhelming—at least ten or twenty to one. The South was not well-prepared even for muscle-powered war. Because of her concentration on export crops food for both men and animals was often scanty. "The real conflict was not between factory and field, but between a

22 See George E. Turner, *Victory Rode the Rails: The Strategic Place of the Railroads in the Civil War* (Indianapolis, 1953); Robert C. Black, *The Railroads of the Confederacy* (Chapel Hill, 1952); and Thomas Weber, *The Northern Railroads in the Civil War, 1861-1865* (New York, 1952). Though Mahan's first book dealt with the Civil War—*The Gulf and Inland Waters* (New York, 1883)—he never returned to his interest in that war. The best book on the pressure of United States' sea power on the Confederacy is A. Lepotier, *Mer contre terre, les leçons de l'histoire, 1861-1865* (Paris, 1945). On the inland waterways in the age of the paddle wheel steamer, see Louis C. Hunter, *Steamboats on the Western Rivers: An Economic and Technological History* (Cambridge, Mass., 1949).

New Orleans, the sixth of America's large cities (168,000 people in 1860), was the only one in the Confederacy. Charleston and Richmond were twenty-second and twenty-fifth with about 40,000 each. Mobile was just under 30,000, Memphis and Savannah just over 20,000. Petersburg, Nashville, Norfolk, and Augusta were under 20,000, about the size of colonial Philadelphia. Five Confederate states (North Carolina, Texas, Mississippi, Arkansas, and Florida) had no cities over 10,000. The population of Atlanta was 9,554.

fairly well coordinated and balanced economy and a distorted, incompetent agriculture." Both governments also failed to deal with many kinds of economic problems—from those of taxation to the kinds of material brought in through the blockade. But if the French government was unable to control the prices of food and fuel in beleaguered Paris, one can hardly blame American statesmen for doing no better. Nineteenth-century Liberal economics was simply unadapted to periods of national emergency. In this respect the men of this age were far less modern than those of the First French Republic.[23]

The rebels of 1861 faced, therefore, somewhat the same difficulties as the rebels of 1776. But they also enjoyed roughly the same advantages. (1) Their armies stood on the defensive in very difficult country, "a wilderness of primeval forest, covering an area twice as large as the German Empire, and as thinly populated as Russia." (2) Britain and France seemed to favor them, a diplomatic advantage which might, as in 1776, prove decisive. (3) They were possibly more united than the Union. The inexperienced Republicans were a minority party even in the North. (4) They were fighting a limited war. They had only to win the independence which many Northerners and the British and French were ready to concede to them. (5) Though they did not enjoy the inestimable advantage of distance, the rebels were almost as well organized as the government. They did not have to face either a large regular army or navy.[24]

Since the United States' military strength was potential rather than actual, much of the credit must go to the political

[23] George Fort Milton, Conflict: The American Civil War (Washington, 1941), 34. "The Confederacy started out with boundless enthusiasm which began sadly to deteriorate as early as 1862. Why? Because of conscription; the progressive decline in the worth of money brought on chiefly by delay in adopting a system of taxation; . . . poor postal service; dissension and factionalism; the raising of false hope of foreign recognition; the battering-ram of rumored victories with the subsequent truth of defeats . . . ; the absence of a concerted effort to maintain morale by spreading among the people proper information; the lack of personable inspiring leadership in Davis, however sound his policies might have been; and during the later period, the false feeling that the old Union might be reentered with all rights guaranteed, which might have come true had Lincoln lived. These factors were fundamental and most of them could have been avoided." Coulter, Confederate States, 566. Excessive localism and individualism were not confined to the South. They were familiar traits of American farmers in wartime.

[24] Henderson, Science of War, 234. "Primeval" is a bit strong, but it shows how the country still appeared to a British observer. With Texas and Florida, the Confederacy was almost as large as Western Europe. Even without them it was as large as Germany, France, and the Low Countries.

leaders who mobilized this strength and drove their armies to victory. Consciously or not, the Union's over-all strategy was very much like that of the British in 1776: to blockade the Confederacy, capture its seaports, and cut it up along the lines of the great rivers. The United States had also to try to hold the border states and Washington in slave territory, and capture Richmond, a little more than a hundred miles from Washington. Here politics profoundly affected strategy. The loss of Washington or of the Army of the Potomac might well have led to foreign recognition of the Confederacy. For the Confederacy Richmond represented the four Mid-South states which had joined it after Sumter. Without them, the Confederacy could hardly claim to represent a Southern nation; it would indeed have been little more than a cotton planters' conspiracy. Those who criticize this mutual fixation on the two capital cities do not realize how vitally both of them affected the "military forces, the country, and the will" of the contenders.[25]

The Union navy, like the Union army, was created after the war began by Northern industry and trained manpower. The little navy of 1861—with twenty-three steamships and seventy-five hundred officers and men—had not been built to blockade a coast as long as that from Hamburg to Genoa. Its best ships were steam frigates to raid British commerce or to show the flag in distant waters. It had no ironclads or armed river vessels, and many of its higher officers were superannuated. At sixty, David Glasgow Farragut, a Tennessean with a Virginia wife, was only fifty-seventh on the list of captains. The navy's Bull Run was the loss of Norfolk navy yard eight days after the beginning of the war. Its elderly commander did not even do a good job of demolition; about three thousand heavy guns went to strengthen the Confederacy's coast and river defenses. Both sides now rushed to buy, charter, or build ships, and the western armies even rustled up navies of their own, like the Eads gunboats, which were designed by a bridge builder, manned by naval personnel, and owned by the United States Army. These ships were armored with anything that came to hand—railroad rails,

[25] In total population the Deep South led the Mid- and Upper South by 4,698-000 to 3,718,000 and 3,628,000 (counting West Virginia and the District of Columbia with the Upper South). But there were 610,000 white males 18 to 45 in the Upper South (Virginia-West Virginia estimated) to 527,000 in the Deep, and 475,000 in the Mid-South. The loss of the Upper South—though many men fought for the Confederacy—was a serious blow. But the loss of the Mid-South would have been catastrophic.

boiler plating, chains, oak, coal, hay, and cotton. A Confederate seagoing ironclad, Confederate Secretary of the Navy Mallory believed, could "traverse the entire coast of the United States, prevent all blockades, and encounter, with a fair prospect of success, their entire Navy." Since no Southern machine shop could build marine engines—a report to United States Secretary of the Navy Welles at this time reported thirty-eight such shops in the North, though some of them were small and in bad financial shape—Mallory decided to armor the hull and utilize the engines of the U.S.S. *Merrimac*, sunk in the debacle at Norfolk. The United States replied with three experimental ironclads—a gunboat, an ironclad like the newly completed French *Gloire*, and John Ericsson's "cheesebox on a raft," the *Monitor*.[26]

The *Monitor*—one of three ships approved by Welles's hastily constituted Ironclad Board—combined light draft, armor, and big guns in a movable turret. The guns could be aimed without turning the ship in the shallow waters which were the circulatory system of the Confederacy. The day before the *Monitor* arrived off Norfolk, the *Merrimac* (now the *Virginia*) destroyed two unarmored ships at the cost of two men to two hundred and fifty. The next day the two ironclads fought for four hours. The *Monitor* fired forty-one heavy shot and was hit twenty-two times. Nobody was killed, though three Yankees and eleven Confederates were wounded. The new ironclads were virtually invulnerable. Their ability to run past all existing coastal defenses was one of the most important factors in the Union's success on Southern waterways. Like all experimental ships, the Union's light draft ironclads had their weaknesses—one whole group of river monitors proved to have "negative flotation"—but they were as remarkable in their day as were the landing craft of the Second World War. After the war one of these "iron sea elephants"—with thirty inches of freeboard for a four-thousand-ton ship—went to Europe and another around Cape Horn.

[26] James M. Merrill, *The Rebel Shore: The Story of the Union Sea Power in the Civil War* (Boston, 1957), and Richard S. West, Jr., *Mr. Lincoln's Navy* (New York, 1957), stress operations. The latter also wrote *Gideon Welles: Lincoln's Navy Department* (Indianapolis, 1943) and *The Second Admiral: A Life of David Dixon Porter* (Annapolis, 1937). Charles Lee Lewis, *David Glasgow Farragut* (2 vols., Annapolis, 1941-1943) and *Admiral Franklin Buchanan* (Baltimore, 1929), and Joseph T. Durkin, *Stephen R. Mallory: Confederate Navy Chief* (Chapel Hill, 1954), are good. The best book on the *Monitor-Merrimac* problem is R. W. Daly, *How the "Merrimac" Won* (New York, 1957). A scholarly edition of Gideon Welles's famous and often tendentious *Diary* is by Howard K. Beale (3 vols., New York, 1960).

None of the smaller ironclads built in the Confederacy seems to have reached the open sea. Like the ships of the Continental Navy, they were mostly lost with the ports they were defending. The *Tennessee*, the largest of these ships (her engines were taken from a river steamer) fought a whole Union squadron in Mobile Bay. Her steering tackle was gone, her funnel broken off inside her, and the shutters jammed so that the gunports would not open. But she lost only two killed and nine wounded.[27]

It is difficult to estimate the real effects of the Northern blockade. Many Southerners agreed with Lord Wolseley: "Had the ports . . . been kept open . . . by the action of any great naval power, the Confederacy must have secured their independence." As in Germany after 1918, it was easy to exaggerate the effects of this almost impersonal force which had beaten down the men who had fought so long and valiantly. This explanation gained added validity from the belief that the war had been won solely by Northern industry. The effects of blockade are always most apparent at the end of a war; people are more conscious of the hardships of the last few months than of conditions in preceding periods. It was also easier to blame the blockade than to examine certain other factors: the disruption of land transportation, the disastrous cotton embargo, and the Confederacy's failure to control imports and stem inflation. Part of the blame could be shifted to Britain and France, who had so cravenly failed to challenge the North's violations of international law.

During the early phases of the war the Confederate cotton embargo did far more damage than the blockade. Obviously related to the Stamp Act boycott and Jeffersonian Non-Intercourse, the aim of the boycott was to force England and France to break the blockade in order to avoid economic collapse, in a period in which one out of every five Englishmen made his living from the textile industry. Southern agricultural products were the chief sources of foreign exchange for the United States. Without such exports, it was argued, the

[27] How many of the 671 United States naval vessels were ironclads depends on the definition. Most lists are in the sixties. There were 16 Confederate ironclads, counting everything finished or unfinished. Their slow rate of fire made the monitors ineffective against forts, although they could run most coast defenses. At Charleston in 1863 the 9 ironclads fired only 139 projectiles and wounded 7 men. The forts fired 2200 times, sinking one ship and putting some of the rest out of action with jammed turrets or other mechanical injuries. Only 3 men were killed. At Lissa in 1866, one ironclad was rammed and another blown up by fire. But only 8 men were killed on the other 17 ironclads in the battle.

North could not pay for imported manufactures. "Satisfied that the three great nations England, France, and the United States [the centers of western industrial civilization] could not live without the southern cotton," the South's leaders, with the almost unanimous support of its people, made the blockade temporarily effective. After the embargo had been abandoned, the Confederates were, for revolutionaries, very well supplied with weapons. During the last phases of the war the Confederacy had more arms than men. Its arsenals were running at a third of their capacity because of the shortage of labor. Largely because of poor internal transportation and the lack of purchasing power and credit, food and clothing were always scarcer than munitions. But $200,000,000 worth of goods were run through the blockade, and at least four-fifths of the supplies actually shipped reached the Confederacy. The blockade running system was costly—a point for the blockaders—and too much of the South's foreign exchange was spent on nonessentials, but contemporary French and British studies of the blockade emphasized its ineffectiveness. Steam, close observers believed, had ended the old-fashioned close blockade for good and all.[28]

The only way to plug the leaks in the blockade was to capture the Southern seaports. Less than ten months after Bull Run, seven of the ten Confederate ports with rail connections

[28] Frank L. Owsley, *King Cotton Diplomacy: Foreign Relations of the Confederate States of America* (2d ed. rev. Harriet Chappell Owsley, Chicago, 1959), 15. The breaking of normal trade with the North, though some traffic continued, hurt the South more than the blockade in the first years of war. For the other side of the coin, see Ludwell H. Johnson, *Red River Campaign: Politics and Cotton in the Civil War* (Baltimore, 1958). Blockade runners got goods in Bermuda or the West Indies, hid along the coast, and ran in at night. With no searchlights and only rocket and lantern signals, fifty blockaders caught a mere third of the ships entering Wilmington in the last months. Francis B. C. Bradlee, *Blockade Running during the Civil War* (Salem, Mass., 1925); Hamilton Cochrane, *Blockade Runners of the Confederacy* (Indianapolis, 1958).

Both armies began with a great variety of weapons, mostly smoothbores. Only a few muzzle-loading rifles had as yet been produced at Springfield and Harpers Ferry, which together could produce 22,000 pieces annually. By the end of 1862 the Union had purchased over 700,000 rifles and muskets and had produced 170,000 rifles. From this time on they depended on home manufacture, producing in all nearly 1,700,000 Springfields. The machinery captured at Harpers Ferry was set up in Richmond. Perhaps 40,000 rifles were made in the South before Gettysburg. Two hundred thousand (out of an eventual total of 600,000) had been imported, and 150,000 captured. Claud E. Fuller and Richard D. Stuert, *Firearms of the Confederacy* (Huntington, W. Va., 1944); Claud E. Fuller, *The Rifled Musket* (Harrisburg, 1958). See also Samuel B. Thompson, *Confederate Purchasing Operations Abroad* (Chapel Hill, 1935), and Frank E. Vandiver, *Ploughshares into Swords: Josiah Gorgas and Confederate Ordnance* (Austin, 1952).

had been captured or neutralized. No Union ironclads were involved except at Norfolk. These victories were won by steam rather than by armor and big guns, though the strong forts below New Orleans had been bombarded by big mortars. The real strength of earthworks was not yet appreciated; most of these victories had been won against little more than token resistance. Mobile, Charleston, and Wilmington might possibly have been taken as easily as New Orleans during this stage of the war, but the Confederates strengthened their defenses until it took whole fleets to capture them. Even so, only 3090 men were lost in all of these operations, more than two-thirds of them in capturing the three remaining seaports. When these losses are compared with Union casualties on land, the value of the Union command of the sea is strikingly apparent.[29]

The most effective Confederate reply to the invulnerable Northern ironclads was the torpedo (a term which was then used for both mines and torpedoes). Torpedoes had been used before, but never as extensively. Floating torpedoes drifted down the rivers. Anchored torpedoes (electrically-detonated "controlled" mines were more successful than contact mines) lurked in the channels. Towed torpedoes were dragged by small boats. Spar torpedoes (mines on the ends of poles) were used by steam launches. Coal torpedoes were hidden in Yankee coal barges. The nature of the coast and the fact that they had little shipping of their own to worry about aided the Confederates, but, considering the state of electricity and chemistry in the 1860's, Confederate torpedo operations were surprisingly successful. They introduced two new elements into naval warfare. For the first time since galley days, a ship could be sunk by attacking her below the waterline. And for the first time a large ship could be attacked by a smaller one. In the 1880's, after the development of the "automobile" torpedo by Robert Whitehead (an Englishman residing in Fiume in Austria-Hungary), a group of French naval officers who called themselves the *Jeune*

[29] Foreign observers were more interested in fortification than in any other aspect of the war, but Viktor E. K. R. von Scheliha, *A Treatise on Coast Defense* (London, 1868) is the only work. See Jay Luvaas, *The Military Legacy of the Civil War: The European Inheritance* (Chicago, 1959). New Orleans cost 335 casualties, an eighth of the British losses in 1815. Ft. Wagner, off Charleston, fell in September, 1863. Farragut entered Mobile Bay the following August. Wilmington, with its direct railroad to Richmond, was sealed off when Fort Fisher—with 48 guns and 1500 men—fell to 5 ironclads, 48 other ships, and 10,000 men in January 1865. For New Orleans see Charles L. Dufour, *The Night the War was Lost* (Garden City, 1960).

Ecole based part of their radically new theory of naval warfare on the torpedo.[30]

Land operations outside of Virginia developed along the lines of the great river systems. The most important land operations of 1861 were the civil wars in the border states of Missouri, Kentucky, and West Virginia. Once the Union had secured the heart of the Mississippi system (the area from which the Missouri, Mississippi, Illinois, Ohio, Wabash, Tennessee, and Cumberland rivers fan out like the spokes of a wheel) the Confederacy was open to attacks along the Mississippi, Cumberland, and Tennessee and along the railroad from Louisville. In February, 1862, the Union gunboats and armies broke through at Forts Henry and Donelson on the Tennessee and Cumberland, in the center of the Confederate position. Tennessee was cut nearly in two and the Union forces advanced against the east-west railroad running along its southern border between Chattanooga and Memphis. This led to the decisive battle of Shiloh in April. Two months later New Orleans was lost and the forces pushing down the Mississippi took Memphis. All this had taken place before McClellan's repulse from Richmond. Lee had taken over the command of the Confederates in front of Richmond only five days before the fall of Memphis. One western army was then based on the river and rail lines leading into west Tennessee; a second Union army was based on the rail and river lines to Nashville. In 1863 the first army under Grant opened the Mississippi by capturing Vicksburg and Port Hudson. The second army defeated a Confederate move into Kentucky (in the fall and winter of 1862), captured Chattanooga in September, 1863, was defeated at Chickamauga in Georgia, and finally opened the way for a Union thrust over the mountains

---

[30] The United States Navy also used torpedoes, but they had fewer targets. The Confederates sank eight armored and eighteen unarmored craft and injured many others. In the operations in which they were used most extensively, no Union ships were sunk by artillery, the heaviest ever used in warfare to that time. The C. S. S. *Hunley*, which sank the U. S. S. *Housatonic*, was a hand-operated submarine. There is some material in Charles Lee Lewis, *Matthew Fontaine Maury: The Pathfinder of the Seas* (Annapolis, 1927) and more in J. T. Scharf, *History of the Confederate States Navy* (Atlanta, 1887). Eugene B. Canfield, *Notes on Naval Ordnance of the American Civil War, 1861-1865* (Washington, 1960), 12-13, lists ships sunk or damaged. This and other pamphlets in this American Ordnance Association series are very important for Civil War buffs. Samuel R. Bright, Jr., *Confederate Coast Defense* (unpublished thesis, Durham, N. C., 1961) and Admiral John D. Hayes forthcoming edition of the correspondence of Admiral Samuel F. Du Pont throw much light on all Civil War naval matters.

in the battles of Lookout Mountain and Missionary Ridge in November.

Sherman's advance to Atlanta in the summer of 1864 was made possible by a combination of rail and water transportation. Sherman used his wagon trains as moving storehouses. They distributed supplies from the railhead to the troops—he later estimated that it would have taken 36,800 six-mule wagons to have hauled supplies for his 100,000 men and 35,000 animals if he had not been able to use the railway—and insured his army against temporary breaks in the railroad. Here the engineering experience of the West Pointers came into play—their wooden "beanpole and cornstalk" railway bridges were as remarkable for their day as their timber fortifications. The bridge over the Chattahoochie before Atlanta, for example, was eight hundred feet long and one hundred feet high, and was built in four and a half days. After Sherman left Atlanta on November 16 he was able to live off the country because he was certain of getting supplies and reinforcements whenever he hit the seacoast. (The rest of his army, under Thomas, had been sent north to watch Hood, who was beaten in the one really Napoleonic battle of the war at Nashville in December.) Meanwhile Grant had slowly moved the Army of the Potomac (in May and June, 1864) around to the east and south of Richmond. His base and one flank were always on the water. In two months he changed his base of operations four times, finally coming out below Petersburg. The result was to place his army across Lee's communications and in a position to capture both Richmond and Lee's army. When Richmond fell and Lee's army was lost with it, the revolution lost all political vitality. In April, 1865, Lincoln, Grant, Sherman, Lee, and Johnston displayed rare statesmanship as well as great military ability.[31]

The only Confederate naval success of the war was the attack on United States merchant shipping, though the South

[31] The term "Anaconda Plan" had been used early in the war to ridicule a letter from Scott to McClellan which outlined the future basis of Northern strategy. How much of this plan was due to Scott and how much to events and geography is impossible to say. One of Sherman's corps in North Carolina had moved by boat from Nashville to Cincinnati, then by rail to Baltimore and Washington, and by ship from Alexandria to Wilmington. The remnants of the Confederate army that had been defeated at Nashville moved south from Tupelo, Mississippi, through Mobile and Macon to Augusta. They then marched through the upper Carolinas to Charlotte, where they took the railway to Smithfield. H. Allen Gosnell, *Guns on the Western Waters: The Story of River Gunboats in the Civil War* (Baton Rouge, 1949), is excellent.

did not accomplish its long-range objective of forcing the United States Navy to lift the blockade. More than half the American merchant marine was driven from the flag. The raiders destroyed about 110,000 tons and 800,000 additional tons were transferred to foreign owners. This was accomplished by about a dozen ships, five of which were responsible for most of the damage. None of these ships was Confederate-built; in this respect the rebels were much weaker than the rebels of 1776. Like the *Bon Homme Richard*, the Confederate cruisers were not particularly good ships; a rebel government usually has difficulty in purchasing very powerful warships. Their success was due to four factors: (1) the ability of the Confederate cruiser commanders, especially Raphael Semmes of the *Sumter* and *Alabama*, (2) the special conditions of the transition from sail to steam, (3) a rather inept Union system of commerce protection, and (4) foreign aid. The raiders combined the range of sail and the speed of steam. All but two of their 261 captures were sailing ships. The Union's refusal to divert ships from the blockade was sound; convoys organized for the Panama route were successful. But the Union failed to prevent transfer to foreign registries by a system of government war-risk insurance. American trade continued under neutral flags; the failure of the transferred ships to return to American ownership after the war was due to long-term economic factors.

The most successful raiders were purchased in Britain, and repaired, coaled, and partially manned in British ports. An international tribunal later awarded the United States $15,500,000 damages for British violations of international law. But the Confederates never ran a foreign ironclad into a Southern port. Many Americans thought that the British were willing to have Confederate raiders cripple the American merchant marine, but were unwilling to risk war with the United States. The Confederate raiders, it was argued, also showed what United States cruisers might do to the British merchant marine in an Anglo-American war. The British paid damages to prevent precedents which would allow the United States to sell raiders to France or Russia. These Confederate successes and Britain's willingness to pay damages were to be major arguments for the *Jeune Ecole's* theories of naval warfare.[32]

32 The best of many studies are George W. Dalzell, *The Flight from the Flag* (Chapel Hill, 1943), and A. Lepotier, *Les Corsaires du Sud et le pavillon étoilé* (Paris, 1936).

Chapter 7

The Years of Uneasy Peace (1871-1914)

Military Organization: The Spread of Prussian Doctrine

IN MANY ways the wars of the mid-nineteenth century had been as important as those of the Great Revolution and the last Great Captain, Napoleon. But while interest in Napoleon still seems unabated, little recent historical work has been done on the military aspects of the Moltkean revolution in Germany. This is probably due to the fact that the German military revolution was a revolution in military organization. It had resulted in a new method of approaching military problems. In addition, Moltke was not a great military writer. His ideas must be studied in the letters and memoranda which he wrote on specific military problems and in the works of his associates, the men who commanded the German army during the late nineteenth century and wrote the books which explained the German method to the world. During the forty-three years of armed peace which followed the wars of the mid-nineteenth century every major power but Britain and the United States adopted the Prussian system of short-service conscription, while every major army set up a General Staff and a system of higher military education more or less on the Prussian pattern.[1]

As the Prussian method of approaching military problems spread, entire schools of military writers replaced the isolated military thinkers of previous generations. Though one of the most interesting of these schools appeared in the once somnolent British army, European military thought can best be studied in Germany and France, where Ferdinand Foch of the newly founded French War College became one of the

---

[1] In the science of war, as in science in general, "the greatest invention of the nineteenth century was the invention of the method of invention, . . . the process of disciplined attack upon one difficulty after another." Alfred North Whitehead, *Science and the Modern World* (New York, 1948), 28.

Moltke remained Chief of the General Staff until 1888, though Count Waldersee had been made Deputy Chief in 1882. Two of Moltke's section chiefs in 1870 became Ministers of War, and wrote major theoretical works. J. A. F. W. von Verdy du Vernois, *Studies in Troop Leading,* trans. W. H. Harrison (2 vols., London, 1872-1877). See also his description of the workings of the staff system, *With the Royal Headquarters in 1870-1871* (London, 1897). Paul Bronsart von Schellendorff, *Der Dienst des Generalstabes* (4th ed., Berlin, 1905). His much franker description of the General Staff's workings is *Geheimes Kriegstagebuch* (Bonn, 1954).

most influential theorists of his generation. Foch's most important work was an attempt to clarify and define the *Principles of War*, "to explain from what necessities they arise, to what results they lead; how, being unchangeable, they can be applied . . . to modern war, the new features of which have so profound an effect." Both Foch and the Germans believed that "history is the base" of all military theory. Officers should study history, in the words of the German strategist Hohenlohe, "not to pass judgment on any given event . . . or general," but as the necessary substitutes for the command experience which they could not otherwise gain in peacetime. "Only those who have passed through the mental struggles which form part of its [strategy's] execution can be sure that their ideas . . . will be just." Since these historical laboratory cases had to be as detailed as possible, Hohenlohe felt that they should be taken only from "the wars of the present century." Though some writers—like the *Jeune Ecole* of naval theorists—wished to limit themselves to wars fought since the introduction of the breechloader, both the French and Germans studied the wars of Napoleon and those of 1859, 1866, and 1870. These were the wars which Clausewitz had analyzed or which his pupils had fought and won. It is not surprising that the conclusions of Foch's chapter on the "Primal Characteristics of Modern War" are based on Clausewitz' statement that "Modern war proceeds from Napoleon's views, as he was the first to throw light on the importance of preparation and on the omnipotence of *mass* multiplied by impulsion, with the object of breaking, in a battle sought from the outset of the war, the moral and material forces of the adversary." "The synthesis we can deduce from history," Foch concluded, "is characterised by three things: preparation; mass; impulsion." [2]

2 *Principles of War*, trans. Hilaire Belloc (London, 1921), Preface to the first ed., 1903, 44-47. Kraft zu Hohenlohe-Ingelfingen, *Letters on Strategy* (2 vols., London, 1898), I, 5-6. Luvaas's important *Military Legacy* shows Europeans studying Civil War logistics and strategy more than tactics, perhaps because of the original inexperience of the armies and the difficult terrain.

On official history see Liddell Hart, "Responsibility and Judgment in Historical Writing" (*Military Affairs*, XXIII, Spring, 1959, 35-36), and W. Frank Craven, *Why Military History?* (United States Air Force Academy, Colorado, 1959). Foch believed that history provided a "practical" means of teaching fixed principles from "particular cases . . . in order (1) to prepare for experience, (2) to teach the *art of commanding*, (3) lastly, to impart the *habit of acting correctly without having to reason*." The aim was "a corps of officers . . . whom the same spirit shall pervade, who shall submit to a common mental discipline, who shall be numerous enough to be able to move and manage the heavy machine of modern armies." *Principles*, 11, 20.

Mass was the central term of Foch's three characteristics of modern war. The Prussian short-service conscription system now spread throughout the European continent. But since Russia, Italy, and Austria-Hungary were still too poor to train and equip all of their available men, the chief phases in the further development of the mass army can best be seen in Germany and France. The greatest concession to German liberalism in the new Imperial constitution had been a popularly elected lower house of parliament. But the *Reichstag* could not force the Chancellor to resign, and its control over the budget was carefully circumscribed. The Imperial revenues were fixed customs and excise taxes; when expenditures exceeded income, the deficit was met by loans or levies on the state governments. The representatives who voted money for arms were not necessarily forced to vote new taxes to pay for them, and many vital aspects of military and foreign policy remained outside this limited parliamentary control. Bismarck first tried to insure the army's financial independence with an "iron budget," linking its numbers and budget to an increasing population. In 1867 the North German parliament had fixed the peacetime army at one per-cent of the total population with an allowance of 225 thalers per man for the next ten years. The first Imperial *Reichstag* renewed this arrangement for three years. In 1874 the army asked for a permanent peacetime force of 401,659 men, but the *Reichstag* refused to vote money for more than a seven-year period. A second "septennate" was adopted in 1880, a year before the expiration of the first one, but Bismarck ran into trouble in 1886 when, on the strength of France's military revival, he again asked for a new army grant before the expiration of the old one. He got his way by dissolving the *Reichstag*, but his successor, General Caprivi, had to accept a five-year military bill in 1893. Even this arrangement—which lasted until the fall of the Hohenzollerns—permitted the German army chiefs to plan on a long-term basis. With Germany's wealth and population increasing rapidly, the generals, after the proper propaganda preparation, usually got just about what they asked for.[3]

[3] Gordon A. Craig, *The Politics of the Prussian Army, 1640-1945* (Oxford, 1945), 217 ff.; Herbert Rosinski, *The German Army* (Washington, 1944); Emil Obermann, *Soldaten, Bürger, Militaristen* (Stuttgart, 1958); Heinrich Meisner, *Militärattaches und Militärbevollmächtige in Preussen und in Deutschen Reich* (Berlin, 1957); Karl Ernst Jeismann, *Das Problem des Präventivkrieges in europäischen Staatensystem mit besonderem Blick auf die Bismarckzeit* (Munich, 1957); Friedrich Hossbach, *Die Entwicklung des*

The French army solved two great problems in the next forty years. It convinced itself that it was as good as the German army. And it got an all-powerful parliament to match these semiautomatic German increases from a less prosperous economy and a static population. Unable to agree on many other things, Frenchmen made their army "the great common denominator" of their hopes and the "symbol of the national revival." Even the conservatives now swung toward the Prussian short-service system, though many of them still believed that an *armée de métier* was politically more reliable. In 1872 all Frenchmen were made liable for five years' active service and the usual reserve duty. Since everyone could not serve five years, eligible men still drew lots and those with the good numbers got only six months' training. Prospective teachers and priests were exempted; men with fifteen hundred francs and certain degrees might volunteer for a year's service and a reserve officer's commission. This compromise law was gradually changed by democratic pressure and German numbers. After 1880 most men were furloughed after serving three years, though this was not made the legal limit until 1889. By the mid-eighties the ultra-nationalistic supporters of General Boulanger were talking of a military dictatorship and a war of revenge on Germany, the situation which produced Bismarck's military bill of 1887. The Germans met the Franco-Russian alliance (1891-1894) by cutting the term of service in the infantry to two years, thus expanding the wartime army without a proportionate increase in peacetime. In the 1890's France and Germany were spending about the same amounts on their peacetime armies, each of which then numbered somewhat less than half a million men.[4]

The Franco-German arms race slacked off a bit during the first years of the twentieth century. Against the wishes of the army, the German Emperor William II (1888-1918) was spending great sums on his new navy. German naval expenditures nearly tripled from 1900 to 1911 while military expenditures rose by only a quarter. In addition, the experts did not agree on future military policy. The General Staff wished to call up more of the available men—in 1911 the Germans

Oberbefehls über das Heer in Brandenburg, Preussen und im Deutschen Reich von 1645–1945 (Würzburg, 1957); and Willi Boelcke, *Krupp und die Hohenzollern: Aus der Korrespondenz der Familie Krupp, 1850-1916* (Berlin, 1956).
[4] See the brilliant works by Richard D. Challener, *The French Theory of the Nation in Arms, 1866-1939* (New York, 1955), Raoul Girardet, *La Société militaire dans la France contemporaine, 1815-1939* (Paris, 1953), and Henry Contamine, *La Revanche, 1871-1914* (Paris, 1957).

were using only 53% of those eligible for service, while the French were calling up 83%—but some of the conservatives in the War Ministry wanted a longer training period. The Military Cabinet, which controlled promotions, feared that a larger army would require too many middle-class officers.

The French Radicals were now pushing for a two-year service law with no exemptions even for theological students, while the great Socialist leader, Jean Jaurès, was evolving a plan for a Swiss-type militia with only six months' training. The future Marshal Lyautey, though a political conservative, believed that the training methods of the old *armée de métier* were outdated. Soldiers were "not brutes but Frenchmen." Their training should strive for *"individual instruction;* each man ought to be inspired to complete his own *individual education."* A republican army needed a republican officers' corps. The Radicals charged that the monarchist generals who had carried over from the Second Empire were not promoting Jewish, Protestant, or even strongly republican officers. The battle was joined in the Dreyfus case of the late 1890's, which the stupidity of certain officers and their conservative political allies turned into the Radical-Socialist electoral victory of 1901. Two-year service with no exemptions was passed in 1905. In the meantime the ardently republican War Minister, General Louis André, attempted to stamp out monarchism and clericalism in the officers' corps by a system of secret political reports from Freemasons, the civilian authorities of the districts in which suspected monarchist officers were stationed, and even from trusted republican officers.[5]

Germany's peacetime army increased by only twenty-five thousand men from 1900 to 1911. In the second Moroccan crisis of 1911 the great powers had moved close to a general war. This crisis and Russia's rapid recovery from her defeat by Japan and the revolution of 1905 finally forced the German army chiefs to resume the march toward really universal conscription. General Colmar von der Goltz had been advocating this policy since his careful study of the French na-

[5] Marshal Louis Lyautey's originally anonymous article was *Du rôle social de l'officier* (Paris, 1946). An abbreviated English translation of Jean Léon Jaurès, *L'Armée nouvelle* (Paris, 1910) is *Democracy and Military Service* (London, 1916). None of the many works on the Dreyfus case deals specifically with the army. Like their German counterparts, many conservative French officers sincerely believed that the Army was the only institution which could prevent complete social and national disintegration. More and more of the nobility now sent their sons into the army because it was the one public service in which the right connections and ideas were still helpful.

tional resistance of 1871. His *Nation in Arms* had greatly influenced such younger officers as Erich Ludendorff, one of the key men in the deployment section of the General Staff, while the superpatriotic Army League, founded early in 1912, imitated the successful German Navy League and flooded Germany with big-army propaganda. Forty thousand men were added to the German army in 1912 and 131,000 in 1913. German army expenditures more than doubled. For the first time Germany pulled ahead of France in per capita arms expenditures. The French had few more men to call up. In spite of the protests of the Radical-Socialists, the only solution seemed to be a return to three-year service. The two active armies each numbered about 800,000 men at the beginning of mobilization in 1914. Nearly every able-bodied man in the proper age groups in France, even workers in the armaments industry, took the field. The men of the Third Republic had carried the *levée en masse* to its logical conclusion.[6]

Mobilization and Intellectual Preparation of the Mass Army

The need for careful *preparation* went along with *mass*. More men were trained by training each one for a shorter time and then placing him in a carefully organized reserve. The mobilization plan was the principal peacetime monument to each General Staff, a complicated set of secret documents to regulate the movement of millions of men, hundreds of thousands of horses, and millions of tons of supplies. The Plan's limits were fixed by the railways. Their capacity and location, in Hohenlohe's words, was "always *the* determining factor for the first deployment." Since each side could estimate the carrying power of the other's railways, strategy became a fairly exact guessing game. The guesses, according to

[6] *The Nation in Arms* was translated by Philip A. Ashworth and published in London in 1887. The tables in A. J. P. Taylor, *The Struggle for Mastery in Europe, 1848-1914* (Oxford, 1954), xxvi-xxix, shows the Germans (4.6%) almost up to France (4.8%) in the proportion of the national income spent on arms. Both were behind poor Austria-Hungary (6.1%) and Russia (6.3%). Britain (3.4%) spent the smallest proportion, though until 1910 she had spent more than any other power, owing to the cost of her volunteer system. Italy (3.5%) was about out of the race. Since 1880 Germany's arms expenditures had more than quintupled. The Russian and British bills had trebled, and that of France had not quite doubled. The various German army bills are discussed in Kurt Jany, *Geschichte der Königlich-Preussischen Armee* (4 vols., Berlin, 1933), IV. For the French see Joseph Monteilhet, *Les Institutions militaires de la France, 1814-1932* (Paris, 1932), and Georges Michon, *La Préparation à la guerre, la loi de trois ans, 1910-1914* (Paris, 1935).

von der Goltz, were based on the enemy's probable objectives, "the locality in which the assembly of his armies must take place, . . . the peacetime distribution of his troops, . . . the railways, roads, or waterways . . . by which they will come up, [and] the natural grouping of the enemy's fighting strength into different armies." Contrary to popular belief, a General Staff did not try to set a timetable for operations after the army's opening moves. The army's objective was usually the very general one, "to invade the theatre of war occupied by the [enemy] army, [to] seek it out, and to force it to battle under the most favorable conditions possible."[7]

The 1914 armies paid surprisingly little attention to long-range strategic reconnaissance or to raids to interfere with the enemy's mobilization. Aircraft, automobile, and even motor-cycle units were still too new for much reliance to be placed on them. Though American horsemen had been used as mounted infantry for long-distance raids and reconnaissance, the German army rejected Alfred von Schlieffen's [Chief of the General Staff—1891-1905] suggestion of an independent cavalry corps to take objectives far ahead of the infantry. Though this idea, which looked forward to the modern armored corps, was supported by the cavalry expert Friedrich von Bernhardi, neither the French nor the German commands attempted to use their cavalry in 1914 to disrupt the enemy's mobilization. The cavalry were either tied to short-range reconnaissance for the advancing infantry or were held in reserve to fight enemy horsemen who never appeared. Cavalrymen could not decide whether the horse was still a valid shock weapon or just a means of locomotion. Though they paid lip service to the irresistible shock of the muscles of men and horses, most cavalry were really trained as mounted infantry.[8]

But this failure to develop long-range reconnaissance was

[7] *The Conduct of War,* trans. Major G. F. Leverson (London, 1908), 126.
[8] Friedrich von Bernhardi's chief work was *Cavalry,* trans. Major G. T. M. Bridges (New York, 1914). The conservatives admitted that horsemen could "get into positions where, if they were infantry and in large numbers, their effect would be most telling." But digging and shooting would be the end of horsemanship. "Every hour devoted by cavalry to shooting which subtracts anything from training in their own proper work . . . weakens them. . . . Shooting ought to be for them always a most subordinate matter." F. Maurice, *War* (London, 1891), 66-67. Sir Evelyn Wood had seen a run-away cab horse knock over an iron lamp post and two stone pillars on Pall Mall. "If it were possible to obtain the same amount of determination from riders, as that which inspired the unfortunate horse, . . . all cavalry charges would succeed, in spite of every sort of missile." *Achievements of Cavalry* (London, 1897), 242.

not wholly due to the weakness of mechanized transport and the confusion of cavalry doctrine. 1914 armies were not particularly interested in upsetting the enemy's mobilization. The right Plan would force him to fight anyhow on ground chosen by the attacker. This belief in the supreme influence of a well-chosen offensive deployment—the central feature of Schlieffen's planning—rested, in turn, on another feature of the mass army—its clumsiness after it had left its original points of concentration. This was the central problem of Foch's third characteristic of modern war—impulsion. Once the staffs had solved the problems of entraining and detraining, men could move several hundred miles by rail as easily as they had once moved ten or fifteen. But once they had left their railheads, they were still primarily dependent on the muscles of men and horses—726,670 of the latter in the mobilized German army of 1914. Hard roads were more common than they had been a century before, but away from the railhead, the highly developed mass army was a less flexible instrument than that of Napoleon. The reservists who were thrown directly into field operations were more likely to be out of condition and such huge numbers could not hope to live off the country.[9]

All armies had now adopted the German (and Sherman's) "staging" system of supply. Just as in the eighteenth century, long wagon trains shuttled between the troops, the magazines, and the all-important railhead. Each man, according to the French regulations of 1887, carried three days' iron rations, which were not to be eaten unless the daily rations failed to arrive. Regimental wagons—with two days' rations—delivered these to the men. "Supply columns"—four hundred wagons per corps—filled the regimental wagons from temporary magazines. Other "reserve supply columns" could be thrown into the shuttle if the troops got too far from the temporary magazines, while a separate supply organization—six hundred

[9] Some motorized units were attached to both the French and German armies in 1914, but there were only 8200 officers and men in all the German truck units. Both the French and German governments paid large premiums (more than $2000 per car in Germany) for automobiles which could be used for military purposes, but the General Staffs were more interested in cycles than in heavier, roadbound vehicles.

As von der Goltz remarked, the 1914 armies represented "the most stupendous emigration of peoples, . . . as though it were a small realm that . . . was wandering to the frontier . . . to pour its whole population over a confined district." *Nation in Arms*, 150. An army corps might march forty-five miles in three days, resting on the fourth to avoid total exhaustion. Forced marches, as always, traded men for time. The men near the rear of the eighteen-mile column were nearly a day's march from its head. The train occupied another nine miles of road.

wagons to each corps—filled the temporary magazines from the railhead and local supplies. The whole system has been compared to an arm pinned from the shoulder to the wrist, with only the fingers free. The army's advance was directly related, of course, to the position of the wrist, or railhead. Its "average daily progress" could never be "greater than the length of field railway that can be . . . completed . . . in one day." And the fingers were so swollen that it was difficult to bring them together against a single point and almost impossible to turn them to either side. Like lemmings, these masses of men and horses would swarm from their trains and push slowly straight ahead. This was the reason for Hohenlohe's maxims that "Deployment at the right spot is the great object of all strategical wisdom" and that "A delay of a single day" or an error "in the original assembly of the army can scarcely ever be rectified."[10]

For this reason, too, it was impossible to be too strong for the first decisive offensive. The army, in Foch's words, must be hurled "with all the means it possesses: guns, rifles, bayonets, swords . . . *as one whole on one objective*." Victory would result from "the *disorder* this manoeuvre produces within the enemy army, and the moral superiority created by the same manoeuvre within one's own army." Bernhardi felt that the importance of the offensive had increased with "the difficulties of moving masses. The counter-measures of the defendant will take all the longer time, the greater the masses he must move, the broader the front, . . . and the more the assailant has succeeded in surprise." Would such a strategic shock end the war? Bernhardi did not know; the Germans had been surprised by the French national resistance after Sedan. But he did not expect the latter phases of a war to be like the first. "The physical efforts made at the beginning of the war are so great, that it is scarcely impossible to increase them, at least in France, which raises its last men on the first day of mobilization." Since most soldiers believed that the next war would be decided in the first battles, the growth of mass armies in an industrial age was not accompanied by

[10] Friedrich von Bernhardi, *On War of Today,* trans. Karl von Donat (2 vols., London, 1913), I, 266. Hohenlohe, *Strategy,* I, 21, 283. Hohenlohe had witnessed the result of two German corps' sudden change of direction in 1870, "the entanglement of wagons making it impossible to move forward or back, and blocking the roads completely." Shaw, *Supply,* 88-92, is excellent. Local supplies were now estimated at no more than a third of the required food and fodder. The marching power of the supply columns was not much greater than that of the infantry.

long-range plans for economic mobilization. This failure to prepare for a long war reinforced, in turn, the belief that such a war could result only in mutual bankruptcy and social revolution. Bernhardi thought the mass army

so enormous and complicated that it [must be] spared great and extensive moral shocks. . . . When large concentrated masses are out of hand, . . . they . . . become a positive danger. . . . War conducted with large armies is therefore . . . a risky game. . . . It is only natural . . . to finish it rapidly and quickly relieve the tension which must arise when the whole nation is called to arms.[11]

So the theorists' picture of the next war was surprisingly like that of the wars of 1866 and 1870, which had been decided by a series of initial shocks from which the defeated armies had never recovered. Then, arguing from these historical examples, these theorists had built mass armies which seemed capable, to their builders, only of fighting the kind of war which had been posited by these historical examples. To this point these theorists can be considered as "scientists," peering at the war of the future by the uncertain light of military history. But many of them also believed that war was necessary to human progress. Philosophical justifications for war were very old—a later writer listed ten different schools of war "ideologists"—the Darwinian hypothesis now enabled these philosophers to draw analogies from natural science. War was as natural as competition between individuals and species. "Modern wars," Foch quoted von der Goltz with approval, "have become the nations' way of doing business." Bernhardi's *Germany and the Next War* held that war was one of the Christian virtues. "The inevitableness, the idealism, and the blessing of wars" should be "repeatedly emphasized to every citizen." Did this glorification of war make better soldiers? Von der Goltz thought that young, enthusiastic conscripts might be better than veterans.

11 Foch, *Principles*, 47, 96. Bernhardi, *War of Today*, II, 28-29, 72-74. Moltke reflected this surprise at the French national resistance when he admitted that, in a two-front war, Germany could not defeat France quickly enough to deal decisively with Russia. See Gerhard Ritter, *The Schlieffen Plan*, trans. Andrew and Eva Wilson (London, 1958). The French even expected to send railway men to the front after mobilization. The Germans, fearing the loss of Russian grain, began to study food supply in 1894. The navy wished to study raw materials supply in 1906, but the army declared itself satisfied when a nine months' supply of food seemed assured. See Friedrich Edlen von Braun, *Kann Deutschland durch Hunger besiegt werden?* (Munich, 1914); Reichsarchiv, *Kriegsrüstung und Kriegswirtschaft* (Berlin, 1930), Vol. I, I Anlage, and Eberhard Scherbening, *Wirtschaftsorganisation im Kriege* (Jena, 1938).

Experience in the short wars of our day, plays but an insignificant rôle for the private soldier. . . . Experience even works injuriously upon courage. . . . It is otherwise with leaders, . . . but in the ranks "veteranism" has lost its former significance. . . . Only the young . . . advance into battle with joy and lightheartedness, and both these are necessary for the bloody work.

Consciously and unconsciously, the men in the ranks in 1914 had been led to believe that the coming war would be short and glorious. The resulting shock was to be one factor in the appearance of the greatest war literature in history.[12]

This glorification of war was one ingredient of German "militarism," however that concept is defined. Others were the lack of parliamentary control over the army and the Junkers' favored position in the officers' corps, though many middle-class scholars and journalists were more chauvinistic than many Junkers. Especially after the election of 1912, conservative politicians tried to exploit the army's popularity to counter rising socialist and democratic sentiment. The military historian Hans Delbrück, the moderate conservative editor of the most influential magazine in Germany, feared that chauvinistic writers like Bernhardi were doing more harm to Germany than the socialists. Their outbursts certainly helped to fix the picture of German militarism in the foreign mind. Yet the Empire was not a military dictatorship. Schlieffen "remained as tolerant of the shortcomings of William [II]'s foreign policy as he was of the egregious mistakes made by the emperor . . . in army manoeuvres." Schlieffen's successor in 1905, the nephew and namesake of Moltke, was equally

---

[12] Foch, *Principles*, 35. Friedrich von Bernhardi, *Germany and the Next War*, trans. Allen H. Powles (New York, 1914), 37. Von der Goltz, *The Nation in Arms*, 17, 18. L. L. Bernard, *War and Its Causes* (New York, 1944), lists biological, psychological or psychiatric, ethical, theological, aesthetic, nationalistic, supernaturalistic, racist, economic, and sociological justifications for war. Both this military propaganda and the processes by which it was injected into the body politic were later to be analyzed as carefully as the battles of 1866 and 1870. Carolyn Playne, *The Pre-War Mind in Britain* (London, 1928), and Carlton J. H. Hayes, *France, a Nation of Patriots* (New York, 1930) are classics. See also Irving Louis Horowitz, *The Idea of War and Peace in Contemporary Philosophy* (New York, 1957); Kenneth N. Waltz, *Man, the State and War: A Theoretical Analysis* (New York, 1959); and Alix Strachey, *The Unconscious Motives of War, a Psycho-analytical Contribution* (London, 1957).

Was the theorists' concentration on one kind of war due to their method of predicting the future from the intense study of the past? Or to too narrow a selection of their historical examples? Or had the general staffs become closed groups of military schoolmen "competent only by definition, . . . out of touch with the living, acting, operating nation?" Douhet, *Command of the Air*, 125.

complaisant. William II was a most difficult monarch to advise. A "combination of military Hohenzollernism and self-hypnotism," he was an easy convert to the new gospels of Social Darwinism, imperialism, and navalism. His "mailed fist" diplomacy was wildly applauded by certain sections of the German public. Waldersee's mild criticisms of William's military genius had been partly responsible for his being replaced by Schlieffen as Chief of the General Staff. Big business, militarist, navalist, and imperialist groups advocated different expansionist policies. Each "had a single enemy and would have liked to make peace with the others. But Germany lacked a directing hand to insist on priorities. It was easier to acquiesce in all the aggressive impulses and to drift with events." Nowhere was this more evident than in Germany's naval policy, William's chief personal achievement as Emperor.[13]

The Race for Colonies and Sea Power

Overseas expansion had been overshadowed before 1871 by such problems as the unification of Italy and Germany. Liberals then advocated colonial home rule, and military conservatives opposed the expense of colonial conquests. After 1880, however, these attitudes sharply changed. Every great power except Austria-Hungary now became involved in the active, conscious colonial expansionism known as imperialism. Their

[13] Craig, *Prussian Army*, 281-282; Fritz Haller, *Philip Eulenberg, the Kaiser's Friend* (2 vols., London, 1930), II, 44; Taylor, *Struggle for Mastery*, 529. See also Joachim von Kurenberg, *The Kaiser: A Life of William II, Last Emperor of Germany*, trans. H. T. Russell and Herta Hagen (New York, 1955), and Hans Hagen, *Wilhelm II als Kaiser und König: eine historische Studie* (Berlin, 1954). Prussian War Minister Karl von Einem did speak out against the Kaiser's naval policy. See *Erinnerungen eines Soldaten, 1853-1933* (Leipzig, 1933). One of Hans Delbrück's most famous articles was his denunciation of *"Die Alldeutschen"* in December, 1913. This is reprinted in *Vor und nach dem Weltkrieg: Politische und historische Aussätze, 1902-1925* (Berlin, 1926), 397-403. See also Annelise Thimme, *Hans Delbrück als Kritiker der Wilhelminischen Epoche* (Düsseldorf, 1955).

Conservative chauvinism goaded the Social Democrats into strong statements, but not votes, against the army. See Milorad N. Drachkovitch, *Les Socialismes français et allemand et le problème de la guerre, 1870-1914* (Geneva, 1955), and Walter Bartel, *Die Linken in der deutschen Sozialdemokratie im Kampf gegen Militarismus und Krieg* (Berlin, 1958). Albert T. Lauterbach sees two kinds of militarism. "The old militarism expected class privileges for the warriors." The new is either "a trend of national policy or a political philosophy" which regards war as the main end of the state. "Militarism in the Western World, a Comparative Study" (*Journal of the History of Ideas*, V, May, 1944, 446-478). On the whole, the Prussian conservatives adapted themselves to the new age with some skill. The middle-class element in the officers' corps was "Junkerized" rather than the reverse.

rivalries were responsible for a number of wars, though six of the wars of this period (1876-1878, 1885, 1887, 1911-1912, 1912-1913, and 1913) involved the perennial Near Eastern problem. One war involved the United States and Spain (1898) and one the British and the Boer republics (1899-1902). There were two major wars in the Far East: the Sino-Japanese War of 1894-1895 and the Russo-Japanese War ten years later. This last war, and to a certain extent the Boer War, were the only ones which seemed to cast some light on the tactics of the new fire weapons. By 1914 there were no less than eleven colonial powers: Britain, France, and Russia, who had steadily increased their holdings; the Netherlands and Portugal; five new entries—Germany, Italy, the United States, Belgium, and Japan; and Spain, who, after losing two hundred thousand men in Cuba, spent $800,000,000 and many more thousands of lives in the conquest of Spanish Morocco.[14]

The imperialist case usually involved one or more arguments—economic, missionary, or strategic—wrapped in the most powerful appeal of all, that of national prestige and glory. The active agents of imperialism were businessmen, army and naval officers, explorers, missionaries, and journalists and politicians who often knew little about the colonies and had even less intention of going there. "Some capitalists," the American historian Carlton J. H. Hayes has written, "undoubtedly promoted imperialism, and more profited by it. But in the last analysis it was the nationalistic masses who made it possible and who most vociferously applauded and most constantly backed it." Since so many of the arguments for colonies were essentially sentimental, it is hard to separate the tangible military fruits of imperialism—such as naval bases, colonial manpower, and strategic raw materials—from the intangibles of national pride and status. Real concern with strategic raw materials did not arise until soldiers began to face the problems of a long war. The same thing was true of colonial manpower. The only colonial forces which were expected to take part in the decisive first battles in Europe were a white Algerian corps and one formed of white long-service colonial troops. Distance and political unrest—the Germans were confident—would cancel out the untrained manpower

14 The military lessons of the "small wars" of this era are discussed in Cyril Falls, *A Hundred Years of War* (London, 1953).

of the British Dominions and the Indian army, still much the largest colonial force in the world.[15]

Navalism—that uncritical demand for sea power which was to spark the greatest warship building boom in history—was closely related to Social Darwinism, imperialism, and militarism. A great state had to have a great battle fleet to protect its great colonial empire whether it could afford or even use it or not. As has been noticed, the Industrial Revolution affected navies even more rapidly than armies; iron ships, armor, steam, big guns, and torpedoes were all introduced in the middle decades of the nineteenth century. The high point of the resulting tactical and strategical confusion was reached in the 1880's when the French *Jeune Ecole* and their followers in other countries argued that torpedo boats had made battleships obsolete and that the wars of the mid-century had shown that the command of the sea was equally useless. For a time during the 1880's battleship construction almost ceased. The House of Commons was told in 1886 that the battleships then building might be the last ever added to the Royal Navy. That same year Admiral Théophile Aube, the leader of the *Jeune Ecole* and Minister of Marine in the cabinet in which General Boulanger was Minister of War, stopped all French battleship construction and put the money into torpedo boats and cruisers. Sea power had, indeed, played little part in the wars of 1859, 1866, and 1870, and the *Jeune Ecole* accepted the general opinion that the next European war would probably follow the same pattern. In such a short war a commercial blockade would not be effective. Amphibious operations—especially considering the small size of the British army—would be too little and too late; though steam—by "bridging the Channel"—had perhaps

15 *A Generation of Materialism, 1871-1900* (New York, 1941), 228. The German colonial empire was of no military value. All that the 1914 French imperialists were able to claim was that the French empire was no longer a positive drain on French manpower. But Colonel Charles Mangin's *La Force noire* (Paris, 1911) was still a project rather than a reality. See Shelby C. Davis, *Reservoirs of Men* (Chambéry, 1934).

The French settlers in Algeria opposed any general arming of the Arabs. Indochina, the most populous French colony, was the farthest from "the hole in the Vosges." Expansion in Indochina had been opposed by many military men as well as by republican and socialist anti-imperialists. Raoul Castex pointed out that Indochina could not possibly be held against Japan. *Le Peril japonais en Indo-Chine* (Paris, 1904) and "L'Expansion coloniale et la stratégie navale" (*Académie de Marine Mémoires et Communications*, IX, 1930). John F. Cady, *The Roots of French Imperialism in Eastern Asia* (Ithaca, 1954), notes that the case for expansion in Indochina rested almost wholly on such intangibles as "pride of culture, reputation, prestige, and influence," 294-296.

made it possible for Continental armies to invade England. The *Jeune Ecole's* trump card against England, however, was commerce destroying. The *Alabama* affair had highlighted Britain's new dependence on imported food and raw materials. Since raiders similar to the *Alabama* could no longer be kept in port, the Royal Navy would have to convoy every ton of a merchant fleet which had become so large that such convoy protection was assumed to be impossible. Since a navy could now perform none of its real functions—blockade, amphibious operations, protection against invasion, and commerce protection—the *Jeune Ecole* argued that the command of the sea was meaningless. Even torpedo boats would sink British shipping in the Mediterranean and the Channel in complete disregard of the recognized rules of cruiser warfare.[16]

The *Jeune Ecole's* decline may be dated by two events: the British Naval Defense Act of 1889 and the publication of Mahan's *Influence of Sea Power upon History*. The Naval Defense Act appropriated huge sums—nearly twice the average annually spent on the whole navy a few years before—for new battleships to bring the British fleet up to a "two-power standard" of equality with France and Russia. The others followed suit, France with a standard to equal the Triple Alliance (Germany, Italy, Austria-Hungary), etc. Since the British Admiral P. H. Colomb's *Naval Warfare: Its Ruling Principles and Practices Historically Treated* (London, 1891) was appearing serially when Mahan's book came out, even the clarification of naval thought now associated with Mahan was doubtless inevitable. At forty-five the latter had been "drifting on the lines of simple respectability" in a navy which traditionally favored the strategy now advocated

---

16 E. M. Winslow, *The Pattern of Imperialism* (New York, 1948); A. P. Thornton, *The Imperial Idea and Its Enemies: A Study in British Power* (New York, 1959). On navies see my chapter in Earle, *Modern Strategy*, Arthur J. Marder, *The Anatomy of British Sea Power: A History of British Naval Policy in the Pre-Dreadnought Era, 1880-1905* (New York, 1940) and his forthcoming sequel volume, his edition of Lord Fisher's letters, *Fear God and Dread Nought*, P. K. Kemp, ed., *The Papers of Admiral Sir John Fisher* (I, London, 1960), Hovgaard, *Modern History of Warships*, and Oscar Parkes, *British Battleships: Warrior 1860 to Vanguard 1950: A History of Design, Construction and Armament* (London, 1958).

Four-fifths of Britain's wheat was now imported; stocks within the country often fell to a six weeks' supply. Much of the damage done by the *Alabama* had been due to transfers to foreign registry. Since proposals for government war risk insurance ran into the usual doctrinaire liberal opposition, it seemed as though Britain's food supply would depend on neutral shipping and on enemy recognition of such wartime transfers.

by the *Jeune Ecole*, when he was assigned to teach naval history at the new United States Naval War College. Mahan had to face the basic issue raised by that group, whether the lessons of the past could be applied "under the changed conditions of naval warfare." Mahan believed that these lessons were still valid, that "History has recorded illustrations, and from those illustrations has formulated principles. . . . Master your principles and then ram them home with the illustrations which History furnishes." Mahan found that such principles had as yet been expressed "entirely" in "works devoted to land strategy," especially those of Jomini. Mahan applied them to naval warfare. "It has since been said . . . that no claim for originality could be allowed me; and that I wholly concede. . . . But no one since [Bacon and Raleigh] had undertaken to demonstrate their thesis [of the importance of sea power] by an analysis of history, attempting to show . . . precisely what influence the command of the sea had had upon definite issues." Mahan's weakness as an historian lay in his uncritical emphasis on this single historical theme and in his equally uncritical acceptance of the extreme Social Darwinist view of international politics. But his acceptance of these popular views of international politics, race, and imperialism was partly responsible for his tremendous influence in his own time. He had hit upon an interpretation of national greatness which linked all of these popular themes together.[17]

By 1914 few people even in France remembered the *Jeune Ecole*, though the failing of sailing raiders did not answer their contention that Britain's economic position was now

[17] *Naval Strategy*, 12, 17. *From Sail to Steam: Recollections of Naval Life* (New York, 1907), 105. "Original research," he admitted, "was not within my scope. . . . I laid my hands on whatever came along, reading with the profound attention of one who is looking for something." *Ibid.*, 277-278. His presidential address to the American Historical Association in 1902 (in *Naval Administration and Warfare*, Boston, 1908) called for history "comprehensible by the mass of men." His views on war are expressed in *Armaments and Arbitration, or the Place of Force in the International Relations of States* (New York, 1912). Like many older officers, Mahan had had no scientific training and his arguments against the dreadnought depended on historical analogies. Colomb's conclusions were similar to Mahan's, but his book was much narrower. An older man, he died in 1899. Mahan, like Jomini, became a world-famous professional military pundit.
Mahan "understood what no other author had quite understood before: the primary importance of the command of the sea and the rôle which it had played in history, . . . that this command . . . and all of the operations which depend on it rest chiefly on an organized force, . . . the importance which must therefore be attached to the destruction of the organized force of the enemy and, therefore, of seeking battle." Raoul Castex, *Théories stratégiques* (2nd ed., 5 vols., Paris, 1937), I, 42.

quite different. And Mahan's German converts had no real answer to the problems of a "second-best" battle force, though they were following Britain's lead in building ever faster and bigger-gunned battleships and battle cruisers (with cruiser speed and armor and battleship guns). The 1905 *Dreadnought* made all her contemporaries, including Britain's own ships, obsolete, and gave her name to all modern battleships. From the 1859 *Warrior* to the 1905 *Lord Nelson* capital ships had increased from 9,210 to 16,500 tons displacement. The *Dreadnought* was 17,900 tons, the 1912 *Queen Elizabeth* 27,500. These increases came from the gunnery revolution which enabled the *Dreadnought* to replace *Lord Nelson's* mixed armament (4-12″ and 10-9.2″ guns) with all-big-guns (10-12″) for long-range firing and the race for still more power (*Queen Elizabeth* had 8-15″ guns) and speed (18.5, 21, and 25 knots respectively) to force an enemy to battle. But a battleship navy was also a prestige symbol—a sentiment which can be seen best in Germany where William II had come to feel that such a navy and a "place in the sun" *ought* to accompany his country's new economic and diplomatic position.[18]

When William II became Emperor his navy was fifth in Europe, substantially behind the British, French, Russians, and Italians. The man who finally persuaded the *Reichstag* to adopt a "High Seas" battleship program was Alfred von Tirpitz, who became Admiralty Secretary in 1897. His Fleet Laws of 1898 and 1900 put the navy on the same secure financial basis as the army, doubled the number of battleships, projected a replacement program (in effect, trading obsolete coastal ships for modern battleships) lasting until

---

[18] Mahan never considered the problems of a second-best navy in detail. To him an Anglo-American war was unthinkable. The United States should not try for "a degree of naval strength of which we have no need; whereas [Britain's] dependence upon it is vital." *Naval Strategy*, 331-332. René Daveluy admitted that "numerical inferiority" was "a plausible objection" to Mahan's formula of "destroy the enemy and . . . secure [everything] . . . at once," but an Anglo-French war was also increasingly unlikely. *The Genius of Naval Warfare*, trans. Philip R. Alger (2 vols., Annapolis, 1910-1911), I, 20, 11.

By 1914 even Argentina, Brazil, Chile, and Turkey had bought dreadnoughts. William II, an avid Mahanite, had been fascinated by the British navy as a child and "attempted to reproduce [it] on a scale commensurate with the resources and interests of my own country." Archibald Hurd and Henry Castle, *German Sea Power: Its Rise, Progress, and Economic Basis* (London, 1913), 98. See also Wilhelm Schüssler, *Weltmachtstreben und Flottenbau* (Witten/Ruhr, 1956), Wolfgang Marienfeld, *Wissenschaft und Schlachtflottenbau in Deutschland, 1897-1907* (Berlin, 1957), and Donald Macintyre's more popular *The Thunder of the Guns: A Century of Battleships* (New York, 1960).

1916, and made Germany's navy second in the world. The German army had opposed so large a fleet, arguing with Mahan that "History has conclusively demonstrated the inability of a state with even a single continental frontier to compete in naval development with one that is insular, although of smaller population and resources." Geographically, Germany, like the Netherlands earlier, was blockaded by the British Isles, an "initial disadvantage of position," which, Mahan thought, could be overcome "only by an adequate superiority of numbers." He believed that the only real danger for Britain would be a Continental coalition against her. Even then, Britain would occupy "an interior position" with "her gates open to the outer world, which maintains three-fourths of her commerce." At the time that the Fleet Laws were passed, with Continental opinion pro-Boer and anti-British, such a coalition seemed to be possible. Britain's isolation between the Franco-Russian and Triple Alliance was the key to the "Risk Theory" which Tirpitz advanced to justify a second-best navy. "It is not absolutely necessary," he explained in the memorandum accompanying the proposed Fleet Law of 1900, "that the German Battle Fleet should be as strong as that of [Britain] . . . for [Britain] will not, as a rule, be in a position to concentrate all her striking forces against us. But even if [she] should, the defeat of a strong German Fleet would so substantially weaken [her] . . . that [her] own position in the world would no longer be secured by an adequate fleet." Britain would rather make concessions to Germany than risk a war which would leave her too weak to face the Franco-Russian Alliance. Conversely, a big fleet would give Germany the balance of naval power (increasing Germany's "alliance value") if war broke out between Britain and France and Russia.[19]

The Fleet Law of 1900 was Tirpitz' major achievement. Later British efforts to halt the naval race were always countered by the bland statement that the German government was legally committed to the 1900 program. In 1914 Tirpitz looked back on his "life's work with satisfaction." His battle fleet was the second largest in the world and technically as good as or better than the British. But, in spite of his boast

[19] Mahan, *Retrospect and Prospect* (Boston, 1902), 167-170. Alfred von Tirpitz, *My Memoirs* (2 vols., New York, 1919), I, 161. These arguments, pro-Boer feeling in Germany, and careful log-rolling were all responsible for the passage of the Fleet Laws. See Eckart Kehr's classic *Schlachtflottenbau und Parteipolitik* (Berlin, 1930).

that, "It was mainly . . . our . . . Fleet that had produced their respectful tone, and had lessened the possibility of a British attack," the Risk Theory had been a failure. As might have been predicted from a really careful study of British history, Britain had met the threat by agreements with her other rivals which enabled her to concentrate against Germany. Britain had withdrawn most of her forces from American waters after the Hay-Pauncefote Treaty of 1901; the Anglo-Japanese Alliance of 1902 had permitted the recall of most of her Far Eastern squadron. And the Anglo-French Entente of 1902-1904 had eventually allowed Britain to weaken her Mediterranean fleet and to shift the home fleet from its traditional bases in the Channel opposite France to new North Sea bases facing Germany. In 1914 all twenty of the British dreadnoughts (against thirteen German) and six battle cruisers (to four) were in the North Sea. The German High Seas Fleet was based on the area from the island of Heligoland (protecting the entrance to the Elbe and Weser, Hamburg and Bremen, and the naval base at Wilhelmshafen) through the Kiel Canal to the Baltic base of Kiel. This complex of naval installations was so strong that it was never to be assaulted from the sea. It was the redoubt from which an admiral was to surrender the remnants of Hitler's Thousand Year Reich. But it was cut off from the Atlantic and offered no chance for the offensive combination of detachments of the German fleet even in the North Sea. In 1914 the Germans expected the British to come close to Heligoland. There Germany's torpedo boats, destroyers, submarines, and minelayers would whittle the British down to size. Then the High Seas Fleet would give battle "under favorable conditions." Ship for ship, because of their shorter range and heavier armor, the Germans expected to be superior. The only weakness of this second version of the Risk Theory was that it depended entirely on the British reacting according to the German plan. Of the British fleet's actual intentions in 1914, the Germans knew almost nothing.[20]

[20] Tirpitz, My Memoirs, I, 313-314. The battleships projected in 1900 gave Germany about two-thirds as many as Britain. Later Anglo-German naval discussions turned on the replacement and German building ahead of schedule. In 1914 the British had three battle cruisers in the Mediterranean and one (Australian) in the Pacific. Elsewhere cruiser squadrons were stiffened by an occasional predreadnought for commerce defense. The Germans knew "next to nothing" of British intentions. See the official account by O. Groos, Der Krieg in der Nordsee (Berlin, 1920), I, 5, and Admiral E. Weniger, "Die Entwicklung des Operationsplanes für die deutsche Schlachtflotte" (Marine Rundschau, Jan., 1930).

William II and his naval advisors had never really faced the strategic problems of a second-best navy. They did not know how to *force* the British fleet to fight under "favorable conditions." They had no plans for an invasion of England, for an all-out attack on English commerce, or even for interfering with the British reinforcement of the French and Belgian armies, though the invasion of Belgium was the key to the success of the Schlieffen plan. In the bitter words of Admiral Hugo von Pohl, the second wartime commander of the High Seas Fleet, Tirpitz' navy was a "Paradeflotte" to bolster William's "Prestigepolitik." German navalist propaganda had been no more Anglophobe than that of the *Jeune Ecole*. But it had been more consistently supported in high places and it had had a most unfortunate effect on Anglo-German political relations. In the words of the British historian E. L. Woodward, Germany's rulers "could not ignore public opinion," but they

seemed to be unconscious that, apart from the deliberate and dangerous stimulation of anti-English feeling, phrases intended to arouse in inland Germany enthusiasm for ships might have an aggressive tone and a sinister meaning in other countries where no such language was necessary. . . . [It may be] that the German people did not give very serious thought to the question whether a navy really added to their security. . . . Bethmann-Hollweg [German Chancellor, 1909-1917] said that Germany wanted a navy not merely for the protection of her sea coasts and her commerce, but for the "general purposes of her greatness." . . . [Such beliefs were common in an age which believed] that a disarmed nation would be at the mercy of other Powers who would at once take advantage of their superior force. This belief was held by the majority of reasonable men, . . . by almost every member of the governing classes, . . . [and] was not effectively disputed by the Socialist minority in any European country.[21]

21 *Great Britain and the German Navy* (Oxford, 1935), 10-11, 31-32, V. Pohl, *Aus Aufzeichnungen und Briefen während der Kriegszeit* (Berlin, 1920), 87-88. Lothar Persius, *Warum die Flotte versagt* (Leipzig, 1929) is trenchantly anti-Tirpitz. Admiral Wolfgang Wegener suggested taking Norwegian bases in *Die Seestrategie des Weltkrieges* (Berlin, 1929). See also Paul Sethe's neglected *Die Ausgebliebene Seeschlacht; die englische Flottenführung, 1911-1915* (Berlin, 1932); Walther Hubatsch, *Die Ära Tirpitz, Studien zur deutschen Marinepolitik* (Göttingen, 1955) and *Der Admiralstab und die Obersten Marinebehörden in Deutschland, 1848-1945* (Frankfurt am Main, 1958). Frederic B. M. Hollyday, *Bismarck's Rival: A Political Biography of General and Admiral Albrecht von Stosch* (Durham, N.C., 1960).

Tirpitz' words are very revealing. "We will have a chance to fight a battle not too far from Heligoland. This . . . is *grounded psychologically* [my italics] in the strong desire of the British Admiralty and government to come to grips as quickly as possible."

Land Tactics with the New Fire Weapons

The German navalists' illusions were not unique. Though all of the great powers were spending large sums on naval armaments in 1914, none of the General Staffs believed that seapower would play a major role in a great Continental war. Such a war would be fought by mass armies on the familiar battlefields of Flanders, the Lorraine gap, and Poland. The most uncertain factor was tactical. Even after the Russo-Japanese War it was hard to predict the effects of the new fire weapons—the repeating rifle, machine gun, and rapid-firing artillery—which had reached maturity after the introduction of smokeless powder. (The new powder did not obscure the field of fire or give away the gun's position. It also made rapid fire more feasible because it did not foul the gun as badly.) Still newer inventions—such as the airplane, the submarine, the automobile, and radio—presented other problems, but one of the most striking features of military thought during this period was the persistent controversy over the tactical effects of the mass army's basic infantry and artillery weapons. The new rifle (such as the 1886 French Lebel) could fire up to twenty shots a minute; its range was limited chiefly by the rifleman's vision. The machine gun (the 1883 Maxim was the first to be widely adopted) could fire from 200 to 400 times a minute, though because of its weight—around 100 pounds for the ordinary heavy machine gun and its mount—it was regarded as a defensive rather than as an offensive weapon. The new field gun (such as the 1897 French "seventy-five") could also fire a more powerful projectile more rapidly (six to ten times a minute) than any of its predecessors. The partisans of the offensive had not ignored the tactical problems created by these new fire weapons, but they hoped that "rapidity and energy of action, as well as surprise" would enable the offensive to overcome a defense armed with a rifle both "terrible in its effect and simple in its manipulation."[22]

22 Von der Goltz, *Conduct of War*, 180, 190. The best work on the machine gun is G. S. Hutchinson, *Machine Guns, Their History and Tactical Employment* (London, 1938). In 1914—contrary to later legends—the German, French, and British armies each had six heavy machine guns per regiment. M. A. Golaz, "L'Armée allemande de 1914-1918 d'après des sources allemandes" (*Révue historique de l'Armée*, April-June, 1948, 101-114, Jan.-Mar., 1949, 38-50).

Rapid fire increased logistical problems. A seventy-five and its ammunition caisson required twelve horses, six gunners, six drivers, and two non-coms. When the supporting columns were included, the total ran to more than fifty men and fifty horses per gun. Paul Lintier, trans. P. D., *My Seventy-five* (London, 1929), 8. Much of "Wagger's" [Cecil W. Longley's] account dealt

The partisans of the offensive also realized that the officers could no longer drive their men forward. "Extension is too great, the noise . . . too loud, the tension . . . too severe. . . . The man as such becomes prominent, yet not the man who is *led* to victory, but the man who wants himself to conquer." Only "this internal power" of an all-pervading offensive spirit could make mass "armies mobile." This problem of the motivation of the common soldier had been the subject of one of the most original and influential works of the century, the posthumous *Battle Studies* of Ardant du Picq, a forty-nine-year-old French colonel who had been killed in 1870.

The human heart . . . is then the starting point in all matters pertaining to war. . . . Centuries have not changed human nature. Passions, instincts, among them the most powerful one of self-preservation, may be manifested in various ways. . . . But at bottom there is always found the same man. . . . The best masters are those who know man best, the man of today and the man of history. . . .
We shall learn from them to distrust mathematics and material dynamics, . . . to beware of the illusions drawn from the range and the manoeuvre field.
There, experience is with the calm, settled, unfatigued, attentive, obedient soldier, with an intelligent and tractable man instrument . . . not with the nervous, easily swayed, moved, troubled, distrait, excited, restless being . . . who is the fighting man from general to private. . . . Let us then study man in battle, for it is he who really fights.[23]

At the time of Du Picq's death he had been circulating a questionnaire among his fellow officers. "The smallest detail, taken from an actual incident in war, is more instructive for me, a soldier, than all the . . . Jominis. . . . They speak . . . for the heads of states and armies, but they never show me . . . a battalion, a company, a squad in action." "How did the fight start?" "At what time, . . . if such a thing did take place, was there but a disordered impulse, whether to the front or to the rear carrying along pell-mell with it both the leaders

---

with horses, which he reckoned at 700 for the 800 to 900 men serving twelve guns. "We . . . have been very lucky; only about ten cases of men kicked and only three of those badly, one in the stomach." *Battery Flashes* (London, 1916), 4, 7.
23 This previously printed pamphlet, his unfinished "Modern Battle," and some other notes were published in 1880. *Battle Studies* (New York, 1921), 39-41. There is a new French edition, with a bibliography (ed. L. Nachin, Paris, 1948). The other quotations are from Bernhardi, *War of Today*, I, 325-326, and von der Goltz, *The Nation in Arms*, 137.

and the men?" Du Picq had coupled this modern scientific approach with a study of the classics—Polybius, Xenophon, Caesar, Thucydides, and Livy—partly because he believed that they had been more outspoken about the primary problem of fear than most moderns.

"Fear! . . . There are . . . soldiers who do not know it, but they are . . . rare. The mass shudders; because you cannot suppress the flesh. . . . The strongest have been those who not only best have understood the general conduct of war, but those who have taken human weakness into greatest account and taken the best guarantees against it.

The Romans had won their victories through discipline and continuity of effort, "engaging only the necessary units and keeping the rest . . . outside of the immediate sphere of moral tension." They had believed in "mass, but from the moral point of view only." The sight of their successive sword lines weakened their enemies' morale and gave their own men "the confidence of being aided and relieved." The same moral principles can be applied to fire weapons. An attack fails when the men, over-awed by a stubborn resistance, will not move forward. It succeeds when the defenders are convinced that their fire cannot halt it. "There is no shock of infantry on infantry, . . . no force of mass. There is but a moral impulse." Troops who make bayonet charges do little "but strike and fire at backs." Most of the defenders flee before any real physical contact.[24]

Du Picq was an officer of the *armée de métier*. He thought that armies should be "commanded by an aristocracy," who have "the firmness and decision of command proceeding from habit and an entire faith in their unquestionable right to command as established by tradition, law and society." Morale was the result of "living together, . . . sharing fatigue and rest, . . . cooperation." "Men do not wish to be alone, they must support and be supported." Good food and warm clothing are more important than "millions . . . squandered . . . for uniforms, gee-gaws, shakos." Du Picq had been greatly depressed by the incompetence of the clique around Napoleon III and by the intellectual laziness of his brother officers, though he was to be killed before his gloomy forebodings were realized. But hundreds of other French officers had returned from German prisons burning to restore their profes-

24 *Battle Studies*, 48-49, 53-54, 148-149.

sional pride and to avenge their defeated country. There was no going back to the *armée de métier*. They had to believe in their own professional competence and in the French conscript's patriotism. Du Picq was read in this spirit. It led his readers to exaggerate his emphasis on morale as they exaggerated the German emphasis on the offensive. Foch quoted the famous maxim of the French philosopher Joseph de Maistre, " 'A battle lost is a battle one thinks one has lost; for . . . a battle cannot be lost physically.' Therefore it can only be lost morally. But then, it is also morally that a battle is won, and we may extend the aphorism by saying: *A battle won is a battle in which one will not confess oneself beaten.*" [25]

Foch's emphasis on the offensive was not unique; in 1914 all of the Continental General Staffs planned immediate strategic offensives. But Foch and some of his followers also advanced the tactical idea that "Any improvement of firearms is ultimately bound to add strength to the offensive. . . . Nothing is easier than to give a mathematical demonstration of that truth." If two thousand men attacked one thousand men with rifles capable of firing once a minute, the "balance in favor of the attack" would be one thousand bullets. With rifles capable of firing ten times a minute, this balance would increase to ten thousand. This would be true if the two forces blazed away at each other in the open. But suppose the defenders took cover, as they had done during the American Civil War, in improvised trenches? Then most of the attackers' bullets would be wasted, while those of the defenders took a fearful toll. This was the view of a self-made Warsaw banker, Ivan S. Bloch, whose six-volume *The Future of War in Its Technical, Economic, and Political Relations* was partly responsible for the Tsar's calling the first Hague Peace Conference in 1899. Bloch was not a military man, but he thought that "the conclusions arrived at by military experts are by no means inaccessible to the general student." Bloch had, in fact,

[25] *Ibid.*, 111, 95-96, 221-222. Foch, *Principles*, 285. Nobody followed up two of the most original features of Du Picq, his interest in the problem of fear and his attempt to find out what men do in battle. Social scientists were still speaking of "the instinct of pugnacity." Though William McDougall admitted that this instinct was not activated by a specific stimulus, he felt that it was triggered by blocking one of the other instincts. He believed too that emulation would gradually replace pugnacity within civilized societies, and "bring to an end what has been . . . probably the most important factor of progressive evolution . . . among both individuals and societies." *An Introduction to Social Psychology* (London, 1908). In spite of two world wars and a generation of new studies, this description of the "instinct of pugnacity" was unchanged in the twenty-fifth edition (London, 1943).

read many of the best military writers of this age. From their works he concluded that better firearms had resulted in "(1) the opening of battles from much greater distances; . . . (2) loose formation in attack; (3) the strengthening of the defense; (4) the increase in the area of the battlefield; and (5) the increase in casualties."[26]

Europeans, like the dervishes who had charged the British at Omdurman in 1898, might test the power of modern fire, but "that one experience was probably sufficient even for" dervishes.

> At first there will be increased slaughter—increased slaughter on so terrible a scale as to render it impossible to get troops to push the battle to a decisive issue. They will try to, thinking they are fighting under the old conditions, and they will learn such a lesson that they will abandon the attempt for ever. . . .
>
> The outward and visible sign of the end of war was the introduction of the magazine rifle, . . . smokeless powder, . . . the quick-firing gun, . . . and higher explosives. . . . The first thing every man will have to do . . . will be to dig a hole in the ground, and throw up as strong an earthen rampart as he can to shield him from the hail of bullets. . . . When you must dig a trench before you can make any advance, your progress is necessarily slow. Battles will last for days, and at the end it is very doubtful whether any decisive victory can be gained.
>
> Every great State would . . . be in the position of a besieged city, and the factor which always decides sieges is the factor which will decide the modern war. . . . The ultimate decision is in the hand of *famine*. . . . I am not speaking so much of the armies, as . . . of the population . . . which is apt to control the policy of which the armies are but the executive instrument. . . . The modern European . . . is much more excitable . . . than his forefathers. Upon this highly excitable, sensitive population you are going to inflict . . . hunger . . . and war. At the same time you will . . . expose your governing . . . classes to more than decimation at the hands of the enemy's sharpshooters. How long do you think your social fabric will remain stable under such circumstances?[27]

26 Foch, *Principles*, 32. Bloch, *Future of War*, trans. R. C. Long of vol. 6 of the original (Boston, 1903), xxxi, lxxix. The whole was translated into French, *La Guerre* (6 vols., Paris, 1898-1900), and German only, *Der Krieg* (6 vols., Berlin, 1899). Bloch thought of himself as an economist and had published works on Russian finance, railways, and local government. In his lantern-slide lectures for the delegates to the Conference, he put forth his "data; the . . . conclusions he leaves to the reason and conscience." *The Memoirs of Bertha von Suttner* (2 vols., Boston, 1910), II, 282. See Merze Tate, *The Disarmament Illusion: The Movement for a Limitation of Armaments to 1907* (New York, 1942), 171-173.

27 Bloch, *The Future of War*, xvi-xvii, xxvii, xl-i.

Bloch's conclusions were simple. "War . . . has become impossible, except at the price of suicide." Since modern states cannot defeat their adversaries on the battlefield, war will "entail, even upon the victorious Power, the destruction of its resources and the breakup of society." "When the impossibility of resorting to war . . . is apparent to all, other means will be devised" to settle international disputes. Bloch died in 1902, two years before the outbreak of the Russo-Japanese War, which seemed to confirm many of his tactical conclusions. This great war, which cost each side about a quarter of a million casualties, was observed by some of the world's ablest professional soldiers. In Kuroki's First Army, for example, Captain John J. Pershing met Lieutenant General Ian Hamilton, Captain Max Hoffman, and three other officers who were to hold important commands in the First World War. If some of their observations were insufficiently appreciated, the reasons were rather similar to those for the insufficient appreciation of some of the lessons of the American Civil War. Both wars were fought in undeveloped areas under conditions quite different from those in Western Europe. And many of the front-line observers were company or field grade officers, whose ideas take time to percolate into the official manuals.[28]

[28] Russia had a larger army and navy than Japan, but Japan had larger forces on the spot, somewhat better equipment, and better leadership. The Japanese surprised the Russian fleet in Port Arthur before declaring war and captured that base before the Russian Baltic fleet could come to the rescue. The main Russian army (supplied over the single-track Trans-Siberian railway) lost Mukden in March, 1905. In May Togo annihilated the Baltic Fleet in the Straits of Tsushima. In August, attempting to head off the growing revolutionary movement in Russia, Nicholas II announced elections for the first Duma and began peace negotiations. Theodore Roosevelt won the Nobel Peace Prize for his part in the negotiations. See John M. Maki's brief *Japanese Militarism, Its Cause and Cure* (New York, 1945); Edwin A. Falk, *Togo and the Rise of Japanese Sea Power* (New York, 1936); Frederick Palmer, *With Kuroki in Manchuria* (New York, 1904) and *John J. Pershing* (New York, 1948); A. Novikov-Priboy, *Tsushima*, trans. Eden and Cedar Paul (New York, 1944); and Richard Hough's popular *The Fleet That Had to Die* (New York, 1958). On the Sino-Japanese War of 1894-1895 and the Boxer Rebellion see Ralph L. Powell, *The Rise of Chinese Military Power, 1895-1912* (Princeton, 1955); Chester C. Tan, *The Boxer Catastrophe* (New York, 1955); and Peter Fleming, *The Siege at Peking* (New York, 1959).

In Europe Russia's defeat temporarily upset the balance between the Triple and Franco-Russian alliances. It led to the Russian Revolution of 1905 and had great repercussions outside of Europe. A non-European great power had decisively defeated a European great power for the first time in centuries, if one does not count the Italian disaster at Adowa in Ethiopia in 1896. See especially Jawaharlal Nehru, *Glimpses of World History* (New York, 1942), 464, and the remarks of Edward Dicey in *The Egypt of the Future* (London, 1907), 139-140.

An American medical officer, Colonel Valery Havard, listed the major lessons of the war as follows:

1. The enormous strength of the active armies. . . .
2. The great length and irregularity of the line of battle. . . .
3. The impossibility for the general commanding an army corps, or larger force, to see more than a very limited part of the battlefield. Hence the necessity of an effective telephone service. . . .
4. The great difficulty or impossibility of successful frontal attacks on account of the number and strength of entrenchments; hence the necessity of flanking or turning movements by wide detours involving a more or less complete separation from bases, much forced marching, and many hardships.
5. The long period of time covered by the series of engagements which constitutes what is conventionally called a battle. . . .
6. The frequent night fighting . . . [in which] the bayonet plays an important part.
7. The almost complete disregard of weather, . . . the most rigorous winter not interfering with active operations.
8. The increased importance of field artillery. . . .
9. The . . . benign or humane [wounding rather than killing] effect of the small caliber, hard-jacketed bullet.
10. The enormous . . . casualties . . . in [units] . . . bearing the brunt of the battle, . . . while the general ratio of killed and wounded . . . is not very much greater than in former wars. . . .[29]

Bloch and Foch can be taken to represent the extremes of the defensive-offensive argument, though the issue was by no means as clear-cut as Foch's absurd mathematical statements would indicate. Foch had combined such arguments with

American observers agreed in effect with Bloch, Captain William V. Judson writing that "When, under present conditions, two countries reasonably well prepared make war, the result is apt to be so near a draw that even victory is extremely unprofitable. This is a splendid fact, as it makes for peace, and may eventually lead to partial disarmament by international convention." *Reports of Miliary Observers Attached to the Armies in Manchuria during the Russo-Japanese War* (Washington, 1906-1907), V, 217.

29 *Ibid.*, II, 5-7. Havard also noted the great importance of the treatment of the wounded, "the full recognition by both belligerents of the . . . Geneva convention," and the importance of the Red Cross. His remarks on the future organization of the medical service are most interesting. General de Négrier, on the other hand, concluded that no revision of the French field manuals was necessary. *Lessons of the Russo-Japanese War*, trans. E. Louis Spiers (London, 1906). New studies of this war and particularly of its effects on European military thought are badly needed.

Frederick Palmer discounted sensational newspaper stories of Japanese fanaticism. Russian overconfidence had boomeranged until they had come to believe that the Japanese were "veritable demons for cunning and shooting." Palmer emphasized Japanese training and teamwork. "By working year in and year out . . . the Japanese officer has set a new standard by sea and land." *With Kuroki*, 360, 351.

some very sensible remarks about reconnaissance, artillery preparation, "making corps less vulnerable and more mobile and . . . utilizing . . . cover." But some of Foch's more extreme statements were exaggerated by his followers as Foch had himself exaggerated some of the ideas of Du Picq and De Maistre. One of Foch's disciples, Louis de Grandmaison, taught that almost any offensive plan is better than any defensive plan and that criticism of the offensive theory was *ipso facto* evidence of moral weakness and of unfitness for future high command. As these firebrands (the "Young Turks") became more influential in the French General Staff, they ruthlessly sidetracked such men as Colonel Philippe Pétain, who had dared to question the official dogma.[30]

The War Plans of the Continental Powers

All of the 1914 war plans of the Continental General Staffs were offensive. All of them were to fail. But the Schlieffen Plan was the most realistic of the lot in its appreciation of the enemy's intentions and of the tactical power of modern rapid-fire weapons. Schlieffen became Chief of the General Staff in 1891, a short time before the conclusion of the Franco-Russian alliance. Italy, the third member of the Triple Alliance, was neither politically nor militarily dependable. Though Germany's and Austria-Hungary's industrial production was greater than that of France and Russia, Germany and Austria-Hungary were inferior in manpower to the new combination. These considerations, however, scarcely entered into Schlieffen's planning, except as additional incentives for a quick decision. Like Bloch, Schlieffen believed that a long European war would be suicidal. As the latter was to write in his anonymous "The War of the Future," "A nation's existence depends upon the uninterrupted continuation of trade and industry, and a quick decision is necessary to start the wheels of industry turning again. A strategy of attrition is impossible when the maintenance of armies of millions requires the expenditure of billions." The search for a quick victory dominated German planning from this point until 1914.[31]

---

[30] Foch, *Principles*, 345-350. Grandmaison, *Deux conférences* (Paris, 1912). Von der Goltz believed that he had been by-passed by William II because his remarks on the value of fortifications had "weakened the offensive spirit of the German army." *Conduct of War*, 52-53; *Denkwürdigkeiten* (Berlin, 1929), 255-257, 277-279. Also Albert Grabau, *Das Festungsproblem in Deutschland und seine Auswirkung auf die strategische Lage von 1870-1914* (Berlin, 1935).
[31] *Gesammelte Schriften* (2 vols., Berlin, 1913), I, 17.

Moltke and Waldersee had worried about a two-front war since 1871 and fear of a Franco-Russian alliance had been Bismarck's main diplomatic preoccupation. Now France and Russia were allies. Schlieffen, a military technician, did not intrude into this political question. The Chief of the General Staff was not a "militarist" in this sense. He accepted the position in which his Emperor's folly and diplomatic advisors had helped to place Germany and the idea of a two-front war as given. The only military solution was to use Germany's central position and the superior striking power of her armies to knock out one of her opponents as quickly as possible. Russia was the weaker of Germany's two opponents, but geography, Russian fortifications along the line of the Narew River, and recent improvements in the Russian railway net made a quick victory on the east very difficult. The first battles would hardly do more than destroy the Russian armies in Russian Poland. Though Schlieffen did not try to calculate the political effects of such a defeat on the Russian monarchy, there would probably be an eastern front of some sort as long as France remained in the field. Since 1871 the French army had grown stronger, thus increasing the possibility of a successful French offensive against the forces which Moltke had planned to leave in the west while dealing with Russia. Schlieffen feared that Moltke's planned counter-offensive against a French attack through Luxembourg and in Lorraine would not find room for maneuver. So Schlieffen set to work on a plan for a single knock-out blow at France, a technical military decision which had tremendous political consequences. Up to this point the Germans had hoped that Germany and France might remain neutral in a war between Russia and Austria-Hungary. Even if it became necessary for Germany to intervene to prevent Russia from destroying Austria-Hungary, there was always a possibility that France would not join Russia or that the French could be checked in the west until the Russians had come to terms. But the decision to concentrate against France made it necessary, according to the British historian A. J. P. Taylor, for the Germans "to attack France at once, even if the war originated in the Balkans. In short, though the prospect of war on two fronts produced Schlieffen's plan of campaign, this plan first made a war on two fronts inevitable. . . . This makes nonsense of the theory that the 'alliances' caused the First World

War. With or without alliances, an Austro-Russian war had to involve the west, once Schlieffen's plan was adopted."[32]

Since the most reckless weakening of their armies on the east would give the Germans only a slight numerical superiority over the French, victory would depend on strategic surprise. Schlieffen found his ideal battle in Cannae (216 B.C.), where Hannibal had destroyed a Roman army half again as large as his own by weakening his own center and attacking the Roman flanks. "In two thousand years weapons and tactics have completely changed, . . . but the principles of war remain unchanged. . . . The enemy's front is not the objective of the principal attack. There is no use massing the main body against it, the reserves will do as well. The soundest strategy is to drive in the flanks." Schlieffen convinced himself that the same principle had been the basis of Frederician and Napoleonic strategy. The wide front of a modern army made its outflanking more difficult, but in other ways it was more vulnerable than ever to a threat to its flanks or rear. The Russo-Japanese War had proved that

Frontal attacks can . . . be pushed through, . . . but the results are small. . . . The enemy is forced back . . . only to renew his resistance. . . . To win a decisive, annihilating victory, he must be attacked on two or three sides, in front and on either or both flanks. . . . But it is difficult to get the necessary numerical superiority to do this under modern conditions. About the only way to find the means for a strong flank attack is by weakening the forces facing the enemy front.

Here the offensive army could take advantage of the defensive power of modern weapons.[33]

[32] *Struggle for Mastery in Europe,* 340 and note 2. It might be noted in Schlieffen's defense (1) that this was the best of the peacetime war plans, (2) that Schlieffen's belief that a great power must, in the last analysis, be prepared to go it alone, was characteristic of this era of intense nationalism, (3) that Italy's position was very precarious and that Austria-Hungary was widely felt to be on the verge of dissolution, and (4) that all of Schlieffen's critics have not solved the problem of how a convinced monarchist should deal with so unstable a sovereign. Resignation might only open the way to an even less able technician.

[33] *Gesammelte Schriften,* I, 29, 17, 18. See also Ludwig von Falkenhausen, *Flankenbewegung und Massenheer* (Berlin, 1911). Ritter notes that Moltke the Elder would not have attempted to find a single historical formula for victory. In this respect Schlieffen's thinking is more reminiscent of Jomini than of Clausewitz. Schlieffen's tactical ideas did not differ greatly from those of Foch. The troops must "try, as in siege-warfare, to [advance] . . . from position to position, day and night, advancing, digging in, advancing. . . . The attack must never be allowed to come to a standstill as happened in the war in the Far East." Ritter, *Schlieffen Plan,* 144. See also Alfred Schlieffen, *Briefe,* ed. Eberhard Kessel (Göttingen, 1958).

The widest and easiest route between France and Germany lay through neutral Belgium. To the east and south of the Belgian coastal plain lay the forested Ardennes, and then the Lorraine gap, where the French had replaced the fortresses lost in 1871. The narrower Belfort gap between the Vosges Mountains and Switzerland was also closed by fortifications. The 1899 version of the Schlieffen Plan called for a frontal-flanking attack by four armies through Belgium and three from Lorraine. The 1905-1906 plan called for a much wider and more daring sweep to the Channel coast and west and south of Paris. The French offensive could be held by the powerful German fortifications in Alsace-Lorraine while the German right wing fell on them from the flank and rear and drove them against the Swiss frontier. Schlieffen hoped that the threatening German troop concentration near the Belgian frontier would force the French to violate Belgian neutrality to deny the Germans the key rail center of Liége, which could then be outflanked by going through the "Maastricht Appendix" of the Netherlands. The younger Moltke felt that Liége was so important to the German plan that the Germans should take it immediately by surprise, without giving France a chance to outrage world opinion. Moltke also decided not to violate Dutch neutrality; a neutral Netherlands would be a useful hole in a British blockade in case of a long war. The plan included two calculated risks. One was the danger of a Russian offensive into East Prussia, a danger which was increased by the Russian army's surprising recovery from defeat in the Russo-Japanese War. The second was the risk of a French breakthrough on the weak German left, particularly at the hinge around Metz. Schlieffen placed his trust in the German fortifications and the developing threat to the French rear. "If the Germans persevere in their operations they can be sure that the French will hastily turn back . . . in the direction whence the greatest danger threatens. The Germans must therefore be as strong as possible on the right wing, because here the decisive battle is to be expected." In 1914 seven German armies pivoted on Metz. Five of them were on the right wing, to which Schlieffen had originally allotted seven-eighths of the German divisions. Moltke, however, had sent enough new divisions to the left to reduce the proportion to three to one.[84]

[84] Ritter, *Schlieffen Plan*, 147-148. The strengthened German left wing consisted of the Seventh and Sixth Armies. Schlieffen had once hoped that a gradual withdrawal of the German left would help to pull the French into his

One weakness of the plan was its demands on men and horses. The right wing was to advance for five to seven weeks, fanning, originally, around Paris. The Belgians and perhaps the British would be locked in Antwerp, a safer place for the latter "than on their island [as] . . . a standing menace." In 1914 Moltke told the navy that it need not hinder the British; he hoped to "settle with the 160,000 English at the same time as the French and Belgians." Worse still, the attackers (with 78 infantry divisions in 1914) were barely superior to the defenders (62 French, 6 Belgian, and, at first, 5 of 6 British divisions). The Germans counted on surprise, on using reserve divisions as frontline troops, and on the usual difficulties of co-ordinating allied armies. But they failed to consider the inevitable "friction" of war. They expected an inexperienced peacetime army to give battle after weeks of marching at the end of improvised supply lines. As the German right wing moved on Paris, it would be moving toward the hub of an intact French communications system. Schlieffen was not responsible, of course, for the younger Moltke's failure to control the German armies in 1914 or for the French command's masterful handling of the bad situation in which their own prewar plans had placed them. Schlieffen did not believe that subordinate commanders should be allowed the leeway which the elder Moltke had given them. "A modern Alexander" ought to make full use of the improvements in communications since 1870, "telegraphs, wireless, telephones, . . . automobiles, and motorcycles." The ailing younger Moltke never really assumed command; only one of the German army commanders' chiefs of staff understood all the details of the plan. German headquarters were located too far from the critical right wing. The Supreme Warlord — to whom

trap, but his 1912 study, which had been sent to Moltke, strengthened the left. He also suggested that the armies might possibly wheel north of Paris rather than taking in that city as in earlier versions. The final 1914 plan followed the earlier version, but Moltke then adopted Schlieffen's idea when he allowed the German First Army to swing east of the city. The plan did not fail because Moltke changed Schlieffen's ideas without consulting the master.

The famous 1905-1906 version was not a plan but "a purely theoretical operational study." *Ibid.*, 46. It called for far geater forces than were then available and was, in effect, a program for the future expansion of the army. Schlieffen had not greatly strengthened the army during his years as Chief of Staff, because of his failure to check the expansion of the navy. Neither the problem of Liége nor the danger of a French offensive against the German hinge had been considered in detail. Ritter also attempts to dispose of the charge that Schlieffen pushed for a preventive war at the time of the First Moroccan crisis, when the Russians were out of the picture. *Ibid.*, 102-138. Craig, *Politics of the Prussian Army*, 283-286, disagrees.

Moltke was only an advisor — did not dare endanger his person and prestige by moving too far forward. Telegraph and telephone lines broke down or were sabotaged. Moltke had to depend on unreliable field radios and personal messengers, while French communications remained intact. Unconsciously the Germans had assumed that the French high command would collapse as it had done in 1870. But Joffre kept his head and managed to rectify errors "in the original assembly of the army" which, by pre-war hypothesis, "can scarcely ever be corrected." This again was part of the predictable friction of combat. The Germans assumed that every break would be in their favor in this tremendous gamble. This is the reason for James E. Edmonds' (the British official historian) conclusion that Schlieffen's plans were "arrogantly based on unjustified contempt for the opposing armies. Germany did not possess sufficient field divisions to carry them out; and they must therefore be accounted bad strategy."[35]

For all its faults, however, the German plan was based on (1) a better appreciation of the tactical effect of modern fire weapons, and (2) a better guess about the enemy's intention than the French Plan XVII. Based on the same general ideas as the Schlieffen plan—i.e., on the supreme importance of the strategic offensive in a short war—Plan XVII was "simple and aggressive, independent of the plans of the enemy and the size of his forces." It had been worked out after the Second Moroccan Crisis of 1911, when the "Young Turks" had taken control of planning. The staff, while recognizing the advantages of the initiative, had previously planned minor

[35] Ritter, *Schlieffen Plan*, 162. Divisions and casualties, unless otherwise noted, are from Edmonds, *A Short History of World War I* (London, 1951), 8-10, 17-18, 26. The British Sixth Division was not present at the Marne. Joffre was no Alexander, but he finally did "control the course of the battle as it raged across the whole of France, . . . coordinating . . . one British and six French armies . . . by the continuous use of the telephone, telegraph, and the trained staff officers whom he dispatched to . . . his leading subordinates." William D. Puleston, *High Command in the World War* (London, 1934), 96.

Schlieffen's remarks about the British apply to an army which had demonstrated its complete incompetence in the Boer War, not to the reformed British army of 1914. The fortifications of Liége had also been strengthened. The Paris problem was more fundamental. Schlieffen himself had suggested that the French might try to use Paris to gather a reserve army which could be thrown against the German flank. Ritter's criticism that Schlieffen was risking the loss of the industries of Silesia and the Lorraine iron ore is not really applicable. No staff was then thinking of economic considerations. This makes Moltke's decision not to go through Holland for economic reason a good example of his tendency to try to hedge Schlieffen's bets. The Schlieffen Plan was "Wilhelminian" in its grandiose naïveté, but the peacetime plans of the other staffs were even more romantic.

offensives until the Germans were open to a decisive counter-offensive. This attitude had been reinforced by the government's refusal to consider a preventive advance into Belgium and the impossibility of holding even defensive staff conversations with the Belgians. The Young Turks' unwitting tool was Adolphe Messimy, a former staff officer who had left the army after the secret police had reported him at a Dreyfusard meeting and who had then been successful in both business and politics. He had become War Minister during the crisis and had found the French army without a real head. The former War Minister, General Brun, was old and lazy. The Council of National Defense had not met for two and a half years because Brun did not think "there was any danger of war." General Michel, the presumptive Commander-in-Chief, seemed to be "crushed" by his responsibilities. Generals Galliéni, Durand, and Dubail, when consulted by Messimy, reported that Michel would not be a good field commander. Michel's fate was decided at a meeting of the Supreme War Council on July 13, 1911. He thought that the Germans would use reserve divisions in their offensive and that their drive through Belgium would thus be much wider and more powerful than the French were then prepared to meet. Michel wished to abandon a possible offensive in the Lorraine gap, to shift his armies west and north toward Belgium and to use French reserve divisions in the front lines. Michel mistakenly opposed building a field gun heavier than the seventy-five. The Supreme War Council voted against Michel on all three counts.[36]

Michel was kicked upstairs. Messimy reorganized the French high command to make the Chief of Staff the presumptive Commander-in-Chief. He offered the post to Galliéni, who refused to accept it because of his age, his own role in Michel's fall, and the probable resentment of some officers at this command's going to an officer of colonial troops. Galliéni recommended Generals Pau or Joffre. Pau asked for absolute control over promotions to general. The cabinet was unwilling to give this power to an outspoken conservative and clerical. Joseph Joffre was a republican, but, as a former engineer, had never served on the General Staff. He accepted the post on the condition that General Castelnau,

---

[36] Douhet, *Command of the Air*, 126-127. The British General Henry Wilson agreed with Michel's analysis. Generals Joffre and Castelnau could not believe that the German General Staff, for whom they had a great deal of professional respect, would gamble on a wide drive through Belgium.

another known clerical, be appointed his deputy. The cabinet took Castelnau to get Joffre. Plan XVII was thus Joffre's in name only. Its keynote was the offensive at all costs. "All attacks are to be pushed to the limit with the firm resolution to charge the enemy with the bayonet, in order to destroy him . . . [even] at the price of bloody sacrifices. Any other conception [is] . . . contrary to the very nature of war." Five French armies (each about the size of the seven German armies because of the German use of their reserves) crowded into the Lorraine gap. One and Two were to drive south of Metz. Three and Four were to attack north of Metz at the Germans coming through Luxembourg. Five was to be held in reserve until the Germans committed themselves about coming through Belgium. It was thus fated to meet the whole right side of the German line. Plan XVII was not, in Joffre's words, a battle plan, but a plan of "concentration. . . . I adopted no preconceived idea, other than a full determination to take the offensive with all my forces assembled." [37]

The Russian plans—such as they were, with four Chiefs of Staff during the six years before the outbreak of war— were governed by two considerations. The first was the French plea for a quick Russian offensive to take some weight from the German drive against France. The French government had guaranteed huge private loans for Russian strategic railways and arms factories. In return the Russians agreed to attack before their forces had completed their mobilization, against roughly equal Austro-German forces. In promising to do this, as Joffre remarked, the Russians gave "proof of great self-denial." The second consideration was the exposed salient of Russian Poland. The Russians had to choose between withdrawing to the present Russo-Polish frontier (then marked by the fortress line Kovno-Grodno-Brest-Rovno) or trying to widen the salient by offensives into East Prussia and Galicia (Austrian Poland). So they sent two armies into East Prussia

---

[37] B. H. Liddell Hart, *Foch, The Man of Orleans* (Boston, 1932), 61. *The Personal Memoirs of Joffre,* trans. Col. T. Bentley Mott (2 vols., New York, 1932), I, 69. Among the most scathing criticisms of Plan XVII are F. E. Gascouin, *Le Triomphe de l'idée* (Paris, 1931) and Arthur Boucher, *L'Infanterie sacrifiée* (Paris, 1930). The most careful study of the Belgian problem is Louis Garros, "Préludes aux invasions de la Belgique" (*Révue historique de l'Armée,* Jan.-March, 1949, 17-37).

Adolphe Messimy was War Minister in 1911 and 1912 and again in August 1914. He was thrown to the wolves after the initial French defeats, but not before he had called Galliéni from retirement. He resigned his seat in the Chamber of Deputies and served with distinction in the army for the rest of the war. See *Mes Souvenirs* (Paris, 1937).

and four into Galicia. Grand Duke Nicholas, who was appointed Russian Commander-in-Chief after war was declared, called on the Poles to rally to the Slavic cause and promised them political autonomy after the war.[38]

Conrad von Hötzendorff, the ambitious and confident Austro-Hungarian Chief of Staff, who had been pushing for a preventive war against Serbia for years, planned to settle with the Serbs immediately. Nearly two-fifths of the entire Austro-Hungarian army was sent against a Serbian army half its size, but with a great deal of recent combat experience in the Balkan Wars of 1912 and 1913. The other three-fifths of the Hapsburg forces formed the Galician part of an Austro-German pincers against Russian Poland. The only thing lacking was the German part of the pincers. Conrad later claimed that he had been deliberately deceived by Moltke, but the Austro-Hungarian Chief of Staff had already proved himself capable of infinite self-delusion. In any case, liaison between the Austro-Hungarians and the Germans was almost as poor as that between the German army and the German navy. Both of Conrad's offensives headed straight for disaster. But so did all of the better-laid plans, the fruits of a generation of careful military speculation.[39]

British Participation in a Continental War

The Boer War played the same role in British military history that was played by the Spanish-American War (1898) in the military history of the United States. The key man in the various commissions which looked into "the many blunders we made in South Africa" was Lord Esher, though the resulting reforms are usually named for Lord Haldane,

[38] *Memoirs*, I, 60. Girard L. McEntee, *Military History of the World War* (New York, 1937), 21-30. In August, 1914, there were 17½ Russian infantry divisions against 14 German in the north, 5 Russian and 2 German in the center, and 38½ Russian against an equal number of Austro-Hungarians in the south. McEntee's map, 90, is based on Nicholas N. Golovine, *The Russian Campaign of 1914* (Fort Leavenworth, 1933). General Golovine, one of the best of the Russian military historians, thinks that one German division was equal to a division and a half of Russians or Austrians, because of German superiority in equipment. See also Louis Garros' important "En Marge de l'alliance franco-russe, 1902-1914" (*Révue historique de l'Armée*, April-June, 1950. 29-44).

[39] Conrad, *Aus Meiner Dienstzeit* (5 vols., Vienna, 1925), I, 403-404. The Austrian official history is *Österreich-Ungarns Letzter Krieg* (7 vols., Vienna, 1930-1938), I, 13-14. See also Oskar Regele, *Feldmarschall Conrad, Auftrag und Erfüllung, 1906-1918* (Vienna, 1955). American and British historians have given Conrad's complaints more credit than they deserve. Similar charges against Schlieffen have even less foundation. Nobody took Beck, the senile Austro-Hungarian Chief of Staff in Schlieffen's time, very seriously.

the able lawyer and philosopher who took the War Office in 1905 after Esher had declined the post. Esher's War Office (Reconstitution) Committee abolished the old office of Commander-in-Chief, established an Army Council modeled on the Board of Admiralty, and recommended the appointment of a Chief of Staff. An Expeditionary Force of six regular infantry divisions was to be backed by a Territorial Army formed from the old Militia, Volunteers, and Yeomanry. Since the British public was not ready to accept conscription —in spite of a campaign led by Lord Roberts, the hero of South Africa—the total of the British land forces remained about the same. But their reorganization made it possible to give real attention to the question of how best to use "the surprise and freedom of movement [which] are pre-eminently the weapons of [the army of a] Power that commands the sea." The first military conversations between the French and British General Staffs resulted from the First Moroccan Crisis of 1905. But the French proposals for the direct reinforcement of the army in France (under a French commander-in-chief) were not reported to the British cabinet or to the Admiralty, where the First Sea Lord, the dynamic Sir John Fisher, had very different ideas of the role of the British army in a continental war. In 1909 Fisher supposedly told the Committee of Imperial Defence:

Continental armies being what they are, . . . the British Army should be absolutely restricted to . . . sudden descents on the coast, the recovery of Heligoland, and the garrisoning of Antwerp. . . . There was a stretch of ten miles of hard sand . . . ninety miles from Berlin. Were the British Army to seize and entrench that strip, a million Germans would find occupation; but to dispatch British troops to the [main] front . . . would be an act of suicidal idiocy.[40]

[40] Henderson, *Science of War*, 385. Admiral Sir R. H. Bacon, *The Life of Lord Fisher of Kilverstone* (2 vols., New York, 1929), II, 182-183. Henderson died at forty-nine, just as the Boer War inquiries were getting under way. Dudley Sommer, *Haldane of Cloan: His Life and Times, 1856-1928* (London, [1960]; J. E. Tyler, *The British Army and the Continent, 1904-1914* (London, 1938); John K. Dunlop, *The Development of the British Army, 1899-1914* (London, 1938); David James, *Lord Roberts* (London, 1954); and Philip Magnus, *Kitchener* (London, 1958) are excellent. See also my "Conscription in Great Britain, 1900-1914" (*Military Affairs*, XX, Summer, 1956, 71-76).

The two Boer Republics—two-fifths of whose 300,000 people were British—put 90,000 men into the field. The British used 450,000. As early as 1858 the Boer commandos used covering fire by picked riflemen over the heads of storming parties. The Boers were superb shots at long ranges and—firing from the hip—at close quarters. Their only regulars were artillerymen, who used their Krupp guns for sniping at long ranges. Their scouting and march disci-

This fundamental difference of opinion between what can be called the "Blue Water" and the "Continental" schools of British strategy—a difference which can be traced back to Elizabethan times—came to a head before the Committee of Imperial Defence on August 23, 1911, during the Second Moroccan Crisis. General Henry Wilson outlined the War Office plan for sending the Expeditionary Force to France, and Admiral Arthur K. Wilson (Fisher's successor as First Sea Lord) outlined a much vaguer plan for a landing somewhere on the German coast. After the meeting Haldane told the Prime Minister (H. H. Asquith) that he would resign the War Office unless the Admiralty was willing to "work in full harmony with the War Office Plans" and began to organize a "Naval War Staff." Sir Edward Grey (the Foreign Secretary), David Lloyd George (the Chancellor of the Exchequer), and Winston Churchill (the Home Secretary) supported Haldane, and Churchill was made First Lord of the Admiralty. This decision did not imply—as "Blue Water" critics have charged—that the Government should immediately have introduced conscription on the Continental pattern. It meant only that Britain should commit her forces at what then appeared to be the decisive point. If Germany had beaten France in the first decisive battles, the British navy might not—in Henry Wilson's famous remark—have been worth more than "500 bayonets" to the Allied cause. A belated British landing in Germany would then have appeared as futile as Walcheren or the abortive Baltic expedition after Friedland. Nor was this decision, as has been suggested, a victory for the army over the navy. Some soldiers might well have favored a well-organized amphibious operation against the German coast. But neither Fisher nor the "Fisher crowd" had a concrete plan. As one younger naval officer commented, "Fisher, supreme in his contempt for history and distrustful of all other men, . . . generalizes about war, saying it is to be made terrible, the enemy is to be hit hard & often, and many

pline were excellent and they made full use of fog, smoke, and night. See Major G. Tylden's short *The Armed Forces of South Africa* (Johannesburg, 1954); J. F. C. Fuller, *The Last of the Gentlemen's Wars* (London, 1937); Ernest Swinton, *The Defence of Duffer's Drift* (new ed., Oxford, 1949); Edgar Holt, *The Boer War* (London, 1958); and Rayne Kruger, *Good-Bye Dolly Gray: The Story of the Boer War* (Philadelphia, 1960). Deneys Reitz' classic *Commando* (London, 1929) was followed by a fine account of the World War, *Trekking On* (London, 1933). There are no military studies of De Wet, Botha, or Smuts, but works on all three men and a new official history are projected. De Wet's *Three Years War* (New York, 1902) and Eric Rosenthal's popular *General De Wet* (Cape Town, 1946) are worth reading.

other aphorisms. These are not difficult to frame. But a logical & scientific system of war is a different matter." The extent of Britain's implied diplomatic commitment to France is still debated. When war came, in any case, the plan for sending the Expeditionary Force to France was immediately set in motion. No better plan emerged from a meeting which Henry Wilson described as "an historic meeting of great men, mostly entirely ignorant of the subject."[41]

The decision to send the small British regular army to the Continent at the outbreak of war was followed by a radical change in British naval strategy. Some British critics, led by the journalist and historian Julian Corbett and the marine painter Fred T. Jane, had taken the *Jeune Ecole's* idea of the impossibility of close blockade seriously. But Germany could still be blockaded and the High Seas Fleet brought to action if it came out—the real aim of the Nelsonian close blockade, as Mahan had noted—from bases well out of range of Germany's underwater forces. Soon after Churchill went to the Admiralty the British navy abandoned its projected close blockade of Heligoland for a far blockade from Scapa Flow in the Orkney Islands or from Rosyth in Scotland. For more than a hundred years, and particularly since the Naval Defence Act, the public had been fed the strong meat of the

[41] Major-General Sir C. E. Callwell, *Sir Henry Wilson, His Life and Diaries* (2 vols., London, 1927), I, 112, 158-159. Arthur J. Marder, *Portrait of an Admiral: The Life and Papers of Sir Herbert Richmond* (London, 1952), 49. Churchill's story is *The World Crisis* (4 vols.. New York, 1923-1929), I. Basil Collier, *Brasshat: A Biography of Field-Marshal Sir Henry Wilson* (London, 1961) is more sympathetic than the scathing view of General Sir Hubert Gough, *Soldiering On* (London, 1954), 171-173. On the more general problem of the Committee of Imperial Defence and the formulation of British strategy see Michael Howard, ed., *Soldiers and Governments* (London, 1957); John Ehrman, *Cabinet Government and War, 1890-1940* (Cambridge, 1958); Franklyn A. Johnson, *Defence by Committee: The British Committee of Imperial Defence, 1885-1939* (New York, 1960); and the memoirs of the heads of that Committee in the two wars, Lord Hankey, *The Supreme Command, 1914-1918* (2 vols., London, 1961) and *The Memoirs of General the Lord Ismay* (New York, 1960).

Schlieffen knew that the British might land 100,000 men at Antwerp or "on the Jutland coast," but was not greatly worried. Ritter, *Schlieffen Plan,* 161, 163. Reviving interest in the amphibious operations is shown in the works of Generals G. G. Aston, *Letters on Amphibious Wars* (London, 1911) and C. E. Callwell, *Military Operations and Maritime Preponderance* (London, 1905), and Franz Freiherr von Edelsheim, *Operations upon the Sea,* trans. Alexander Gray (New York, 1914). Brigadier Bernard Fergusson, *The Watery Maze* (London, 1961) is a fascinating capsule history of the problem, very important for British operations in the Second World War. Alfred Vagts' voluminous *Landing Operations* (Harrisburg, 1946) stressed American incompetence in 1898 without noting that the French had done no better in Tunisia and Madagascar. The best-managed amphibious operations of this era were those of the Japanese.

Nelson tradition. With the hostile fleets only a few hundred miles apart, they had come to believe that the command of the sea would be quickly determined in gladiatorial combat in the middle of the North Sea. Instead, the world's most powerful battle fleets steamed in opposite directions and were to spend the next four years in a gigantic game of cat and mouse, a game which was to be as vigorously criticized by some of the victorious cats as by the defeated mice. This new and "un-Nelsonian" distribution of the British fleet was due to three "un-Nelsonian" conditions: the new vulnerability of even the most powerful surface ships to underwater attack, Britain's new dependence on her overseas commerce, and the decision to risk the small British army in the decisive Continental battle. From its positions in Scotland and the Channel the British fleet cut all of Germany's shipping lanes except those with Scandinavia, which could hardly be interfered with, and protected British shipping from German surface attack, except for the routes into the Baltic. Any large German invading force would either be intercepted or face a crushing blow to its communications. The overly large forces which were to be kept in Britain against such an invasion were more of a tribute to a century of invasion scares than to the power of the High Seas Fleet to carry one out. Finally, the Expeditionary Force's short cross-Channel communications were protected by destroyers and old battleships and the Grand Fleet's threat to the High Seas Fleet's line of retreat to its single North Sea base. Togo had annihilated the Russians at Tsushima under somewhat similar strategic circumstances and the High Seas Fleet was to be constantly hampered by this fear of interception.[42]

The Royal Navy's "defensive" dispositions secured the basic aim of strategy, defined by the *Jeune Ecole* as "the specific powerlessness of a given enemy." Plan XVII and the later Maginot Line, on the other hand, are monuments to the tyranny which the words "offensive" and "defensive" may

[42] Nelson hagiography reached its peak with the Trafalgar Centennial. Corbett's views are in *Some Principles of Maritime Strategy* (London, 1911) and *Naval Operations* (*History of the Great War Based on Official Documents*, 5 vols. in this series, IV-V by Henry Newbolt, London, 1920-1931), I, 2-3. Jane's are in *Heresies of Sea Power* (London, 1906). His *Fighting Ships* dates from 1897, Lord Brassey's *Naval Annual* from 1886. For the Grand Fleet's two commanders see Admiral Sir R. H. Bacon, *The Life of John Rushworth, Earl Jellicoe* (London, 1936) and Admiral W. S. Chalmers, *The Life and Letters of David, Earl Beatty* (London, 1951). Fisher's alleged favoritism to Jellicoe and Beatty was partly responsible for the bitterness of the later Jutland controversy.

exercise over strategic thinking. The Grand Fleet's defensive strategy has also been criticized as affecting its tactics. Its first wartime commander, John Jellicoe, thought that its superior numbers, speed, and long-range firepower assured its decisive superiority in good weather. But he would not close with the Germans at night or in bad weather when their lighter guns would not be outranged and their heavier armor and superior torpedo strength might give them the advantage. His superiors had approved his decision not to leave *"anything to chance in a Fleet action, because our Fleet was the one and only factor that was vital to the existence of the Empire."* As Churchill put it, Jellicoe was the only man who could lose the war in an afternoon. When the two fleets met on the foggy afternoon of May 31, 1916, they exchanged pawns and broke off. The British lost twice as many men and nearly twice as much tonnage as the Germans, but the Grand Fleet's command of the sea remained unshaken. It had not won a super-Tsushima, but the High Seas Fleet did not take that chance again.[43]

[43] *The Grand Fleet, 1914-1916: Its Creation, Development and Work* (New York, 1919), 397-398. The German commander at Jutland was Reinhard Scheer, *Germany's High Seas Fleet in the World War* (London, 1920). See also Langhorne Gibson and Admiral J. E. T. Harper, *The Riddle of Jutland* (New York, 1934), Commander Holloway H. Frost, *The Battle of Jutland* (Annapolis, 1936), Admiral Sir Frederic Dreyer, *The Sea Heritage* (London, 1955), Captain Donald Macintyre, *Jutland* (London, 1958), and Commander Georg von Hase, *Kiel and Jutland,* trans. Arthur Chambers and F. R. Holt London, 1921).

Scheer hoped to lure the British into submarine traps or to defeat them in detail. Beatty's battle cruisers were brought into contact with the German main body, but turned and lured Scheer into contact with Jellicoe, deployed across Scheer's line of retreat. Scheer turned away twice, covering his second turn with a battle cruiser sortie and destroyer torpedo attack. Jellicoe's ships turned away from the torpedoes. The Germans forced their way home through the British rear at night. The German ships were better compartmented and their damage control was better, but the decisive factor was the explosion of British cordite powder when flash reached a magazine; 3309 of their 6097 killed were on the three battle cruisers which blew up in action. One German battle cruiser had to be sunk and the other four were badly hit, but only 382 of their 2545 killed were on these ships. The dreadnoughts on both sides were hardly engaged. The German pre-dreadnought *Pommern* was torpedoed during the night with the loss of 840 lives.

THE AGE OF VIOLENCE

Chapter 8

The First World War

The Opening Battles (1914)

AUSTRIA-HUNGARY declared war on Serbia on July 28, 1914. Within a week Serbia, Russia, France, Belgium, and Britain were arrayed against Austria-Hungary and Germany. Few of the shouting citizens who thronged the streets of Europe's cities during that week had any experience of war, but the armies' mobilization demonstrated the results of years of general staff planning. Millions of men left their normal occupations, and industry and commerce came almost to a standstill. Two ministers resigned from the British cabinet, but the powerful parties of the Second Socialist International all voted for the necessary war loans and taxes. There were no strikes or acts of sabotage; even deserters who had been living abroad came back to defend their respective Fatherlands. Charles de Gaulle later described this as a social revolution,

. . . the culmination of long years of change, suddenly brought to a head by the cataclysm. For generations universal suffrage, compulsory education, . . . industrialization and city life, . . . the press, . . . political parties, trade unions, and sport [had] all fostered the collective spirit. . . . The mass movements and mechanization to which men and women were subjected by modern life had preconditioned them for mass mobilization and for the brutal, sudden shocks which characterized the war of peoples.[1]

The Germans invaded Belgium on August 3. Two days later they got behind the Liége forts, which were then battered into submission. On Tuesday, August 18, their First Army (on the right end) drove the Belgian army into Antwerp. On Thursday their Sixth and Seventh Armies (on the left end) defeated the two French armies advancing south of Metz, and began battering the French fortifications in that area in an attempt to turn a single into a double envelopment. Even if he had wished to do so, the limited rail facilities in the Liége bottleneck would have kept Moltke from shifting many men from his left to his right wing. On Saturday the

---

[1] *France and Her Army*, 90. For the British mood in the opening months see James Cameron, *1914* (London, 1959).

German Fourth and Fifth Armies defeated the two French armies advancing north of Metz and the exposed French Fifth Army met the whole right side of the German line. But Bülow of the German Second Army bungled a Cannae by attacking too soon. The German Third Army could not get into a flanking position in time, and the First Army was distracted by the appearance of the British Expeditionary Force. By Monday, August 24, the Allied armies in the west were retreating everywhere. In this Battle of the Frontiers "the whole French strategic plan was upset by the enemy's vast enveloping movement and by his use of his reserves. On the tactical plane, the revelation of the enemy's fire power made nonsense of the accepted theories. Morally, the illusions behind which the soldiers had taken refuge were swept away in a trice." But Joffre did not panic. General Bertholet suggested attacking the German center, but Joffre decided to shift troops from his right to his left to try to outflank the German right wing. Many northern French industrial cities had to be abandoned, but neither high command was thinking of anything except *the* decisive battle. On the same day Moltke detailed twelve divisions to the east to meet the surprisingly strong Russian invasion of East Prussia. The four which were finally sent—all from the right wing, a force almost as large as the B. E. F.—missed the decisive battles on both fronts.[2]

Joffre formed a new Sixth Army northwest of Paris. The British were to the south of them with the French Fifth and a new Ninth Army around the corner to the east. By the end of the next week there were twenty-nine divisions in the three armies on the German right; the Allied forces facing them had been increased from less than twenty to more than fifty divisions. The German First and Second Armies were also out of line. Bülow had asked Kluck of the First Army to swing inward to hit the French Fifth Army's flank and had again ruined the operation by attacking before Kluck was ready. Bülow then halted, but Kluck continued to cut across his front, ignoring the British, whatever forces might be gathering in Paris, and a specific order from Moltke to guard Bülow's flank. Discovering this on Friday, September 4, Moltke sent a staff emissary, Lieutenant Colonel von Hentsch (chief of the intelligence section for France) to order Kluck back. That afternoon Joffre ordered the Sixth, British, and Fifth Armies to "take advantage of the exposed position of the

German First Army," while his other armies turned to attack along the rest of the line. The Battle of the Marne began the next day. Kluck, hastening back into position, ran into part of the French Sixth Army northwest of Paris. He recklessly tried to outflank it by drawing troops from his left wing, next to Bülow's army, thus opening a gap in the German line opposite the British and part of the French Fifth Army. Moltke saw the danger and sent Hentsch on another inspection mission on Tuesday. Though he was not given written instructions, Hentsch was empowered to order a general retreat if he found it necessary. Hentsch found Bülow thoroughly scared. They agreed that Bülow should retire if the British were found to be across the Marne River in force on Wednesday, September 9. Hentsch saw Kluck's chief of staff the next morning and ordered the retirement of the First Army when news of Bülow's retreat arrived. The Germans halted at the formidable barrier of the Aisne River, about forty miles back of their previous positions. On Monday, September 14, Moltke was secretly replaced as Chief of the General Staff by the Prussian War Minister, Erich von Falkenhayn.[3]

The Allies had won "a psychological rather than a physical victory" from "a jar . . . causing a crack in a weak joint of

[3] William II was Supreme War Lord, but the Chief of the General Staff issued "operative commands" and was the "bearer of the authority of the Supreme Command." Falkenhayn, *General Headquarters, 1914-1916 and Its Critical Decisions* (London, [1919]), 4. In the confusion the Germans had not exploited a near break in the French center, where Foch's Ninth Army recklessly attacked and was defeated. Contamine, *La Revanche,* thinks that the Germans' initial superiority came from better and more uniform peacetime training. Some French units were too bold, others too passive. But the French learned to fight by fighting. As long as their morale and communications remained intact, they were soon as good as the Germans. See also Pierre Varillon, *Joffre* (Paris, 1956), and M. G. Gamelin, *Manoeuvre et victoire de la Marne* (Paris, 1954). Cyril Falls, *The Great War* (London, 1959), C. R. M. F. Cruttwell, *A History of the Great War* (Oxford, 1934), and Harvey A. DeWeerd, *Great Soldiers of the First World War* (Washington, 1943), are good. Liddell Hart's views of the same personalities are condensed in *Through the Fog of War* (New York, 1938). Jean de Pierrefeu, *French Headquarters, 1915-1918,* trans. Major C. J. C. Street (London, 1924); Robert Blake, *The Private Papers of Douglas Haig* (London, 1952); John W. Wheeler-Bennett, *Hindenburg: The Wooden Titan* (London, 1936); and Karl Tschuppik, *Ludendorff: The Tragedy of a Specialist* (London, 1932), are important works in English.

Anyone interested in a particular campaign should look at Douglas W. Johnson, *Battlefields of the World War* (New York, 1921). Major-General Sir Frederick Maurice, *Lessons of Allied Cooperation, Naval, Military, and Air, 1914-18* (London, 1942), is a basic work. James T. Shotwell, ed., *Economic and Social History of the World War* (200 projected volumes, New York, 1921-   ), was one of the most successful international historical projects ever attempted. Albrecht Mendelssohn-Bartholdy, *The War and German Society: The Testament of a Liberal* (New Haven, 1937), may be the best of the many fine volumes in this series.

the German line, and the penetration of this physical crack in turn producing a moral crack in the German command." Perhaps Foch had been right after all. The Allies had won because their commanders would not admit that they were beaten. The Battles of the Frontiers and of the Marne had cost each side half a million men, more than the whole Prussian army in 1866. The Allies were too exhausted to pursue the retreating Germans. The British had crawled, rather than raced through the gap in the German line. Some British infantrymen had averaged only four hours of sleep for thirteen consecutive days. The great battle had ended in mutual exhaustion. Yet the Marne, like Valmy (which the Germans had taken and then abandoned in their great effort), had been one of history's decisive battles. Germany's bid for quick victory in the west had failed, the first disappointment in the war which the brilliant strategist Max von Hoffman was to call *The War of Lost Opportunities*. After the German retreat to the Aisne, the lines ended near Compiègne (the scene of the signing of the Armistices of 1918 and 1940) about fifty miles northeast of Paris. To the north and west lay the unoccupied triangle of Picardy, Artois, and Flanders—about 125 miles north to the western tip of the neutral Netherlands and roughly the same distance west to the mouth of the Seine River. This triangle contained the important Channel ports of Dieppe, Boulogne, Calais, Dunkirk, and Ostend—the objects óf scores of historic sieges and battles. The Germans had ignored this area during their drive, though the British had evacuated the coast to Le Havre (south of the Seine) and had even prepared to transfer the base of the B. E. F. to St. Nazaire on the Bay of Biscay.[4]

Each commander now attempted to turn the other's open flank in a mis-named "Race to the Sea." Though Joffre was always "a day or a division too late" to outflank the German line, he saved most of this open triangle and all of the Channel ports except Ostend and Zeebrugge in Belgium. During these operations the B. E. F. was transferred to the north end of the line to reinforce that part of the Belgian army which had broken out of Antwerp and a small British force which had been landed to help them. In November the Germans tried to break through to the Channel near Ypres, the

[4] B. H. Liddell Hart, *A History of the World War, 1914-1918* (London, 1934), 87, 111. Hoffman's book, trans. A. E. Chamot (London, 1924), was reprinted in his *War Diaries and Other Papers*, trans. Eric Sutton (2 vols., London, 1929).

strategic center of the "Flanders Mountains," a range of low clay hills commanding wide stretches of the coastal plain. The Belgians had opened the dikes south of Ostend to form an impregnable water barrier to a German advance along the coast. The Germans assaulted Ypres with new divisions of reservists and volunteers, many of them students between seventeen and twenty. They were beaten back at Langemarck with fearful losses in an assault which became as famous in German war literature as the later British attack at Passchendaele five miles away. After the Guards had also failed to break the British-Belgian lines, the First Battle of Ypres flickered out in mid-November. Now there were no flanks to go around. Improvised trenches ran from Switzerland to salt water. When these were reinforced with barbed wire and concrete, the war in the west became a war of attrition, one of the longest and the bloodiest in history. As J. F. C. Fuller was to put it,

Their carefully planned war was . . . smashed to pieces by firepower . . . so devastating that . . . there was no choice but to go under the surface . . . like foxes. Then, . . . to secure these trenches from surprise, . . . each side . . . spun hundreds of thousands of miles of steel web around its entrenchments. . . . Armies, through their own lack of foresight, were reduced to the position of human cattle. They browsed behind their fences and occasionally snorted and bellowed at each other.

Like so many good similes, this one is not quite true. The cattle recklessly charged the fences as soon as they felt able to do so.[5]

5 *War and Western Civilization* (London, 1932), 227-228. Blake's Introduction to Haig's *Private Papers* is one of the best single works on the British army at this time. Lord Beaverbrook, no supporter of Haig, says that Haig "committed suicide 25 years after his death." *Men and Power, 1917-1918* (London, 1956), xvii. Haig claimed that he knew that Britain should prepare *"for a war of several years"* from the first and had grave doubts about Sir John French's fitness to command the B. E. F. After Langemarck Haig noted "The Germans, quite young fellows, came on with great gallantry. One mounted officer kept encouraging his men to go forward, until within 400 yards of our firing line, when he was killed." He reported the British "7th Division reduced to inefficiency through ignorance of their leaders in having placed them in trenches on the *forward* slopes where enemy could see and so effectively shell them." He found the King "very cheery but inclined to think that all our troops are by nature brave" and "ignorant of all the efforts which commanders must make . . . to enable [men] . . . to go forward as an organised unit in the face of almost certain death. I told him of the crowds of fugitives who came back down the Menin Road from time to time during the Ypres Battle having thrown . . . their rifles and packs . . . with a look of absolute terror on their faces." *Private Papers*, 69-79.

Meanwhile the sixty-seven-year-old Paul von Hindenburg, called from retirement to check the Russians in East Prussia, had annihilated one Russian army at Tannenberg the day after Moltke's decision to take troops from the west to shore up the east, and had beaten a second Russian army at the Masurian Lakes two weeks later. To the south, however, the Russian steam-roller had flattened the Austro-Hungarians. By the onset of winter the Central Powers had traded the western part of Russian Poland for most of Austrian Poland, and three Austro-Hungarian drives into Serbia had been turned back with heavy losses of men and equipment. The prophets had been correct. The Germans were better than the Russians (who had lost 700,000 men and a quarter of their artillery), but the latter were superior to the Austro-Hungarians. German and Hungarian units (each about a quarter of the Hapsburg army in 1914) fought well until the end of the war, but the rest of this polyglot army never again fought more than half-heartedly.[6]

Not much seemed to have happened at sea. Most of the German cruisers or merchant cruisers in non-European waters had been run down or bottled up by December 8, when British battle cruisers destroyed Admiral Spee's small squadron near the Falkland Islands. All of the German colonies except East Africa had fallen to the British, French, and Japanese (who had entered the war in August). In the Mediterranean two German cruisers had escaped to neutral Turkey, and had helped to bring that power into the war in November on the German side. This closed the Dardanelles, the only good sea route from the western Allies to Russia. It also forced Russia to open a new front in the Caucasus. An Indian force was landed in Mesopotamia (modern Iraq was then part of the Ottoman Empire) and substantial Indian, Australian, and New Zealand forces were sent to Egypt to protect the Suez Canal. The Sultan had proclaimed a Holy War which might cause trouble among the millions of Moslem subjects of the Russian, French, and British Empires. Italy had not joined her allies of the Triple Alliance. Montenegro had thrown in her lot with Serbia, but the remaining

---

[6] The Germans had planned to meet an invasion of East Prussia by using their superior rail net and interior lines to beat the Russians in detail. Most of the arrangements for Tannenberg had been made by Hoffman and François before Hindenburg and his chief of staff Ludendorff arrived. The standard English study of this classic "Cannae" battle is Edmund Ironside, *Tannenberg: The First Thirty Days in East Prussia* (Edinburgh, 1925).

Balkan states (Rumania, Greece, and Bulgaria) were still neutral.

At the beginning of the winter of 1914-1915 everyone was running short of supplies. Even Germany had not stocked ammunition for a long war or correctly estimated the enormous ammunition requirements of the new rapid-fire weapons. No army had enough machine guns or enough material for siege warfare—high-angle mortars and howitzers to kill men in deep dugouts, barbed wire, hand grenades to lob into the opposing trenches, and star shells for night fighting. The new British Secretary of State for War, Lord Kitchener, had scrapped Haldane's plan for expanding the British army through the Territorials. He was raising a new volunteer army, which had to be equipped with everything. Poorly industrialized Austria-Hungary, Russia, Turkey, and Italy (who was to join the Allies in April, 1915) were not ready for anything. The Russian guns fired as many shells in a day as their factories could make in a month. Neither the Russian nor the Austro-Hungarian railways could supply their armies in the Carpathians; even German troops in that area had no winter clothing or equipment. Disease and bad weather were chiefly responsible for the Turks losing all but 12,400 of 190,000 men in the Caucasus. In this situation the German conquest of most of Belgium and forty percent of France's coal and ninety percent of her iron ore was very important. The Germans could still trade with Scandinavia, Switzerland, and the Netherlands, but were cut off from overseas food and raw materials. The Allied command of the sea—which enabled them to draw supplies from their empires and the neutral United States—had become a major, perhaps even the predominating, factor in a European war.

Deadlock in the West (1915-1916)

Falkenhayn still believed that France would have to be beaten and that no victory over Russia could be decisive. But he was overruled by the "easterners" (Hindenburg, Ludendorff, and Conrad—who, as an ally, could appeal directly to William II). In 1915 the Central Powers thus virtually revived the plan of the elder Moltke, going over to the offensive against Russia, then suffering the worst of its munitions crisis, while standing generally on the defensive in the west. This decision resulted in great German victories in Russia and the Balkans, but it gave the British a chance to raise Kitch-

ener's new army. The belief in the tactical offensive died hard.
What was needed were heavy guns and ammunition to blast
a gap. Douglas Haig, now commanding the British First
Army, told the Military Correspondent of *The Times* on
January 22, 1915, that, "as soon as we were supplied with
ample artillery ammunition . . . we could walk through the
German lines at several places." He did not realize that the
key word was "walk." After the failure of the British offensives in March and May he wrote, "The defences in our front
are so carefully and so strongly made, and mutual support
with machine-guns is so complete, that in order to demolish
them a *long methodical bombardment* will be necessary . . .
before Infantry are sent forward to attack." But in spite of
heroic sacrifices, of new hopes as fantastic as the old ones,
the lines did not move more than ten miles for twenty-eight
months (a period which would have covered the American
Civil War from Fredericksburg to Appomattox). The French
and British offensives of 1915 were all much alike. After air
reconnaissance of the German positions, artillery pounded
their wire, machine gun nests, and trenches. After the barrage
had been "lifted" to the rear (later "creeping barrages" were
used in front of the infantry), the men went "over the top"
in waves about a hundred yards apart, with the men in each
wave six to eight feet from each other. The only German
offensive during this period in the west was launched at Ypres
with the help of chlorine gas. The Allies had been warned,
but thought that they were ready for gas. Two divisions
broke, but the Germans were not ready to exploit the gap.[7]

The attackers usually carried the first line and often the
second before being halted by the enemy's reserves. In all of
1915 the British and French did not gain more than three
miles at any one point. The French lost 1,430,000 men compared to a mere 955,000 for five months in 1914 and 900,000
in 1916. On June 14, 1915, one of Joffre's aides told Haig
that "the French people are getting tired of the war."

The tremendous cost of the war, the occupation of a very wealthy
part of France . . . and the cessation of trade and farming operations were affecting them. Everything was practically at a standstill and the whole of the manhood of the nation was concentrated

---

[7] *Private Papers*, 84, 93. The best short account of gas warfare is by the later
Major-General Alden H. Waitt, *Gas Warfare* (New York, 1942). For its
further development and the reasons why it was not used in the Second World
War see Leo P. Brophy *et al.*, *The Chemical Warfare Service* (2 vols., *U. S.
Army in World War II*, Washington, 1959-1961).

on this frontier. *There was a general wish that a vigorous effort should be made to end the war by the autumn.*

The new British armies, in proportion to their numbers, suffered even more. At the end of the year the B. E. F.'s commander, Sir John French, was replaced by Haig. As Hubert Gough, one of their subordinates, put it,

We all fell into these mistakes, friend and foe alike, in the early days of the War. . . . We were always looking for the GAP, and trying to make it, hoping that we would pour through it in a glorious exciting rush, and so put an end to any more heavy fighting. But war against a great, efficient and brave enemy is not so quickly ended as this. Under such conditions, war is a matter of hard blows, heavy loss, long, stern and desperate struggles, and victory will not be gained until the *morale* of one side or the other be broken.[8]

Trenches were not new, but the trench systems in the west during the First World War were the most elaborate in history. One British officer described them as follows:

Trenches, properly speaking, could not long exist in Flanders, where the country is scientifically irrigated. . . . Farther to the south in Picardy, very neatly designed trenches could be cut to any depth in the hard chalk. In most parts of the line the trenches varied between these two extremes, and life was a struggle to dry and drain and dig what the weather and the enemy's bombardment were continually destroying. . . .

When a position was occupied for any length of time . . . [there were] at least two parallel trenches perhaps two hundred yards apart, a front line occupied by sentry posts, and a support line where most of the men off duty lived in dugouts. Communications trenches would be dug . . . from the front line back to the support line, and then farther back still until they reached a point invisible to the enemy. . . . Some . . . were three miles long. . . . Dugouts began as mere cavities scooped into the side of a trench. . . . Lined with boards, strengthened with beams and courses of sandbags, . . . they became more or less proof against splinters of shell. The only dugouts safe from a direct hit . . . were underground chambers . . . made like . . . a coal mine.

[8] Haig, *Private Papers*, 95-96. Gough, *The Fifth Army* (London, 1931), 129-130. The best defense of Haig is by his D. M. O., Major-General Sir John Davidson, *Haig, Master of the Field* (London, 1953). John Terraine, *Mons: The Retreat to Victory* (London, 1960) and Alan Clark, *The Donkeys* (London, 1961) are readable popular accounts of the old British army. Haig thought that "Foch and Co. . . . are a queer mixture of fair ability . . . and ignorance of the practical side of war. . . . They never seem to think of what the enemy may do, . . . and take steps to meet it." *Private Papers*, 91.

To complete a trench system two more things were required: barbed wire and "strong points" . . . little fortresses [to] . . . hold out even if the main trench lines were taken. . . . [With kinks in the line] every five or ten yards . . . [one walked] in a maze, squeezing past people at narrow bends, paddling through mud and water, climbing over obstructions . . . usually in the dark . . . with a load of pit props, barbed wire, sandbags, and corrugated iron.[9]

In 1916 Falkenhayn decided to renew the offensive in the west. Russia had been beaten, but Russian communications were so bad that the Germans would bog down before reaching Petrograd or Moscow. So Falkenhayn would finish with France, aided by the defeatism already being spread in France by German agents (including some members of the Chamber of Deputies). Falkenhayn planned to hit the partly surrounded and partially dismantled old fortress of Verdun at the hinge of the French line with an irresistible artillery bombardment. The loss of this supposedly impregnable position might cause a French collapse. Joffre was similarly determined to attack, this time on the Somme River. Essentially both sides had accepted the French staff's conclusion that "breakthrough followed by exploitation is impossible until the enemy has been so worn down that he has no reserves available to close the gap." The battle for Verdun, an area about the size of New York City, lasted ten months. The Germans lost fewer men (336,000 to 362,000) but failed to win their propaganda victory. The defender of Verdun, Pétain, became a national hero. Hindenburg, with Ludendorff as his chief collaborator, replaced Falkenhayn in August. The Allies lost fewer men than the Germans on the Somme (614,-000 to 650,000), but also failed to break through. The fighting on the Italian-Austrian front had been just as indecisive. The main Italian objective was Trieste, only thirty miles from the frontier. By September, 1917, at the end of the eleventh Battle of the Isonzo, the Italians were less than half-way to Trieste and had lost nearly a million men. One cabinet had been forced out, but General Cadorna was still in command of the army. Colonel Douhet, an artillery officer interested in motor transport and in air power, had been court-martialed and imprisoned for circulating criticism of Italian tactics.

[9] Charles Edmonds [Carrington], *A Subaltern's War* (London, 1930), 213-216. The best work on tactics is P. M. H. Lucas *The Evolution of Tactical Ideas in France and Germany during the Wars of 1914-1918* (London, 1925).

Never a great general, Joffre had kept his head in one supreme crisis, but the French army had suffered terribly from a high command which had first adopted Plan XVII and then had recklessly resumed the offensive after the Miracle of the Marne. The French government had given Joffre enormous power. His headquarters dabbled in diplomacy and economic warfare while Joffre tried to do the work of the War Minister and of his own chief of staff, Castelnau. Even his aide thought Joffre had gone too far when he would not let the War Minister visit the front. "It might be well and good," the aide wrote, "to forbid access to the indiscreet, but it is unthinkable to try and prevent the *government* from going there." Joffre's critics finally brought down the cabinet, and Galliéni became War Minister. But Joffre ignored repeated warnings of the impending German attack on Verdun, appointing Pétain to hold that point but refusing to give him additional troops because this would weaken his own projected Somme offensive. Finally the Chamber of Deputies met in secret session to discuss Joffre's policies and Joffre's critics, led by André Maginot, who had been wounded at Verdun in 1914, carried the day. When the Somme offensive failed, Lyautey became War Minister. Joffre was forced out in December, 1916, after having alienated both the politicians and some of the ablest generals in the French army. The French government's mistake was not in recovering control of its army, but in choosing Robert Nivelle—a good republican with a good press and a good combat record—as his successor. He optimistically promised to "rupture" the German front in a single massive thrust in the spring of 1917. Lyautey thought this "insane," but, fortunately for Nivelle, Lyautey was forced to resign as War Minister over another matter.[10]

The cult of the offensive still had many followers. Many generals could not see that these tremendous artillery bombardments sacrificed mobility and surprise for mass and concentration. The guns destroyed all communications in the GAP—roads, paths, even the topsoil—leaving crater-pocked deserts as bad as the barbed wire and trenches and making

[10] Emile Herbillon, quoted in Jere C. King, *Generals and Politicians: Conflict between France's High Command, Parliament and Government, 1914-1918* (Berkeley, 1951), 58. Joffre's most recent defender is General Desmazes, *Joffre, la victoire du caractère* (Paris, 1955). Sewell Tyng admits "Joffre's arbitrary exercise of the powers confided to him ' while trying to prove that he was not the "Papa Joffre" of the legend—"carried along . . . by forces utterly incomprehensible to him and ending up as a hero, almost in spite of himself." *The Campaign of the Marne, 1914* (London, 1935), 347-351.

surprise impossible. War was mechanized behind the lines; reserves brought up in trains or trucks could plug the GAP while the attackers were laboring through it. The nineteen-day British bombardment at Third Ypres (1917) used 321 train loads of shells, a year's production for 55,000 war workers. The whole battle area reverted to a swamp in which the British army took 45 square miles in five months at a cost of 370,000 men, or 8,222 per square mile. Never had so many men been so long under such fire. The shock—to men whom society had taught that war would be short and glorious—produced the greatest of all war literatures.[11]

Its "wellspring," Edmund Blunden noted thirty years later, was "the compassion" of educated, sensitive men who "were themselves for a time 'common soldiers' and . . . constantly in touch with, and in the position of guardians of, those millions," whom the nineteen-year-old Henry Williamson had seen dying in the wide and shattered country of the Somme, . . . among the broad, straggling belts of rusty wire smashed and twisted in the chalky loam, while the ruddy clouds of brick-dust hang over the shelled villages by day, and at night the eastern horizon roars and bubbles with light.

And everywhere in these desolate places I see the faces and figures of enslaved men, the marching columns pearl-hued with chalky dust on the sweat of their heavy drab clothes; the files of carrying parties laden and staggering in the flickering moonlight of gunfire; the "waves" of assaulting troops lying silent and pale on the tapelines of the jumping-off places.

I crouch with them while the steel glacier rushing by just overhead scrapes away every syllable, every fragment of a message bawled into my ear. . . . I go forward with them . . . up and down across ground like a huge ruined honeycomb, and my wave melts away, and the second wave comes up, and also melts away, and then the third wave merges into the ruins of the first and second, and after a while the fourth blunders into the remnants of the others, and we begin to run forward to catch up with the barrage, gasping and sweating, in bunches, anyhow, every bit of the months of drill and rehearsal forgotten.

We come to wire that is uncut, and beyond we see grey coalscuttle helmets bobbing about, . . . and the loud crackling of machine-guns changes to a screeching as of steam being blown off by a hundred engines, and soon no one is left standing. An hour

11 J. F. C. Fuller, *On Future Warfare* (London, 1928), 61-62, 130. Iwo Jima's eight square miles were to cost *both* armies 5,500 casualties per square mile. Leon Wolff, *In Flanders Fields* (New York, 1958), Brian Gardner, *The Big Push* (London, 1961), and John Harris, *Covenant with Death* (London, 1961) are good popular accounts.

later our guns are "back on the first objective," and the brigade, with all its hopes and beliefs, has found its grave on those northern slopes of the Somme battlefield.[12]

German Victory in the East (1915-1916)

While the armies on the west remained deadlocked, a decision had been reached in the east. In 1915 the Central Powers conquered Russian Poland. The shallow Russian trenches had little wire and no deep dugouts. The German guns blew them to bits; the few smoke-blackened, shell-shocked survivors gave up when the infantry reached them. Here, where the attackers had more room to maneuver, gaps were exploited as rapidly as infantry and horse-drawn artillery could move through them. The retreating Russians, with little confidence in their leaders and still less in their artillery, often pulled back at the first threat to their flanks. All told, Russia was to mobilize over fifteen million men, a hopeless mass of human flesh against the steel glacier. Falkenhayn stopped his offensive while the tired German army still had time to prepare for winter. Russia itself had not been invaded, but Falkenhayn believed the Russians incapable of launching another major offensive. Nicholas II took over the field command from his uncle, the Grand Duke Nicholas, thus leaving the home front to the unbalanced Tsarina and her favorites. In 1916, as has been noted, the Germans concentrated their efforts on the west, while the Russians again tried to relieve the pressure on their French allies. The most successful of their efforts, General Brusilov's offensive against the Austro-Hungarians, led Rumania to join the Allies (in August) and to be conquered by the Germans (September through December). Perhaps another million Russians, an equal number of Austro-Hungarians, and half a million Rumanians were casualties. Austro-

12 Blunden, *War Poets, 1914-1918* (London, 1958), 13. Williamson, *The Wet Flanders Plain* (London, 1929), 14-16. Cyril Falls' superb *War Books: A Critical Guide* (London, 1930), 182-183, remarked on the failure of taste which made Blunden's masterpiece, *Undertones of War* (London, 1928), less influential than the translation of Erich Maria Remarque, *All Quiet on the Western Front* (Boston, 1929). Blunden is the only recent guide. The others are Eugene Löhrke's sensitive anthology, *Armageddon: The World War in Literature* (New York, 1930) and H. M. Tomlinson, "A Footnote to the War Books" (*Out of Soundings*, London, 1931, 223-254).
For Williamson's attitude after a second War compare the savage anti-patriotism of *The Patriot's Progress* (London, 1930) with his last Philip Maddison volumes, *Love and the Loveless* (London, 1958) and *A Test to Destruction* (London, 1960). And listen to the wartime shift from the poignant patriotism of the dying Debussy's *musicien francais* to Rave 's "Le Tombeau de Couperin." Ravel was only thirteen years younger than Debussy, but he had driven a truck at Verdun.

Hungarian Slavic conscripts had deserted to the Russians by the thousand. Various revolutionary committees were now recruiting among these war prisoners and asking for Allied diplomatic recognition. After the death of the aged Hapsburg Emperor Francis Joseph in 1916, Germany was "fettered to a corpse," but her ally's desperate political situation had permitted Germany to set up a new command structure which, in effect, gave Hindenburg the command of all the Central Powers' armies. In Russia the Empress' favorite, Rasputin, was surrounded by charlatans and traitors. The Russian army was now a "militia of peasants" under company officers drawn from outside the old privileged classes. The chief remaining question was whether revolution would come from above or below—from the complete collapse of the incompetent monarchy or from mutiny (a million deserters were already at large) in the army.[13]

Great Britain, like the United States in the Second World War, was the only Allied power which still held the initiative, not because she was better prepared, but because all of her forces had not been committed and the command of the sea gave these forces mobility. Or so it had seemed to the First Lord of the Admiralty, who had asked on December 24, 1914, "Are there not other alternatives than sending our armies to chew barbed wire in Flanders? Further, cannot the power of the Navy be brought more directly to bear upon the enemy? . . . Ought we not, as new forces come to hand, to engage him on new frontiers, and enable the Russians to do so too . . . ?" Lord Kitchener, the most influential member of the War Council, accepted the French view that men and

[13] The classic account is Winston Churchill, *The Unknown War* (New York, 1931). Churchill's favorable estimate of the Grand Duke Nicholas is not shared by many historians. Alfred W. Knox, *With the Russian Army, 1914-17* (New York, 1921), is a major source. The best military accounts are Nicholas N. Golovine, *The Russian Army in the World War* (New Haven, 1932), and Y. Danilov, *La Russie dans la guerre mondiale* (Paris, 1927).

Michael T. Florinsky, *The End of the Russian Empire* (New Haven, 1931), and Bernard Pares, *The Fall of the Russian Monarchy* (New York, 1939), agree in essentials. The inadequate Russian railways could barely haul these masses around; industry and even agriculture began to run short of manpower. The Russian medical services could provide only three doctors for every four thousand men. A unit might lose three-quarters of its men in three or four hours. Pares "saw an English surgeon, with one unqualified Russian assistant, deal with three or four hundred cases . . . under fire in . . . four days; he had scarcely any anaesthetics and no litters; the men lay in the late autumn mud—only a few of them had the shelter of a tent. . . . Most of our wounded had gangrene before they reached the base hospital. There were points on the front where anyone with a stomach or leg wound was a lost man, as transport was impossible and the nearest hospital was miles away." Bernard Pares, *Russia* (New York, 1941), 80.

guns should not be diverted from the west, but finally declared himself willing to go along with one of Churchill's several schemes for the capture of Constantinople. The resulting Dardanelles fiasco has been studied from every possible angle. The Allies hoped to open a way to Russia, end Turkish pressure in the Caucasus, Egypt, and Mesopotamia, reinforce Serbia, influence then neutral Bulgaria, Rumania, and Greece, and possibly precipitate an Austro-Hungarian collapse. Such stakes justified speed, surprise, and careful political planning. The Greeks offered to take Constantinople if Russia would keep Bulgaria out of the war, but Russia demurred. The French and British were equally unwilling to ask the Russian Black Sea fleet for aid, though it was closer to Constantinople than any force in the Mediterranean. As so often before and since, the Turks were to hold their capital because of jealousy among the Christians. The Dardanelles' defenses were obsolete. The Turkish army (after the 1908 revolution and three wars in three years) was not ready for a major enemy. Liman von Sanders, the able head of the German military mission to Turkey, feared that the Dardanelles could be forced by ships alone, a plan which appealed to Churchill because it would not take large ground forces and because he exaggerated the effects of naval gunfire. But the Anglo-French fleet warned the Turks by bombarding the forts on February 15, 1915, and failed to push its expendable pre-dreadnoughts past them a month later.[14]

At the end of April a mixed, inexperienced force of 80,000 men—the Anzac (Australian-New Zealand) corps, British marines, Indian troops, and French colonials—won a beachhead on the Gallipoli peninsula on the European side of the Dardanelles. But they failed to exploit their initial successes, and trench warfare developed. More men were thrown in— 480,000 in all—until October. In December the force was

[14] *The World Crisis,* II, 30-31. Fisher, again First Sea Lord at seventy-three, wanted to land a Russian army "within striking distance of Berlin." He "would . . . sow the North Sea with mines on such a scale that naval operations in it would become impossible." The 612 ships which he ordered included 200 barges, 37 monitors, and 5 light draft battle cruisers, 3 of which, with 4—18" guns, were later converted to carriers. Though he opposed the diversion of his "unparalleled Armada . . . to the damned Dardanelles," Fisher saw Churchill's "fighting qualities: . . . Courage, audacity, celerity, imagination." *Fear God and Dread Nought,* III, 45-46, 422, 364.

The best books are Alan Moorehead, *Gallipoli* (London, 1956), C. F. Aspinall-Oglander's superb official account, *Gallipoli* (2 vols., London, 1929-1932), Ian Hamilton, *Gallipoli Diary* (2 vols., London, 1920), and Liman von Sanders, *Five Years in Turkey* (Annapolis, 1927).

withdrawn after suffering 252,000 casualties. It was the worst British defeat between Saratoga and Singapore. By failing to rescue Russia before the outbreak of revolution, it may well have been as decisive as those battles. It also convinced many military men that the *Jeune Ecole* had been correct: amphibious operations had become impossible. What it actually proved was that nobody in either the prewar British army or navy had done the staff work necessary to make that army a "projectile fired by the navy." The Liberal cabinet was replaced by a coalition, in which Churchill was given a post normally reserved for politicians "in the last stages of unmistakable decrepitude." Lloyd George was advanced to Minister of Munitions and, after Kitchener's death in June, 1916, to Secretary of State for War.[15]

Meanwhile, Bulgaria had joined the Central Powers. In a vain attempt to rescue Serbia, the Allies had violated Greek neutrality by landing another force at Salonika. Though part of the Serbian army escaped to Corfu, the Central Powers now controlled a solid block of territory from Belgium to Mesopotamia and Palestine. The Salonika force could not be withdrawn without abandoning all Allied influence in the Balkans. Greece was finally forced into the Allied camp in 1917—after the Allies' 1916 disaster in Rumania—but this dormant front still tied up 600,000 Allied troops (not counting Greeks, but including Italians, British, French, Russians, and Serbs) at the end of the long submarine-infested sea route through the Mediterranean. The seeming futility of these Allied efforts of 1915 through 1917 was to have considerable effect on postwar Balkan politics. Even after the Central Powers' defeat, the Balkan states retained a healthy respect for German industrial and military prowess. The Turks had stamped out Armenian unrest by wholesale deportation and massacre, but a great British-sponsored "Revolt in the Desert" had begun among the Arabs of the Hedjaz in 1916. Both sides were now deliberately playing with revolution. The Germans were spreading defeatist propaganda and making promises to the Poles, Finns, and Irish. The Allies were making even more effective promises to the more numerous subject nationalities of the Hapsburg and Ottoman Empires. By the end of 1916—as a result of military defeat and nationalistic

---

[15] C. G. Brodie, *Forlorn Hope, 1915* (London, 1956) is good on British submarine operations. The Near Eastern campaigns were all costly, with 554,000 British Empire casualties, mostly from disease, in Egypt and Palestine. The best book is Lord Wavell, *Allenby: A Study in Greatness* (New York, 1941).

and social discontent—the old-fashioned, multinational, agrarian Hapsburg, Romanov, and Ottoman Empires were close to collapse. Italy was shaky, but had not been in the war as long. Japan had contented herself with taking the German Pacific colonies north of the Equator and dipping into troubled China.

The war had begun as a quarrel between the Hapsburgs and the Romanovs. It was to be finished by the four great industrial powers of the west: Germany, Britain, France, and the United States. Germany, Britain, and France were in better shape than the other three European powers, but two years of attrition had taken a heavy toll even in the west. The Hindenburg-Ludendorff team arranged for the call-up of boys of 18 and men previously regarded as fit only for garrison duty, expanding the German army from 176 to 230 divisions by May 1, 1917. Reversing Falkenhayn's suicidal order "not to abandon a foot of ground," Hindenburg also prepared for a withdrawal to a shorter semi-permanent series of defenses in depth (the Hindenburg Line) twenty odd miles back of the Somme battlefield, which could be held by 13 fewer divisions. The retiring Germans then completed the desert begun by Allied shellfire, wrecking houses, cutting down trees, and filling in or polluting every well. After the Battle of Jutland (May 31-June 1, 1916) the High Seas Fleet had again retired behind its minefields. The third High Seas Fleet commander in less than two years had failed to shake the strangling British blockade. Germany was now on increasingly short rations; everything from clothing to railway cars was wearing out. From necessity Germany led the way in economic planning, with Walter Rathenau, the son of the Jewish founder of the electrical trust, becoming an economic dictator. The German chemical industry developed substitutes for many overseas imports, its most significant achievement—which won Fritz Haber the Nobel prize for chemistry in 1918—being the manufacture of nitrates from the air, for guns which used more explosives in one battle than the whole army had used in 1870-1871. Lloyd George became British Prime Minister in December, 1916. Owing to his previous work as Minister of Munitions, the army now had enough munitions and 1,200,000 men in France (its peak strength on that front). But the British people were also becoming war-weary and shipping losses to German submarines were mounting. Everything considered, however, France was more exhausted than either Britain or Germany. Both the soldiers and the civilians who had ousted Joffre now spoke of the "last army of France" being mustered for Nivelle's "final" offensive in the spring of 1917.[16]

Instead of causing a business collapse, war had become a national business enterprise. The distinctions between the fighting and home fronts (a significant new term) tended to disappear as governments discovered that housing, fair rationing, and price controls were important factors in production and that military morale (another military term now applied to civilians) was affected by the care given soldiers' wives and children. The citizens of both the western democracies and the Hohenzollern monarchy also had to be persuaded as well as compelled to change their normal peacetime habits. Taxes, loans, manpower conscription, price controls, and rationing were reinforced by positive centrally-directed propaganda. Doubt and lethargy became as treasonable as dissent. Advertisers, artists, newspapermen, historians, and clergymen pooled their skills in the common propaganda effort. Advertisers had sold soap and sewing machines long before they sold war bonds; the new factor was the conscious use of these specialized techniques by governments. Temporarily, all of the contending states became more or less "totalitarian" and "socialistic," these experiments in "War Socialism" later proving as significant in the development of centralized state planning as the propaganda of the Marxist parties. "The four fundamental lessons," J. F. C. Fuller later wrote,

emerging out of this great conflict were that the business of industrialized war demanded . . . (1) political authority; (2) economic self-sufficiency; (3) national discipline; and (4) machine weapons. Further still . . . both the winning and the losing of the war clearly showed that these lessons must be applied during peacetime in order to be ready for war.[17]

16 The increase in German divisions, the building of the Hindenburg Line, the Allies' mistakes, and the later shifting of German forces from the east were crucial in the events of 1917-1918. Edmonds, *Short History*, 211, reckons 186 Allied divisions in the west early in 1917. The German forces rose from 122 to 170 divisions during 1917, most of the increase coming from new units. There is little on German-sponsored revolutions, except in Russia. The classics on the Arab revolt are T. E. Lawrence, *Seven Pillars of Wisdom: A Triumph* (Garden City, 1936) and *Revolt in the Desert* (New York, 1927). His admirers should also look into *The Mint* (London, 1955).

17 *Machine Warfare* (London, 1943), 35. Major works are Frank P. Chambers, *The War behind the War* (New York, 1939); Max Schwarte, *Die Technik im Weltkriege* (Berlin, 1920); Marion C. Siney, *The Allied Blockade of Germany 1914-1916* (Ann Arbor, 1957); G. Beyerhaus, *Einheitliches Ober-*

The United States and the War (1917)

By the end of 1916 the United States had become an Allied arsenal. American exports to the western Allies had quadrupled; American investors had lent over two billion dollars to Allied governments. American public opinion had always been more sympathetic to the Allies than to the Central Powers. To many Americans Germany stood for militarism and autocracy. Close historical and cultural ties with Britain and France predisposed them to believe Allied, rather than German, propaganda. Trouble had arisen with both belligerents over the rights of American shipping. The British had steadily expanded their contraband list (goods which can be taken from neutrals on the high seas) and interfered with American trade with Scandinavia and the Netherlands. The resulting Anglo-American controversies might have led to serious trouble—in 1916 Congress voted a large capital ship program to make the United States Navy "Second to None"— if they had not been overshadowed by even greater difficulties with Germany over submarine commerce destroying.[18]

In spite of some early successes, the Germans had failed to whittle down the Grand Fleet by underwater action. But they had also discovered (1) that the submarine's range made her an ideal commerce destroyer, and (2) that she could not follow the usual rules of cruiser warfare. If she surfaced to examine suspects, even a small gun could sink her. She could not carry prize crews to take her captures into port. If she sank them, she could not take their crews and passengers to a

befehl: ein Problem des Weltkrieges (Munich, 1938); Harold Lasswell, *Propaganda Technique in the World War* (New York, 1927); and Paul M. A. Linebarger's standard *Psychological Warfare* (2d ed., Washington, 1955).

Even such great scholars as Werner Sombart gave way to the tides of nationalist sentiment in Germany. But G. F. Nicolai, professor of physiology at the University of Berlin, was jailed for pointing out that warfare was a human act and that the trend toward unlimited war was rendering war obsolete. *The Biology of War* (New York, 1918). See also the conclusions of the Dutch author Rudolf Steinmetz, *Soziologie des Krieges* (Leipzig, 1929).

[18] The Irish-American inventor John P. Holland had built a workable submarine in 1875, and the French had launched the *Gymnote* in 1888, partly as a result of the *Jeune Ecole's* interest in such craft. But the submarine did not become a real threat until about 1905, when the Diesel was adapted to submarine propulsion. The Germans had built very few of the early gasoline boats. Tirpitz was willing to let other navies spend their money for experiments. The 1914 German submarine force was only fifth in the world, though its boats were exceptionally well constructed. Little attention had yet been paid to antisubmarine devices. The *Jeune Ecole* had envisaged torpedo boat attacks on merchantmen, but the Germans had not considered submarine commerce raiding. The best survey is R. H. Gibson and Maurice Pendergast, *The German Submarine War, 1914-1918* (New York, 1931).

"place of reasonable safety." On February 4, 1915, the Germans had declared that British ships would be sunk without warning in certain waters. Neutrals were warned that they might be mistaken for British. This had brought immediate American protests, but the first neutral ship, a Norwegian, had been sunk on February 19. As incident had followed incident—the most famous being the sinking of the British liner *Lusitania* with the loss of over a hundred Americans—the American public had become steadily more irritated. When it had also become clear that Germany did not have enough U-boats to be decisive, the first unrestricted submarine campaign had been abandoned in September, 1915. By the end of the next year, however, Hindenburg and Ludendorff could see no other hope of defeating Britain. With fifteen ships being sunk for every submarine destroyed, the German naval staff informed the government that they now had enough submarines to defeat Britain within five months after the resumption of unrestricted warfare. President Wilson would not back up his diplomatic notes by force; he had just been re-elected on a peace platform. In any case, Britain would be starved out before the Americans could get an army to Europe. William II and the Chancellor, Bethmann-Hollweg, had no alternative proposals for victory. Germany resumed unrestricted submarine warfare on February 1, 1917, and the United States declared war on Germany on April 6.[19]

Though its navy—now third in the world—was stronger in capital ships than in antisubmarine craft, the United States was better prepared than for any previous war in its history.

[19] See Karl E. Birnbaum, *Peace Moves and U-Boat Warfare* (Stockholm, 1958), the works listed in Thomas A. Bailey, *A Diplomatic History of the American People* (6th ed., New York, 1958), Walter Millis, *Road to War: America 1914-1917* (Boston, 1935), H. C. Peterson, *Propaganda for War: The Campaign against American Neutrality, 1914-1917* (Norman, 1939) and *Opponents of War, 1917-1918* (with Gilbert C. Fite, Madison, 1957), and Ernest R. May, *The World War and American Isolation, 1914-1917* (Cambridge, Mass., 1959).

George Kennan, *American Diplomacy, 1900-1950* (Mentor ed., New York, 1952) refines Walter Lippman's notion that the war should have been presented to the public as one to preserve the balance of power. Lippman, *U. S. Foreign Policy, Shield of the Republic* (Boston, 1943), at least did not think it possible for the United States to have then been armed to the teeth, an argument which Kennan concedes, but goes on to speak of our diplomatic influence anyway. The grand alliance against Germany eventually numbered twenty-four states, two of which (Russia and Rumania) did not last out the war. There were nine other European states (Serbia, Montenegro, France, Belgium, Luxembourg, Britain, Italy, Portugal, and Greece), nine from the Americas, and Japan, China, Siam, and Liberia. Not all were at war with all of the Central Powers.

The army, with some 133,000 men, was still very small, but it was five times the size of the Indian-fighting army which had entered the Spanish-American War less than twenty years previously. That war had resulted in two key reforms: the establishment (under another name) of a General Staff and the standardization of the equipment and training of the militia (now known as the National Guard). The occupation of the Philippines and other "police" operations had also given the army much administrative and some combat experience outside the Continental United States. The outbreak of war in Europe had precipitated a long debate over "preparedness," resulting in June, 1916, in a compromise National Defense Act providing for a regular army of 186,000 men and a National Guard of 425,000 to be reached in five annual increments, plus an Officers Reserve Corps and a Reserve Officers Training Corps in colleges. At 4 p.m. on February 4, 1917, the day after breaking diplomatic relations with Germany, President Wilson called on Secretary of War Newton D. Baker, unattended and without a previous appointment. Half an hour later Baker sent for the Judge Advocate General, Enoch Crowder, and asked him to have a conscription bill by 10 o'clock the following morning. Crowder's Selective Service Act of 1917—which passed without any really restrictive amendments after a vigorous Congressional fight—remains the foundation of American conscription legislation. Many of its chief provisions came from the army's unhappy experience with Civil War conscription. Though this American version of Kitchener's new army was conscript rather than volunteer, the new National Army was to supply three times as many men as the United States Army and the National Guard combined. The Navy and Marine Corps remained volunteer. The United States Army and the National Guard could use conscripts if they failed to recruit up to strength. The provisions for local administration sold the bill to the governors and mayors, who had been among the bitterest opponents of the Civil War conscription.[20]

20 After the Civil War the United States returned to the military system of 1812. Nothing came of a plan of the Burnside Commission of seven Representatives and Senators in 1878 for a special national volunteer force which they incorrectly compared to the *Landwehr*. The 28,000 man regular army of 1898—the smallest in proportion to total population in the history of the Republic—did not even have a paper divisional organization. Congress again tried to triple the regulars and recruited another separate army of 125,000 volunteers for two years or the duration. Some of these units—like Theodore Roosevelt's Rough Riders—were recruited from scratch and others from the

Four million men eventually served in the Army of the United States (the three armies were consolidated in August, 1918) and eight hundred thousand in the Navy, Marines, and Coast Guard. The American industrial contribution is difficult to assess because of the Allies' previous orders from the American munitions industry. In general the United States provided food, raw materials, ammunition, and small arms, while the Allies turned out heavy equipment. In 1918 the Allies needed men more desperately than equipment, and men had to be given shipping priority. About a quarter of the two million men who went to France were transported in American ships. Another quarter went in interned German ships; Allied ships (most of them British) carried a bit more than half. The average American soldier was given six months of training in the United States, two months more overseas, and a month in a "quiet" sector of the trenches. Even regular units were heavily diluted with recruits. Captain George C. Marshall, a First Division staff officer, "discovered that of two hundred men to a company, approximately one hundred

militia. Unfortunately for the reputation of Secretary of War Alger, the war ended before the Bull Run stage was over. See Walter Millis, *The Martial Spirit: A Study of Our War with Spain* (Boston, 1931), Frank Freidel, *The Splendid Little War* (Boston, 1958), and Uldarico S. Baclagon, *Philippine Campaigns* (Manila, 1952).

Elihu Root pushed through the resulting reforms. See Elbridge Colby, "Elihu Root and the National Guard" (*Military Affairs*, XXIII, Spring, 1959, 28-34), Elihu Root, *The Military and Colonial Policy of the United States* (Cambridge, Mass., 1916), and William A. Ganoe, *History of the United States Army* (Washington, 1942). Emory Upton's *The Military Policy of the United States* (Washington, 1917) was originally written for the Burnside Commission. For the National Guard, see William H. Riker, *Soldiers of the States: The Role of the National Guard in American Democracy* (Washington, 1957). The United States Army's concept of the position of the General Staff is explained in Otto Nelson, *National Security and the General Staff* (Washington, 1946). Theodore Roosevelt's ideas are studied in Howard K. Beale, *Theodore Roosevelt and the Rise of America to World Power* (Baltimore, 1956).

Former Chief of Staff Leonard Wood, who had Presidential ambitions, lent the preparedness advocates his office and an aide. Ex-President Roosevelt talked of raising his own division of mounted infantry. Volunteers took summer training in Wood's "Plattsburg" camps for reserve officers and talked of an "American Legion" of 250,000 men. The army wanted more regulars and a "Continental Army" of 400,000 volunteers to take two months' summer training for three consecutive years, with three additional years as reservists, a scheme bitterly opposed by the National Guard's supporters. In 1917 Wilson was given the authority to raise 500,000 volunteers under such officers as he wished to appoint, but he took care never to use this authority. The day of the Rough Riders or Jefferson Davis' Mississippi Rifles was over. The best book is David A. Lockmiller, *Enoch H. Crowder* (Columbia, Mo., 1955). The British experience with conscription, which was not finally adopted until 1916, has not yet been systematically studied. There is no evidence that Crowder's bill was influenced by this experience.

and eighty were recruits. . . . The people with the Stokes mortars and 37 mm. cannon not only did not have the weapons, but the men themselves had never even heard of them. . . . Everything [was] begged, borrowed, or stolen—certainly not manufactured in America." Only 100 of the 2250 field guns used by the Americans in battle were American-made. Still, a great army was raised and half of it sent to France. American intervention tipped the balance in favor of the Allies and may have speeded up the German collapse by as much as a year. There were no Bull Runs. With very limited training and combat experience, American forces successfully attacked one of the strongest parts of the German lines. But this success had its drawbacks. Congressmen, undoubtedly, reflecting the views of their constituents, still underestimated the time required to train men for modern combat and to provide them with heavy equipment. The old militia theory— the plow left in the furrow and the long rifle taken from the wall—was to be reinforced by the idea that industrial capacity alone guarantees adequate preparation for modern mechanized war.[21]

Years of Decision (1917-1918)

By the end of 1916 both sides had been successful in shaking the other's morale and, incidentally, the foundations of European society. Late that year Wilson had asked both sides to state their war aims in the hope of bringing them together. But Wilson's "peace without victory" had little appeal to the leaders of the warring peoples. His own war message was to declare that the United States was entering the war "to vindicate the principles of peace and justice . . . and to set up amongst really free and self-governed peoples . . . such a concert of purpose and action as will henceforth ensure the observance of these principles." The United States sought "no conquest, no dominion, . . . no indemnities, . . . no material compensation." Whatever else could be said about it, Wilson's idealism was superb propaganda. It encouraged the dreams of those, both inside and outside Germany, who hoped to build a better world on the ruins of the old one.

[21] *Selected Speeches and Statements of General of the Army George C. Marshall* (Washington, 1945), 32-33. See also *The United States Army in the World War, 1917-1919* (17 vols., Washington, 1948) and Leonard P. Ayres, *The War with Germany: A Statistical Summary* (2d ed., Washington, 1919). Richard O'Connor, *Black Jack Pershing* (New York, 1961) supplements Frederick Palmer, *Pershing*.

When the Tsar's government collapsed in March, 1917, and was replaced by a provisional government of moderate parliamentarians, even Russia seemed to be on the way to a democratic government. Like the European peoples of 1914, the Americans entered the war in a mood of patriotic exaltation. The democratic grand alliance would make short work of Europe's last autocracies. These high hopes proved to be quite unjustified. Instead of winning the war in 1917, the Allies nearly lost it. Though the battle lines did not move very far, crisis followed crisis.

The first crisis was caused by the German submarines, which sank nearly four times as much shipping in April as in January. When Admiral W. S. Sims, the American naval commander, reached London, Jellicoe told him that Germany would " 'win, unless we can stop these losses—and stop them soon.' " The only possible answer was convoy, and, without American naval help, the Allies could not have organized an effective convoy system. But the convoys were not fully organized until September; shipping replacements did not catch up with losses until early in 1918. In all, 15,053,000 gross tons of Allied and neutral shipping were lost during the war, against building and captures of 13,241,000 tons. The submarine war further dislocated the Allies' war-strained economies. The volume of British imports was cut by over a third (mostly food and raw materials for civilian industry), while British exports fell even more sharply. The Mediterranean was so dangerous that British shipping was routed around the Cape of Good Hope, and half of the Italian merchant marine was put out of action. Many Italian factories were shut down for lack of fuel or raw materials. A shaky economy was to help to undermine the equally shaky Italian political structure. The damage was done by about 100 to 140 submarines on active service. Since a third of these were usually refitting and another third were coming from or going to their stations, only 30 to 50 U-boats were operating on the shipping lanes at any given time.[22]

A second crisis was caused by the near collapse of the sorely tried French army. Lyautey, the former War Minister, had already expressed doubts about Nivelle's promised "rup-

[22] Sims, *The Victory at Sea* (New York, 1920), 9. C. Ernest Fayle, *Seaborne Trade* (3 vols., London, 1920-1924), III, 467. For the crisis and Sims's earlier gunnery reforms, see Elting E. Morison, *Admiral Sims and the Modern American Navy* (Boston, 1942). Fifteen to twenty times as many ships and men eventually fought the submarines as the Germans used in submarine warfare.

ture" of the German line. Other complications were introduced by the surprise German withdrawal to a shorter line, imminent American intervention, the fall of the Russian monarchy, and the German capture of part of Nivelle's plan. The offensive would have to be launched without a Russian diversion or American aid, but things might be even worse if Russia collapsed completely. When questioned, all of Nivelle's army group commanders expressed doubts about the plan, which eventually was to throw 48 French divisions against 42 strongly entrenched German divisions. Nivelle offered to resign, but his resignation was not accepted, the French chiefs deciding to commit their reserves if a break was made but to break off if this did not occur. The British attacked near Arras on April 9. The French attacked along the Aisne on April 16 and lost from 96,000 to 187,000 men in the first nine days. They pushed a salient four miles deep and sixteen miles across the base into the German lines, a major success by 1916-1917 standards, but no "rupture." The Minister of War charged the high command with " 'more fantasy than judgment and more audacity than method' " and replaced Nivelle with Pétain. The latter immediately announced that " 'it is absolutely necessary to await the arrival of the American divisions and the provision of [more] heavy artillery material.' " Meanwhile, units of the five armies which had taken part in the offensive had begun a series of sit-down strikes. More than a hundred cases of "collective indiscipline" affected 54 divisions, half of those in the French army. Nearly 25,000 men were court-martialed, though only 55 were shot and a few hundred sent to penal colonies. Some infantry had refused to move into front line trenches, and a few officers had been attacked.[23]

The French soldiers themselves had finally ended the cult of the reckless offensive, though Pétain repeatedly urged Haig to continue the British offensives to tie down the German reserves during the French army's recuperation. Pétain also followed Du Picq's neglected advice. The men got longer leaves, better food and quarters, and larger allowances for their dependents. As De Gaulle put it, Pétain "taught his army to distinguish the real from the imaginary and the possible from the impossible. . . . When a choice had to be made between ruin and reason, Pétain received promotion." In November the seventy-six-year-old "Tiger," Georges Clemen-

23 Edmonds, *Short History*, 211-238.

ceau, became Premier and War Minister. Hindenburg and Ludendorff, faced with a major political crisis of their own, did not take advantage of the French mutinies. They secured the replacement of Bethmann-Hollweg, Germany becoming a disguised military dictatorship. If Germany won, she would dominate Europe. If she lost, the army, the Hohenzollern family, and the extreme Pan-Germanists would go down together. On the eastern front, the Russian Provisional Government tried a last offensive against the Austro-Hungarians. When this was checked by the usual German rescue squad, the Russian soldiers "voted with their feet" for peace, deserting by the million. The Bolsheviks took over in November; both Russia and Rumania made peace with the Central Powers early in 1918. The Central Powers annexed or dominated Russian Poland, Finland and the Baltic states, Rumania, the Ukraine, and Transcaucasia. If Germany could also win in the west (where the Pan-Germans proposed to annex Belgium, northern France, and additional African colonies), postwar Germany would unite the industry of Western Europe with the oil and agricultural resources of Rumania and southern Russia.[24]

At the end of October the Italians had been routed at Caporetto in the *Twelfth* Battle of the Isonzo. Picked German and Austrian troops had captured 275,000 prisoners. Another 400,000 Italians had deserted or lost their arms before the line was restored in front of Venice. Eleven French and British divisions had to be rushed to Italy. The Italian commander, Luigi Cadorna, was replaced by Armando Diaz on the day of the Bolshevik coup in Russia. Meanwhile Haig had been hammering away at Passchendaele. The British armies were nearly as war-weary as the French, though there were no mutinies. In spite of Pétain's careful husbandry, the French were still losing 40,000 men a month and infantry divisions were being broken up for replacements. Haig had to take over part of the French line during the winter of 1917-1918, though he had fewer combat troops (1,097,906) on January 1, 1918 than on January 1, 1917 (1,192,668). There were

[24] De Gaulle, *France and her Army*, 103. Henri Carré, *Les grandes heures du Général Pétain: 1917 et la crise du moral* (I, Paris, 1952). The standard work in English on Brest-Litovsk (the most important of these treaties) is John W. Wheeler-Bennett, *The Forgotten Peace, Brest-Litovsk, March 1918* (New York, 1939). For the political situation and the Pan-Germans see Hans W. Gatzke, *Germany's Drive to the West: A Study of Germany's Western War Aims during the First World War* (Baltimore, 1950), and Hans Peter Hanssen, *Diary of a Dying Empire* (Bloomington, 1955).

607,403 trained men (exclusive of administrative personnel) in Britain, and 888,315 men were in Italy, the Balkans, and Mesopotamia, and Palestine. This division of the British forces in the face of an expected German offensive in the west in the spring of 1918 was only partially due to the demands of the overseas theatres and the German invasion bogey. It was also the result of Lloyd George's deliberate policy. The Prime Minister

was determined to avoid a repetition of . . . Passchendaele. . . . But he not only considered himself too weak to dismiss Haig, he even doubted his own ability to overrule Haig if the latter were to propose a renewal of the offensive. . . . The only way of escaping this dilemma was to keep the Commander-in-Chief so short of troops that he could not even suggest a renewal of the British offensive. [In so doing, the Prime Minister] was endangering the entire existence of the British armies in France. The cleavage between the civil and the military power could scarcely have been more profound.

Some British politicians and soldiers had joined with the French in massive resistance to the cult of the offensive, at least until the Americans arrived.[25]

[25] Edmonds, *Short History*, 275-277; Blake, Introduction to Haig, *Private Papers*, 46-47. The manpower crisis of 1917-1918 was rather like that of 1944. Infantry replacement projections from previous losses were very high. Men were needed for new artillery units and to replace men released to industry. See General E. L. M. Burns, *Manpower in the Canadian Army, 1939-1945* (Toronto, 1956), H. D. M. Parker, *Manpower: A Study of Wartime Policy and Administration (History of the Second World War, United Kingdom Civil Series*, London, 1957), and Byron Fairchild and Johnathan Grossman, *The Army and Industrial Manpower (U. S. Army in World War II*, Washington, 1959).

These figures (except for men in Britain) include the Dominion and Indian armies, which together furnished three and a quarter million men and lost over 200,000 dead as a result of battle, four times as many as the United States. Conscription for foreign service was a major issue. It was adopted in Great Britain (except for Ireland) and New Zealand in 1916 and again in the second war. It was not applied to Ireland (including Ulster) in either war; a proposal to do so was a big factor in the rise of Sinn Fein. It was not adopted in South Africa in either war; Afrikaner fear of conscription for the invasion of German Southwest Africa partly sparked the 1914 rebellion (put down by largely Afrikaner forces). Australia rejected conscription in two referenda (partly on the Irish vote) in the first war, but applied it to certain Pacific areas in the second. A coalition of Conservatives and conscriptionist Liberals won the 1917 Canadian election on this issue, but there were riots and passive resistance in French Canada. The Government was empowered to send conscripts overseas in 1942, but a decision to do so in 1944 split the cabinet. There is no general work on these nationalist stirrings, or on Canada, Ireland, or South Africa in the first war. D. W. Krüger, *The Age of the Generals: A Short Political History of the Union of South Africa, 1910-1948* ([Johannesburg], 1958), and Elizabeth H. Armstrong, *The Crisis of Quebec, 1914-1918* (New York, 1937) are excellent.

Hindenburg and Ludendorff opened their final "Victory Drive" on March 21, 1918, using tactics developed in the east and at Caporetto. To insure surprise, troops were moved to the attack area at the last possible moment. Picked assault teams "infiltrated" the soft spots in the opposing lines after a short four-hour barrage. Special retraining with live ammunition had given these teams practice in following a rolling barrage. Each team was to drive as far as it could, ignoring threats to its flanks. Weaker in infantry than a British division, a German division was considerably stronger in trench mortars (50 to 36) and heavy machine guns (350 to 64). Using their railways to shift their forces from east to west, Hindenburg and Ludendorff achieved about the same numerical superiority on that front as in 1914. Infantry rifle strength on April 1 has been estimated at 1,559,000 German to 1,245,000 for the Allies. Still more remarkable, the Germans again managed to achieve strategic surprise, striking farther south than Allied intelligence had anticipated and with one-third larger forces. Not counting troops normally holding the line, the Germans succeeded in throwing 62 divisions against 26 British, and 2,508 heavy guns against 976. The first German drive—at the junction of the British and French armies— pushed the British back and away from the French toward the railway center of Amiens. Pétain wanted to swing his flank back toward Paris. Haig proposed that the French army "be taken out of Pétain's" hands by the appointment of a French general—who could *order* Pétain to keep contact with the British—as Allied supreme commander. Haig's choice was Foch, who had been kicked upstairs and was now military advisor to the French cabinet.

Some historians have ascribed to unity of command all the victories which followed in the summer and autumn of 1918. Its importance, however, can be exaggerated. It was an *ad hominem* arrangement dictated not by its theoretical merit, but by the need to overrule the defeatism of Pétain. It served the purpose for which it was intended, but did not greatly influence events after the Germans had ceased to be dangerous.

The gap was closed, but the British had lost 150,000 men (90,000 of them prisoners). In April the Germans attacked near Ypres. In May, June, and July they hit the French and again reached the Marne only thirty-seven miles from Paris. In these five offensives they won ten times as much ground as the Allies had won in 1917 and caused a million casualties. But they had lost a million of their own men, many of them the picked soldiers in the assault divisions.[26]

On July 18 Foch began to attack, not in a single "Big Push" but in a series of smaller drives to keep the Germans from recovering the initiative. These attacks were directed against the sides of the salients which the Germans had pushed in the Allied lines, where the Germans were now at a corresponding strategic disadvantage. Nine double-strength American divisions took part in Foch's first offensive. The American army in France had doubled between March and May, doubled again in May, and was to double again by the end of August. By August 1 the Germans had definitely lost their numerical superiority in the west. Infantry rifle strength was now estimated at 1,682,000 Allied to 1,395,000 German. The Allies now made increasing use of "tanks"—armored vehicles which could (1) resist the "Storm of Steel," (2) roll over the craters and wire on caterpillar tracks, and (3) support the advancing infantry with mechanically- rather than hand-carried machine guns or light artillery. Both armored vehicles and caterpillar tractors had been developed before the war, but their combination seems to have been first suggested by E. D. Swinton, a British staff observer in Flanders in 1914. His idea had received no support from the War Office, then wholly occupied with Kitchener's new army, but it had appealed to the First Lord of the Admiralty, who had already suggested steam rollers to flatten barbed wire. So the first tanks—so labeled to confuse the Germans into thinking they were water storage devices—were developed by a navy "Landships" committee, a name which Churchill thought

26 Blake, Introduction to Haig, *Private Papers*, 50. Blake continues, "The victories of 1918 were won principally by the British Army directed not by Foch, but by Haig. No doubt Haig subordinated his strategy to French requirements, but then he had always done so. . . . Unity of command was well justified by the . . . March [crisis], but it . . . made little difference in the final stages." On Pétain see the important memoirs of General Serrigny, *Trente Ans avec Pétain* (Paris, 1959).

Golaz, "L'Armée allemande de 1914-1918," published after the second war, corrects earlier French official accounts, which underestimated tactical doctrine. The Germans' use of the initiative and better machine gun and artillery tactics, rather than their numbers, were key factors in both 1914 and 1918. As in 1940, the French command tended to blame their weapons, for which the government could be held partly responsible. On artillery see Aubrey Wade, *Gunner on the Western Front* (London, 1959, reissue of *The War of the Guns*, 1936). *The Times Literary Supplement*, LVIII, Oct. 30, 1959, 631, remarked on "the great use still made of the horse, even in the great battles of 1917 and 1918. This adds a touch of archaic horror to a shocking authentic narrative."

might reconcile officials to naval experiments with armored land vehicles. The first machines were slow (four miles per hour) and short-ranged. The early French tanks and half of the British tanks used machine guns, the rest of the British tanks carrying naval guns from the Admiralty's stocks.[27]

The first tanks were used, or misused, in 1916, moving behind a rolling barrage and ahead of the infantry against machine gun nests which had outlasted the bombardment. A breakthrough was achieved at Cambrai in November, 1917, when 324 tanks assaulted the German lines without a warning preliminary bombardment. Each wedge of three machines was followed by an infantry platoon. The idea was to saturate the defenses with more tanks than they could handle, while heavy artillery concentrations were directed at the German artillery batteries. The tanks broke through the Hindenburg Line for nearly four miles, though 179 of them were put out of action the first day by fire, ditching, and mechanical failure. These tactics were elaborated by the French, whose Renault light tanks proved well suited to the job of helping the infantry deal with isolated machine guns. The French planned to supplement their light tanks with superheavy breakthrough machines, but none of these was finished by the end of the war. The Americans were to be equipped with French-type light tanks and British heavy tanks powered by the famous Liberty airplane engines. Some British theorists, however, took up another idea, the use of longer-range, faster medium tanks as armored cavalry to exploit the GAP which the light and heavy tanks had created. Horsed cavalry had not been able to deal with even scattered machine guns. The medium tank could survive in the GAP and then move to exploit it. For the campaign of 1919, the chief of staff of the British Tank Corps, an "Unconventional Soldier," who seems to have been assigned to the Tank Corps to get him out of the way, worked out a plan to combine tanks with armored personnel carriers. The Germans seldom met tanks with tanks—the first such fight was at Villers-Bretonneux on April 24, 1918—because materials were short and tanks did not get first priority

27 Swinton's best book is *Eyewitness* (London, 1932). His *Over My Shoulder* (Oxford, 1951) deals with other matters. *Storm of Steel*, trans. Basil Creighton (London, 1929), was by Ernst Jünger, who became a Nazi hero. For these continuing "militaristic" currents in German war literature see S. D. Stirk, *The Prussian Spirit: A Survey of German Literature and Politics, 1914-1940* (London, 1941), H. K. Pfeiler's fine *War and the German Mind* (New York, 1941), and Hanna Hafkesbrink, *Unknown Germany* (New Haven, 1948).

until that summer. They also did little to develop antitank weapons, partly because the staff thought that it would be bad for morale to show concern over this new Allied weapon. The Germans used only forty-five machines, some of them captured from the enemy, in twelve engagements. The British built over three thousand tanks, and the French were turning out fifty light tanks a week by the middle of 1918.[28]

While tanks were crossing the man-made deserts of France and Flanders, planes and dirigibles had been flying over them —first to reconnoiter and photograph and then to attack troops, railroad centers, factories, and cities. There had been over a hundred German air raids on England. Three hundred tons of bombs had killed 1400 people and had cut the output of some factories by three-quarters. The Germans had once commanded the air; here, too, the balance was finally tipped against them. By the end of 1918 the British air force, the most powerful in the world, had expanded nearly a hundred and fifty times to a force of nearly 300,000 men. Allied tactics for 1919 called for tank-plane co-operation, and the British had formed an "Independent Air Force" of planes which could reach Berlin, though the war ended before it could carry out that particular mission. The war was always an infantry-artillery war—by the end of the war both the Germans and the Allies had developed infantry-artillery tactics which could create the GAP—but the tank and plane were clearly weapons to be reckoned with in the future.

A British attack on August 8, supported by 415 tanks, had killed or captured 18,000 men and 400 guns in an eight-mile breakthrough. A German divisional staff had been captured at breakfast, and retreating troops had tried to prevent reserves from moving to the front. This, in Ludendorff's words, was the "Black Day of the German Army." A crown council

---

[28] Two of J. F. C. Fuller's most interesting works are his *Memoirs of an Unconventional Soldier* (London, 1936) and *The Army in My Time* (London, 1935). Swinton spent a part of 1917 and 1918 on a mission to the United States. There was little future for him in the army since he had not been to the staff college. He was sent to the Ministry of Labour, resigned from the army, went to the Air Ministry, and finally became Chichele Professor of Military History at Oxford. The great work on tanks is now B. H. Liddell Hart, *The Tanks: The History of the Royal Tank Regiment and Its Predecessors Heavy Branch Machine-Gun Corps, Tank Corps, and Royal Tank Corps, 1914-1945* (2 vols., New York, 1959). Another pioneer, Giffard Le Q. Martel, wrote the interesting *In the Wake of the Tank: The First Fifteen Years of Mechanization in the British Army* (London, 1931), *Our Armoured Forces* (London, 1945), and *An Outspoken Soldier* (London, 1949). Richard M. Ogorkiewicz, *Armor: A History of Mechanized Forces* (New York, 1960) is interesting and ill-organized.

a week later decided that Germany should open peace negotiations while the army was still on French soil; the new Austro-Hungarian Chief of Staff reported that his armies could not "hold out over the winter." The Central Powers faced a hungry winter; workers in munitions plants had already lost up to a quarter of their body weight, and were listless, apathetic, and hopeless. In mid-September the British routed the Turks in Palestine; the Salonika forces knocked Bulgaria out of the war on September 29. This, rather than Foch's new offensive of September 26, was the straw that broke Ludendorff, whose aides found him on the floor with foam on his lips and who that night recommended an immediate armistice. "The immediate issue of the war was decided," Liddell Hart wrote, "in the mind of the German command. Ludendorff and his associates had then 'cracked,' and the sound went echoing . . . throughout the whole of Germany. Nothing could catch it or stop it. The Command might recover its nerve, the actual military position might improve, but the moral impression, as ever in war, was decisive."[29]

What of the art of generalship in this Great War? The German generals' apologists blamed everyone else and claimed that the generals had changed their tactics to meet new situations and had, after all, almost won "The War of Lost Opportunities." The general impression in the western democracies, however, was summed up in Clemenceau's famous phrase that "war is too important to be left to the generals." Plan XVII was a monument to their stupidities. The French high command had failed even to develop effective infantry tactics and had persisted in their errors long after many soldiers and civilians had been aware of their futility. "Brass hat" was not a term of respect in Britain. David Low's Colonel Blimp, conceived in the thirties "as a symbol of stupidity, not of colonels," had to be buried by his creator because he could never overtake

his military legend. Sometimes, when, twenty years after his invention, I come across his name . . . used as a synonym for military or administrative incompetence, I wonder how he might have turned out if in that Turkish bath of 1934 I had chosen to christen him Dr. Blimp, or Bishop Blimp, using the same aphorisms.

[29] *History of the World War*, 590. The blockade's effect must be estimated; the rise in wholesale prices is one index of strain. American and British prices more than doubled, French and Italian more than trebled, German more than quadrupled. The increases in 1790-1812, 1913-1920, and 1939-1948 were about the same. A. J. Brown, *The Great Inflation, 1939-1951* (Oxford, 1955), 18.

The answer is clear. The clichés about the "military mind" which Blimp personified were based, in part, on direct observation of men whose professional rigidity was matched, in all too many cases, only by their social conservatism. Citizen soldiers who had seen some officers practicing the profession for which they were presumably prepared were alternately amused and appalled by their ineptitude and their lack of contact with—as Douhet put it—"the living, acting, operating nation." Some military critics—Liddell Hart, Fuller, and some air power proponents—were expert polemicists. Their attacks undoubtedly strengthened this public image of the "military mind."[30]

This picture of universal military incompetence was as overdrawn as that of the German apologists. The generals had been wrong in 1914, yet some military men had learned from experience. General G. M. Lindsay, the author of the 1918 British tactical manual on machine guns, spent some of the darkest days of the Second World War—between December 1, 1941, and February 1, 1942—on an excellent analysis of the tactical lessons of that first conflict.

(a) The attack complex during the early stages of the last war caused a useless waste of life in all the armies concerned. For that war showed that large-scale attacks only succeeded where the attacker had: (i) Great superiority of material. (ii) Superiority of morale. (iii) Effective surprise. . . . For example: CAMBRAI (20 November 1917). Here we had some hundreds of tanks, . . . and we effected surprise, . . . elements (i) and (iii). But we had not the mobility to exploit success. . . . 21 MARCH 1918. Here the Ger-

[30] *Low's Autobiography* (London, 1956), 270, 275. For the civilians and Lloyd George's machinations see Geoffrey Brunn, *Clemenceau* (Cambridge, Mass., 1943), General Mordacq, *Le Ministère Clemenceau, journal d'un témoin* (4 vols., Paris, 1930-1931), Lloyd George, *War Memoirs* (6 vols., London, 1933-1937), Thomas Jones, *Lloyd George* (Cambridge, Mass., 1951), and S. Maccoby, *English Radicalism: The End?* (London, 1961). Haig's *Private Papers* show much friction between British and Dominion officers, but his support of Sir John Monash, the engineer who commanded the Australians in France in 1918, shows that Haig was not prejudiced against all civilian soldiers. C. E. W. Bean, *Anzac to Amiens: A Shorter History of the Australian Fighting Services in the First World War* (Canberra, 1952), 458. This summary of the official history and his *Two Men I Knew: William Bridges and Brudenell White, Founders of the A. I. F.* (Sydney, 1957) are excellent. For the bitter criticism of the Canadian commander (a former businessman) see Hugh M. Urquhart, *Arthur Currie: The Biography of a Great Canadian* (Toronto, 1930). The same feeling against the professionals appeared during the Crimean, American Civil, Spanish-American, and Boer Wars, for similar reasons. Its apparent decline since the Second World War surely reflects the increased competence of many professionals. William Haynie Neblett still proclaims *No Peace with the Regulars* (New York, 1957), but the danger may now be uncritical acceptance of "competence by definition."

mans effected surprise, had great superiority in numbers and material, were assisted by fog which blinded our machine guns, achieved a complete initial success, . . . but lacked mobility. . . . GERMANS AT AISNE, 1918. They had great superiority in numbers and material, they were opposed by weak formations of tired troops. But they again lacked mobility. . . . FINAL PALESTINE BATTLE. Here we again had everything in our favour and we achieved all but complete success. Yet note one outstanding lesson. . . . Those Germans and Austrians who kept together in a compact body and never lost cohesion or morale were never defeated and escaped destruction and capture. . . .

(b) It is now the fashion to say that these lessons are of no value and that while the last war proved the supremacy of the defence over the attack this one has proved the reverse. . . . When the attacker has everything in his favour, . . . he wins. So (within limits) he did in the last war. This advantage the Germans have enjoyed in every campaign up to the Russian, . . . [when] for the first time they met an opponent who was their equal, if not their superior, in numbers, who was reasonably their equal in equipment, and who . . . [had] a High Command who did understand modern war, both on the political and military fronts, and who had prepared themselves for it.[31]

On October 4 Prince Max of Baden, supported by the Center, Social Democratic, and Progressive parties, became Chancellor and asked Wilson to negotiate a peace on the basis of the Fourteen Points. Wilson insisted that the Allies would negotiate only with a democratic German government. On October 24 the Italians broke the Austro-Hungarian armies in the Battle of Vittorio Veneto. Turkey signed an armistice on October 30; part of the German fleet mutinied on November 3, the day that Austria-Hungary quit the war. By this time the Allies had recovered most of northern France and a third of Belgium; in some sectors they were advancing three to five miles a day, hindered chiefly by the incessant rain and the German destruction of communications. These facts are important because many die-hard Germans later claimed that the German army had not been "defeated in the field." It had been betrayed by Wilson's promises, its leaders' "failure of nerve," and the "stab in the back" of the revolution which began in Munich on November 7. The next day a German armistice commission, headed by the leader of the Center party, entered the Allied lines. Hindenburg had insisted that the civilian government, rather than the military leaders, sign

31 *The War on the Civil and Military Front* (Cambridge, 1942), 42-43.

the armistice. Three days later William II fled to the Netherlands. The Hapsburg emperor abdicated and hostilities ended on November 11. Though sporadic fighting continued in the Baltic states, Russia, and the Near East, Armistice Day is usually taken as the end of a war which had cost the lives of some ten million soldiers. An equal number of noncombatants may have died of disease, privation, and the revolutions which had gripped Central and Eastern Europe and the Near East.

Many of Europe's finest young men had been killed. Many of those who survived had been profoundly shocked by the horror and seeming futility of the war and by the incompetence of their military and civilian leaders. What came to be the conventional western literary view of the war was expressed in F. Scott Fitzgerald's description of the Somme battlefield, published in the spring of 1934, just before Adolf Hitler's "Blood Purge" of his own followers.

See that little stream—we could walk to it in two minutes. It took the British a month to walk to it—a whole empire walking very slowly, dying in front and pushing forward behind. And another empire walked very slowly backward a few inches a day, leaving the dead like a million bloody rugs. No European will ever do that again in this generation. . . . The young men think they could do it but they couldn't. They could fight the first Marne again but not this. This took religion and years of plenty and tremendous sureties and the exact relation that existed between the classes.

Fitzgerald was an infantry lieutenant who had never gotten to the front. A more thoughtful comment had been made thirteen years before by the great journalist, C. E. Montague, who at forty-seven had dyed his grey hair to enlist as a private. He saw that these attitudes of mingled horror and disgust might make it far more difficult to preserve the peace which had been won with such suffering.

Civilization itself . . . wears a strange new air of precariousness. Even before the war a series of melancholy public misadventures had gone some way to awake the disquieting notion that civilization, the whole ordered, fruitful joint action of a nation, a continent, or the whole world, was only a bluff. When the world is at peace and fares well, the party of order and decency, justice and mercy and self-control, is really bluffing a much larger party of egoism and greed that would bully and grab it if it dared. . . . The bad men are not held down by force; they are only bluffed by the pretence of it. They have got the tip now. . . .

The plain man, so far as I know him, is neither aghast nor gleeful at this revelation. For the most part he looks somewhat listlessly on. . . . A sense of moral horror does not come easily when you have supped full of horrors on most of the days of three or four years. . . . Some new god, or devil, of course, may enter at any time into this disfurnished soul. Genius in some leader might either possess it with an anarchic passion to smash . . . all the old institutions or fire it with a new craving to lift itself clear of the wrack. . . . For either a Lenin or a St. Francis there is a wide field to till, cleared, but of pretty stiff clay.[32]

---

[32] Fitzgerald, *Tender Is the Night* (New York, 1934), 117-118. Montague, *Disenchantment* (London, 1922), 195-197. The day after the Armistice Fisher wrote Viscount Mersey, "Mr. C. P. Scott [proprietor of the Manchester Guardian and Montague's father-in-law] wrote me a few days ago saying that had my strategy been adopted, the War would have been over two years ago! . . . But . . . 'At that date we would not have got rid of these Emperors and Kings'! HOW TRUE!!! *For peace, we want republics!* No one man, no set of men, can in a republic make war!" *Fear God and Dread Nought*, III, 558.

For the war's effects in Nyasaland, see George Shepperson and Thomas Price, *Independent African: John Chilembwe and the Origins, Setting and Significance of the Nyasaland Native Rising of 1915* (Edinburgh, 1958). The language of Chilembwe's teacher, Joseph Booth, might have been taken from the New Zealand *Maoriland Worker*. The fantasies which sparked that rising can be compared with those which sparked the South African rising, a rebellion which needs a more impartial study than G. D. Scholtz, *Die Rebellie, 1914-1915* (Johannesburg, 1942). Any such study must take account of F. A. van Jaarsveld, *The Awakening of Afrikaner Nationalism* (Cape Town, 1961).

Chapter 9

The Long Armistice (1919-1939)

The Peace Settlements

THE victorious Allies established a League of Nations, disarmed Germany, redistributed the chips in the colonial game, and recognized the results of the nationalist revolutions in Eastern Europe. Though the United States Senate rejected the German treaty and the League Covenant, it did ratify treaties to limit naval armaments and stabilize the international situation in East Asia. Members of the League accepted "obligations not to resort to war," and Article XVI outlined specific sanctions against such behavior. Any member resorting to war "in disregard of its covenants . . . shall ipso facto be deemed to have committed an act of war against all other Members, . . . which hereby undertake immediately to subject it to the severence of all trade or financial relations." The League's council might also ask members for "military, naval, or air force . . . to protect the covenants." France wanted international supervision of armaments and a careful legal definition of aggression, but on paper the League, like the old Concert of Europe, was a formidable body.

Germany lost her colonies and about an eighth of Bismarck's Empire, but Wilson blocked a French effort to split off the area west of the Rhine, roughly the size of Belgium. Germany was not to fortify or militarize this area or the territory fifty kilometers east of the Rhine, an area which included the Ruhr, the heart of German heavy industry. Like Prussia in 1808, Germany was also disarmed, as the first step toward "a general limitation of the armaments of all nations." Conscription and the General Staff were abolished. The new German Republic was limited to an *armée de métier* of 100,000, with twelve-year service for the men and twenty-five year service for officers. Germans could not enlist in other armies except in the French Foreign Legion; border, forest, and coast guards and police were carefully regulated. "Educational establishments, the universities, societies of discharged soldiers, . . . and . . . associations of every description . . . must not occupy themselves with any military matters." The new republican army was not to have poison gas,

275

tanks, or planes. Arms factories were dismantled, and the importation or exportation of war material forbidden. Existing stocks of arms were to be surrendered; the Germans could keep 102,000 rifles and carbines (but, originally, no bayonets) and 1,926 machine guns. They were allowed six old battleships to balance the Russian Baltic fleet, but were not allowed to build submarines or to replace their old battleships with ships larger than 10,000 tons with eleven-inch guns. The fortifications of Heligoland and all other works "commanding the maritime routes between the North Sea and the Baltic" were to be demolished. Allied commissions were to supervise the execution of these stringent terms, and Allied armies were to occupy parts of the Rhineland for five-, ten-, or fifteen-year periods. In the preamble to the reparations section of the treaty Germany was made to accept "the responsibility for . . . all the loss and damage to which the Allied . . . governments and their nationals have been subjected as a consequence of the war imposed upon them by the aggression of Germany and her Allies." This "war guilt" and certain other clauses needlessly irritated German opinion, while the failure to detach the Rhineland left Germany's war-making potential relatively unimpaired. The treaty was neither a peace of reconciliation nor one of vengeance, but a compromise which may have been worse than either.[1]

In return for leaving the demilitarized Rhineland to Germany, Wilson and Lloyd George promised to defend France against any future German attack. This special guarantee treaty never reached the floor of the United States Senate and was, as a result, never ratified by the British. To replace it (and the shattered Anglo-French Entente) France armed the four largest of the new East-Central European states which had arisen out of the debris of the Hapsburg, Romanov, and Hohenzollern empires. When the conference met the armies of the victorious Big Four of this area—Poland, Czechoslovakia, Jugoslavia, and Rumania—were already in possession of many disputed areas. The vanquished Germans, Hungarians, and Bulgarians were correspondingly dissatisfied with the final treaty arrangements. The Allies also half-heartedly supported the anti-Bolsheviks in the Russian Civil

---

[1] See Jere Clemens King, *Foch versus Clemenceau: France and German Dismemberment, 1918-1919* (Cambridge, Mass., 1960). William II was charged with "a supreme offense against international morality," but the Dutch would not extradite him. Twelve persons were tried in German courts; six were convicted.

War (1918-1920) and the border states' efforts to enlarge their territory at Russia's expense. Poland tried to take the entire Ukraine. When the Russians drove them back toward Warsaw, the French rushed aid to the Poles to prevent contact between a possible Red Germany and the Bolsheviks. In the end Russia lost more territory than Germany, but she did not lose the Ukraine, the oil-rich Caucasus, or her empire in Asia. The Allies' Russian policies—hamstrung by inter-Allied jealousies and the fear of involvement in another of those "little" campaigns which had proved so costly at Gallipoli— had resulted in another unsatisfactory compromise. Russia's potential military capacity remained relatively unimpaired. The Reds were still in power, more suspicious than ever of their former capitalistic and imperialistic Allies. France's new "Eastern Barrier" was directed against both Germany and Russia. Czechoslovakia, Jugoslavia, and Rumania formed a "Little Entente" to prevent a Hapsburg restoration, but these alliances were shaky before Hitler came to power.[2]

In 1914 Japan had taken the Caroline and Marshall Islands and the German concessions on the Shantung peninsula in China. In 1915 she had presented the Chinese government with "Twenty-One Demands" which would have made China into a Japanese protectorate. In 1918 Japanese troops had moved into eastern Siberia; a small American force which was sent there was as anxious to watch the Japanese as the Bolsheviks. To get Japan into the League, Wilson had agreed

2 See Harold Nicolson, *Peacemaking, 1919* (Boston, 1933); Edward Hallett Carr, *The Twenty Years Crisis, 1919-1939: An Introduction to the Study of International Relations* (London, 1939) and *The Soviet Impact on the Western World* (New York, 1947); James T. Shotwell, *What Germany Forgot* (New York, 1940); W. M. Jordan, *Great Britain, France, and the German Problem, 1918-1939: A study of Anglo-French relations in the making and maintenance of the Versailles settlement* (London, 1943); Louis A. R. Yates, *The United States and French Security, 1917-1921* (New York, 1957); and Alexander DeConde, ed., *Isolation and Security* (Durham, N. C., 1957). There is no study of the fear of another Gallipoli as a factor in the Allies' Russian and Turkish policies. When the Turkish nationalists refused to accept the treaty, the Greeks, encouraged by Lloyd George, marched on Ankara and were routed. When the Turks neared the Straits Lloyd George's appeal to " 'the might of this great Empire' . . . set . . . opinion irresistibly against him," and resulted in his resignation. Esme Wingfield-Stratford, *The Harvest of Victory, 1918-1926* (London, 1935), 230. The Turks accepted the loss of their non-Turkish territories, and a demilitarized Straits, but paid no reparations. Greece and Turkey exchanged minorities. For other cases of British fear of further involvement see Gerda Richards Crosby, *Disarmament and Peace in British Politics, 1914-1919* (Cambridge, Mass., 1957), Stephen Richards Graubard, *British Labour and the Russian Revolution, 1917-1924* (Cambridge, Mass., 1957), and Titus Komarnicki, *Rebirth of the Polish Republic* (London, 1957).

that she could keep Shantung, but the United States battle fleet had been moved back into the Pacific and the two countries were threatening a full-scale naval race. Though the British could not afford to build battleships just to keep up with their allies, their 1921 Estimates included four 48,000 ton battle cruisers and projected 18" gun 48,000 ton battleships. The 41,200 ton battle cruiser *Hood* (begun after Jutland and completed in 1920) was more than twice as big as the *Dreadnought* and more than three times as costly. This new "bigger and better" race would cost the three powers $1,234,000,000 for capital ships alone. Like the *Dreadnought*, these giants would make the rest of the British fleet obsolete and could not dock in any British base outside of Europe. The British had not modernized any of their overseas bases since "the recall of the legions" to face Germany. In addition the Anglo-Japanese Alliance was due for renewal in 1922. Its renewal would be almost as unpopular in the British Dominions as in the United States. Its rejection would deeply offend Japan at a time when Britain's Far Eastern interests were almost defenseless and Bolshevism was threatening to spread throughout Asia.

The United States Navy was now second in the world. Its 1916 program of ten battleships and six battle cruisers would give it equality with Britain by 1924. During the war this program had been sidetracked for antisubmarine craft, but Wilson had presented an additional ten-six program in 1918 to make the navy "incomparably the greatest in the world." At Paris Wilson had agreed to delay his supplementary program to get Britain into the League; soon afterward Wilson's physical collapse involved the League, the treaty, the Democratic party, and his naval program in common ruin. Congress was not afraid of a war with Britain or convinced that the United States needed a larger navy than Great Britain. When Harding became President in 1921, only four of the 1916 battleships were more than barely begun and appropriations for new construction had fallen from $135,000,000 in 1919 to $90,000,000. Some Congressmen were talking of scrapping all the incomplete ships, whether a disarmament conference met or not. Some American naval officers were opposed to battle cruisers, which the United States Navy had not built before the war. The 1916 battle cruisers, these officers claimed, had been designed on the basis of the misleading British victory claims after Jutland. These officers believed that the still experimental aircraft carrier might do the battle cruiser's job better. Other air power enthusiasts—led by the controversial General William Mitchell—had revived the *Jeune Ecole's* claim that all battleships were now obsolete. On July 21, 1921, a group of army bombers under Mitchell's command had sunk the old German dreadnought *Ostfriesland* with six one-ton bombs. Mitchell had deliberately broken the rules of the test—which he claimed had been rigged against the airmen—but the public had been mightily impressed. The United States fleet was also poorly balanced. It was strong in battleships and antisubmarine craft, but had commissioned no cruisers since 1908. The ten incomplete 7,500-ton cruisers and nine large submarines of the 1916 program were quite inadequate for a war against an island power across the Pacific. The British naval critic, Hector C. Bywater noted that

The modern United States Navy is exceptionally strong in heavy armoured ships and exceptionally weak in fast cruising ships. . . . American naval policy . . . has been guided by considerations of Atlantic and Caribbean strategy; . . . very little attempt has been made [to prepare for] . . . war in the Pacific, where the considerations would be fundamentally different.[3]

Japan's China adventure had proved unprofitable. She could not hope to compete with the United States in an all-out naval race. All of these considerations led to compromise at the Washington Conference of 1921-1922. The three major naval powers agreed to scrap most of their older ships and blueprints to reach a 5/5/3 capital ship tonnage ratio (after replacing obsolete ships—525,000/525,000/315,000 tons). France and Italy accepted the status quo (1.67 or 175,000 tons each). Except for two ships which Britain might build to reach her quota, no capital ships could be built for ten years. None, except the *Hood*, could then be larger than 35,000 tons or carry larger than sixteen-inch guns. The new battleship race—the most dangerous feature of the old Anglo-German race—was stopped before it was well started. The Conference failed to "outlaw" the submarine, though an agreement, which France did not ratify, prohibited its use as

[3] *Sea Power in the Pacific* (New York, 1921), 128-129. On the tests, see Harry H. Ransom, "The Battleship Meets the Airplane" (*Military Affairs*, XXIII, Spring, 1959, 21-27). For the earlier period see William Reynolds Braisted, *The United States Navy in the Pacific, 1897-1900* (Austin, 1958); George T. Davis, *A Navy Second to None* (New York, 1940); and Outten Jones Clinard, *Japan's Influence on American Naval Power, 1897-1917* (Berkeley, 1947).

a "commerce destroyer." Cruisers were limited to 10,000 tons, cruisers and aircraft carriers to eight-inch guns. Carriers could not be larger than 27,000 tons, except for the 33,000 ton *Lexington* and *Saratoga*, which the United States Navy built on the hulls of two of its "scrapped" battle cruisers. Britain and the United States were allowed 135,000 tons of carriers, Japan 81,000, and France and Italy each 60,000. These rather high limits allowed the American and Japanese navies to develop the carrier as a striking weapon—a far more significant contribution to the development of air power than Billy Mitchell's theories. After the failure of the Geneva Conference of 1927, the London Conference of 1930 gave Japan a 10/7 cruiser tonnage ratio and parity in submarines. The Second London Conference (1935-1936) was a failure. Since Japan had already given the required two years' notice, the Washington tonnage agreements formally ended on December 31, 1936, not quite five years before the Japanese attack on Pearl Harbor.[4]

The three major Pacific powers also agreed to stabilize the status quo in naval bases in a vast triangle west of Hawaii and Alaska, north of Singapore and Australia, and south of Japan proper. The United States could not build new bases in the Aleutians, Guam, or the Philippines; the British could not modernize Hong Kong; and Japan could not build bases in the Kuriles, Ryukyus, Formosa, the Bonins, or the Carolines and Marshalls. This agreement was as unsatisfactory to American naval officers as the 3/5 ratio was to the Japanese, but the Congress which had taken the axe to the 1916 naval program had shown even less interest in bases in the Western Pacific. The Anglo-Japanese Alliance was dissolved. France, Britain, Japan, and the United States agreed to respect each others' "insular possessions," and a Nine Power Pact (signed by all the Pacific powers except Russia, which had not been invited) reaffirmed the Open Door in China. The Washington

[4] The United States Navy's General Board had wanted a 10/10/6 ratio, which would have meant completing the ships of the 1916 program. Two nearly completed *West Virginias* (the newest battleships of the Pacific Fleet when Japan attacked Pearl Harbor) were saved when Japan would not scrap the new *Mutsu*. The two new British battleships (completed in 1927) were cut-down 48,000 ton battle cruisers. This building "holiday" made the completion dates of post-Washington Conference ships a major factor in World War II. In May, 1941, Britain had only five ships as fast as the new *Bismarck:* two new battleships (the *Prince of Wales* still shaking down), the twenty-one-year-old *Hood*, and the last Fisher battle cruisers, the *Repulse* and the *Renown*. The *Hood*, paired with the *Prince of Wales*, blew up in ten minutes in their fight with the *Bismarck*. The *Repulse* was paired with the *Prince of Wales* six months later when both were sunk by Japanese planes off Kuantan.

Treaties contained no sanctions. In ratifying them, the Senate specified that the United States was making "no commitment to armed force, no alliance, no obligation to join in any defence."[5]

Less than a year after the close of the Washington Conference the Reparations Commission declared Germany in default for the third time. French and Belgian troops marched into the Ruhr in a unilateral attempt to collect reparations. The German government ordered passive resistance and deliberately inflated the currency to pay the idle workers. This completed the ruin of the mark and raised the specter of Communist or monarchist revolution in Germany, while the French toyed with a movement for an independent Rhineland republic. With the franc also going down disastrously, British and American bankers worked out the reparations settlement known as the Dawes Plan. The political agreement which followed the French and Belgian withdrawal from the Ruhr was known as the Locarno Pact (1925). Its signatories (Britain, Italy, Germany, France, and Belgium) promised "immediately" to aid the victim of "an unprovoked act of aggression . . . or the assembly of armed forces in the demilitarized zone." In 1926 Germany joined the League with a permanent Council seat; the disarmament control commission was abolished the next year. The French Foreign Minister, Aristide Briand, and the American Secretary of State, Frank B. Kellogg, then sponsored a general peace pact of two articles. "I.

[5] The best single works are Harold and Margaret Sprout, *Toward a New Order of Sea Power* (2d ed., Princeton, 1946), and John Chalmers Vinson, *The Parchment Peace: The United States Senate and the Washington Conference, 1921-1922* (Athens, Ga., 1955). The naval base agreement left each power free to build bases in the area of its most vital interest. Britain and the United States together enjoyed a crushing naval superiority over Japan and fleet bases at Pearl Harbor and Singapore for a long-range naval blockade. Japan did not directly attack the two powers until the Second Anglo-German War had drawn most of the British fleet and half of the United States fleet into the Atlantic. Nobody could have predicted that the entire United States battle line would be sunk in its base in a single sneak attack or that the great new base at Singapore would be taken in two months.

Bywater, *Sea Power in the Pacific*, 288-289, 318-319, predicted the general course of a Pacific War with considerable accuracy. "Within a fortnight . . . the United States would find herself . . . without a single base [in the Western Pacific]. . . . Japanese strategists . . . have satisfied themselves that . . . the United States would [then] negotiate for peace. . . . The wish is probably father to the thought. . . . It is scarcely conceivable that public opinion in the United States would . . . own defeat. . . . If, as is all but certain, the struggle were to be protracted, no facile successes achieved in the beginning could avert the most ruinous consequences to the Island Empire, . . . [from] a militarist gamble more reckless even than that which caused the ruin of the German Empire."

The High Contracting Parties . . . condemn . . . war, . . . renounce it as an instrument of national policy, [and] . . . II. . . . agree that the settlement of all disputes . . . shall never be sought except by pacific means." Sixty-five states, including all of the great powers, eventually ratified this new Pact of Paris, which went into effect on July 24, 1929, just halfway between the signing of the Treaty of Versailles and the outbreak of the Second World War in Europe. A month later, after Germany had accepted a new reparations agreement (the Young Plan), the Allied occupation forces began to withdraw from all German territory ahead of schedule.

These peace settlements were to prove as ephemeral as Napoleon's Empire. Today, the Briands and the Kelloggs are the "hollow men," who optimistically believed that they could return to the stable, peaceful world of the late nineteenth century. The shock of the First World War had been so great that it was only natural to try to forget it, especially when it was followed by a very rapid economic recovery in the 1920's. The most obvious political reason for the failure of the peace was the Big Three's failure to stick together and the inability of their peoples and leaders to choose either collective security or adequate armaments. But this combination of American "isolationism" and Anglo-French "appeasement" with inadequate armaments had been overemphasized; peace depended on many factors outside the Big Three's immediate control. The stability of the German Republic was very important, especially after the break-up of Austria-Hungary into its mutually hostile nationalistic components. Russia, a former Ally, remained hostile and suspicious, and the rise of a strong China, one aim of the Washington agreements, was to threaten the whole position of Japan, another Ally, as a great power. Finally, the nationalistic, antidemocratic Fascist party had overthrown the parliamentary regime in Italy in 1922, potentially alienating the last of the Big Five of the Paris conference. The pessimists—Oswald Spengler, Ortega y Gasset, and the earlier Arnold Toynbee—had correctly discerned that the First World War had aggravated many of Western civilization's most difficult problems. The war had inflamed nationalistic ambitions and animosities, especially in Eastern Europe, where the Second World War was also to begin. Outside Europe, opposition to European domination was still increasing, and Europe's war-weary peoples were both less willing and less able to use force to maintain their controls. The world-wide economy of the late nineteenth century had been seriously disrupted and Northwestern Europe's position within it gravely weakened. Still higher tariffs now protected uneconomic wartime industries; new frontiers had severed old economic connections. Many of Northwestern Europe's investments had been lost; markets had been invaded by Japan and the United States. Russia had withdrawn from the international economy, and the United States, in economics as in politics, was not prepared to assume the leadership so hastily thrust upon her.

Most important of all, a decade of violence had profoundly shaken old political ideas. Within twenty years of the Russian Revolution, two additional European powers became totalitarian dictatorships and Japan and a number of other states changed their pseudo-democratic clothing for pseudo-totalitarian trappings. The "pattern of interrelated traits of the totalitarian dictatorship consists of an ideology, a single party typically led by one man, a terroristic police, a communications [education and propaganda] monopoly, a weapons monopoly, and a centrally directed economy. . . . The last two are also found in constitutional systems, . . . all modern states possess a weapons monopoly." The major totalitarian states were all dissatisfied with the peace settlements; all proved to be as willing to use force in international relations as in domestic policy. One of the chief aims—either open or covert—of the totalitarian state was military efficiency; most of them were militaristic in their glorification of war as one of the chief purposes of human society.[6]

Soldiers had to evaluate the lessons of the war and make a place for the new weapons—especially the tank and plane— which had finally helped to break the deadlock. The military

[6] Carl J. Friedrich and Zbigniew K. Brzezinski, *Totalitarian Dictatorship and Autocracy* (Cambridge, Mass., 1956), 9. A major weakness of this work is its deliberate failure to include such pseudo-totalitarian states as Poland, Jugoslavia, and Rumania. The Polish dictator Joseph Pilsudski, like Mussolini a former socialist turned nationalist, may well have doubted the applicability of parliamentary institutions to Poland's precarious situation. But he failed to see that only forced-draft industrialization might make it possible for Poland to develop the strength to withstand the temporarily impotent great powers on her eastern and western frontiers. Or, as in Mussolini's case, Pilsudski may not have been strong enough to force such a policy on the industrialists and landed proprietors who supported him. Pilsudski's successors both exaggerated Poland's military capabilities and allied themselves to Hitler, whom Colonel Beck confessed that he had believed would be "a real partner, not one who would jump through the window in the course of negotiations." See Hans Roos, *Polen und Europa: Studien Zur Polnischen Aussenpolitik, 1931-1939* (Tübingen, 1957). For what Poland did accomplish see *Pologne, 1919-1939* (3 vols., Neuchatel [1946-1947]).

theorists of the victorious powers saw these lessons—in Fuller's analysis, the need for political authority, national discipline, economic self-sufficiency, and machine weapons—as clearly as those of the totalitarian states. But, perhaps inevitably, the defeated or dissatisfied powers, all of which eventually became more or less totalitarian, applied these lessons more resolutely than the defenders of the new status quo. Fuller himself thought that a liberal state could not meet these requirements. An American political scientist, Samuel P. Huntington, feels that military security requires

a shift in basic American values from liberalism to conservatism. . . . [to] permit American military leaders to combine the political power which society thrusts upon them with the military professionalism without which society cannot endure. . . . West Point embodies the military ideal at its best. [It] is a community of structured purpose, . . . governed by a code, the product of generations, . . . [with] little room for presumption and individualism, . . . a bit of Sparta in the midst of Babylon.

On the other hand, the revolutionary totalitarianisms of the Long Armistice were also antithetical to certain elements in the old military code. The army was often what the authors previously quoted call an "island of separateness" (with the churches, the family, and the universities and the sciences) in the totalitarian dictatorships.

Most of the traditional dictatorships of our age, . . . not only based their power on the army, but had actually come to power from the army, . . . [which] tended to remain in a sacrosanct position, jealously watching its many prerogatives and privileges, and retaining a distinct political identity. . . . In a totalitarian system, this relationship is startlingly reversed. The totalitarian movement is the source of the dictator's power, despite occasional expedient compromises. . . . As soon as power is seized, efforts are made to neutralize, and then to integrate the armed forces into the totalitarian fabric. [Ideally, they become] a sort of totalitarian militia, supporting the external policies of the regime in much the same way the totalitarian secret police buttresses the regime's domestic policies.[7]

In this respect the Russian Bolsheviks were more successful than the German National Socialists or the Italian Fascists,

[7] Huntington, *The Soldier and the State: The Theory and Politics of Civil-Military Relations* (Cambridge, Mass., 1957), 464-465. Friedrich and Brzezinski, *op. cit.*, 273-274.

while Japan was not totalitarian at all. Huntington claims that "Japan had the form, the external shell, of military professionalism, but not the substance. . . . The ideal officer was a warrior—a fighter engaged in violence himself rather than a manager directing the employment of violence by others." The problem of the German General Staff is more complex, since Huntington feels that "Imperial civil-military relations between 1871 and 1914 reflected an extraordinary degree of objective civilian control and military professionalism. . . . The German military probably came closer to approximating the ideal-type military ethic than those of any other officer corps in history." Yet Giulio Douhet felt that these professionals had caused the Empire's downfall.

A wall was erected between the civil and the military. . . . And because the people on the inside . . . were engaged in something which seemed mysterious, . . . those on the outside considered that something as beyond their comprehension and bowed to it with a respect almost religious. . . . Having taken into consideration only the military angle, . . . the German General Staff had concluded that a decisive victory could be gained quickly. . . . It was accepted in political circles without careful examination because it had come from the organ competent by definition. . . . Had the shrewd men who governed Germany . . . examined the reality, . . . very likely they would have gained clearer insight into the situation, the unlikelihood of victory, and the prodigious cost of the game. And perhaps they would have refrained from throwing the dice.[8]

The Totalitarian State: Bolshevik Russia

By the Darwinian test of survival Bolshevik Russia was the most successful of the new totalitarian autocracies. Fuller's principles of political authority, national discipline, economic self-sufficiency, and machine weapons can be followed through-

[8] Huntington, *op. cit.*, 126, 99-100. Douhet, *Command of the Air*, 125-126. In some respects the Japanese constitution, which provided for the independence of the Supreme Command under the Emperor, was rather like that of the German Empire. General Hideki Tojo, premier at the time of Pearl Harbor, later commented, "I am not saying that the independence of the Supreme Command is a bad thing, . . . for example, being able to conduct operations without political interference. It was a good thing in 1890, . . . but in these days when the influence of a single action is felt around the world, a certain amount of control by the political authority is necessary. . . . The independence of the Supreme Command is good . . . only if fighting is the only thing considered, but fighting today is also a part of politics. . . . If I and the other men had fully understood this, the Supreme Command would have taken account of the political aspect of things and adjusted military operations accordingly." Quoted in Yale Candee Maxon, *Control of Japanese Foreign Policy: A Study of Civil-Military Rivalry, 1930-1945* (Berkeley, 1957), 218.

out the history of the Soviet state. The Bolsheviks were not hampered by racist or nationalist limitations on Party membership, and none of these principles was incompatible with Marxist writ. Unlike many revolutionaries of the 1840's, Marx had accepted the Industrial Revolution. Socialism was, to him, the inevitable final phase in the evolution of an industrial society. Marx and Engels had also studied Clausewitz, and both were first-rate military journalists. Naturally enough, they stressed the relations of politics and war and the impact of the Industrial Revolution on warfare. Still more important, they did not commit their followers to any specifically Marxist military theory, such as the natural superiority of a people's militia to any form of professional military organization. Lenin had also studied and annotated Clausewitz. Discipline, unity, and tactical flexibility are as important in class warfare as in war in general. This Clausewitzian emphasis on (1) the close relations between politics and war and (2) orthodox principles of command and discipline can be followed throughout the entire Leninist-Stalinist era (1917-1953).[9]

The Red Army of the Civil War was thrown together from any elements which could be used to retain the Party's control over defeated Russia. The Germans—and Red revolutionary propaganda—had smashed the army of the tsars. Leon Trotsky, the Red Carnot, augmented his proletarian militia (the Red Guard) and existing peasant partisan bands with all the conscripts the governments could catch, though members of the former middle class or the upper peasants (kulaks) were placed in separate labor battalions. This amalgam was commanded by former tsarist officers, such as Michael Tukhachevsky or the scholarly staff officer Boris Shaposhnikov, noncoms such as the cavalryman Simeon Budenny, and professional revolutionaries such as Trotsky himself or his successor, Michael Frunze. The Bolsheviks had studied revolutionary history. Political commissars tried to inspire men and

[9] See Sigmund Neumann's fine discussion in Earle, *Modern Strategy*. "Advances in technique," Friedrich Engels believed, "as soon as they become usable in the military sphere, . . . immediately produced changes in the methods of warfare . . . often even against the will of the army command. . . . Nowadays any zealous subaltern could explain . . . how greatly the conduct of a war depends on the productivity and means of communication of the army's own hinterland as well as of the arena of war." *Herr Eugen Dühring's Revolution in Science* (1878, New York, 1935), 198.

Engels, like Jaurès, thought that all workers should be trained to defend the revolution, but this idea cannot be divorced from the general trend of late nineteenth-century military thought. The mass conscript army *was*, in some respects, a people's militia. Engels' support of such an army underlines the conservatives' fear that it might well prove politically unreliable.

alleviate their sufferings, watched the officers for signs of treason or incompetence, and sometimes protected them against unfounded calumnies. Though far inferior to the armies of the west, the Red Army was able to outlast the equally ramshackle White and Polish forces and the half-hearted efforts of the Allies.[10]

During the crises which followed the death of Lenin, the Party never relaxed its grip upon the army. The demobilization of the 1920's enabled it to get rid of many incompetents and some of the holdovers from the old regime. It also packed workers into the key arms and pushed young proletarians—such as the leather-worker Gregory Zhukov or the Polish stonecutter Konstantin Rokossovsky—into command positions. The commissars were now subordinated to the unit commanders. During the early 1930's they were chiefly concerned with morale and the indoctrination of the peasant conscripts in Marxist ideology. The bitter struggle with the peasants over collective farming was not marked—as far as we know—by mutinies among the peasant soldiers. The commissars were again made equal to the unit commanders in 1937, when Stalin executed or removed perhaps half of the officers and as many as three-quarters of the higher commanders, including most of the Civil War holdovers, in the high command. Secret police agents now watched both the commanders and the commissars, and the secret police built up its own separate elite units. Except for Shaposhnikov, who was in a staff position, the surviving Civil War commanders—Timoshenko, Budenny, and Voroshilov—did not measure up to the Germans during the Second World War. The outstand-

---

10 Though the Red Army may have reached 5,000,000 men in 1920, the largest field armies of the Civil War numbered about 100,000 each. "On paper it looked like the Great War. . . . In fact it was only its ghost. . . . [The Whites] advanced . . . till they had scarcely one man to the mile. When the moment came the Bolsheviks, lying in the center, equally feeble, . . . gave a prick or a punch at this point or that. Thereupon the balloon burst and all the flags moved back . . . and horrible vengeances were wreaked on helpless people." Churchill, *World Crisis*, IV, 240-241. George Stewart, *The White Armies of Russia: A Chronicle of Counter-Revolution and Allied Intervention* (New York, 1933).

The Reds never lost the transportation and industrial centers of Petrograd and Moscow. They were supported by most of the industrial workers, many of the poorer peasants, and even by some nationalistic members of the middle class. The Party had a "concise program . . . comprehensible to the most illiterate worker . . . [and] the 'darkest' peasant, . . . [and] ability, will power, and indefatigable application. . . . Whoever they were, commissars, commanders, rank and file soldiers, their will to victory provided the unifying cement, the iron frame, that held the Red Army together, despite its internal conflicts." D. Fedotoff White, *The Growth of the Red Army* (Princeton, 1944), 125-126.

ing Soviet field commanders were to be the younger men—mostly in their early forties—who had been promoted as a result of the 1937 purge.[11]

These controls were supplemented by all of the economic and psychological incentives which the Soviet Union's rulers could command. Common soldiers, like skilled factory workers, were given somewhat better food, housing, clothing, and cultural opportunities than ordinary citizens. The progressive professionalization of the officers was marked by a widening gap between them and their men, the gap which was also widening between the new managerial classes and the workers. Orderlies, salutes, uniforms, vacations, cars, housing, and even educational privileges for their children were given to faithful and fortunate specialists in all fields which the Party considered important. Though some of these trappings made the Red Army as "militaristic" as any in the world, the Party remained vigilant against real militarism: "Bonapartism" or the establishment of a "Praetorian Guard." On the whole the army remained loyal during the Great Patriotic (Second World) War. Whether this was due to the Party's elaborate system of incentives and controls, revolutionary idealism, the Stalinist-encouraged revival of Russian nationalism, or Nazi racist-inspired cruelty toward the conquered population is as hard to determine as it is to evaluate some of the same elements in the age of Carnot. Soviet military education was based on the German classics; some German officers lectured in Russia and some Russians studied in Germany. The Red Army blended rigorous political indoctrination with military conservatism and technological pragmatism. Fuller's and Douhet's theories of mechanization and air power were rejected as too radical. Russian armored tactics were basically French. They "represented the most highly developed system derived directly from the methods of the First World War and the most elaborate form of tank employment under the control of infantry." The Russian tank forces were theoretically strong enough to push through the enemy's defense

[11] Raymond L. Garthoff's figures of nine-tenths of the generals and eight-tenths of the colonels are, as he indicates, probably too high. *Soviet Military Doctrine* (Glencoe, 1953), 220-221. Friedrich and Brzezinski, *Totalitarian Dictatorship*, 281, believe that "It is the Soviet handling of the army which comes closest to the model image of the complete integration of the military into the totalitarian movement." For a longer study see the latter author's *Political Controls in the Soviet Army* (New York, 1954). Another doctrinal study is Berthold C. Friedl, *Les Fondaments théoriques de la guerre et de la paix en U.R.S.S.* (Paris, 1945).

system, but "the overall tempo and depth of the attack were still governed by the foot-fighting infantry. . . . Although tank brigades or even tank corps existed, in battle they hardly operated as such." Russian artillery tactics were possibly more advanced than those of the Germans, and all training was quite realistic.[12]

Stalin's program for "Socialism in One Country" placed great emphasis on heavy industry. Russia had been beaten by Germany because of her lack of arms. The Five Year Plans stressed the industrialization of areas away from the exposed western frontier and close to the undeveloped resources of the Urals and Western Siberia. The First Five Year Plan (1928-1932) was almost wrecked by inexperience, incompetence, and peasant opposition to collective farming. During the Second Five Year Plan (1933-1937) people got a little more to eat, but the Party was racked by the great purges. During the Third Five Year Plan (1938-1942) still greater stress was placed on arms production to meet the growing German danger. By 1940 Russian steel production had passed that of Great Britain and was close to that of Germany. Whole new industries—machine tools, aviation, and automobiles—and new industrial areas had been created. With the rapid industrialization of Japan, the industrialization of Soviet Russia was a major factor in the changing balance of international forces during the Long Armistice. Dictatorships may invent crises for propaganda purposes, but the dangers facing the Soviet Union in the thirties were real, rather than imaginary.

12 Ogorkiewicz, *Armor*, 118-119. The Russians studied Fuller rather than his less radical followers—who could not follow his independent "land battleship" concept—because he developed his ideas early and systematically, especially in his *Lectures on Field Service Regulations III: Operations between Mechanized Forces* (London, 1932). On Fuller's downgrading of artillery see Fred K. Vigman, "The Theoretical Evaluation of Artillery after World War I" (*Military Affairs*, XVI, Fall, 1952, 115-118). G. A. Deborin, ed., *Istoriia Velikoi Otechestvennoi Voiny Sovetskogo Soiuza, 1941-1945* (I, Moscow, 1960) also shows that the Russians had not studied disengagement and withdrawal, had taught that their counteroffensives would immediately take the war to enemy soil, and that Stalin ignored commando and air incursions as well as foreign warnings of the impending German attack.

All social organizations formed "transmission belts" for directives from above and "barometers" for testing public opinion. The Party did not glorify war as such; its guiding philosophy remained Jaurès's idea of the proletarian nation in arms. Military training began in the fifth grade and civilian paramilitary organizations trained millions of citizens in rifle-shooting, gliding, parachute jumping, and other skills. Since the Red Army was not able to train all of its eligible conscripts until the late 1930's, these premilitary and paramilitary activities were to prove very important. One of the best descriptions is still Julian Towster, *Political Power in the U.S.S.R., 1917-1947* (New York, 1948).

The struggle with the peasants coincided with a revival of the German danger. The purges were deliberately used to heighten Soviet nationalism, and the Communist Third International was even more openly subordinated to the needs of Soviet foreign policy. At the end of the purges the American ambassador reported Stalin in "complete control of the army, the secret police, the newspapers, the radios, and the schools. . . . Barring accident or assassination . . . the present regime will persist for some time. . . . It is supremely confident that it could successfully resist simultaneous attack by Japan and Germany." Other observers were not so sanguine. Who could trust leaders who had just shot most of their army's high command and might reveal all of their secrets at the next state trial? This distrust was one factor in the British and French decision to allow Hitler to partition France's ally Czechoslovakia in 1938. Munich, in turn, confirmed the Communists' worst suspicions of their erstwhile allies (Russia had joined the League in 1934 and had signed a five-year alliance with France the next year), and paved the way for Stalin's own appeasement of Hitler in 1939, the deal which precipitated the Second World War.[13]

Italian Fascism and the Theories of Giulio Douhet

Italian Fascism stressed the need for political authority and national discipline and glorified the life of the warrior. But Mussolini seems to have been chiefly interested in the decorative aspects of military life; his armed forces were not ready for a major war in 1939. Supplies had been stolen or used up during his Ethiopian and Spanish adventures; his "eight million bayonets" were not supported by modern heavy weapons. Though the Germans were often unfair in their judgments of their allies of the "Pact of Steel," Erwin Rommel's analysis of the weaknesses of the Italian army was essentially correct. "Its tanks and armoured vehicles were too light. . . . The army had too few anti-tank and anti-aircraft guns and even its rifles and machine-guns were . . . obsolete. . . . A great part of the Italian army consisted of non-motorised infantry . . . of practically no value" in North Africa.

[13] Joseph E. Davies, *Mission to Moscow* (New York, 1943), 364-365. On German-Russian relations see Gustav Hilger and Alfred G. Meyer, *The Incompatible Allies: German-Soviet Relations, 1918-1941* (New York, 1953), and the documents published in *Nazi-Soviet Relations, 1939-1941* (Washington, 1948). On Munich see John W. Wheeler-Bennett, *Munich, Prologue to Tragedy* (New York, 1948), and Boris Čelovsky, *Das Müncher Abkommen von 1938* (Stuttgart, 1958).

After their early defeats, the Italians, "with good reason, lost all confidence in their arms and acquired a very serious inferiority complex. . . . Psychologically, it is particularly unfortunate when the very first battle of a war ends with such a disastrous defeat, especially when it has been preceded by such grandiose predictions."[14]

Unlike Russia or Germany, Italy possesses few of the raw materials for modern war, and there are none to be conquered in the Central Mediterranean. Her geographical position with respect to her old allies was rather like that of Japan. She could threaten limited Anglo-French interests; they could always launch an unlimited counterstroke. Many French armies have invaded northern Italy since 1494, no vital French interests are open to Italian land attack. The Italian fleet could threaten French communications to North Africa, but France developed an alternative Atlantic route to this area in the 1930's. The British could confine the Italian naval forces to the Mediterranean, while still retaining an alternative route around the Cape of Good Hope. Sicily, Sardinia, Naples, Genoa, and even Rome remained open to naval attack or amphibious assault. Italy's weakness against France had been a factor in her decision to join the Triple Alliance, at a time when Britain was attempting to check French and Russian ambitions in the Mediterranean. But after Britain and Germany became diplomatic rivals, Italy's position in the Triple Alliance became very difficult. Mussolini did not enter the Second World War until Germany's victory over the Anglo-French allies seemed certain. He succeeded only in proving the truth of the old axiom that Italy could not challenge British sea power in the Mediterranean. The Italian army and people had suffered heavily during the First World War, and air power had been spectacularly successful on the deadlocked Italian front. Eighty tons of bombs—more than the Germans had dropped on London—had nearly destroyed

[14] *The Rommel Papers*, ed. B. H. Liddell Hart (New York, 1953), 91-97. The Duce's son-in-law, Galeazzo Ciano, wrote just before a big Fascist review in 1939 that Mussolini "spends many a half-hour at the window of his office, concealed behind the blue curtains, looking at . . . units [practicing the goose step or Roman step]. . . . He . . . chose the band-leader's baton . . . [and changed its] proportion and design. He is a strong believer that in the armed forces it is the form that determines the substance." *The Ciano Diaries, 1939-1943*, ed. Hugh Gibson (New York, 1946), 18-19. Three of the most interesting of the many works of explanation are Umberto Spigo, *Premesse techniche della disfatta (dell' euforia al disastro)* (Rome, 1946), Amadeo Tosti, *Da Versailles a Cassabile* (Bologna, 1954), and Carmine Senise, *Quando ero capo della polizia, 1940-1943* (2d ed., Rome, 1947).

the little Italian city of Treviso, and Venice and the Austrian naval base of Pola had been bombed repeatedly. The three outstanding examples of air action against a retreating enemy —in Palestine, on the Bulgarian front, and after Vittorio Veneto—had taken place on fronts where communications were far more constricted than in the west. These were some of the general conditions which helped to produce the theories of Giulio Douhet, the greatest military writer of the Long Armistice.[15]

Douhet was forty-six when Italy entered the war in 1915. That year, while serving as chief of staff in an infantry division, he proposed an independent bombing force of five hundred tri-motored Capronis to attack Austrian communications. He became head of the Central Aeronautical Bureau after his release from prison in 1918 and published *The Command of the Air* in 1921, when he retired from the army. He became Commissioner of Aviation after the Fascist Coup, but soon retired again to devote his time to writing. He died in 1930, the year of his last work, the fictional *War of 19—*. His works did not attract attention abroad until after his death, when parts of them were translated into French, English, German, and Russian. The general lessons which Douhet drew from the war paralleled those of General Fuller. "Integral" war involves every aspect of life and must be directed by a single authority. A "Fascist of the First Hour," Douhet supported the unified command set up in 1925 and called for a "War Academy" in which representatives of the three services "could study these formidable new forces together." The war had proved the tactical difficulties of a land offensive, particularly in the Alps, where tanks could be easily contained by antitank defenses. The Italian navy's strategic situation was even worse than that of the Germans. Germany had not been "satisfied with a minimum [surface ship] program," and had failed to concentrate on submarines until too late. Since Italy must stand on the defensive on land and sea, her only offensive weapon is in the air. Two proposi-

[15] Lord Trenchard, a key man in the development of R.A.F. doctrine, published little, but P. R. C. Groves, Director of Flying Operations in 1918, wrote many articles on strategic bombing. Mitchell was chiefly a polemicist. Douhet was the first to advance a full-scale theory of air power. The British official account of these battles is H. A. Jones, *The War in the Air*, VI (Oxford, 1937), 225-226, 292, 311-312. J. C. Slessor, *Air Power and Armies* (Oxford, 1936), 102-106, did not mention Douhet, but used a British account of Vittorio Veneto. See the fine anthology by Eugene M. Emme, *The Impact of Air Power: National Security and World Politics* (Princeton, 1959).

tions are the heart of Douhet's doctrine. (1) "The aeroplane is the offensive weapon *par excellence* . . . because of its independence of surface limitations and its superior speed." (2) "The disintegration of nations [which] in the last war was brought about [indirectly] by the actions of the armies in the field [and blockade] . . . will be accomplished directly by . . . aerial forces." Douhet did not claim to have found "a general recipe for victory," but this formula seemed to fit Italy's situation in the twenties. "A doctrine of war must simply correspond to the realities of war obtaining at the time and to the peculiar characteristics of the nation it refers to." "In all probability, if I were specifically considering a conflict between Japan and the United States, I would not arrive at the same conclusions."[16]

Douhet's program of *"A progressive decrease of land and sea forces, accompanied by a corresponding increase of aerial forces until they are strong enough to command the air,"* was not designed to win popularity with the other services. The air force should be "organically self-sufficient and independent of land and sea forces in its operation." An independent air force could give tactical support to the army and navy after it had won command of the air, auxiliary army and naval air forces diverted part of the nation's air power from the primary mission of destroying the enemy's air power. In 1921 Douhet had been willing to allow the army and navy to have such auxiliary forces. Five years later he explained that he had adopted this view only because

I thought that when a really worth-while auxiliary aviation had been organized and the army and navy compelled to pay for it out of their own budgets, and their authorities had been obliged seriously to study the organization and employment of it, they would automatically come to the conclusion that such auxiliary aviation was useless—and therefore not only superfluous, but contrary to the public interest.

He opposed diverting fighter forces to defensive purposes, though he favored passive defense supported by other funds. Some enemy bombers would always get through. *"We must therefore resign ourselves to the offensives the enemy inflicts*

16 *Command of the Air,* 18-19, 200-201. Douhet's ideas were also spread by an able French disciple, Colonel Pierre Vauthier, whose *La Doctrine de guerre du Général Douhet* (Paris, 1935) is still the best study. Louis A. Sigaud, *Douhet and Aerial Warfare* (New York, 1941), was a good popular account in its day, but full-scale scholarly biographies of Douhet and studies of his influence are badly needed.

upon us, while striving to put all our resources to work to inflict even heavier ones upon him." These principles—the primacy of air power, the necessity of an Independent Air Force, and dependence on passive civil defense and "massive retaliation"—still play a large role in air doctrine.[17]

Douhet had little immediate influence. Italy was the first power to devote its greatest effort to the air arm, but official Italian air doctrine came from Britain and the British development of an independent air service. Italy's ultimate failure in the air power race does not prove Douhet wrong; it is only additional evidence of Italy's economic and geographical limitations, Douhet himself admitting that Italy was more vulnerable to French bombers than France was to Italian air raids. Perhaps Italy should not have tried to become a great military power. But that dream had accompanied the struggle for national unification in every European people, and the frustration of Italy's hopes after all of her sacrifices, and Allied promises, of the First World War had been a powerful factor in the rise of Italian Fascism. Douhet's technical ideas were soon outmoded. He was fifty-two when he published *The Command of the Air*, older than Mahan at the time of *The Influence of Sea Power*, a year older than Clausewitz at the time of the latter's death. Douhet was not an engineer, as Mahan had not been a naval architect. Douhet's all-purpose "battleplanes suitable for both combat and bombing" have never proved satisfactory; the balance between over- and under-specialization remains one of the most difficult problems of mechanized warfare. Douhet also overemphasized civil aviation, though the principle that interest in civil aviation stimulates the development of air power is still sound. Like Mahan and Clausewitz, Douhet formulated ideas which were already in the air. That was one reason for his influence, though his works, like those of Clausewitz and Du Picq, were to become more famous after their author's death than during his lifetime. His books, too, are still very much worth reading as the products of a powerful mind and personality.[18]

The Military Recovery of Germany

The German army was saved from total destruction by the skill of some of its leaders and Allied and republican fear of

[17] *Command of the Air*, 30-31, 64, 81, 50.
[18] In spite of some inaccuracies and its dependence on Soviet propaganda handouts, Max Werner, *The Military Strength of the Powers* (New York, 1939) is an acute survey of doctrine and armament in the late thirties.

Bolshevism. Wilhelm Groener, the last Chief of the General Staff and Defense Minister from 1928 to 1932, helped the Socialist Chancellor, Friedrich Ebert, crush the Spartacist (pro-Bolshevik) revolt in Berlin in January, 1919, and protected the republican constitutional convention. The next year the Berlin garrison joined an abortive monarchist revolt, but the republicans did not dismiss the officers who had refused to move against their former comrades. They needed the army to suppress a second Spartacist uprising in the Ruhr. Hans von Seeckt, chief of the army command from 1920 to 1926, did not tolerate overt monarchism. He felt that the army must keep out of politics if it were not to endanger its own existence. In return, the republican Defense Ministers tried to protect the soldiers from parliamentary "meddling." Seeckt was no partisan of a Swiss militia or of the *armée de métier* allowed by the Versailles Treaty. The republican army was to provide the framework for a new mass conscript army whenever Germany should be strong enough to get away with one. Every officer was to be prepared to jump at least two grades; every enlisted man was considered as a potential noncommissioned officer. Sections of the outlawed General Staff functioned in various civilian ministries. Flying clubs and civil aviation formed the framework of a future air force. Some arms were concealed and some manufactured abroad, but research was considered more important than the stockpiling of obsolete or obsolescent equipment. The Krupp factories, for example, were almost fully converted to "peaceful" production, but a large research department developed weapons which were then manufactured and tested by dummy corporations in Holland, Sweden, and Russia.

The army's political role during the last years of the republic was largely negative. As Professor Gordon Craig has put it, the army chiefs

heartily disliked Hitler . . . but also admired the disciplined forces which stood behind him, and had no desire to destroy them. Instead they set out to . . . seduce these forces from their Leader. . . . But . . . the generals were far more successful in weakening those political parties . . . opposed to National Socialism than . . . in dividing Hitler's party; and, as intriguers, they were hopelessly outclassed. . . . When all their elaborate schemes had proven to be bankrupt, they were still, however, able to persist in their old delusions. . . . Hitler would allow himself to be managed and, if he did not, he could be disposed of. Of all the mistakes made by political generals in the long history of the Prussian army, this was the greatest and, for the nation, the most tragic.[19]

After Hitler had obtained control of the state, he overwhelmed the army chiefs with displays of esteem, appointing Werner von Fritsch to the army command rather than the outspokenly pro-Nazi Walther von Reichenau. Some officers approved the Blood Purge of June 30, 1934, though Generals von Schleicher and von Bredow had been among its victims, since the main target had been the brown-shirted Storm Troops, whom the generals feared might dominate German rearmament. A month later President Hindenburg died and Hitler became both President and Chancellor. The next day, apparently at the suggestion of Defense Minister Werner von Blomberg, every officer and man swore "unconditional obedience" to Hitler, an oath which later made it almost impossible to organize a substantial officers' resistance. The reintroduction of conscription in 1935 swamped the army with men who had been subjected to intense Nazi propaganda and also opened the way to rapid promotion, though the army chiefs began to fear that Hitler was going too fast and was too enthusiastic about mechanization and the new air force. Hitler came to feel that the generals had no imagination, especially after their opposition to his march into the demilitarized Rhineland in 1936. When Hitler's intuition proved correct— as he had said in *Mein Kampf*, ten guns in the hands of a coward are of less value than a club in the hands of a brave

19 *Prussian Army*, 486-487. Other fine English works are Harold W. Gordon, Jr., *The Reichswehr and the German Republic, 1919-1926* (Princeton, 1957); John W. Wheeler-Bennett, *The Nemesis of Power: The German Army in Politics, 1918-1945* (London, 1953); Hans W. Gatzke, *Stresemann and the Rearmament of Germany* (Baltimore, 1954); J. H. Morgan, *Assize of Arms: The Disarmament of Germany and Her Rearmament, 1919-1939* (New York, 1946); and for the Party's praetorian guard, Gerard Reitlinger, *The SS: Alibi of a Nation, 1922-1945* (New York, 1957).

The French were well aware of Germany's rearmament. See Eugène Carrias's second volume, *Le Danger allemande, 1866-1945* (Paris, 1952), and General Georges Castellan, *Le Réarmement clandestin du Reich, 1930-1935* (Paris, 1954), and G. Gauché, *Le Deuxième bureau au travail, 1935-1940* (Paris, 1954). On Groener see Dorothea Groener-Geyer, *General Groener, Soldat und Staatsman* (Frankfurt, 1955), and his own *Das Testament des Grafen Schlieffen* (Berlin, 1927) and *Lebenserrinnerungen* (Göttingen, 1957). The General Staff is generally defended by Waldemar Erfurth, *Die Geschichte des deutschen Generalstabes von 1918 bis 1945* (Göttingen, 1957). An excellent survey of the Austrian army is Ludwig Jedlicka, *Ein Heer im Schatten der Parteien: Die Militärpolitische Lage Österreichs, 1918-1938* (Vienna, 1955). One of the most slashing criticisms of the officers' corps by one of its members is Moriz von Faber du Fahr, *Macht und Ohnmacht: Errinnerungen eines alten Offizier* (Stuttgart, 1953).

man—he increasingly discounted the generals' gloomy predictions. Hitler purged the high command in January, 1939, a month before his invasion of Austria. Blomberg and Fritsch and sixteen other generals were retired; forty-two more were transferred to other commands. Hitler became Defense Minister and appointed Wilhelm Keitel and Walter von Brauchitsch to the chief posts in a reorganized command. From this time on the German generals, like the parvenu Red Army commanders, were mere military technicians, while Hitler's own acts were never subject even to the approval of a Fascist Grand Council or a Communist Party Central Committee. He was outstandingly successful in meeting the first two of Fuller's conditions for modern warfare: political authority and national discipline. As he told his generals a few days before he began the Second World War, "Probably no one will ever again have the confidence of the German people as I have."[20]

The aim of National Socialist economic planning, to use the terminology of *Geopolitik*—the study of states in their geographical environment—was the creation of a self-sufficient economy (*Autarkie*) through the conquest of additional space (*Lebensraum*) and raw materials. In 1927, partly as a result of Allied postwar private loans, German steel production was back to its 1913 level. By 1938 it was a fifth larger, and most of the increase was being put into finished weapons. Military men like Ludendorff—whose *Der Totale Krieg* came out of Munich in 1935—stressed Germany's neglect of economic preparedness before 1914. National Socialist economic planning was based on the example set by Rathenau, who had been murdered by nationalist fanatics in 1922. Businessmen, some of whom had supported Hitler, welcomed the Party's efforts to hold down wages and eliminate strikes, but soon found themselves subjected "to an evertightening rule of the new bureaucratic machinery, whose power stemmed from

[20] Alan Bullock, *Hitler: A Study in Tyranny* (London, 1953), 482. Some of the many books on the opposition are Gerhard Ritter, *The German Resistance: Carl Goerdeler's Struggle against Tyranny*, trans. R. T. Clark (New York, 1959), Constantine Fitzgibbon, *The Shirt of Nessus* (London, 1956), Günther Weisenborn, ed., *Der hautlose Aufstand* (Hamburg, 1955), Helmut Lindemann, *Generäle machen Politik: Eine Studie* (Bonn, 1952), Helmut Krausnick, *Vorgeschichte und Beginn des militärischen Widerstandes gegen Hitler* (Munich, 1956), Ludwig Beck, *Studien* (Stuttgart, 1955), and Wolfgang Foerster, *Ein General Kämpft gegen den Krieg* (rev. ed., Munich, 1953). There are two important surveys in the *Révue d'histoire de la deuxième guerre mondiale:* F. Boudet, "L'Ecroulement militaire et l'opinion allemande" (July, 1952, 13-28), and M. Adler-Bresse, "Jugements allemandes sur la Wehrmacht" (April, 1956, 10-22).

and was largely based upon uprooted classes and (from their own viewpoint) irrational ideologies." Like disillusioned army officers, "disappointed businessmen, however, found it impossible to overthrow such a regime once it was firmly established." The decision to concentrate on finished weapons ("armament in width") rather than on the longer-range projects ("armament in depth") favored by the high command was the logical complement of Hitler's desire to strike while his opponents were divided and unprepared. Some of these factors—particularly the shortage of oil—affected preparations for the "lightning war" or *Blitzkrieg*. Only the cutting edge of the army was mechanized, the air force lacked oil reserves to plan for sustained strategic bombing, and the navy was given last priority. A series of quick victories would also increase German war potential, while the Party had implicitly promised the people that they would be spared the agony of another war of attrition. Hitler's first victories seemed to vindicate these policies. Only in 1943 was it realized that the German economy was unequal to a war with the world's three greatest remaining industrial powers.[21]

Geopolitik wrapped the biological theory of the state, the Nordic myth, Antisemitism, and the Social Darwinist glorification of war into one package. Its prophet was Karl Haushofer, a Bavarian General Staff officer born in 1869, who had gone to the Far East in 1909 to study the Japanese army. During a long leave caused by illness in 1912, he had written a popular study of Japanese expansion and "The German Share in the Geographical Opening of Japan and the Sub-Japanese Earth Space, and Its Advancement through the Influence of War and Military Policy," which won him a Ph.D.

[21] Albert T. Lauterbach, *Economics in Uniform: Military Economy and Social Structure* (Princeton, 1943), 114; Burton H. Klein, *Germany's Economic Preparations for War* (Cambridge, Mass., 1959). On the United States see George A. Lincoln *et al.*, *Economics of National Security* (2d ed., New York, 1954), and R. Elberton Smith, *The Army and Economic Mobilization* (*U. S. Army in World War II*, Washington, 1959). Rathenau opposed the Armistice and wanted a *levée en masse* in 1918. He later counseled fulfilment of the treaty terms, while showing the Allies that Germany could not meet their reparations demands. Rathenau's "socialism" was rather like British Labour's "Fair Shares for All." Like Keynes, Rathenau also thought that big business had often failed to recognize important investment opportunities. For the diehard nationalists who murdered Rathenau see Robert G. Waite, *Vanguard of Nazism: The Free Corps Movement in Post War Germany, 1918-1923* (Cambridge, Mass., 1952), and *The Answers of Ernst von Salomon to the 131 Questions in the Allied Military Government "Fragebogen"* (London, 1954), 55-66. Hitler's relations with business are discussed in George W. F. Hallgarten, *Hitler, Reichswehr und Industrie: zur Geschichte der Jahre 1918-1933* (Frankfurt, 1952).

in geography, geology, and history "with the highest distinction" at the University of Munich. After the Armistice, like many other former officers, Haushofer continued to work for a Greater Germany, as professor of geography and director of the Geopolitical Institute at Munich, the intellectual seat of National Socialism. The Institute's products combined abstruse terminology—such as *Geopsyche*—the influence of climate on the soul—minute research, and propaganda maps and charts which were as simple as its jargon was complicated. Even the stupidest member of the Master Race could understand the big black arrows directed at surrounding states or the solid bars representing encircling alliances. Haushofer held that Germany's future lay in the area which the British geographer Halford MacKinder had in 1904 called " 'The Geographical Pivot of History'—that vast area of Euro-Asia which is inaccessible to ships, but in antiquity lay open to the horse-riding nomads, and is today to be covered with a network of railways." Fifteen years later MacKinder called this area the "Heartland" of the "World Island" formed by Eurasia and Africa. In order to dramatize his fear that Germany might eventually conquer Russia and become invulnerable to Allied sea power, MacKinder suggested that "some airy cherub should whisper . . . this saying: 'Who rules East Europe commands the Heartland: who rules the Heartland commands the World-Island; who rules the World-Island commands the world.' "[22]

Haushofer's version of MacKinder's ideas gave the proper scientific color to Germany's revival of the traditional *Drang nach Osten* (Drive to the East). The army had always opposed William II's disastrous naval and colonial policies; during the First World War they had actually set up a great mid-European empire. Its re-establishment was Hitler's primary aim. The states which now occupied the *Trümmerzone*

[22] MacKinder, *Democratic Ideals and Reality* (reissue, New York, 1942), 150. MacKinder and Haushofer survived the war, the former having the last word in a striking reassessment of his theory in 1944: "The Round World and the Winning of the Peace," reprinted in Hans W. Weigert and Vilhjalmur Stefansson, eds., *Compass of the World* (New York, 1944). At the very time MacKinder had been calling British attention to the development of land power, one of Haushofer's predecessors at Munich, Friedrich Rätzel, had just written a book on the sea, *Das Meer als Quelle der Völkergrösse* (Munich, 1900).

Typical effusions in other related fields are General Horst K. A. von Metzsch, *Wehrpolitik, Wegweiser und Winke* (Berlin, 1939), and Walther M. Schering, *Wehrphilosophie* (Leipzig, 1939). See also Edmund F. Szczot, *Die deutsche Doktrin des totalen Krieges von der Machtübernahme Hitlers bis zum Ausbruch des Zweiten Weltkrieges* (Vienna, 1946).

(Debris Zone) between Germany and Russia were weak and divided. Russia had been pushed back and the Bolsheviks (in the mid-1920's) were quarreling among themselves. In the 1930's Stalin was starving his own peasants and killing many of his remaining technicians and the high command of the Red Army. Eastern Europe contained the agricultural land necessary for the *Völkisch* state (Nazi racial scientists taught that the peasant was the source of racial strength). Large German minorities were found as far east as the Volga; they were especially easy to organize because they had belonged to the ruling classes of the old Hapsburg and Hohenzollern empires and of the former Baltic provinces of Russia. As Hitler explained it in the second volume of *Mein Kampf* in 1927:

> *We finally terminate the colonial and trade policy of the pre-War period, and proceed to the territorial policy of the future.* But if we talk about new soil . . . in Europe today, we can think primarily only of *Russia* and its vassal border states. . . . In the surrender of Russia to bolshevism, the Russian people was robbed of [its] . . . Germanic nucleus . . . of leaders. . . . The Jew has replaced it, [and this Jewish-Bolshevik] . . . state is now ripe for collapse.[23]

Since J. F. C. Fuller was one father of the *Blitzkreig*, the first, or tactical, stage in its development is best described by him, especially since we have used his description of the difficulties which had caused the failure of previous efforts

> to drill a hole through the enemy's front by massed artillery fire, and then pass an army through the gap. At . . . Cambrai in November, 1917, all these difficulties were overcome by . . . tanks. . . . Though this battle ended in failure, . . . it clearly demonstrated that the forward battle area could rapidly be penetrated and the rear or inner command . . . area be attacked. . . . The German armies were strung out along a five hundred mile . . . zone, the forward area of which was approximately five miles deep and the rear area fifteen. . . . This linear distribution not only favoured [penetration], but hindered the Germans frustrating it. . . . I put forward a project . . . to attack the enemy's command prior to attacking his fighting body, so that his fighting body, when attacked, would be paralyzed through lack of command. The

23 (New York, 1939), 950-952. Haushofer visited Hitler in prison after the failure of Hitler's and Ludendorff's Beer Hall coup. This chapter and such sections as that on "Japan and Jewry" may have been directly influenced by Haushofer.

means was to pass powerful columns of fast-moving tanks, strongly protected by aircraft through the forward areas . . . on to the German . . . Headquarters.

After Fuller began to apply his ideas to strategical objectives, he found Douhet's theories somewhat similar. The latter held that

the vital area . . . was the will of the civil population; for were it broken by terror, the whole machinery of government and with it of military direction would collapse. . . . Though, in idea, these two theories ran parallel, in application they differed radically. Whereas the first demanded the integration of army and air force, the second was based on their separation, the army becoming a police force which did no more than occupy a country . . . subdued by air attack.[24]

By forbidding fixed fortifications and a mass army the Allies had pushed the new German army toward mechanization. The *Blitzkrieg*, as Heinz Guderian of the Motorized Transport Division of the new army put it, came from "Fuller, Liddell Hart, and Martel," and especially from Liddell Hart's emphasis on "long-range strokes . . . against communications, and . . . armoured division[s] combining panzer and panzer-infantry units." As Liddell Hart describes it, "The *Blitzkrieg* was aimed to cut the enemy's main arteries of supply far back, and thus produce the collapse of his army, while spreading demoralization [with the help of subversion and terror propaganda] in the hinterland—and in the opposing government. . . . The essential elements were: combination of low-flying attack with the armor; keeping up a continuously fast pace by a torrent-like process of by-passing resistance or varying the thrust-point; pushing on by night without pause; keeping the enemy puzzled as to the real objective by threatening several simultaneously." The Air Force (*Luftwaffe*), though organized as a separate service, had the primary task of aiding the ground forces by paralyzing the enemy's air power, communications, and command structures, and by attacking tactical objectives. The infantry specialized in the infiltration tactics advocated in Erwin Rommel's *Infanterie Greift An* of 1937. Since "there could be no question for the time being of even approaching [the Allies'] standard of equipment," the Germans, Guderian noted, had to rely on

24 *The Second World War, 1939-1945: A Strategical and Tactical History* (London, 1948), 36-39.

"superior organization and leadership. A tight concentration of our limited forces in large units . . . would, we hoped, compensate for our numerical inferiority." The high command originally opposed a separate armored arm, but Hitler backed it and mechanization.[25]

The Germans rejected the infantry tank idea and went beyond the official British cavalry tank doctrine. The German Panzer division was a striking force of tank brigades, motorized infantry, artillery, and engineers with much more power and mobility than those of similar armored formations in other armies. The Panzer divisions struck suddenly on comparatively narrow fronts, the tanks generally pushing through with only occasional aid from their accompanying infantry and engineers. The infantry, the later Panzer grenadiers, were usually used against remaining enemy strongpoints while the tank spearheads attempted to turn tactical into strategic success. Artillery was replaced, insofar as possible, by the dive bomber. The fairly small artillery components of the Panzer divisions were used as antitank forces or against enemy antitank defenses. German armored doctrine had its weaknesses, but it was far in advance of that of the French or the Russians, whose tanks were tied to the infantry. On land, as in the air, somewhat sounder British doctrine did not offset existing weapons deficiencies and shortages. The same situation existed in the political field, where Hitler's early lead in the rearmament race enabled him to take advantage of his hesitant, unready, and divided enemies. Like Napoleon, Hitler had gained control of the greatest European power of his time. Though he could not have won his victories without Germany's industries and military skills, it was he

who provided the indispensable leadership, the flair for grasping opportunities, the boldness in using them. . . . Luck and the disunity of his opponents will account for much of Hitler's success as it will of Napoleon's—but not for all. . . . His abilities [were]: his mastery of the irrational factors in politics, his insight into the weaknesses of his opponents, his gift for simplification, his sense of timing, his willingness to take risks. An opportunist entirely

[25] Guderian, *Panzer Leader,* trans. Constantine Fitzgibbon (New York, 1952), 20, 35; Letter from Liddell Hart, August 26, 1959. The Germans refer to Guderian as the "creator" of their armored forces and doctrine. Rommel, *Infantry Attacks,* trans. G. E. Kiddé (Washington, 1944). Also the Austrian L. R. von Eimansberger, *Kampwagenkrieg* (Munich, 1934); Eddy Bauer, *La Guerre des Blindés* (Paris, 1947), and Telford Taylor, *The March of Conquest* (New York, 1958).

without principle, . . . he retained an unshaken belief in his historic role and in himself as a creature of destiny.[26]

The Three Democracies

During the twenties and thirties France built the most elaborate fortifications of modern times, the Maginot Line, a symbol of the failures of the French offensives of 1914 to 1917 and of the war weariness which had affected the victors even more deeply than the vanquished. France had forced Germany to adopt the *armée de métier*; she reduced her own armaments expenses by the now traditional method of reducing active service for her conscripts to eighteen months in 1923 and to twelve months in 1928. A long service nucleus of 100,000 men—roughly equaling the *Reichswehr*—protected France against a sudden attack and trained the conscripts. Two year service was restored in 1935, for the "lean years" when the number of conscripts would be cut in half. The French standing army of 1939 was about half the size of the French army of 1914 and a bit more than a third as large as Hitler's army. France was markedly inferior to Germany in both industry and population; the Maginot Line was a shield to protect the slow mobilization of Allied arms and manpower before the counteroffensives into Germany. There is no doubt that this was the kind of army the average Frenchman wanted, or that, as Jaurès had predicted, this short-term citizens' army was thoroughly defensive-minded. The Third Republic—in spite of certain deep social and political weaknesses—continued to spend large sums on armaments, but this money was spent for the wrong things at the wrong time or—in the case of the sums lent to France's new eastern allies—thrown away by appeasement. The French army relied on steel and concrete and old-fashioned infantry-artillery offensives with tanks supporting the infantry. Mass armies would again fill up the whole Franco-German frontier; both commands, the French believed, would be forced to use the slow hole-punching tactics of 1918. The French tanks were not far inferior in numbers to the Germans, and Charles de Gaulle, whose later political role has caused him to be rather overrated as a military thinker, had proposed six very large armored formations—with 500 tanks each—in 1934.

---

[26] Bullock, *Hitler*, 735-736. For German army organization see B. Mueller-Hillebrand, *Das Heer, 1933-1945* (Darmstadt, 1955). The best book on the "Strategy of Terror" is by Louis de Jong, *The German Fifth Column in the Second World War* (Chicago, 1956).

But De Gaulle's proposals and those of other tank experts such as General Emile Alléhaut found little support. De Gaulle's major premise—a return to the *armée de métier*—was as unacceptable to the high command as to French public opinion. His six divisions would have required 3000 tanks at a time when French heavy tank production was about four per month. The high command began to form tank divisions in 1938. By 1940 they had three light mechanized and three tank divisions with 220 and 150 tanks each. Their heavy tanks were about as fast as the German mediums, and their light tanks were better armored than those of the Germans. But they had few mobile antitank guns or land mines. Their command procedures were geared to the infantry. Their attempted counterattacks were hours or even days too late.[27]

French Air Minister Pierre Cot later admitted that Germany had about three times as many first-line planes as France and about four times as many combat planes, but claimed that "The French Air Force was . . . all that it possibly could have been, if one remembers the relative power of production and foreign supply facilities of France and Germany." The French aircraft industry was nationalized in 1936, partly as a matter of Socialist policy and partly because it was in desperate need of capital and modernization. But nationalization seems only to have added new red tape, though a visiting American industrialist reported that French machine tools and workers were excellent. French designers had toyed too long with Douhet's all-purpose fighter-bomber. Too much attention had been paid to prototypes and too little to production. After reluctantly consenting to the formation of a separate Air Force in 1933, the French high command successfully hobbled its thinking. In Cot's words,

[27] On French military thought as a whole see Eugène Carrias, *La Pensée militaire française* (Paris, 1960). Vivian Rowe, *The Great Wall of France* (London, 1959) supplements General A. G. Pretelat, *Le Destin tragique de la ligne Maginot* (Paris, 1950) and Colonel Rodolphe, *Combats dans la ligne Maginot* (Paris, 1949). Key pre-war works were Generals N. Chauvineau, *Une Invasion est-elle encore possible?* (Paris, 1938), G. Debeney, *Sur la Sécurité militaire de la France* (Paris, 1930), and Jean Mordacq, *Les Leçons de 1914 et la prochaine guerre* (Paris, 1934), and De Gaulle's *The Edge of the Sword*, trans. Gerard Hopkins (1932, New York, 1960) and *The Army of the Future* (1934, Philadelphia, 1941). Alléhaut's major works were *La Guerre n'est pas une industrie* (Paris, 1925) and *Être Prêts* (Paris, 1935). Key postwar studies are by Generals Georges Ferré, *Le Défaut de l'Armure* (Paris, 1948), Gaston Roton, *Années cruciales* (Paris, 1947), and Tony Albord, *Pourquoi cela est arrivé: ou les responsibilités d'une génération militaire (1918-1939)* (Nantes, 1946).

French aviation was merely a juxtaposition of small aerial units.
. . . In peacetime, for convenience of administration and command, these small units were organized into air fleets. . . . But after . . . mobilization, . . . 86 per cent of the air fleets . . . were to be dissolved into pursuit groups and observation escadrilles, at the disposal of the commanders of the land armies.

In spite of their defensive-mindedness, or rather because they had placed too much of their trust in fixed land defenses, the French air defense system was very weak. It relied on observers using civilian telephones and was very short of antiaircraft guns and fighters. In 1940 these weaknesses led to constant French pressure for more British fighters and against British bombing which might provoke German retaliation. In the words of the British official history, "The French had no effective and reasoned body of air doctrine. . . . Not to put too fine a point upon it, our Allies were desperately afraid of the *Luftwaffe;* and in truth the state of their air defenses gave them every reason to be." [28]

Britain and United States reverted to their traditional military policies, tempered by a new respect for research and military theory. The services' chief problem was to extract funds from reluctant legislators. The strong Anglo-American antimilitary tradition had been reinforced by war weariness, postwar disillusionment, and concern with pressing economic problems. The command of the sea remained all important to both countries. President Franklin D. Roosevelt was a big-

---

[28] Cot, *Triumph of Treason* (Chicago, 1944), 278, 441. Denis Richards, *The Fight at Odds (Royal Air Force, 1939-1945,* ed. Denis Richards and Hilary St. George Saunders, I, London, 1953), 111. L. F. Ellis, *The War in France and Flanders, 1939-1940 (History of the Second World War, United Kingdom Military Series,* ed. J. R. M. Butler, London, 1953), 25, gives the French 549 fighters (131 of them old), 186 bombers (all but 11 old), and 377 reconnaissance and observation planes (of which 316 were old). General Jean Hébrard's figures in *Vingt-cinq années d'aviation militaire* (2 vols., Paris, 1946) are similar.

Pétain, who had been Inspector-General of Aerial Defense from 1931 to 1934, thought that bombing raids might shake enemy morale at the outbreak of war. Then the planes should be parceled out to aid the infantry. One Air Force theorist called for two separate air forces: one to delay the enemy's approach to the Line (*d'arrêt*) and one to co-operate with the infantry and armor in counterattacks. In short, the French army's ideas of *couverture* (the main function of the Line), linear defense, and counteroffensives can be found in French air literature. Many wartime surveys of French doctrine failed to see the importance of the 1918 type of counteroffensive in French military thought. The high command of 1940 had not prepared defenses in depth. It did not stand on the defensive, but sent its mobile forces into Belgium and exposed them to a surprise flank attack through the Ardennes.

navy man, though the first naval bill of his administration was disguised as relief for the hard-pressed steel and shipbuilding industries. The United States did not match Japan's forced-draft construction after the expiration of the Washington treaties in 1936, but the United States Navy never fell far below the 5/3 ratio. That ratio, however, had tacitly assumed Anglo-American naval supremacy in the North Atlantic. Congress did not begin a "two ocean" naval program until after the fall of France in June, 1940. The previous year it had rejected a proposal for dredging for a submarine base on Guam. The navy of the 1930's, like all peacetime military organizations, was weak in some elements and strong in others. Its torpedoes were inferior to those of the Japanese, but its system of high-pressure, high-temperature steam propulsion was the best in the world. The navy had led in aircraft carrier development. Marine Corps' amphibious doctrine was to develop "the most far-reaching tactical innovation of the war." The Fleet Train was to become a floating base for that combination of floating air power, floating gun power, and floating army which won the Pacific War. As usual, the weakest component of United States sea power was merchant shipping.[29]

The Anglo-French navies began the Second World War where the First had ended, in control of the bottlenecks at Scapa Flow, Dover, Gibraltar, and Alexandria. They had seventeen battleships and battle cruisers to two German battle cruisers and three "pocket battleships." Neutral Italy had two modernized battleships completing and two others being modernized. The German and Italian navies were weak in the air; for most operations they had to borrow planes from their independent air forces. The Germans had only fifty-six submarines, thirty of which were small coastal boats which could not operate outside the North Sea. Admiral Karl Doenitz'

[29] Fuller, *Second World War*, 207. "The fate of the Philippines is . . . indissolubly connected with that of Guam, . . . indeed, . . . the issue of an American-Japanese war would primarily be decided by the fate of Guam." Bywater, *Sea Power in the Pacific*, 265. Earl S. Pomeroy, *Pacific Outpost: American Strategy in Guam and Micronesia* (Palo Alto, 1951); Jeter A. Isely and Philip A. Crowl, *The U. S. Marines and Amphibious War: Its Theory and Its Practice in the Pacific* (Princeton, 1951). On naval research see Harold G. Bowen, *Ships, Machinery, and Mossbacks* (Princeton, 1954), and William Frederick Durand, *Adventures in the Navy, in Education, Science, Engineering, and in War* (New York, 1953). For British amphibious developments see L. E. H. Maund, *Assault from the Sea* (London, 1949) and Fergusson, *The Watery Maze*.

later statement that Germany was "never prepared for war against England. . . . A realistic policy would have given Germany nearly a thousand U-boats from the beginning" was both strategically sound and politically naïve. Something had to be left to diplomacy, considering Hitler's need for keeping the jump on Allied and Russian preparations. The Munich agreement of 1938 had certainly confirmed Hitler's old belief that Britain would give him a free hand in Eastern Europe. The British had spent large sums on naval rearmament, but a proposed "two-power standard" of equality with Germany and Japan proved too expensive. Air power had to be given a higher priority. So the British navy was ready for war in Europe, but was below strength in the Pacific. The naval staff was chiefly concerned with German surface raiders. It had told the Shipping Defense Advisory Committee in 1937 that its Asdic submarine detection device was so efficient that "the submarine should never again be able to present us with the problem we were faced with in 1917." [30]

The creation of the Royal Air Force, the world's first separate air force, had been partly the result of two daylight raids on London in that year. The public had demanded the permanent withdrawal of certain air units from France under a separate Air Ministry and the formation of an Independent Air Force to retaliate against German cities. As General William Robertson, then Chief of the Imperial General Staff, later wrote, the excitement generated by these raids proved that "Home Defence whether on land, on sea, or in the air, will, except perhaps in . . . a great crisis . . . invariably have to be given precedence over operations abroad." The War Cabinet finally turned the problem over to its trouble shooter, Jan Christian Smuts, the former Boer general who was one of the greatest self-taught soldiers of the twentieth century. He reported on August 17, 1917, that

[30] S. W. Roskill, The War at Sea, I (History of the Second World War, United Kingdom Military Series, London, 1954), 34, 41-62. On research see Dreyer, The Sea Heritage (London, 1956), on the general situation, Admiral Sir Herbert Richmond, Sea Power in the Modern World (New York, 1934). Hitler told his admirals in 1938 that there would be no war with Britain before 1944. They planned to have 10 battleships and battle cruisers, 4 carriers, and 270 U-boats by that time. See Karl Doenitz, Memoirs: 10 years and 20 days, trans. R. H. Stevens, in collaboration David Woodward (Cleveland, 1959), and Erich Raeder, Struggle at Sea, trans. Edward Fitzgerald (London, 1959). Anthony Martienssen, Hitler and His Admirals (New York, 1949), and F. H. Hinsley, Hitler's Strategy (Cambridge, 1951), are based on the Fuehrer Conferences on Matters Dealing with the German Navy (3 vols., Washington, 1946).

The position of an air service is quite different from that of the
artillery [which] . . . could never be used . . . except as a weapon
in military or naval or air operations. . . . Air service on the contrary can be used as an independent means of war operations . . .
and for that reason the creation of an Air Staff for planning and
directing independent air operations will soon be pressing. . . . In
settling in advance the types to be built the operations for which
they are intended apart from naval and military use should be
clearly kept in view. . . . Otherwise engines and machines useless
for independent strategical operations may be built. . . . Continuous and intense [aerial] pressure against the chief industrial
centres of the enemy as well as on his lines of communication
may form an important factor in bringing about peace. . . . The
progressive exhaustion of the man-power of the combatant nations
will more and more . . . [make] this war . . . one of arms and
machinery rather than of men. . . . The submarine has already
shown . . . startling developments . . . in naval warfare. Aircraft
is destined to work an even more far-reaching change in land
warfare.[81]

Though the war had ended before the Independent Air
Force could bomb Berlin, Hugh Trenchard, the R. A. F.'s
Chief of Staff in 1918 and from 1919 to 1929, had become a
major proponent of strategic bombing. The first major step
toward British air rearmament in the thirties resulted from
Hitler's attempted Austrian coup of 1934. "Since the day of
the air," Prime Minister Stanley Baldwin told the House of
Commons, "the old frontiers are gone. When you think of
the defences of England, you no longer think of the chalk
cliffs of Dover; you think of the Rhine." Winston Churchill,
then out of office and out of favor in the Conservative party,
thought that Baldwin's proposal to double the R. A. F. by
1939 was not enough. The illegal *Luftwaffe* was already two-
thirds as large as the British home defense force; if Germany
forged ahead, she might never be overtaken because of her
large reserve of trained civilian pilots. London was very vulnerable to air attack, "a tremendous fat cow . . . tied up to

[81] H. A. Jones, *The War in the Air, Appendices* (Oxford, 1937), 10-11. The
problem of co-ordination with the two older services did not appear insupera-
ble. Smuts thought that "all Air units detailed for naval or military work
should . . . come directly under the orders . . . of the commanders of the
forces with which they are associated, . . . and that a considerable number of
officers of both Navy and Army should be attached . . . to the Air Service in
order that naval and military commanders . . . may be . . . able to utilize
. . . the contingents of the air forces which will be put at their disposal."
The quotation from Robertson is from *Soldiers and Statesmen* (2 vols., London, 1926), II, 18. His *From Private to Field Marshal* (Boston, 1921) is most
interesting.

attract the beasts of prey." By 1938 the Germans were well ahead of the British in the air, though they may have exaggerated their lead for propaganda purposes. The R. A. F. had been given top priority in 1937, but fighters were not to be given priority over bombers until after war was declared, thus emphasizing Robertson's point that home defense requirements will almost always be given precedence by a representative government. British plane production passed that of Germany in 1940; the new British Hurricane and Spitfire fighters were excellent. But the R. A. F. lacked heavy bombers—though its four-engined bombers had been designed in 1935—dive bombers, and transports, except on paper.[32]

The United States Army Air Corps, like other branches of the army, paid much attention to weapons development and plans for industrial mobilization, partly to avoid obsolescence and fruitless requests for funds. In January, 1939, when Roosevelt asked Congress for a rapid build-up of American air power, the Air Corps was a skeleton force of less than 20,000 officers and men and 1,700 planes. But it had developed a "well-defined doctrine" and the "most advanced bomber in the world"—the four-motored B-17 (Flying Fortress), which had been designed in 1934 and flight-tested in 1935. These factors and "its gigantic production possibilities . . . were to allow the United States to build, in a few years, the most powerful air army in the world." Meanwhile the public had been treated to the usual argument about a separate air force and the colorful Billy Mitchell. The airmen had not won the first argument, though a General Headquarters Air Force had been formed by consolidating several tactical air units. The public's interest in defense against seaborne invasion had led Mitchell to stress the big bomber as the best means of meeting this essentially bogus threat and had involved him in much wrangling with the navy. In public the airmen stressed defense and the interdiction of possible enemy bases within range of the United States. But the doctrine taught at the Air Corps Tactical School was closely related to that of Douhet, though it emphasized industrial war-

---

[32] Many experts assumed that the next war would begin with a shattering gas and incendiary attack on London, the world's largest metropolis. See the writings of J. M. Spaight, an Air Ministry civil servant, especially *Air Power and the Cities* (London, 1930), and *Air Power and War Rights* (3d ed., London, 1947). On the development of the R. A. F. see Lord Templewood [Samuel Hoare], *Empire of the Air* (London, 1956), Philip Joubert de la Ferté, *The Third Service: The Story behind the Royal Air Force* (London, 1955), and J. C. Slessor's autobiography, *The Central Blue* (New York, 1957).

fare rather than the breaking of enemy morale through indiscriminate bombing.

The special mission of the air arm . . . should be to attack the whole of the "enemy national structure." . . . The military, political, economic, and social aspects of a nation's life are closely and absolutely interdependent, so that dislocations in any one will bring sympathetic disturbances . . . in all. . . . Modern war . . . places an especial importance upon a nation's "industrial web." . . . A moral collapse brought about by disturbances in this close-knit web may . . . force an enemy to surrender, but the real target is industry itself, not national morale.[33]

The ground forces were comparatively neglected in both the United States and Britain. Neither country adopted peacetime conscription, but the United States National Defense Act of 1920 authorized plans for industrial mobilization and the largest peacetime army in the history of the United States. The regulars—with a ceiling of 280,000 enlisted men—were to garrison overseas bases, form striking forces for immediate duty, and provide the cadres for wartime expansion. The paper strength of the National Guard was set at 425,000. The reserves—originally recruited from veterans and then from college and summer volunteers—were to be somewhat more numerous than the Guard. But Congress never appropriated enough money to bring the land forces even close to these ceilings. The regulars were reduced to 132,000 men in 1922 and remained well under that figure until 1936. The Guard was also less than half as large as that contemplated in 1920 and many reserve units simply went out of existence. Douglas MacArthur, the Chief of Staff during the depression (1930-1935), scaled these targets down to 165,000 regulars and 235,000 National Guard. The army reached its new goal in 1937, but the National Guard had not made it when it was federalized in 1940. There were only three fully-organized (but under strength) infantry and two half-strength cavalry divisions in the United States in 1939. All were armed with a combination of samples and obsolete First World War material. An Armored Force was not organized until July 10, 1940, nearly a month after the French government had surrendered to Hitler. The Armored Force then fell heir to 400

[33] Wesley Frank Craven and James Lea Cate, eds., *The Army Air Forces in World War II* (7 vols., Chicago, 1948-1958), I, 51-52, 71. Thomas H. Greer, *The Development of Air Doctrine in the Army Air Corps* (Maxwell Field, 1956).

light tanks and 18 old mediums. A new medium tank was in production, but only 66 such tanks—instead of the 1500 promised—were to be ready by June, 1941.[34]

The British protagonists of mechanization—Swinton, Fuller, Liddell Hart, and Martel, the only one to hold a high command during the Second World War—were more honored abroad than at home, partly because of the British army's lack of money and partly because of the belief that Britain would not send a large army to the Continent. The aims of Baldwin's "limited liability" rearmament program of the middle thirties were primarily political—to warn aggressors, particularly Italy and Japan, and to assure the British public that Britain would support the League. The function of the divisions to be re-equipped under the Baldwin program were officially defined as "the defence of imperial commitments, including anti-aircraft defence at home." The mechanized cavalry and motorized artillery were designed for colonial service; they were given no heavy armor or special tactical aircraft. Britain's Continental friends were to be specifically told to expect no help from British land forces. Though French pressure for British troops in 1914 had been perfectly understandable, the French would have been better off if the British "Continentalists" had not promised them troops. They might then have abandoned the *offensive à outrance* and Joffre's suicidal continuation of that strategy after the Marne. Now France was protected by the Line and Hitler had formally promised to respect Belgian neutrality. This reversion to a "blue-water" strategy had found typical expression in Liddell Hart's *The British Way in Warfare* of 1932, before the German danger became obvious. Its author then advocated a return to the

distinctive British practise of war . . . based on economic pressure exercised through seapower. This naval body had two arms; one financial, . . . the subsidizing and military provisioning of allies; the other military . . . seaborne expeditions against the enemy's

[34] Mark S. Watson, *Chief of Staff: Prewar Plans and Preparations (The United States Army in World War II: The War Department*, I, Washington, 1950), chap. ii. One account of tank theory is Mildred Hanson Gillie, *Forging the Thunderbolt: A History of the Development of the Armored Force* (Harrisburg, 1947).

Lockmiller, *Crowder*, and Palmer, *America in Arms* discuss the Act of 1920. The Selective Service Act of 1940, though prepared by the General Staff, was pushed by private pressure groups to avoid the charge of War Department "militarism." See Henry L. Stimson and McGeorge Bundy, *On Active Service in Peace and War* (New York, 1948), 377-379.

vulnerable extremities. . . . In the last war the conditions of industrial civilization had made her enemy more susceptible to economic pressure than in the past. And because of her geography her navy was better able to apply it. Yet for the first time in her history she made it a subsidiary weapon, and grasped the glittering sword of Continental manufacture.[85]

In addition, the tank experts did not always agree with each other. Fuller stressed what Liddell Hart has called the land-battleship concept. "Battle Cruiser" tanks were to be the core of a "floating mechanical army" launched from "our floating mechanical base. . . . This force propels itself ashore, crawls up the beach and moves straight inland. . . . Freed from railways, . . . it can spread havoc . . . and, when threatened by a superior force, it can make for the coast, . . . swim out to the fleet and re-embark." Planes could never hit targets as small as tanks; bombers could do no more damage than armored forces unless they used poison gas. Liddell Hart emphasized armored infantry or "tank marines," night attacks, combined air and tank operations, and deep strategic penetrations, but neither Fuller nor Liddell Hart was satisfied with the compromise Mobile Division of 1937. Most of its tanks were light cavalry tanks armed with machine guns. Its accompanying infantry—in unarmored trucks and tracked troop-carriers— were not numerous enough, though the Division might have been very useful against the even lighter Italian tank forces. Such a force was not even consistent with a "limited liability" program, since Liddell Hart felt that "the help we should give to our Allies was with the air force and a high quality armoured force [of powerful gun-armed tanks], rather than an infantry mass." Hitler's march into Prague was the turning point. In 1939 Britain began to prepare for all-out war. But the army had to be remodeled, as well as expanded, before it would be ready to face the Germans. It raised its sights from five to thirty-two divisions, but this absorbed money and facilities which were needed to implement the 1938 decision to create more armored divisions. Conscription was reintroduced. The Mobile Division was split into two armored divisions and a third was being formed in Egypt, though new names did not automatically mean more tanks. When war began the British had only 146 fairly modern

[85] (London, 1932), 7, 37, 41. One of the most vigorous critics of the tank school was Victor W. Germains, *The Mechanization of War* (London, 1927). The Dominions heartily favored "limited liability." See the very important work by Lord Hankey, *Diplomacy by Conference* (New York, 1947).

tanks and 1,002 light reconnaissance machines. Before Dunkirk 437 more modern tanks were built, but 210 were lost in Flanders. Thirteen British infantry divisions (three of them only partially equipped) were in France when the Germans struck in May, 1940, but the First Armoured Division was just leaving for Cherbourg. Part of the division was then diverted to Calais, and it never fought as a unit.[36]

[36] Fuller, *On Future Warfare*, 142-143, 101. Letter from Liddell Hart, August 25, 1959. Seventeen years younger than Fuller and seven years younger than T. E. Lawrence or Guderian, Liddell Hart was an infantryman who had revised the British infantry regulations before being invalided out of the army in 1924. His first large book after his conversion to the tank was *The Remaking of Modern Armies* (London, 1927), although he believes that *Paris, or the Future of War* (London, 1925) "had a bigger effect because of its impact on the new C. I. G. S., Milne. It was made the textbook for the Experimental Mechanised Force which he then decided to create . . . [and] taken up by Trenchard as a textbook for the R. A. F. Indeed it was Trenchard who introduced it to Milne by presenting him (and the First Sea Lord) with a copy of it." *Ibid.* On all army policy questions in the immediate pre-war period see R. J. Minney, *The Private Papers of Hore-Belisha* (London, 1960).

For tank production see M. N. Postan, *British War Production (United Kingdom Civil Series*, London, 1952), 183-195. Although British tanks, type for type, were superior in armor and fire power, their infantry tanks were inferior in speed and maneuverability, and the division between mobile brigades and heavily armored infantry tanks was unnecessarily complex. But German superiority was due as much to doctrine as to design. Too many British tanks were misused to support static defenses or in poorly prepared counterattacks. Ellis, *France and Flanders*, 353.

It is still hard to assess the "dress rehearsals" of the interwar era, but much can be learned from Hugh Thomas, *The Spanish Civil War* (London, 1961) and David H. Zook, *The Conduct of the Chaco War* (New York, 1960). On Latin America generally see Edwin Lieuwen, *Arms and Politics in Latin America* (New York, 1960). Che Guevara, *Guerrilla Warfare* (New York, 1961) is something more than a Latin American popularization of Mao Tse Tung.

Chapter 10

The Second World War

The Opening Battles

THE First World War was a world war insofar as hundreds of thousands of non-Europeans participated in the major campaigns at sea and around the Central Powers' territories in Europe and the Near East. Its strategy was in large part determined by the Germans, who headed an empire rather than a real coalition. The Second World War consisted of four related major wars, each presenting separate military-political problems. Some British historians call it the Second German War, with Italy joining the Germans. Its outcome was partly determined by the outcome of a Russo-German War or, more accurately, the Great Patriotic War of the Soviet Union. Less than three-fifths of the Soviet peoples were Great Russians, and this proportion was perhaps even lower at the time when their armies finally checked Hitler's 1942 offensive. The United States' defeat of Japan in the Great Pacific War gave the Chinese, though not the Chinese Nationalists, victory in the War for East Asia. This war, though the United States did not recognize the fact until too late, lasted for a bit over seventeen years, and ended with the victory of the Chinese version of national Communism as the Russo-German War had resulted in victory for the Soviet version. The Western Allies did not accomplish their original war aim, a free Poland; and the United States did not accomplish its aim, the kind of China predicated by the Washington Conference. By the end of the War for East Asia, the four powers which had signed the Munich Agreement—Britain, France, Italy, and a new German Federal Republic, which became sovereign on May 5, 1955—were jointly rebuilding their military power for protection against Russia, and the United States had signed a Mutual Security Pact with Japan on September 1, 1951. There had been little fighting during the Second World War in the Asian territories of the old Ottoman Empire, the scene of the most extensive Asiatic campaigns during the first conflict. After 1954 the Near East was possibly the softest spot between the two blocs into which the Big Five of the Second World War were now divided.[1]

The details of the Anglo-French decision to guarantee Poland, Rumania, Greece, and Turkey after Hitler's violation of the Munich Agreement are still obscure, but military considerations seem hardly to have entered the picture. As Chamberlain's biographer noted, "If Chamberlain and Halifax were innocents, they were innocent of playing power politics." Chamberlain reintroduced conscription to show that Britain meant business and opened negotiations with Russia, the only Eastern European power with a large land army. The approach to Russia failed for reasons which Chamberlain had secretly noted before it began. "I have no belief whatever in

[1] There are few "revelations" in the material still pouring from the presses. *The Memoirs of Field-Marshal the Viscount Montgomery of Alamein, K. G.* (Cleveland, 1958) said little that he had not said before and are no better than Omar Bradley, *A Soldier's Story* (New York, 1951). Fuller's *Second World War* and Liddell Hart, *Strategy, the Indirect Approach* (New York, 1954) are important. The closest approach to the Shotwell series is Arnold and Veronica Toynbee, eds., *Survey of International Affairs, 1939-1946* (11 vols., London, 1952-1958). The only account of great events by a participant comparable to Churchill's *Second World War* (6 vols., Boston, 1948-1953) is Trotsky's *History of the Russian Revolution*, trans. Max Eastman (3 vols. in one, New York, 1936), or *The Russian Revolution*, ed. F. W. Dupee (Garden City, 1959). De Gaulle's *War Memoirs* (3 vols., New York, 1952-1960) are supplemented by Arthur Layton Funk, *Charles de Gaulle: The Crucial Years, 1943-1944* (Norman, 1959). *The Fall of Mussolini*, trans. Frances Frenaye, ed. Max Ascoli (New York, 1948) is vintage *Duce*.

Desmond Flowers and James Reeves' anthology, *The Taste of Courage: The War, 1939-1945* (New York, 1960) and William L. Shirer, *The Rise and Fall of the Third Reich* (New York, 1960) are better than Louis L. Snyder, *The War: A Concise History, 1939-1945* (New York, 1960). Raymond Aron, *The Century of Total War* (New York, 1955), may survive. Cyril Falls, *The Second World War* (3d ed., London, 1950), needs revision. Marc Bloch, *Strange Defeat* (New York, 1954), is one of several remarkable works produced by the scholars of German-occupied Europe. The most nearly comparable German work is Friedrich Meinecke, *Die Deutsche Katastrophe* (Wiesbaden, 1947). There are also a number of excellent journalistic accounts. George H. Johnston, *The Toughest Fighting in the World* (New York, 1943), is as good as Jack Belden, *Retreat with Stilwell* (New York, 1943) and *Still Time to Die* (Philadelphia, 1945), and Chester Wilmot's opinionated *The Struggle for Europe* (London, 1952) is still good reading.

Other outstanding memoirs are Robert L. Eichelberger, *Our Jungle Road to Tokyo* (New York, 1950), Howard Kippenberger, *Infantry Brigadier* (New York, 1951), Charles B. MacDonald, *Company Commander* (Washington, 1947), and *The Stilwell Papers*, ed. Theodore H. White (New York, 1948). The personality of one Japanese general emerges from Frank Reel, *The Case of General Yamashita* (Chicago, 1949). Many of the novels of this war are thin and derivative. Their authors were only too familiar with the classics of the First World War. As a colleague once remarked, one can be only so naked and so dead. Theodore Plivier and Erich Maria Remarque were among the few novelists to write about both wars. Bill Mauldin, *Up Front* (New York, 1945), is a remarkable work, but Mauldin was one of the few really untutored observers of the Second World War.

her ability to maintain an effective offensive, even if she wanted to. And I distrust her motives, which seem to me to have little connection with our ideas of liberty. . . . Moreover, she is both hated and suspected by many of the smaller States, notably by Poland, Roumania, and Finland." Hitler had more to offer Stalin. Their Nonaggression Pact of August 23, 1939, sealed the fate of Poland, gave Stalin a free hand in the Baltic states and Bessarabia, and nullified the Western Allies' faint hopes of a "long, solid and durable front" in the east and the denial to Germany of Eastern Europe's resources. In the spring British and French staff representatives had agreed that they must hope for another war of attrition, a war in which their only immediate weapon would be blockade, which depended upon their only immediate asset, their command of the sea. Their enemies

would be more fully prepared for war, . . . would have superiority in air and land forces, but would be inferior at sea and in general economic strength. . . . We must be prepared to face a major offensive directed against either France or Great Britain or against both. To defeat such an offensive we should have to concentrate all our initial efforts, and during this time our major strategy should be defensive. Nevertheless, Italian action in North Africa . . . [and] our control of Italian communications to East Africa [may present opportunities for] obtaining, without undue cost, successes against Italy which might reduce her will to fight. Our subsequent policy should be directed to holding Germany and to dealing decisively with Italy, while . . . building our military strength to a point at which we shall be in a position to undertake the offensive against Germany. During these stages the steady and rigorous application of economic pressure would be reducing the powers of resistance of our enemies . . . [while] all the resources of diplomacy should be directed to securing the benevolent neutrality or active assistance of other powers, particularly the United States of America.[2]

In a later appreciation the staff representatives saw little hope for Poland, but hoped that her resistance might give the

[2] Keith Feiling, *The Life of Neville Chamberlain* (London, 1947), 403-409. J. R. M. Butler, *Grand Strategy, Volume II: September 1939-June 1941* (*United Kingdom Military Series,* London, 1957), 10-11. Volume I, on the prewar period, has not appeared. The author continues, "When allowance is made for the initial non-belligerency of Italy, for the collapse of France, and for the extension of the struggle in 1941, it is remarkable how faithfully the main lines of this strategy of 1939 were followed: the early defensive phase, the elimination of Italy after the conquest of Italian East and North Africa, and the final defeat of Germany, with the active assistance of the United States."

Western Allies up to six months' time (it proved to be three weeks) and perhaps blunt Germany's striking power. Poland's fate, they concluded, "'will depend upon the ultimate outcome of the war.'" Hitler attacked Poland nine days after his deal with Stalin. The Germans cut up the Polish army in ten days with tank-plane teams operating under ideal weather and terrain conditions. Only two-thirds of the Polish army of 1,700,000 men was mobilized; less than half the men reached their concentration areas. The Germans lost some 10,000 killed, the Poles about 66,000. Russia then occupied her share of Poland and the Baltic states. Finland resisted and was defeated in the Winter War of 1939-1940; the Red Army's poor showing in the early stages of this war was seemingly due to political miscalculation. An Allied expedition to aid Finland never got started. The French had hoped to divert Hitler's attention, the British to interfere with iron ore shipments through the Norwegian port of Narvik. On April 8 the Allies mined Norwegian waters; the next day German sea and airborne forces, aided by Norwegian fifth columnists, occupied Denmark and the four major Norwegian cities. Allied counterattacks failed, though Narvik was captured and then abandoned after the Battle of Flanders. Norway gave the Germans naval bases on the North Atlantic and a protected sea route for Swedish ore, but the German surface fleet had no major warship fit for sea at the end of the campaign. The Norwegian campaign finished Chamberlain, who was replaced by Churchill on May 10, the day that Hitler struck at three other neutrals: Belgium, Luxembourg, and the Netherlands. Curiously enough, the dynamic First Lord of the Admiralty had been among those most responsible for these various northern schemes, which had resulted in fiasco in the field, the weakening of British prestige, and even to less damage to the German surface fleet than might otherwise have been the case.

The main characteristic of his cherished products was audacity, and in his impatience he was apt to mistake [professional] criticism . . . for timidity and inertia. He seemed not always to remember that . . . what is operationally desirable may not be administratively possible . . . [and] was much too inclined to consider boldness a sufficient qualification for high command. . . . His greatness lay elsewhere, as a national leader in critical times. . . . He possessed in a supreme degree the qualities needed by the hour:

vigilance, drive, joy of battle, love of responsibility, resounding eloquence, and above all courage and faith.[3]

West of the Maginot Line lay the forested Ardennes, which the French believed impassable for armor, and then the Flanders Plain. Belgium had denounced her alliance with France in 1937 in return for a German promise to respect her neutrality. Though they spent eight months preparing temporary defenses just south of the Belgian border, the Allies never considered not aiding Belgium. They planned to move up to the Dyle River with about twenty-three infantry and three French light armored divisions, while the twenty-two Belgian and eight Dutch divisions blunted the German attack. The German forces in this area were in two groups: Group B (as it happened, for Belgium) under Fedor von Bock and Group A (Ardennes) under Gerd von Rundstedt. The first German plans—which would have been followed in November, 1939, and January, 1940, when attacks were cancelled because of the weather—gave Group B up to forty-three divisions, eight of them armored, and Group A twenty-two divisions with no armor. These plans, which the Allies had captured to confirm their previous view of German intentions, were radically changed in February. Hitler had been thinking of striking through the Ardennes in the rear of the Allied armies and forced such a plan on the high command after Rundstedt and his chief of staff, Erich von Manstein, had developed it on their own and had proved that it was practicable. The proportions of the two army groups were almost reversed. Group B was now given twenty-eight divisions, three of them armored. Group A struck with forty-four divisions, seven of them armored, against twelve French reserve and four cavalry divisions in the Ardennes hinge. Rundstedt broke through to the Channel in ten days. Six days later the Belgians surrendered and the British government ordered the evacuation of the B. E. F. The last British and French forces left Dunkirk on June 4; the Battle of France began

[3] *Ibid.*, 562-563. The best study of the Polish campaign is Robert Jars, *La Campagne de Pologne* (Paris, 1949). On Finland see C. Leonard Lundin, *Finland in the Second World War* (Bloomington, 1957), Waldemar Erfurth, *Der Finnische Krieg* (Wiesbaden, 1950), and Lothar Rendulic, *Gekämpft, gesiegt, geschlagen* (Heidelberg, 1952). Marshal Carl Mannerheim, *Memoirs*, trans. Count Eric Lewenhaupt (New York, 1954), estimated that the Finns lost 25,000 killed in the Winter War and the Russians four times as many. On Norway see T. K. Derry, *The Campaign in Norway* (*United Kingdom Military Series*, London, 1952), and Walther Hubatsch, *Die Deutsche Besetzung von Dänemark und Norwegen, 1940* (Göttingen, 1952).

the next day. The Germans took Paris in nine days, and the French government, now headed by the eighty-four-year-old Pétain, asked for an armistice three days later. The Maginot Line had been left like a stranded battleship by the defeat of the Allied armies in Flanders. The French may have lost 100,000 killed, the other Allies 20,000. Hitler admitted 45,000 killed and missing. In any case, the *Blitzkrieg* was cheap by World War I standards.[4]

The "Miracle of Dunkirk," like the "Miracle of the Marne," was the result of many factors. The Allies had hoped to rescue 45,000 men. They saved 366,000, about two-thirds of them British, partly because the Royal Navy had begun preparations for evacuation the day the Germans reached the Channel. Fog and smoke hindered the *Luftwaffe*. The R.A.F. threw in parts of every available air squadron to cover the evacuation, though German losses in the Dunkirk area had been only half the hopeful British estimate. The battered German surface navy did not intervene, and Allied ground forces had fought desperately to protect the beachhead. Neither high command had believed that the Allies could rescue so many men "from a half-destroyed harbour and a few miles of open

---

[4] The incomplete French estimate is 123,639 killed, missing, and captured and 200,000 wounded. *Révue historique de l'Armée*, April-June, 1950, 45. The official study is *La Campagne de France* (Paris, 1953). A. Goutard, *The Battle of France, 1940*, trans. A. R. P. Burgess (London, 1958), supplements Ellis, *France and Flanders*. See also Jean Vidalenc, *L'exode de mai-juin 1940* (Paris, 1957); Pierre Lyet, *La Bataille de France* (Paris, 1948); Louis Marin, "Gouvernement et commandement (mai-juin 1940)" (*Révue d'histoire de la deuxième guerre mondiale*, Oct., 1952, 1-28; Charles-Leon Menu, *Lumières sur les ruines* (Paris, 1953). Bauer's unreliable *Guerre des blindés* thinks that Weygand's antitank measures were more effective than Hitler would admit and that he may have lost up to 100,000 killed. Edward L. Spears, *Assignment to Catastrophe* (2 vols. New York, 1954-1955), *Liaison, 1914* (London, 1930), and *Prelude to Victory* (London, 1939) are good on both wars. Other major works on armor are Generals J. Boucher, *L'Armée blindée dans la guerre* (Paris, 1953) and F. W. von Mellenthin, *Panzer Battles, 1939-1945*, trans. H. Betzler, ed. L. C. T. Turner (London, 1955).

On the Belgians see Jane K. Miller, *Belgian Policy between Two Wars, 1919-1940* (New York, 1951); R. F. C. van Overstraeten, *Albert I-Leopold III: Vingt ans de politique militaire belge, 1920-1940* (Bruges, 1950); Marcel Chambord, *Ombres et clartés de la campagne belge de 1940* (Brussels, 1946), and "Sur la Belgique pendant la guerre" (Special number 31, July, 1958, *Révue d'histoire de la deuxième guerre mondiale*).

The best German general history is Kurt von Tippelskirch, *Geschichte des zweiten Weltkrieges* (Bonn, 1951). On the high command see Helmuth Greiner, *Die Oberste Wehrmachtführung, 1939-1943* (Wiesbaden, 1951); Hermann Teske, *Die silbernen Spiegel* (Heidelberg, 1952); Gunther Blumentritt, *Von Rundstedt, the Soldier and the Man*, trans. Cuthbert Reavely (London, 1952); Erich von Manstein, *Lost Victories*, ed. and trans., Anthony G. Powell (Chicago, 1958) and *Aus einem Soldatenleben, 1887-1939* (Bonn, 1958); and Hans-Adolf Jacobsen, *Fall Gelb: Der Kampf um den deutschen Operationsplan zur Westoffensive 1940* (Wiesbaden, 1957).

beach . . . in spite of all that the strongest army and air forces in the world at that date could do to stop it." Dazed by success and anxious to regroup his forces for the coming Battle of France, Hitler had refused to use his armor in an area which some of his generals (especially Rundstedt) felt unsuited for tank warfare. Even so, the disaster to the B. E. F. had left Britain with few effective ground forces. At the end of May the Home Forces included twenty-two infantry divisions and an incomplete armored division. The infantry divisions were less than half strength, with a sixth of the field and antitank guns to which they were entitled. There were 69 cruiser, 85 infantry, and 387 light tanks operational, and 236 training and other tanks. The men rescued at Dunkirk made "equipment, not manpower, . . . the ruling factor." With additional equipment manufactured during the summer, the Home Forces could only hope to " 'prevent the enemy from . . . tearing the guts out of the country as had happened in France and Belgium.' " Meanwhile "there seemed good ground for the opinion" of Air Chief Marshal Hugh Dowding of Fighter Command that, " 'the continued existence of the nation . . . depends upon the Royal Navy and the Fighter Command.' Indeed, the Chiefs of Staff admitted that, 'should the Germans succeed in establishing a force with its vehicles in this country, our army forces have not got the offensive power to drive it out.' "[5]

The Battles of Flanders and France set the stage for the Battles of Britain, the Atlantic, and the Mediterranean. Germany now controlled a half-circle of air and naval bases from North Cape to the Spanish border. Mussolini had entered the war without consulting Hitler, and Japan had taken a major step toward war in Southeast Asia with the occupation of French Indochina. Italy's entrance into the war raised the possibility that the combined German, Italian, and French

[5] Ellis, *France and Flanders*, 248. Basil Collier, *The Defence of the United Kingdom* (*United Kingdom Military Series*, London, 1957), 109-120. See also W. S. Chalmers, *Full Cycle: The Biography of Admiral Sir David Home Ramsay* (London, 1959) and popular accounts by David Divine, *The Nine Days of Dunkirk* (New York, 1959) and Richard Collier, *The Sands of Dunkirk* (London, 1961). Hitler's hope for peace with Britain was only incidental to his decision. A third of the already inadequate British destroyer force was lost during this and other operations in the first year of the war. This was the background for the Anglo-American bases for destroyers trade in September, 1940. Though half of the ships known to have taken part in the Dunkirk evacuation were private craft, the navy saved the most men and took the heaviest losses. The R. A. F. had not stopped the German armor, which it had not been prepared to fight, but its forces remained substantially intact at the end of the Battle of France.

surface fleets might equal the British. Japan could be checked only by the United States, which now began full-scale rearmament. Almost nothing is known about the effect of these events in Russia or of the discussions which followed the then Colonel Rotmistrov's plea for a radical revision of Russian armored tactics. Germany now controlled most of the resources of the European Continent, and the Russian and Spanish leaks in the British blockade had become torrential. During 1940 Germany received more than three million tons of supplies from Russia and nearly a quarter of a million tons more by way of Russia from the Far and Middle East. The *Blitzkrieg* had more than paid for itself and the German army was not to consume large quantities of material again until the invasion of Russia. The manpower situation was just as favorable; the use of collaborationist or slave labor was eventually to allow Germany to put two-thirds of her male population between the ages of eighteen and forty-five into the armed forces. During the first phases of the Russian war, everything was again to go according to plan. As a result Hitler was to order a cut-back in arms production in September, 1941. From the fall of France to mid-1942 or even later, "Germany's war production was not limited by . . . resources, . . . but by demand— . . . the notions of the German war leaders of what was required to win." As a result of German overconfidence both British and Russian production of tanks and planes may have topped Germany's during this period.[6]

Britain, the Mediterranean and the Atlantic

Hitler had always wished to avoid William II's mistake of adding Britain to Germany's "natural" enemies—France and Russia. He hoped that the Churchill government would be replaced by one willing to accept his terms and postponed his victory speech on rumors of a British cabinet reshuffle. The

[6] United States Strategic Bombing Survey, *Over-All Report (European War)* (Washington, 1945), 31. Garthoff, *Soviet Military Doctrine,* 308-315, discusses the available materials on Russian tank doctrine during this crucial period. A career officer's discussion of German forced labor is Konstantin Hierl, *Im Dienst für Deutschland, 1918-1945* (Heidelberg, 1954). In July, 1944, there were about eight million foreigners working in Germany and ten million men in the German armed forces. *Bilanz des zweiten Weltkrieges* (Oldenburg, 1953), 215-221, 267-285. The British hope that the exploitation of the Continent would strain the German economy may "have done less harm than an overdose of the harsh truth would have done." W. K. Hancock and M. M. Gowing, *British War Economy (United Kingdom Civil Series,* London, 1949), 100. W. N. Medlicott, *The Economic Blockade* (2 vols., *United Kingdom Civil Series,* London, 1952, 1959).

navy had been studying the invasion of Britain since November, 1939, but Raeder did not mention it to Hitler until the German army reached the Channel. Hitler did not direct the army and *Luftwaffe* to begin planning for an invasion until July 2. Two weeks later he told them that, "Since England, in spite of her militarily hopeless situation, shows no signs of coming to terms, I have decided to prepare a landing operation . . . and, if necessary, to carry it out." The German navy had to plan to ferry the army across in whatever shipping it could hastily collect. The British fleet was to be bombed in its bases and the invaders covered by light craft, minefields, and coastal guns. The *Luftwaffe* had first to win command of the air, an operation for which it was ill-prepared. Douhet's prophecies were untested. Large-scale bombing was still experimental.[7]

Most of the German bombers were poorly protected twin-engine machines carrying one to two tons of bombs. Their experiences in Spain, Poland, and France had convinced the Germans that the average bomber had little to fear from fighters, and the lessons of the air battles over Dunkirk were too recent to have been assimilated. About 800 German long-range and 250 dive-bombers and 820 fighters could be sent into action on a given day. The Germans expected to face up to 675 single-engined fighters, but pilot shortages cut this number to about 600 on any single day. The defenders were also short of antiaircraft guns and searchlights. Their decisive advantage—as so often in war—came from the command and control made possible by their still untried radar (radio detection—or direction-finding—and ranging) warning net. In the first phase of the Battle of Britain—which began on August 12—heavily escorted German bombers attacked coastal targets. The Germans lost 290 planes to 114 British fighters. During the second phase—August 24 to September 6—the Germans badly damaged fighter bases and communications around London, but failed to knock them out. Convinced that the British reserves were gone and pressured by Hitler to retaliate for British raids on Berlin, the *Luftwaffe* turned

[7] Many German officers hold that the invasion project was never taken seriously, but the older services did not want to be caught short if the *Luftwaffe* won command of the air. Elements of thirteen—later nine—divisions would land on a "narrow front" west of Dover. Admiral Walter Ansel's *Hitler Confronts England* (Durham, N. C., 1960) replaces Ronald Wheatley, *Operation Sea Lion* (Oxford, 1958), Peter Fleming, *Operation Sea Lion* (New York, 1957), Duncan Grinnell-Milne, *The Silent Victory* (London, 1958), and Karl Klee, *Das Unternehmen "Seelöwe"* (Gottingen, 1958).

on the "tremendous fat cow" of London. The metropolis was hit hard by night bombers, but heavily escorted daylight raiders failed to destroy Fighter Command. In this phase of the battle its losses fell from 286 to 242 planes. The *Luftwaffe's* rose from 380 to 433. Hitler had already put off the invasion until October. On October 12 it was postponed until spring. The Germans had lost five planes for every three lost by the defenders, but these losses had been replaced on both sides. In this respect only the Battle of Britain had been a draw.[8]

On July 31, two weeks before the beginning of the Battle of Britain, Hitler had told his officers that he would invade Russia the next May. Even if the invasion of England, which the conference had been discussing, did not take place immediately, the British could be kept on the ropes by a combination of bombing and submarine, surface, and air attacks on their shipping. The British might make peace in the meantime or after Russia had been conquered. If not, German industry could then turn its full strength to the production of submarines and bombers. Germany's leaders were not alarmed by the apparent failure of their improvised air assaults on Britain. And they did not plan for more planes or pilots for Barbarossa (the code name for the invasion of Russia), partly because they also underestimated Red air strength. Even their failure in Russia was not to shake their self-confidence. In November, 1941, when General Eberhard Milch was placed in charge of aircraft procurement, his superiors vetoed his plan for a thousand fighter planes a month by the end of 1943. General Jeschonnek, the chief of the German air staff,

---

[8] Collier, *Defence of the United Kingdom*, 161-162, 456-460, 491-492. Drew Middleton, *The Sky Suspended: The Battle of Britain* (New York, 1960), Air Vice-Marshal Peter Wykeham, *Fighter Command* (London, 1960), Werner Baumbach, *The Life and Death of the Luftwaffe*, trans. Frederick Holt (New York, 1960), Adolf Galland, *The First and the Last: The Rise and Fall of the German Fighter Forces, 1938-1945* (New York, 1954), Rudolfo Gentile, *Storia delle operazioni aeree nella seconda guerra mondiale* (Florence, 1952), Georg W. Feuchter, *Geschichte des Luftkriegs* (Bonn, 1954), and Theo Weber, *Die Luftschlacht um England* (Frauenfeld, 1956).

For British scientists and radar see C. P. Snow, *Science and Government* (Cambridge, Mass., 1961), Roy F. Harrod, *The Prof: A Personal Memoir of Lord Cherwell* (London, 1959), and Robert Watson-Watt, *Three Steps to Victory* (London, 1957). For some of the same problems in the United States see A. Hunter Dupree, *Science in the Federal Government: A History of Policies and Activities to 1940* (Cambridge, Mass., 1957), James Phinney Baxter, 3d, *Scientists Against Time* (Boston, 1946), and Don K. Price, *Government and Science* (New York, 1954). For a much smaller country there is James P. Mellor, *The Role of Science and Industry* (*Australia in the War of 1939-1945*, Canberra, 1958).

told Milch that the *Luftwaffe* would not know what to do with more than 360 fighters a month. At that time combined British and American plane production was about 2000 a month and was to rise to 3500 planes monthly during 1942.[9]

In the course of the war German bombing raids killed 51,509 British civilians and did enormous property damage, but, like everyone else at the time, the Germans had overestimated bomb damage and underestimated civilian resilience. In 1938 the Committee of Imperial Defence had judged Germany capable of delivering a "knock-out blow" of 3,500 tons of bombs on London during the first twenty-four hours of war, with 600 tons a day thereafter. The Committee anticipated fifty casualties (including gas casualties) for each ton of bombs and feared that psychiatric casualties might be three times as numerous as physical casualties. During the German *Blitz* of September, 1940, to May, 1941, some 18,000 tons of bombs fell on London, killing about 20,000 people. Though gas was not used, these casualties were only a fourteenth of those expected. The British people and their government kept going, there was no increase in mental disorders, and drunkenness declined by more than half. "The young found a considerable stimulus in the excitement, and even a sense of freedom; in most young people there is a happy streak of anarchy. For the middle-aged it was a dreary, exhausting, but just tolerable ordeal. It was the old who suffered most, since for them adjustment is always more difficult." In a military sense, the Germans had also neglected the principle of concentration. "Saturation" raids do more damage than raids of attrition, while the *Luftwaffe* did not concentrate on a single industry—such as power or aircraft—or on such key targets as seaports and shipping. The final German aerial blows against England were to be made by the V (*Vergeltungswaffe*—retaliation weapon) weapons after the Allied landing in France in June, 1944. The V-1 was a pilotless jet plane with a warhead of about a ton of high explosive. The Germans had hoped to produce 5,000 V-1's a month, but Allied bombers so interfered with their manufacture and launching that only about 10,500 were finally sent against Britain. About a third of them reached their target—

[9] Milch had succeeded the First World War ace Ernst Udet, who had committed suicide. An ardent Nazi of Jewish origin, Milch was a personal favorite of Goering. See Willi Frischauer, *The Rise and Fall of Hermann Goering* (Boston, 1951), for the efforts to make the *Luftwaffe* the most Party-minded of the three services.

though large numbers of guns, balloons, and fighter planes were diverted against them—killing 6,194 civilians. The V-2 was a single-stage supersonic rocket against which no defense was then possible. Of these weapons, 1,115 fell in Britain and killed 2,754 people. This marked the beginning of pushbutton warfare, a threat so deadly that Eisenhower believed that it would have seriously hampered Allied preparations for the invasion of France if it had been available six months earlier.[10]

War had caught the German navy with a few long-range surface ships and a small submarine flotilla. The Battle of the Atlantic began with successful small-scale U-boat operations supported by surface raiding, minelaying, and improvised air operations. In May, 1941, the battleship *Bismarck* was destroyed on her first Atlantic sortie at a time when Hitler, already deep in his Russian project, had about decided to concentrate his remaining surface forces on the Murmansk route to Russia. By this time—after twenty-one months of war—7,200,000 gross tons of Allied and neutral shipping had been sunk, more than twice the total lost during the corresponding months of the previous conflict. Of this total, aircraft had accounted for 1,312,000 tons, mines 876,000, and surface raiders 886,000—nearly twice as much as the latter had sunk during the entire First World War, highlighting the damage which such raiders might have done if they had so supported their submarines in 1917. The Germans were to destroy many ships on the Murmansk run, but Hitler's fear of losing more big ships, an acute shortage of fuel oil, and poor air-surface co-ordination hampered German operations even in these favorable waters. Only the heavy cruiser *Prinz Eugen*—mined once, bombed, and torpedoed—was to survive the war and was to be used in the atomic bomb tests at Bikini. By the end of the war the Allies had re-established something like the Nelsonian close blockade. A surface ship which was forced into port for repairs was doomed. Such ships could no longer get to sea against a power which controlled both the air and the surface.[11]

10 Terence H. O'Brien, *Civil Defence (United Kingdom Civil Series,* London, 1955), 678. Collier, *Defence of the United Kingdom,* 523, 527. Constantine Fitzgibbon, *The Winter of the Bombs* (New York, 1958), 7-10, 131-132. Richard Collier, *The City that Wouldn't Die* (London, 1960).
11 Roskill, *War at Sea,* I, Appendix R. See also Ian Campbell and Donald Macintyre, *The Kola Run: A record of Arctic convoys, 1941-1945* (London, 1958), Dudley Pope, *73 North: The Battle of the Barents Sea* (London, 1958). The official summaries of British operations are P. K. Kemp, *Key to Victory:*

The Allies and neutrals eventually lost 23,506,000 gross tons of shipping, half again as many as during the First World War. German submarines accounted for 14,155,000 tons, 3,000,000 tons more than during the previous war. Over a third of this tonnage was sunk in 1942 (8,330,000), the crisis of the Battle of the Atlantic. Sinkings in 1940 (3,992,000), 1941 (4,329,000), and 1943 (4,065,000) were about half those in 1942. Only 1,495,000 tons were to be lost in 1944, at the peak of the Allied war effort. In 1939 the Allies had been short of escort craft, the R. A. F. Coastal Command had been starved to help the Fighter Command, and the Admiralty had dissipated some of its forces to hunt U-boats. The Admiralty had forgotten that convoy is essentially an offensive measure. The convoy has the advantage of secrecy and surprise and attracts submarines to places where, as Admiral Beatty noted during the First World War, it is "easier to find and destroy them." The fall of France had also changed the strategic situation in the Atlantic. The U-boats began to move into the mid-Atlantic from French bases at a time when the British had only enough escorts to reach five hundred miles west of Ireland. By the end of 1940 the Germans had also begun to concentrate their submarines, which operated in "wolf-packs" of eight to twenty. The first submarine to find the convoy sent its position to a shore command post, which ordered the rest of the pack into action. The submarines approached the convoy on the surface at night, attacked it, and then maneuvered at night into new positions. The escorts were too few to counterattack without leaving the convoy.[12]

The Triumph of British Sea Power in World War II (Boston, 1957) and S. W. Roskill, White Ensign: The British Navy at War, 1939-1945 (Annapolis, 1960). The best one volume history of the whole naval war is Friedrich Ruge, Der Seekrieg: The German Navy's Story, 1939-1945, trans. M. G. Saunders (Annapolis, 1957). See also Donald Macintyre, Fighting Admiral: The Life of Admiral of the Fleet Sir James Somerville (London, 1961), the memoirs of Admirals Andrew B. Cunningham, A Sailor's Odyssey (London, 1951) and Philip Vian, Action this Day (London, 1960), and W. S. Chalmers, Max Horton and the Western Approaches (London, 1954).

The battleship Gneisenau (allegedly 26,000 tons, but 38,100 tons full load) was damaged in February, 1942, when she and the Scharnhorst returned from Brest to Germany, and never put back into service. The latter ship was sunk attacking a Murmansk convoy in December, 1943. A year later the Bismarck's sister ship Tirpitz (52,600 tons full load, 8,000 tons larger than any British battleship finished during the war)—which had been repeatedly damaged by submarines, midget submarines, and bombers—was destroyed by R. A. F. heavy bombers.

[12] Roskill, War at Sea, I, Appendix R, and Samuel Eliot Morison, The Battle of the Atlantic, September 1939-May 1943 (History of United States Naval

This second Battle of the Atlantic had gradually drawn the United States into the war. The first American aid to Britain "short of war" was the destroyer-for-bases deal in September, 1940. This was followed by American naval protection for shipping to Iceland, where the British had established themselves after the German invasion of Denmark and Norway. By July, 1941, when American ground forces relieved this garrison, the United States Congress had passed the Lend-Lease Act, American and British staff talks had been held, British warships had been repaired in American bases, American officers had chosen bases in Britain, and the Western Hemisphere "Security Zone" extended to 26 degrees West Longitude, 18 degrees east of Pope Alexander VI's line of 1493. A postwar Geopolitical revision was to declare, by special protocol, that the Mediterranean and Asia Minor are also part of the North Atlantic. In September, 1941, the United States Navy began to convoy ships to its new bases, shipping of any nationality being free to join the convoy. At the time of Pearl Harbor the United States Navy was convoying British troops to Cape Town. German submarines sank one American destroyer and damaged another during this period, but Hitler avoided open war with the United States until Japan forced his hand by attacking Pearl Harbor. His submarines then struck at American coastal shipping, which was almost unprotected because escorts were more badly needed in other waters. After convoys had cut these losses, the submarines moved back into the mid-Atlantic beyond the reach of land-based planes. November, 1942, saw the heaviest tonnage losses of the war, but was to be the last month in which losses exceeded new construction. Another turning point was reached in May, 1943, when 41 U-boats were lost and only 26 were constructed. Nearly two-fifths of the U-boats then at sea had been lost. They had sunk less than half as much tonnage in the Atlantic and Arctic as in March. Hitler had replaced Admiral Raeder with Doenitz, a sub-

---

Operations in World War II, I, Boston, 1947), Appendix I, and The Atlantic Battle Won, May 1943-May 1945 (United States Naval Operations, X, Boston, 1956), Appendix I. See also Wilhelm Fahrmbacher and Walther Matthiae, Lorient: Entstehung und Verteidigung des Marine-Stützpunktes, 1940-1945 (Weissenburg, [1958], S. W. Roskill's brilliant "CAPROS not CONVOY: Counter-Attack and Destroy!" (United States Naval Institute Proceedings, LXXXII, Oct., 1956, 1047-1053), David D. Lewis, The Fight for the Sea (Cleveland, 1960), Donald Macintyre, U-Boat Killer (New York, 1957), Philip Joubert de la Ferté, Birds and Fishes (London, 1960), and Bodo Herzog, Die Deutschen U-boote, 1906-1945 (Munich, 1959).

marine specialist, in January, but Doenitz was able to fight only a holding operation, sinking as much tonnage as possible until greater submarine production, the new snorkel breathing device, and new tactics would enable him to regain the initiative. Though the snorkel was to change submarine tactics and more U-boats were to be built in 1944 than in any other year, the Germans had already lost the Battle of the Atlantic.

The convoys had finally been given enough escorts to enable them to attack the wolf packs. Scores of small escort carriers and hundreds of destroyer escorts and destroyers enabled each convoy to become a little fleet with its own air cover. Since patrol bombers discovered many submarines and escort craft directed many land planes to their kills, the percentages of submarine sinkings ascribed to each of these various weapons are almost meaningless. Many submarines were sunk by mines and some by Allied submarines. Though bombing of U-boat bases was much less effective than had been anticipated, the campaign against German industry and transportation had serious effect on U-boat assembly and manufacture. Science also contributed to the submarine's defeat by developing key detection and killing devices. The United States, Britain, and Canada built over 40,000,000 tons of shipping. Four-fifths of these ships were built in the United States; more than a third of them were "Liberty" ships—an old-fashioned British design adapted for quick construction by the extensive use of welding. The greatest emergency cargo carrier ever built, the Liberty was thrown into the balance at the critical period when ships were being sunk faster than they could be constructed. Contrary to popular belief, the American historian Samuel Eliot Morison has concluded that "the Axis submarines never came within measurable distance of victory. In World War I, largely because of the Allies' tardiness in setting up merchant convoys, the U-boats almost won the decision before the United States entered the war. In World War II, the German submarine campaign may have postponed, but did not affect the outcome."[13]

[13] *The Atlantic Battle Won*, 64. On shipbuilding see H. Duncan Hall, *North American Supply* (London, 1955), 425, and C. B. A. Behrens, *Merchant Shipping and the I emands of War* (London, 1955, both in the *United Kingdom Civil Series*). Other American accounts are Richard M. Leighton and Robert W. Coakley, *Global Logistics and Strategy, 1940-1943* (*U. S. Army in World War II*, Washington, 1956), Frederick C. Lane, *Ships for Victory* (Baltimore, 1951), and Emory Scott Land, *Winning the War with Ships* (New York, 1958).

At the beginning of the Battle of Britain, the British boldly decided to send some of their scarce armor to Egypt, before the vastly superior Italian armies (the British had only 36,000 men in Egypt in May) could wipe out the forces stranded there by the French collapse. In June Force H (under Admiral James H. Somerville) had been sent to Gibraltar to operate in either the Atlantic or the Western Mediterranean. After neutralizing part of the French fleet at Oran, it passed reinforcements through the Central Mediterranean bottleneck —under the noses of the much stronger Italian fleet and air force—to Admiral Andrew D. Cunningham's Mediterranean Fleet operating from Alexandria, helped to cover an abortive attack on Dakar, and remained on guard against rumored German attempts on the Azores, Cape Verde, and Canary Islands. Both Goering and Rommel felt that the Germans should have then taken Gibraltar by attacking through Spain, but Franco remained coy and Hitler only talked of taking various Atlantic islands. The Italians, ignoring Malta, finally pushed into Egypt and proposed to partition Jugoslavia. When Hitler refused, they invaded Greece from Albania on October 28. The British sent troops to Crete and an air contingent to Greece. On November 11 Cunningham's carrier planes heavily damaged half the Italian battle line in its base at Taranto. The Greeks drove the Italians back into Albania with heavy losses, and General Archibald Wavell counterattacked from Egypt. In the ensuing ten weeks Wavell's two divisions, one of them armored, advanced five hundred miles, destroying ten Italian divisions and capturing 130,000 prisoners at a cost of 555 men killed and missing. Other British forces conquered Italian East Africa, where 371,000 troops, many of them native auxiliaries, had been holding Mussolini's recently conquered and rebellious Empire.[14]

[14] The seven generals who wrote *The Fatal Decisions*, ed. Seymour Freidin and Williams Richardson (New York, 1956), did not list the failure to take Gibraltar. See also I. S. O. Playfair et al., *The Mediterranean and Middle East* (I-III, *United Kingdom Military Series*, London, 1954-1960), Don Newton and A. Cecil Hampshire, *Taranto* (London, 1959), J. F. MacDonald, *Abyssinian Adventure* (London, 1957), Robert John Collins, *Lord Wavell* (London, 1947), Roger Woolcombe, *The Campaigns of Wavell, 1939-1943* (London, 1959), Adrienne Doris Hytier, *Two Years of French Foreign Policy: Vichy, 1940-1942* (Geneva, 1958), and Paul Auphan and Jacques Mordal, *The French Navy in World War II*, trans. A. J. C. Sabalot (Annapolis, 1959). Pétain had promised that the French fleet would not fall into German hands; its heavy ships had been moved to British or French colonial ports. The British disarmed three old battleships and another was sunk at Oran. Another and two new light battleships escaped to Toulon and were scuttled in November, 1942. The new *Jean Bart*—without her main battery—was at Casablanca; an

These Italian defeats drew Hitler into the Mediterranean. In January, 1941, *Fliegerkorps X* was sent to Sicily to seal the Central Mediterranean, and an *Afrika Korps* of an armored and a light armored division was sent to help the Italians in Libya under Erwin Rommel. The Greeks, with the concurrence of the Jugoslav Government, refused an offer of additional British troops, fearing that this would provoke a German invasion. In April the Germans overran both countries—and a British force hastily sent to Greece—from bases in Hungary and Bulgaria, and Rommel's forces recovered all of Cyrenaica except the by-passed port of Tobruk. In May German air and sea-borne forces captured Crete, but the British defeated a coup in Iraq. The British and Free French occupied Syria just as Hitler invaded Russia after waiting for good weather and possibly the end of this Balkan campaign. He had done what he "set out to do. Italy was still in the war, though greatly dependent on German help, and the British, driven off the territory of Greece, could do nothing to take the pressure off their Russian ally." During the fall and winter of 1941-1942 Wavell's successor, Claude Auchinleck, relieved Tobruk and recaptured Benghazi, but was driven back to a line just in front of Tobruk by Rommel's counterattack. These battles were less significant, however, than the Allied naval crisis which accompanied the Japanese attack on Pearl Harbor. The only carrier in the Mediterranean was sunk on a plane-carrying sortie toward Malta, one of the three British battleships in the Eastern Mediterranean was sunk by a submarine, and Italian manned torpedoes damaged the two remaining battleships in their base at Alexandria. Force H was sent to the Indian Ocean to face the Japanese. Malta was dependent on planes flown from carriers and on supplies brought in by submarines, two fast minelayers, and occasional convoys. Ten of thirty ships sent in convoy to Malta in the first seven months of 1943 were sunk. Ten were turned back. Three were sunk after they arrived.[15]

---

earlier attack at Dakar had immobilized her sister *Richelieu*. The carrier *Béarn* was at Martinique. The Dakar fiasco led to much recrimination, but De Gaulle got control of French Equatorial Africa, a major aid in establishing the Allied Trans-African air route from the Gold Coast to the Sudan.

15 Playfair, *Mediterranean*, II, 325. See also W. G. McClymont, *To Greece* (*Official History of New Zealand in the Second World War, 1939-1945*, Wellington, 1959), D. M. Davin, *Crete* (Wellington, 1953), and the Australian official volume by Gavin Long, *Greece, Crete and Syria* (Canberra, 1953). For the Greeks use Alexander Papagos, *The Battle of Greece, 1940-1941*, trans. Pat. Eliascos (Athens, 1949), and Ehrengard Schramm-von Thadden, *Griechenland und die Grossmächte im Zweiten Weltkrieg* (Wiesbaden, 1955).

The crisis in the desert began on May 26, 1942, when Rommel—who had been reinforced during the fall by another German motorized division—assaulted the British lines near Bir Hacheim in front of Tobruk. Auchinleck's Eighth Army was considerably superior in tanks and tank reserves, but his badly co-ordinated counterattacks enabled Rommel to fall on him with such effect that the British infantry were practically left without tank protection. The Germans recaptured Tobruk and pushed on toward El Alamein, fifty-five miles from Alexandria. While the British prepared to abandon that base, Egyptian politicians prepared to rush to the aid of the winners. But Rommel was stopped at El Alamein. The German armies were now pushing toward the Caucasus and Rommel got almost no reinforcements. The Italian fleet was almost immobilized by lack of oil; two-fifths of the ships and three-fifths of the oil sent to Rommel in October was lost in transit. Much of the damage was done by planes or ships from Malta. The forces earmarked for its capture in the spring had been diverted to Rommel, whose supply line to Tobruk—the Germans had thought—could be protected from Crete. As F. W. von Mellenthin, one of Rommel's staff officers, later wrote, "Our presence at Alamein was producing a tremendous reaction by the Anglo-American war machine, . . . [which was] gaining a decisive lead in the . . . build-up . . . to the Middle East." Rommel's new opponent, Bernard L. Montgomery, was "a great tactician—circumspect and thorough in making his plans, utterly ruthless in carrying them out. He . . . illustrated once again the vital importance of personal leadership, . . . strongly reminiscent of Wellington's."[16]

Montgomery struck in October, 1942. The next month an Anglo-American force seized Morocco and Algeria and al-

---

See also Correlli Barnett, *The Desert Generals* (London, 1960), Anthony Heckstall-Smith, *Tobruk: The Story of a Siege* (London, 1960), and Robert Crisp, *The Gods were Neutral* (London, 1960).

[16] *Panzer Battles*, 138, 135. Auchinleck (commanding in the Middle East, but personally commanding the 8th Army after June 25) "failed in tactical detail, or perhaps [in making] . . . his subordinates do what he wanted." See John Connell, *Auchinleck* (London, 1959), Robert Crisp, *Brazen Chariots* (London, 1959), and Neil McCallum, *Journey with a Pistol* (London, 1959). Harold Alexander and Montgomery took over in August. The best study of these battles is J. A. I. Agar-Hamilton and L. C. F. Turner, *Crisis in the Desert, May-July 1942* (Cape Town, 1952). Another good German account is Hans Gert van Esebeck, *Afrikanische Schicksaljahre* (Wiesbaden, 1956). On Montgomery see the account by his Chief of Staff, Francis de Guingand, *Operation Victory* (New York, 1947), and Alan Moorehead, *Montgomery* (New York, 1946).

most reached Tunis. Rommel's retreating army joined the German and Italian forces which had been hastily thrown into Tunisia; in May, 1943, the whole Axis army was captured. In July the Allies invaded Sicily and the Fascist Grand Council overthrew Mussolini. The new Italian government surrendered itself and most of its fleet, though the Germans sank the new battleship *Roma*, rescued Mussolini, and occupied the remainder of Italy. Like Poland and France, Italy had now become a battleground between the Allies and the Germans. The desert war had also captured the public's imagination. With able commanders on both sides and few civilians to get in the way, this was true armored war with land battleships. The early British feats of arms in the Mediterranean were worthy of Nelson, in the sea which had brought out the best and the worst sides of his character. The British had "without undue cost" almost destroyed Italy's "will to fight." Churchill also appears at his best and his worst in the Mediterranean. His hasty honoring of the British commitment to Greece had cost Britain the forces which might have held both Crete and Cyrenaica. And his simultaneous underestimation of the Japanese threat—in which he clearly ignored the advice of his professional advisors—was supported by arguments which remind one British official historian of "those which the weird sisters gave Macbeth." They may have helped to cause the loss of Singapore and resulted in the Australian Government's losing all confidence in Churchillian strategy. Wavell was partly the victim of his superiors' improvisations and poorly calculated risk taking, but it should be remembered that Rommel's successes were equally due to a boldness which frightened his superiors almost as much as the British.[17]

[17] Butler, *Grand Strategy*, II, 497. The relevant volumes, sharply critical of the Anzio operation, in Samuel Eliot Morison's *United States Naval Operations* are II, *Operations in North African Waters, October 1942-June 1943* (Boston, 1947), and IX, *Sicily-Salerno-Anzio, January 1943-June 1944* (Boston, 1954). Mark Clark's defense of Allied strategy is *Calculated Risk* (New York, 1950). On the naval war see also Raymond de Belot, *The Struggle for the Mediterranean 1939-1945*, trans. James A. Field, Jr. (Princeton, 1951), and Marc' Antonio Bragadin, *The Italian Navy in World War II*, trans. Gale Hoffman (Annapolis, 1957). Two interesting comments by important naval theorists are Romeo Bernotti, *La Guerra sui mari, nel conflitte mondiale* (2 vols., Leghorn, 1948-1950), and Giuseppe Fioravanzo, "Italian Strategy in the Mediterranean" (*United States Naval Institute Proceedings*, LXXXIV, Sept., 1958, 65-72). The official United States Army volume is George F. Howe, *Northwest Africa: Seizing the Initiative in the West* (Washington, 1957).

Robert Jars, *La Campagne d'Italie* (Paris, 1954), is good. The Italian apologias are very extensive. Among the better works are Ugo Cavallero, *Com-*

The Russo-German War

To paraphrase Clausewitz' comments on Napoleon's critics, a plan which succeeds is bold and one which fails is reckless. Two weeks before the beginning of the Battle of Britain, Hitler had told his officers of his decision to invade Russia. He involved the German armies in their second two-front war in a generation on June 22, 1941, the day before the anniversary of Napoleon's invasion of a country which, Clausewitz had believed, could only be subdued "by its own weakness, and by the effects of internal dissension." Hitler believed that he could beat the Red Army in three months with forces which enjoyed about the same slight numerical superiority as the Germans had held in the west in 1914. The theater of operations was larger and the Russians had larger reserves, but the Germans had been combat tested on a much larger scale than the Russians. The directive for Barbarossa stated that

The bulk of the Russian Army stationed in western Russia is to be destroyed in a series of daring operations spearheaded by armored thrusts. The organized withdrawal of intact units into the vastness of interior Russia is to be prevented. . . . A fast pursuit up to a line . . . along the . . . Volga and thence . . . toward Archangel [would render] the Russian air force . . . incapable of attacking German territory. Thus, if necessary, the German Air Force would be in a position to neutralize the last industrial region . . . in the Urals. [During the decisive first phases] any effective interference by the Russian Air Force will be eliminated by . . . decisive blows at the very beginning.

This looked like the *Blitzkrieg* formula, but it planned old-fashioned envelopments rather than deep strategic thrusts against the main Russian communications. Though Hitler admitted that Stalin was an "intelligent, . . . careful . . . ice-cold blackmailer," he clearly hoped that the destruction of the Red Army in western Russia would lead to the collapse of Stalin's regime. His major miscalculation—but one which seemed to be supported by the upheavals in Russia in the mid-thirties—was, like Napoleon's, political.[18]

mando Supremo (Bologna, 1948), Francesco Rossi, *Mussolini e lo stato maggiore* (Rome, 1951), and Giacomo Carboni, *Più che il dovere: Storia di una battaglia italiana. 1937-1951* (Rome, 1952). Even more partisan is Pietro Pallotta, *L'Esercito italiano nella seconda guerra mondiale attraverso i giudizi dei commandanti avversari et alleati* (Rome, 1955), and Roberto Battaglia, *Storia della Resistanza italiana* (Turin, 1953).
18 Guesses of Russian numbers—including, as for France and Italy, untrained reserves and obsolescent tanks and planes of little use if the government col-

The invaders seem to have been slightly superior in numbers and greatly superior in armored doctrine, though not in numbers of tanks. Their chief weakness—as in 1914—was in logistic preparation, though the *Luftwaffe* also tended to separate tactical and strategical operations into too rigid chronological phases. Wilhelm von Leeb's Northern Army Group— the smallest of three such groups—and the Finns advanced on Leningrad. Bock's Central Army Group—the largest— took Napoleon's route to the Stalin Line covering Smolensk and Moscow. Rundstedt's Army Group South and the Rumanians drove into the Ukrainian pocket formed by the bend of the Dniepr River. "The strength of the Russian military organization," the German command told its men, "is based on the mass of its personnel and equipment, . . . on the simplicity, hardness, and bravery of the human material, as well as on the vastness of the area. Its weakness resides . . . in . . . incomplete training, in mental slowness, and dislike of responsibility on the part of its leaders." Stalin may have been surprised—he later told Churchill, "I thought I might gain another six months or so"—or he may have overestimated the efficiency of his massive forces. Many Russian planes were destroyed on the ground, the Russian light tanks could not match the German medium tanks, and the Red Army was too far forward in its newly-acquired territories. The Russian infantry had been well trained for fighting at night, in woods, in swamps, and in bad weather, but its transport and communications often broke down in the early fighting. In the first five months the Germans officially reported 743,112 men killed, wounded, and missing in action. Russian official sources admit casualties of 2,122,000, about three times the German figure. But the Russians have admitted only 520,000 men missing, while the Germans claim to have taken 3,006,867

lapsed—are in Wladyslaw Anders, *Hitler's Defeat in Russia* (Chicago, 1953), 16-19. Augustin Guillaume, *La Guerre Germano-Sovietique, 1941-1945* (Paris, 1949) is fuller than *Soviet Arms and Soviet Power* (Washington, 1949). Ernest Lederrey, *La Défaite allemande à l'est: les armées sovietiques en guerre de 1941 à 1945* (Paris, 1951) and Gert Buchheit, *Hitler der Feldherr* (Rastatt, 1958), are good. The Barbarossa directive is translated by George E. Blau, *The German Campaign in Russia, Planning and Operations, 1940-1942* (Washington, 1955), 22-25, the most sober study. The Germans attacked with 145 divisions, 19 of them armored, and 13 Finnish divisions were also available. The Rumanian divisions were of little immediate help. German intelligence finally gave the Red Army 118 infantry and 20 cavalry divisions in western Russia, plus 46 armored and motorized brigades, forces roughly equivalent to the German armor. On the organization of German intelligence see Paul Leverkuehn, *German Military Intelligence*, trans. R. H. Stevens and Constantine Fitzgibbon (London, 1954).

prisoners. Even so, these figures are comparable to Polish, French, and Italian losses under rather similar circumstances. The mass army, as Bernhardi had predicted, was both powerful and fragile.[19]

The German Chief of Staff Franz von Halder wrote in his diary on July 3, 1941,

> On the whole, then, it may be said even now that the objective to shatter the bulk of the Russian Army this side of the Dvina and Dnieper, has been accomplished. . . . The Russian Campaign has been won . . . in two weeks. Of course, this does not yet mean that it is closed. The sheer geographical vastness of the country and the stubbornness of the resistance . . . will claim our efforts for many more weeks to come.

By the end of July Bock was driving through the Stalin line to Smolensk and was closing his second big trap. Leeb was approaching Leningrad and Rundstedt was about to bag the entire Russian army in the Ukraine. This embarrassment of riches brought on the first serious disagreements among the German generals. According to their apologias, Brauchitsch (the Commander-in-Chief), Bock, and Guderian (commanding Bock's Second Armored Group) wanted to drive on to Moscow to bring the forces defending the Red capital to a super-Borodino. Hitler decided, instead, to detach some forces from Bock's wings to aid Leeb and Rundstedt. In the Ukraine Rundstedt captured Simeon Budenny's whole group of armies. This was Hitler's greatest single victory and, perhaps, his greatest blunder. September, 1941, slipped away. Napoleon

[19] "Russia's Fighting Methods and Ability as seen by the Wehrmacht" (a translation and digest of a German article by Lt. Col. M. Waibel, *The Military Review*, XXVI, Feb., 1947, 95-99). Blau, *German Campaign in Russia*, 88. Fuller thinks that the Germans should have planned "several campaigns, covering two or possibly three summers," with their main drive in the Ukraine combining with a force reaching the Caucasian oil fields through Turkey. *Second World War*, 117. Anders agrees that quick victory was impossible, but holds that Moscow was the main objective. Runstedt and Admiral Ruge think that the German command of the Baltic made Leningrad the most promising objective. See *Das Kriegstagebuch des Oberkommandos der Wehrmacht* (4 vols., Frankfurt, 1960), Frido von Senger und Etterlin, *Krieg in Europa* (Cologne, 1960), *Die Deutsche Panzer, 1926-1945* (Munich, 1959), *Die Panzergrenadiere* (Munich, 1961), and *Der Gegenschlag* (Neckargemünd, 1959), Otto Wilhelm Förster, *Das Befestigungswesen* (Neckargemünd, 1960), Hermann Hoth, *Panzer-Operationen: Die Panzergruppe 3 und der operative Gedanke der deutschen Führung Sommer 1941* (Heidelberg, 1956), Eike Middeldorf, *Taktik im Russlandfeldzug* (Darmstadt, 1956), and Maximilian Fretter-Pico, *Missbrauchte Infanterie, Deutsche Infanteriedivisionen im osteuropäischen Grossraum 1941 bis 1944: Erlebnisskizzen, Erfahrung und Erkenntnisse* (Frankfurt, 1957).

had fought Borodino on September 7 and had entered Moscow a week later.[20]

The Germans had not underestimated their superiority over the first-line strength of the Red Army, but they had miscalculated the numbers and fighting ability of its poorly trained reserves and the political solidity of Stalin's dictatorship. This seems an odd mistake for one totalitarian state to make about another, but it was one which was quite consistent with Hitler's views on Bolshevism. Many Russian troops had been forced to surrender, but the only real collapse had occurred in the Ukraine, long a center of disaffection and a major German political target. But the Germans' ruthlessness soon turned the Ukraine against them, while news of the sufferings of those who were dying of neglect in German prison camps spread throughout the rest of Russia. On August 11—little more than a month after his optimistic diary entry of July 3—Halder had written

The whole situation makes it increasingly plain that we have underestimated the Russian Colossus, who consistently prepared for war with that utterly ruthless determination so characteristic of totalitarian states. This applies to organizational and economic resources, . . . communications, . . . and, most of all, to the strictly military potential. . . . We reckoned with about 200 enemy Divisions. Now we have already counted 360, . . . not armed and equipped . . . to our standards, and their tactical leadership is often poor. But . . . if we smash a dozen of them, the Russians simply put up another dozen. . . . Time . . . favors them, as they are near their own resources, while we are moving farther and farther away from ours. And so our troops, sprawled over an immense frontline, without any depth, are subjected to the incessant attacks of the enemy. Sometimes these are successful, because too many gaps must be left open in these enormous spaces.[21]

Hitler resumed his drive on Moscow on October 2, the day before the anniversary of Napoleon's decision to retreat from that city. The Germans gained another one hundred and fifty miles in three weeks; the Russian government left for Kuibyshev on the Volga. Budenny and Voroshilov—on the northern front—had already been relieved of their commands. Timo-

[20] *The Halder Diaries* (7 vols., Washington, 1950), VI, 196. Napoleon, too, had reached Smolensk at the end of July, where some critics, though not Clausewitz, have suggested that he should have erected winter quarters. Hitler followed the rules by deciding that the Russian armed forces were more important than the capital.

[21] *Ibid.*, VII, 36. He does not mention the fact that the enemy's communications and resources might be hit by air power.

shenko, the last of the original Russian commanders, was now sent to the southern front and replaced by Zhukov in the center. When bad weather slowed the German drive, Rundstedt favored going into winter quarters. With German advance units only forty miles from Moscow, Hitler decided that there would be no failure of nerve and renewed the offensive on November 17, on which day Russian troops from the Far East were discovered on the central front. The southern prong of the Moscow drive was finally halted by wide rivers and the big factory city of Tula. The heavily wooded marshes to the north and the new Russian T-34 tanks proved more than a match for Guderian's armor. Like Paris, Moscow was also a major communications center, while German lateral communications were snow-covered mud tracks unsuitable for their wheeled (instead of tracked) infantry transport. The first real German defeat took place in the south, where the First Panzer Army had taken Rostov on the Don. German propaganda had magnified this success and Hitler refused to permit Rundstedt to abandon the city in the face of Timoshenko's counterattacks. Rundstedt then asked to be relieved of the command of Army Group South and was officially replaced on December 3, two days after Hitler had permitted his designated successor to abandon the city. Two days later Zhukov attacked on the Moscow front and eventually drove the Germans back from fifty to a hundred miles. Hitler took over the army command from von Brauchitsch and relieved both of the other army group commanders and droves of lesser generals. By the end of the year the invaders had lost more than a quarter of their men and horses; their tank and plane losses had increased because of inadequate winterizing, and the generals had forbidden the circulation of Caulaincourt's memoirs of Napoleon's campaign. Moscow had been the Marne of the Russo-German War, though Hitler's losses were still small by First World War standards or compared to those of the Russians. And the final stabilization of the German front later enabled Hitler to resist all suggestions for strategic withdrawal.[22]

[22] A. M. Samsonov, *The Great Battle of Moscow, 1941-1942* (Moscow, 1958). Halder, *Hitler as War Lord*, trans. Paul Finlay (London, 1950) is less dramatic than the *Journal*. Nov. 22: Bock compared it to "the Marne, where the last Bn. that could be thrown in turned the balance." On Nov. 29 Bock reported, "if the current attack on Moscow from the north is unsuccessful . . . the operation will become another Verdun, . . . a brutish chest-to-chest struggle of attrition." On the day before Pearl Harbor and the day after the beginning of Zhukov's counteroffensive, Halder noted that

Stalin's critics have not detailed all of his military errors, but Hitler's critics have told all. Since Hitler's target was political and he knew that his opponent would seek to trade space for time, his postponement of Barbarossa for a month in the late spring—whether this was due to the Balkan campaign or the weather—and his August postponement of the drive on Moscow cannot be defended. In any case—as with the Schlieffen Plan—delays should be regarded as part of the inevitable friction of war. All of Hitler's other errors are related to his political underestimation of the Stalinist dictatorship or to racist underestimation of Russian tactical improvisation at the company level, which often compensated for the inexperience of the Russian commanders. Stalin and his generals, like the French high command in 1914, saved themselves by refusing to be panicked, though they proved to be no more expert in their first counteroffensives than the French had been in their first counteroffensives in 1914 and 1915. Timoshenko's counteroffensive toward Kharkov in May, 1942, threatened to upset Hitler's plans for a summer offensive further south but cost the Russians heavily in what was to become the decisive theater. During the previous campaign the Germans' transportation problems had become critical only after their big initial victories had failed to destroy the Stalinist dictatorship in the three to five months which Hitler had promised, though German armor had sometimes been forced to wait for the infantry during the early battles. The *Luftwaffe* had also been handicapped by inadequate transportation and air base construction. It continued to think that strategic bombing could be separated from tactical operations and failed to hit the Russian rail net hard enough at the proper time, when such action might have hindered the evacuation of Russian war plants to the east and the arrival of

---

Hitler "cannot be bothered with strength ratios. To him the PW figures are conclusive proof of our superiority." The day after Pearl Harbor Bock reported, "Unless we can form reserves, we face the danger of a serious defeat." On the next, "Guderian [who was to be relieved of his command] reports that the condition of his troops is . . . critical. . . . 'Serious break of confidence in the field commands.' Reduced fighting strength of his Infantry! He is scraping together in the rear whatever forces he can get hold of (in one Armd. Div. 1,600 rifles!); tank gunners and drivers of course are not used as Infantry." On Dec. 19, Hitler told his generals: "(1) The notion of 'rear positions' was installed into the lower echelon commands. Such positions do not exist and cannot be created. (2) Provisions against extreme cold were inadequate. Army works too mechanically. Air Force . . . has been educated in entirely different spirit by the Reich Marshal [Goering]. (3) Orders to hold present positions. Not worried about any threats to flanks." VII, 176-233.

reinforcements from the interior. Russian mud and the early winters were known strategic factors. Gambling on victory before bad weather, the German command had ordered winter clothing only for the sixty divisions which were to be required for occupation duties. Guerrilla opposition surprised the prophets of the New Order throughout Europe. The Germans were not prepared for such operations even in the Balkans, where the Serbs, in particular, had a long record of nationalist intransigence. For theorists who placed Nationalism ahead of Socialism, this is as surprising as their underestimation of a sister totalitarianism.[23]

Hitler took personal charge of the offensive in 1942, the last year in which he was able to concentrate most of his forces on one front. Halder claims that Germany should have remained on the defensive and waited for the increased production promised by Albert Speer, the able architect who became the Rathenau of the Second World War. Though American aid to Britain and Russia might be cut by Doenitz' submarines, Hitler saw that Italy was in trouble and that he must take advantage of the Japanese diversion in the Pacific. Halder favored wheeling on Moscow from the south to force the Russians to fight where further retreat would be impossible. Hitler decided to hit the area between the Don and the Volga and then southeast toward the Caucasian and Caspian oil fields. This would increase Germany's war potential; the Russians, who were thought to be too short of steel to raise new armored units, would have to fight for their oil reserves and the transportation system between the Caspian and Moscow. The German armor and motorized divisions had been brought up to strength, but the new German infantry divisions and most of the satellite divisions were short of equipment. Since Hungary had helped Hitler partition Rumania, German, Italian, and other satellite divisions were interspersed between the twenty-seven Rumanian and thirteen Hungarian divisions which were to be available. German officers and propagandists were to be particularly careful of the sensibilities of

[23] The tenor of much German criticism is indicated by the title of Karlheinrich Rieker's *Ein Mann verliert einen Weltkrieg* (Frankfurt, 1955). On the partisans see C. Aubrey Dixon and Otto Heilbrunn, *Communist Guerilla Warfare* (New York, 1954); Edgar M. Howell, *The Soviet Partisan Movement, 1941-1944* (Washington, 1956); and *German Antiguerrilla Operations in the Balkans, 1941-1944* (Washington, 1954). A New Zealand surgeon who worked Lindsay Rogers, *Guerilla Surgeon* (London, 1957). Equally fascinating is Lena A. Yovitchitch, *Within Closed Frontiers: A Woman in Wartime Yugoslavia* (London, 1956).

the other national components of this increasingly polyglot army. The main offensive began on June 28. Part of Timoshenko's front on the Don collapsed, though the Germans did not destroy all of his forces in the pocket. The Germans then failed to follow up their first successes as they had planned. Armor which had been ordered to strike for Stalingrad was uselessly diverted to back up the Caucasus drive and did not swing back toward Stalingrad until the Russians were dug in. The Germans then advanced toward the city on a comparatively narrow front in an assault which drew troops from the Caucasus, where the German drive flickered out a hundred miles from the Caspian because of the terrain, Russian resistance, and lack of fuel and reinforcements. Halder was removed as Chief of the General Staff—for worrying over the long northern flank of the Stalingrad salient, where the satellite armies had failed to liquidate a number of Russian bridgeheads over the Don and one just south of Stalingrad. Hitler saw the danger—Halder's warnings were repeated by his successor, Kurt Zeitzler—but interpreted Russian activity in these bridgeheads and on the Central and Northern fronts as diversionary. His prestige was now irretrievably engaged at Stalingrad.[24]

Stalin's reorganization of the Red Army in the summer of 1942 may have been the turning point in the Russo-German War. The political commissars were again down-graded, younger generals—Vatutin, Eremenko, Rokossovsky, and Golikov—got the southern commands, while Stalin allegedly planned a counteroffensive with the help of Zhukov, Voronov, and Vasilievski. Stalingrad was a new Verdun, not only because of the nature of the fighting but also because of its moral importance. Some units had panicked on the Don, and the Germans had found widespread unrest among the Cossacks and the Moslems of the Caucasus. At the end of 1942, one of Stalin's younger generals, Andrei A. Vlasov, who had

24 The best book is Hans Doerr, Der Feldzug nach Stalingrad: Versuch eines operativen Überblicks (Darmstadt, 1955). On the Russians see Ronald Seth, Stalingrad: Point of Return (London, 1959) and Alexander Werth, The Year of Stalingrad (New York, 1947). Theodore Plievier's novels, Moscow, trans. Stuart Hood (London, 1953) and Stalingrad, trans. H. Langmead Robinson (London, 1948) are good. Among the best of many German personal accounts are Heinz Schröter, Stalingrad, trans. Constantine Fitzgibbon (London, 1958), Hans Dibold, Doctor at Stalingrad, trans. H. C. Stevens (London, 1958), Heinrich Gerlach, The Forsaken Army, trans. Richard Graves (London, 1958), Peter Bamm, The Invisible Flag, trans. F. Hermann (London, 1956), Benno Zieser, In Their Shallow Graves, trans. Alec Brown (London, 1956), and Helmut Pabst, The Outermost Frontier, trans. Andrew and Eva Wilson (London, 1957).

been captured during the summer on the Volkhov front, announced the formation of the Russian Liberation Committee which was to become the most conspicuous of the committees which tried to enlist Soviet war prisoners and other citizens in the New Order's armies. The final number of such *Osttruppen* was between half a million and a million; some Moslems and Cossacks were used in front-line units, and increasing numbers were used in fighting Communist or anti-Communist partisans on all fronts as the tide of battle changed. Though the majority of the *Osttruppen* were used in construction work, where they were hard to distinguish from ordinary slave labor, this was a considerable departure from Hitler's original insistence that no Slav be allowed to bear arms. But the enlistment of large numbers of *Osttruppen* in the winter of 1942-1943 and the use of many satellite divisions during the Stalingrad campaign clearly shows that the war had become a war of attrition and that the morale of both sides was a major consideration in the struggle for Stalingrad.[25]

On November 9, a week after Montgomery had driven through the German lines in Egypt and the day after the Anglo-American landings in French North Africa, Hitler promised that "Stalingrad will be won . . . by new shock tactics." The staff of the exhausted Sixth Army listened in silence to Hitler's further announcement that "not one square yard of ground will be given up." Ten days later the Russians broke through the Rumanians. The Sixth Army's commander, Friedrich Paulus, wished to break out of the trap, but Hitler ordered him to hold and Goering promised to supply him by

25 The best accounts are Alexander Dallin, *German Rule in Russia, 1941-1945: A Study of Occupation Policies* (London, 1957), and George Fischer, *Soviet Opposition to Stalin: A Case Study in World War II* (Cambridge, Mass., 1952). Other good works are Adolf von Ernsthausen, *Wende im Kaukasus* (Neckargemünd, 1958), John A. Armstrong, *Ukrainian Nationalism, 1939-1945* (New York, 1955), Ihor Kamenetsky, *Hitler's Occupation of Ukraine, 1941-1944* (Milwaukee, 1956), and Robert L. Koehl, *RKFVD: German Resettlement and Population Policy, 1939-1945: A History of the Reich Commission for the Strengthening of Germandon* (Cambridge, Mass., 1957). The most interesting account of French units in German pay is not Roger Nimier, *Le Hussard bleu* (Paris, 1950), but Sergeant Labat, *Les Places étaient chères* (Paris, 1951).

This was the summer in which the Russians allowed the Polish army to be evacuated through Iran. Its story is told by General Wladyslaw Anders in *An Army in Exile* (London, 1949). The Germans did not discover the Katyn murders until April, 1943, provoking the long-simmering break between the Polish and the Soviet governments and the eventual establishment of the rival Communist-sponsored Bierut government. Its troops had been organized with Russian officers in key positions. The best account is now Edward J. Rosek, *Allied Wartime Diplomacy: A Pattern in Poland* (New York, 1958).

air. Hitler, who had never been to that front, now directed operations from his East Prussian headquarters, fifteen hundred miles away. The Russians finally captured the whole Sixth Army, the first German army to be captured in the field since the Napoleonic wars. Hitler had expected Paulus, whom he had recently promoted to Field Marshal, to commit suicide and ascend "into eternity and national immortality, but he prefers to go to Moscow." During the winter and spring of 1942-1943, the Germans stabilized their front about where it had been a year before, except for a Russian salient around Kursk. Its losses and redeployment against Anglo-American bombing had cost the *Luftwaffe* air superiority on the east. Returned soldiers spread the news of these defeats throughout the Axis countries and prepared the public for the surrender of the Axis armies in Tunis on May 12, 1943.[26]

Hitler began his last offensive in Russia on July 5. Perhaps half the armor in the German army was squandered against the Kursk salient in an offensive reminiscent of those of the First World War, with up to one hundred and sixty tanks per mile assaulting defenses nearly sixty miles deep. The Russians counterattacked on July 12, two days after the Allies landed in Sicily. Russian operations "increasingly came to resemble those of the Allies' 1918 counter-offensive— . . . an alternating series of strokes . . . each temporarily suspended when its impetus waned, . . . each so aimed as to pave the way for the next, and all close enough in time and space to have a mutual reaction. . . . [The Germans rushed] their scanty reserves to the points that were struck, . . . [thus] restricting their power to move . . . to the points . . . about to be struck . . . [and paralyzing] their freedom of action, while progressively decreasing their balance of reserves. . . . Each time the Germans were tied to the defence of a fixed point by Hitler's orders, an eventual collapse was the costly penalty." By November 1, the Russians were across the Dnieper and had cut the land escape routes from the Crimea. On November 7, in a speech on the twenty-second anniversary of the Beer Hall

[26] Recent Soviet accounts of the Stalingrad battle naturally play down Stalin's and Zhukov's roles in the battle, without doing more than credit Khrushchev, who was chief political officer on that front, for good work. The front commanders now get the credit. One of the few works on Paulus' later collaboration with the Russians is by Bismarck's grandson, Heinrich von Einsiedel, *I Joined the Russians: A Captured German flier's diary of the Communist Temptation* (New Haven, 1953). On the Italians see Giovanni Messe, *La Guerra al fronte russe* (Milan, 1947), Aldo Valori, *La Campagna di Russia* (Vol. I, Rome, 1951), and the caustic account by P. Giuffrida, *L' A. R. M. I. R., Il Generale, La Ritirata* (Rome, 1953).

coup, General Alfred Jodl estimated Axis strength in Russia at 4,183,000 men (3,900,000 of them Germans, the rest Hungarians and Rumanians). There were 176,800 men in Finland. The Russians, whose strength had fallen to between 2,000,000 and 3,000,000 in December, 1941, now had 5,500,-000 men. Fifty additional divisions were in process of formation. About a fifth of the German forces, 1,370,000 men, were in France and the Low Countries. Another 612,000 men were tied down in the Balkans, and there were 412,000 men in Italy. The 486,000 men in Norway and Denmark reflected German fears of an Allied landing in Scandinavia. Jodl did not estimate the number of men occupied in the air defense of Germany, but aptly compared the situation in the east to that on the west in 1917 and 1918. Hitler's armies were scattered the length and breadth of Europe and were inferior in numbers and equipment on every front.[27]

The Russian offensives of 1944 followed the same pattern. By mid-September, the line ran through the Baltic states to the tip of East Prussia, south to the Vistula near Warsaw and the Carpathians, and around them to Sofia. Finland, Rumania, and Bulgaria had quit. The Hungarian government was kidnapped in October to prevent its surrender. "At the Teheran Conference [in December, 1943], Stalin [had said] . . . that his margin of superiority . . . was about sixty divisions which could be shifted . . . to provide massed power for a breakthrough in areas of their own choosing. It is impossible to conceive how these divisions could have been moved . . . [without] American trucks to ride in, American shoes to march in, and American food to sustain them." Western aid had been far less important in stopping the German drives than in enabling the Russian counteroffensives to flow around the river crossings, cities, and road and rail junctions which were the key points in Eastern Europe's plains, marshes, and forests. The Western supplement to Russian munitions production—which equaled that of Germany from 1941—was never more than about a tenth of the total. Russian ground forces munitions production was about equal to that of the United States, though it had to be spread much more thinly.[28]

[27] Liddell Hart, *Strategy*, 295-297. *Trial of the Major War Criminals before the International Military Tribunal* (42 vols., Nuremberg, 1947-1949), XXXVIII, 630-639. Georges Blond, *The Death of Hitler's Germany*, trans. Frances Frenaye (New York, 1954) is a splendid popular summary.
[28] John R. Deane, *The Strange Alliance* (New York, 1947), 87. Her Allies sent Russia 400,000 trucks, 22,000 planes, and 12,000 tanks. A sixth of the 17,500,000 long tons of cargo from Western Hemisphere ports to Russia left

The Russo-German war was the greatest land war in history. It was accompanied by the massacre of about 5,000,000 Jews and the greatest forced migrations of modern times. Military casualties were as great as those of the First World War; civilian casualties were greater. The Germans lost about 3,500,000 military dead and about 525,000 civilians, a figure which does not include 280,000 Jews. Deaths during the migrations may bring the total lost to the Master Race to 6,500,000 *Volksdeutsche*, roughly eight per cent of the total. The Soviet Union lost from 7,000,000 to 40,000,000 people; Russian losses were certainly heavier than for the First World War and Civil War combined. A recent German estimate is 20,000,000 military and civilian dead, a tenth of the population. The Russo-German war was a war of attrition in which the contestants were always more evenly balanced than in Western Europe. The scale of military casualties is indicated by Finnish losses of 82,000 dead in an army of 500,000, Rumanian 350,000 out of 650,000. The peoples living in the battleground suffered terribly. Poland, Czechoslovakia, Rumania, Jugoslavia, Greece, Bulgaria, and Hungary lost 1,070,-000 military dead, 3,855,000 civilians, and 3,860,000 Jews. Counting losses during the migrations, these states also lost about a tenth of their populations, the heaviest losses falling on Poland, with its large Jewish population, and on faction-rent Jugoslavia. Though property damage was much heavier, Western Europe's losses were much less than during the First World War. France, the Low Countries, Denmark, and Norway lost 284,000 soldiers and 610,000 civilians, more than a third of them Jewish. France and Belgium had lost 1,371,000 dead during the First World War. Italy's 330,000 military

in 1941-1942. T. H. Vail Motter, *The Persian Corridor and Aid to Russia* (*U. S. Army in World War II*, Washington, 1952), 139, 481-483. Robert W. Coakley, "The Persian Corridor as a Route for Aid to the U. S. S. R." (Kent Roberts Greenfield, ed., *Command Decisions*, New York, 1959, 154-181). This is a fine sampling of the work of army historians. The worst losses—equal to those of a major land or air battle—were in the early convoys: 430 of 594 tanks and 210 of 297 planes were lost in convoy PQ 17. Roskill, *War at Sea*, II, 143. About three-fourths of American Lend-Lease went to the British Commonwealth, whose reverse Lend-Lease was about as large a portion of its production, though not overall.

Raymond W. Goldsmith, "The Power of Victory; Munitions Output in World War II" (*Military Affairs*, X, Spring, 1946, 69-80), suggests that the Russians were about 3/2 superior in munitions to the Germans during their counteroffensives and that the Allies were 5/1 superior in Western Europe and the Pacific. Russian generalship, like that of Eisenhower and Montgomery, has been criticized as overcautious, but so little is known of its details that it is impossible to judge it. A good general picture is in Francis Tuker, *The Pattern of War* (London, 1948), 100-101.

and 80,000 civilian dead can be compared to 650,000 dead in the First World War. The United Kingdom and Malta lost 326,000 soldiers and 64,000 civilians, a bit more than half their losses during the earlier war. American deaths from all causes were three times as numerous (389,000 to 130,000) in the Second World War, but were a smaller fraction of those mobilized (15,513,000 to 4,609,000). About two-thirds of the casualties were in the European theater, where mechanized Anglo-American land, sea, and air forces finally tipped the balance between the Russian and German land juggernauts.[29]

Allied Deployment: Decision in Western Europe

The chief United States Army planning officer and future Allied Supreme Commander in the Mediterranean and then in Northwest Europe was a product of the new system of American higher military education. After serving in staff positions from 1929 to 1935, Dwight D. Eisenhower had accompanied Douglas MacArthur to the Philippines and had been made chief of the reorganized War Department's Operations Division—the "personal command post" for Chief of Staff George C. Marshall—on March 9, 1942. Without the command of the sea it was impossible to reinforce MacArthur; in the first three months of the Great Pacific War the Japanese had captured Singapore, Rangoon—the port feeding the Burma Road and north and central Burma—and the islands lying ten degrees north and south of the Equator from Sumatra to Rabaul in New Britain. On February 28 Eisenhower wrote that " 'We must differentiate sharply between those things . . . *necessary* to the ultimate defeat of the Axis

[29] Gregory Frumkin places Russian military dead at 13,600,000. *Population Changes in Europe* (London, 1951). More modest estimates are in *Bilanz des Zweiten Weltkrieges;* Xavier Lannes, "Les Conséquences démographiques de la guerre en Europe" (*Révue d'histoire de la deuxième guerre mondiale,* July, 1955, 1-14); and L[ouis] H[enry], "Au Sujet des pertes de guerre" (*Population,* VIII, April-June, 1953, 372-373). Canada mobilized nearly a tenth of her population in the Second World War and less than a twelfth in the First, but casualties among those mobilized were more than twice as large in the First World War.

The war crimes are summarized by Lord Russell of Liverpool, *The Scourge of the Swastika* (New York, 1954) and *Knights of Bushido: The shocking history of Japanese war atrocities* (New York, 1958). The best criticism of the trials is Lord Hankey, *Politics, Trials and Errors* (Oxford, 1949). August von Knieriem, *The Nuremberg Trials,* trans. Elizabeth D. Schmitt (Chicago, 1959), analyzes the twelve trials before tribunals of American judges in 1946-1949. A splendid study of the great migrations is Malcolm J. Proudfoot, *European Refugees, 1939-1952: A Study in forced population movement* (Evanston, 1956).

. . . [and] those which are merely *desirable*.' " The *necessary* list, in addition to the security of the " 'continental United States and Hawaii, the Caribbean area, and South America north of Natal [the eastern tip of Brazil],' " included " 'the United Kingdom, which involves relative security of the North Atlantic sea lanes, . . . retention of Russia in the war as an active enemy of Germany, . . . [and] a position in the India-Middle East Area which will prevent physical contact of the two principal enemies, and will probably keep China in the war.' " The *desirable* list included " 'Alaska, . . . bases west and southwest of Hawaii [such as Midway to the west and southwestern islands on the way to Australia], . . . Burma, particularly because of its influence on future Chinese action, . . . South America south of Natal, . . . Australia, . . . [and] bases on West African coast and trans-African air route.' " [30]

All but the most necessary American reinforcements were to go to Europe and the Atlantic, a joint Anglo-American responsibility. The Middle and Far East (in fact, the Indian Ocean to Singapore) was a British area. Chiang was responsible for China Theater. The United States was primarily responsible for the Pacific. The United States Navy was given three Pacific commands: North (roughly from Canada to the Kuriles), Central (to Japan and the China coast), and South (the islands to New Zealand and Australia) under Chester W. Nimitz, who commanded the Pacific Ocean Area. MacArthur was given the Southwest Pacific from Rabaul to Java, with a bulge into the Central Pacific to the Philippines. His first decision was to hold Port Moresby on the southern coast of the eastern tail of New Guinea, a thousand miles north of Brisbane, from which the Australians had planned to defend their settled southeastern coast. This decision in effect committed the South Pacific command to preventing a Japanese attack around the New Guinea tail through the Coral Sea in the rear of Port Moresby. MacArthur protested this division of the Coral Sea, but this was less serious than the fact that the Australian and American forces assigned him were "only a small fraction of those he would need" to return to the

[30] *Crusade in Europe*, 16-48. Maurice Matloff, *Strategic Planning for Coalition Warfare* (2 vols., I with Edward M. Snell, *U. S. Army in World War II*, Washington, 1955-1960), I, 157-158. On the American soldier and his education see Morris Janowitz, *The Professional Soldier: A Social and Political Portrait* (Glencoe, Ill., 1960), John W. Masland and Laurence I. Radway, *Soldiers and Scholars: Military Education and National Policy* (Princeton, 1957), and Gene M. Lyons and John W. Masland, *Education and Military Leadership: A Study of the R.O.T.C.* (Princeton, 1959).

Philippines. In any case, his problems were small in comparison to those handed to Joseph W. Stilwell, a comparatively unknown infantryman three years younger than MacArthur and seven years older than Eisenhower. Stilwell was joint (Allied) chief of staff for China Theater (under Chiang, with the Chinese army retaining its own chief of staff and commanders), commander (under the British, but responsible to Chiang) of the small Chinese force which had moved into Burma too late to save Rangoon, and commander of the small American forces (under the British or Chiang, but responsible to the American joint chiefs of staff) in China-Burma-India. Stilwell knew the Far East and seemed to be a good choice to help the Generalissimo build up his ground forces to reopen the Burma Road and to defend the bases from which the Allies hoped to launch an air offensive against Japan, though he was hardly qualified to direct such an offensive. His known and "monumental absence of tact" and "contempt of Chinese [and British and American] officialdom" made him even less qualified to reconcile the divergent interests of the three Allies to which he was subordinate. The Americans wanted to help Chiang, but could spare only a few airmen and engineers and some lend-lease equipment for this purpose. The British were primarily interested in Rangoon and Singapore. Chiang was primarily interested in the East Asian War with the Japanese and the Chinese Communists. The Allies planned an immediate offensive in Europe and hoped for four eventual concentric offensives against Japan: from Hawaii across the Central Pacific, from the South and Southwest Pacific to the Philippines, from India toward Rangoon and Singapore, and from China toward Canton.[31]

No major military critic claims that the Allies should have concentrated against Japan. The amphibious strength for such

[31] Matloff and Snell, *Strategic Planning,* 157-173. By December, 1942, 8 United States Army divisions and 27 air groups (less than half the total in each case) were in Europe. By October, 1944, there were 40 divisions and 149 air groups deployed against Germany, and 27 divisions and 57 air groups against Japan. In December, 1942, the Central Pacific had 4 divisions and 4 air groups and much of the Navy's air power. The South Pacific had 4 divisions (one of them a Marine division) and 5 air groups and additional naval air power. MacArthur had 3 divisions (a Marine division included) and 10 air groups, plus Australian forces. An Australian division and a New Zealand division had been left in the Middle East. There were 7 United States Army air groups in the Middle East, 7 in Latin America, 2 in Alaska, and only 4 in China-Burma-India. For the Western Hemisphere see two volumes in the *U. S. Army* series: Byron Fairchild and Stetson Conn, *The Framework of Hemisphere Defense* (Washington, 1960) and Stanley W. Dzubian, *Military Relations between the United States and Canada, 1939-1945* (Washington, 1959).

concentration did not then exist, no major help could be expected from either Britain or Russia, and Japan did not threaten the existence of any of the major Allies. As Marshall wrote on April 2, 1942, "The bulk of the combat forces of the United States, United Kingdom, and Russia can be applied simultaneously only against Germany, and then only if we attack in time." The Western Allies' deployment was based on a correct appreciation of their enemies' strength and objectives, the length of the Allies' own communications and the nature of their forces, and the relative importance of the Western Allies' political objectives. But the public did not realize how these decisions would affect the political settlements of the four wars then in progress. In retrospect, at least, it is hard to see how their comparatively small mechanized forces could have advanced much farther into the Heartland than they were to advance by the end of 1945: to the boundaries of Charlemagne's and the Byzantine Empires at the end of the eighth century, to the mountain wall from the Caucasus to central Indochina, and into the Pacific islands and those parts of Korea which had not been part of the Chinese Empire of the Han period. In any case, the Western Allies had tipped the balance in the Russo-German War, and had won the Second German and Great Pacific Wars. Their contributions of air power, military equipment, and advice seemed to have enabled Chiang to triumph in the continuing War for East Asia. As in all coalition wars, there were the usual controversies over strategical and political details and the personalities of the various commanders and their military subordinates and political superiors.[32]

The controversies over Western Allied strategy in Europe turn on four major issues: the distribution of forces between a "Second Front" in Northwest Europe and what Churchill called the "soft underbelly" in the Mediterranean, the timing of the Second Front and Eisenhower's alleged timidity in the operations which followed the liberation of France, the role of strategic bombing, and the Americans' alleged neglect of political objectives and the Allies' demand for unconditional surrender by both Germany and Japan. Montgomery, for example, does not think that Eisenhower was a great soldier. He believes that he was essentially a military statesman whose genius for compromise enabled him to command a truly

[32] *Ibid.*, 185. The best study is Louis Morton, "Germany First: The Basic Concept of Allied Strategy in World War II" (Greenfield, *Command Decisions*, 3-38).

multi-national army. The American planners, from the beginning, had pushed for a Second Front in France. In Eisenhower's words,

To use American forces . . . through the Russian front was impossible. . . . Plans for attacking through Norway, through Spain and Portugal, and even for . . . depending exclusively on . . . sea and air superiority, were [rejected]. . . . The difficulty of attacking Germany through the mountainous . . . southern and southeastern flanks was obvious [geographically, the underbelly is not soft], while the full might of Great Britain and the United States could not be concentrated in the Mediterranean. . . . The land armies and, above all, the air and naval strength required for the defense of England could be employed offensively only . . . across the Channel.

The British accepted the American proposals for a beachhead in France in 1942 as a basis for further planning, but then correctly vetoed this scheme and replaced it by the landing in North Africa. The Allies did not have the landing craft for the build-up necessary to break out of the beachhead, though their assaulting forces would have met less resistance in 1942 than in 1944. The Russians had taken their hopes and public statements of Allied solidarity as a promise of an immediate Second Front. Their propaganda, if only for internal purposes during the desperate Stalingrad struggle, and their well-meaning friends in the West demanded immediate action. The North African campaign "showed both originality and daring" and gave the Allied armies much needed experience, but the Russians and some Americans thought they had been more or less deliberately deceived. When the North African campaign opened the way to further Mediterranean campaigns and caused the Second Front to be delayed until 1944, many people thought that Churchill had never favored a cross-Channel assault.[33]

Churchill's further insistence on driving up the mountains

[33] Eisenhower, *Crusade in Europe*, 42-45. Fuller *Second World War*, 241. Fuller agrees with Ralph Ingersoll that Eisenhower was "a shrewd, intelligent, tactful, careful chairman, . . . neither bold nor decisive." Ingersoll, *Top Secret* (New York, 1946), 219. Only fifty-one when the United States entered the war, Eisenhower had not seen front-line service during the First World War. Montgomery, who was three years older, had been badly wounded at First Ypres. He had commanded a division in the Flanders battle. Actually, Eisenhower was a decisive commander, but did not always decide in favor of Montgomery. Clausewitz had closed his study of the "Genius for War" with the words, "Searching, rather than creative minds, comprehensive minds rather than such as pursue one special line, cool, rather than fiery, heads are those to which . . . we should . . . trust . . . the honor and safety of our country." *On War*, 46.

of Italy to the Po River valley after the Mediterranean had been reopened—a decision which, Fuller says, resulted in "a series of Somme-Ypres battles, among mountains instead of swamps" in "a campaign which for lack of strategic sense and tactical imagination is unique in military history"—heightened American suspicions that Churchill was still trying to divert forces from the main European and Pacific assaults at the very time when "the political problem [of the division of Europe between Russia and the West] had become paramount." This is the background for the Americans' refusal to switch the final Mediterranean landing operation (in August, 1944) from southern France to Trieste and to attempt to beat the Russians to Berlin in the spring of 1945. The Western Allies' demand for "unconditional surrender" (at the Casablanca Conference in January, 1943) may have been a concession to Western opinion for their failure to open a Second Front before 1944 and a necessary reassurance to Stalin that they were not contemplating a deal with the Germans. But the Morgenthau plan (adopted at Quebec in September, 1944) for de-industrializing Germany was a useless concession to wartime nationalist passion. As Edmund Burke had once noted, "Frenzy does not become a slighter distemper on account of the number of those who may be infected with it." Unconditional surrender, which the American critic Hanson Baldwin and many others regard as "perhaps the biggest political mistake of the war," may have delayed the Italian surrender by about a month. But it is hard to believe that the Germans, who were on the spot, would have allowed Italy north of Rome to slip away. Unconditional surrender and Allied "terror bombing" may have solidified German opinion behind Hitler, but Germany's fanatical resistance seems to have been determined rather by the very nature of the Nazi regime. The ablest of the German generals began to toy with

The Second Front controversy could hardly have increased the distrust between Stalin and his Allies, but it may have enabled Communist resistance groups in Western Europe to play on old suspicions of perfidious capitalist Albion. See Herbert Feis, *Churchill-Roosevelt-Stalin: The War They Waged and the Peace They Sought* (Princeton, 1957); Trumbull Higgins, *Winston Churchill and the Second Front, 1940-1943* (New York, 1957); Samuel Eliot Morison, *Strategy and Compromise* (Boston, 1958); Wynford Vaughan-Thomas *Anzio* (New York, 1961); for Roosevelt as a strategist, Ernest R. May, ed., *The Ultimate Decision: The President as Commander in Chief* (New York, 1960); Elting E. Morison, *Turmoil and Tradition: A Study of the Life and Times of Henry L. Stimson* (Boston, 1960); and Maurice Matloff, "The ANVIL Decision: Crossroads of Strategy (1944)" (Greenfield, Command Decisions, 285-302).

the opposition only after the Allies' victories had shown them the hopelessness of Germany's situation and the plotters were unable to strike soon enough to deliver the armies in the west to the Allies.[34]

Eisenhower later listed the pre-conditions for the cross-Channel assault as follows:

[1] that our Air Force would be, at the chosen moment, overwhelming in strength; [2] that the German air forces would be virtually swept from the skies and that our air bombers could practically isolate the attack area from rapid reinforcement; [3] that the U-boat could be so effectively countered that our convoys could count on . . . a safe Atlantic crossing; [4] that our supporting naval vessels would . . . batter down local defenses and [5] that specialized landing craft could be available in such numbers as to make possible the pouring ashore of a great army through an initial breach.

Victory in the Atlantic helped to meet the third and fourth conditions. The fifth—the shortage of landing craft—was the last condition to be met chronologically, but by 1944 the

[34] Fuller, *Second World War*, 261, 271, 324. Hanson W. Baldwin, *Great Mistakes of the War* (New York, 1949), 24. Burke, *Letter . . . on the Affairs of America, 1777 (The Works of Edmund Burke*, World's Classics ed., London, 1924), II, 263. See also John L. Snell, *Wartime Origins of the East-West Dilemma over Germany* (New Orleans, [1959]), and Eugene Davidson, *The Death and Life of Germany: An Account of the American Occupation* (New York, 1959). Military victory, Clausewitz once noted, is sound psychological warfare. "1. Warfare has three main objects: (a) To conquer and destroy the armed power of the enemy; (b) To take possession of his material and other sources of strength; and (c) To gain public opinion. 2. To accomplish the first purpose, we should always direct our principle operation against the main body of the enemy army or at least against an important part of his forces. For only after defeating these can we pursue the other two objects successfully." *Principles of War*, trans. and ed. Hans W. Gatzke (Harrisburg, 1942), 45. The British Government, incidentally, had suggested that unconditional surrender be applied to Italy. Paul Kecskemeti, *Strategic Surrender: The Politics of Victory and Defeat* (Stanford, 1958), concludes that unconditional surrender did not significantly affect German resistance. He tends to discount the actual military situation in Italy in 1943.

Churchill's many critics will use Arthur Bryant, *The Turn of the Tide: A History of the War Years Based on the Diaries of Field-Marshal Lord Alanbrooke, Chief of the Imperial General Staff* (Garden City, 1957) and *Triumph in the West* (Garden City, 1959), but Alanbrooke, like Haig, does not increase his stature by his memoirs. John Kennedy, *The Business of War* (London, 1957) is more temperate. Some of Churchill's ideas—such as the proposal to switch Anvil from Toulon to the Bay of Biscay without additional shipping or air cover—display the amateur touch to the end. John Ehrman, *Grand Strategy, VI* and *VII (United Kingdom Military Series*, London, 1956), like all volumes in this series, discuss the differences between the politicians and the generals, but do not reveal "individual differences within the War Cabinet," which might be of prime importance in political matters as the war approached its climax. The American side is covered in Forrest C. Poge, *The Supreme Command (U. S. Army in World War II*, Washington, 1954).

trickle of munitions of all kinds had become a torrent, a fact which enabled the Western Allies to launch their decisive offensives in Western Europe and the Pacific simultaneously, a major revision of their basic "Germany first" strategy. The most difficult strategical problem was that presented by the first and second conditions. It is easy to forget that all air operations were still experimental. The German failures in the Battle of Britain must be judged accordingly, and comparison between the R. A. F. and U. S. A. A. F. is useless because of the ways in which the latter benefited from the former's experiments. The R. A. F.'s 1939 raids on German naval bases had shown the difficulty of unescorted daylight bombing. From this time on the British had concentrated on night "area" bombing, though they might have developed new daylight bombers if the United States had not entered the war. The R. A. F. stressed bomb tonnage. American heavy bombers flew at higher altitudes (for better protection against antiaircraft guns) and American designers placed greater faith in precision bombsights and the defensive power of heavier guns used in tight flying formations.[35]

From 1940 to 1943, to quote Eisenhower's Deputy Supreme Commander, Air Marshal Arthur W. Tedder, "it is almost impossible to disentangle the strategic and economic from the political, technical, and tactical factors" as Allied bombers attacked "oil, power, chemicals and explosives, aircraft factories and airfields, aluminium plants, docks and ports, and communications." This dispersion of effort was due, in part, to the theory already mentioned, that Germany's economy was stretched to capacity and that damage to any sector of it would indirectly cut arms production. But Germany's earlier failure to go all-out had left her with reserve factories and labor. German arms output rose sharply from its January/February, 1942 (pre-Stalingrad), base of 100 to 232 in May, 1943 before Kursk), and 322 in July, 1944 (after the Normandy landings). But continuous Allied pressure had also made it impossible for Speer to concentrate on any single weapons program—atomic, V-weapons, snorkel submarines, or jet aircraft. Everything was done "piecemeal, . . . as urgent military needs made . . . high output essential, now in tanks, now in guns, or ammunition. The last industry to be so tackled was the aircraft industry, during the first half of 1944." But the increase in German aircraft production

85 Eisenhower, Crusade in Europe, 45-46.

even before that date was of prime importance to Carl Spaatz, the later Commander of the U. S. Strategic Air Forces in Europe with the job of co-ordinating the strategic operations of the Eighth Air Force in England and the Fifteenth Air Force in Italy. Spaatz later wrote that many people had underestimated "two prime necessities for success in modern war: first, control of the air as the essential condition for the advance of all forces; second, strategic use of air power [a definition not generally used in this connection] as the means to gain that control against an enemy equipped with equal or nearly equal, replacement capacity." The Americans never lost their faith in daylight bombing. Their vast material commitment to planes for this type of attack finally led to its success, though not by the means—unescorted precision attacks—on which this faith had originally been based.[36]

The *Luftwaffe* refused to

commit its fighters . . . against bombers making shallow penetrations under heavy fighter protection. . . . The only way to draw the German air force up to combat was to attack sensitive targets, which were for the most part deep in Germany. When the American heavy bombers . . . began deep penetration, . . . they were met by fierce resistance. In the many air battles of the ensuing months our aircraft losses were heavy but replaceable. The German losses were also heavy, but they were not so easily replaced.

Unlike the *Luftwaffe* during the Battle of Britain, the U. S. A. A. F. won the command of the air by deliberately forcing battle. Like most battles of attrition, Pointblank—the code word for the Air Battle of Germany from June, 1943 to the end of March, 1944—was won by Perseverance and Superiority in Numbers, though Stratagem (scientific ingenuity)— to borrow some headings from Clausewitz' discussion of Strategy in General—had something to do with it. In October, 1943, the bombers struck four targets deep inside Germany.

[36] Tedder, *Air Power in War* (London, 1948), 99-100. U. S. Strategic Bombing Survey, *Over-all Report (European War)*, 32. Spaatz, "Strategic Air Power Against Germany" (*Newsweek*, XXXIII, March 7, 1949, 28). On radar see Dudley Saward, *The Bomber's Eye* (London, 1959), on German research, Leslie E. Simon, *German Research in World War II* (New York, 1947) and Rudolf Lusar, *German Secret Weapons of the Second World War*, trans. R. P. Heller and M. Schindler (London, 1959). See also Arthur Harris, *Bomber Offensive* (New York, 1947), J. M. Spaight, *Air Power Can Disarm* (London, 1948), Stefan T. Possony, *Strategic Air Power: The Pattern of Dynamic Security* (Washington, 1949), Asher Lee, *Air Power* (New York, 1955), Fred Charles Iklé, *The Social Impact of Bomb Destruction* (Norman, 1958), and Admiral Gerald Dickens' critical *Bombing and Strategy* (New York, 1949).

On the last of these raids—on the ball-bearing plants at Schweinfurt—60 out of 291 planes were lost, 17 wrecked, and 121 damaged. In six days the Eighth Bomber Command had lost nearly a quarter of the bomber crews assigned to it. The American official history notes that "The Eighth Air Force had . . . lost air superiority over Germany [and] could not . . . [regain it] until sufficient long-range escort became available." The German fighters were still increasing in numbers, but the Americans had learned "how to drop bombs accurately in unnerving circumstances, how to cope with . . . the weather, above all how to outwit the Luftwaffe." These lessons were applied during the "Big Week" of February 20-25, 1944. Almost 10,000 tons of bombs were dropped on German aircraft plants with the loss of only 226 planes in 3,800 sorties. R. A. F. bombers had dropped 9,198 tons of bombs on five industrial cities, losing 157 bombers in 2,351 sorties. The Germans were forced to disperse their entire aircraft industry; their fighter losses had been so heavy that they no longer opposed every major attack. In Spaatz' words:

When our ground forces stormed the beaches, . . . our fighters were not needed to form a protective umbrella . . . and could be used almost exclusively as fighter-bombers against enemy troops. Our armies were thus assured of freedom of movement by day or night, whereas the German troops were continuously harried. . . . These advantages . . . were gained through the strategic use of air power to destroy the German air force.[37]

The invasion coast—that part of the Atlantic Wall within fighter range of England—was about twice the length of the Maginot Line. The Dutch and Belgian beaches were too far from the ports from which the assault would be launched. Britanny (originally chosen) was too far from Germany. Since the nearest beaches—in the area from Dunkirk to Le

[37] Spaatz, "Strategic Air Power." Craven and Cate, *Army Air Forces, II,* 70-75, 718; III, 44-45. The problem of the Assembly of Forces in Space and in Time, which the Germans had failed to solve during the Battle of Britain, was brilliantly solved. The biggest daylight raid on Berlin (March 18, 1945) involved 1,250 bombers and about the same number of fighters. This was equivalent to assembling an infantry division squad by squad from dozens of separate points over a target 600 miles away.

Perseverance is the means by which a commander overcomes the friction of war, the "constant surge of false and true information, of mistakes committed through fear, through negligence, . . . from ill will, a true or false sense of duty, indolence or exhaustion." Perseverance "becomes obstinacy" as soon as "resistance to an opposing judgment proceeds not from a better conviction or reliance upon a higher principle, but from a feeling of opposition." Clausewitz, *On War,* 41, 136.

Havre—would be most heavily defended, the Allies chose the area between Caen in Normandy and the base of the Cotentin peninsula to land elements of five infantry and three airborne divisions, a force about the size of that contemplated in the German Sea Lion plan. The British were to take Caen while the Americans cut off the Cotentin peninsula and captured the port of Cherbourg at its tip. Rundstedt, the German commander, talked of a mobile defense in depth, but his subordinate, Rommel, wanted his reserves well forward. His African experiences had convinced him that "there could be no question of ever moving large formations . . . as a result of the enemy's air supremacy." Rundstedt had thirty-three reserve divisions, fifteen good infantry divisions, and ten armored divisions. Rommel had four of the latter, two north and two south of the Seine. Three were watching the Bay of Biscay and the Mediterranean, and the other three were controlled by the Army high command in Germany. The key Allied strategems were Churchill's scheme for towing two temporary harbors across the Channel and a fake landing near Dunkirk. The Germans hesitated to move south of the Seine because of the latter threat; even the Mediterranean divisions were not ordered north. The only armored division in the assault area lost its chance to attack by waiting for an order from Rommel; other units moved in daylight and suffered heavily or were thrown into areas under Allied naval gunfire.[38]

Cherbourg fell on June 26, but the British had hard going at Caen against most of the German armor and the Americans were stuck in the hedgerow country at the base of the Cotentin peninsula. But Rommel had been disabled and Rundstedt temporarily removed, and the plotters almost killed Hitler on July 20. The Americans broke out at the end of July. The armor which tried to cut them off was trapped at Falaise, and the landing in southern France added to the rout. By the first week in September the Allies were approaching Germany by the traditional routes: the Russians through the Polish plain and the Balkans, the Western Allies through the low-

[38] Guderian, *Panzer Leader*, 330-331. A storm wrecked one of the temporary harbors on June 19, but 629,000 men and 218,000 tons of supplies were already ashore. Gordon A. Harrison, *Cross-Channel Attack (U. S. Army in World War II*, Washington, 1951), 387. Frederick E. Morgan, *Overture to Overlord* (New York, 1950) discusses planning. See also David Howarth, *D Day: The Sixth of June, 1944* (New York, 1959), Cornelius Ryan. *The Longest Day* (New York, 1959), and John Frayn Turner, *Invasion '44: The First Full Story of D-Day in Normandy* (New York, 1949). The best German accounts are *The Rommel Papers* and Ruge, *Der Seekrieg*.

land plain and the Lorraine and Belfort gaps. Montgomery's Army Group (the 1st Canadian and 2nd British Armies) had taken Antwerp, but the Germans held its approaches. Omar Bradley's Army Group screened the Ardennes, with the 1st U. S. Army approaching the Rhine through the lowland plain and George S. Patton's 3rd U. S. Army going into the Lorraine gap. Still further south the 7th U. S. and 1st French Armies (later another Army Group) were approaching the Belfort gap. But most supplies were still coming in over the beaches or through Cherbourg. The Germans still held Le Havre and most of the smaller Channel and the Atlantic ports. Bombing had wrecked the railroads; the Allied spearheads depended on truck and even air transport. But the Combined Intelligence Committee (which had seen similar portents in 1943) thought that Germany might collapse by "1 December 1944, [or] . . . even sooner," an idea shared by much of the Allied public and by Eisenhower's colorful subordinates, Montgomery and Patton. By September 8, however, the Allied thrust to the Rhine had been checked, and Churchill told his Chiefs of Staff

One can already foresee the probability of a lull in [our] magnificent advances. . . . Will [our] forces be so limited by supply conditions and the lack of ports as to enable the Germans to consolidate on the Siegfried Line? . . . The . . . consolidating effect of a stand on . . . native soil should not be underrated. It is at least as likely that Hitler will be fighting on the 1st January as that he will collapse before then. If he does collapse before then the reasons will be political rather than purely military.[39]

Eisenhower had already rejected Patton's and Montgomery's separate offers to end the war by "pencil-like" thrusts into Germany. Though his intelligence chief had seen no

[39] Pogue, *Supreme Command*, 245. Ehrman, *Grand Strategy*, V, 401-402. The Germans escaped from France with "little more than their rifles." Eleven armored divisions now "amounted to eleven regimental combat teams, each with five or ten operationally fit tanks and a few batteries of artillery." Pogue, *Supreme Command*, 217. Also Martin Blumenson, "General Bradley's Decision at Argentan (1944)" (Greenfield, *Command Decisions*, 303-319). The best of many accounts of the French underground is "Aspects de la Résistance française" (entire November, 1950, issue of the *Révue d'histoire de la deuxième guerre mondiale*). On the French army see Marcel Vigneras, *Rearming the French (U. S. Army in World War II*, Washington, 1957) and the memoirs of Marshals Juin, *Mémoires* (2 vols., Paris, 1959-1960) and Lattre de Tassigny, *History of the French First Army*, trans. Malcolm Barnes (New York, 1953). For the Paris plot see Wilhelm von Schramm, *Conspiracy among Generals*, trans. and ed. R. T. Clark (New York, 1957). For psychological warfare at this time see Daniel Lerner, *Sykewar, Psychological Warfare against Germany, D-Day to VE-Day* (New York, 1949).

signs of imminent victory, Patton, through Bradley, claimed that his Third Army could drive through the Lorraine gap if it was given enough gasoline. Bradley was sure that this would require the help of the First Army, which Montgomery wanted for his thrust through the lowland plain. In the temperate words of the British official history—neither Patton nor Montgomery being teetotalers with words—Eisenhower and Montgomery agreed that

the pace of operations must be everywhere reduced, to conform to the supplies; or they must be concentrated on one sector and virtually halted elsewhere. . . . Montgomery believed that the Germans might well collapse . . . [under] a concentrated offensive . . . [to] the Rhine on either side of the Ruhr, or the Rhine between Frankfurt and Karlsruhe [opposite Patton] . . . [He preferred the former, which] would strike at the industrial heart of Germany; and in an area beyond the Rhine where armour could best be deployed. But whichever section was chosen . . . must enjoy absolute priority, and enough forces must be massed and placed under a single command. . . . Eisenhower . . . was not so sure either that a concentrated offensive could be maintained or that the enemy was so near to collapse. . . . To halt Patton . . . and to leave the armies in southern France with virtually nothing to do, might be to sacrifice the amity of the Command—possibly of the Alliance—to a controversial venture which might well not succeed.

He ordered a "broad front" approach. The First Army would help Montgomery secure the Rhine approaches, but Patton would also push ahead. Both thrusts were already in trouble, but events never shook their commanders' faiths that they could have won the war in 1944.[40]

Patton soon faced "the strongest of all the German armies in the West." The ensuing Lorraine campaign cost the Americans more casualties than Normandy.

The earlier drive across western France had seen the fortunate combination of a dashing armored commander, ground suited for tank action, and an almost complete demoralization and disorganization . . . of the enemy. The subsequent German stand at the Moselle line [and Montgomery's failure to take a bridgehead over the Rhine at Arnhem] benefited, it is true, from the logistical lag in Allied operations, but [also] . . . typified the Germans' amazing powers of recuperation.

[40] Ehrman, Grand Strategy, V, 379-380. Roland G. Ruppenthal, "Logistics and the Broad-Front Strategy (1944)" (Greenfield, Command Decisions, 320-328). Montgomery, Normandy to the Baltic (Boston, 1948), 196-198. Ingersoll, Top Secret and Charles R. Codman, Drive (Boston, 1957) give Patton's side. His printable comments are in War As I Knew It (Boston, 1947).

These powers were demonstrated during the early winter by German counteroffensives in the Ardennes, in Alsace, and to relieve Budapest. The Ardennes offensive "inflicted much damage, . . . [but cost the Germans more] than they could afford. . . . It brought home to the German troops their incapacity to turn the scales, and thereby undermined such hopes as they had retained." In the meantime Allied bombing had reached its peak. If it "had been better designed—to dislocate supplies rather than to devastate populated areas—it could have produced a quicker paralysis, . . . [but] it did spread a creeping paralysis." Half of the 2,697,473 tons of bombs dropped by the Western Allies during the war fell on Germany; about three-quarters of the tonnage dropped on Germany fell during the last ten of the sixty-eight months of the war. The campaign against oil fuel was "decisive within less than a year." The Germans had more planes than fuel to fly them; tanks were hauled into action on the east by oxen. Chemical production was cut so sharply that shells were three-quarters filled with rock salt, and the attack on German transportation was so effective that the German economy was headed for collapse by the end of the winter. The United States Strategic Bombing Survey concluded "that even a first-class military power—rugged and resilient as Germany was—cannot live long under full-scale and free exploitation of air weapons over the heart of its territory." By spring the Germans, like the Poles and French in 1939 and 1940, were fighting from fixed positions against overwhelming mechanized power.[41]

The Red Army crossed the Oder about thirty miles from

[41] H. M. Cole, The Lorraine Campaign (U. S. Army in World War II, Washington, 1950), 604-605. Liddell Hart, Strategy, 324, 300. Craven and Cate, Army Air Forces. III, 794. U. S. Strategic Bombing Survey, Over-all Report (European War), 107. See also Charles B. MacDonald, "The Decision to Launch Operation MARKET-GARDEN (1944)" and Charles V. P. von Luttichau, "The German Counteroffensive in the Ardennes (1944)" (Greenfield, Command Decisions, 329-357), Robert E. Merriam, Battle of the Ardennes (London, 1959), S. L. A. Marshall et al., Bastogne (Washington, 1946), and R. E. Urquhart and Wilfried Greatorex, Arnhem (London, 1958). Montgomery's thrust received "logistical support which [Montgomery then] . . . thought 'a great victory;' . . . and the operation failed." C. P. Stacey, The Victory Campaign (Official History of the Canadian Army in the Second World War, 3 vols., Ottawa, 1955-1960, III), 322. G. W. L. Nicholson, The Canadians in Italy, (II in the same series) is equally fine. The airmen Lewis H. Brereton, The Brereton Diaries (New York, 1946), 339, and H. H. Arnold, Global Mission (New York, 1945), 520-522, blame the Supreme Command. Fuller, Second World War, 345, holds the airmen responsible for the shortage of transport planes and notes that the Allies "overlooked the sea, or were incapable of calling it to their assistance."

Berlin in February, 1945. The Allies crossed the Rhine in March and the U. S. Ninth Army, which had been sand-wiched between the British Second and the U. S. First Armies in the fall, reached the Elbe, about fifty miles from Berlin, on April 11. The Anglo-American plan for occupying Germany dated from January, 1944; Stalin had agreed to it at Yalta in February, 1945. Eisenhower now rejected Churchill's suggestion that the Ninth Army be placed under Montgomery to beat the Russians to Berlin. Bradley feared "It might cost us . . . 100,000 casualties. 'A pretty stiff price to pay for a prestige objective, . . . especially when we've got to fall back and let the other fellow take over.' " Hitler committed suicide two days after the lynching of Mussolini on April 28. Doenitz surrendered the remnants of the Thousand Year Reich on May 7 (armies in Italy, Denmark, Holland, and parts of Germany had already surrendered), though fighting con-tinued in Czechoslovakia for another week.[42]

The East Asian and Pacific Wars: The Japanese Raid

Japan had taken over Manchuria in 1931, but the East Asian War really began on July 7, 1937, when the Japanese attack on the Marco Polo Bridge led to the capture of Peiping and to an expedition to Shanghai and the Chinese capital of Nanking. The Japanese smashed most of Chiang's German-trained divisions, but failed to destroy his government, which retreated to Chungking on the upper Yangtze. This was "The Last, Lost Good Chance" to stop Japan, but again "the only concurrent action was to do nothing." By the winter of 1938-1939 the Japanese held the major ports and railway centers and the Nationalists were dependent on supplies brought in through Indochina, Burma, and Russia.

An undeclared truce existed along the front, broken occasionally when the Japanese forces advanced to break up Chinese troop concentrations or to train their own troops. . . . About thirty [of three hundred] Chinese divisions were . . . primarily [loyal] to the

[42] Bradley added "Berlin was to be . . . a symbol of unity among the Allies. Although I . . . was no less beguiled than the others on the Soviet's friendly postwar intentions, . . . I would never have assumed responsibility for a sector unless I was certain I could have supplied it." *A Soldier's Story*, 535-536. See also *The Testament of Adolf Hitler: The Hitler-Bormann Documents*, ed. François Genoud, trans. R. H. Stevens (London, 1960) and Herbert Feis, *Between War and Peace: The Potsdam Conference* (Princeton, 1960). The Berlin matter may not have been "presented to Mr. Roosevelt, who was then at Warm Springs, . . . where he was to die in less than a week." Pogue, *Supreme Command*, 444-445, and "The Decision to Halt at the Elbe (1945)" (Greenfield, *Command Decisions*, 374-387).

Generalissimo. . . . The Chinese said they had about 1,000,000 rifles, 83,000 machine guns, . . . 7,800 trench mortars, . . . [and] 1,330 cannon . . . of diverse calibers and origins. . . . Soldiers were unpaid, poorly fed, . . . poorly clad, [and diseased]. . . . Trucks and motor fuel were almost nonexistent . . . and there was no organization for keeping up a steady flow of rations to troops on the march.

Contrary to American press reports, the Japanese were living off the country rather than bleeding to death in China, and the Communists were gradually extending the areas under their control.[43]

Japanese production quintupled from 1930 to 1941; the army air forces were nearly tripled; combat naval tonnage had increased by about the same amount since the Washington Conference. Still more important, about half of the United States fleet and most of the British fleet were occupied with Germany and Italy. In December, 1941, the Japanese had ten older battleships (the 18" gun, 71,659 ton full load *Yamato* was commissioned after December 7, the *Musashi* a year later), six carriers, and four light carriers to nine older battleships and three carriers for the United States Pacific Fleet. The new *Prince of Wales* and the old battle cruiser *Repulse* made Singapore on December 2, but the carrier which was to accompany them had grounded in Jamaica. Western observers of the East Asian War had accurately reported the Japanese skill in landing operations, but these and other favorable observations "had not sunk very deeply into the consciousness of European officer corps accustomed to regard Asian military leaders generally as deficient in first-rate organising and technical ability, and the rank and file as lacking the fibre and initiative of their own men." An Australian booklet which was printed too late to be used in Malaya described Japanese tactics as " 'a vigorous advance using the roads until contact is gained; a direct frontal attack is avoided. Small parties carry out attacks on flanks and rear . . . through the jungle, river and sea, . . . usually caus[ing] a general withdrawal . . . and exert[ing] considerable moral effect on troops who may be attacked in the rear.' " Years of mobile operations against poorly armed, but clever and stubborn, Chinese forces had led the Japanese to depend increas-

[43] Herbert Feis, *The Road to Pearl Harbor* (Princeton, 1950), 9. Charles F. Romanus and Riley Sunderland, *Stilwell's Command Problems (U. S. Army in World War II.* Washington, 1956), 3-4. The best account is F. F. Liu, *A Military History of Modern China, 1924-1949* (Princeton, 1956).

ingly on light mortars, light tanks, bicycles, and local transport and supplies in areas with poor ground communications.[44]

The European war provided the opportunity both for the Japanese conquest of Southeast Asia and for the development of the local nationalist and Communist groups which had sparked occasional rebellions (in 1927 in the East Indies, in 1930 in Burma, in 1935 in the Philippines, and at various times in Indochina) during the interwar years. With France and the Netherlands in German hands and Britain and the United States involved in Europe, the Western states had been unable to send "adequate forces from outside, in the old style imperialist tradition," and had failed, except in the Philippines, to give "the resident peoples enough of a stake in the country to make it worth their while to defend Western rule." The Indian Army's size was deceptive; the Auchinleck Committee of 1938 had judged it " 'unfit to take the field against land or air force equipped with up-to-date weapons,' " and the expansion of both the British and Indian Armies had spread experienced personnel very thin. An Indian recruit was not likely to develop strong personal loyalty for a newly-arrived officer who knew only a few words of Urdu. Malaya was defended by 37,000 Indians, 19,600 British, 15,200 Australians, and 16,800 local volunteers with a few planes, little antitank or antiaircraft equipment, and no tanks. The Australians had refused to put down striking rubber workers; the Malayan authorities had objected to the recruiting of labor battalions because of its effect on wages, and the wages had then been fixed so low that nobody had enlisted. The 14,500 men at Hong Kong, including Canadians sent out in October to deter the Japanese, had four planes. Burma had the equivalent of two divisions, mostly Indian and Burmese, four old bombers and thirty-two old fighters. Support was expected from the Chinese and the twenty-one fighters of the American Volunteer Group who were to defend the Burma Road. The Dutch East Indies—whose population was about as large as that of Japan—were defended by about 40,000 Dutch and 100,000 native troops.[45]

[44] Lionel Wigmore, *The Japanese Thrust (Australia in the War of 1939-1945,* Canberra, 1957), 109-117. See also the fine book by Saburo Hayashi and Alvin D. Coox, *Kogun: The Japanese Army in the Pacific War* (Quantico, 1959).

[45] Virginia Thompson, *Postmortem on Malaya* (New York, 1943), 313. She is the co-author, with Richard Adloff, of *The Left Wing in Southeast Asia* (New York, 1950). Strength figures from Wigmore, *Japanese Thrust,* 103-108.

The only national army under Western auspices in East Asia was in the Philippines, which were to become an autonomous republic in 1946. After retiring from the United States Army, MacArthur had become Military Advisor to the Commonwealth and Field Marshal of the new army. His subordinates, Majors Eisenhower and James B. Ord, had planned an army of 200,000 men, with six months' compulsory training for privates, by 1946. It was to be trained by the Philippine Constabulary and men on loan from the Philippine Scouts, the Filipino component of the United States Army. Though he admitted that he would need the help of God and the United States, MacArthur hoped to make the Islands an "Asiatic Switzerland," strong enough to make an attack too costly in men and money to be worth it. When the Japanese attacked, 31,095 regulars were backed by 100,000 men of the Philippine Army, the small U. S. Asiatic Fleet, strong only in submarines, 35 modern bombers and 107 fighters. Reinforcements were on the way, but were to be diverted elsewhere. Guam, the key to the Western Pacific, and Wake were almost undefended. In both Malaya and the Philippines

an initial policy of holding only the naval base area had been replaced by a policy of holding a wider area. At length a Commander-in-Chief had been appointed in both areas [MacArthur, not quite 62 when the Japanese attacked, for U. S. Army Forces Far East, and Air Chief Marshal Robert Brooke-Popham, aged 63, as British Commander-in-Chief Far East]. The naval forces in both areas were inadequate, and the policy was to rely largely on air defense; but too few aircraft were available. Both commanders possessed a relatively small force of well-trained troops and a larger body of less well-trained ones. Both commanders were excessively optimistic; and both were gravely short of equipment.[46]

Japan had made great strides toward self-sufficiency, but was still very short of oil, the prime mover of mechanized warfare. This was the major factor in turning her attention toward the nearly undefended resources of Southeast Asia. In September, 1940, Japan became a member of the Axis and took over northern Indochina, leaving the Burma Road (which the British had agreed to close for three months in

Why the cautious Mackenzie King went along with this bit of brinkmanship is not yet clear. There are many books on the various nationalist movements. Malcolm D. Kennedy, *A Short History of Communism in Asia* (London, 1957) is a survey.

[46] Louis Morton, *The Fall of the Philippines* (U. S. Army in World War II, Washington, 1953), 8-50. Wigmore, *Japanese Thrust*, 90.

June) as China's only remaining line to the Western powers. In April, 1941, Japan signed a Neutrality Pact with Russia, the later German attack on Russia surprising the Japanese as much as the Russians. Foreign Minister Yosuke Matsuoka, who had just negotiated the Neutrality Pact, proposed attacking Russia, but War Minister Tojo felt that there was no point in helping Germany and that Japan should turn south to take advantage of this new Allied crisis. Japan occupied southern Indochina on July 24, and the Allies froze all Japanese assets two days later. This forced the Japanese to decide whether to bargain for the resources necessary for war or to try to take them at once. Before the Allies would reopen trade, they demanded promises of no further Japanese aggression or participation in the war on the Axis side. American military power was increasing; delay, Tojo insisted, would deplete the stockpiles which Japan had already collected. Prime Minister Fumimaro Konoye and many naval officers were reluctant to challenge the United States, but Konoye finally agreed that preparations for war should be completed in October. Tojo became Premier, Minister of War, and Minister of Internal Affairs on October 16, but was persuaded to extend the deadline until the end of November, while Ambassadors Kichisaburo Nomura and Saburo Kurusu attempted to trade southern Indochina for an end to American aid to China and the resumption of trade with the Allies. But American public opinion made a Far Eastern Munich impossible. The United States asked Japan to sign a non-aggression pact with Great Britain, the Netherlands, the Soviet Union, and the United States, and to withdraw from all of her recently acquired territories except Manchukuo. Japan's forces were now in position; the order to attack was sent out on December 2.[47]

[47] The best accounts are Feis, *Road to Pearl Harbor* and Louis Morton, "Japan's Decision for War (1941)" (Greenfield, *Command Decisions*, 63-87). Also William L. Langer and S. Everett Gleason, *Challenge to Isolation* (New York, 1952) and *The Undeclared War, 1940-1941* (New York, 1953), Richard N. Current, *Secretary Stimson: A Study in Statecraft* (New Brunswick, N. J., 1954), Paul W. Schroeder, *The Axis Alliance and Japanese-American Relations, 1941* (Ithaca, 1951), Frank W. Iklé, *German-Japanese Relations, 1936-1940* (New York, 1956), Mamoru Shigemitsu, *Japan and Her Destiny*, ed. F. S. G. Piggott, trans. Oswald White (New York, 1958), Richard Storry, *The Double Patriots* (London, 1958), Maxon, *Control of Japanese Foreign Policy*, and on all economic matters, Jerome B. Cohen, *Japan's Economy in War and Reconstruction* (Minneapolis, 1949). F. C. Jones, *Japan's New Order in Asia: Its Rise and Fall, 1937-1945* (London, 1954), 450. His idea that the United States might then have made fewer "concessions at the expense of China than were later to be made to Stalin at Yalta" ignores American opinion.

The Japanese had studied simultaneous attacks on Malaya and the Philippines with the Indies to be taken later, a raid on the Indies followed by assaults on these bastions, a counter-clockwise campaign from the Philippines through the Indies to Malaya, and a clockwise drive with Malaya first and the Philippines last. The army thought that this last plan might delay American intervention. The timing of the Philippines' assault and the question of attacking other American positions were, like the question of attacking Russia, primarily political. It is hard to believe that isolationist sentiment against pulling British and Dutch imperialist chestnuts out of the fire would have prevailed over a government which was already engaged in a shooting war in the Atlantic. The isolationists made much of the duplicity of both candidates' anti-war promises during the presidential campaign of 1940, but few voters believed that this was more than the traditional homage to the ancestral isolationist gods. In a military sense, Isoroku Yamamoto, the commander of the Combined Fleet, correctly objected that these plans ignored the principal force of the prospective enemy, the United States Pacific Fleet. He proposed to cripple it by a surprise carrier raid on Pearl Harbor, in conjunction with simultaneous landings on Wake, Guam, Hong Kong, Malaya, the Philippines, and the Northern Indies, and the occupation of Thailand. The Japanese hoped to take the Philippines in two months, Malaya in three, and to control the area bounded by the International Date Line and the chain of islands from New Britain to Sumatra and central Burma in about five.

The Japanese planned a limited war for specific economic objectives. The Allies' positions lay in two rings about fifteen hundred and three thousand nautical miles from Yokohama. The inner ring included Hong Kong, Manila (1,782 miles), Guam (1,352 miles), and Wake. The outer ring included Singapore, Batavia, Soerabaja, Rabaul in New Britain (2,526 miles), Tarawa in the Gilberts, and Pearl Harbor (3,397 miles). Possible objectives beyond this ring were another fifteen hundred miles away, such points as Calcutta, Colombo, Sydney, Auckland (4,789 miles), San Francisco, or Vancouver (4,262 miles). Panama (7,682 miles) was only a bit more than a hundred miles closer than the southern entrance of the Suez Canal. The original Japanese plan did not include a few minor positions within the three thousand mile ring: Kiska in the Aleutians (1,977 miles), Midway (2,250 miles), and points in the islands beyond Rabaul, from which it might be possible to operate against shipping from the United States to Australia. These positions in the Southwest Pacific might be taken in short jumps, with carrier cover supplemented by land-based planes. Operations against Midway or in the Aleutians could not be supported by land-based planes. In no case, however, could Japan threaten the national existence of Great Britain or the United States. Britain's Mediterranean and Cape of Good Hope lifelines were only the lifelines of part of her Empire; her own lifeline ran to North America. In challenging the world's greatest seapowers, Japan could hope only for a favorable political settlement, and then only in the event of a German victory or a stalemate in Europe. Immediately, the Japanese planned to throw up strong perimeter defenses around her prospective conquests, in the hope that these defenses—backed by mobile air and sea power—would make Allied counterattacks so expensive that their peoples would force their governments to a compromise peace.

On December 7 Japanese planes sank five of the eight battleships in Pearl Harbor and destroyed most of the United States Army's planes in the Philippines. Three days later land-based planes sank the *Prince of Wales* and the *Repulse*. "In all the war," Churchill later wrote, "I never received a more direct shock. . . . There were no British or American capital ships in the Indian Ocean or the Pacific except the American survivors of Pearl Harbor, who were hastening back to California. Over all this vast expanse of waters Japan was supreme, and we everywhere were weak and naked." Singapore fell on February 15, 1942, well ahead of schedule. In April Force H—sent from Gibraltar to the Indian Ocean—withdrew to East Africa after losing a carrier and two heavy cruisers in a brush with Chiuchi Nagumo's Carrier Striking Force off Ceylon. Since Pearl Harbor Nagumo "had operated . . . one third of the way around the world. . . . He had sunk 5 battleships, 1 aircraft carrier, 2 cruisers and 7 destroyers; . . . and disposed of thousands of tons of fleet auxiliaries and merchant ships. . . . Yet *not one ship* of his Striking Force had been sunk or even damaged by Allied action." Resistance in the Philippines had surprised the Japanese but had not changed the issue of a series of campaigns which had destroyed whatever remained of the legend of innate Western military superiority. "In five months the Japanese had . . . [become] the new overlords of more than 100,000,000 people, . . . [capturing] about 250,000 troops, mostly Asian, but including an Australian division, a British division, and the equivalent of a division of Americans. . . . This had been achieved with comparatively modest land forces and at relatively small cost —about 15,000 killed and wounded." The Japanese had also lost 272,000 tons of shipping—just four times the tonnage they had built during the first four months of war—but had captured more than they had lost. They stepped up merchant shipbuilding, but built only 89 destroyers and escort craft during the next three fiscal years. They had grossly under-estimated the strongest 1941 submarine force in the world; 202 American submarines were to be commissioned after Pearl Harbor, and Japan's submarines failed to strike effec-tively at Allied shipping. Japan's underestimation of the sub-marine—a curious mistake for an island empire which had challenged two great sea powers to obtain sea-borne supplies —was one of those errors which could "never be rectified."[48]

The Japanese might possibly have followed up the capture of Singapore by landing in India, Ceylon, or the Vichy French base of Diego Suarez in Madagascar, but time, distance (Cal-cutta and Colombo were some sixteen hundred nautical miles from Singapore and Diego Suarez was more than twice that distance), and their lack of shipping and land forces worked

[48] Churchill, *Second World War*, III, 55. Samuel Eliot Morison, *The Rising Sun in the Pacific, 1931-April 1942 (United States Naval Operations*, III, Bos-ton, 1951), 385-386. Wigmore, *Japanese Thrust*, 407-408. Also A. E. Percival, *The War in Malaya* (London, 1949), S. Woodburn Kirby *et al., The War Against Japan* (I, II, *United Kingdom Military Series*, London, 1957-1958), and Bisheshwar Prasad *et al., Campaigns in the Eastern Theatre* (6 vols., *Official History of the Indian Armed Forces in the Second World War*, Cal-cutta, 1953-1959).

On Pearl Harbor use Walter Millis, *This Is Pearl* (New York, 1957), and the documents edited by Hans Louis Trefousse, *What Happened at Pearl Har-bor?* (New York, 1958). None of MacArthur's biographers say much about his attempts to create a national army in the Philippines. These include the pro-MacArthur books by Clark Lee and Richard Henschel, *Douglas MacAr-thur* (New York, 1952); Courtney H. Whitney, *MacArthur: His Rendezvous with History* (New York, 1956); and Charles A. Willoughby and John Cham-berlain, *MacArthur, 1941-1951* (New York, 1954). The anti-MacArthur work is by Richard H. Rovere and Arthur M. Schlesinger, Jr., *The General and the President, and the Future of American Foreign Policy* (New York, 1951).

The best study of the Allied naval crisis is Roskill, *War at Sea*, II. A con-nected account of Japanese naval operations is Emmanuel Andrieu d'Albas, *Death of a Navy*, trans. Anthony Rippon (New York, 1957). Figures on Japanese escort construction and merchant shipping are in Cohen, *Japan's Economy*, 267, and in United States Strategic Bombing Survey, *The Effects of Strategic Bombing on Japan's War Economy* (Washington, 1946), 214-215. See also Mochitsura Hashimoto, *Sunk: The Story of the Japanese Sub-marine Fleet, 1942-1945*, trans. E. H. M. Colegrave (London, 1954), and Y. Horie, "The Failure of the Japanese Convoy Escort" (*United States Naval Institute Proceedings*, LXXXII, 1956, 1073-1081).

against them. Only a fifth of their fifty-one active divisions had been assigned to the Southern Army, to twenty-two divisions for China and Indochina, five for Japan, and fourteen (a quarter of the army) for Manchukuo and Korea. The Chief of Staff of the Combined Fleet suggested expeditions against Midway and Hawaii to force the remnants of the Pacific Fleet to battle. When this was reported too risky, he had turned to Ceylon, but the army refused to draw the necessary troops from the forces watching Russia. He then suggested a "Midway only" plan, but an "Australian first" group in the Naval General Staff argued that Australia was more dangerous because of the threat of land-based plane raids against the Southwest Pacific Islands. The army refused to release divisions for a full-scale invasion of Australia, but agreed to let the South Seas Detachment participate in the first move against Australia's supply lines by taking Port Moresby and Tulagi in the Solomons. The two divisions which had taken Rangoon and two additional divisions from Singapore were driving the British and Stilwell's Chinese forces out of Burma. Four Indian divisions and part of a British division held Madras and Bengal against invasion or an Indian revolt. The Congress Party leaders, who had not been consulted on India's entrance into the Second German War, finally turned down a British offer of postwar independence—with the proviso that defense remain a British responsibility—as "a post-dated check on a bank that was obviously crashing." Ceylon had to be reinforced. Nagumo's carriers had successfully attacked the British fleet, but had lost many planes and pilots to land-based fighters at Trincomalee.[49]

The Japanese had their minds made up for them by the carriers which Nagumo's six carriers had failed to find in Pearl Harbor. The *Enterprise* and *Lexington* had been ferrying planes to Wake and Midway. The *Saratoga*, then off Cali-

[49] The discussion of future Japanese strategy is summarized in Mitsuo Fuchida and Matasake Okumiya, *Midway, the battle that doomed Japan: The Japanese Navy's Story,* ed. Clarke H. Kawakami and Roger Pineau (Annapolis, 1955). Stilwell told the Burma story in his diary entry of May 10. "Hostile population; no air service; Jap initiative; inferior equipment; . . . stupid, gutless command; interference by CKS [Chiang]." Charles F. Romanus and Riley Sunderland, *Stilwell's Mission to China (U. S. Army in World War II,* Washington, 1953, 148. See also Belden, *Retreat with Stilwell,* John Smyth, *Before the Dawn* (London, 1957), William Slim, *Defeat into Victory* (London, 1957) and *Unofficial History* (London, 1959). On later events in India see William Ennis, *The Great Bombay Explosion* (New York, 1959) and the fine study of Chandra Bose by Hugh Toye, *The Springing Tiger: A Study of a Revolutionary* (London, 1959).

fornia, had since been torpedoed, but the *Yorktown* had been sent from the Atlantic to help raid positions from New Guinea to Wake. On April 18 sixteen land bombers, commanded by James H. Doolittle and ferried from the Atlantic by the *Hornet*, hit Tokyo and crash landed in China in a propaganda raid whose moral effects proved to be as profound as the physical damage had been negligible. The Japanese allowed the Port Moresby-Tulagi operation—which was to be covered by two of Nomura's carriers—to proceed, but threw everything else into the drive for Midway and minor objectives in the Aleutians, the most important points within the three thousand mile outer ring of their conquests. The Allied decisions to fight for Port Moresby and Midway and the Americans' knowledge of the Japanese code—an advantage which had so signally failed to benefit them in December —now enabled the four American carriers to win the first carrier battles in history and the decisive naval battles of the Pacific War. In the Coral Sea (May 4-8, 1942) the *Yorktown* and *Lexington* turned back the Port Moresby force and sank the light carrier accompanying it before tangling with the other two carriers. The Japanese sank the *Lexington* and damaged the *Yorktown*, but one of their carriers was damaged and both of them lost many planes and pilots. The Tulagi landing was successful. Much more important, only four of Nomura's carriers were ready for Midway, but the Japanese hoped that they had sunk the *Yorktown* and had perhaps lured the *Enterprise* and *Hornet* to the Coral Sea area. The Americans knew that the next drive would be at Midway. The repaired *Saratoga* did not arrive in time, but the *Yorktown* was patched up and joined the other two carriers. During the first moves of the Coral Sea battle, the British had taken Diego Suarez to end the threat of a hostile submarine base on the route from the Cape to the Middle East and Ceylon and to give them a base to balance Singapore.[50]

50 See Samuel Eliot Morison, *Coral Sea, Midway and Submarine Actions, May 1942-August 1942 (United States Naval Operations, IV*, Boston, 1949). The difference between strategical and tactical intelligence—insofar as such distinction can be made—is vital to the understanding of the events from Pearl Harbor to Midway, the Schlieffen plan, or Jutland. The Allies knew the enemy's general intentions, but not his exact plans. Only in a few instances, as in the case of the Nivelle offensive, is the latter possible; a change in the enemy's plans, as in 1940, may make such prior knowledge worse than useless. In the case of the Jutland, Pearl Harbor, the Coral Sea, and Midway, the Allies knew that something was up, but nothing more. In the case of Pearl Harbor, the American leaders assumed that the main Japanese drives would be at Guam, the Philippines, and Southeast Asia. Even on this assump-

The Midway operation threw the remaining capital ships in the Japanese navy—eleven battleships, Nagumo's four operational carriers, and four light carriers—at forces estimated at no more than two or three carriers and the land-based planes on Midway, which had been considerably reinforced. Four Japanese forces were involved. The Aleutians force, covered by two light carriers, secured its objectives, but this diversion came too late to pull any American forces out of position. The next day, June 4, Nagumo's Striking Force, with two accompanying battleships, was to soften up Midway for the Midway invasion force which, supported by two battleships and a light carrier, was approaching from the southwest. The fourth light carrier was with the seven battleships of the Main Body, which was to trap any American heavy forces in the area. The three Japanese forces approaching Midway proved to be too far apart for mutual support. Nagumo's carriers ran into heavy land-based plane opposition at Midway and were then hit by planes from the American carriers. The Japanese sank the *Yorktown*, but lost their four carriers. The Midway invasion force retired, and Admiral Raymond A. Spruance did not attempt to close with the Japanese battleships. "Keeping in his mind the picture of widely disparate forces yet boldly seizing every opening, . . . [he] emerged from this battle one of the greatest fighting and thinking admirals in American naval history." Midway was the decisive battle of the Pacific war, unless the Battles of Britain, Moscow, and Stalingrad can be said to have doomed the entire Japanese enterprise. Contrary to all pre-war expectations, the fate of the Japanese Empire had not been decided

---

tion, however, "the pertinent question is whether or not he [Husband E. Kimmel, commanding the Pacific Fleet, and other commanders] used the means available to him to the best advantage. In my opinion, he did not. The fault lay in the fact that he was not fully informed by the Navy Department of what was known as to probable Japanese intentions and of the tenseness of the situation, and further, that his judgment was to some extent faulty and that he did not fully appreciate the implications of the information that was given to him." Admiral Ernest J. King, Commander in Chief, United States Fleet and Chief of Naval Operations, Nov. 6, 1944, "Second Endorsement to Record of Proceedings of Pearl Harbor Court of Inquiry" (*Hearings before the Joint Committee on the Pearl Harbor Attack*, 39 parts, Washington, 1946), Part 39, 342. Fifty marines got into Diego Suarez from the rear and took the naval depot after the first assault had failed. The submarine danger had been underlined on May 30, when a midget submarine from the Japanese I-20 torpedoed a battleship and a tanker. See the account in the British popular official history by Christopher Buckley, *Five Ventures: Iraq-Syria-Persia-Madagascar-Dodecanese* (London, 1954).

within the inner ring of the Japanese position, but within fifteen hundred miles of Hawaii. "The dominance of the Japanese navy in the Pacific had lasted for a few days short of six months. At Midway it was destroyed in a few hours ... [a result, with the Coral Sea] almost wholly accomplished by the four pre-war American carriers *Lexington*, *Yorktown*, *Enterprise*, and *Hornet*. Rarely can such rich benefits have been derived from so few ships." The next day was the turning point in the battle for Bir Hacheim. There was no chance for a Japanese drive in the Indian Ocean when Rommel reached El Alamein.[51]

The Japanese commander in Burma was told not to move into India or China without specific orders, though he was later allowed to plan operations into Assam to cut the Allied air route to China. The strain on Japanese shipping was to be relieved by hacking a link through the jungles and mountains between the Burmese and Siamese railways, a link which was to cost 325 deaths per mile among the 62,000 war prisoners and 270,000 coolies who were forced to build it. The Indian nationalists wavered between Nehru's "resolve that the Japanese must be resisted," Ghandi's "total pacifism," and sabotage. Rioting broke out in August, but "what was at one time feared would become the most serious rebellion since the Sepoy Mutiny of 1857 fizzled out." Some Indians joined a Japanese-sponsored Indian National Army to fight alongside a similar Burma Defense Army, but the Japanese, like the Germans, used these collaborators chiefly to help them plunder the country. A Burmese nationalist and Communist Anti-Fascist People's Freedom League joined the Burma Defense Army against the retreating Japanese in March, 1945, and then refused to accept the officials whom the British brought back from India. Britain recognized Burma's independence in 1948. In 1958, after ten years of warfare against two Communist groups, Karen and Kachin tribesmen, and Chinese Nationalists who stayed in Burma after Chiang's defeat, the Chief of Staff of the old Burma Defense Army took over the government. In the meantime, the British had won a six-year (1948-1954) anti-Communist war in Malaya, which had tied down more than 30,000 troops, 75,000 full-time police, and more than 250,000 Home Guards. In neighboring Thailand, the western-trained military oligarchy which

[51] Morison, *Coral Sea, Midway*, 158. Roskill, *War at Sea*, II, 41.

had taken power in 1932 survived both the Japanese occupation and numerous postwar plots.[52]

The Allied Counterattack in the Pacific

MacArthur was one of the few high ranking officers of 1930—when he had become the youngest Chief of Staff in the history of the United States Army—to win success in the field in the Second World War. Good connections had helped him, but his brilliance is attested both by his outstanding record at West Point and by his mastery—during his sixties— of the art of amphibious war. His relations with the Australians and with the naval officers under his command were excellent; those with his superiors, who insisted on Germany first, and with those naval officers who wanted to fight their private war with Japan in the Central Pacific were tempestuous. MacArthur's record and flair for propaganda had made him the most famous of American generals. He was able to count on anti-British, anti-New Deal, formerly isolationist elements in the United States which, playing on the strong emotions which had long governed American Far Eastern policy, also wished the United States to concentrate against Japan. MacArthur's decision to hold Port Moresby had already helped to touch off the Battle of the Coral Sea. After Midway both the Americans and the Japanese turned their attention back to unfinished business in this area. The Japanese prepared to work over the Owen Stanley Mountains

---

52 Romanus and Sunderland, *Stilwell's Mission*, 232-233. Churchill, *Second World War*, IV, 191-196. The Malayan Communists were chiefly armed with Japanese weapons and recruited from the Chinese, who were disliked by the other elements of the population. See Lucien W. Pye, *Guerrilla Communism in Malaya* (Princeton, 1956). The British used some conscripts—see Arthur Campbell's fine *Jungle Green* (London, 1953)—but most of the fighting was done by regulars. See M. C. A. Henniker, who commanded 63 Gurkha Infantry Brigade, *Red Shadow over Malaya* (London, 1955). For the Kenya Mau Mau see Ian Henderson, with Philip Goodhart, *The Hunt for Kimathi* (London, 1958). Lawrence Durrell, *Bitter Lemons* (New York, 1957) is a superb account of the changes which affected both governors and governed in an analogous situation in Cyprus. The French did not send conscripts to Indochina. In Algeria conscripts turned on the professionals to save De Gaulle.

Though the occupying Japanese in East and Southeast Asia had "ensured that the old order of Western political domination would never return . . . [by attacking] the whole Occidental way of life [and] . . . democratic ideas, . . . they had nothing positive to offer. . . . The pre-existing Communist groups were quick to seize their opportunity of stimulating, and, as far as possible, dominating active resistance movements. Thus Japanese aggression, . . . Communist calculation and also American [and British] anticolonialism created . . . the possibility of another 'New Order' for East Asia—that of Communism." Jones, *Japan's New Order*, 399-400.

from Buna on the northern coast opposite Port Moresby, to land at the tip of the tail near Milne Bay, and to build an airstrip on Guadalcanal, a few miles from Tulagi. MacArthur had strengthened the defenses of Milne Bay and proposed an immediate drive on Rabaul along the northern coast of New Guinea. The Navy insisted that Tulagi be taken first and objected to MacArthur's commanding the first phase of a purely amphibious operation. The South Pacific Command was finally given the job of taking Tulagi with the First Marine Division, while MacArthur's naval forces and land-based planes prevented Japanese reinforcement of the Solomons and prepared for the next phases of the operation. The Japanese struck first by landing at Buna in July, the Marines landed on Guadalcanal on August 7, and the Japanese attempted to take Milne Bay at the end of August.[53]

The Guadalcanal landing touched off a series of naval and air battles which cost the Japanese two old battleships and a light carrier to two American carriers. One of the two Japanese carriers which had fought in the Coral Sea was damaged; the other retired to the north. After the naval Battle of Guadalcanal (November 12-15, 1942) the Japanese pulled their capital ships out of this campaign of attrition for an objective outside of their original defensive perimeter. For the next nineteen months they held these ships in reserve for a decisive battle. They evacuated Guadalcanal in February, 1943, after losing about 28,600 of the 37,700 men they had committed to action. The 60,000 Americans had lost 1,752 men killed or missing, plus at least as many naval dead. In January MacArthur's Australian and American forces had taken Buna after a campaign which—contrary to his press releases—"had been neither cheaply won nor conducted on the supposition that there was 'no necessity of a hurry attack.' . . . [It] had been rather one in which the troops suffered heavy casualties while being hastily pressed forward on prepared enemy positions with little more in the way of weapons than their rifles, machine guns, mortars, and hand grenades."

[53] Operations from August, 1942, to April, 1944, are covered in Morison, *U. S. Naval Operations*, V-VII (Boston, 1950-1951); *History of U. S. Marine Corps Operations in World War II* (I, 1958), which is replacing *Operational Narratives of the Marine Corps in World War II* (15 vols., Washington, 1947-1955); and John Miller, Jr., *Guadalcanal: The First Offensive* (1949) and *CARTWHEEL: The Reduction of Rabaul* (1959), Samuel Milner, *Victory in Papua* (1957), and Philip A. Crowl and Edmund G. Love, *Seizure of the Gilberts and Marshalls* (1955) in the *U. S. Army in World War II* series (Washington).

It had cost his ground forces 3,085 dead, more than two-thirds of them Australians. The three combat teams of the 32nd Division, a Wisconsin-Michigan division "quite unprepared and untrained for the miseries and terrors of jungle warfare" had suffered battle and sickness casualties of almost ninety per cent. "The Southwest Pacific Area was exactly where it would have been the previous July had it been able to secure the beachhead before the Japanese got there." But these campaigns which General Charles A. Willoughby later described as "a race . . . [with] the Marines . . . to see who would turn in the first important 'land' victory of the Pacific war" had taught the Allies "the new water-land-air use of the old tactic of envelopment, the go-around-them-and-get-astraddle-on-their-supply-lines-and-flank that was the where-withal of the pay-off." The Japanese had lost about three-fourths of their 16,000 men. As one Japanese officer later described MacArthur's later tactics, " 'The Americans attacked and seized, with minimum losses, a relatively weak area, constructed air fields and then proceeded to cut the supply lines to our troops. . . . The Americans flowed into our weaker points . . . as water seeks the weakest entry to sink a ship.' " [54]

Rabaul was isolated by amphibious operations. The North Pacific forces recaptured Attu and Kiska in the Aleutians, which proved to be poor bases for further operations against Japan. In November, the Central Pacific forces took Tarawa in the Gilbert Islands in an assault in which everything seemed to go wrong, but took Kwajalein in the Marshall Islands in January with much smaller losses. By this time the United States' "two-ocean" navy was nearing completion. Its major elements included: (1) a striking force of fast carriers —26 of which were commissioned from Pearl Harbor to the end of the war—and 8 new battleships to win the command of the sea, conduct preliminary air strikes, and isolate the attack area; (2) a force of old battleships and escort carriers —114 of the latter were commissioned—to give the landing forces direct fire support and air cover; and (3) tremendous numbers of cruisers—48, destroyers and destroyer escorts—

[54] Milner, *Victory in Papua*, 369-378. Willoughby and Chamberlain, *MacArthur*, 92, 104-105. See also three volumes in *Australia in the War of 1939-1945*, Dudley McCarthy, *South-West Pacific Area—First Year: Kokoda to Wau* (Canberra, 1959), David Dexter, *The New Guinea Offensives* (1961), and Volume III in Allan S. Walker's Medical Series, *The Island Campaigns* (1957).

850, submarines—203, and mining and patrol craft—2,703. These ships were supported by (4) the Fleet Train—1,541 vessels were commissioned as fleet auxiliaries—a mobile base and repair force as large as the prewar navy, and (5) Naval Construction Battalions ("Seabees") with as many men as the Marine Corps, who specialized in projects such as the reconstruction of captured airfields, an important factor in freeing carrier planes for other operations. Increasing numbers of (6) landing and district craft—105,398 of them—and (7) land-based planes enabled the growing ground forces to undertake the decisive offensive which was to force Japan to surrender fourteen months after the landing on Saipan in the Marianas near Guam on June 15, 1944.[55]

Fifty-five per cent of Japanese naval armaments expenditures went to aircraft, and much of the sixteen per cent devoted to combat ships went to replace the carriers lost in 1942. Nine carriers (only two of them large fleet carriers) were finished in 1942-1943. Since six fleet carriers and another light carrier were to be completed in 1944, the Americans hoped to force the Combined Fleet to fight before these ships and their air groups were fully ready. These ships were supported by chains of "unsinkable" but immobile airfields throughout the Central and Southwest Pacific islands, but the construction of these defenses was hampered by general shortages of ships and planes and by heavy losses of both men and equipment in transit. The tempo of the American offensives surprised the Japanese, whose thirty-two thousand men on Saipan (almost double the estimate of American intelligence) had not finished their planned defenses. Japanese war production reached its peak in September, 1944—two months after the peak for Germany—but could not match American production, even for the Pacific theater. In January, 1943—at the end of the battles for Guadalcanal and Papua—American and Japanese army and navy air strength in the Pacific had been about equal; a year later the Japanese were outnumbered nearly three to one. Though the battles in the South and Central Pacific had cost the Japanese many ships and planes, American submarines had done even greater damage. By the end of March, 1944, the Japanese merchant marine was less than two-thirds as large as it had been at the

[55] Ernest J. King, *United States Navy at War* (Washington, 1945), Appendix B. See also Duncan S. Ballantine, *U. S. Naval Logistics in the Second World War* (Princeton, 1947), and Robert H. Connery, *The Navy and Industrial Mobilization in World War II* (Princeton, 1951).

time of Pearl Harbor. Admiral Soichi Takagi of the Naval General Staff told former Navy and Prime Minister Admiral Mitsumasa Yonai that Japan was losing the war. The shipping crisis, Japan's vanishing stockpiles, and the possibility of air attack on Japan itself had convinced Takagi that Japan should try peace negotiations, even at the price of her conquests in China, Korea, and Formosa.[56]

The May, 1943, "Strategic Plan for the Defeat of Japan" had envisaged MacArthur's forces driving toward South China through the Celebes Sea in conjunction with a Chinese offensive and British operations through the Strait of Malacca. The Central Pacific force would secure "MacArthur's right flank by seizing the Gilberts, Marshalls, and Truk; after which it was assumed, at least by General MacArthur, that the Pacific Fleet and amphibious forces would come under his command and support his major advance." MacArthur thought that an advance through the Central Pacific would be too dependent on carrier planes and that the Marianas were too far from Japan for effective strategic bombing. This plan had been drastically modified by the time of the Cairo Conference in November, when the British postponed their operations toward Singapore and Chiang lost interest in Burma. The success of the carrier-supported operations in the Gilberts and Marshalls showed what could be done in the Marianas, in which the Army Air Forces became increasingly interested as their prospects of secure bases in China declined. Some naval officers still felt that the "relentless pressure of sea power could defeat Japan short of invasion" and that the use of their carriers in "narrow seas commanded by land-based planes would be idiotic." The path through the Marianas was shorter; the Japanese could deploy fewer men and planes on the small, scattered Central Pacific islands than on the larger islands of the Southwest Pacific. And an attack on the Marianas—within the Japanese inner ring— might force the Combined Fleet to fight far from its oil sup-

[56] Cohen, *Japan's Economy*, 267. U. S. Strategic Bombing Survey, *Japan's Struggle to End the War* (Washington, 1946), 3. Only two of the 1944 carriers took part in the fleet actions of that year, and both were lost. Two were sunk by submarines after Leyte. The other three were never fully operational because of shortages of escorts, planes, and fuel. Only *Yamato*, a light cruiser, and 8 destroyers were sent against the Allies off Okinawa in 1945, although there were 2 other battleships, 2 battleship-carriers, and 5 carriers in Japan. The Americans lost 16 men to 2498 men in *Yamato* alone. On mine warfare see Arnold S. Lott, *Most Dangerous Sea: A History of Mine Warfare, and an Account of U. S. Navy Mine Operations in World War II and Korea* (Annapolis, 1959).

plies and major bases. These considerations forced a compromise. On March 12, 1944, the Southwest and Central Pacific forces were ordered to co-operate in a two-pronged advance against the southern Philippines. MacArthur's forces were to jump to Hollandia on the northern coast of New Guinea on April 15 and to be ready to land on Mindanao by November 15. The Central Pacific forces would bypass the big Japanese base at Truk, support MacArthur at Hollandia (which was beyond the range of his land-based fighters), and assault the Marianas on June 15. Their fast carriers and battleships would thus cover both the Southwest and Central Pacific landings and keep the Japanese guessing.[57]

MacArthur's landing at Biak on May 26 convinced the Japanese that the next blow would fall on the Palaus in the Southwest Pacific. But when the Central Pacific forces hit the Marianas instead, Admiral Jisaburo Ozawa's Mobile Fleet (3 carriers, 6 light carriers, and 5 battleships to 7 carriers, 8 light carriers, and 7 fast battleships for Spruance's Fifth Fleet) moved into action. On June 19, 330 Japanese carrier planes were destroyed over the American carriers or attempting to land on Guam, 50 land-based planes were wrecked on Guam, and two carriers were sunk by Admiral Charles A. Lockwood's brilliantly handled submarines. Spruance's carriers did not find the remaining Japanese carriers until the following afternoon. A light carrier was sunk and the remaining big carrier and two light carriers damaged by a strike at such long range that many American planes were lost on the return flight from lack of fuel. The Japanese had lost 426 carrier planes and 445 airmen to 130 planes and 76 airmen in a battle which marked the real end of their carrier force. A few days after this second Midway in the Battle of the Philippine Sea, Marquess Koichi Kido, the Emperor's closest advisor, told Foreign Minister Mamoru Shigemitsu that the Emperor wished a compromise peace. Tojo fell on July 18, and General Kuniaki Koiso, with Admiral Yonai as his deputy, was given the dual task of making peace and stiffening the defenses of the Philippines. MacArthur now wished to speed up the Mindanao landing and to land on

[57] Morison, *New Guinea and the Marianas, March 1944-August 1944 (United States Naval Operations,* VIII, Boston, 1953), 3-10. Philip A. Crowl, *Campaign in the Marianas (U. S. Army in World War II,* Washington, 1957) and, in the same series, Robert Ross Smith, *The Approach to the Philippines* (1953) and the same author's "Luzon versus Formosa (1944)" (Greenfield, *Command Decisions,* 358-373).

Leyte to the north by November 15. William F. Halsey relieved Spruance in August. The success of his September air operations in support of the Central Pacific forces' Palau Islands and MacArthur's Morotai landings convinced him that the Philippines were "a hollow shell. . . . I began to wonder . . . whether MacArthur [might] shift to Leyte the invasion [of] . . . Mindanao, and advance the date." This was done, and Leyte moved up to October 20.[58]

Within nine minutes of American Ranger landings on the approaches to Leyte, the rest of the Japanese navy began to move toward Leyte Gulf. Ozawa's remaining carriers (a veteran of Pearl Harbor and 3 light carriers) and 2 battleship-carriers came from Japan; his green pilots were to attack and fly to land bases on Luzon. Ozawa's mission was to lure Halsey out of position while Takeo Kurita, with the main Japanese force of 5 battleships (including the giant *Musashi* and *Yamato*) broke through San Bernardino Strait north of the twin islands of Leyte and Samar and a smaller force built around 2 old battleships tried Surigao Strait to the south. Halsey's 5 carriers, 6 light carriers, and 6 fast battleships (3 carriers and 2 light carriers were refueling) were running interference to the north. Admiral Thomas C. Kinkaid's 6 old battleships and 18 slow escort carriers—a similar support force had not had to take part in the Philippine Sea battle—

---

[58] Morison, *New Guinea and the Marianas,* 213-321. William F. Halsey and J. Bryan, III, *Admiral Halsey's Story* (New York, 1947), 199. Halsey had been in the South and Southwest Pacific since the middle of the Guadalcanal campaign and had become a warm friend and admirer of MacArthur. See also M. Hamlin Cannon, *Leyte: The Return to the Philippines (U. S. Army in World War II,* Washington, 1954).

Spruance's submarine tactics made up for poor air search and communications. Lockwood's submarines, watching the bottlenecks from which the Japanese might approach the Marianas, had discovered two Japanese forces on June 15 and had made another contact on the night of June 17-18, though darkness prevented a discovery that the two forces had united. Spruance's carrier commander, Mark A. Mitscher, who had been hitting the Bonin Islands staging bases for planes flown from Japan, wanted to move west toward the Japanese. But Spruance feared an "end run" by the now non-existent second force. " 'We could not gamble. . . . The way Togo had waited at Tsushima for the Russian fleet to come to him has always been in my mind.' . . . The situation was almost the reverse . . . of Midway. Ozawa knew where Spruance was, but Spruance as yet had no certain intelligence of Ozawa's position." Morison, *New Guinea and the Marianas,* 253-254. Admirals Nagumo, demoted from the command of the fast carriers, and Takeo Takagi, commanding the Japanese submarine fleet, were lost in the Marianas. Yamamoto had been killed in April, 1943. All but 8 of 25 Japanese submarines operating from the Marianas were lost. See also Lockwood's *Sink 'Em All* (New York, 1951), and two volumes by Theodore Roscoe, *United States Submarine Operations in World War II* (Annapolis, 1949) and *United States Destroyer Operations in World War II* (Annapolis, 1953).

were covering MacArthur's landing. Neither Halsey nor Kinkaid was certain of the other's exact responsibility. Halsey thought that Kinkaid would stick close to the beachhead; Kinkaid thought that Halsey would cover him to the north. Owing to Halsey's impetuousness and somewhat contradictory orders and poor American communications, the Japanese plan nearly worked. Kinkaid destroyed the smaller Japanese gun force in Surigao Strait, but Kurita, after the loss of the *Musashi*, penetrated San Bernardino Strait, which Halsey had left unguarded while he concentrated against Ozawa's carriers. But Kurita failed to follow up his advantage and retired without pressing his attack against the shipping in Leyte Gulf. The Japanese lost all of Ozawa's carriers and 3 battleships. Ozawa's force sank a light carrier and Kurita an escort carrier, while land-based suicide planes, unknown to Kurita, sank another American escort carrier and damaged three others. The largest, though not the most significant, naval battle of the war, Leyte was the Japanese Navy's Trafalgar. It had been forced to fight two decisive battles on the outside rather than on the inside of major land masses. MacArthur was able to penetrate the central Philippines to Mindoro (December 15) and Luzon (January 9, 1945) to cut Japan off from her "Southern Resources Area" with only Kamikaze (suicide) opposition.[59]

Exaggerated reports of the success of suicide attacks at Leyte "caught the fancy of military leaders as well as the [Japanese] public—and the craze was on. . . . Headquarters [ordered] . . . all armed forces [to] . . . resort to suicide attack." On November 11, 1944, B-29's had raided Tokyo from bases in the Marianas, but the results of the first daylight precision raids were disappointing. Many planes had been lost on the long return flight; the Japanese were using the Bonin Islands as fighter and early warning bases. On February 19 the Marines assaulted Iwo Jima to win a base for emergency landings and fighter cover. Its eight square miles of volcanic ash were finally taken by nearly 70,000 men "inching forward with hand weapons" in a battle which lasted for nearly a month instead of the expected five days. The last major Allied landing was on Okinawa on April 1. Four times the size of

[59] Morison, *Leyte: June 1944-January 1945, The Liberation of the Philippines,* and *Victory in the Pacific, 1945 (United States Naval Operations,* XII-XIV, Boston, 1958-1960). James A. Field, Jr., *The Japanese at Leyte Gulf* (Princeton, 1947).

Malta and 350 miles from Japan, Okinawa would enable land-based planes to cut Japanese communications with China.

For the assault echelon alone, about 183,000 troops and 747,000 measurement tons of cargo were loaded. . . . After the landings, maintenance had to be provided for the combat troops and a continuously increasing garrison force that eventually numbered 270,-000. . . . The West Coast, which furnished the bulk of resupply, was . . . 26 days sailing time [away]. Allowing 30 days to prepare and forward the requisitions, 60 days for procurement and loading, . . . and 30 days for sailing to the target, the planners were faced with a 120-day interval between the initiation of their calculations and the arrival of supplies.

During the next two months Kamikazes sank 36 ships, none larger than a destroyer, and damaged 368, including 10 battleships and 13 carriers. American forces lost 12,610 dead. The Japanese lost 110,000 dead; 7,401 soldiers and 3,339 unarmed laborers surrendered. Generals Mitsuru Usajima and Isamu Cho committed hara-kiri on June 22. " 'Our strategy, tactics, and technics . . . were used to the utmost and we fought valiantly, but it was as nothing before the material strength of the enemy.' "[60]

On March 9 General Curtis E. LeMay, now commanding the lagging bomber campaign, had ordered the first large low-level night fire raid on Tokyo.

The area attacked was . . . four by three miles . . . with 103,000 inhabitants to the square mile, . . . wood-bamboo-plaster . . . home industries and feeder plants. 267,171 buildings were destroyed—about one-fourth of the total in Tokyo—and 1,008,000 persons were rendered homeless, . . . [with] 83,793 dead and 40,918 wounded. . . . In some of the smaller canals the water was actually boiling. . . . Destruction . . . exceeded that of any of the great conflagrations of the western world. . . . No other air attack of the war, either in Japan or Europe, was so destructive.

[60] Admiral Toshiyuki Yokoi (with the assistance of Roger Pineau), "Kamikazes and the Okinawa Campaign" (*United States Naval Institute Proceedings*, LXXX, May, 1954, 505-514). Roy E. Appleman, *et al.*, *Okinawa: The Last Battle (U. S. Army in World War II*, Washington, 1948), 36, 470, 489. The Kamikazes used planes, motorboats, one- and two-man torpedoes, two-and five-man submarines, and piloted rockets; 2,409 Kamikaze pilots lost their lives. Rikihei Inoguchi and Tadashi Nakajima with Roger Pineau, *The Divine Wind, Japan's Kamikaze Force in World War II* (Annapolis, 1958), 234, for naval planes only, lists 1,228 planes lost for 34 ships sunk and 283 damaged in Kamikaze attacks.

With four more such raids in the next ten days, three times as much bomb tonnage was dropped as in the whole previous campaign, the savings on fuel and ammunition permitting each plane to carry twice its previous bomb load. Only 20 planes had been lost in 1,595 sorties.[61]

The Japanese industrial economy was destroyed twice, "once by cutting off of imports and secondly by air attack." After a pause while the bombers supported the Okinawa landing, the fire raids were supplemented by precision bombing, air minelaying, and carrier and surface ship bombardments. An atomic bomb destroyed Hiroshima on August 6 and another was dropped on Nagasaki three days later. Perhaps 300,000 Japanese civilians were killed, to 1,555,000 dead in the armed forces. Twenty-two million people—almost a third of the population—sought shelter "in the countryside . . . or shanties amidst the rubble." Though the last Japanese shipping was used to bring in salt, cereals, and soy beans, the cities faced starvation. "With the lowest relative consuming power, and the least reserve to fall back on . . . the Japanese civilian was hit harder by the war than his counterpart even in Germany." In his last statement as head of the Army Air Forces, General H. H. Arnold concluded:

Even before the . . . atomic bomb, . . . mass air raids were obliterating the great centers of mankind. . . . The Twentieth Air Force was destroying Japanese industrial cities at . . . [a] cost to Japan [which] was fifty times the cost to us. . . . Atomic bombing is [even] . . . more economical. . . . Destruction is too cheap, too easy. . . . No effort spent on international cooperation will be too great if it assures the prevention of this destruction.[62]

Study of the factors which resulted in the Japanese leaders' decision to surrender has been complicated by the intricacies of the Japanese political structure, the conflicting claims of the American armed services, and the controversies over Far Eastern policy, the decision to use the atomic bomb, and Russia's entrance into the War for East Asia. Both MacArthur and the Joint Chiefs of Staff had long wished to draw Russia into the war, but they had nothing to do with the price

[61] Craven and Cate, *Army Air Forces*, V, 615-617.
[62] Cohen, *Japan's Economy*, 107. Arnold, *Report . . . to the Secretary of War, 12 November 1945* (Washington, 1945), 35, and "Air Force in the Atomic Age," 26-27. *Japan Statistical Yearbook, 1949*, 1056-1058.

for Russia's entrance. With Russia well-informed of the Japanese leaders' state of mind and large Russian forces on the spot, it is hard to see how the Russian occupation of Manchuria and North Korea could have been prevented. The United States Strategic Bombing Survey listed the major factors as the blockade, the operations which had cut the Empire to pieces, strategic bombing, and the German surrender. The atomic bomb "permitted the Prime Minister to bring the Emperor overtly . . . into a position . . . to override the remaining objectors." Fear of invasion and Russia's entrance into the war two days after the Hiroshima bomb were "not significant."[63]

When Japan surrendered there were only twenty-seven American divisions in the Pacific. As late as the Battle of the Philippine Sea, American ground forces had been no more numerous than the British Commonwealth forces facing the Japanese. At the end, the Japanese army had been little more than a spectator in the war for which its leaders had been primarily responsible. As MacArthur was to explain it on May 3, 1951:

Japan had . . . nearly 80 million people, crowded into 4 islands, . . . the factories, . . . [and] the labor. . . . The basic materials, they seized with the advantage of preparedness and surprise. . . . Their general strategic concept was to hold . . . the islands of the Pacific, so that . . . we would ultimately . . . allow them to control the basic products . . . they had captured. . . . We evolved an entirely new strategy . . . to evade those [bastions]. . . . We crept up and crept up, and crept up, always approaching the lines of communications which led from those . . . conquered countries to Japan. By the time we had seized the Philippines, we were enabled to lay down a sea and Navy blockade so that the supplies for the maintenance of the Japanese armed forces ceased to reach Japan. . . . At least 3,000,000 of as fine ground troops as I have ever known . . . laid down their arms because they didn't have the materials to fight with . . . and the potential to gather them . . . where we would attack. . . . The ground forces that were available in the Pacific were probably at no time more than one-third of the

[63] United States Strategic Bombing Survey, *Japan's Struggle to End the War*, 10-13. The conclusions of Robert J. C. Butow, *Japan's Decision to Surrender* (Stanford, 1954), and Kecskemeti, *Strategic Surrender*, differ only in details. On the atomic bomb see the letter from Harry Truman to James L. Cate, Jan. 12, 1953, in Craven and Cate, *Army Air Forces*, V, following page 712, and Louis Morton, "The Decision to Use the Atomic Bomb (1945)" (Greenfield, *Command Decisions*, 388-410).

[Japanese] ground forces; but . . . when we disrupted their entire economic system, . . . they surrendered.[64]

The War for East Asia

The failure of Stilwell's difficult mission may have been inevitable. As has already been suggested, his personality, the demands of grand strategy, and differences between the Allies and within the American command worked against him. The Chinese had expected a high ranking officer, but Hugh A. Drum, whom Stilwell described as "pompous, stubborn, new to them, high rank," had shown no enthusiasm for the job, partly because he had expected the European command and partly because he had not been told that Chiang would take an American as his chief of staff for China Theater. The Chinese "remember me," Stilwell noted, "as a small-fry colonel that they kicked around. They saw me on foot in the mud, consorting with coolies, riding soldier trains. . . . The old gag about 'they shall offer up a goat for a burnt sacrifice' is about to apply to my own case." The Chinese did not give Stilwell a staff, so he set to work with an interpreter and a stenographer to build "an elite force, . . . [equipped] by lend-lease, . . . to retake all Burma and reopen . . . communications. . . . Once this had been done, and a powerful Chinese Army created, . . . a powerful air offensive [might be launched] against . . . the Japanese homeland." While Stilwell focused on the Burma Road or a substitute road from Ledo, the terminus of the narrow gauge Bengal and Assam Railway, Claire L. Chennault, who had won Chiang's confidence as leader of the American Volunteer Group of airmen, proposed to "defeat Japan with a small air force, operating under a tactical system designed by him to exploit the relative strengths and weaknesses of American and Japanese aircraft and pilots." The British were more interested in Rangoon and Singapore than in north Burma and China, which Churchill thought was "not a world-power equal to Britain, the United States, or Russia." His Allies, Chiang complained, looked on China "not as an equal, . . . but as a ward. . . . If we are thus

---

[64] *Hearings on . . . the Relief of General . . . MacArthur* (Washington, 1951), Part I, 57-58. David James estimated Japanese forces at about 5,000,-000: 2,115,000 in Japan, Sakhalin, and the Kuriles, 1,310,000 in Manchuria, North China, and Korea, 953,000 in South and East China, Malaya, Burma, and Indochina, and 772,000 in Formosa, the Philippines, the Mandated Islands, and Indonesia. *The Rise and Fall of the Japanese Empire* (New York, 1951), 246.

treated during the stress of war, what becomes our position during the peace conference?"[65]

Stilwell held that his main job was to strengthen the Chinese army and that " 'Chinese troops if well trained, equipped and led can match the valor of soldiers everywhere.' " He formed the Chinese forces in India into two divisions (X force) to reopen the Burma Road with the help of thirty divisions from Yunnan (Y force). Another force (Z) was to be formed in the east near Kweilin for an eventual drive to the sea near Canton. In May, 1943, the Combined Chiefs of Staff approved a "Strategic Plan for the Defeat of Japan" in which the new long-range B-29 bombers, based in India and refueled in China, would destroy the Japanese steel industry. Stilwell feared that any effective air offensive "would bring a strong [Japanese] reaction. . . . The first essential [was a Chinese] . . . force capable of seizing and holding air bases." But Chiang told Roosevelt "that the existing Chinese forces could defend the east China airfields." The two men met Churchill in Cairo in November to plan to reopen the Burma Road from Ledo to Myitkyina and Yunnan, a campaign in which "the logistical preparations, the planning, and the fighting proceeded simultaneously." Chiang was told that the British planned a "major amphibious operation in the Bay of Bengal," though Churchill had just told Lord Mountbatten (the Supreme Allied Commander in Southeast Asia, to whom Stilwell was also Deputy) that unless the landing were on Sumatra, "he would take away all SEAC's landing craft." Chiang agreed that Y force would move toward Myitkyina, reversed himself, and then accepted. Churchill and Roosevelt then met Stalin at Teheran, where the latter again promised to enter the Pacific war, but insisted that no landing craft be diverted from Europe. Chiang then refused to commit Y force. In Stilwell's words, "Results of reneging on Burma. . . . I can go ahead and fight with the Ledo [X] force."[66]

[65] *Stilwell Papers*, 19, 30. Churchill, *Second World War*, IV, 837. Matloff and Shell, *Strategic Planning*, 204-205. *The Brereton Diaries*, 129. Romanus and Sunderland, *Stilwell's Command*, 3-4.

[66] *Ibid.*, 5, 10, 65-68, 110-111. *Stilwell Papers*, 262-265. "The command set-up is a Chinese puzzle, with Wavell ['Bumble,' Viceroy of India since his failure to retake Akyab], Auk [Auchinleck, British commander in India since his defeat by Rommel], Mountbatten, Peanut [Chiang], Alexander [Middle East] and me . . . mixed beyond recognition." *Ibid.*, 219. For Chennault see his *Way of a Fighter* (New York, 1949) and Robert Lee Scott, *Chennault of China* (Garden City, 1959). "From Ledo to Myitkina was 263 miles. . . .

Sixty years old and nearly blind, Stilwell took personal command of the Ledo force just before Christmas, 1943. On May 17, 1944, the remnants of X force, 300 Kachin tribesmen, and 3,000 American infantry raiders took Myitkyina airstrip. Chiang had allowed Y force to move, but the Japanese defended Myitkyina until August 3. Stilwell wrote three weeks later, "It was a bitch of a fight. . . . FIRST SUSTAINED OFFENSIVE IN CHINESE HISTORY AGAINST A FIRST-CLASS ENEMY." The first convoy for Chungking reached the Chinese border on January 31, 1945. On August 1, 1944, Stilwell had been promoted to general, a rank he then shared only with Marshall, Craig, MacArthur, Eisenhower, and Arnold. Patrick Hurley, Roosevelt's personal envoy to Chiang, thought that Stilwell might be given command powers to meet the Japanese offensive against the east China air bases and Z force training centers. But Chiang refused to take troops from the Communist blockade and publicly asked for Stilwell's recall on October 2. "Reasons given by Gmo. Incompetent, non co-op, lack of respect, . . . unwarranted diversion of munitions and men to Burma. Responsibility for disaster in South China." The air bases were lost and the B-29's, which had been raiding Japan since June 15, withdrawn. "Not three months after . . . Stilwell's recall, Roosevelt . . . adopted [an attitude toward China at Yalta which] suggests that the Generalissimo's triumph of October 1944 was one of the steps that led to the Manchurian partition." Before he died in 1946 Stilwell wrote, "If a man can say he did not let his country down, and if he can live with himself, there is nothing more he can reasonably ask for."[67]

The overall distance to the Chinese border was 478 miles, . . . [and] Chungking, nearly 2,000 miles away. . . . October 1943 found the road no farther than Milestone 42 when Brigadier General [Lewis A.] Pick, a famous American engineer, arrived. Seventy-five per cent of the men working were in hospital with malaria. . . . Stilwell . . . wanted at least a track built to Shinbiyang by the end of the year. . . . Pick [built] . . . a highway of 54 miles in 60 days." Roy McKelvie, *The War in Burma* (London, 1948), 69-72.

[67] *Stilwell Papers*, 313, 349. Romanus and Sunderland, *Stilwell's Command*, 469-470. By June 4 Frank D. Merrill's "Marauders" had lost 131 dead or missing, 203 wounded, and 1,970 sick. See Charlton Ogburn, Jr., *The Marauders* (New York, 1959). The idea for this force came from the British General Orde Wingate, who had been killed in March. The best book is Christopher Sykes, *Orde Wingate* (London, 1959). Meanwhile, the British and Japanese had struck at each other in campaigns which, for a time, threatened the line to Ledo. A million men finally recovered Burma in "the largest single action fought against the Japanese." Its failure to re-establish Western power in much of this area may justify the American prejudice against "political" campaigns. Liddell Hart, *Strategy*, does not mention it. Fuller thinks

When Japan surrendered, thirty-nine Chinese divisions had American equipment. But only sixteen had completed training and there was no pool of trained, healthy replacements. Stilwell's able successor, Albert C. Wedemeyer, was directed to "support" the Nationalists unless "they engaged in civil war." His request for seven American divisions to assist the overextended Nationalists in disarming the Japanese in Manchuria fell foul of the American rush to demobilize and Secretary of State Marshall's attempt to unify China by "peaceful, democratic methods." The Communists (with Japanese weapons left them by the Russians, who carted off everything else of value) reverted to guerrilla warfare. Chiang's troops, like the Japanese before them, were confined to the cities and railroads. Chiang fled to Formosa in 1949, the year in which American occupation forces left South Korea. MacArthur and Stilwell had correctly felt that the Japanese were not the only Asiatics who could be made into good soldiers, a fact which the Indian Army had long since demonstrated. The Chinese Communist armies, like the Japanese, depended perforce on "weight of numbers," but they now "possessed all the qualities . . . of a modern army [without] . . . the 'long administrative tail' which eats up the manpower, and hampers the manoeuvrability, of Western troops."[68]

On June 25, 1950, a North Korean army—89,000 combat troops with a core who had fought with the Soviet or Chinese Communists—invaded South Korea, whose 65,000 combat troops were being trained for internal security purposes by

that it was technically "one of the most remarkable campaigns of the entire war. . . . Besides leadership and soldiership, the three outstanding [factors] . . . were air power, medical care, and engineering." Second World War, 372-373. The Australians were equally reluctant to be used for the recapture of Singapore, preferring to be in on the invasion of Japan. See Ehrman, Grand Strategy, VI, 224-233.

Chiang was not present at Yalta. Stalin agreed to go to war with Japan "two or three months after" the German surrender, in return for the preservation of the status quo in Outer Mongolia, the annexation of the Kuriles and southern Sakhalin, and the restoration of Tsarist Russia's rights in Dairen, Port Arthur, and the Chinese Eastern and South Manchurian Railways. Roosevelt agreed to "take measures to obtain" Chiang's "concurrence on advice from Marshal Stalin."

[68] Charles F. Romanus and Riley Sunderland, Time Runs Out in CBI (U. S. Army in World War II, Washington, 1959), 368, 395. C. N. Barclay, The First Commonwealth Division (Aldershot, 1954), 33-34. See also Liu, Military History, 226-270, L. M. Chassin, La Conquête de la Chine par Mao Tse-Tung, 1945-1949 (Paris, 1952), and Wedemeyer's Wedemeyer Reports (New York, 1958).

an American military mission. The North Koreans had 150 Russian tanks, a small tactical air force, and greatly superior artillery. Two days later the United Nations Security Council asked all U. N. members to aid South Korea and the United States ordered its Seventh Fleet to "neutralize" Formosa to save Formosa for Chiang or, Chiang claimed, to save the Communists from his counteroffensive. His offer of 33,000 ground troops was rejected by the U. N. Supreme Commander, MacArthur. The latter's forces made a stand at Pusan, across the Straits of Tsushima from Japan. In September they destroyed the North Korean army by an amphibious assault on the Inchon-Seoul area and a counteroffensive from Pusan. On September 27 the U. S. Joint Chiefs of Staff ordered MacArthur not to use non-Korean ground forces near the Russian or Manchurian borders or to support such forces by "air or naval action against Manchuria or U. S. S. R. territory." A week later the Chinese Communists warned the Indian Ambassador that they would intervene if non-Korean forces advanced into North Korea, but the U. N. General Assembly approved such action on October 7. A week later MacArthur told President Truman that there were 300,000—a figure raised to 400,000 by October 20—Chinese Communist troops in Manchuria. How many could enter North Korea without being detected? Would the Communists risk them—the chief support of the "new China"—in a peninsular trap against U. N. air power? "Only 50,000 to 60,000," MacArthur thought, "could be gotten across the Yalu River [against a U. N. ground combat force of about 230,000 and a still larger number in service, air, and naval units]. They have no Air Force. Now that we have bases for our Air Force in Korea, if the Chinese try, . . . there would be greatest slaughter." No political, intelligence, or military echelon of the U. N. Command doubted that massive Chinese forces could be detected and defeated in North Korea. Mid-November U. N. estimates of Chinese "volunteers" in North Korea varied from 44,851 to 76,800. The Chinese actually "moved 300,000 men into position in October and November and none of them was ever discovered by the U. N. Command prior to actual contact," because of their extraordinary march discipline and camouflage.[69]

[69] Roy E. Appleman, *South to the Naktong, North to the Yalu (June-November 1950)* (*United States Army in the Korean War*, ed. Stetson Conn, Wash-

MacArthur began his final offensive on November 24. When the Chinese counterattacked, he announced "an entirely new war." His forces were driven back to about the 37th parallel, but his proposals for a blockade of China, naval and air action against Chinese cities, and the use of Nationalist troops in Korea and from Formosa were rejected. His forces counterattacked to the 38th parallel in March. On the 24th, he publicly offered to meet the enemy commander in the field to realize the United Nations' political objectives in Korea, under the threat of "an expansion of our military operations to its [China's] coastal areas and interior bases." That day President Truman reminded him of the Joint Chiefs' previous warnings about public statements on military or foreign policy. Four days previously, MacArthur had written House Republican Leader Joseph W. Martin, to explain his views. Martin published this letter on April 6; MacArthur was relieved of all his commands on the 11th. The resulting Congressional investigation coincided with two Chinese offensives and a counteroffensive along the 38th parallel. "With the Russians' colossal error in starting the Korean conflict [assuming that the North Koreans had not jumped the gun themselves] having been erased through the efforts of the Chinese Communists—the Soviet Union made a formal bid to end the fighting." Armistice negotiations—punctuated by little battles—began on July 10 and ended more than two years later on July 27, 1953. South Korea was persuaded to accept the armistice line (generally a bit above the 38th parallel) by offers of American military and economic aid, an American alliance, and a policy statement by the sixteen states which had sent combat units (the United States, five British Commonwealth states, France and the three Benelux states, Greece and Turkey, Colombia, Ethiopia, and Thailand and the Philippines) that "a breach of the armistice terms would be so grave that, in all probability, it would not be possible to confine hostilities within the frontiers of Korea." United Nations' casualties have been estimated at 44,000 South Koreans, 27,000 Americans, and 3,000 others killed

ington, 1961), 7-18, 605-607, 760-770. See also Carl Berger, *The Korea Knot: A Military-Political History* (Philadelphia, 1957), 93-121, John W. Spanier, *The Truman-MacArthur Controversy and the Korean War* (Cambridge, Mass., 1959), Trumbull Higgins, *Korea and the Fall of MacArthur: A Précis in Limited War* (New York, 1960), and Allen S. Whiting, *China Crosses the Yalu: The Decision to Enter the Korean War* (New York, 1960).

and 250,000 wounded. Estimates of 1,350,000 enemy dead and wounded may be much too high.[70]

In Indochina, two thousand miles to the south, the Japanese had replaced the Vichy French authorities in March, 1945, with governments headed by the Emperor of Annam, Bao Dai, and the Kings of Laos and Cambodia. The Communist-dominated Vietminh, under Ho Chi Minh, which had proclaimed a united front against both the Japanese and the French, overturned Bao Dai and set up a Republic of Vietnam in September. Chiang's occupation force in the north favored Ho, but the British handed authority back to the French in the south. After the French recovered the north, they proposed an autonomous federation of Indochina within the French Union, a plan rather like that which the Dutch were to propose to the Indonesian Republic to which the Japanese had handed power when they surrendered. The Indonesians made good their independence by combining appeals to the United Nations and the United States with guerrilla warfare, though they agreed to a paper union with the Netherlands in 1949 and dissolved it in 1954, leaving the Dutch in control of New Guinea. Fighting between the Vietminh and the French broke out in the fall of 1946. The latter, who finally brought back a reluctant Bao Dai, were strongest in the south, in the cities, and along the lines of communication. The Vietminh began to get Communist Chinese aid after the latter's victory in 1949; the United States—who eventually paid four-fifths of the cost of the war —agreed to aid the French just before the Korean War. The French almost pacified the north in 1951, but the Korean stalemate permitted increased Communist aid to the Vietminh. On May 7, 1954, they captured the force which had been air-lifted to Dienbienphu to cut this supply line and caused a French governmental crisis. The United States would not commit its forces and the Geneva Agreement of July 21 partitioned Vietnam, neutralized Laos and Cambodia, and temporarily ended seventeen years of land combat in East

70 Berger, *Korea Knot*, 131-137, 171-177. U. S. Department of the Army, *American Military History, 1607-1953* (Washington, 1956), 485. The three Scandinavian states, India, and Italy contributed medical personnel. Other good accounts of the fighting are Barclay, *First Commonwealth Division;* Russell A. Gugeler, *Combat Actions in Korea: Infantry, Artillery, Armor* (Washington, 1954); two works by S. L. A. Marshall, *The River and the Gauntlet* (New York, 1953), and *Pork Chop Hill* (New York, 1956); and the series by Lynn Montross and Nicholas A. Canzona, *U. S. Marine Operations in Korea, 1950-1953* (Washington, 1954-   ).

Asia. For the moment the great powers preferred two Chinas, two Koreas, two Vietnams, and two Germanies to either nuclear or "conventional" war.[71]

The Second World War demonstrated the soundness of Fuller's formula of political authority, economic self-sufficiency, national discipline, and machine weapons. The East Asian War proved only that states with a high degree of political authority can produce weapons on a fairly slender industrial base and that inexperienced Western troops might be too dependent on mechanized equipment and unfamiliar with perimeter defense and combat patrolling. The United States had not adopted a consistent policy or trimmed its aspirations to the forces which it was willing to commit during many stages of the War for East Asia. The need for political authority and national discipline is clear enough, though the known mistakes of the four dictatorships show that authority and discipline for their own sakes are not the solutions. The forms of political authority and national discipline, as Montesquieu had insisted two centuries before, depend on the spirit of a particular society. The collaboration, during the Korean War, of one American prisoner out of three with his captors, and the death of another in captivity—more from inertia than from maltreatment—may prove that the totalitarian stick and carrot technique was highly effective, that the soldier was too soft, or only that many prisoners had not been in service long enough to develop any sense of group solidarity. In any case, neither the military nor the political

[71] Frank N. Trager, ed., *Marxism in Southeast Asia* (Stanford, 1959), Ellen J. Hammer, *The Struggle for Indochina* (Stanford, 1954), Jean Marchand, *L'Indochine en guerre* (Paris, 1955), Littleton B. Atkinson, *Communist Influence on French Rearmament* (Maxwell Field, 1955), Nguyen Tien Lang's fictional *Les Chemins de la révolte* (Paris, 1955), and Bernard B. Fall, *Street Without Joy: Indo-China at War, 1946-1954* (Harrisburg, 1961) all throw light on this war and on the importance of professional infantry in such operations. The French profesisonals' efforts to adapt Communist techniques prepared the way for their active intervention in the internal politics of the Fourth and Fifth Republics.

For wider discussions of some of these problems see Reinhold Niebuhr, *The Structure of Nations and Empires* (New York, 1959), James D. Atkinson's fine *The Edge of War* (Chicago, 1960), Cyril Falls, *The Art of War: from the age of Napoleon to the present day* (London, 1961), and the irregular warfare issue of *Military Affairs* (XXIV, No. 3, Fall, 1960). Mao's *Strategic Problems of the Anti-Japanese Guerrilla War* and *On the protracted War*, both 1938, are in his *Selected Works* (4 vols., London, 1954-1956), II. Other interesting works are James F. Downs, *Thoughts on Cavalry, Guerrilla Warfare, and the Fall of Empires* (Berkeley, 1960), G. M. C. Sprung, *The Soldier in Our Time* (Philadelphia, 1960), Joseph Maxwell Cameron, *The Anatomy of Military Merit* (Philadelphia, 1960), and Brian Crozier, *The Rebels: A Study of Post-War Insurrections* (Boston, 1960).

events of these four wars seem to have changed Clausewitz's idea that war is as complex a business as politics, and that it is impossible to find a simple formula.[72]

[72] Homesickness had been clearly recognized as a potentially fatal disease in the eighteenth century. See Marcel Reinhard's excellent, "Nostalgie et service militaire pendant la Révolution" (*Annales historiques de la Révolution française*, Jan.-Mar., 1958, 1-15). See also William L. White, *The Captives of Korea: An Unofficial White Paper on the Treatment of War Prisoners* (New York, 1957), Eugene Kinkead, *In Every War but One* (New York, 1959), Murray Dyer, *The Weapon on the Wall: Rethinking Psychological Warfare* (Baltimore, 1959), Eli Ginzberg *et al.*, *The Ineffective Soldier* (3 vols., New York, 1959), and the materials in William E. Doughtery and Morris Janowitz, *A Psychological Warfare Case Book* (Baltimore, 1958).

Much attention is paid to the new relationship between industrial and military power in Fritz Sternberg, *The Military and Industrial Revolution of Our Time* (New York, 1959), Robert Strausz-Hupé *et al.*, *Protracted Conflict* (New York, 1959), Oskar Morgenstern, *The Question of National Defense* (New York, 1959), Michael R. D. Foot, *Men in Uniform: Military Manpower in Modern Industrial Societies* (London, 1961), James R. Schlesinger, *The Political Economy of National Security: A Study of the Economic Aspects of the Contemporary Power Struggle* (New York, 1960), and the present Pentagon Bible, Charles J. Hitch, Roland N. McKean, *et al.*, *The Economics of Defense in the Nuclear Age* (Cambridge, Mass., 1960). The theory of games has been applied to military situations by Thomas C. Schelling in his influential *The Strategy of Conflict* (Cambridge, Mass., 1960).

On Israel's shoestring war see the fine work by S. L. A. Marshall, *Sinai Victory: Command Decisions in History's Shortest War, Israel's Hundred-Hour Conquest of Egypt East of Suez, Autumn 1956* (New York, 1958). A more sober account of the political and military consequences of this adventure is Edgar O'Ballance, *The Sinai Campaign of 1956* (New York, 1960).

EPILOGUE

Epilogue

"To PREPARE for war," Douhet wrote a generation ago, "demands, then, exercise of the imagination."

We shall glance at the war of the past long enough to retrace its essential features; we shall ask of the present what it is preparing for the future; and, finally, we shall try to decide what modifications will be made in the character of war by the [consequences of the] causes at work to-day.

A 1958 survey found that the "outstanding characteristic" of the period since 1945 was "spectacular" technological change. The systematic application of science had increased the power of various destructive "agents" and the range and speed of their "delivery." The last stages of the Second World War, like the last stages of the First, had produced such new agents as the atomic bomb and such improved means of delivery as the snorkel submarine, a true underwater rather than a submersible ship, jet planes, long-range rockets, and new guidance and navigation systems. The same survey found "four trends of particular significance":

1. Weapons technology will become increasingly complex with a corresponding increase in the difficulty of choosing the most effective combination of weapons [the problem of military organization]. . . . 2. The rate of technological change will increasingly complicate the tasks of the defense relative to the offense. . . . 3. The U.S.S.R. will continue to gain in over-all military strength greatly aided by Communist China and some of its other allies [a major political result of the Second World War was the potential unification of the Heartland]. . . . 4. The concept of "scarcity" in nuclear weapons will disappear from the calculations of the U.S., the U.S.S.R., and to a lesser extent Great Britain. . . . Other countries will in due course have their own atomic arms if on a more limited scale.[1]

The first atomic bomb had an estimated power of twenty kilotons (20,000 tons) of TNT. In a typical western city, some 400,000 people would have been rendered homeless, though half of them could have returned after minor repairs.

[1] Douhet, *Command of the Air*, 119-120. Rockefeller Brothers Fund, *Prospect for America* (their collected reports, Garden City, 1961), 103-104. Harrison Brown and James Real, *Community of Fear* (Center for the Study of Democratic Institutions, Santa Barbara, 1960) is equally cogent.

"About 50,000 of them," a British mission reported, "would be dead or would die within eight weeks, and a comparable number [equalling the hospital beds in New Jersey] would require extended hospital treatment." The gulf between this bomb and the fifteen megaton (15,000,000 tons) hydrogen bomb tested at Bikini on March 1, 1954, was about equal to that between the atomic bomb and a ten ton (by 1960 the American nuclear stockpile was equal to one of these for everyone in the world) Second World War "blockbuster." The 1954 bomb showered radioactive coral over an area as big as New Jersey or Wales, an area which included Rongelap Atoll and the Japanese tuna boat *Lucky Dragon*, eighty-five miles from Bikini and twenty miles outside the official danger zone. Seventy-four Rongelapians and the twenty-three Japanese fishermen fell ill, though the latter had immediately washed the faintly-audible five-hour dust fall from their boat and headed home. On March 31 Admiral Lewis L. Strauss said that the bomb could "take out" any city in the world. President Eisenhower announced a week later that there was "no military requirement that could lead us into the production of a bigger bomb." Radioman Aikichi Kuboyama died on September 23. Seven years after his death and a three-year testing moratorium, Russia resumed testing and both superpowers announced that they could build hundred megaton bombs. An American claim that such bombs were less efficient than smaller bombs from heavy or fighter bombers, rockets (some of them small enough to be trucked), or submarines was modified by estimates that a hundred megaton bomb might burn out an area six times as big as the New York-New Jersey metropolitan area (with about 15,000,000 people), half again as large as New Jersey, or the size of Belgium. The bomb's incendiary effects would be much greater than those from blast (destroying frame houses eighteen miles away) or direct radiation (as in the proposed "neutron" bomb). Basement fall-out shelters might only trap families in their burning homes.[2]

Bombs could be "dirtied" by cobalt casing (radioactive cobalt is 320 times as powerful as radium and loses half its

[2] *The Effects of the Atomic Bombs at Hiroshima and Nagasaki* (London, 1946), 19. The United States gave Mrs. Kuboyama $2,800 and the Japanese fishing industry $2,000,000. Ralph E. Lapp, *The Voyage of the Lucky Dragon* (New York, 1958). For this era see Ansley J. Coale, *The Problem of Reducing Vulnerability to Atomic Bombs* (Princeton, 1947); and Augustin M. Prentiss, *Civil Defense in Modern War* (New York, 1951).

radioactivity every five years) or "cleaned." "Tactical" atomic weapons were now "conventional." Bombs might spread the radioactive by-products of atomic production. Geneticists tried to predict the increased mutation rates from increased radioactivity and the genetic damage from the absorption of radioactive strontium in animal bone marrow. There was no agreement on the viability of agreements on testing or weapons, and no agreements were reached. By 1956 General James M. Gavin, the United States Army's Director of Research and Development, put Russian casualties from "an assault in force with nuclear weapons" at "several hundred million deaths." A northwest wind would extend them "into the Japanese and perhaps . . . the Philippine area. If the wind blew the other way they would . . . back up into Western Europe." As the Russians increased their capacity to reach Western Europe and North America, machines computed the casualties which various societies could bear. Their operators produced a massive literature which may be classified as science fiction.[3]

The problems of radioactive fall-out, with its grave dangers to attackers, defenders, and neutrals, are analogous to those of biochemical warfare. Bacteriological agents are cheap, light, and to some extent, self-spreading and self-propagating. They may "hang fire" for weeks or months after delivery, and by wounding rather than killing men and their domesticated plants and animals, could tie up both manpower and

[3] *Hearings Before the Subcommittee on the Air Force of the Committee on Armed Services United States Senate* (Washington, 1956), Part X, 860-861. On these problems see J. Schubert and R. E. Lapp, *Radiation: What It Is and How It Affects You* (London, 1957), Arnold Kramish, *Atomic Energy in the Soviet Union* (Stanford, 1959), Royal Institute of International Affairs, *On Limiting Atomic War* (London, 1956), Philip Noel-Baker, *The Arms Race* (London, 1958), Seymour Melman, ed., *Inspection for Disarmament* (New York, 1958), Hedley Bull, *The Control of the Arms Race* (London, 1961), Bernard G. Bechhoefer, *Postwar Negotiations for Arms Control* (Washington, 1961), and Louis Henkin, ed., *Arms Control: Issues for the Public* (New York, 1961). Herman Kahn, *On Thermonuclear War* (Princeton, 1960) and Lewis F. Richardson, *Arms and Insecurity: A Mathematical Study of the Causes and Origins of War* and *Statistics of Deadly Quarrels* (both Chicago, 1960) are mathematical fiction.

The scientist's moral problems are explored in Linus Pauling, *No More War* (London, 1958), Robert Jungkh, *Brighter than a Thousand Suns: The Moral and Political History of the Atomic Scientists* (London, 1958), Fletcher Knebel and Charles Bailey, *No High Ground* (New York, 1960), for Britain's part, Ronald W. Clark, *The Birth of the Bomb* (London, 1961), and Paul Ramsey, *War and the Christian Conscience* (Durham, N. C., 1961). For current topics follow *Brassey's Annual*, the *Bulletin of the Atomic Scientists*, *Foreign Affairs, Military Affairs, Current Thought on War and Peace*, and the *Journal of Conflict Resolution*.

equipment. Large quantities of "nerve" gases were made during the Second World War. Like some insecticides, they affect the bridge chemicals between the nerve endings and the muscles, resulting in muscular disorders called the "D.D.T.'s" by British pathologists. Odorless, tasteless liquids which can be spread like commercial insecticides, they quickly penetrate ordinary clothing. Their vapor kills within a few minutes, a drop on the skin within half an hour. Doses are cumulative. Like gunpowder, they are weapons for the weak. Patience and intelligence are the chief research requirements. Two fine recent surveys ignored them. The editor of another noted, "While public attention has been focused primarily on the destructive power of long-range guided missiles, sustained research and development has been carried out on another class of weapons whose destructive power may very well be as extensive as that of nuclear explosives." This work has no chapter on chemical warfare. The author of the chapter "On the Feasibility of Control of Biological Weapons" thinks that large scale production and field trials might be detected, but that "It is entirely possible for any nation to carry out an extensive research and developmental program in biological warfare that even the most astute inspection team would find almost impossible to detect."[4]

Research on the means of delivery of these agents was concentrated on manned planes, atomic submarines, and on unmanned torpedoes and rockets. The size of the bull's-eye for either a ballistic or a guided missile—the former discards its rocket engine and, like an arrow or bullet, follows a "free flight" path to its target—could be increased because a nuclear agent can damage a larger area. The Russian earth satellites of 1957 turned the public's attention to missiles. Both the U. S. S. R. and the United States developed short, medium-ranged, and intercontinental missiles (accurate within a mile at 8,000 miles), but the U. S. S. R. had more powerful rocket engines. Like pre-1914 dreadnoughts, missiles,

[4] "Chief Characteristics of Nerve Gas" (*British Medical Journal*, August 9, 1952). Melman, *Inspection for Disarmament*, 25, 185-190. Vincent Groupé's chapter lists a 1942 report on the subject by Theodor Rosebury, brought up to date in his *Peace or Pestilence: Biological Warfare and How to Avoid It* (New York, 1949). The Office of Civil and Defense Mobilization, "Interim Statistical Report" (Battle Creek, December 31, 1960), 36, 50, notes that detection of such agents "requires the development, procurement, and implementation of electronic and laboratory type equipment and the training of highly specialized technical personnel," and that "equipment for the detection and identification of BW agents" is not commercially available.

earth satellites, and big bombs were also prestige factors. Russian medium-ranged missiles could cover Western Europe, Japan, and the Middle East. Their American counterparts could be launched from the Arctic and other oceans from nuclear-powered submarines and from European and Far Eastern land bases.[5]

Europe was politically divided along the lines reached by Western and Soviet forces in 1945. During the next ten years the Western Allies restored Western Europe's shattered industries and democratized many of its Communist and Fascist fellow-travelers by re-education, judicious purging of the civil services, and a higher standard of living, but were much less successful in rebuilding the traditional mass conscript armies of Italy, France, and West Germany. Poverty, local Communist obstructionism, the fear that a resurgent Germany might either try to dominate its neighbors or drag them into another anti-Soviet crusade, apathy, war-weariness, and France's colonial wars in Indochina and Algeria worked against massive Western European land rearmament. After 1954 these factors were reinforced by the conviction that modern nuclear warfare requires professional forces or conversely, that the use of tactical atomic weapons would surely "escalate" and finish whatever was left of Western Europe. The North Atlantic Treaty Organization built a massive base and communications "infrastructure" and a complex command superstructure, but failed to reach either its original ninety-six division (a few more than for France alone in 1940) or its later thirty division targets. The resulting forces, critics felt, were too small for a shield and too large for a "trip wire" for nuclear retaliation. Their best ground components were still the Anglo-American forces—or "hostages" —in West Germany. In 1954 Marshal Slessor proposed to reorganize the whole force around its "armoured . . . [and] tactical air forces," and supplement them with "local semi-static forces" which could not take "the strategic offensive,"

5 Nels A. Parson, Jr., *Guided Missiles in War and Peace* (Cambridge, Mass., 1957). Philip Joubert de la Ferté, *Rocket* (New York, 1958); I. J. Galantin, "The Future of Nuclear-Powered Submarines" (*United States Naval Institute Proceedings*, LXXXIV, June, 1958, 23-35), Anthony E. Sokol, *Sea Power in the Nuclear Age* (Washington, 1961), F. I. Ordway and R. C. Wakefield, *International Missile and Spacecraft Guide* (New York, 1960), and Karl W. Deutsch, "The Impact of Science and Technology on International Politics" (*Daedalus*, LXXXVIII, Fall 1959, 669-685) on these prestige factors. Critics of the American missile program could remember that the technologically backward Japanese had used less advanced infantry weapons most effectively in the Pacific War.

i. e., attack each other or Russia's East European satellites. Such forces would combine the "peaceful" features of Juarès's national militias with the counteroffensive power of De Gaulle's "Army of the Future." Four years later Field Marshal Montgomery proposed combining international forces for service outside the NATO area with national forces for local defense and protection against fifth columnists.[6]

Russia had recovered the buffer zone lost in the First German War and had added a wide belt of satellite states. The Red Army retained its great numerical superiority by reverting to normal peacetime conscription and by rebuilding the Polish and other satellite armies along similarly traditional lines. The inherent political dangers of such armies—which should be deprived of all but light weapons until they are thoroughly indoctrinated—was again demonstrated in 1957, when part of the Hungarian army sided with the rebels against the police and some Russian units supposedly refused to help in suppressing the rebellion. The Russian mobile forces, on the other hand, were equal to their task, and the rebels received little but good wishes from the West. In 1945 the Russians had to rebuild their own industries, integrate the satellites into their economy, and send whatever assistance they could to the Communist forces in the unfinished war in East Asia. Their primary military problems were in the air and at sea, the Anglo-American monopolies of strategic air power and atomic weapons obviously being the most pressing. The Western powers already possessed air bases within range of much of the Soviet Union. Their naval and air strength was increasingly concentrated in the Near East near the exposed Caspian oil fields. The Russians had simultaneously to

[6] Slessor, *Strategy for the West* (New York, 1954). Montgomery, *Memoirs*, 468-473. See also Ben T. Moore, *NATO and the Future of Europe* (New York, 1958) and Alastair Buchan, *NATO in the 1960's* (New York, 1960). In 1959 NATO had 22 divisions in Western Europe and 24 Greek, Italian, and Turkish divisions. The multiplication of nuclear weapons and the closer coordination of all forces, so that navies, for example, can deliver megaton bombs 1,500 miles inshore, make divisional figures increasingly meaningless. The choice of forces, as in the Middle Ages, depends on political, geographical, and psychological circumstances.

The "fundamental principles" of war and *Realpolitik* are now seen as no more than the pooled experiences of the Iron Age and its Great Empires and Great Captains from Ashurbanipal to Bonaparte. As its maxims, "loud cries," and "shining objects" and the idea that military or political history can furnish useful guides to policy or do more than satisfy that "passion for knowledge" which Einstein compared to the "passion for music," seem ever less applicable, we are left with the Greek beliefs in reason as a social tool and that men are much the same everywhere and Tolstoy's belief in man's "unwavering, irrefutable consciousness of freedom."

build up their fighter and radar defenses, create a Strategic Air Command and an effective submarine force, and produce atomic weapons and guided and ballistic missiles. Their ground forces were not rearmed and modernized until the late fifties. Russian science and industry met these multiple challenges brilliantly, though the Soviet economy was strained almost to the breaking point. Jugoslavia, the one satellite which the Red Army had not occupied in force during the last stages of the Russo-German War, broke away from Stalinism and was discreetly supported by the United States. Stalin's successors tried to patch up the quarrel, but revolts broke out in East Germany, the Caucasus, and Poland, as well as in Hungary. These events were accompanied by grave defections from the Western Communist parties—even among the party leaders—and by signs of unrest among the Soviet intellectuals and technocrats.[7]

The political situation in East Asia in 1945, as has already been noted, was reminiscent of that in East-Central Europe in 1918. The Big Three, the Russians included, held only the center and parts of the perimeter of the Japanese Empire at the end of the Great Pacific War. The Communist victory in the war for East Asia was due less to the outside forces exerted by the Big Three than to local conditions. In the Near East Anglo-American power forced Stalin to honor his pledge to withdraw from northern Iran and shored up a "northern tier" of Iran, Turkey, and Greece. Behind this tier, however, rampant nationalism forced Britain and France to withdraw from Libya, Israel, the Sudan, Egypt, Iraq, Cyprus, Syria, Lebanon, Tunis, and Morocco, while Algerian nationalists crippled French power in Europe and indirectly brought down the Fourth Republic. Almost all of colonial Africa, except for Portuguese Africa, became independent, and the Union of South Africa left the Commonwealth.

The United States Army was hard hit by the traditional

[7] See Raymond L. Garthoff, *Soviet Strategy in the Nuclear Age* (New York, 1958), Herbert S. Dinerstein, *War and the Soviet Union* (New York, 1959), and the symposia edited by Asher Lee, *The Soviet Air and Rocket Forces* (New York, 1959), M. G. Saunders, *The Soviet Navy* (London, 1958), and Liddell Hart, *The Red Army: The Red Army, 1918 to 1945, the Soviet Army, 1946 to the Present* (New York, 1956). The historical sections of the last work are excellent.

For Russian views of atomic weapons see Raymond L. Garthoff, *The Soviet Image of Future War* (Washington, 1959), his translation of Major General G. I. Pokrovsky, *Science and Technology in Contemporary War* (New York, 1959), and Major General Nicolai N. Talensky, "On the Character of Modern Warfare" (*Atlas*, II, March, 1961, 28-33).

demobilization of 1946. The Air Force concentrated on super-bombers and the Navy on supercarriers, though the airmen were publicly skeptical of the latter's value in a war with a landlocked state already surrounded by land air bases. Congress turned down a plan for universal military training; by June, 1948, the United States Army was down to 525,000 men and 10 skeleton divisions. Conscription was then revived to stimulate volunteering, a system which funneled the unlucky and the unwary into the infantry and kept industry and educational institutions in a state of perpetual confusion. The armèd forces' strength was then set at 2,005,000. Because of the lack of new reserves, many veterans of the supposedly ended Second World War were recalled when the entire United States Army and Marine Corps—except for 2 divisions in Germany—were sent to repel the North Korean attack on South Korea. The United States armed forces rose to 3,630,000 men in 1952, fell to 2,476,000 in early 1961, and rose again during the Berlin crisis of that year. About half of the ground forces remained overseas near the main forces of numerically superior potential enemies. The most trenchant critics of the post-Korean "more bang for a buck" policy were James M. Gavin and Maxwell D. Taylor. In addition to routine criticisms of Defense Department organization and the lack of tactical and transport aircraft controlled by the ground forces, General Gavin insisted that nuclear warfare would require larger, rather than smaller, ground forces because of the great difficulties of supply and communications for dispersed mechanized forces. General Taylor, on the other hand, thought that even tactical atomic weapons should not be used in defending Western Europe. Russia's forces included the traditional conscript reserves, but the trend of American—as well as British—policy was away from compulsory service. How civil defense organizations could function without large numbers of persons with some preliminary training was hardly considered in some American works on defense policy. At the time of the Berlin crisis civil defense planning still called for massive automobile evacuations. Citizens had traded their traditional muskets for automobiles which the state trained them to drive, but it did not train them in other survival techniques.[8]

---

[8] Gavin, *War and Peace in the Space Age* (New York, 1958). Taylor, *The Uncertain Trumpet* (New York, 1960). F. O. Miksche, *The Failure of Atomic Strategy* (New York, 1959) supports Taylor. Henry Kissinger, *The Necessity*

On April 4, 1957, a British White Paper outlined "the biggest change in military policy ever made in normal times." During the next five years the Government planned to cut the number of men in the armed forces almost in half to 390,000, or about the number in 1937, and to abandon peacetime conscription. All three services were to be equipped with nuclear weapons and guided or ballistic missiles. Since "There is at present no means of providing adequate protection for the people of this country against . . . nuclear weapons—" a platitude which was regarded in Washington as top secret—"the only existing safeguard against major aggression is the power to threaten retaliation with nuclear weapons." The reduced tactical air forces would be armed with such weapons, and fighters would be first concentrated for the defense of nuclear launching sites—manned bombers being replaced by ballistic missiles—and then replaced by guided missiles. The army's contingent in Germany would be reduced and reorganized into independent brigades armed with nuclear weapons. A similar reduction of forces "to defend British colonies and protected territories against local attack, and to undertake limited operations in overseas emergencies" had been one aim of British military policy since the time of George III. "A Central Reserve . . . in the British Isles" would gain mobility from "a substantial fleet of transport aircraft." The navy

for Choice: Prospects of American Foreign Policy (New York, 1961), Gordon B. Turner and Richard D. Challener, eds., National Security in the Nuclear Age: Basic Facts and Theories (New York, 1960), and Bernard Brodie, Strategy in the Missile Age (Princeton, 1959) are brilliant surveys. The one part of the Compton Commission's Program for National Security (Washington, 1947) rejected by Congress was peacetime compulsion. On organization see Paul Y. Hammond, Organizing for Defense: The American Military Establishment in the Twentieth Century (Princeton, 1961). The Rockefeller report devoted nine pages to organization and three to civil defense. "While it may be impossible to protect the population against the blast and heat of an atomic explosion," it stressed early warning and shelter against fall-out, "tax incentives . . . for the location of new [industrial] facilities away from main concentrations, . . . [and] understanding . . . [of] the effects of modern weapons to respond with discipline [but not compulsory civil defense training] and effectiveness to a surprise attack." Prospect for America, 139-140.

Other key works were Kissinger, Nuclear Weapons and Foreign Policy, Paul L. Peeters, Massive Retaliation: The Policy and Its Critics (Chicago, 1959), George C. Reinhardt and William R. Kintner, The Haphazard Years: How America Has Gone to War (New York, 1960), Hanson W. Baldwin, The Great Arms Race (New York, 1958), Robert Endicott Osgood, Limited War: The Challenge to American Strategy (Chicago, 1957); William W. Kaufmann, ed., Military Policy and National Security (Princeton, 1956), Washington Platt, Strategic Intelligence Production: Basic Principles (New York, 1957), and Alfred Vagts, Defense and Diplomacy: The Soldier and the Conduct of Foreign Relations (New York, 1956).

would retain "a small number of carrier groups," while reducing its forces for commerce protection. This last part of the program was later modified, but the White Paper admitted that "The role of naval forces in total war is somewhat uncertain. It may well be that the initial nuclear bombardment and counterbombardment . . . would bring the war to an end within a few weeks or even days. . . . On the other hand, there is a possibility that it would be of great importance to defend Atlantic communications against submarine attack." Though Washington feared that this plain talk about the implications of its own nuclear-oriented "more bang for a buck" policies would encourage neutralism and apathy in Western Europe, the White Paper's emphasis on air transport and mobile combinations of local forces and powerfully-armed regulars against subversion became major features of later American programs.[9]

The superpowers' refusal to wage total war after 1945 was not due to lack of arms or courage. Danger, Clausewitz noted, "dominates the leader, not only by threatening him personally, but also by threatening all those entrusted to him. Who could advise, or resolve upon, a great battle, without feeling . . . more or less . . . paralyzed by the danger and responsibility which such a great act of decision carries in itself?" Brigadier C. V. Barclay defined the "New Warfare" as "the means by which a nation (or group of nations) seeks to impose its will . . . by all means short of total war, and without disturbing its own economy to an extent which is unbearable, or unacceptable, to its people." Its time-tested, cheap, and effective methods (governments have been overthrown for less than the cost of a radio station or a ballistic missile) include propaganda, obstruction, planned mischief,

[9] *Outline of Future Policy on Defence*, Command 124. The Home Secretary was forced to announce that the Government was going to do its best for civil defense, but would not propose compulsory training for this purpose. On the abolition of nuclear weapons, disengagement, or an agreed withdrawal of NATO and Soviet forces from Céntral Europe see Michael Howard, *Disengagement in Europe* (Harmondsworth, 1958), J. C. Slessor, *The Great Deterrent* (New York, 1957), E. J. Kingston-McCloughry, *Global Strategy* (New York, 1957) and *Defence: Policy and Strategy* (London, 1960), Eugene Hinterhoff, *Disengagement* (London, 1959), Patrick Lort-Phillips, *The Logic of Defence* (Purley, 1959), and Liddell Hart's masterly *Deterrent or Defense: A Fresh Look at the West's Military Position* (New York, 1960).

De Gaulle has not discussed the future of war, but has devoted himself to France's immediate problems. His goals are the disengagement of the Mediterranean and then of Western Europe from American tutelage and the formation of a Western European Third Force. The key military work is General Pierre Gallois, *Strátegie de l'age nucleaire* (Paris, 1960).

underground war, sabotage, intimidation, bribes, armed threats, limited war, and war by proxy. The operative phrase is Clausewitzian—"seeks to impose its will." The limitations— "short of total war, and without disturbing its own economy" —come from the scientific, social, and economic revolutions of the last century. In MacArthur's words:

You have got to understand the history of war. . . . With the scientific methods which have made mass destruction reach appalling proportions, war has ceased to be a sort of roll-of-the-dice. . . . The integration of the world . . . has outlawed the very basic concepts upon which war was used as a final word to settle international disputes. . . . The last two wars have shown it. . . . If you have another world war . . . only those will be happy that are dead. . . . I understand . . . that you cannot abolish war unless others do it. . . . If . . . one great power . . . keeps armed and threatening, the only way that you can meet force is by force, . . . and you have to provide for that. But sooner or later, if civilization is to survive, . . . war must go.[10]

MacArthur was then seventy-one. His statement does not seem to justify Barclay's fear: "As it is the customary order of things that we should be governed, and guided, mostly by very elderly people, there is a very real danger of . . . authoritative opinion lagging behind realities." In fact, many authorities—statesmen, soldiers, and scientists—saw the realities before they were seen by the public and agreed with Bloch that total war had "become impossible, except at the price of suicide." The key question was simple—in war "everything is very simple, but the simplest thing is difficult"—could war now be considered a political act? No philosopher, in any case, defines politics as the art of mutual suicide. On March 1, 1955—twenty-two years after Liddell Hart gave the lectures which provided the theme for this book—the eighty-year-old Winston Churchill told the House of Commons that,

We live in a period . . . when the whole world is divided intellectually and to a large extent geographically between the creeds of Communist discipline and individual freedom . . . [both armed

10 Clausewitz, *On War,* 73-74. Barclay, *The New Warfare* (London, 1953) 18. *MacArthur Hearings,* 148-149. W. Philips Davison, *The Berlin Blockade: A Study of Cold War Politics* (Princeton, 1958), Hugh Seton-Watson, *Neither War nor Peace: The Struggle for Power in the Post-War World* (New York, 1960), John W. Spanier, *American Foreign Policy since World War II* (New York, 1960), and Kenneth W. Thompson, *Political Realism and the Crisis of World Politics* (Princeton, 1960) are excellent. The implications of cheap and secret war were hardly discussed before the Cuban fiasco.

with] obliterating weapons . . . Russia['s and America's] enormous
spaces . . . [will soon be] on an equality or near equality of vulnerability with our small, densely-populated island and with Western Europe. . . . It may well be that we shall by a process of
supreme irony have reached a stage in this story where safety will
be the sturdy child of terror, and survival the twin brother of annihilation. . . . In the past, an aggressor has been tempted by the
hope of snatching an early advantage. In future, he may be de-
terred by the knowledge that the other side has the certain power
to inflict swift, inescapable and crushing retaliation. . . . All de-
terrents will improve and gain in authority during the next ten
years. By that time, the deterrent may well . . . reap its final
reward. The day may dawn when fair play, love for one's fellow
men, respect for justice and freedom, will enable tormented generations to march forward serene and triumphant from the
hideous epoch in which we have to dwell. Meanwhile, never flinch,
never weary, never despair.'[1]

11 *Parliamentary Debates*, 5th Series, Vol. 537, Cols. 1893-1905. What books
to begin with? The author's students use Earle, *Modern Strategy*, Fuller,
Military History, or Spaulding *et al.*, *Warfare* on some topics, sample
Clausewitz, Mahan, Fuller, *Machine Warfare*, Liddell Hart, *Strategy*, and
Douhet, and read Wavell, *Generals* and *Generalship*, and either Brodie,
Strategy in the Missile Age, or Turner and Challener, *National Security in the
Nuclear Age.*
Or work back to Caesar, Xenophon, and Thucydides from novels and
memoirs, classifications which are impossible to separate. *War and Peace*, *The
Red Badge of Courage*, and Euclides da Cunha, *Rebellion in the Backlands*,
tr. Samuel Putnam (Chicago, 1944) lead through Du Picq and Bloch to the
great literature of the First World War, examples of which have already been
noted. Its writers came from all walks of life, though many had already tried
writing. Hans Carossa, *A Roumanian Diary*, tr. Agnes Neill Scott (New York,
1930), Francis Brett Young, *Marching on Tanga* (London, 1918), and Georges
Duhamel, *The New Breed of Martyrs*, tr. Florence Simmonds (New York,
1918) were doctors. The last two works, like Ian Hay, *The First Hundred
Thousand* (London, 1915), Henri Barbusse, *Under Fire*, tr. Fitzwater Ray
(New York, 1917), and Fritz von Unruh (a former officer from an old
Junker family), *Way of Sacrifice*, tr. C. A. Macartney (New York, 1928)
were more than contemporary war or peace propaganda. *Verdun*, tr. Gerard
Hopkins, is the best of Jules Romains, *Men of Good Will* (14 vols., New
York, 1933-1946) series. Arnold Zweig, *The Case of Sergeant Grischa*, tr.
Eric Sutton (New York, 1928) is the best of a shorter, better German series.
R. H. Mottram, *The Spanish Farm Trilogy* (New York, 1927) and Jaroslav
Hasek, *Schweik: The Good Soldier*, tr. Paul Selver (Garden City, 1930) were
bank clerks. This was the only volume of Hasek's Czech saga that was trans-
lated into English. Mottram, John Easton, and Eric Partridge *Three Personal
Records of the War* (London, 1929) is, like Falls, *War Books*, hard to find;
many of the best books are out of print. Ford Maddox Ford's fine *The Good
Soldier* (New York, 1951) and Robert Graves, *Good-Bye to All That* (new ed.,
Garden City, 1957) are available, but this may not be the case with Siegfried
Sassoon, *Memoirs of George Sherston* (New York, 1937) or C. S. Forester's
best work, *The General* (Boston, 1936). Mikhail Sholokhov, *And Quiet Flows
the Don*, tr. Stephen Garry (New York, 1935) deals with the Russian Civil
War. Ernest Hemingway's best war book is surely *For Whom the Bell Tolls*
(New York, 1940). But the best of the American books may be John W.
Thomason, Jr., *Fix Bayonets* (New York, 1926) or E. E. Cummings's descrip-
tion of a prison, *The Enormous Room* (New York, 1922).

Index

Abell, Westcott, 71
Accomb, Evelyn M., 97
Adams, G. W., 170
Adcock, F. E., 19
Adloff, Richard, 361
Agar-Hamilton, J. A. I., 331
Ahnlund, Nils, 40
Alanbrooke, Lord, 351
Albion, Robert G., 71
Albord, Tony, 304
Alden, John Richard, 81, 87, 88
Aldington, Richard, 132
Alexander I, 56, 120-121, 126, 148
Alexander, Harold, 331, 383
Anders, W., 334-335, 341
Anderson, Bern, 75
Anderson, Eugene N., 154
Anderson, R. and R. C., 64
Anderson, Troyer S., 94
Andre, Louis, 41, 199
Andrieu d' Albas, Emmanuel, 366
Ansel, Walter, 322
Anson, George, 75
Appleman, Roy E., 379, 386
Armstrong, Elizabeth H., 265
Armstrong, John A., 341
Arnold, Benedict, 89
Arnold, Henry H., 13, 358, 380, 384
Aron, Raymond, 146, 315
Arthur, Sir George, 146
Artz, Frederick B., 139
Asher, Eugene L., 73
Ashley, Maurice P., 78
Aspinall-Oglander, C. F., 253
Asquith, H. H., 232
Aston, Sir George, 165, 233
Athearn, Robert G., 177
Atkinson, James D., 389
Atkinson, Littleton B., 389
Aube, Théophile, 208
Auchinleck, Claude, 330, 331, 361,
   383
Auphen, Paul, 329
Ayalon, David, 28
Ayers, James T., 176
Ayers, Leonard P., 261

Baclagon, Uldarico S., 260
Bacon, Eugene H., 92, 231
Bacon, Reginald H., 234
Bacquet, Louis H., 98
Bailey, Charles, 395
Bailey, Thomas A., 258
Bainville, Jacques, 119

Baker, Newton D., 259
Baldwin, Hanson, 350-351, 401
Baldwin, Stanley, 308, 311
Ballantine, Duncan L., 374
Bamford, Paul W., 71
Bamm, Peter, 340
Bao Dai, 388
Barbussi, Henri, 404
Barclay, C. N., 385, 388
Barclay, C. V., 402-403
Barnett, Correlli, 331
Barrett, John G., 183
Bartel, Walter, 206
Barthell, Edward E., 176
Battaglia, Roberto, 333
Battershaw, Brian, 156
Bauer, 319
Baumbach, Werner, 323
Baurmeister, Carl L., 88
Baxter, James P., 164
Baxter, James Phinney, III, 323
Baxter, Stephen B., 78
Bayley, C. C., 28
Bazaine, François A., 172, 174
Beaglehole, J. C., 75
Beale, Howard K., 188, 260
Bean, C. E. W., 271
Beatty, David, 234-235, 326
Beaverbrook, W. M. Aitken, 243
Bechhoefer, Bernard G., 395
Beck, Ludwig, 230, 283, 297
Behrens, C. B. A., 328
Beirne, Francis F., 92
Belden, Jack, 315, 367
Bell, Douglas H., 128
Bell, Sir George, 128
Belot, Raymond de, 332
Bender, Averam B., 177
Benedek, Ludwig von, 147, 169-170,
   173
Bengtsson, Frans G., 41
Beresford, Lord, 130
Berger, Carl, 387-388
Berlin, Isaiah, 135
Bernadotte, Jean, 120, 124
Bernard, Henri, 11
Bernard, L. L., 205
Bernardo, C. Joseph, 92
Bernhardi, Friedrich von, 201, 203-
   205, 216, 335
Bernotti, Romeo, 332
Berthier, Alexandre, 97, 150
Bertholet, General, 240

405

Bethmann-Hollweg, Theobald von, 214, 258, 264
Beyerhaus, G., 256-257
Bickel, W., 23
Bill, Alfred Hoyt, 90
Billias, George Athan, 90
Birnbaum, Karl E., 258
Bismarck, Prince, 154, 170, 197, 198
Black, Robert C., 185
Blackford, W. W., 180
Blackmore, Howard L., 33
Blair, Claud, 21
Blake, Robert, 241, 243, 265, 267
Blakeless, John, 90
Blau, George E., 335
Blease, W. Lyon, 134
Bliven, Bruce, 90
Bloch, Ivan S., 218-222
Bloch, Marc, 315, 403-404
Blomberg, Werner von, 296
Blomfield, Reginald, 44
Blond, Georges, 343
Blücher, G. L. von, 132
Blumenson, Martin, 356
Blumentritt, Gunther, 319
Blunden, Edward, 250-251
Bock, Fedor von, 318, 335, 337-338
Bodart, Gaston, 44
Boelcke, Willi, 198
Bolton, Charles K., 90
Bonnai, H., 170
Bonsal, Stephen, 97
Booth, Joseph, 274
Botha, 232
Bouchard, Georges, 109
Boucher, Arthur, 229
Boucher, J., 319
Boudet, F., 297
Boulanger, Georges, 198, 208
Bourcet, Pierre de, 101
Bourdet-Pléville, Michel, 63
Bourgin, Georges, 149
Bourne, Ruth, 76
Bouthoul, Gaston, 13
Bovill, E. W., 38
Bowen, Harold G., 306
Boxer, C. R., 62
Boyen, Leopold von, 138, 153
Braddock, Edward, 83-84
Bradlee, F. B. C., 190
Bradley, Omar, 315, 356, 357, 359
Bragadin, Marc' Antonio, 332
Braisted, W. R., 279
Brassey, Lord, 234
Brauchitsch, Walker von, 335, 337
Braun, Friedrich Edlen von, 204
Bredow, Adelbert von, 296
Brenan, General, 149
Brereton, Lewis H., 358
Brett-James, Antony, 132, 138

Briand, Aristide, 281-282
Briggs, John Henry, 144
Bright, Samuel R., Jr., 192
Brodie, Bernard, 61, 164, 401
Brodie, C. G., 254
Brogger, A. W., 63
Bronsart von Schellendorf, Paul, 195
Brooke-Popham, Robert, 362
Brooks, Charles R., 92
Brophy, Leo P., 246
Brown, A. J., 270
Brown, Harrison, 393
Bruce, R. V., 164
Brun, General, 228
Brunet-Moret, Jean, 174
Brunswick, Charles, Duke of, 106
Brusten, Charles, 25
Brunn, Geoffrey, 119, 271
Bryan, J., 377
Bryant, Arthur, 351
Brzezinski, Zbigniew K., 283-284, 288
Buchan, Alastair, 398
Buchheit, Gert, 334
Buckley, Christopher, 369
Budenny, Simeon, 286-287, 335-336
Bugeaud, Thomas Robert, 129, 149
Bühlow, 240-241
Bull, Hedley, 395
Bullock, Alan, 297, 303
Bullocke, John G., 73
Bundy, McGeorge, 311
Burgess, A. R. P., 319
Burgoyne, John, 94-95
Burke, Edmund, 33, 350-351
Burne, Alfred H., 21, 78, 121, 179
Burns, E. L. M., 265
Butler, J. R. M., 316, 332
Butow, Robert J. C., 381
Bywater, Hector C., 279, 281

Cadorna, Luigi, 248, 264
Cady, John F., 208
Caemmerer, Rudolf von, 152
Callwell, C. E., 233
Cameron, James, 239
Cameron, Joseph Maxwell, 389
Camon, Hubert, 119
Campbell, Arthur, 371
Campbell, Ian, 325
Canestrini, Giovanni, 33
Canfield, Eugene B., 192
Cannon, M. Hamlin, 377
Canzona, Nicholas A., 388
Caprivi, General, 197
Carboni, Giacomo, 333
Carman, W. Y., 33
Carnot, Lazare, 43, 108-109, 112, 113, 124, 125, 287-288
Carossa, Hans, 404
Carr, E. H., 277

Carré, Henri, 264
Carrias, Eugene, 151, 153, 296, 304
Case, Lynn M., 152
Casson, Lionel, 63
Castellan, Georges, 296
Castelnau, Edouard de C. de, 228-229, 249
Castex, Raoul, 69, 208, 210
Castle, Henry, 211
Cate, James Lea, 310, 354, 358, 380, 381
Catton, Bruce, 178, 179
Caulaincourt, Armand de, 136, 337
Cavaignac, Godefroyde, 139
Cavallero, Ugo, 332
Celovsky, Boris, 290
Challenger, Richard D., 198, 401, 404
Chalmers, W. S., 234, 320, 326
Chalmin, P., 149
Chamberlain, John, 366, 373
Chamberlain, Neville, 315-316, 317
Chambers, Arthur, 235
Chambers, Frank P., 256
Chambord, Marcel, 319
Chapelle, Howard I., 93
Chapman, H. P., 184
Chapperon, Alessio, 143
Charles I, 76-77
Charles II, 78
Charles V, 28, 36-37, 56
Charles VII, 24-25
Charles VIII, 26, 29
Charles XII, 41, 47
Charles, Archduke, 132
Chassin, L. M., 385
Chauvineau, N., 304
Chennault, Claire L., 382
Chiang Kai Shek, 346-348, 359-360, 367, 370, 375, 382-385, 386, 388
Cho, Isamu, 379
Choiseul, Duc de, 98-99
Chorley, Katharine, 104
Chudoba, Bohdan, 40
Churchill, Winston, 41, 232-233, 235, 252-254, 287, 308, 315, 317, 321, 332, 334, 348, 349-355, 359, 365, 366, 371, 382, 383, 403
Ciano, Galeazzo, 246, 259-260, 290
Civil War, 161-164, 169, 175-194, 218, 220, 246, 259-260
Clark, Alan, 247
Clark, Sir George, 41
Clark, Matt, 332
Clark, Ronald W., 395
Clark, William Bell, 90
Clausewitz, Karl von, 12, 14, 15, 121, 127, 132, 135, 136, 138, 150-152, 158-160, 196, 224, 286, 333, 336, 349, 351, 353, 354, 390, 402, 403, 404

Claver, Scott, 57
Cleaves, Freeman, 179
Clemenceau, Georges, 263-264, 270-271, 276
Clinard, O. J., 279
Clinton, Henry, 95
Clode, C. M., 79
Clowes, William L., 75
Coakley, Robert W., 328, 344
Coale, Ansley J., 394
Cobden, Richard, 145
Coblentz, Stanton H., 14
Cochrane, Hamilton, 190
Codman, Charles R., 357
Cohen, Jerome B., 363, 366, 375, 380
Coignet, Jean-Roch, 116
Colbert, Jean Baptiste, 41, 66
Colby, Elbridge, 53, 260
Cole, H. M., 358
Colegrave, E. H. M., 366
Coles, Cowper, 164
Colin, Jean, 47, 119
Collier, Basil, 233, 320, 323, 325
Collier, Richard, 320, 325
Collins, Robert John, 329
Colomb, Philip Howard, 209, 210
Commager, Henry Steele, 88, 180
Conn, Stetson, 347
Connell, John, 331
Connery, Robert H., 374
Conrad von Hötzendorff, Franz, 230, 245
Contamine, Henry, 198, 241
Cooper, Samuel, 177
Coox, Alvin D., 361
Corbett, Julian S., 66, 69, 70, 85, 118, 233, 234
Cornish, Dudley Taylor, 176
Cot, Pierre, 304-305
Coulter, E. Merton, 176, 186
Courville, Xavier de, 150
Craig, Gordon A., 197, 206, 226, 295-296
Crane, Stephen, 184
Craven, Wesley Frank, 196, 310, 354, 358, 380, 381
Creswell, John, 61
Crimean War, 145, 164-169
Crisp, Robert, 331
Croker, John Wilson, 115, 129
Cromwell, Oliver, 30, 34, 72
Crosby, Gerda R., 277
Crouzet, François, 123
Crowder, Enoch, 259-260
Crowl, Philip A., 306, 372, 376
Crozier, Brian, 389
Cruickshank, C. G., 66
Cruttwell, C. R. M. F., 241
Cuneo, John R., 85
cummings, e. e., 404

Cunningham, Andrew B., 326, 329
Cunningham, H. H., 176
Curling, Henry, 128
Current, Richard N., 363
Curtis, Edward E., 87
Curtiss, John Shelton, 148

Dallin, Alexander, 341
Daly, R. W., 188
Dalzell, George W., 194
Danilov, Y., 252
Daveluy, Rene, 211
Davidson, Eugene, 351
Davidson, Sir John, 247
Davidson, R. L. D., 81
Davies, Godfrey, 128
Davies, Joseph E., 290
Davin, D. M., 330
Davis, George T., 279
Davis, Jefferson, 176, 187, 260
Davis, Shelby C., 208
Davison, W. Philips, 403
Deane, John R., 343
Deborin, G. A., 289
Debussy, Claude, 251
DeConde, Alexander, 277
De Forest, John W., 180
de Gaulle, Charles, 55, 125, 239, 263-
  264, 303-304, 315, 371, 398, 402
de Grasse-Tilly, Marquis de, 96-97
Delbrück, Hans, 11, 53, 205, 206
Denison, George T., 33
Derry, T. K., 19, 318
Desbrière, Edouard, 48, 118
Desmaret, Jacques, 175
Desmazes, General, 249
D'Estaing, Jean Baptiste, 95-96
Deutsch, Harold C., 118
Deutsch, Karl W., 397
De Weerd, Harvey A., 241
DeWet, General, 232
Dexter, David, 373
Diaz, Armando, 264
Diaz del Castillo, Bernal, 33
Dibold, Hans, 340
Dicey, Edward, 220
Dickens, Gerald, 353
Dickerson, O. M., 67
Dickinson, G., 32
Diffie, Bailey W., 62
Dinerstein, Herbert S., 399
Divine, David, 320
Dixon, C. Aubrey, 339
Dodge, Ernest S., 75
Dodge, Theodore A., 11, 119
Doenitz, Karl, 306-307, 327-328, 339,
  359
Doerr, Hans, 340
Donald, David H., 178, 180
Donat, Karl von, 152, 203
Doolittle, James H., 368

Dorn, Walter, 44, 84
Dorson, Richard M., 88
Douhet, Guilio, 12, 60, 205, 228, 248,
  271, 285, 288, 290-294, 301, 304,
  309, 393, 404
Dowding, Hugh, 320
Downey, Fairfax, 88, 183
Downs, James F., 389
Drachkovitch, Milorad N., 206
Dreyer, Frederic, 235, 307
Drum, Hugh A., 382
Du Picq, Ardant, 149, 216-218, 222,
  263, 294
Dubail, General, 228
Dufour, Charles L., 191
Dumouriez, Charles François, 106-108
Dunlop, John K., 231
du Pont, Samuel F., 192
Duportail, Louis, 90
Dupuy, Trevor N., 92
Durand, John, 103
Durand, William Frederick, 306
Durkin, Joseph T., 188
Durrell, Lawrence, 371
Dyer, Murray, 390
Dzubian, Stanley W., 347

Earle, Edward Meade, 12, 28, 102,
  160, 209, 286
Edmonds, Charles, 248
Edmonds, James E., 227, 256, 263,
  265
Ehrman, John, 68, 351, 356, 357, 385
Eisenhower, Dwight D., 158, 325,
  344-346, 347, 348, 349, 351, 352,
  356, 357, 359, 362, 384, 394
Elizabeth I, 38-39, 65
Ellis, L. F., 305, 313, 319, 320
Erfurth, Waldemar, 296, 318
Ergang, Robert, 40, 46

Falkenhayn, Erich von, 241, 245, 248,
  251, 255
Falls, Cyril, 66, 207, 241, 251, 315,
  389, 404
Farragut, David Glasgow, 187, 188,
  191
Feis, Herbert, 350, 359, 360, 363
Ferdinand of Aragon, 26, 28
Fisher, John, 159, 209, 231-232, 234,
  253, 274
Fitzgerald, F. Scott, 273-274
Fitzgibbon, Constantine, 297, 325, 334
Fleming, Peter, 220, 315
Foch, Ferdinand, 195-197, 202-205,
  218, 219, 221-224, 229, 241-242, 247,
  266-267, 270, 313
Folard, Jean Charles, 51-52
Forester, C. S., 93, 127, 404
Fortescue, John W., 42, 82, 128, 146
Franco-Prussian War, 144, 161, 168

Frederick II of Prussia, 44-53, 85, 90, 99-100, 133, 150, 151, 155-156, 224
Frederick William I, of Prussia, 45-46, 54, 156
French, John, 243, 247
Friedrich, Carl J., 283-284, 288
Fuller, J. F. C., 11, 14, 19, 59, 85, 179, 232, 243, 250, 256, 269, 315, 335, 349, 350, 351, 358, 389, 404

Gage, Thomas, 87-88, 93
Galliéni, Joseph S., 228, 249
Garros, Louis, 229, 230
Garthoff, Raymond, 288, 321
Gatzke, Hans W., 264, 351
Gavin, James M., 395, 400
Geyl, Pieter, 39, 119
Goering, Hermann, 324, 329, 338, 341
Golaz, M. A., 215, 267
Golovine, Nicholas N., 230, 252
Goltz, Colmar von der, 199-202, 204, 205, 215-216, 222
Grant, Ulysses S., 178-179, 192, 193
Greenfield, Kent R., 344, 348, 356-359, 363, 376, 381
Groener, Wilhelm, 295, 296
Guderian, Heinz, 301-302, 313, 335, 337, 338, 355
Guibert, Jacques de, 98, 100-102
Gustavus Adolphus II, 39, 42, 46, 155

Haig, Douglas, 241, 243, 246-247, 263, 264-266
Haldane, Richard Burdon, 230-232, 245
Halder, Franz von, 335-336, 337-340
Hall, A. R., 49, 112
Hamilton, Ian, 220, 253
Hamley, Edward, 164-165, 166
Hankey, Maurice, 233, 312
Hart, B. H. Liddell, 11, 59, 128, 138, 160, 180, 196, 229, 241, 242, 269-271, 291, 315, 343, 358, 384, 399, 402, 403, 404
Haushofer, Karl, 298-300
Hayes, Carlton J. H., 205, 207
Heckscher, Eli F., 67, 123
Henderson, George F. R., 121, 165, 173, 179, 186
Henry, Robert S., 177, 178
Hentsch, Richard von, 240, 241
Hindenburg, Paul von, 241, 244, 245, 248, 252, 255, 258, 264, 266, 268, 272, 296
Hitler, Adolf, 213, 273, 277, 283, 290, 295-299, 300-303, 307, 310-312, 315-320, 321, 322, 323-325, 327, 329, 330, 333, 335, 336, 337, 338, 339, 341, 342, 343, 350, 355, 359
Hoche, Lazare, 110, 113
Hoffman, Max, 220, 242, 244

Hohenlohe-Ingelfingen, Kraft zu, 196, 200, 203
Hovgaard, William, 164, 209
Howard, Michael, 175, 233
Howe, William, 93-95
Hubatsch, Walther, 214, 318

Ingersoll, Ralph, 349, 357

James II, 68, 78
James, W. M., 96, 115
Jars, Robert, 318, 332
Jaurès, Jean Léon, 199, 286, 289, 303
Jellicoe, John, 234-235, 262
Joffre, Joseph, 227-229, 241-242, 248-249, 256, 311
Johnston, Joseph E., 178, 193
Jomini, Antoine Henri, 110, 118, 124, 127, 137, 150-151, 158-160, 178, 210, 216, 224
Jones, H. A., 292, 308
Joubert de la Ferté, Philip, 309, 327, 379

Kecskemeti, Paul, 351, 381
King, Ernest J., 369, 374
Kissinger, Henry A., 59, 143, 400-401
Kitchener, Horatio Herbert, 245, 246, 252, 254, 259, 267
Kluck, Alexander von, 240-241
Kurita, Takeo, 377-378

La Fayette, Marquis de, 104-106
Lane, Frederick C., 63, 328
Lapp, Ralph E., 394, 395
Lauterbach, Albert T., 206, 298
Lee, Asher, 353, 399
Lee, Robert E., 178-183, 192-193
Leeb, Wilhelm von, 334-335
Lefebvre des Noëttes, 30, 63
Lenin, Nicolai, 286-287
Lepotier, A., 185, 194
Lewis, Charles Lee, 97, 188, 192
Lewis, Lloyd, 179-180
Lewis, Michael, 62, 66, 73, 75, 114
Lincoln, Abraham, 176, 179, 186, 188, 193
Livy (Titus Livius), 27, 217
Lloyd, Christopher, 65, 85, 144-145
Lloyd, E. M., 32, 130
Lloyd George, David, 232, 254-255, 265, 271, 276, 277
Lockmiller, David A., 260, 311
Lockwood, Charles A., 376, 377
Longstreet, James, 178, 182
Louis XIV, 40-44, 45-46, 53, 58, 68, 78-79
Louis XVI, 102-103, 105-107
Louvois, Marquis de, 41, 57
Low, David, 270-271
Ludendorff, Erich von, 200, 241, 244,

245, 248, 255, 258, 264, 266, 269, 270, 297, 300
Luvaas, Jay, 179, 191, 196
Lyautey, Louis, 199, 249, 262

MacArthur, Douglas, 310, 345-347, 362, 371-373, 375-376, 377, 378, 381, 384, 385, 386, 387, 403
McClellan, George B., 178-179, 183, 192-193
MacDonald, Charles B., 315, 358
Machiavelli, Niccolo, 22, 27, 28, 32, 44, 45, 71
MacMahon, M. E. P. M. de, 149, 172
Mahan, Alfred Thayer, 60-61, 67, 69-70, 83, 93, 115, 118, 158, 185, 209-212, 233, 294, 404
Maistre, Joseph de, 139, 218, 222
Marder, Arthur J., 159, 209, 233
Marlborough, John Churchill, Duke of, 41, 46, 78, 83, 121
Marshall, George C., 260-261, 345, 348, 385
Marshall, S. L. A., 30, 358, 390
Martel, Giffard Le Q., 269, 301, 311
Marx, Karl, 286-287
Matloff, Maurice, 346-347, 350, 383
Maurice, Frederick, 146, 201, 241
Maxon, Yale Candace, 285, 363
Mellenthin, F. W. von, 319, 331
Melman, Seymour, 395, 396
Merriman, Roger B., 34, 38
Messimy, Adolphe, 228-229
Millis, Walter, 79, 258, 260, 366
Milner, Samuel, 372-373
Mitchell, William, 279-280, 292, 309
Moltke, Helmuth von (the Elder), 157-158, 169-170, 173, 182, 195, 204, 224, 226, 245
Moltke, Helmuth von (the Younger), 205-206, 223, 225-227, 230, 239-241, 244
Montague, C. E., 273-274
Montesquieu, Baron de, 32, 45, 102
Montgomery, Bernard L., 315, 331-332, 341, 344, 348, 349, 356, 357, 359, 398
Moorehead, Alan, 253, 331
Morison, Samuel Eliot, 63, 93, 326, 328, 332, 350, 366, 368, 370, 372, 376, 377, 378
Morton, Louis, 81, 362-363
Mussolini, Benito, 283, 290-291, 320, 329, 332, 359

Nagumo, Chiuchi, 365, 367, 369, 377
Napoleon I, 34, 39, 46-48, 51-52, 97, 98-139, 148-151, 159-160, 162, 170-171, 180-181, 193, 195-196, 202, 224, 282, 288, 302, 333, 335-336, 337
Napoleon III, 148-153, 168-174, 217

Nassau, Maurice of, 39, 43
Nef, John U., 14, 25, 28, 40, 42, 44, 47
Nehru, J., 220, 370
Nelson, Horatio, 71, 72, 74, 75, 114-115, 233-234
Nicholas I, of Russia, 56, 148, 167
Nicholas, Grand Duke, 230, 251, 252
Nickerson, Hoffman, 11, 59
Nimitz, Chester W., 62, 346
Nivelle, Robert, 249, 256, 262-263

Oman, Carola, 115, 128
Oman, Charles W. C., 20, 25, 34, 128, 130
Ozawa, Jisaburo, 376-378

Pabst, Helmut, 340
Packard, Francis R., 28
Paget, Henry W., 138
Palit, D. K., 12
Pallotta, Pietro, 333
Palmer, Frederick, 220, 221, 201
Palmer, John M., 91, 177
Palmer, Robert R., 102, 109, 110, 111
Papagos, Alexander, 330
Pares, Bernard, 252
Pares, Richard, 76
Pargellis, Stanley M., 82
Parker, H. D. M., 265
Parkes, Oscar, 209
Parkman, Francis, 85
Parry, J. H., 63
Parson, Nels, A., Jr., 397
Patterson, A. Temple, 97
Patton, George S., 356-357
Pauling, Linus, 395
Paullin, Charles O., 93
Paulus, Friedrich von, 341
Peckham, Howard H., 86, 88
Peeters, Paul L., 401
Pendergast, Maurice, 257
Penn, C. D., 68
Penn, Geoffrey, 164
Penrose, Boies, 63
Percival, A. E., 366
Perroy, Edouard, 21
Persius, Lothar, 214
Pétain, Philippe, 222, 248-249, 263-264, 266, 267, 305, 319, 329-331
Pershing, John J., 220, 261
Peter I (the Great), 44, 134
Peterson, H. C., 258
Peterson, Harold L., 33
Petrie, Sir Charles, 132
Petty, William, 66, 67
Pfeiler, H. K., 268
Philip II, 36, 37-39, 65
Phillips, Thomas R., 51
Phipps, Ramsay W., 110
Pichené, René, 152

Pick, Lewis A., 384
Pieri, Piero, 28, 41
Pierrefeu, Jean de, 241
Piggot, F. S. G., 363
Pilsudski, Joseph, 283
Pineau, Roger, 379
Pitt, William (the Elder), 83-85
Platt, Washington, 401
Playne, Carolyn, 205
Playfair, I. S. O., 329, 330
Plivier, Theodore, 315, 340
Pogue, Forrest C., 351, 356
Pohl, Hugo von, 214
Pokrovsky, G. I., 399
Pomeroy, Earl S., 306
Pope, Dudley, 118, 325
Porter, Robert Ker, 133
Possony, Stefan T., 353
Postan, M. N., 313
Potter, E. B., 62
Potter, G. R., 28
Powell, Ralph, 220
Powley, E. P., 68
Prasad, Bisheshwar, 366
Prentiss, Augustine M., 394
Preradovich, Nikolaus von, 147
Prescott, William H., 33
Presland, John, 147
Preston, Richard A., 5-6, 11
Pretelat, A. G., 304
Price, Don K., 323
Price, Thomas, 274
Proudfoot, Malcolm J., 345
Prucha, Francis P., 177
Puleston, William D., 60, 227
Pullen, John F., 178
Putnam, Peter, 134
Pye, Lucien W., 371

Quimby, Robert S., 98, 130

Radetsky, Joseph, 147
Radway, Laurence I., 346
Raeder, Erich, 307, 322, 327
Ramsay, David Home, 320
Ramsay, Paul, 395
Rasputin, 252
Rathenau, Walter, 255, 297, 298, 339
Rätzel, Friedrich, 299
Ravel, Maurice, 251
Redlich, Fritz, 42
Redlich, O., 41
Reel, Frank, 315
Reeves, James, 315
Regele, Oskar, 147, 230
Regnault, J., 158
Reichenan, Walther von, 296
Reinharat, George C., 401
Reinhard, Marcel, 109, 390
Reitlinger, Gerard, 296
Reitz, Deneys, 232

Remarque, Erich-Maria, 251, 315
Rendulic, Lothar, 318
Ribbing, Olof, 40
Richards, Denis, 305
Richardson, Lewis F., 395
Richmond, Herbert, 66, 307
Rieker, Karlheinrich, 339
Riker, William H., 260
Rippon, Anthony, 63, 366
Ritcheson, Charles R., 88
Ritter, Gerhard, 46, 154, 204, 224, 225-227, 233, 297
Ritter, E. A., 81
Roberts, Lord, 231
Roberts, Michael, 40
Robertson, E. Arnot, 67
Robertson, Frederick Leslie, 72
Robertson, William, 307-309
Robinson, C. N., 73
Robson, Eric, 94
Rocca, M. de, 127
Roddis, L. H., 74
Rodolphe, Colonel, 304
Rodgers, William L., 36, 63
Rogers, H. C. B., 33
Rogers, Lindsay, 339
Rokossovsky, Konstantin, 287, 340
Romains, Jules, 404
Romanus, Charles F., 360, 367, 371, 383-385
Rommel, Erwin, 290-291, 301-302, 329-331, 355, 370
Roon, Albrecht von, 157
Roos, Hans, 283
Roosevelt, Theodore 72, 220, 259, 260, 359, 383, 384, 385
Roosevelt, Theodore 72, 220, 259, 260, 366
Root, Elihu, 260
Roscoe, Theodore, 377
Rosebury, Theodor, 396
Rosek, E. J., 341
Rosenthal, Eric, 232
Rosinski, Herbert, 197
Roskill, S. W., 307, 325, 326, 327, 344, 370
Rossi, Francesco, 333
Rothenberg, Gunther Erich, 99
Rothfels, Hans, 160
Rotmistrov, Colonel, 321
Roton, Gaston, 304
Rovere, Richard H., 366
Rowe, Vivian, 304
Ruge, Friedrich, 326, 335, 355
Runciman, Steven, 20
Runstedt, Gerd von, 318, 319, 320, 334, 335, 337, 355
Ruppenthal, Roland G., 357
Russell, Carl P., 81
Russell, P. E., 21
Russell, Lora, of Liverpool, 345

Ryan, Cornelius, 355

Saint Cyr, Gouvion, 100, 149
Saint Germain, Comte de, 98, 100
Saxe, Maurice de, 42, 47, 51, 53-55, 98, 101
Scharnhorst, Gerhard Johann, 132-133, 153, 155-156, 158
Schaumburg-Lippe, Wilhelm von, 132
Schering, Walther M., 160, 299
Schlesinger, Arthur M., Jr., 366
Schlesinger, James R., 390
Schlieffen, Alfred von, 201-202, 205-206, 214, 222-227, 230, 233, 338, 368
Scott, Winfield, 176, 193
Ségur, Philippe-Paul de, 136
Sen, Surendra Nath, 147
Senger und Etterlin, Frido von, 335
Seton-Watson, Hugh, 403
Shanahan, William O., 133
Shannon, Fred A., 176
Shaposhnikov, Boris, 286-287
Shaw, G. C., 29, 203
Shaw, W. A., 78
Shepperson, George, 274
Sherman, William T., 179-183, 193, 202
Sherrard, O. A., 85
Shetelig, Haakon, 63
Shields, Joseph W., Jr., 49
Shigemitsu, Mamoru, 363, 376
Shirer, William L., 315
Sholokhov, Mikhail, 404
Shotwell, James T., 241, 277
Sigaud, Louis A., 293
Silberner, Edmond, 55
Simon, Leslie E., 353
Simon, Walter M., 139
Sims, W. S., 262
Siney, Marion C., 256
Singer, Charles J., 19
Singletary, Otis A., 176, 177
Six, Georges, 125
Slessor, John C., 292, 309, 402
Slessor, Marshal, 397-398
Slim, William, 367
Smail, R. C., 20
Smelser, Marshall, 93
Smith, Adam, 145
Smith, Dennis Mack, 168
Smith, Edgar C., 164
Smith, John, 81
Smith, Justin H., 176
Smith, Louis, 79
Smith, Robert Ross, 376
Smuts, Jan Christian, 232, 307-308
Smyth, John, 367
Snell, Edward M., 346-347, 351
Snow, C. P., 323
Snyder, Louis L., 315

Sokol, Anthony E., 397
Solt, Leo F., 78
Sombart, Werner, 14, 257
Somerville, Boyle, 75
Somerville, James H., 326, 329
Sommer, Dudley, 231
Soutai, Maurice, 48
Spaatz, Carl, 353-354
Spaight, J. M., 309, 353
Spanier, John W., 387, 403
Spanish-American War, 230, 259
Spaulding, Oliver L., 11, 19
Spee, Admiral, 244
Speer, Albert, 339
Spengler, Oswald, 282
Sprigge, Cecil J. S., 169
Sprout, Harold and Margaret, 93, 281
Spruance, Raymond A., 369, 376-377
Sprung, G. M. C., 389
Stacey, Charles P., 82-83, 85, 358
Stadelmann, Rudolf, 133, 170
Stalin, Joseph, 287, 289, 290, 300, 316, 333, 334, 336, 338, 340, 341, 342, 343, 359, 363, 385
Steinmetz, Rudolf, 257
Sternberg, Fritz, 390
Stevin, Simon, 43
Stiere, Edward, 182
Stilwell, Joseph W., 315, 347, 361
Stimson, Henry L., 311, 350
Stirk, S. D., 268
Stoffel, Baron de, 152, 170
Storry, Richard, 363
Strauss, Lewis L., 394
Strausz-Hupé, Robert, 390
Stuart, Brian, 128
Sumner, B. H., 44
Sunderland, Riley, 360, 367, 371, 383-385
Suvorov, Alexander, 133, 134
Swinton, Ernest, 232, 267-269, 311
Sykes, Christopher, 384
Szczot, E. F., 299

Taine, Hippolyte A., 103, 152
Tan, Chester C., 220
Tarlà, Eugène, 119, 135
Taylor, A. J. P., 200, 223
Taylor, E. G. R., 63
Taylor, F. L., 28
Taylor, Frank, 41
Tedder, Arthur W., 68, 352-353
Thompson, Virginia, 361
Timoshenko, Semyonk, 287, 337
Tirpitz, Alfred von, 211-214, 257
Todleben, Franz E., 166
Togo, Heihachiro, 220, 234
Tojo, Heaeki, 285, 363, 376
Toynbee, Arnold, 282
Tolstoy, Leo, 56-57, 135, 167, 398

Trenchard, Hugh, 292, 308, 313
Trend, J. B., 39
Trevelyan, George O., 95
Trochu, Louis J., 152, 173-174
Trotsky, Leon, 286
Truman, Harry, 381, 386-387
Tucker, Glenn, 92
Turenne, Henri, Vicomte de, 141
Turner, E. S., 58
Turner, Gordon B., 11-12
Tyng, Sewell, 249

Urquhart, Hugh M., 271

Vagts, Alfred, 233, 401
Vandiver, Frank E., 178, 179, 190
Vauban, Sebastien le Prestre de, 41, 43-44
Vegetius (Flavius Vegetius Renatus), 31-32, 51
Verdy du Vernois, J. A. F. W. von, 195
Vigny, Alfred de, 149
Voltaire, 54, 56
Voroshilov, Klementy, 287, 336

Wade, Aubrey, 267
Waibel, M., 335
Waite, Robert G., 298
Waitt, Alden H., 246
Wakefield, R. C., 397
Waldersee, Alfred von, 195, 206, 223
Walker, Allan S., 373
Wallace, Willard M., 88
Wallace, William A., 88
Wallenstein, Albrecht von, 39
Walter, Gérard, 108
Walton, C. E., 79
Waltz, K. N., 205
Ward, Christopher, 88
Ward, Ned, 70
Ward, S. P. G., 129
Warner, Oliver, 115, 118
Washington, George, 88-90, 94-97
Waters, David W., 63
Watson, Mark S., 311
Watson, S. J., 109, 119
Watson-Watts, R., 323
Wavell, Lord, 14, 254, 329-330, 332, 404
Way, Katharine, 14
Weber, Theo, 323
Weber, Thomas, 185
Wedemeyer, Albert C., 385
Wedgwood, C. V., 40, 78
Wegener, Wolfgang, 214
Weigert, Hans W., 299
Weigley, Russell F., 176
Weisenborn, Günther, 297
Welles, Gideon, 188
Wellington Arthur Wellesley, Duke of, 115, 128-132, 145, 146, 151

Weniger, E., 213
Werner, Herman O., 11
Werner, Max, 294
Werstein, Irving, 176
Werth, Alexander, 340
West, Richard S., 188
Weygand, Maxime, 41, 319
Wheatley, Ronald, 322
Wheeler-Bennett, John W., 241, 264, 290, 296
White, D. Fedotoff, 287
White, William L., 390
Whitehead, Alfred North, 195
Whitehead, Robert, 191
Whiting, Allen S., 387
Whitney, Courtney H., 366
Whitton, F. E., 87, 170
Whitworth, Rex, 83
Wigmore, Lionel, 361-362, 366
Wijn, Jan Willem, 39
Wiley, Bell I., 178
Wilkinson, Spenser, 53, 119, 158
William I, of Germany, 153-154, 156-157
William II, of Germany, 198, 205, 206, 211, 214, 222, 241, 245, 273, 299, 321
William of Orange, 68, 78-79
William the Silent, 38, 39
Williams, Kenneth P., 179
Williams, Trevor I., 19
Williams, T. Harry, 92, 179
Williamson, Henry, 250-251
Williamson, James A., 66
Willoughby, Charles A., 366, 373
Wilmot, Chester, 315
Wilson, Arthur K., 232
Wilson, Charles, 67
Wilson, Henry, 228, 232-233
Wilson, Robert T., 134
Wilson, Woodrow, 258-259, 260, 261, 275-278
Wingate, Orde, 384
Wingfield-Stratford, Esme, 277
Wintringham, Tom, 14
Winslow, E. M., 209
Wise, Jennings C., 183
Wise, Sydney F., 11
Wolf, John B., 41
Wolff, Leon, 250
Wolseley, Garnet J., 146, 179, 189
Wood, Evelyn, 201
Wood, Leonard, 260
Woodham-Smith, C. B. F., 167
Woodroofe, Thomas, 66
Woodruff, Philip, 147
Woodward, E. L., 214
Woolcombe, Roger, 329
World War I, 29, 181, 220, 223-224, 282, 288, 291, 294, 299, 306, 310, 314, 325, 326, 342, 344-345

World War II, 30, 34, 61, 188, 246, 252, 276, 282, 287, 288, 290, 291, 297, 306, 311, 314-390
Wright, Gordon, 152
Wright, John W., 11
Wright, Quincy, 13
Wykeham, Peter, 323

Yamashita, General, 318
Yamamoto, Isoroku, 364, 377
Yates, Louis A. R., 277
Yokai, Toshiyuki, 379
Yonai, Mitsumasa, 375, 376

Yorck von Wartenburg, Hans, 118-119, 132, 136
Young, Francis Brett, 404
Young, H. A., 95
Young, Peter, 78
Yovitchitch, Lena A., 339

Zeitzler, Kurt, 340
Zeller, Gaston, 44
Zieser, Benno, 340
Zhukov, Gregory, 287, 337, 340, 342
Zieser, Benno, 340
Zook, David H., 313